Women in Utah History

Paradigm or Paradox?

Two women selling the *Herald Republican* newspaper at 167 South Main Street, Salt Lake City, January 31, 1911.

Women in Utah History

Paradigm or Paradox?

edited by

Patricia Lyn Scott
and Linda Thatcher

Susan Allred Whetstone, photograph editor

A Project of the Utah Women's History Association
Cosponsored by the Utah State Historical Society

Utah State University Press
Logan, Utah
2005

Utah State University Press
Logan, Utah 84322–7800
www.usu.edu/usupreses

All royalties from the sale of this book will be donated to the Utah Women's History Fund at the Utah State Historical Society to promote women's history.

Manufactured in the United States of America
Printed on acid-free paper

An earlier version of "Gainfully Employed Women" by Miriam Murphy was published in the *Utah Historical Quarterly* 50 (Spring 1982): 139–59.

Cover photos used by permission, Utah State Historical Society, all right reserved.
Front, top to bottom:
      Osbourne auto party, April 7, 1909.
      Women at work, 1944.
      Mrs. J. W. Fowles working in her Victory Garden, May 6, 1945.
Back:
      Unidentified group of Japanese Americans, ca. 1920.

Library of Congress Cataloging-in-Publication Data

Women in Utah history : paradigm or paradox? / edited by Patricia Lyn Scott and Linda Thatcher.
    p. cm.
 Includes index.
 ISBN-13: 978-0-87421-625-7 (pbk. : alk. paper)
 ISBN-10: 0-87421-625-7 (pbk. : alk. paper)
 ISBN-13: 978-0-87421-624-0 (cloth : alk. paper)
 ISBN-10: 0-87421-624-9 (cloth : alk. paper)
 1. Women--Utah--History. 2. Women--Utah--Social conditions. 3. Utah--History. 4. Utah--Social conditions. I. Scott, Patricia Lyn. II. Thatcher, Linda, 1946-
 HQ1438.U8W66 2005
 305.4'09792--dc22
                   2005020065

Contents

Illustrations

For our mothers.

Introduction

Linda Thatcher and Patricia Lyn Scott

The chief goal of this book is to integrate Utah women of all ethnic and religious backgrounds into the broader field of women's studies. Readers will find that these historical essays show women in Utah as sharing much with other American women, particularly in the West—in other words, as not unique. But they are also diverse and distinctive—in other words, not as expected.

The title *Utah Women's History: Paradigm or Paradox?* recognizes the stereotypes normally associated with Utah's largest group of women: Mormon, polygamous, Caucasian, under-educated, male-dominated, etc. On the one hand, Utah women are seen as a paradox (contradictory to the national norm) for embracing polygamy and submitting to hierarchal Mormon Church authority. On the other hand, they can be seen as paradigm (an example or model) for forging their own way with self-reliance and industry. Perhaps the paradox is that Utah women were both representative of national women (a paradigm) and distinctive. Few realize that Utah was the second territory to grant women the franchise (1870), and Utah's women often sustained themselves and their families both economically and emotionally for long periods of time, while their husbands were away on church assignments or dividing their time among multiple households. Julie Roy Jeffrey wrote concerning polygamy: "With its peculiar tensions and freedoms, polygamy did, of course, shape the Mormon female life on the frontier. Mormon women were different from women on other frontiers in a number of ways which were related to their religion. Yet they also shared with other pioneer women common frontier experiences and even common ideas about woman's place in the world. To be a Mormon woman on the Utah frontier was, therefore, to be both the same as, and different from, pioneer women elsewhere."[1]

Utah was also a mixing ground of cultures. Native American women of many tribes led lives that having changed little over centuries, were shattered within a generation when a great flood of white settlers washed over their traditional territories. Mormon missionaries proselyted in European countries, and new members journeyed to Utah from Great Britain, Germany, and the Scandinavian countries by the thousands. Emigrants who continued to embrace their traditional religions followed from Italy, Greece, and Asia during the late nineteenth and early twentieth centuries, brought for economic reasons, not religious ones, to work in Utah's mines and industries.

By taking a historical perspective, these essays capture the process of the social, religious, political and economic changes that Utah women experienced. In so doing, it is the first booklength attempt to appraise Utah women of all religions, ethnicities, and social classes. Such an approach, we believe, will move the history of Utah's women into the academic mainstream of women's history. Although Utah history is rife with female stereotypes, we believe that the depth and variety of involvement of Utah women in the life of the state will surprise readers.

TWELVE THEMATIC APPROACHES

The book is arranged thematically and explores varied women's activities such as agriculture, education, law, literature, and the arts. Each chapter focuses on a particular period, usually identified in the title. The dates are not meant to be all-inclusive. Underlying each chapter is our keen recognition that Utah women played an important but largely invisible—by today's standard—role in Utah's history. This book allows their contribution to be documented and celebrated.

The dominant stereotype associated with Utah women, is the subject of the book's first chapter: "Polygamous and Monogamous Mormon Women: A Comparison" by Jessie L. Embry, associate director of the Charles Redd Center for Western Studies, Brigham Young University, and Lois Kelley, a graduate student in history at Utah State University at the time of her death. This practice put Mormon women at odds with their American sisters. While they considered plural marriage a God-given commandment and believed it was a Constitutionally guaranteed exercise of religious freedom, American women in general were horrified. Harriet Beecher Stowe viewed polygamy as "a slavery which debases and degrades womanhood, motherhood, and family."[2] American legislators agreed with them. The authors discuss briefly the colorful and unique pre-Utah history of this practice and its complex and increasingly intense legislative and judicial contest, resulting finally in the Mormon Church's withdrawal of approval for the practice. Their focus, however, is neither political nor religious but domestic. How did plural families live their lives, conduct their courtships, arrange their households, share the work, raise their children, and, finally, disentangle those households to conform to federal legislation? Embry's and Kelley's chapter is based on autobiographies and diaries from the participants and, interestingly, on two series of interviews and oral histories conducted with participants during the 1930s and with the adult children of polygamists during 1976–82.

Embry and Kelley explore stereotypes concerning polygamy and sources of discord in polygamous families—such as the unequal division of financial resources, living arrangements, shared goods and equipment, and personality. However, the chapter balances this discussion with descriptions of several instances of harmony and love within plural families. Some of the questions that they address are: "How did Mormon women react to these events [the Manifesto announcing an end to polygamy in 1890]? How did they feel about sharing their husbands? What motivated them to say yes (when they did)? And then when that policy changed, how did they feel about giving up the practice of plural marriage?"

"Innovation and Accommodation: The Legal Status of Women in Territorial Utah, 1850–96" is written by Lisa Madsen Pearson and Carol Cornwall Madsen—an attorney daughter and a historian mother. The authors find that the main influences on the legal status of women in Utah territory were "the liberalizing tendencies of frontier development, and most important, the necessity of protecting Mormon control and practices, including plural marriage, and ultimately defending them against the counter measures of the federal government." Utah Territory was mired from its beginning with legal problems that arose from conflicts between federal and local courts, and Utah Territory's effort to reject common law and polygamy. Pearson's and Madsen's chapter examines the many years of conflict and conciliation that it took for Utah and the federal government to arrive at an agreement so that Utah could finally obtain statehood.

"Conflict and Contributions: Women in Churches, 1847–1920" by John Sillito, university archivist at Weber State University, broadens the book's religious focus beyond Mormonism, documenting religion's important role for most women in Utah's history. Despite a stereotype of Utah as exclusively Mormon, "the zeal of American Protestantism" readily launched missions throughout the Mormon stronghold. Protestants enriched education in Utah through several academies and schools, usually headed by men but staffed by devout women. "Mormon-controlled, territorial schools were woefully characterized even by the *Deseret News* in an 1855 editorial as having teachers who 'had no other qualifications excepting they were out of employ,' and also by overcrowding, inadequate facilities, and high tuition," observes Sillito. As a result, Mormons were willing to take a chance on turning their children over to non-Mormons to be educated.

Various churches also promoted early social, medical, and charitable work in Utah. The Episcopal and Catholic churches made important contributions to Utah's medical care by opening St. Mark's Hospital in 1872 and Holy Cross Hospital (the first hospital founded in the United States by the Sisters of the Holy Cross) in 1875. At the end of the nineteenth and the beginning of the twentieth century, non-Mormon churches and schools were prolific in Utah. But as public education improved and polygamy was officially outlawed, the Protestant missionary and education effort lost its momentum and many schools closed, leaving Episcopal, Catholic, and Presbyterian institutions to add their enduring contributions to Utah's religious landscape.

"Ethnic Women, 1900–1940" is a summary by Helen Z. Papanikolas, a Greek-American whose efforts to reclaim Utah's ethnic minorities were monumental. She sketches the experiences of American Indians, African Americans, Balkans, and Asians from 1900 to the 1940s. Papanikolas's chapter especially provides a tangible sense of the transitions of immigrants. They built solidly traditional homes; preserved, often with heroic efforts, traditional values, and launched a new generation of "hyphenated" Americans, who inevitably cherished some of these values but relinquished others. Not well recognized at the time was the great bond forged among immigrant women by the similar circumstances they experienced after arriving in Utah. Most left their homelands reluctantly for a new land—sometimes to marry a husband whom they did not know—to live in a strange community, often isolated from their fellow countrymen and customs and facing lives of hard work and discrimination. Often only dire poverty in their native countries and prospects of an even bleaker future motivated them to make the long journey to America. Papanikolas uses census records and oral histories to examine immigrants' roles in communities, the impact of federal immigration laws, hostility toward their cultural groups, and the difficulties of the Depression years.

"The Professionalization of Farm Women, 1890–1940" by Cynthia Sturgis, a teacher, discusses the changes in rural Utah women's roles from producer to consumer between 1890 and 1940. Strongly influencing this change was the domestic arts program offered by Utah Agricultural College (Utah State University) in Logan. Inaugurated in 1903, the school of home economics focused on improving young women's skills in the home. The university's extension program also disseminated educational programs at the grassroots level throughout the state, and such publications as *Utah Farmer* (1912–97; originally the *Deseret Farmer,* 1905–1912) had sections devoted particularly to women's concerns. Later, electricity played an even more important role in the way that rural women accomplished their daily chores. As women gained more education and as communication increased, housekeeping on the farm and in the city grew to resemble each other more closely. Sturgis notes, "The farmwife had become a 'household manager,' a consumer, and a believer in planning and education."

"Gainfully Employed Women, 1896–1950" by Miriam B. Murphy, retired associate editor of the *Utah Historical Quarterly,* traces the role of women as wage earners during the nineteenth century when Utah had "a frontier economy based primarily on agriculture" to the twentieth century's "mixed economy of a developing agricultural-commercial-industrial state." This article refreshingly reconsiders the image of Utah's women as housewives and farm-wives. Although both of these roles were important ones for Utah's hard-working women, they sought and accepted opportunities for paid employment in Utah's "mixed economy of a developing agricultural-commercial-industrial state. The role of women in that transformation resembled that of women in other parts of westerning America." Women's employment opportunities, which began primarily with domestic service, expanded to keep pace. By the turn of the twentieth century, national events and trends dominated Utah's economic life. Even though Utah was not a major manufacturing state, it boasted a larger and more diverse list of manufacturers than most states of the Mountain West. Many young Utah women worked in seasonal canning operations, candy factories, textile mills, and clothing factories. Self-employed women were dressmakers, milliners, and boarding house operators. Depression-era government projects also provided significant employment to Utah women, while record numbers, like their sisters elsewhere in the nation, entered the workforce during World War II. Against this context, Murphy also discusses the Mormon Church's traditionally conservative views on working women.

"From Schoolmarm to State Superintendent: The Changing Role of Women in Education, 1847–2004" by the late Mary R. Clark, a former doctoral student at the University of Utah, and Patricia Lyn Scott, a section manager at the Utah State Archives, focuses in greater detail on women's contribution to education in Utah. Mary Jane Dilworth began Utah's first school in a tent on October 24, 1847, only three months after the pioneers entered the Salt Lake Valley. In early Utah, the first public structure in most pioneer communities was a combination school/church house. The schools were an early battlefield in the national contest to end Mormon control of daily life in Utah. This chapter also discusses the role of women in public education through Mormon ward schools, private schools, and non-Mormon mission schools, the development of teacher education, increased numbers of women in the profession, the end of discriminatory pay and rules, the marked increase of women administrators during the 1990s, and finally the appointment of a women state school superintendent in 2004.

"Scholarship, Service, and Sisterhood: Women's Clubs and Associations, 1877–1977," by Jill Mulvay Derr, managing director of the Joseph Fielding Smith Institute for Latter-day Saint History at Brigham Young University, analyzes the significant role of Utah women's clubs and associations from 1877 to 1977. Derr writes: "The history of Utah women's clubs and associations is best understood within the context of the ongoing national discussion about women's role in the public sphere. . . . The question of appropriate roles of women emerged as a burning topic." Clubwomen's strategy was to espouse "the ladylike ideal" with the goal of encouraging women's status and respect and encouraging them to seek self-improvement. Derr discusses three important time periods: 1877–1917, "when women began establishing a new network of clubs and associations"; 1917–45, "when both new and well-established organizations for women addressed the challenges of war, depression, and peace"; and 1945–77, "an age of discontent and discovery informed by the twentieth-century women's movement." She focuses particularly on the significant civic contributions associations of Utah women have always made to their communities.

"Women of Letters: A Unique Literary Tradition" by Gary Topping, archivist of the Catholic Diocese of Utah, explores the topic of Utah women in literature. "The harshness of frontier life, though poignantly present in early Utah, seems to have been generally less of a factor in inhibiting cultural development than elsewhere," he comments. "An important factor was Mormonism's characteristic gregariousness. Mormon migration and colonization were movements of an entire society rather than a diffusion of individuals. Thus, while the poet behind the plow and the historian in the haymower are to be found on the Utah frontier as elsewhere, Mormon society from the beginning sought a degree of specialization that potentially included the arts, sciences and letters." He examines the contributions of individual writers and women's literary societies along with their contributions to the genres of the novel, poetry and short story. Utah has produced several nationally known authors including Maurine Whipple, Juanita Brooks, Fawn Brodie, May Swenson, and Judith Freeman. Today many of the state's nationally known authors are noted for their environment-oriented writings and include Terry Tempest Williams, Ann Zwinger, and Ellen Meloy (1946–2004), who was nominated for a Pulitzer Prize in nonfiction in 2003.

"Women in the Arts: Evolving Roles and Diverse Expressions" by Martha Sonntag Bradley-Evans, associate professor in the College of Architecture and Planning at the University of Utah, surveys Utah women in dance, theater, music, the visual arts and handicrafts, motion pictures, and popular entertainment. Since the Victorian ideal encouraged cultural/artistic activities for women as appropriately "refining" activities, it is not surprising that women participated from the 1850s, beginning with Brigham Young's organization of the Deseret Musical and Dramatic Society soon after their arrival in the valley. Unlike many conservative religious movements, Mormonism encouraged dramatics, singing, and dancing as wholesome recreations, while the later Mutual Improvement Associations had strong drama, music, singing, and dancing programs (sports were confined largely to men) that continued broad community sponsorship of such activities. Thus, Utah added to the nation's actresses such women as Maude Adams, famous for her Broadway role as Peter Pan, and Hazel Dawn, an early Hollywood film star. Maud May Babcock, the first woman professor at the University of Utah, dominated theater and dance, directing more than 800 productions. Artists Mary Teasdel, Rose Hartwell, Florence Ware, and Myra Sawyer and a host of less well-known Utah women fine artists benefitted from the far-sighted Alice Merrill Horne's sponsorship in 1899 of a bill that created the first state arts council in the United States.

"Women in Politics: Power in the Public Sphere" by Kathryn L. MacKay, associate professor of history, Weber State University, discusses the three major issues that activated women in the political sphere in the nineteenth century: "abolition of slavery, temperance, [and] woman suffrage." She focuses on women's place in Utah politics from 1847 to 2003, beginning with the suffrage movement, women's achievement of suffrage in 1870, disfranchisement as a side effect of the polygamy fight between 1887 and 1895, and the regranting of the vote by the state constitution—but only after a monumental struggle. MacKay positions these events against their national context, noting where the Utah experience follows or diverges from national trends. MacKay brings her chapter into the twenty-first century with her discussion of former Governor Olene Walker's recent role in Utah politics.

Jessie L. Embry authors a second chapter in our book: "Women's Life Cycles: 1850–1940." Embry uses Gerda Lerner's *The Female Experience: An American Documentary* as her model. Embry proposes: "Studies like Lerner's consider that the life elements that most women share are of greatest importance and seek those patterns rather than writing from an assumption of uniqueness." To gain an understanding of Utah women's life patterns, Embry read more than three hundred oral histories and one hundred published life sketches. She discusses the "typical" life cycle (daughter, wife, childbearing and child rearing, aging, and usually widowhood), along with such variations as employment outside the home and the options available for single women.

A History of the History

The introduction to this book would be incomplete without a brief discussion of the project's history—in itself a glimpse of Utah women from the last quarter of the twentieth century to the present. The book traces its beginnings to April 1977 when a group of women historians and women working in history-related fields organized themselves as the Task Force on Women in Utah History of the Utah Commission for the Observance of International Women's Year (IWY). For the Utah state IWY meeting in June 1977, the task force presented a workshop that included a slide-sound lecture and a photographic exhibit.

The workshop was so successful and the relationships formed so rewarding that several of the women decided to continue their association with the formation of the Women's History Association with the dual goals of encouraging women in the history professions and also promoting the study, teaching, and writing of women's history. In 1978 the group's name changed to the Utah Women's History Association. The association's initial focus was a combination of support group and network—a place where women in history could share common concerns, network with each other, exchange ideas, and report successful methodologies. The organization also envisioned promoting women's history by organizing and sponsoring public programs and conferences on women's history and encouraging the researching and writing of women's history.[3]

On October 29, 1983, the first planning meeting was held at the Salt Lake City Public Library to discuss the possibility of writing and publishing a history of Utah's women. Those in attendance included: Patricia Lyn Scott, Lavina Fielding Anderson, Sharon Arnold, Peggy Lee, Helen Papanikolas,

Fred Buchanan, Lois Kelley, Linda Thatcher, Kathryn MacKay, Jill Mulvay Derr, and Lori Hefner. The editors selected were Patricia Lyn Scott and Linda Thatcher (current and incoming presidents), with Lavina Fielding Anderson as production editor and the late Cary Stevens Jones as photograph editor (Susan Whetstone has stepped into that role).

This group developed the list of topics that would form the table of contents and also proposed authors. An impressive number of outstanding Utah historians agreed to author chapters.[4] The organization successfully applied for a grant from the Utah Endowment for the Humanities (Utah Humanities Council) to sponsor a lecture series where the chapters were presented as papers. During the fall and winter of 1985–86, all sixteen authors presented their lectures in Salt Lake City and repeated them in Utah communities outside the Wasatch Front. This series proved to be very successful with several hundred people in attendance.

For multiple reasons, the project lost momentum, but the editors never lost their belief that the eventual goal of publishing the book was a worthwhile project. In 2004 the editors regrouped and asked those authors who were still interested in participating to update their chapters. All were—all did. The chapters presented in this book are somewhat different than those initially envisioned, but they still reflect the original intent—that of telling the history of Utah's women.

Significantly, during the intervening years, several important biographical works on Utah women have been published, but no thematic book has appeared devoted to Utah women as a whole.[5] The need for such a book envisioned during the 1970s has only become more acute with the passage of time, particularly as women's history has assumed its place in the broader historiographical landscape. This book's primary objective is to make the history of Utah's women more visible, to celebrate their achievements, to appreciate their struggles and sacrifices, and to see more clearly the work that still remains to be done.

Acknowledgments

Finally, we acknowledge with deep appreciation the individuals and institutions who made this project possible. Lavina Fielding Anderson, more than a technical editor, provided assistance and direction at crucial points of our project. The quality of this publication is largely due to her editing skills.

We also express sincere appreciation to the Utah Humanities Council, which provided the initial funding for writing the first papers/lectures in 1985. This sponsorship played a critical role in the development of the project. Cynthia Buckingham encouraged this project throughout its long gestation.

Various institutions played an important role in this project, most notably the Utah State Historical Society, which provided consistent support. We are especially appreciative of its sponsorship of the publication, thus allowing dozens of photographs to be used and allowing the services of Linda Thatcher as an editor and Susan Whetstone as photograph editor. The society's director, Philip F. Notarianni, was not only supportive but enthusiastic about the project. Other very helpful institutional support came from the Giovale Library, Westminster College and its director David Hales; photo curator Dan Davis at Utah State University's Merrill Library; Janet Burton Seegmiller at Southern Utah University's Sherratt library; University of Utah's Special Collections at Marriott Library; Utah State archivist Patricia Smith-Mansfield and the Utah State Archives; Catholic Diocese of Salt Lake City; Kennecott Utah Copper; and countless other archivists and manuscript curators throughout Utah.

We also acknowledge the support of our families, friends and institutions, who believed in this project. Thanks to them and their persistent reminders that it needed to be done, we could not give up.

Our most sincere tribute goes to our authors. In the two decades that have passed since the project began, the young enthusiasts have become seasoned scholars and the mature scholars have produced an important body of historical studies. Demands on their time have multiplied mercilessly, but their commitment to women's history and the bonds of friendship have remained intact, motivating them to move this project through its many iterations repeatedly to the head of their priority list.

It is with sorrow and gratitude that we acknowledge four who finished their journey and have passed from our circle: Lois J. Kelley and Mary R. Clark died before the project's completion was assured, leaving their work and their encouragement to able co-authors. We recognize the support of Mary's and Lois's families in allowing us to use their work in this project, especially that of Mary's daughter, Alice Clark. The remarkable Helen Zeese Papanikolas died as we were completing revisions. We will always remember her supportive e-mails, her grace in her final illness, and the stature of her legendary reputation, lent so willingly to this project. Cary Stevens Jones, the project's first photo editor, devoted hours to the project. We remember her positive nature and mourn her loss.

This is a project that would not die, because the story of Utah's women has a right to be told and shared with all Utahns. We thank John Alley and Utah State University Press for making it a reality.

Notes

1. Julie Roy Jeffrey, *Frontier Women: The Trans-Mississippi West, 1840–1880* (New York: Hill and Wang, 1979), 150.

2. Harriet Beecher Stowe, "Introduction," in *Tell It All: The Tyranny of Mormonism; or, an Englishwoman in Utah, by Mrs. T.B.H. Stenhouse* (1880; reprint, New York: Praeger Publishers, 1971). See also the front page of each *Anti-Polygamy Standard* starting April 1880.

3. "Origins and Purposes," *Women's History Association Newsletter*, 1, no. 1 (Winter 1977): 1.

4. The original authors were Jeffery O. Johnson, Jessie L. Embry, Lois Kelley, Davis Bitton, Cynthia Sturgis, John Sillito, Frederick S. Buchanan, Martha Bradley, Gary Topping, Kathryn L. MacKay, Jill Mulvay Derr, Miriam B. Murphy, Carol Cornwall Madsen, Helen Z. Papanikolas, Loretta Hefner, and Lisa Madsen Pearson.

5. In the past two decades, there have been four types of biographical studies published on Utah women. First, there are the traditional biographies. They include Levi S. Peterson's *Juanita Brooks: Mormon Woman Historian* (Salt Lake City: University of Utah Press, 1988) and Judy Dykman and Colleen Whitley's *The Silver Queen: Her Royal Highness Suzanne Bransford Emery Holmes Delitch Englitcheff, 1859–1942* (Logan: Utah State University Press, 1998). Second are the compiled biographical works. They include Colleen Whitley's two volumes, *Worth Their Salt* (Logan: Utah State University Press, 1996) and *Worth Their Salt, Too* (Logan: Utah State University Press, 2000) containing the biographical essays of thirty-four Utah women; and the Daughters of Utah Pioneers' four volume *Pioneer Women of Faith and Fortitude* (Salt Lake City: International Society of Daughters of Utah Pioneers, 1998) which contains hundreds of biographical entries on women who arrived in Utah between 1847 and 1869. Third are the documentary works, the edited diaries, letters, and other records of Utah women. They include *The Personal Writings of Eliza Roxcy Snow*, edited by Maureen Ursenbach Beecher (Salt Lake City: University of Utah Press, 1995); *Letters from Exile: The Correspondence of Martha Hughes Cannon and Angus M. Cannon,* edited by Constance L. Lieber and John Sillito (Salt Lake City: Signature Books, 1989); and *A Widow's Tale: The 1884–1896 Diary of Helen Mar Kimball Whitney*, edited by Charles M. Hatch and Todd Compton (Logan: Utah State University Press, 2003). The fourth are material culture studies which examine the lives of women through what they produced domestically. Examining quilts and their makers has become an important segment of this type of study. They include Mary Bywater Cross's *Quilts and Women of the Migration: Treasurers of Transition* (Nashville, Tenn.: Rutledge Hill Press 1996) and Kate Covington's *Gathered in Time: Utah Quilts and Their Makers: Settlement to 1950* (Salt Lake City: University of Utah Press, 1997).

1

Polygamous and Monogamous Mormon Women

A Comparison

Jessie L. Embry and Lois Kelley

For many people throughout the world, the words *Utah* and *Mormons* automatically bring associations of polygamy even though members of the Church of Jesus Christ of Latter-day Saints have not officially practiced plural marriage for at least a century. I[1] realized this when I knocked on a door as a Mormon missionary in Fredericton, New Brunswick, in 1974. The man who answered the door asked, "Isn't that the Church where you can have more than one wife? Would both of you be available?" Utah historian Thomas G. Alexander frequently reminds me that I should not be surprised by such comments, explaining that for many the interesting aspects of history are sex and violence. For many, the most interesting part of polygamy is: "How did the women respond?"

Views of Mormon plural wives have changed over the years. Nineteenth-century contemporaries like author Harriet Beecher Stowe described Mormon polygamy as "a slavery which debases and degrades womanhood, motherhood, and family," reflecting the nineteenth-century view that "polygamy destroyed the family and women's unique place in it and made women unfit for their moral and social responsibilities."[2]

While Stowe had a negative view of polygamy, recent scholars who have studied elite Mormon polygamous wives declare them the forerunners of modern feminists—especially in finances. According to one study, "Polygamy developed independent women who bore much of the financial responsibility for their families because husbands were often away on missions and even when they were home the wives were often left to manage their homes alone."[3]

Based on the conclusions of nineteenth-century contemporaries and some twentieth-century studies, Mormon plural wives were unique. Yet a study of Mormon polygamous and monogamous wives in Utah during the late nineteenth and early twentieth centuries shows little difference in their lifestyles. As historian Julie Roy Jeffrey explained, "With its peculiar tensions and freedoms, polygamy did, of course, shape the Mormon female life on the frontier. . . . Yet Mormon women . . . shared with other pioneer women common frontier experiences and even ideas about woman's place in the world. To be a Mormon woman on the Utah frontier was therefore, to be both the same as, and different from, pioneer women elsewhere."[4] This chapter examines the experiences of Utah women who lived in polygamous households and those who lived in monogamous families.[5]

SAMPLE

Our study is based on our examination of interviews, autobiographies, and diaries. Sociology professor Kimball Young and two graduate research assistants, James Hulett and Fay Ollerton, conducted the first set of interviews in the late 1930s. Hulett used them to write his dissertation, "The Sociological and Social Psychological Aspects of the Mormon Polygamous Family," and Young used them extensively in his book *Isn't One Wife Enough?*[6] The Kimball Young Collection is in the L. Tom Perry Special Collections and Manuscripts, Harold B. Lee Library, Brigham Young University. It contains Hulett's and Ollerton's notes from interviews with thirteen husbands, fifty wives, five husbands and wives, and eighty-three children of polygamous families. A second data source is the Charles Redd Center for Western Studies's LDS Polygamy Oral History Project (1976–82), also housed in Perry Special Collections. Included are the transcriptions of interviews with more than 250 men and women who were children in plural marriages contracted before the Second Manifesto of 1904. In 1982 the Redd Center project added interviews with 150 men and women who were children in monogamous families from the same period, thus forming a comparison group.

Other interviews, diaries, and autobiographies are housed in both Archives of the Family and Church History Department, Church of Jesus Christ of Latter-day Saints, Salt Lake City (hereafter LDS Church Archives) and in the L. Tom Perry Special Collections, Harold B. Lee Library, Brigham Young University. Altogether, this essay looks at the experiences of approximately 400 plural wives and 150 monogamous women.

Informants' observations in oral histories are the most severely limited in scope. Most children, especially in the nineteenth century, never asked their parents why they married in polygamy, how they divided money and goods, and how often they had sexual relations. Elsie Chamberlain Carroll, a daughter of Thomas Chamberlain and Eleanor Hoyt Chamberlain, who grew up in Kane County, added another reason: "I guess it is just natural to remember the pleasant things and forget the unpleasant."[7] However, often, their memories are the only sources available, and they provide valuable data that cannot be found elsewhere.

A Historical Overview of Mormon Polygamy

Religious values underlie any discussion of Mormon polygamy. Latter-day Saints believe that the church Joseph Smith Jr. founded in 1830 restored truths lost from Christianity during a "great apostasy," which followed the death of Christ's apostles. As part of this restoration, he revised the Bible to correct errors in translation and recorded many revelations, often in answer to his questions. These revelations were canonized in the Doctrine and Covenants. As part of the restoration of all things, he received a revelation recorded as:

> Prepare thy heart to receive and obey the instructions which I am about to give unto you; for all those who have this law revealed unto them must obey the same. . . .
>
> If any man espouse a virgin, and desires to espouse another, and if the first give her consent, and if he espouse the second, and they are virgins, and have vowed to no other man, then is he justified; he cannot commit adultery for they are given unto him; for he cannot commit adultery with that that belongeth to him and to no one else.[8]

Smith had already been "sealed" to several plural wives before he recorded this revelation in July 1843, apparently at the request of his brother, Hyrum, who hoped to reduce the opposition of Joseph's wife, Emma Hale Smith. He reportedly received this revelation as much as a decade earlier and, although the evidence is circumstantial, married his first plural wife, Fanny Alger, in 1835.[9] However, he was never able to persuade Emma, except for two brief periods in 1843, to accept this practice.[10]

Before Joseph and Hyrum Smith's assassinations in June 1844, only a few of the people in Nauvoo's elite circle knew of or entered into the practice of polygamy. They used code words in an attempt to conceal the practice from the enemies of the church and from most church members and issued public statements denying that they were practicing polygamy. However, the rumors surfaced repeatedly. After the disaffection of John Cook Bennett, one-time mayor of Nauvoo, in the summer of 1842, he published a detailed exposé. Even more significant were the defections of William Law, a member of the First Presidency (consisting of the church president and two counselors), and his brother Wilson. With other dissidents, they organized a separate church and published the *Nauvoo Expositor* whose primary theme was opposition to polygamy. After the first number appeared in June 1844, Joseph Smith as mayor and the Nauvoo City Council ordered the press destroyed, an act that led to Smith's arrest and death in Carthage, Illinois, later that month.[11]

In 1846, the Mormons evacuated Nauvoo. By July 1847, they had reached the Great Basin and founded Salt Lake City. Brigham Young had energetically pursued Joseph Smith's doctrine of polygamy, and its practice was an open secret in Utah. Brigham Young decided to publicly announce the practice of plural marriage. In August 1852, Orson Pratt, an apostle who had left the church for a short time when Joseph Smith proposed marriage to Pratt's wife, made the announcement at a church conference and made a systematic defense of the practice as a religious principle with social benefits.[12]

Hosea Stout, an early Mormon who was involved in church and civic affairs, recorded in his diary: "Orson Pratt preached today on the subject of polygamy or plurality of wives as believed and practiced by the Latter day Saints. In the after noon the Revelation on the subject given to Joseph Smith . . . was publicly read for the first time to the great joy of the saints who have looked forward . . . for the time to come when we could publickly declare the . . . greatest principles of our holy religion."[13]

While Stout appreciated the public announcement, Americans in the larger society were shocked. Two years later in 1854, the Republican Party termed polygamy and slavery the "twin relics of barbarism." Opponents petitioned Congress to pass laws; and in 1862, Representative Justin S. Morrill of Vermont, introduced a bill that prohibited plural marriage in the territories, disincorporated the church, and restricted the church's ownership of property to $50,000. Although Abraham Lincoln signed the bill, the nation was in the midst of the Civil War and he reportedly said, "You tell Brigham Young if he will leave me alone, I'll leave him alone."[14]

The Utah Territorial Legislature asked Congress to repeal the Morrill Act in 1867. Some federal officers saw this petition as an attempt to legalize polygamy, and the House Judiciary Committee asked why the law was not being enforced. Illinois Representative Shelby M. Cullom introduced a bill in late 1870 that called for greater federal control in Utah Territory. Women in Utah could vote; and three thousand Mormon women immediately signed a petition protesting the bill as unjust and asserting that they were not oppressed, as non-Mormons commonly believed. The Cullom Bill passed in the House of Representatives but failed in the Senate. Congress introduced several bills against polygamy during the 1870s; but only the Poland Act (1874), introduced by Vermont's Lake P. Poland, passed. It gave district courts all civil and criminal jurisdiction and limited the Mormon-controlled probate courts to estate settlement, guardianship, and divorce.[15]

Mormons continued to perform polygamous marriages and to live as plural families because they believed it was a religious practice protected by the freedom of religion clause in the First Amendment. To test the constitutionality of the laws, George Reynolds, Brigham Young's private secretary, agreed to become the test case in 1875. After a series of appeals, in January 1879 the U.S. Supreme Court upheld the Morrill Act's constitutionality. According to the court's opinion, "Laws are made for the government of actions, and while they cannot interfere with mere religious belief and opinion, they may with practices."[16] John Taylor, who had become church president after Brigham Young's death in 1877, responded to the Reynolds ruling: "We are between the hands of God and the hands of the Government of the United States. God has . . . commanded us to enter into these covenants with each other. . . . I know they are true, . . . and all the edicts and laws of Congress and legislators and decisions of courts could not change my opinion."[17]

Three U.S. presidents—Rutherford B. Hayes in 1880 and James A. Garfield and Chester A. Arthur in 1881—spoke against the "barbarous system" of polygamy. Petitions against the practice flooded Congress during 1881 and 1882. In response, Congress passed the Edmunds Act in 1882, introduced by Senator George F. Edmunds, a Vermont Republican. A series of amendments to the Morrill Act, it restated that polygamy was a felony punishable by five years of imprisonment and a $500 fine.

Because of the difficulty in establishing that a marriage ceremony had occurred (plural marriages were not registered in public records), the act made a misdemeanor of "unlawful cohabitation," which merely required that the couple lived in the same dwelling. It was punishable by six months' imprisonment and a $300 fine. The law disenfranchised polygamous men and prohibited them from holding political offices. Those who practiced polygamy could not be on a jury, and those who professed a belief in the practice could not serve in a polygamy case. A board of five commissioners replaced the registration and election officers. Male voters had to take an oath that they did "not live or cohabit with more than one woman in the marriage relation." In 1885 the U.S. Supreme Court upheld the disenfranchisement of polygamists but voided the test oath. The commission replaced the oath by a new one that left out the terms "marriage relation."[18]

The Edmunds Act did not succeed in suppressing polygamy, and after three years of debate, in 1887 it passed what one historian called the "hodge-podge Edmunds-Tucker Bill." It required plural wives to testify against their husbands, dissolved the Perpetual Emigrating Fund (a revolving loan system institution to help Mormons immigrate to Utah from Europe), abolished the Nauvoo Legion (Utah militia), and provided a mechanism for acquiring the church property already disincorporated by the Morrill Act. Congress debated the Cullom-Struble Bill with even stricter measures in 1889; but it was seen as unnecessary after Wilford Woodruff, John Taylor's successor as church president, issued the Manifesto in September 1890 withdrawing official support for new plural marriages.[19]

In the fifty years between the 1840s and the 1890s, all of these pressures affected the church, though they did not compel the Latter-day Saints to abolish polygamy. Each church president, including John Taylor and Wilford Woodruff, publicly affirmed the continual practice of polygamy. Even after the Manifesto, the church abandoned the practice but did not repudiate the religious doctrine of polygamy. During the late 1870s and especially during the 1880s when federal marshals and deputies flooded Utah Territory, raiding each community to arrest polygamous men, both husbands and wives went

Joseph F. Smith's (1838–1918) family that included five wives, forty-eight children, including five adopted children. The photograph was taken on Smith's sixty-fourth birthday, November 13, 1904. Smith was the sixth president of the Church of Jesus Christ of Latter-day Saints.

into hiding, on the "underground" to avoid arrest or to prevent testifying. John Taylor, who had argued he was not violating the law because he had not married a plural wife since before the Morrill Act, operated the church from hiding. Some polygamous groups who still practice plural marriage ("fundamentalists") claim that Taylor, while he was in hiding, received a revelation that the practice of polygamy should continue and ordained several men to continue it outside official sanction. Acting on his new understanding, Taylor married an eighth wife, Josephine Roueche, in 1886. He died the next year.[20]

As might be imagined, the transition away from authorized plural marriage was a time of enormous tensions, especially given the immense efforts and sacrifices of church leaders and members to continue living the "higher law" as federal pressures intensified. Wilford Woodruff initially supported the continued practice of polygamy; but the confiscation of the church's economic resources and especially the threat of seizing the church's four temples (the forty-year project of building the Salt Lake Temple came to fruition during his presidency in 1893), faced him with intolerable alternatives. In 1889, he told Salt Lake reporters that he had refused to authorize any new plural marriages since becoming church president.[21]

A year later on September 15, 1890, he recorded in his journal: "I have arrived at a point in the history of the Church of Jesus Christ of Latter-day Saints where I am under the necessity of acting for the temporal salvation of the Church." The next day, after consultation with some but not all of the apostles, he issued a press release, the Manifesto: "I publicly declare that my advice to the Latter-day Saints is to refrain from contracting any marriages forbidden by the law of the land." Federal officials would not accept the declaration as binding without a sustaining vote by the church membership. They did so a week later at the general conference on October 6, 1890.[22]

Reasons for Living "the Principle"

How did Mormon women react to these events? How did they feel about sharing their husbands? What motivated them to say yes (when they did). And then when that policy changed, how did they feel about giving up the practice of plural marriage? According to written accounts, Mormon women and men were shocked when they first heard that they would be expected to accept a new marriage pattern. The underlying reason that Mormons accepted this practice was they believed that God spoke to a prophet. Annie Richardson Johnson of the Mormon colonies in Mexico, and also a child of a polygamous family, explained, "Like Joseph Smith, polygamists had sealed their testimony, not only with their blood but with the power of acceptance when the principle of Plural Marriage was revealed. . . . This extreme test was possible only because they knew that theirs was the revealed Church of Jesus Christ directed by his priesthood and by revelation and that its blessings came through daily obedience to its principles."[23]

The Mormons gave other reasons for accepting polygamy, but they were justifications of the religious motivations. One was having children who would then grow up in righteous homes. Mormons frequently claimed that children who grew up in polygamous families were more likely to serve missions, marry in the temple, and remain faithful Mormons.[24]

Another reason was that polygamy solved the social problem of prostitution. Orson Pratt explained in his 1852 announcement speech that prostitution could be "prevented in the way the Lord devised in ancient times; that is by giving to his faithful servants a plurality of wives by which a numerous and faithful posterity can be raised up, and taught in the principles of righteousness and truth."[25] When Mormon women held a mass meeting in January 1870 to protest the Cullom Bill, they resolved: "We . . . are believers in the principle of plural marriage or polygamy . . . as an elevating social relationship and a preventative of many terrible evils which afflict our race."[26] Ida Stewart Pacey of Provo contended in a 1937 interview that polygamy cured the "social evil" of prostitution and that some men might not have been faithful husbands if they had not married plural wives.[27]

However, as already noted, the primary motivation was religious. Eunice Stewart Harris summarized the way most polygamous men and women felt about the practice: "I want to bear testimony to my children, my grandchildren, and my great grandchildren, that I know to the very depth of my being that this order of marriage is true, that it was revealed from God, and I thank my Heavenly Father for my testimony."[28]

Sociologist Kimball Young reached the same conclusion, "While we examine the wide range of motives which appear in our records of polygamous families, we note that there is nearly always a basic faith in the principle of plurality of wives. . . . Secondary motives . . . emerged, but since the deeper motives are hidden below the surface of our daily habits, it is not expected that writers of personal documents or informants in interviews would be able to expose their deeper desires in these matters."[29]

Women's Reactions to Polygamy's Commencement and Termination

Despite profound religious motivation, accepting or living polygamy was seldom easy. In 1880 one apostle's wife recalled her initial reactions to polygamy: "I went into the cellar and prayed, but it seemed that the more I prayed, the more my feelings became wrought up. But I did not give up. I stayed there. First I'd weep; then I'd rage in anger and then I'd pray. So I struggled until I was about exhausted. When I was about to give up the effort a great calm settled on my soul. Then I knew . . . polygamy was a true principle of the Lord."[30]

Mormons also had mixed reactions to the Manifesto, although most accepted it as revelation. Annie Gardner, the second wife of John Gardner of Pleasant Grove, spent time in Salt Lake City and Bountiful "on the underground" during the 1880s. She explained, "I was there in the Tabernacle the day of the Manifesto and I tell you it was an awful feeling. There President Woodruff read the Manifesto that made me no longer a wife and might make me homeless. I sat there by my mother and she looked at me and said, 'How can you stand this?' But I voted for it because it was the only thing to do. I raised my hand and voted a thing that would make me an unlawful wife."[31]

Annie Clark Tanner of Farmington, Utah, whose mother was a plural wife and who married into polygamy herself, was on the underground in Franklin, Idaho, when the Manifesto was issued. She said:

> With the long years of sacrifice just back of me, I was easily convinced that it was from the Lord. . . . It was just a coincidence that the doctrine of polygamy was abandoned on my birthday. My first birthday was an event made possible by it; my whole life had been shaped according to it. . . . I can remember so well the relief that I felt when I first realized that the Church had decided to abandon its position. For all of my earliest convictions, a great relief came over me. . . . I suppose [the Church's] leaders may have realized, at last, that if our Church had anything worthwhile for mankind, they had better work with the government of our country rather than against it.[32]

Although it is customary to see the announcement of the Manifesto as a decisive turning point, for Mormons at the time, it ushered in a transitional period that brought its own stresses and trials. At least part of the problem was the complexity of the situation. Even if no new plural marriages were authorized, what was the status of existing marriages? And, during the next fourteen years, other plural marriages *were* secretly authorized by leading church officials, a mixed message that created great confusion. As D. Michael Quinn, who has done the most detailed research on that period, states: "For both the hierarchy and the general membership of the LDS Church, the Manifesto inaugurated an ambiguous era in the practice of plural marriage rivaled only by the status of polygamy during the lifetime of Joseph Smith."[33]

On October 7, 1890, the day after the general conference had voted to accept the Manifesto, the First Presidency and Quorum of the Twelve Apostles met with all of the stake presidents. "President Woodruff drew the attention of the brethren to the fact that the Manifesto did not affect our present family relations but it simply stated that all plural marriages had ceased." Woodruff's counselor George Q. Cannon stated, "A man who will act the coward and shield himself behind the Manifesto by deserting his plural wives should be damned."[34]

Yet in June 1891, the church-owned *Deseret News* published an interview with Woodruff and Cannon. When asked whether they or any officer of the church would authorize a polygamous marriage or countenance unlawful cohabitation, they replied that they would not authorize marriages that did not obey the law.[35]

In October 1891, when Woodruff testified on oath before Judge Charles F. Loofbourow, appointed to decide the fate of church property, he asked Woodruff if the Manifesto covered "living or associating in plural marriage by those already in the status." Woodruff replied, "I intended the proclamation to cover the ground, to keep the law—to obey the law myself and expect the people to obey the law." The judge thus had every reason to believe that the church also expected its members to dissolve plural marriages contracted before the Manifesto. However, on November 12, 1891, Woodruff told the First Presidency and the Twelve that "he was placed in such a position on the witness stand that he could not answer other than he did. Yet any man who deserts and neglects his wives or children because of the Manifesto, should be handled [tried] on his [membership]."[36]

Some couples did separate after the Manifesto. John Brown was a bishop in Pleasant Grove. According to his daughters, "At the time of the Manifesto Father deeded the two homes to the wives. The Church recommended that. Men were supposed to give up their wives (plural) but they were supposed to support them and for safety the Church asked the men to deed the property equally to the wives."[37] Elizabeth Ann Schurtz McDonald of Heber City, a second wife, said that her husband, William McDonald, deeded some of his property to her and provided for her as he had before but did not live with her until after the first wife had died. At that point he married Elizabeth as a legal wife. She explained, "He would have lived with both women, but he had an old country respect for law and his first wife determined that he give the second one up."[38]

Others interpreted the Manifesto as applying only to new marriages. All polygamous General Authorities (church leaders including the First Presidency, Council of the Twelve Apostles, church patriarch, First Council of Seventy, and Presiding Bishopric) continued to cohabit with their wives. Based on impressionistic evidence from family histories and records of births, "most" polygamists followed the General Authorities' example.[39] Conover Wright, the son of Amos Russell Wright and his second wife, Martha Loella Weaver Wright, of Bennington, Idaho, commented in 1938: "After many years of practicing polygamy, it was unreasonable to expect the thing to cease immediately after the Manifesto. Of course, it was never intended that plural wives should stop having children but only that no more marriages should be contracted."[40] This perspective reflects the private statements of General Authorities, not their public statements.

A few children reported that their fathers had specific sanction from church leaders to continue plural relationships. Lorin "Dutch" Leavitt of Bunkerville, Nevada, explained that his father had grown up with Anthony W. Ivins, who first served as a stake president in the Mormon colonies in Mexico and in 1907 was ordained an apostle. Because of this long-standing friendship, Leavitt's father, Thomas Dudley Leavitt, asked his advice during the post-Manifesto period: "'Now, Tony, you know I have the two families and two wives. What am I going to do? Am I going to give one of them up?' . . . He said, 'No, I don't think the Lord intended you to give them up. But I can promise you that if you do keep them and take care of them the Lord will bless you for it.'"[41]

Nor did all new plural marriages end in 1890. Mormon church leaders authorized new plural marriages in both Mexico and Canada, although polygamy was against the law in both of these countries. Because the Canadian government threatened to enforce the law strictly, husbands lived with only one wife in that country, essentially having one legal wife in the United States and one in Canada. The Mexican government wanted colonists and chose to ignore the Mormon marriage practices, so plural families lived together openly.[42]

Apostles also performed authorized marriages in the United States during the transitional period, although it led to difficult adjustments. For instance, Apostle Matthias Cowley was disfellowshipped in 1911 by the First Presidency and Council of the Twelve for performing plural marriages after 1904. He explained as his defense: "I was never instructed to go to a foreign land to perform those marriages. President Cannon told me to do these things or I would have never had done it."[43] George Q. Cannon had been an assistant counselor to Brigham Young and was first counselor in three successive First Presidencies: John Taylor, Wilford Woodruff, and Lorenzo Snow. He had died in 1901, ten years before Cowley's trial.

In March 1904 Joseph F. Smith, who had succeeded Lorenzo Snow as church president in 1901, testified before the Senate Committee on Privileges and Election, admitting his own continued cohabitation with his plural wives and the births of children to them. Then in consultation with the Quorum of the Twelve, Smith presented what historians have called the "Second Manifesto" at April general conference in 1904. It states: "Inasmuch as there are numerous reports in circulation that plural marriages have been entered into contrary to the official declaration of President Wilford Woodruff, . . . I . . . do hereby affirm and declare that no such marriages have been solemnized with the sanction, consent, or knowledge of the Church of Jesus Christ of Latter-day Saints." He stiffened the terms of the Manifesto by announcing a punishment: "If any officer or member of the church shall assume to solemnize or enter into any such marriage he will be deemed in transgression against the church and will be liable to be dealt with according to the rules and regulations thereof and excommunicated therefrom."[44]

It was for his disregard of this Second Manifesto that Cowley was disciplined in 1911. John W. Taylor, another apostle and son of John Taylor, had also continued to perform plural marriages and had, in fact, taken plural wives after the Manifesto. He was also excommunicated in 1911. Both men were replaced in the quorum by men who were monogamously married.[45]

In 1909 a committee of apostles including Francis M. Lyman, John Henry Smith, Heber J. Grant, and George F. Richards met to investigate post-Manifesto polygamy. By 1910, church leaders had a new policy for dealing with polygamists. Those married after 1904 were excommunicated, and those married between 1890 and 1904 were not to have church callings where the members would have to sustain them.[46]

With these more conspicuous efforts to comply with the law, a tacit agreement seemed to develop to let the passage of time and the death of the polygamous generation end the practice. However, many plural husbands and wives continued to cohabit until their deaths in the 1940s. Some plural wives were still living during the 1970s.[47] As the practice died out in the official church, however, it gathered strength and took more definite form among the fundamentalists, who are now estimated to number about 10,000.[48]

Number of Polygamous Families

No definitive study has determined how many Mormons practiced polygamy between the 1840s and 1904. Stanley S. Ivins, the son of Anthony W. Ivins, studied 2,300 polygamous marriages and estimated that 15–20 percent of Mormon women entered plural marriage. He also pointed out that plural marriages were highly responsive to official encouragement from leaders, leading to a somewhat wavelike effect in numbers.[49] Historians Leonard J. Arrington and Davis Bitton estimated that about 12 percent of Mormon wives were plural wives.[50] Larry Logue, who did an intensive study of St. George, documented that as many as two-thirds of the married women's years and one-half of all child years until 1880 occurred in polygamous families.[51] Historian Dean L. May's 1976 study of Kanab found that nearly a quarter (24 percent) of all the town inhabitants—men, women, and children—were members of polygamous families.[52]

Geographer Lowell "Ben" Bennion examined households in the 1880s census and found that the numbers of plural families varied dramatically by community. In Washington County alone, the figure varied from almost 40 percent in St. George to just over 11 percent in Harrisburg/Leeds. In Kane County, the figures went from 10 percent in Rockville to 67 percent in Orderville. In Davis County slightly more than 5 percent practiced polygamy in South Weber in contrast to nearly 30 percent of the families in Bountiful. Springville in Utah County had 15 percent polygamous families. Bennion suggested that the higher percentage of polygamists in St. George reflected greater religious commitment in general since many Mormons had accepted calls from church leaders to settle there and had struggled hard in the harsh environment to fulfill their mission. Those in Orderville lived a United Order and were also committed to follow LDS Church leaders. Other areas might not have been as devout.[53]

POLYGAMY STEREOTYPES

Was there a typical Mormon polygamous family? During the nineteenth century, cartoons showed Brigham Young in bed with many wives, fixing an image in the American mind of Young with his numerous wives as a typical plural husband. Maurine Whipple likewise helped fix more stereotypes in place in her popular 1941 novel *The Giant Joshua.* The family in her novel had three wives: the first wife, a second wife whom the husband married because she was a widow who needed someone to take care of her, and a much younger and prettier third wife. The husband both lusted for the third wife, who had grown up as an orphan in his household, and resented her for being so appealing. He married her when she was sixteen and he was in his forties. As elements of the plot, Whipple portrayed a brief romance between the third wife and the oldest son of the first wife (it ended when he was killed in an accident) and constant tensions between the first and third wives. The second wife rarely stood up for herself and was content to be a sort of servant in the first wife's home. Despite these difficulties, the wives shared a home for years until the third wife demanded a space of her own and started building it herself.[54]

While Whipple described problems that did occur in some families, they were never the norm. In fact, it is difficult to identify a "typical" Mormon polygamous family. Time of marriage, location, and personality, for example, all played major roles in a plural household, just as they did in a traditional monogamous home. For example, the respondents in the LDS Polygamy Oral History Project described turn-of-the century polygamy with its many hardships. A generation earlier, those who lived "the principle" between 1852 and 1880 had to deal with poverty and internal dynamics but not with the added burden of formal and intense opposition from the government.

Maureen Whipple (1903–92), author of *The Giant Joshua,* published in 1941 depicting the settlement of the St. George, Utah, area.

The sources used in this study question some stereotypes. For example, over half of Mormon polygamous men had only two wives. The majority did not charitably marry old maids and widows who needed financial support or lustfully wed young girls. Rather, a husband married his first wife usually when he was in his early twenties and the woman was in her late teens, the same pattern as most monogamous marriages. The second marriage occurred when the groom was in his late twenties to early thirties and the bride was again in her late teens. For the few men who married a third wife, he was typically in his late thirties and the wife again was in her late teens. Thus, the age difference between husband and wife increased but the brides remained about the same age.[55]

Plural wives had about the same number of children as their monogamous counterparts, and first wives usually had more children than the other wives. This pattern was also true when a man monogamously married a second wife after his first had died. The second wife was usually younger than he was, but had fewer children than his first wife. However, even though plural wives had fewer children on average than monogamous wives, plural husbands clearly had more total children than monogamous husbands.[56]

LIFE IN A POLYGAMOUS FAMILY

Since Mormons lived in polygamy for barely half a century and much of that time in secret, there was no time to establish accepted understandings or broadly applied rules of how families should be set up and how family members should react to each other. In contrast are long-term polygamous societies where many decisions are culturally modeled. For example, anthropologist Pamela Blakely found that Bahemba wives in eastern Zaire had separate homes with front doors that faced each other so they could visit while working; but in one case where the wives did not get along, the doors faced in opposite directions. Other African societies had cultural patterns developed over many years that standardized courtship patterns, living arrangements, and husband-visiting patterns.[57] But Mormonism's experience with polygamy lacked such a foundation, so most plural marriage patterns were minor adaptations of monogamous U.S. and European traditions.

Courtships and Proposals

The decision to marry a plural wife, the proposal, and her agreement may be considered a courtship stage. Nineteenth-century society, while it valued romantic love, did not see it as either a requirement or a justification for contracting marriage, whether monogamous or polygamous. As one nineteenth-century marriage manual explained, "A married couple should feel love for each other, . . . [but] the love should grow out of the relationship rather than be the cause of it." Religious motivations, temperance, family-centeredness, and physical considerations including beauty, intelligence, and health to ensure good offspring, the manual continued, were more important than love.[58]

First wives most often cited religious reasons as their motivation in agreeing to a plural marriage. Sometimes the first wife even initiated the decision because she felt so strongly that accepting the principle was essential for her salvation and that of her husband. According to Emma Hoth McNeil of Logan, the second wife of William McNeil, "The first wife sanctioned it! She was more anxious about it than he was."[59]

In a few cases, the first wife accepted polygamy because she had no children and wanted her husband to have offspring, an important element in LDS doctrine. After childless Wealthy Clark of Bountiful agreed to let her husband marry a plural wife, she had a child and considered its birth as a reward for her obedience, the fulfillment of a promise given to her by a Mormon church leader.[60]

Young women who looked forward to marriage also had to decide if they would be willing to and capable of sharing their husbands. Most, though not all, were motivated by religious considerations as they contemplated marrying already-married men. Lula Roskelley Mortensen of Smithfield, Utah, said that, although her mother's parents were not polygamists, all of their children married in the principle because "that's when polygamy was flourishing the most." She was responding to the stress laid on the principle in official church teachings. Also, she grew up in a plural household, since her father had married two sisters, Margaret and Agnes Wildman.[61] Laura Fackrell Chamberlain, the second wife of Thomas Chamberlain of Orderville said, "I accepted polygamy just as natural as anything. My own father had three wives and I believed in the Principle. I wanted to live it so I could get the blessings."[62] For some polygamy was just the norm. Sigrid Hockenson Skanchy, the third wife of Anthon Skanchy of Logan observed that "a girl would judge the man and if he suited her she would take him in those days and not pay attention to polygamy"—meaning that she did not rule out a married man.[63]

Mary Minerva Clark Bennion of Farmington, Utah, prayed that she would be guided to the man that she should marry. She dreamed of meeting people after church; as she shook one man's hand, a dove landed on his shoulder. Later as she was shaking her husband-to-be's hand, that dream flashed back and she accepted it as her confirmation, even though he was already married.[64]

Others had more practical motivations. Heber C. Maughan pointed out that his mother, Elizabeth Prater Maughan, married Peter Maughan of Cache Valley because she was unhappy living with her brother and being financially dependent on him.[65] According to Winnifred Harker Smith, her mother, Sarah Elizabeth Carter Harker, agreed to be a plural wife because the first wife, Alice Jane Bennion of Taylorville, was ill and unable to care for her children. She said, "I had a boyfriend I could have married, but I saw the need of somebody to take care of a family."[66]

While the belief is widespread that church leaders had to "call" men to marry polygamously or at least give permission before a man could contract a plural marriage, these examples show that the decision to marry in polygamy did not come from one source. Based on my research, there was not a typical courtship and marriage for polygamy just as there is not for monogamous marriages. Some indeed married because Brigham Young (or another church leader) instructed them to. Others heard general advice that polygamy was an important gospel principle and applied it personally. Some had deep personal convictions, reinforced by spiritual experiences, that polygamy was essential for their salvation in the next life. There probably were some men who lusted after a young woman. Although documentation on such cases is rarer, it is clear that the motivations for plural marriage ranged from the pure to the not-so-pure.

Living Arrangements and Visiting Schedules

After a plural marriage occurred, those involved had to determine household arrangements. As in other aspects of Mormon polygamy, no one pattern controlled where wives lived and how often husbands visited. However, some of the more common patterns can be identified. Often the wives shared a home just after a second marriage; but when it became financially possible, the husband provided a separate dwelling for each wife. Usually the wives lived in the same community, but schooling arrangements, economic conditions, pressure from law enforcement, and personal preference sometimes determined that wives lived in different towns. As children were born, grew, and left home, living arrangements also changed. Another frequent cause of change was when a wife, particularly one who was pregnant or who had a new baby, had to go on the underground to avoid being forced to testify against her husband.

Because most plural wives lived separately, husbands developed rotating schedules so that they visited each family at regular intervals. Sometimes when wives did not live in the same community, the husband visited irregularly, or only on weekends or at harvest time.

In 150 cases of couples from the Redd Center oral histories, 47 percent of the wives shared homes for a while after the husband married an additional wife. Nearly one-quarter of the wives lived in separate homes in the same town, and 19 percent lived in different towns.

A small fraction of the wives continued to share homes once they started having children. But 55 percent had separate homes in the same town after children arrived. Caroline Pederson Hansen shared a two-room home with her husband's first wife, Bengta, after her marriage in 1878 but prayed secretly for a separate house. After her husband returned from a seven-month mission, her father gave her some land, and her husband built a small adobe house. She later wrote, "I shall never forget how happy I was, and as soon as we were in and I was alone, I bowed down before the Lord and poured out my soul in prayer and gratitude for having a house of my own."[67]

James Carson Allen had separate homes for his wives, Betsy and Ellen, in Cove, Cache County, until the children were old enough to go to high school. Then Betsy moved to Logan to keep house for the children who were attending Brigham Young College in Logan, while Nellie remained in Cove about fifteen miles away with the younger children. Evan B. Murray, the son of William Archibald Murray and his second wife, Amanda Bailey Murray, of Wellsville, said that both the children's needs and economics determined where his father's two wives, Amanda and Sara Jane Park Murray, lived. "One house was on the farm where most of the boys from both families lived, and one house was in town which served as a place for children to live who were working or going to school."[68]

Just as there was no standard living arrangement in plural homes, there was no predetermined plan for how much time the husband spent with each wife, although he was expected to establish some pattern of visiting each family. Of the 156 families used in this study, 27 percent of the husbands changed homes nightly, 21 percent moved every week, 8 percent had no routine, and 21 percent stayed primarily with one wife. Douglas Cannon recalled that his father, David Henry Cannon, "used to be in our home every third night, regular as clockwork. He stayed at one house one night, the next house the next night, and our house the third night." David worked in the St. George Temple all day, "but he was home at one or the other of these homes every night," all of which were easily accessible in St. George. Douglas also recalled it was his responsibility each day to take his father's shaving kit to the home where he would be staying.[69]

Wives were sometimes lonely. Martha Hughes Cannon, the fourth wife of Angus Cannon of Salt Lake City, wrote in February 1888 that she had "a thorough knowledge from God, that the *principle* for which we are battling and striving to maintain in purity upon the earth is ordained by Him, and that we are chosen instruments in His hands to engage in so great a calling." Still, she acknowledged: "Even with this assurance grounded in one's heart, we do not escape trial and temptations, grievances at times in our nature."[70] Emmeline B. Wells, the sixth wife of Daniel H. Wells of Salt Lake City, lamented: "Oh if my husband could only love me even a little. . . . He is surrounded by love on every side, and I am cast out."[71] Julia Winter Smith, the second wife of Samuel Smith of Salt Lake City, commented, "He didn't spend his time equally with us. He had to be where his business was and other interests. There were months at a time when I was down on that ten acre lot alone with the children."[72] Children occasionally disagreed on why their fathers adopted a certain schedule. Meda Lucille Jenkins Parker said that her father, John Jenkins of Newton, stayed mainly with her mother, the third wife, Anna Marie Jensen Jenkins, because "there was more room down there for animals."[73] Archie Jenkins, a son of the second wife, Annie Clarke Jenkins, said that, when his father stayed more with another family, "we felt sometimes maybe there was a little more fatherly love in the first family than we were receiving. . . . My mother was a very unselfish woman. She never complained, and she just took things in stride as the days went on."[74] He did not mention the need to take care of animals.

Sometimes the decision to stay with only one wife was based on family income. When George Conrad Naegle and his families left Mexico during the revolution in 1912, Sabra Naegle Foremaster's mother (third wife Maggie Romney Naegle) was dead, and Sabra was living with her father's other families. Sabra said, that during the 1920s when her father decided to move from St. George to Salt Lake City to sell insurance, his fifth wife, Jennie Dora Jameson, insisted that he take her and her family because she was tired of the criticism about polygamy and the other surviving wife (fourth wife Philinda Keeler Naegle) could support herself with tailoring and teaching. "Father hoped to be able to support both families, but after three years he was not able to help Linnie." Eventually Linnie moved to New Mexico to be near her parents.[75]

Age and children were also considerations in deciding where a husband would live. An older husband sometimes "settled down" with just one wife. Ida Stewart Pacey of Provo said of her father, Andrew J. Stewart, Jr., "A man has his 'gallivanting' when he can be interested in more than one woman. That is until he is about 50 years old. After then, even the polygamist, in my experience

Polygamist home located in Lake Shore, Utah, ca. 1890. (Note the entrances on both sides of the house.)

seems to settle down at one place."[76] Franklin Lyman Stout said his father, David Fisk Stout, of Mexico and then Logan, lived with the youngest wife in his later years because she had a younger family who needed his help. The children of his other three wives were grown at that point.[77]

On a rotational schedule, it was natural that a husband/father's visit was something of an occasion. Wasel Black Washburn of Blanding was thrilled when her father's visit fell on Christmas. Elna Cowley Austin, a daughter of Mormon Apostle Matthias Cowley said that, when he came to see her mother, Luella Smith Parkinson in Logan, "his visits were marvelous. We prepared for them. Mother was just singing and so thrilled. 'Oh, Papa is coming. Now all of you be just as nice as you can, for Papa will be here.'" In contrast, other families were relieved when the man left. Alma Elizabeth Mineer Felt of Salt Lake City, the second wife of Joseph Felt, said, "He spent a week with each one of us, and I tell you, I was as glad to see his back as I was to see his face. As I grew older, more and more I valued my independence and my personal freedom."[78]

Relationships of Plural Wives

In addition to working out a relationship and schedule with the husband, plural wives also had to determine how they would relate to their husband's other wives. In a modern context where romantic love and sexual relationships constitute an exclusive bond in marriage, polygamy elicits the emotional question of how one woman regarded another woman who had her church's sanction for sharing her husband's affections and bed. As might be expected, the reports range from idyllic harmony in a shared conviction of doing God's will to open jealousies and tensions. Marital relationships caused some problems; but others, while ultimately stemming from sharing a husband resulted more from economic pressures, personality differences, and unfulfilled expectations, which were similar to any family's problems.

Mary E. Croshaw Farrell of Smithfield, the fourth wife of George H. Farrell, felt that most domestic disagreements in polygamous families were caused by financial problems.[79] Charles Smith Merrill, a son of Clarence Merrill and his first wife Bathsheba Smith Merrill, added, "Polygamy is ideal for a celestial personage because you are not worrying ever about something to eat or something to buy or if one wife's skirt is made of silk and the other of cotton. . . . Aunt Julia and my mother didn't get along too well because my mother had money and [Aunt Julia] . . . didn't have any money to buy her a new dress or anything for herself. There was a lot of black air around there." He did not explain how his mother got more money than Julia.[80] Julia was a daughter of George A. Smith, a counselor in the First Presidency, and Bathsheba Wilson Bigler Smith, his first wife; thus, she may have inherited some money after her father's death in 1875; or her mother, who lived until 1910, may have given her presents. Clarence's plural wife divorced him, citing his unwillingness or inability to provide for her and her children. She explained, "My trouble wasn't polygamy. That was nothing. Bathsheba was a lovely, kind person and we got along. She was good to me. . . . But . . . he could not support me and I could not endure it because I was ambitious for myself and children."[81]

When money was tight, personality differences could exacerbate jealousies. Julia Bateman Jensen, a daughter of Samuel Bateman and his first wife, saw the second wife as a "petty, whimper kind." When her mother had a new dress, the second wife insisted she should have one. She continued to complain even when Julia's mother was living away from Samuel and being supported by Julia. Even then, if Julia bought her mother a new dress, the second wife also got one.[82] Mary Jane Rigby Roskelley of Smithfield complained of being "very poor." She felt that the five wives had to get everything on their own. Their husband provided the "stuff" such as "land, and cows, and sheep" to earn a living but they had to do the work. She felt that her sister and co-wife, Maggie, had an advantage because she had a millinery store and "didn't have to milk cows like we did."[83]

What appeared to be unequal divisions of financial resources and time often led to disputes. William Roskelley of Smithfield married two sisters, Margaret and Agnes Wildman Roskelley. The children's combined stories show that William may have favored Margaret. When William filed on a homestead in Weston, Idaho, he settled Margaret on the claim in a one-room log house. There she struggled with crop failures, visiting tramps, and new babies, but she stayed until William acquired title. In return, William promised to build Margaret a new home. He did; but because of financial setbacks, it took him five years to complete the eleven-room house. Agnes, in contrast, lived in smaller homes. The first family recognized that the second family resented them for having a larger home, but they justified the difference because Margaret had twelve children while Agnes had only four; and Margaret had earned the house by living on the homestead.[84]

Living arrangements were not the only area of dispute. According to Zina Roskelley Bell, a daughter of the first wife, Margaret, her father felt that he should not live with both wives openly after the Manifesto. Instead he spent the night occasionally with Agnes but lived most of the time with Margaret. Zina continued, "I felt bad . . . because I felt like my aunt was neglected as a wife when my mother had my father most of the time." William also allowed Margaret to divide the fruit and other produce that he provided. Margaret split the supplies according to the number of children in each family so she got more. Rebecca Roskelley Lewis, Margaret's daughter, said, "They tried to be fair, really!" But Agnes's daughter, Lula Roskelley Mortensen, felt that Margaret tried to control her mother. "The pantry window [at Margaret's home] had so many memories attached, . . . the peg for the milk pail, the bucket for the eggs and the mail and other things that were meant for us. This was sort of a watch tower to observe the happenings at our home and to keep a tab on everything."[85]

Shared goods and equipment could create hard feelings, but most families worked out ways to resolve their differences. Ann Amelia Chamberlain Esplin said that her father's five wives had to share the washing tubs and each wife had her own washing day. But rather than resenting this schedule, the wives learned to share. She cited as an example one day when Laura asked to use the washing machine when it was Ann's turn. Ann dumped her water out and sent the equipment over. "One of the other ladies said, 'I wouldn't do it if I were you. She knows what her washday is.' . . . [Ann] said, 'I can wash tomorrow and it may not be convenient for her to do that.'" Daughter Ann explained: "That's the spirit they carried through. They'd have to live in peace."[86]

The issue of sexual jealousy was difficult to identify in the sources because of their reticence to talk of such matters. Isabel McFarland Bingham of Smithfield, the second wife of Parley Pratt Bingham and the younger sister of Margaret, the first wife, married Parley because she was "dead in love" with him. She explained, "Certainly she [Margaret] was jealous sometimes. So was I. It's natural enough to be jealous and my sister was human. Yes, I'm sure she had a pretty hard time in the early days. But we understood the situation and did everything we could to make her feel all right. She was the first wife and she had a right to be jealous." She continued, "I guess she shed buckets of tears, and I shed plenty, too. We knew she was going through an awful trial. I never did get cross with her. No, I don't feel as if the second wife has as much right to be jealous as has the first."[87]

Elizabeth (Lizzie) Adams McFarland, the third wife of John M. McFarland of St. George, acknowledged the pressures of polygamy: "Looking back I can't blame either of his wives for any of their actions towards me. I'd have done the same or worse. They had the harder lot to bear, seeing me, a young woman, come into the family. I know if that had come to me I'd have made a lot of trouble. We were jealous. No woman can help being jealous, if she loves her husband. But we went into it knowing what to expect. I have heard women say that when their husband was spending their times with the other wives, that they spent the night in agony. We weren't like that. We knew it had to be and we knew that he loved us all. . . . In a few years we got over the jealousies, and we were happy together, but for all that, the only real happiness of its kind I had was when I was alone with my husband in Mexico."[88]

Equally important were the women's personalities and how they adjusted to the polygamous lifestyle or how adept they were at schooling or concealing their feelings. Ruth May Fox of Salt Lake City said that her husband Jesse Fox's second wife "was a good woman, but we were not alike in many ways. I was more reserved."[89] Margaret and Agnes Wildman Roskelley had very different personalities. Lula Roskelley Mortensen, Agnes's daughter, said, "Aunt Maggie was a small woman with a fierce scowl, piercing black eyes and a shrill voice. . . . I was scared to death of both her and Dad." Even Margaret's children recognized that their mother had some less than desirable characteristics. Her daughter, Roxey Roskelley Rogers, explained that her mother "could just turn you off. She didn't know you existed." Another of Margaret's daughters, Rebecca Roskelley Lewis, felt that her mother was strong willed. "She didn't argue or cause any trouble, but I think she had her own mind about things." In contrast, Lula said Agnes was a "gentle, quiet, submissive, wonderful woman (too gentle for own good). . . . She never asserted her rights or desires, always trying to 'get along' and 'be agreeable' especially in this situation of plural marriage." Her half-sister, Rebecca, explained it as: Agnes "didn't have spunk as she should have had."[90]

Given the many opportunities and motivations for disagreement, Mormon plural wives seem surprisingly congenial. Of 197 families for which information was available, almost half the wives had only minor disputes. Only about 13 percent reported jealousy so intense that a wife left her husband or avoided the other wives completely. About 30 percent did not show jealousy. Since much of this information came from children, they might not have known about minor disputes or their mothers' hidden feelings, and some acknowledged that they had no way of knowing what their mothers really thought or felt. Still a commitment to the institution of plural marriage and the religious commitments that led the wives into polygamy also motivated them to overcome jealousies. Although there were differences and even jealousies between wives, most were minor and easily resolved or suppressed.

Mary Elizabeth Woolley Chamberlain, the sixth wife of Thomas Chamberlain, explained how personality and religious commitment combined to lead to good relationships. "Right now I want to pay a tribute of love and appreciation to those wives. . . . A better set of women never lived. If they ever had any ill feeling or jealousy toward me, it was locked in their hearts, and never came to the surface, for they have always treated me with the greatest love and respect. I love them as dearly as my own sisters, and there is nothing I would not do to help them if I could."[91] Alma Elizabeth Mineer Felt recalled visiting the third wife in California when they were both older. During a gin rummy game, a non-Mormon player, in casual conversation, wondered how plural wives got along. "I pointed to my rummy partner and said that we were polygamists and had lived in the same house together. They thought it quite remarkable that polygamist wives could play rummy peacefully together."[92]

Women in plural marriage had ample opportunity and motive to fight for increased status, gain a greater share of their husbands' affections, acquire greater power in the family, or dominate a greater share of the family resources. Yet the wives got along remarkably well. Kimball Young pointed out that only 23 percent of the marriages in his study showed considerable to severe conflict. Some disagreements led to formal divorce, although, given the ambiguous status of plural marriages during much of this period, it is sometimes difficult to tell when a separated couple felt that their marriage was "over." A liberal territorial divorce law made a split easy for the first wife.[93] David Osborne, a polygamist from Hyrum, separated from his second wife after they wrote and signed their own agreement of settlement.[94]

Plural wives, like other women in the nineteenth century, united particularly over the common tasks of women: childbirth and illness. One historian called this special effort "the sisterhood of the sickbed."[95] Elizabeth Ann Schurtz McDonald, the second wife of William McDonald said, "I nursed a great many of [the first wife's] children. She had trouble with her milk and I didn't so when we had children together, I always helped to take care of them. When she was sick, I went right into her home and stayed with her."[96]

In a few cases, the wives became even closer than husband and wife. Cynthia and Kesiah Allen, the two wives of Ira Allen, shared a home in Hyrum for thirty years. After Allen returned from serving time in the penitentiary for unlawful cohabitation, he felt he was under a legal obligation to live with only one. He reportedly said, "Two women who have lived together for 30 years in such peace and harmony and reared their children under one roof and eaten at one table, shall never be separated by me." He moved to a vacant house where he lived alone.[97] The 1870 and 1880 census reports verify that Cynthia and Kesiah Allen lived in the same house.

As these examples demonstrate, plural marriage could intensify the conflicts that would occur in any marriage. Mormon polygamy did not endure for enough generations to normalize patterns of behavior. As a result, co-wives modeled their relationships on other female relationships common from their European American background: mother-daughter (especially if there was an age difference), friends, and most commonly, sisters. In 25 percent of the families sampled for this study, the wives were biological sisters. Kimball Young reported that 20 percent of the men in his study married sisters, following an Old Testament pattern. But even if the wives were not related, the sister pattern seemed to fit, since it accommodated both affection but also competition and jealousy commonly found among siblings.[98]

WOMEN'S ROLES

Courtships, living arrangements, husbands' schedules, and relationships with co-wives were distinctive elements in polygamy, but they fit into an already existing social framework that accommodated plural marriages. A comparison of the plural and monogamous wives documented in the Kimball Young collection and the LDS Polygamy and LDS Family Life Oral History Projects at the Redd Center show that polygamous and monogamous wives did the same work. Rather than being forced from the home as Harriet Beecher Stowe suggested or seizing opportunities to establish feminist careers, plural wives, like their monogamous counterparts, departed from the traditional work norm only when pressing circumstances required it, returning to these roles whenever possible. In a parallel situation, historians have found that women performed masculine tasks primarily while crossing the plains.[99]

For the most part, wives worked within their homes, gardens, and yards. Women made virtually every household item except furniture—soap, clothes (often carding, spinning, and weaving), and rugs. They also raised or processed almost all the food their families ate except wheat and flour. They grew extensive gardens and tended orchards. To provide the cash to buy sugar, baking powder, or other items that they could not produce, some sold the excess butter, eggs, and other produce, sold weaving, laundered, cooked, or took in boarders. A few worked outside the home, but usually only for short periods of time during economic emergencies and then only in occupations such as teaching children and nursing that were an "extension of the domestic expressive role."[100]

Polygamy has produced two economic stereotypes. One is that polygamous men were well-to-do church and community leaders who could afford to support plural wives. Their wives were "proto-feminists," involved in activities outside the home and frequently with careers like doctor, editor, midwife, and social reformer. It is true that prominent church leaders usually were more affluent. David Cannon said that the families of his father, George Mousley Cannon, were not "a real example of how polygamy was because I think we were better off than a lot of polygamous families."[101]

It is also true that many plural wives were involved in church auxiliaries, clubs, and the suffrage movement. Scholars frequently refer to Ellis Shipp and

Romania Pratt who went to the eastern United States to study medicine and Martha Hughes Cannon who was a doctor and became a member of the Utah State Senate, winning in a multi-candidate race that also included her husband. According to these studies, these elite women could be both mothers and careerists because their sister wives helped care for their children.

It is true that Ellis Shipp sometimes left her children with a sister wife while she went to medical school. But the question remains: Did polygamy prompt Shipp to become a doctor? Or was Shipp simply like other talented and ambitious women throughout the United States at the turn of the century who found a way to be active in the community and in the home? In other words, did polygamy liberate the elite women or was it simply another factor in a complex formula that allowed certain women the luxury of stepping out of their traditional roles?

Probably this "either/or" question is really a "both/and" one. Many women who served on the general boards of the Relief Society, Young Ladies Mutual Improvement Association, and Primary, who became active in the women's club movement around the turn of the century, and who supervised the women suffrage movement in Utah were the daughters and wives of Mormon church leaders who were, more frequently than "ordinary" members, likely to be polygamists. But just as in other areas of the United States, these women probably would have had leadership positions without polygamy because of their education, comparative affluence, and social position, largely derived from their fathers' and husbands' status. Like the elite women who formed clubs in Memphis, Tennessee, Mormon plural wives were active in social reform in Utah.[102] But if they had been the monogamous wives of their husbands, they would have still occupied a privileged social position.

The second economic stereotype is that polygamous men were not able to support their large families so many wives were forced to provide for themselves. While some plural wives like Belle Harris Merrill Nelson Berry felt that their husbands did not provide adequately for them and their children, polygamy was not the only cause. Some Mormon families struggled economically because of poor land, crop failures, and many other problems common across the frontier. Some wives, both monogamous and polygamous, described their poverty and the need to provide some of their own support. Monogamous wife Molly Law Jacobs gleaned wheat so that she could earn money for bacon.[103] Lydia Hall Turner, the daughter of a monogamous marriage, said, "Mother made straw hats to sell. We would glean the wheat, cut the heads off, and soak the straw in water. I braided the straw while she sewed."[104] Rose Brown Haynes and Mrs. Clark, daughters of John Brown's second and third wives, recalled that one wife took in washings and spent the money on "all of us." They added, "Each wife did whatever she could."[105] Plural wife Sarah Jardine Shumway of Clarkston kept boarders so she could buy the things she wanted for her home.[106]

Although polygamy raised the level of need, it also increased the number of hands to do the work, generally an advantage in a labor-intensive economy. Mary Ann Mansfield Bentley, the wife of Israel Bentley of St. George, divided the workload with her co-wives. Isabel, the first wife, had no children, so twice a year she traveled from southern Utah to Salt Lake City to trade the family's molasses, dried fruit, and other goods for needed materials. Joan, the second wife, wove cloth. Margaret, the third wife, kept their communally occupied home. Marie, another wife and Mary Ann's full sister, dried fruit to sell for supplies. Mary Ann also helped Joan with the weaving and Margaret with the housework. She added, "Besides these heavier duties there was [sic] always carpet rags to sew, quilts to make, stockings to knit, clothing to sew, and in fact so many things to do that our recreation usually consisted in a change of occupation only."[107]

With no established pattern on how to divide work, each family adapted its monogamous traditions to meet its specific needs. For example, in the Nathaniel Morris Hodges family, the first two wives, sisters Louisa and Anna Weston, usually lived together on the family ranch near Bear Lake. Louisa, who liked working outside, took charge of the cows. Anna did most of the housework. Charlotte Hancock, the third wife, had her own home.[108]

A variation of the financially independent plural wife involves the absent missionary-husbands. While married men with young children are not called on missions now, it was a common practice at the turn of the century whether they were polygamous or monogamous. Usually these missions lasted two or three years. Just as wives crossing the plains sometimes stepped out of their traditional roles to take on masculine chores, so did the wives of missionaries. But they returned to their domestic roles as soon as possible after their husbands returned. Polygamy was not a factor in this temporary change of work assignments.[109]

There was no typical way that the wives of missionary husbands cared for their families. Quite frequently, the women became as self-sufficient as possible. Caroline Pederson Hansen, speaking for herself and her co-wife, wrote in her autobiography, "We were very thankful and proud of our husband that he was considered worthy to go on another mission. The Lord has blessed us greatly during the past three years. We had no debts, we each had our own comfortable little home, we were well provided with clothing, we had our cows to milk, some chickens and pigs. The same farms we had gave us some income. We had wood stacked up to last us and we got along happily."[110] Joseph Gibbons and his first wife, Mercy Weston Gibbons, moved from Ogden to Laketown near Bear Lake. When Joseph went on a mission, Mercy took over the farm and reported proudly that Joseph was "kind of surprised when he came back and found what a nice farm we had built up while he was gone."[111]

Other families of missionaries received help from the church or from neighbors. Arthur O. Chapman, a son in a monogamous family, recalled that the stake quorum of seventies helped support his father while his mother took

Dr. Ellis Reynolds Shipp (1847–1939) with one of her graduating classes in obstetrics and nursing, ca 1899.

in laundry to support the family.[112] When John Brown of Pleasant Grove went on a mission, his two wives, one of them pregnant, were about to move into a new home. "The people in the community helped." The cobbler gave shoes and the storekeeper let the family have what they needed. Other neighbors let them stay in their home during the winter while the men finished the new house.[113] Marianne Stettler of Logan, the only wife of Samuel Stettler, had neighbors and friends who helped with the farm work.[114] Henry Earl Day remembered his mother stepping into the gap left when his father went on a mission. "[She] still had the chores. She still had a team of horses. . . . We had some cows, and she had to milk the cows every day." Fortunately, however, "my Uncle Arza took over the farm and ran the farm when Father left."[115]

ECONOMIC INFLUENCES ON WOMEN

A prolonged agricultural depression between 1890 and World War II also changed economic conditions for both monogamous and polygamous families. Monogamous child Vera Christensen recalled constant moves to find work between Richfield and Elsinore between 1910 and 1913, when she was born because "the cattle and sheep business was going downhill." The family then moved to Pima, Arizona, and to farming communities in Idaho. As the children grew, "it became a series of moves from one farm to another ranch to another farm. We would move out to a farm in the summer and back into the town where the schools were because both my father and mother wanted us children to have good advantages with a good education. By the time my father and mother had reached their twenty-fifth anniversary we had moved twenty-six times." During the 1930s, her father started working at Ironton Steel Plant near Provo so that Vera's brothers could attend Brigham Young University. When her father was laid off, he tried to find carpentry jobs. Her mother went back to school and completed a teaching certificate. Utah did not allow married women to teach, so the family returned to Idaho. Later they lived in Logan so that her mother could work in Idaho and her father could find jobs in Cache Valley.[116]

The polygamous families forced to leave Mexico in 1912 suffered sometimes irreversible financial losses. Charles Edmund Richardson, an attorney in Mexico, wanted to keep all of his families together in Thatcher, Arizona. His second wife, Sarah, however, saw little hope of breaking out of the spiral of poverty and moved to Snowflake, Arizona, where she could be near her brothers. Initially the other three wives stayed in Thatcher, but Edmund had trouble finding work. Sadie, the first wife, and Becky, the third, could earn extra money, but Daisie, the fourth, was so crippled with arthritis that she was unable to provide for herself. Finally, acting on the advice of the stake president, she moved to Logan where her father helped care for her and her children.[117]

The death of a husband had profound negative effects on the family's economic condition. Lizzie McFarland, the third wife of John M. McFarland of St. George recalled that, after her husband died in 1900, the wives divided the property equally. The other wives had children who could help them, but Lizzie's children were too small. She cleaned the schoolhouse, then worked in hotels, and also did washing, ironing, and cooking.[118]

Thomas Chamberlain of Orderville, who died in 1918, left each of his six wives with a good home but no ready money. Mary Elizabeth Woolley Chamberlain, the sixth wife, recalled that her sons worked in the fields, while Mary made and sold butter. She baked cookies, which she sold to tourists, and she also made and sold hats.[119]

Monogamous wives also had to provide from themselves during widowhood. Lula A. Rigby Larsen's father, William Frederick Rigby Jr., died when she was four, leaving her mother, Sarah Angeline Clarke Rigby, to care for twelve children. She recalled, "We did not have a lot of money, but we always had good food because we grew big gardens. We had our own chickens. We had milk, and we had meat." Her mother sold butter. "People in town would request that they got Sarah Rigby's butter because they had used it year after year and liked it." The family also sold eggs. Lula remembered her mother would let her use one egg to spend for candy. But although Sarah took care of her children and provided a happy home life, Lula said her mother took William's death "very hard. She had been president of the Primary and president of the Relief Society and had been very active in the Church. I suppose it was because of the sorrow, strain and all. After that I don't remember her going out too much."[120]

Summary

Did Mormon polygamy move Utah women into a lifespan pattern different than those women who were monogamous? While some nineteenth-century contemporaries of those women argued that polygamy destroyed the family and later scholars applauded the plural wives' independence, my conclusion, based on the data reported here, is that neither case was typical. Individual situations and personalities were important in how plural wives responded to their situations.

Since the Mormon church did not have established rules on how to set up a plural household, wives and husbands adapted monogamous traditions to create a new lifestyle. Such distinctive elements as courtship, marriage, and living arrangements required variations from the monogamous pattern; but as the many examples show, no uniform pattern existed. In the same way that no two monogamous families are ever exactly the same, no two polygamous families were either. Plural wives had to relate to another wife or wives and to her children (and also to her husband's relationship to that other wife and children). They modeled those relationships on relationships inherited from the larger monogamous culture. Because of their religious commitment and their acceptance of polygamy as God's commandment, many plural wives overlooked or suppressed the expected jealousies and worked hard on adapting themselves to their new marriage style.

A focus on how polygamy was different from monogamy overlooks the many ways in which women's lives were the same in both polygamous and monogamous households. Women did the same type of work in both. They depended on similar resources when the husband was absent, whether he was working out of the community, serving a mission, or dead. Polygamy did not create a unique family style but rather adapted traditional nineteenth- and early twentieth-century women's roles.

Notes

1. Lois Kelley was writing the original article on polygamy for this volume. Unfortunately, her death prevented her from finishing it. Her friends attempted to complete the chapter as a memorial to her but it was not sufficiently close to completion. While Lois would not have agreed with all of my conclusions, I have tried to use some of her material to give her a voice in this book. —Jessie L. Embry

2. Harriet Beecher Stowe, quoted in Julie Roy Jeffrey, *Frontier Women: The Trans-Mississippi West, 1840–1880* (New York: Hill and Wang, 1979), 149.

3. Joan Smyth Iverson, "Feminist Implications of Mormon Polygyny," *Feminist Studies* 10 (1984): 502–22; see also Stephanie Smith Goodman, "Plural Wives," in *Mormon Sisters,* edited by Claudia L. Bushman (Salt Lake City: Olympus Publishing, 1976), 104–5.

4. Julie Roy Jeffrey, *Frontier Women: Civilizing the West?: 1840–1880,* (New York: Hill and Wang, 1979), 182; rev. ed. (New York: Hill and Wang, 1998), 150. This quotation combines the wording from both editions.

5. My focus here is the experiences of plural wives and how they compare to those of monogamous wives during the same time period in Utah. While this paper provides some historical background, interested readers should turn to other sources for a more complete background, beginning with the two bibliographic essays, Martha Sonntag Bradley, "Out of the Closet and into the Fire: The New Mormon Historians' Take on Polygamy," and Todd Compton, "The New Mormon Women's History," in *Excavating Mormon Pasts: The New Historiography of the Last Half Century,* edited by Newell G. Bringhurst and Lavina Fielding Anderson (Salt Lake City: Greg Kofford Books, 2004), 303–23, and 273–303 respectively; Davis Bitton, "Mormon Polygamy [1907–77]," *Journal of Mormon History* (1977): 1-118; Patricia Lyn Scott, "Mormon Polygamy: A Bibliography, 1977–92," *Journal of Mormon History* 19 (Spring 1993): 1993–55); and Patricia Lyn Scott, "Mormon Polygamy: A Bibliography, 1900–2004," in *Wrestling with the Principle: Essays from the Journal of Mormon History,* edited by Lavina Fielding Anderson, introduction by Larry Foster (Salt Lake City: Signature Books, forthcoming).

6. James Edward Hulett, Jr., "The Sociological and Social Psychological Aspects of the Mormon Polygamous Family" (Ph.D. diss., University of Wisconsin, 1939); Kimball Young, *Isn't One Wife Enough?* (New York: Henry Holt and Co., 1954).

7. Elsie Chamberlain Carroll, interviewed by James Hulett, 1937, 4, Kimball Young Collection, Perry Special Collections, Harold B. Lee Library, Brigham Young University, Provo, Utah.

8. Doctrine and Covenants (Salt Lake City: Church of Jesus Christ of Latter-day Saints, 1981), section 132, verses 3, 61; hereafter parenthetically in the text as D&C by section and verse.

9. Todd Compton, "Fanny Alger Smith Custer," *Journal of Mormon History* 22 (Spring 1996): 174–207; and his *In Sacred Loneliness: The Plural Wives of Joseph Smith* (Salt Lake City: Signature Books, 1997), 25–43.

10. Emma's opposition is referred to in verses 51–57 of this revelation and, when Hyrum read it to her, she not only rejected its content but burned it. Richard S. Van Wagoner, *Polygamy: A History* (Salt Lake City: Signature Books, 1986), 4, 6; Danel W. Bachman, "New Light on an Old Hypothesis: The Ohio Origins of the Revelation on Eternal Life," *Journal of Mormon History* 5 (1978), 19–32; Linda King Newell and Valeen Tippets Avery, *Mormon Enigma: Emma Hale Smith: Prophet's Wife, "Elect Lady," Polygamy's Foe* (New York: Doubleday and Co., 1984), 152, also see 95–105, 130–56, 297–98.

11. Van Wagoner, *Polygamy: A History,* 22–23, 65–69.

12. Orson Pratt, August 29, 1952, *Journal of Discourses,* 27 vols. (Liverpool and London: Latter-day Saint Book Depot, 1843–86), 1:53–66.

13. Juanita Brooks, *On the Mormon Frontier: The Diary of Hosea Stout,* 2 vols. (Salt Lake City: University of Utah Press, 1964), 2:449–50.

14. Quoted in Gustive O. Larson, "Government, Politics, and Conflict," in *Utah's History,* edited by Richard D. Poll, Thomas G. Alexander, Eugene E. Campbell, and David E. Miller (Provo, Utah: Brigham Young University Press, 1978), 244.

15. Van Wagoner, *Polygamy: A History,* 107–9; Larson, "Government, Politics, and Conflict," 250–52.

16. Van Wagoner, *Polygamy: A History,* 108.

17. Quoted in Van Wagoner, *Polygamy: A History,* 111; Larson, "Government, Politics, and Conflict," 254; Bruce A. Van Orden, *Prisoner for Conscience Sake: The Life of George Reynolds* (Salt Lake City: Deseret Book, 1992); Sarah Barringer Gordon, *The Mormon Question: Polygamy and Constitutional Conflict in Nineteenth-Century America* (Chapel Hill: University of North Carolina, 2002); Sarah Barringer Gordon and Kathryn M. Daynes, *Prosecution of Mormon Polygamists in Utah Territory* (forthcoming).

18. Larson, "The Crusade and Manifesto," in *Utah's History,* 259–60.

19. Ibid., 267.

20. D. Michael Quinn, "LDS Church Authority and New Plural Marriage, 1890–1904," *Dialogue: A Journal of Mormon Thought* 18 (Spring 1985): 29–30; Van Wagoner, *Polygamy: A History,* 132.

21. Van Wagoner, *Polygamy: A History,* 138.

22. Official Declaration 1, Doctrine and Covenants; Van Wagoner, *Polygamy: A History,* 147.

23. Annie Richardson Johnson, *Heartbeats of Colonia Diaz* (Mesa, Ariz.: n.pub., 1972), 294.

24. Quoted in Jessie L. Embry, *Mormon Polygamous Families: Life in the Principle* (Salt Lake City: University of Utah Press, 1987), 45–46.

25. *Journal of Discourses,* 1:60–62.

26. Van Wagoner, *Polygamy,* 109.

27. Ida Stewart Pacy, interviewed by Hames Hullett, 1937, Kimball Young Collection.

28. Eunice Stewart Harris, Life Story, n.d.

29. Young, *Isn't One Wife Enough,* 118–19.

30. Quoted in Nels Anderson, *Deseret Saints* (Chicago: University of Chicago, 1942), 131–32. H. H. Bancroft, whom Anderson is quoting, identifies her as "wife #1 of a leading apostle."

31. Annie Gardner, interviewed by James Hulett, n.d,, 3, Young Collection.

32. Annie Clark Tanner, *A Mormon Mother* (Salt Lake City: Tanner Trust Fund, University of Utah Library, 1976), 129–30.

33. Quinn, "LDS Church Authority and New Plural Marriage," 48–49.

34. Ibid., 49; Van Wagoner, *Polygamy: A History,* 147.

35. Quinn, "LDS Church Authority and New Plural Marriage," 49.

36. Thomas G. Alexander, *Things in Heaven and Earth: The Life and Times of Wilford Woodruff, a Mormon Prophet* (Salt Lake City: Signature Books, 1991), 271–73.

37. Rose B. Hayes and Mrs. [full name not given] Clark, interviewed by Fay Ollerton, 1936, 7, Young Collection.

38. Elizabeth Ann Schurtz McDonald, interviewed by James Hulett, 1936, 1, Young Collection.

39. Quinn, "LDS Church Authority and New Plural Marriage," 51.

40. Conover Wright, interviewed by James Hulett, 1938, 2, Young Collection.

41. Lorin "Dutch" Leavitt, Oral History, interviewed by Leonard Grover, 1980, 5, LDS Polygamy Oral History Project, L. Tom Perry Special Collections, Harold B. Lee Library, Brigham Young University, Provo, Utah (hereafter Polygamy Oral History Project).

42. Embry, *Mormon Polygamous Families,* 14–15.

43. Quoted in Van Wagoner, *Polygamy: A History,* 161.

44. Ibid., 169, 174.

45. B. Carmon Hardy, *Solemn Covenant: The Mormon Polygamous Passage* (Urbana: University of Illinois Press, 1992), 265, 326.

46. Van Wagoner, *Polygamy: A History,* 169, 174; Thomas G. Alexander, *Mormonism in Transition: A History of the Latter-day Saints, 1890–1930* (Urbana: University of Illinois Press, 1986), 67–68.

47. In 1979, Maude Taylor Bentley, the third wife of Joseph D. Bentley, died, prompting Eugene E. Campbell, BYU professor of history, to suggest that the Redd Center interview the children of polygamous families who were senior citizens. The Redd Center contacted one plural wife who refused to be interviewed. Edward Christian Eyring and his wives, Caroline Romney Eyring and Emma Romney Eyring, are just one example of a plural husband and wives who died in the 1940s. Soon afterward, the Charles Redd Center launched its LDS Polygamy Oral History Project.

48. The only comprehensive treatment of contemporary plural marriage with Mormon roots is Brian C. Hales, *Modern Polygamy and Mormon Fundamentalists: The Generations after the Manifesto* (Salt Lake City: Greg Kofford Books, forthcoming), which spends more than two-thirds of its pages on post-1904 developments. Martha Sonntag Bradley, *Kidnapped from That Land: The Government Raids on the Short Creek Polygamists* (Salt Lake City: University of Utah Press, 1993), focuses on one group. Attorney Ken Driggs has written several significant legal articles: "After the Manifesto: Modern Polygamy and Fundamentalist Mormons," *Journal of Church and State* 32 (Spring 1990): 367-89; "Twentieth-Century Polygamy and Fundamentalist Mormons in Southern Utah," *Dialogue: A Journal of Mormon Thought* 24 (Winter 1991): 44-58; "Utah Supreme Court Decides Polygamist Adoption Case," *Sunstone* 15 (September 1991): 67-68; and "Who Shall Raise the Children?: Vera Black and the Rights of Polygamous Utah Parents," *Utah Historical Quarterly* 60 (Winter 1992): 27-46. Three anthropological/sociological studies are Irwin Altman and Joseph Ginat, *Polygamous Families in Contemporary Society* (New York: Cambridge University Press, 1996), and two works by Janet Bennion: *Women of Principle: Female Networking in Contemporary Mormon Polygamy* (New York: Oxford University Press, 1998), and *Desert Patriarchy: Mormon and Mennonite Communities in the Chihuahua Valley* (Tucson: University of Arizona Press, 2004). The LDS Church considers fundamentalists schismatics.

49. Stanley Ivins, "Notes on Polygamy," *Utah Historical Quarterly* 35 (Fall 1967): 311–17.

50. Leonard J. Arrington and Davis Bitton, *The Mormon Experience: A History of the Latter-day Saints* (New York: Alfred A. Knopf, 1979), 199.

51. Larry Logue, "A Time of Marriage: Monogamy and Polygamy in a Mormon Town," *Journal of Mormon History* 11 (1984): 3–26.

52. Dean L. May, "People on the Mormon Frontier: Kanab's Families of 1874," *Journal of Family History* 1 (Winter 1976): 169–89.

53. Lowell "Ben" Bennion, "The Incidence of Mormon Polygamy in 1880: 'Dixie' versus Davis Stake," *Journal of Mormon History* 11 (1984): 30–31, 36–37; Lowell "Ben" Bennion, "The Geography of Polygamy Among the Mormons in 1880," Paper presented at the Mormon History Association annual meeting, May 11, 1984, Provo, Utah. A forthcoming book by Lowell "Ben" Bennion, Kathryn M. Daynes, Charles "Chuck" Hatch, with Thomas Carter, *Plural Wives and Tangled Lives: Polygamy's Place in Mormon Society, 1850s-1880s* is examining Utah communities (one per county) and will answer many questions about the numbers of polygamists in the state.

54. See Jessie L. Embry, "Overworked Stereotypes or Accurate Historical Images: The Images of Polygamy in *Giant Joshua,*" *Sunstone* 14 (April 1990): 42–46.

55. Embry, *Mormon Polygamous Families,* 31, 35–36.

56. See charts in Embry, *Mormon Polygamous Families,* 37.

57. Pamela A. R. Blakely, "Co-Wives in Africa: A Discussion of Polygyny in Eastern Zaire," Lecture presented for the Women's Research Institute, Brigham Young University, January 23, 1985.

58. Michael Gordon, "The Ideal Husband as Depicted in the Nineteenth-Century Marriage Manual," in *The American Man,* edited by Elizabeth H. Pleck and John N. Pleck (Englewood Cliffs, N.J.: Prentice-Hall, 1980), 150–54.

59. Emma Hoth NcNeil, interviewed by James Hulett, 1938, 2, Young Collection.

60. Bryant R. Clark, Oral History, interviewed by Chris Nelson, 1981, 5–6, Polygamy Oral History Project.

61. Lula Roskelley Mortensen, Oral History, interviewed by Jessie L. Embry, 1976, 13, Polygamy Oral History Project.

62. Laura Fackrell Chamberlain, Oral History, interviewed by James Hulett, 1935, 1–2, Young Collection.

63. Sigrid H. Skanchy, interviewed by James Hulett, 1937, 1–2, Young Collection.

64. Theodore C. Bennion, Oral History, interviewed by Jessie L. Embry, 1976, 3, Polygamy Oral History Project.

65. Heber C. Maughan, interviewed by James Hulett, 1937, 2, Young Collection.

66. Winnifred Harker Smith, Oral History, interviewed by Jessie L. Embry, 1982, 15, Polygamy Oral History Project.

67. Caroline Pederson Hansen, "Autobiography," in *Our Pioneer Heritage,* compiled by Kate B. Carter, 20 vols. (Salt Lake City: Daughters of the Utah Pioneers, 1958–77), 12:71.

68. Clarence Allen, Oral History, interviewed by James Comish, 1979, 2–3, LDS Polygamy Project; Evan B. Murray, interviewed by Hulett, 1937, Young Collection.

69. Douglas Cannon, oral history, interviewed by Leonard Grover, 1980, 1, 6, Polygamy Oral History Project.

70. Quoted in Jean Bickmore White, "Dr. Martha Hughes Cannon: Doctor, Wife, Legislator, Exile," in *Sister Saints,* edited by Vicky Burgess-Olson (Provo, Utah: Brigham Young University Press, 1978), 391–92.

71. Quoted in Patricia Rasmussen Eaton-Gadsby and Judith Rasmussen Dushku, "Emmeline Blanche Woodward Wells: 'I Have Risen Triumphant,'" in *Sister Saints,* 467.

72. Julia Winter Smith, interviewed by James Hulett, 1936, 4, Young Collection.

73. Meda Lucille Jenkins Parker, Oral History, interviewed by Jessie L. Embry, 1980, Polygamy Oral History Project, 5.

74. Archie L. Jenkins, Oral History, interviewed by Leonard Grover, 1980, 5, Polygamy Oral History Project.

75. Sabra Naegle Foremaster, Oral History, interviewed by Jessie L. Embry, 1982, 18–19, Polygamy Oral History Project.

76. Ida Stewart Pacey, interviewed by James Hulett, 1937, 2, Young Collection.

77. Franklin Lyman Stout, Oral History, interviewed by Stevan Martin Hales, 1982, 2, Polygamy Oral History Project.

78. Wasel Black Washburn, Oral History, interviewed by Amy Bentley, 1983, Polygamy Oral History Project, 4; Edna Cowley Austin, Oral History, interviewed by Leonard Grover, 1980, Polygamy Oral History Project, 11; Alma Elizabeth Mineer Felt, interviewed by James Hulett, 1935, 5–6, Young Collection.

79. Mary E. Croshaw Farrell, interviewed by James Hulett, 1937, 9, Young Collection.

80. Charles Smith Merrill, Oral History, interviewed by Amy Bentley, 1984, 10, 14, Polygamy Oral History Project.

81. Bell Harris Merrill Nelson Berry, interviewed by Fay Ollerton, 1935, 2, 8, Young Collection.

82. Julia B. Jensen, interviewed by James Hulett, 1935, 1, Young Collection.

83. Mary Jane Rigby Roskelley, interviewed by James Hulett, 1937, 2, Young Collection.

84. Zina Roskelley Bell, Oral History, interviewed by Jessie L. Embry, 1976, 5–6, Polygamy Oral History Project.

85. Ibid.; Rebecca Roskelley Lewis, Oral History, interviewed by Leonard Grover, 1980, 3, Polygamy Oral History Project; Lula Roskelley Mortensen, Oral History, Appendix, 8, Polygamy Oral History Project.

86. Ann Amelia Chamberlain Esplin, Oral History, interviewed by Ronald K. Esplin, 1973, 20, James Moyle Oral History Program, LDS Church Archives.

87. Isabel McFarland Bingham, interviewed by James Hulett, 1937, 2, Young Collection.

88. Elizabeth (Lizzie) Adams McFarland, interviewed by James Hulett, 1936, 2–3, Young Collection.

89. Ruth May Fox, interviewed by James Hulett, 1935, 4, Young Collection.

90. Mortensen, Oral History, Appendix, 8; Roxey Roskelley Rogers, Oral History, interviewed by Jessie L. Embry, 1976, 10, Polygamy Oral History Project; Lewis, Oral History, 5.

91. Mary Elizabeth Woolley Chamberlain, Autobiography, 106, typescript, 1936–39, Perry Special Collections, Lee Library.

92. Felt, interviewed by James Fulett, 7.

93. Young, *Isn't One Wife Enough?* 56–57; R. Collin Mangrum, "Further the Cause of Zion: An Overview of the Mormon Ecclesiastical Court System in Early Utah," *Journal of Mormon History* 10 (1983): 79–90; Eugene E. Campbell and Bruce L. Campbell, "Divorce among Mormon Polygamists: Extent and Explanations," *Utah Historical Quarterly* 46 (Winter 1978): 4–23. See also chap. 2.

94. Elvera Manful, "Biography of David Osborn, Sr.," Federal Writer's Project, October 25, 1939, 39, Utah State Historical Society, Salt Lake City.

95. John Mack Faragher, *Men and Women on the Overland Trail* (New Haven, Conn.: Yale University Press, 1979), 138, 140.

96. Elizabeth Ann Schurtz McDonald, interviewed by James Hulett, 1936, 3–4, Young Collection.

97. Alvin Allen, *Ira Allen: Founder of Hyrum, the Story of a Mormon Pioneer* (Hyrum, Utah: n.pub., 1946), 61.

98. Young, cited in Embry, *Mormon Polygamous Families,* 137, 141.

99. Carl N. Degler, *At Odds: Women and the Family in America from the Revolution to the Present* (New York: Oxford University Press, 1980), 47–48.

100. D. H. J. Morgan, *Social Theory and the Family* (London: Routledge and Kegan Paul, 1975), 141.

101. David Cannon, Oral History, interviewed by Laurel Schmidt, 1981, 15, Polygamy Oral History Project.

102. For information see Anne Firor Scott, "Mormon Women, Other Women: Paradoxes and Challenges," *Journal of Mormon History* 13 (1986–87): 2–20; Marsha Wedell, *Elite Women and the Reform Impulse in Memphis, 1875–1915* (Knoxville: University of Tennessee Press, 1991).

103. Molly Law Jacobs, Interview, 1, Utah Historical Survey, Bancroft Library, University of California-Berkeley, Berkeley, California.

104. Lydia Hall Turner, typescript, 2, Utah Historical Survey, Bancroft Library.

105. Hayes and Clark, interviewed by Ollerton, 4.

106. Charles M. Shumway and Sarah Jardine Shumway, interviewed by James Hulett, 1937, 1, Young Collection.

107. Mary Ann Mansfield Bentley, *Life Sketch* (Provo, Utah: BYU Library, 1938), 9, 11, 12, quotation from p. 12.

108. Joseph Hodges, interviewed by James Hulett, 1937, 1, Young Collection; Morris Hodges, oral history, interviewed by Jessie L. Embry, 1979, 3, Polygamy Oral History Project.

109. For another view of missionary wives, see Linda Thatcher, "Women Alone: The Economic and Emotional Plight of Early LDS Women," *Dialogue: A Journal of Mormon Thought* 25 (Winter 1992): 45–57.

110. Hansen, "Autobiography," 71.

111. Mercy Weston Gibbons, interviewed by James Hulett, 1938, 2, Young Collection.

112. Arthur O. Chapman, interviewed by Martha C. Martin, 1983, 11, LDS Family Life Oral History Project, Charles Redd Center for Western Studies, Manuscript Division, Harold B. Lee Library, Brigham Young University, Provo, Utah (hereafter Family Life Project).

113. Hayes and Clark, interviewed by Ollerton, 5.

114. Elmer Stettler, Oral History, interviewed by Jessie L. Embry, 1987, 2, LDS German-Speaking Immigrants Oral History Project, Charles Redd Center for Western Studies, Manuscript Division, Harold B. Lee Library, Brigham Young University, Provo, Utah.

115. Henry Earl Day, Oral History, interviewed by Marsha C. Martin, 1983, 3, Family Life Project.

116. Vera Christensen, Oral History, interviewed by Stevan Hales, 1982, 8–10, 22, 24, 33–34, Family Life Project.

117. Jessie L. Embry, "Charles Edmund Richardson Families: A Case Study of Mormon Polygamy," *Richardson Family History* (Provo, Utah: Charles Redd Center for Western Studies, 1982), 16–17.

118. McFarland, interviewed by Hulett, 9.

119. Chamberlain, Autobiography, 227–29.

120. Lula A. Larsen, Oral History, interviewed by Rochelle Fairbourn, 1982, 1, 6–8, Family Life Project.

2

Innovation and Accommodation

The Legal Status of Women in Territorial Utah, 1850–1896

Lisa Madsen Pearson and Carol Cornwall Madsen

The story of the legal status of women in territorial Utah (1850–96) weaves together three historical strands: the expansion of women's legal rights nationally, the liberalizing tendencies of frontier development, and most important, the necessity of protecting Mormon control and practices, including plural marriage, and ultimately defending them against the counter measures of the federal government. While influenced to varying degrees by the first two developments in American history, the third most clearly defined the focus of early Utah territorial law with respect to women.

Creating territorial law to support Mormon ideology and practice, particularly by providing a legal identity for plural wives and their children within the framework of American jurisprudence, required innovative and imaginative measures by Utah lawmakers. Polygamy (the popular name) or polygny (the technically correct term for marriage between a man and multiple wives) was a basic tenet of Mormonism. By any name, it was a system of female enslavement, according to its critics and was designated an illegal practice after 1862 by federal decree. According to its defenders, it was a God-given commandment that should have been protected as a free exercise of religion by the U.S. Constitution. Paradoxically, this system forced a consciousness of women's legal rights by Utah's territorial legislature and put Utah in the vanguard of efforts to improve the legal status of women.

Some of these innovative measures, however, were casualties of the escalating assertion of federal power, aimed at destroying polygamy and Mormon political hegemony in the territory. The process of accommodation that followed federal anti-polygamy legislation eventually led to the discontinuation of the practice by the Mormon Church and opened the way to statehood. It also removed any recognition of legal rights of plural wives; but in some other areas of the law, the legal advances experienced by Utah women survived the transition to statehood.

The National Struggle for Woman's Rights

In the first half of the nineteenth century, women's legal status was still defined in large measure by common law, a form of British jurisprudence transported to the American colonies. While some of its provisions were dropped in transit, the principle of "coverture" remained intact.[1] Under the doctrine of coverture, upon marriage a woman's "very being or legal existence [was] suspended during the marriage or at least incorporated or consolidated into that of the husband," according to William Blackstone, the seventeenth-century compiler of the common law.[2]

Because under the law a husband and wife were considered one person (and that person was the husband), they could not testify for or against each other in court. Furthermore, married women were denied such civil rights as the right to sue or be sued in their own name or keep any judgment recovered on their behalf, to manage or control their real property, to own personal property, to keep their wages, or to make a contract or will. Nor could they act as independent legal guardians of their children.[3]

In exchange for the surrender of her legal identity and her property to her husband, the common law granted a married woman two rights: the right of support (to be fed, clothed, and sheltered) and the right of dower (a right to the income and use of one-third of the real estate that her husband owned during the marriage if she survived him). She received no protected interest in her husband's personal property, including that which originally belonged to her. In practice, some of the harsh consequences of the common law were ameliorated by (1) prenuptial contracts which reserved property rights to the wife, often in lieu of her dower interest; (2) trust arrangements which gave a third-party trustee legal title to property to hold for the wife; (3) court settlements of the wife's property on the husband only after some provision was made for the wife; and (4) the doctrine of *feme sole* where women widowed or abandoned by their husbands were given power to act as if they were single or where women who ran mercantile establishments were given power to act independently with respect to their businesses.[4] Nevertheless, the consequences of coverture were far-reaching for the majority of women.

The common law thus reflected cultural assumptions about male and female relationships in society as well as in marriage. Women were under the control and protection of men, and the law recognized the husband as the sole legal representative of a family, particularly in the public realm. Blackstone acknowledged the disabilities which the wife lived under but claimed that they "were for the most part intended for her protection and benefit; so great a favourite is the female sex of the law."[5]

Instrumental in eroding the harsh effects of the common law on women was the rising importance of state and territorial legislatures. The common law was a collection of legal precedents, distilled and compiled in Blackstone's

Commentaries. Legislatures, however, created and formulated laws, sometimes paralleling and sometimes differing with common-law precedents. Women's emergence from the common-law "legal fiction," or legal construct, of marital unity began primarily with state legislation, notably the passage of Married Women Property Acts, beginning in 1835, which granted women the right to their own property.[6] Initially, the rationale for the Married Women's Property Acts was not economic equity or relief of women's economic dependence. Rather, they reflected the "male response to such major economic dislocations as panics and depressions," according to historian Joan Hoff. Land transfers and business transactions were also facilitated by these acts, which could help support the family economy by protecting married women's assets from the husband's creditors during periods of personal or general economic depression.[7]

But after these first acts were passed, women began to actively campaign for such reform in their own behalf. One consequence of these acts, according to some legal historians, lay in demonstrating the effectiveness of statutory revision on the state or territorial level as a major instrument of legal change for women. By 1865 twenty-nine states had property acts that modified, in varying degrees, the common-law doctrine of coverture.[8] Throughout the rest of the nineteenth century, these acts would be amended and enlarged in varying degrees to include essential aspects of women's economic independence. This relatively quiet feminist success in altering the law, which accompanied the economic rationale for change, provided impetus to the movement for greater political rights that followed the close of the Civil War.[9]

The Liberalizing Effect of the West

A further national trend that affected the development of Utah law for women was the protracted struggle for woman suffrage—most successful in the western United States. Political reform followed immediately on the heels of domestic legal reform, and the two soon became intertwined. Among the grievances listed in the "Declaration of Sentiments," drawn up by Elizabeth Cady Stanton and presented to the first women's rights convention held in Seneca Falls, New York, July 1848, was not only the lack of women's legal identity but also denial of the vote.[10] Political reform proved to be far more challenging, divisive, and controversial, however, than legal change, since it impinged even more directly on the dicta of coverture.

Following the Civil War, the drive toward equal political rights began in earnest. The national campaign kept the issue before the national conscience and found its initial success in the West, where the expansiveness of its lands and resources matched the breadth of its attitudes and vision. While Congress debated the question of granting suffrage to the territories "as an experiment," both Wyoming and Utah territories passed statutes enfranchising their women, Wyoming in 1869 and Utah in 1870. Both acts reenforced the ability of legislative means to effect legal change for women. Well before the 1920 passage of the Nineteenth Amendment granting all U.S. women the vote, thirteen western states had enfranchised their women. In addition to Wyoming, they were Colorado (1893), and Utah and Idaho (1896) at statehood. (See also chap. 11.)

This adventurous and entrepreneurial spirit of western settlers, along with the endless promises the West offered, conspired to soften the social and legal restrictions on women dominant in Eastern society. The initial absence of a formal judiciary allowed local justice to rule in many areas. Legal practices based on the common law were suspended or transformed as the natural and social characteristics of the various western territories dictated a unique application and development of the law. The scarcity of women, the interdependence so essential during the frontier period, the physical labor required to establish homes and communities that of necessity ignored traditional gendered divisions of labor, and the homesteading laws that allowed women to own and develop property in their own names, all contributed. Western women came to enjoy more legal rights, greater political power, and more employment opportunities much earlier than their Eastern counterparts. All of these factors were also appealing motivations for female migration.[11]

The Development of Utah Law

Though influenced by these national developments, Utah responded to an even stronger social force shaping the legal and political status of women in the territory. Settled by Mormon pioneers and populated largely by Mormons during the nineteenth century, Utah was an anomaly among the states and territories. Driven out of their former settlements in the East and Midwest, Mormons hoped to establish a spiritual kingdom of their own making in the pristine West. Their mission was to establish "the kingdom of God" on earth in preparation of the Second Coming of Jesus Christ under the direction of their prophet, at that time (1847), Brigham Young. He was their spiritual head but also their economic and political leader. His spiritual and secular leadership blurred the line between the temporal and the eternal. "We are trying to establish the Kingdom of God on the earth," he declared, "to which really and properly everything that pertains to men [and women]—their feelings, their faith, their affections, their desires, and every act of their lives—belong, that they may be ruled by it spiritually and temporally."[12] With this overriding mission, the spiritual equality of men and women, a concept that underlay their theology, translated in many respects to various forms of social equality.[13] While the prevailing notion of "separate spheres" for men and women constituted a type of ideal division of labor in Mormon Utah, the exigencies of their mission rendered the boundaries between the two extremely permeable. Even the parameters of what constituted the "public sphere" underwent considerable transformation in Mormon practice, as women assumed numerous economic, professional, and community responsibilities individually or as members of their local Relief

Society. Establishing the territory of Utah did not fit the settlement pattern that prevailed elsewhere in the West, being founded on a religious rather than an entrepreneurial base.

Added to this distinguishing feature were the communal fervor of Mormons, the solidarity of their interests, their united commitment to the faith, and their shared distrust of the federal government that resulted from its failure to intervene when Mormons were forced repeatedly from their homes and communities before settling in Utah. From the beginning, all of these peculiarities made other Americans suspect Mormon loyalty to the government.

But nothing could match the opprobrium that followed the public announcement of the LDS Church's practice of plural marriage in 1852. This religious practice formed the basis for an innovative departure from the common law to protect its adherents and, in many respects, aligned it with the national movement for women's rights. The basis for law in Utah was established the day Brigham Young entered Salt Lake Valley in 1847. As that first exploratory pioneer company met together, Mormon Apostle Wilford Woodruff recorded that, among other principles Young announced, "the ten commandments and the Christian ethics were practically proclaimed to be in force."[14] The statutory form of these principles closely paralleled those of the Mormon ecclesiastical court system which the pioneers had used during their sojourn in Winter Quarters, Nebraska, on the trek to Utah. It was no great change to establish them in Utah.[15]

The first Legislative Assembly in Utah met in 1849 and sent a memorial to Congress to recognize the provisional "State of Deseret." Congress rejected that first appeal and Utah became subject to a Congressional organic act giving it territorial status and providing its governing law two years later. Within the general framework of that law, the new territorial legislature adopted the enactments passed previously by the "State of Deseret."[16]

When the first federally appointed officials arrived in Utah, the conflict with the federal government began. "Their [Mormon] judicial economy," Utah writer Edward Tullidge wrote, "was after the pattern of the New Testament rather than Blackstone. It was this that made the Mormon rule so obnoxious to the federal judges and Gentile [non-Mormon] lawyers."[17] Throughout the territorial period, that contest influenced the development of law in a variety of ways. Congress had the power to review and approve or disapprove laws as well as enact legislation for the territory,[18] and federally appointed territorial judges interpreted and applied laws passed by the territorial legislature.[19] Consequently, Utah jurisprudence often represented a compilation of unique legal expedients and innovations designed to sustain Mormon practices and doctrines carefully constructed to fit within federal guidelines.

A primary point of conflict centered on the jurisdiction of the federal and local courts. The Mormon legislature granted unusual legal powers to

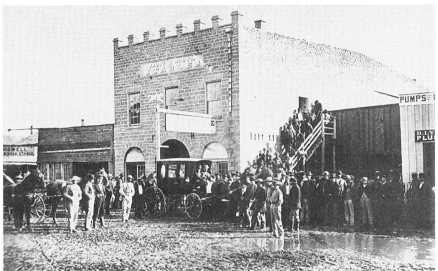

Faust & Houtz Livery Stable, Salt Lake City, 1871. In Judge James B. McKean's Third District Court on the second floor, many violations of the Morrill Anti-Bigamy Act of 1862 were prosecuted, including Brigham Young's.

county probate courts presided over by local officers. Besides conducting matters relating to estates, guardianship of minors, and divorces, the territorial legislature also granted probate courts jurisdiction over all civil and criminal cases and the drawing of jury lists. It created the locally filled offices of territorial marshal and territorial attorney with powers paralleling those of their federal counterparts. Later, the legislature extended their power by giving the probate courts the same original jurisdiction as the federally governed district courts.[20] Many litigants, particularly Mormons, took their cases to the probate courts rather than before the federally appointed judge of the district court. The effect was to displace the federally appointed courts with a judiciary under local control. The probate courts thus provided an alternative legal system and allowed Mormons to appear in locally administered and thus more sympathetic courts.[21] Moreover, the Mormon ecclesiastical court system entertained a wide variety of civil suits, thus offering a second locally governed legal avenue to church members. Concerned that the probate courts gave extensive judicial power to the LDS Church and, in effect, thwarted the prosecution of polygamists, Congress reacted by placing the judiciary firmly under federal control. The Poland Act of 1874 stripped the probate courts of all civil, criminal, and chancery (equity) jurisdiction and transferred to federal officials the duties of the territorial attorney general and marshal. It also gave federal judges wide latitude in the selection of jurors.[22] Probate courts were restricted to matters of estates, guardianship, and divorce.

A second point of discord was Utah Territory's effort to reject the common law. In 1852 Brigham Young declared: "We have not adopted the common law of England, nor any other general law of old countries, any further than the extending over us the constitutional laws of the United States by Congress, has produced that effect."[23] This disclaimer took statutory form in 1853: "All questions of law, the meaning of writings other than laws, and the admissibility of testimony shall be decided by the Court: and no laws nor parts of laws shall be read, argued, cited or adopted in any court, during any trial, except those enacted by the Governor and Legislative Assembly of this Territory, and those passed by the Congress of the United States when applicable; and no report, decision or doings of any Court shall be read, argued, cited or adopted as precedent in any trial."[24]

In 1874 the chief justice of the Utah Supreme Court, James McKean, expressed his incredulity at the legislative attempt to exclude from Utah the authority of Coke, Blackstone, Mansfield, Kent, Story and Marshall (authors of widely used treatises which compiled cases involving the common law in certain areas of the law). "What can be said?" he queried. "Language fails properly to characterize such legislation."[25] Despite the 1842 statute, the applicability of the common law was recognized in a variety of local court cases beginning in 1855. In 1889 the U.S. Supreme Court ruled that the common law operated in Utah by virtue of the Organic Act, which declared in section 9 that the courts of the Territory possessed "chancery as well as common law jurisdiction." It was also operative as a result of the territorial legislature's enactment of a statute in 1852, which provided that all courts should have "law and equity jurisdiction."[26]

The third and most persistent Mormon-federal conflict focused on polygamy.[27] The need to provide legal protection for plural wives generated several legal advances for women. Congress responded with legislation to abolish the practice, however, beginning with the Morrill Act in 1862, followed by the Poland Act in 1874, the Edmunds Law in 1882, and the Edmunds-Tucker Law in 1887.[28] The severity of the last, with even more crushing measures promised, led to an accommodation by LDS Church President Wilford Woodruff, who issued a manifesto in 1890 withdrawing public support for new plural marriages and advising members to abide by the laws of the land. The civil and criminal sanctions and disabilities imposed by these federal laws substantially altered the legal status of Utah's women, especially plural wives and their children.[29]

These three social forces were instrumental in shaping Utah law in the nineteenth century and had long-range influence on how the law related to women. The national trend toward women's rights along with the more innovative attitude of western lawmakers is clearly discernible in the development of domestic law in Utah during this period. But the impact of the struggle to assert a Constitutional right against escalating federal intervention had a far more perceptible and pervasive effect than the first two. Utah's bumpy ride to statehood left its innovative measures far behind as it accommodated itself to the expectations of becoming the forty-third state in the Union.

Elias Smith (1804–84) was a cousin of the Prophet Joseph Smith. He was an early pioneer of Utah as well as editor and publisher of the *Deseret News.* He also held the position of probate judge in Salt Lake County from 1852 to 1882.

Marriage and Divorce Laws

The lack of legislation regulating marriage and Utah's lenient divorce law (1852), provoked major political and legal controversy and clearly demonstrated the influence of Mormon beliefs on the formulation of Utah law. The first territorial legislature in 1852 authorized officers of the Church of Jesus Christ of Latter-day Saints "to solemnize marriage" and required that "a registry of marriages" be kept in every branch or stake [ecclesiastical units] of the church.[30] For Mormons, marriage was a religious covenant properly solemnized only by ecclesiastical authority and enduring beyond the deaths of the partners. Therefore, the legislature made no provision for the civil recording of marriages nor did it pass any other regulatory measures. As a result, the only documentation of the numerous marriages civilly or ecclesiastically during most of Utah's territorial period appears in the personal records of judges and justices of the peace, church records, diaries and journals, and temple sealing [marriage] records.[31] Federally appointed governors exhorted the legislatures in 1872, 1874, 1876, and 1878 to pass statutory provisions regulating marriage, but none was adopted until 1887.[32]

The Mormon-dominated territorial legislature did not enact a civil marriage law, not only because of the Mormon concept that only LDS marital rites were binding, but also because of the need to avoid public records of plural marriages, especially after passage of the Morrill Act (1862), criminalizing bigamy. The force of this act stemmed from Congress's power to regulate marriage in the territories as legislatures did in the states.[33] It had no provisions for enforcement, however. Not until passage of the far more stringent anti-polygamy Edmunds-Tucker Act in 1887, which provided for the certification of marriages, did the territorial legislature enact a parallel marriage statute outlawing polygamy and requiring the registration of all marriages, including the names of the parties, and the officiator, to be filed with the probate court.[34]

In contrast to its failure to enact a marriage law, the first legislative assembly in 1852 established a liberal divorce law, which, paradoxically, appeared to permit the easy dissolution of marriage by a religious community committed to the sanctity and eternity of marriage.[35] The Utah law allowed anyone who was or "wished to become" a resident of Utah to invoke the jurisdiction of the court. This act was influenced both by Utah's location in the West and by a basic premise of Mormon theology. During this period, the Western population was rapidly increasing with migrants, especially in Utah. Moreover, the amount of mobility between the western territories begged the question of what constituted residency. With the constant influx of new settlers and frequent change of domicile, a long period of residency was impractical for many reasons and often worked hardship for new westerners seeking legal separation from spouses unwilling to join them.[36]

The traditional grounds for divorce were impotency, adultery, desertion, habitual drunkenness, felony conviction, and abusive treatment. Significantly, the Utah statute added a seventh cause: "when it shall be made to appear to the satisfaction and conviction of the court, that the parties cannot live in peace and union together and that their welfare requires a separation."[37] Only six other states and territories had a similar law.[38] The circumstances giving rise to these lenient statutes, however, differed in each jurisdiction and particularly in Utah.

Utah's divorce statute gave legal force to a social and religious principle that governed divorce in LDS Church courts. Mormons valued social unity and harmony, qualities that family life was meant to exemplify and foster. Divorce provided a way to remove a source of social contention and permitted the innocent party to remarry and ideally create a more harmonious and peaceful family relationship.[39] Thus, divorce for Mormons did not "destroy" home and family but was in reality a safety valve, a means of preserving the institution of the family by dissolving those alliances that abused its peace and harmony.

Moreover, since civil marriage ceremonies were neither eternally binding nor valid in the eyes of the church, divorce was merely a rhetorical exercise in compliance with the demands of a temporal legal system. Marriage was a religious covenant, its eternal duration entirely dependent on the faith and commitment of the marital partners. Spiritually, it would have no force if either partner disregarded the covenants he or she had made. As early as 1842, according to diarist John D. Lee, Mormon prophet Joseph Smith declared that couples "were married to each other only by their own covenants, and if their marriage relations had not been productive of blessings and peace, and they felt it oppressive to remain together, they were at liberty to make their own choice, much as if they had not been married . . . . It was a sin for people to live together and raise and beget children in alienation from each other."[40]

In 1861 Brigham Young acknowledged the desire of couples to have tangible evidence of their separation. In a ruling that clearly favored women, he announced: "When a woman becomes alienated in her feelings and affections from her husband, it is then his duty to give her a bill [of divorcement] and set her free." In other words, to live together without natural affection from whatever cause was a violation of the marriage covenant. Moreover, if a man proved to be an "unworthy" husband and father, according to Young, he automatically forfeited his marriage covenants, and his wife or wives were "free from him without a bill of divorcement."[41] Young issued divorce certificates only reluctantly, complaining, "You might as well ask me for a piece of blank paper." He charged husbands whose wives requested a divorce ten dollars, not for his services, he said, but for their "foolishness."[42] In Mormon terms, marriage ideally endured only on the basis of mutual affection and righteous behavior and was automatically dissolved when either partner failed to meet his or her religious commitments. This position had, needless to say, numerous practical problems—hence the development of written certificates of divorce.

More than two thousand extant bills of divorce, granted by Brigham Young and his successor, John Taylor, provide evidence that women, particularly those in plural marriages, were not bound in relationships that proved undesirable, contrary to the assertions of anti-polygamists. Though the records do not indicate, it can be assumed that most of the applicants were plural wives dissolving their marriages through ecclesiastical courts.[43] This easy access to divorce, either through probate or ecclesiastical courts, coupled with the liberal attitude toward the dissolution of unharmonious marriages, stood in marked contrast to the conservative views of marriage and divorce that dominated American society in the nineteenth century.[44] In fact, for some Mormon critics, it was as undesirable as polygamy. While divorce has never been treated as a desirable social institution in American life, it was the only remedy for women legally bound to dissolute, abusive, and irresponsible husbands. And for disillusioned plural wives, it offered ready escape. A *Deseret News* article explained: "Polygamy would be considered a system of bondage, if women desiring to sever their relations with a husband having other wives, were refused the liberty they might demand."[45]

Despite this apparent permissiveness toward divorce, Brigham Young and other church leaders consistently advised against it, admonishing couples to overlook personality flaws and other personal irritations. Nevertheless, while urging husbands to be more patient and long-suffering, Young seldom refused a woman who expressed dissatisfaction with her husband. A letter to Frederick Kesler explains Young's position. "Your wife Abigail called upon me, stated her feelings and requested a bill [of divorce], which under the circumstances we thought proper to grant her, as is usual when a woman insists upon one." He also made other statements expressing this preferential status of wives in divorce actions: "When women tease for a divorce, and are determined to have one what can be done better than to give them one?" Or "I should feel a little ashamed to require a wife to ask me twice for a bill of divorce, or to refuse signing and paying for it at once." Or "If the brethren were but a small part as anxious, diligent and prompt in this particular [acceding to divorce] as they are in having women sealed to them, it would prevent much needless annoyance and perplexity to the sisters." Grievances ranged from "an abusive tongue" to desertion.[46]

Church divorces for first wives were not accepted by the civil courts as legal, nor could plural wives appeal to the civil courts for the termination of their marriages. Since Mormon bishops presided over many of the county probate courts, the jurisdiction of the bishops' ecclesiastical courts and the civil probate courts was sometimes invoked incorrectly. First wives occasionally obtained divorces in church courts, and some plural wives received divorces in probate courts, causing them later legal difficulties.[47] A noted jurisdictional dispute involved John R. Park, first president of the University of Utah and first state superintendent of public instruction. Park married Annie F. Armitage in 1872 on her supposed deathbed in a church marriage, which was considered legal at that time; but when she unexpectedly recovered, the couple, evidently changing their minds, decided to obtain a church divorce, which was not legally recognized. While Park never remarried, Armitage, on the basis of her church divorce, married William Hilton in 1875 and gave birth to ten children. At Park's demise in 1900, Armitage successfully sued for a dower interest in Park's property, claiming her right as his widow, since she had been his only wife and since their church divorce was not recognized by the court.[48] Legal readjustment of such marital relationships continued well into the twentieth century.

An unforeseen result of Utah's lenient divorce statute occurred after the completion of the transcontinental railroad in 1869. Eastern lawyers used the liberal residency and grounds provisions to obtain quick and easy divorces for their clients. In the eight years between 1869 and 1877, Utah's civil divorces increased from 75 in one year to as many as 914 in 1877, while the general population had slightly less than doubled. Nearly all of these divorces were initiated by nonresidents.[49]

The federally appointed governor, George W. Emery, strongly urged the legislature to amend the divorce laws in 1876; but the legislature did not act until after a grand jury investigation in 1877 and another appeal by Emery in 1878.[50] Divorces dropped to 122 that year. Although Mormon ecclesiastical courts continued to grant divorce for incompatibility, civil law could no longer embrace a religious concept too liberal for prevailing social norms and policies. Once again Mormon theology and practice met and were forced to yield to federal authority. Mormon legal theory, however, continued to focus on the *quality* of the marital relationship rather than the institution of marriage itself, putting Utah on the liberal side of this nationally debated social issue.[51] Though even more controversial than woman suffrage, liberalizing divorce laws was on the agenda of many social activists of this time.[52]

Custody and Guardianship

The common-law approach to guardianship vested custody and guardianship rights exclusively in fathers. Children were considered dependents entitled to support but were also essentially the property of their fathers, who were entitled to their children's services and wages.[53] Early Utah territorial law likewise affirmed that the father was the guardian of his minor children during their lifetimes and had the power to appoint another guardian upon his death. Thus, mothers became guardians only if their husbands became incapacitated, appointed them guardians, or died without appointing another guardian.[54] In the case of divorce, common law also awarded custody to the father.[55]

The first law in Utah, however, recognized that women could be awarded custody of children when the legislature granted probate courts authority to make provision for maintaining the wife and children who were placed in her custody. The law further allowed for the divorcing parties to mutually agree on the disposition of the children; children age ten or older could designate their choice of custodial parent.[56]

If a minor child owned property that did not derive from either parent, the courts were empowered to appoint a guardian to manage the property. No express preference was statutorily conferred upon fathers. Rather, the law provided that either the mother or father (or other adult) could be appointed and that children over fourteen could select the guardian.[57]

Utah law was consistent with early attempts in other jurisdictions nationally to accord greater custody rights to women. These changes were influenced in part by the reform efforts of women's rights advocates. The 1848 Seneca Falls "Declaration of Sentiments" described the male-authored laws of custody and guardianship as being in total disregard of the "happiness of women" and kept these issues at the forefront of the women's rights campaign. Nineteenth-century ideology assigned the proper sphere of women to the home and defined their primary role as motherhood, a view that contributed in some instances to the judicial acceptance of expanded legal rights for women within the home. Finally, the emergence of the role of the courts as arbiters and protectors of the "best interests of the child" led to an erosion of the paternal custody rights and an increase in maternal ones. The power shifted away from husbands and fathers, not directly to women, however, but to the state. While the law did begin to recognize women's legal capacity for custody and guardianship, the ability to enjoy those rights still depended on a discretionary determination by a male-dominated judicial system.[58]

Utah's unique family situation—where one man fathered many children with multiple wives—however, clearly necessitated some circumvention of the common-law decree on guardianship. When Isaiah Cox of St. George moved to Mexico to escape federal prosecution, his plural wife, Martha Cragun Cox, became, in effect, the primary guardian of her children. She taught school to provide for them, while her young sons assisted by carrying the mail. Their wages became Martha's to control.[59] Without paternal influence, sometimes for years at a time, plural wives were thrust into decision-making roles regarding their children. In some cases, plural wives' situations were tantamount to divorce since they lived apart from their husbands throughout their married lives, often in separate cities, and frequently received little or no maintenance from them. They were in fact, if not in law, the primary guardians of their children. Moreover, a plural wife would sometimes give one of her children to a childless sister-wife to rear, a decision between the women rather than by the father. The reality of life in Mormon society obviated the rule of common law and its assumptions about parent-child relationships.

PROPERTY RIGHTS: CONTROL OF REAL ESTATE AND WILLS

When the Mormon pioneers first arrived in the Salt Lake Valley, they surveyed the area and divided it into lots, which were distributed at a drawing. Forty-one women were allocated lots in that initial distribution. Some were single, some were widowed, some were plural wives, and some were married but were considered "heads of households" because their husbands were away with the Mormon Battalion, then on its way to California, or serving church missions.[60]

Federal land laws successfully sought to encourage female migration to the West by allowing women land ownership rights beginning with the Oregon Donation Act of 1850.[61] Passage of the federal Homestead Act of 1862 entitled the "head of a family" to obtain title to 160 acres by living on the land for five years and improving it. If the original settler died, his widow or his or her heirs could continue in possession and make the claim.[62] The Townsite Act of 1867 gave city dwellers the means to obtain title to property within the boundaries of cities and towns by filing and establishing their right to it.[63] Not until 1868 were federal land laws extended to Utah, with a federal land office following the next year.

The combined property laws had a unique effect in practice in Utah. While married women generally were not able to make claims under the Homestead or Townsite Acts, because most of them were not "heads of families" or the primary "occupant," married women who were de facto heads of families or the main adult occupant apparently made such claims successfully, giving them legal control of the property. For example, Orson Pratt and his first wife, Sarah Marinda Bates Pratt, occupied a lot in Salt Lake City for some time prior to 1861 and made improvements on it. They moved to St. George and Brigham Young took possession. Sarah returned in the winter of 1867–68, and Young relinquished possession. She resided on the property with her children, with little or no aid from her husband and with no agreement, express or implied, to pay rent to Young. When the time came to file claims under the Townsite Act, both she and Young sought title. The court held that, though she was married, as head of the household and actual occupant of the land, Sarah Pratt was entitled to the deed.[64]

The property claims of plural wives did not go unchallenged, however. In 1879, the acting secretary of the Interior Department denied a plural wife's homestead claim. His decision asserted that plural wives were, to all intents and purposes, subject to the control and governance of their husbands. If all plural wives made claims under the homestead laws, he asserted, a husband could gain control of multiple tracts. His ruling apparently gave no weight to the 1872 passage in Utah of the Married Person's Property Act giving women control of their own property, nor did it recognize that many plural wives were independent heads of households. That the practice was extensive enough to elicit notoriety is suggested by a critical article by Schuyler Colfax published in the *Chicago Advance*, December 22, 1881: "Nor should these surplus wives be allowed to claim land as the 'head of a family' to help enrich their husbands,—a right denied to legal wives anywhere. . . . Such a practice holds out a premium in power and in possession to polygamy as against law abiding citizens."[65] Though Utah's property laws mirrored those elsewhere, in Utah they carried implications beyond their original intent.

Once "legal" ownership of land was possible, the same social imperative which led to the passage of married women's property acts in other jurisdictions motivated passage of "An Act Concerning the Property Rights of Married Persons" by the Utah legislature in 1872.[66] The law provided "that all property owned by either spouse before marriage, and that acquired afterwards by gift, bequest, devise or descent with the rents, issues and profits thereof, is that separate property of that spouse by whom the same is owned or acquired and separate property owned and acquired as specified above may be held, managed, controlled, transferred and in any manner disposed of by the spouse so owning or acquiring it, without any limitation or restriction by reason of marriage."[67]

This statute, similar to married women's property acts in other states, represented a departure from the common law by allowing married women to keep their personal property and to control their real property. It took another quarter century before all states recognized married women's right to their property.

But there was still resistance. Conservative legislators in several states interpreted married women's property acts as undermining the institution of marriage and the concept of marital unity. Some of the earliest acts entitled women to *hold* their own property but not to *use* it by conveying it in any way. Such provisions, they assumed, would assist husbands acting on behalf of or together with their wives.[68] During the 1895 convention to draft the constitution for the state of Utah, the debate on this issue demonstrated ambiguity in defining the act's intent as well as its extent. Delegate Charles S. Varian, representing one point of view, proclaimed himself "in favor . . . of incorporating in this Constitution a recognition of the community system . . . which enables the wife to participate equally with the husband in all the earnings and accretions derived by either of them during the marriage."[69] Under the community property system, developed in states and territories of Spanish heritage, each spouse retained ownership of his or her property owned before marriage. All money and property acquired during the marriage was jointly owned, although the husband enjoyed the right of sole management and control. Upon the husband's death or divorce, the wife received one-half interest. It thus went beyond the provisions of the Utah Married Person's Property Act by giving women joint ownership of property acquired by either marital partner. This measure was too liberal for the delegates, who rejected it.

On the other end of the spectrum was Representative William Howard, described by a colleague as "a man too much married [who] wished to take away some of the liberties of women." He proposed that the constitution provide that a woman could sell, devise or mortgage her separate property but that "such sale, or alienation . . . shall not be valid, without the signature of her husband to the same." That amendment met only laughter and failed for lack of a second. The delegates were clearly no longer bound to the principle of coverture. The final draft of Utah's constitution gave women rights over their separate property but stopped short of including control over marital property or earnings.

The Married Person's Property Act of 1872, which allowed women to "transfer" or "dispose of" their own property "in any manner," seemed to include the power to dispose of property by will.[70] In an atypical response to the "liberating" features of the Married Person's Property Act, the legislature passed an act in 1876 providing that a married woman could *not* dispose of her property by will without her husband's consent.[71] Its intent may have been to protect a husband's interest in the property of his wife, especially if he were a polygamist. Governor George W. Emery did not sign the bill because he found it inconsistent with both the Married Person's Property Act and with national progress in this area. The legislature reconsidered and within months passed a law that allowed a married woman to dispose of her separate estate by will.[72] While Utah was already progressive in passing a Married Person's Property Act, this extension of its provisions reflected national goals in women's legal rights.

Women's right to control their property by will not only effectively challenged the underlying premise of coverture but contributed to the growing legal independence of women as well as to their individual wealth. As more states adopted Married Women's Property Laws, women's financial holdings grew proportionately throughout the century.[73] Women's wills thus provide some measurement of the extent of their individual wealth and the control they exercised over it. In Utah, for example, plural wife Elizabeth Hoagland Cannon used this newly clarified legal right by willing all her property to her husband but requested that he use it to rear and educate *her* children and that upon his death he assign her property or the equivalent to *her* children and heirs so that, in her words, "said children and heirs may stand upon the same footing as my said beloved husband's other children and heirs and not suffer any loss because I have bequeathed to him . . . all the property, real and personal, which I possess."[74] This property included an inheritance from her father and gifts from her husband, including stock in ZCMI (a church-owned cooperative retail store in Salt Lake City), the Deseret National Bank, the Provo Woolen Factory, Salt Lake City Railroad Company, and some real estate.

Like Elizabeth Cannon, Eudora Shaugnessey, in 1889, bequeathed her property to her husband in trust for the support, maintenance, and education of her children, and provided that each child was to receive his or her share of the estate when reaching the age of majority.[75] In 1894, Jane McKay Smith executed a will which appointed two of her children as trustees and directed them to sell one parcel of her property and to use the proceeds to build a house on another lot for the use of her husband and unmarried children, the husband to have the use and benefit of the house (including the right to lease it) for his lifetime. The property then passed to her daughter.[76] These women had extensive land and stock holdings whereas many other women had only small sums of money and a few personal effects to bequeath.

Rather than to their children, some women chose to leave their small inheritances to friends, their church, or to charities. Sophie Ramzell's will in 1876 bequeathed to "her sisters in the faith," Margaret Blyth, $100; Olivia Rosengreen, $100 and her "steam box"; Maria Lagergran, $100 and her "black worsted dress"; Julie Sophie Weinerholm, $100; Sarah P. Heywood, her "black silk dress," all as "tokens of remembrance." In addition, she bequeathed $200 to the Trustee-in-Trust of the Church for the temple in St. George, $200 for the temple in Salt Lake City, and all the rest, including land, buildings, notes, mortgages or furniture, to George Q. Cannon, a member of the LDS First Presidency.[77] In 1881, Sarah Cunningham willed to her niece all her wearing apparel and keepsakes, to the Female Relief Society her house and lot, "to assist the poor," and the rest to her bishop to "dispose of as proper."[78] Lydia Blinde's will of 1890 left what appeared to be all her household property to Emma Elizabeth Wilson: one "feather bed weight," three quilts, three comforters, four pillows, a cookstove, furniture, one side board, one eight-day clock, one carpet, one leaf table, a sewing machine, pictures, household furniture and dishes, books, clothes, and garden tools.[79]

However small the bequest, women clearly enjoyed designating the beneficiaries of their own property, a legal development that also provided historical insight into women's individual wealth, their personal and household possessions, and their relationship to family, friends, and community. Women's right to control their own property became a necessary corollary to the growing economic independence of women nationally throughout the nineteenth century and reflected not only changing economic realities but social attitudes as well.

Right to Sue or Be Sued

The Utah Married Person's Property Act also allowed married women to sue or be sued in their own names.[81] However, the 1884 Code of Civil Procedure required that a married woman's husband be joined in suit except "when the action concerns her separate property or her right or claim to the homestead property, . . . when the action is between herself and her husband, . . . or when she is living separate and apart from her husband by reason of his desertion of her, or by agreement in writing entered into between them."[81]

Husbands and wives did in fact bring suit together in cases which concerned only the wife. In *Oliphant v. Fox,* Mrs. Oliphant, who had recently married Mr. Oliphant, sued her former husband, Mr. Fox, to modify the divorce action which gave Fox custody of some of the children. In fact, all the children had chosen to live with Mr. and Mrs. Oliphant, and the Oliphants sued for more support.[82] This was but one of a number of cases in which husband and wives sued together to recover for injuries sustained by the wife.[83]

A few territorial statutes gave women specific rights in certain classes of cases. For example, one territorial statute granted a married woman the right to "institute and maintain, in her own name, a suit [on a bond posted by persons licensed to manufacture, dispense, or sell liquor] for all damages sustained by herself and children, or either, on account of the [liquor] traffic, and the money when collected, [was to] be paid over for the use of herself and children, or either."[84] Wrongful death actions for the loss of a child could be brought only by the father, however, unless he had died or deserted the family.[85] In either of those cases, the mother could sue for the seduction of a minor daughter, and an unmarried woman could sue her seducer in her own behalf.[86]

In the right to sue or be sued, Utah law cases resembled those in other states with Married Women's Property Acts. Through a series of amendments to the basic property acts, married women gradually acquired a legal identity independent of their husbands and important to their concurrent claims to independent political representation.

Inheritance Laws

Throughout the territorial period, the inheritance rights of wives, especially plural wives, had a stormy history under inheritance laws. A review of local court proceedings shows that many estates went to the widow and minor heirs by virtue of statutes which reserved homestead and personal property for their benefit. An 1852 law provided that the homestead (the home occupied by the family) was to be set apart for their benefit despite will provisions to the contrary or creditors' claims (both during life and upon death). The homestead exemption laws (not to be confused with the federal homestead legislation which regulated grants of public land to those who lived on and improved it for a specified period of time) were a unique American legislative innovation of the early nineteenth century. Like the bankruptcy laws of the same period and the later Married Women's Property Acts, these laws were aimed at preserving family financial stability by insulating the basic properties that a family needed to survive from imprudent financial actions by the head of the family.[87]

Initially, no specific dollar amount of the real estate was designated, but the law did outline specific items of personal property to be reserved for the use of the head of the household, or upon his death for the widow and children such as clothing, furniture, tools of trade, livestock, household effects, farm implements, and sewing machines.[88] Later enactments allowed the court to award the family additional funds from the estate, but provided that, if the widow had a sufficient, independent maintenance, the homestead would go to the minor children.[89] Under the 1852 law, the widow had only a life interest in the use of the property, her share passing to the children on her death.[90] In 1888 the law was amended to give the widow absolute ownership of all the homestead property if there were no children or one half the property if there were.[91]

In the early territorial period, these provisions were applied to both the legal and plural wives; and the whole estate was often set aside for their use as a result. The welfare of plural wives and their children had prompted the passage of these provisions. For example, when William Nixon died intestate, the court ordered that a house then under construction be completed and set aside as the homestead for two of the wives to occupy and that a third wife be given a homestead interest in the house she occupied. In addition, the court awarded amounts for the support and maintenance of all the wives and their children.[92] At J. M. Woolley's death, his estate was divided, giving one wife, Maria, and her six children the homestead on which she resided, worth $3,000, and additional property including cows, stoves, buffalo robe, dishes, beds, linens, all worth an additional $1,000, and $500 in additional personal property. Another wife, Anna Woolley, who apparently had no children, did not have a home or the necessary furnishings for housekeeping. The administrators were ordered to purchase a cooking stove and other essential furniture for her and to provide for her support and maintenance.[93]

In later enactments, the homestead was limited to a specific value ($1,000 which was later raised to $1,500) plus additional support for the wife and each child.[94] Where property remained in the estate after the homestead allowance was awarded and there was no will, the laws of intestacy determined the distribution of the balance of the estate. Possibly in recognition of the legal challenge posed by multiple wives, in 1852 the territorial legislature enacted a somewhat ambiguous law providing for the estate of a husband who died intestate:

> If there be other property remaining after the liabilities of the estate are liquidated, then it shall, in the absence of other arrangements by will, descend in equal shares to his children or their heirs; one share to such heirs through the mother of such children, if she shall survive him, during the natural life, or during her widowhood; or if he has had more than one wife who either died or survived in lawful wedlock, it shall be equally divided between the living and the heirs of those who are dead, such heirs taking by right of representation.[95]

Under this law a monogamous wife shared equally with her children. In *Cain Heirs v. Young,* the court held that the widow took "a child's part during her life or widowhood" which then descended to the children. In that case there were two children who each took a one-third interest immediately and one-half reversionary interest in the widow's one-third interest.[96] It is not clear whether the statute meant to cover cases where the decedent had more than one wife simultaneously, as in polygamy, or simply consecutively. Nor does the term "survived in lawful wedlock" necessarily specify the first wife, rather than the plural wife, since the Morrill Act outlawing such marriages had not yet been enacted. Nevertheless, no territorial court cases appear to have granted plural wives property under this statute.

Both church courts and individual informal arrangements, however, attempted to equalize the claims of all surviving wives and children, as in the case of Mary Ann Maughan of Cache Valley, the first of Peter Maughan's plural wives. When her husband died intestate, she selected local leaders to handle the settlement. She was not entirely happy with the decision, however: "January 1872. I chose G. L. Farrell and Francis Gunnell to assist in settling the estate. The Brethren thought it best for all to share alike, so [plural wife] Lissy's little boy 2 ½ years was awarded just as much as I was."[97]

A separate provision of the 1852 law, however, allowed "illegitimate children and their mothers" to inherit from the father, whether acknowledged by him or not, if it could be demonstrated that he was the father.[98] Cases later in the territorial period suggest that the probate courts elected to include plural families under this provision, so worded as to pass Congressional scrutiny while covering the justifiable if illegal claims of plural families.

In 1872, ten years after passage of the Morrill Act, a plural wife's right to inherit under the second provision of the 1852 statute was challenged. In the case of *Chapman v. Handley,* the probate court had denied any distribution from the estate of George Handley to his second wife, Sarah Chapman, and her children, ruling that the Utah statute was nullified by the Morrill Act, which made bigamy a crime and invalidated all laws which "establish, support, maintain, shield or countenance polygamy."[99] The Utah Supreme Court agreed, and plural wives and their children were left unprovided for by intestacy laws. They became dependent on the largesse of the first or legal wife or the willingness of all parties to allow ecclesiastical leaders to distribute the property. Like other cases where first wives were unwilling to share their inheritance, the plural wives of Francis Gunnell experienced economic hardship when the husband died intestate. Gunnell's plural wife Emma "wept uncontrollably for now she would have to stay in a little one-room cabin with her five children," according to a granddaughter. "She and Jane [another plural wife] were left nothing, not being recognized by law as a wife. Everything was left to the first living wife, Esther, except some property which was divided among the children."[100] To avoid this situation, Anne Leischman, aware of the precarious financial position that her father's second wife would face at his death, urged him to make a will. "My mother would come in all right if he dies for a home and things," she explained, "but Aunt Betsy would only be treated as a child. . . . She can't write a check, she can't sign a deed, she can't do anything."[101]

In 1876 Governor Emery urged the legislature to *require* that the father acknowledge illegitimate heirs before they inherit to avoid the possibility of fraudulent claims.[102] The legislature added the suggested provision to the statute while reluctantly removing any inheritance rights of mothers of illegitimate children. One year after the *Chapman v. Handley* decision, the issue of the inheritance rights of children of polygamous unions was again raised in *Cope v. Cope,* a case that went all the way to the U.S. Supreme Court. Four years after the Edmunds-Tucker Act reinforced anti-polygamy measures and one year after LDS Church President Wilford Woodruff issued his manifesto suspending the authorized performance of new plural marriages, the Supreme Court ruled that the legislature was free to provide for illegitimate children to inherit from their mother, father or both since it was "unjust to visit the sins of the parents on the heads of the children."[103] The Court disagreed with the determination of the Utah Supreme Court that the Morrill Act, which invalidated laws that supported polygamy, applied to this statute which provided inheritance rights for offspring of polygamous unions. The Court noted that subsequent federal anti-polygamy legislation had been particularly solicitous of the rights of children of polygamy, specifically legitimating any such offspring born before 1883[104] and expressly disallowing inheritance rights only of illegitimate children born twelve months after passage of the Edmunds-Tucker Act in 1887. This act provided that

> the laws enacted by the legislative assembly of the Territory of Utah which provide for or recognize the capacity of illegitimate children to inherit, or to be entitled to any distributive share in the estate of the father of any such illegitimate child, are hereby disapproved and annulled; and no illegitimate child shall hereafter be entitled to inherit from his or her father, or to receive

The Salt Lake City and County Building was dedicated in 1894 and has been in continuous use for government offices since its construction ca. 1900.

any distribute share in the estate of his or her father: Provided, That this section shall not apply to any illegitimate child born within twelve months after the passage of this act, nor to any child made legitimate by the seventh section of the [Edmunds] act.[105]

Despite the legislature's initial attempt to provide legal protection for plural wives, these later legislative and judicial decisions annulled their efforts. Intestate husbands thus left their plural wives in straitened economic circumstances. The only legal safeguard for plural wives was a will.

Occasionally some husbands designated their wives as guardians of their property but often only until their children reached maturity. For example, in 1874 John Proctor left his wives their respective homes and lands only until their youngest child reached the age of sixteen, when the property was to be sold and the proceeds divided as he specified.[107] Some men, however, entrusted full control of their estates to their surviving wives. John McDonald gave his wife a lifetime interest in his property for her own use and that of her daughters and the right to designate the distribution of the property to the daughters after her death with the provision that she eliminate from her will any daughter who married a non-Mormon.[107] Albert Merrill, with little to leave behind, willed his lot and house to his first wife but reserved the two back rooms for his second wife.[108]

At common law, if a husband either disinherited his wife or disposed of all his property in some other way, the common law right of dower, or one-third interest in his real property, protected her. In Utah, however, prohibiting dower was necessary to avoid the impracticability or even impossibility of granting multiple one-third dower interests to plural wives. While granting married women the right to control their own property, the Utah Married Person's Property Act of 1872 formally disallowed dower in property settlements. Monogamous marriages were thus seriously affected. Absence of dower effectively diminished a legal wife's claim by withdrawing her contingent, prospective interest in one third of her husband's property during his lifetime, which he could not transfer away without her consent, and granting her only an equal share with all of her husband's direct heirs at his death. While non-Mormons complained, Mormon wives declared that dower was a form of "vassalage" and a "relic of the old common law" and claimed that the property rights granted women were far more progressive and reflective of social and economic change.[109] After signing the legislation, however, Governor George L. Woods reconsidered and urged the legislature to repeal it at the next session.[110] The legislature did not. One polygamy critic, U.S. Vice-President Schuyler Colfax, after visiting Utah, argued: "The right of dower which has been abolished by the Utah legislature (so as to render a polygamous wife slavishly dependent on the husband's favor for any share of his property after his death for herself or her children) should be reenacted by national legislation and carefully guarded for the legal wife, who, in polygamy is not the favorite as a general rule. This would greatly discourage women from marrying a polygamist."[111]

In 1887 the federal government entered the controversy over the dower. Despite a growing national trend to rescind dower, passage of the anti-polygamy Edmunds-Tucker Law that year reinstated in Utah a dower interest for married women in all of their deceased husband's land held any time during the marriage.[112] Five years later Utah legislation provided rules for claiming dower, and for releasing dower interests, and created a cause of action for the wrongful withholding of dower property.[113] Court cases addressed various aspects of the right of dower, including the inability of plural wives to claim dower even when the first wife had died.[114] The court ruled essentially that "once a plural wife, always an unlawful plural wife."[115] The dower right became part of Utah law in 1896 when the first Utah state legislature enacted a dower provision which mirrored the language of the Edmunds-Tucker Act.[116]

By the end of the territorial period, because Utah was in the forefront of the homestead exemption movement and construed the right rather generously along with the federal ruling to reinstate dower rights, monogamous wives in Utah enjoyed greater protections than most women in the country. The restrictions on inheritance of polygamous children that were imposed by the final, most drastic piece of anti-polygamy legislation, the Edmunds-Tucker Act, were removed upon statehood. Plural wives, however, were left without any legal protection if not provided for by will.

Women in Non-Domestic Work

Despite the prevailing cultural value of domesticity, Brigham Young enunciated a progressive view of women in the trades and professions. For example, in 1869 he issued a call to women to expand their social usefulness:

> We have sisters here who, if they had the privilege of studying, would make just as good mathematicians or accountants as any man; and we think they ought to have the privilege to study these branches of knowledge that they may develop the powers with which they are endowed. We believe that women are useful, not only to sweep houses, wash dishes, make beds, and raise babies, but that they should stand behind the counter, study law or physic, or become good bookkeepers and be able to do the business in any counting house, and all this to enlarge their sphere of usefulness for the benefit of society at large.[117]

Out of necessity or by choice, women acted on this invitation and found employment in a variety of professions. As noted by Elizabeth Kane, wife of Brigham Young's friend, Thomas L. Kane, during a visit to Utah in 1872: "They close no career on a woman in Utah by which she can earn a living."[118] Because of polygamy, widowhood, and their husbands' missionary service, many women acted as heads of their households, including the role of breadwinner for themselves and their children—and, not infrequently, for their husbands as well. Some did so in traditional ways: domestic service, sewing, millinery, and managing boarding houses. Less traditional occupations in which Utah women were employed included typesetting and printing, bookkeeping, clerking, and accounting. Some women became telegraph operators, nurses, and midwives, and doctors. In the area of vocational choice, Utah was in advance of many other states and territories, including actively finding ways to train women in their chosen field.[119] Even the field of law was open to women, although such progressivism is ironic, considering Mormon distrust of lawyers during the early territorial period.[120] It was this very disdain for professional lawyers that opened the door for women to enter the legal profession.

To avoid the necessity of requiring licensed lawyers to protect one's legal interest when challenged, the 1852 legislature provided another route for litigating cases, a statute that appeared to allow women as well as men to act as their own legal counsel or to choose any person, male or female, of good moral character to represent them.[121] While a few courageous women were struggling to assert their admission to various state bars elsewhere, largely unsuccessfully, Utah's provision, which allowed men *and women* to act not only in their own behalf but also as counsel for others, was markedly advanced. Although the provision was seldom invoked by women, in 1874 a Provo woman, Martha

Jane Coray, may have assisted a sick friend in a legal capacity during several days of court hearings in a custody suit.[122] She was at least an active participant in the case. To further protect individuals from exorbitant legal fees, the same act prohibited attorneys from compelling payment through the courts.

Despite these provisions for non-professional legal service and an early denigration of the profession, there were attorneys in Utah territory, including women. Rather than legal expertise or academic credentials, admission to the Utah bar was based on good moral character, a favorable report of an examining committee, or admission to practice in the highest courts of other states or territories:

> Applicants for admission to practice as attorneys and counselors of this court, shall be admitted on proof, presented at the time of applications, of good moral character, and on the favorable report of an examining Committee appointed for that purpose; or on the production of a certificate or proof of previous admission to practice in the highest Court of any State or other Territory of the United States. A person admitted to practice in this Court shall be entitled to practice in all Courts of this Territory.[123]

In 1872, Utah formally admitted two women to the bar: Phoebe Couzins, a graduate of the Washington University Law School in Missouri, who had previously been admitted to practice in Missouri state and federal courts and in the Arkansas state court but had been denied admission by several other state bars; and Georgiana Snow, daughter of Zerubbabel Snow, a former attorney general of Utah Territory, who had clerked in her father's law office for three years. In welcoming Couzins and Snow "as sisters at the bar," the court expressed an unusually favorable view of the prospect of having women members of the bar: "It has been said by a learned writer that law is the refinement of reasoning. Perhaps it is natural to infer that those who have the most refinement ought to be very clear, perhaps intuitive reasoners. Certainly no gentleman of this bar would deny that, in social life, woman's influence is refining and elevating. May we not hope that the honorable profession of the law be made even more honorable by the admission of women to the bar?"

And in welcoming Miss Snow the court stated: "It may be pertinent for the court to remark that Miss Snow will find in Utah an ample field for the exercise of her professional talent . . . . The fact that she has long resided here, and that she is the daughter of a lawyer, will be of great service to her, giving her much advantage over strangers who come here, and especially in listening to the complaints of her own sex."[124]

Far from being impediments to this traditionally male profession, Judge James B. McKean, chief justice of Utah, asserted, their womanly characteristics would prove advantageous. Myra Bradwell of Illinois, however, found those same characteristics grounds for denying her entry into law. In 1869, after studying law in her husband's office, she applied for admission to the Illinois

Bar. Denied admission, Bradwell carried her case to the U.S. Supreme Court. When the Court finally heard her case in 1873, it ruled against her, declaring, among other reasons, that "the natural and proper timidity and delicacy which belong to the female sex evidently unfits it for many of the occupations of civil life." Viewing the legal profession as outside the domain of women's "natural sphere," it declared that "the constitution of the family organization, which is founded in the divine ordinance, as well as in the nature of things, indicates the domestic sphere as that which properly belongs to the domain and function of womanhood."[125] This attitude prevailed in the majority of states and territories, although this strong bastion of male dominance was beginning to fall through the agitation and determination of women activists. Mormon women concurred with this social norm, but they also created a uniquely female public domain that intersected philosophically with the private and expanded their opportunities for non-domestic activities. Moreover, though Utah's rationale behind its approach to the legal profession did not result from female agitation, it put Utah in the vanguard of states to remove this impediment to women's vocational rights.

However, the admission of Couzins and Snow did not herald a surge of female lawyers in Utah Territory. Both women eventually left Utah and proved to be ineffective role models for other women in that profession although both became politically active. But in 1892, Utah territory admitted Josephine Kellogg of Provo to the bar, and records show that several other Utah women studied law before the turn of the century, although no evidence is available that they were admitted to the bar.[126]

Jury Duty

In Wyoming, a woman suffrage statute was passed a month before Utah's, which also allowed women to sit on juries, As soon as Wyoming women began acting in that capacity, however, men organized to take away that right, and it was not restored until the 1940s.[127] Unlike the Wyoming law, Utah's first woman suffrage law, passed in 1870, did not expressly cover the public duty of jury service or the right to hold public office. Before that time women did not sit on juries in the territory, although the law was less than clear in excluding them. Utah's first general code of civil procedure provided that if either party requested a jury, the court should issue an order to the proper officer requiring him to summon for that purpose, not less than three nor more than twelve "judicious persons," which suggests the possibility of including women.[128] However, the code of criminal procedure enacted in the same session required grand juries of "judicious *men*."[129] Despite the gender-neutral wording of the civil statute, there is no evidence that women ever served on juries in civil cases nor sought to do so. All enactments concerning petit, grand, and special juries expressly required men, although some women occasionally served on coroners' juries.[130] After the Civil War, Utah's jury statutes were amended to omit the "free" and "white" requirements, but the "male" requirement remained.[131]

A case in which the defendant claimed that the exclusion of members of his religion from the jury was a denial of equal protection illustrates the prevailing interpretation of "a jury of one's peers" of particular importance to women. In pointing out the illogic of the defendant's argument, the court stated: "The correctness of this theory is contradicted by every day's experience. Women are not allowed to sit on juries; are they thereby denied the equal protection of the laws?"[132] Many women, like Susan B. Anthony, would have answered, "Yes!" In 1872, following a suggestion by the National Woman Suffrage Association, women were urged "to apply for registration" and if that failed to bring suit in order "to secure general and judicial recognition" of their cause. Their plan was to test the Fourteenth Amendment in relation to women's right to vote, who were U.S. citizens. Anthony and fifteen of her friends in Rochester, New York, succeeded in voting but were thereafter arrested for violating the Enforcement Act. Anthony promptly sued. Before the verdict was delivered the judge gave Anthony opportunity to speak. She responded with a lengthy diatribe against the discriminatory legal system which denied her a jury of her peers, since no women were in the jury box. Though she lost her case, the judge imposed neither a fine nor imprisonment.[133]

In many states, jury service was tied to voter status, and women hoped that the opportunity to serve on juries would follow the grant of suffrage. In the decade prior to passage of national suffrage for women by the Nineteenth Amendment in 1920, Washington, Kansas, California, New York, and Michigan gave women the right to serve on juries along with voting rights. Most other states, however, did not.[134]

While many men and women slowly accommodated themselves to the notion of women in the political realm, jury service still appeared to be more appropriately and exclusively a male duty.

Even in those states where jury service was allowed, exemption provisions led to curtailment of women's presence in the jury box. As late as 1961, the U.S. Supreme Court upheld a state's power to automatically exempt women from jury service.[135]

A defendant's right to have a jury drawn from a pool that included women was not recognized until 1975, and the practice of using peremptory challenges to exclude female jurors on the basis of gender was not ruled unconstitutional until 1994. Indeed for most women in the United States, the right to be considered for jury service was not fully vouchsafed until the last decade of the twentieth century.[136]

The right to serve on juries became an issue for Utah women after statehood in 1896. Although the state constitution allowed women all civil and political rights and privileges, this provision was at first not construed to include jury service.[137] The point was debated and passed in the first state legislative session in January 1896. Utah thus became the first state to have a permanent statute that allowed women to serve as jurors. However, Utah women could also claim exemption from doing so. Utah's first governor, Heber M. Wells, so indicated in his 1902 report on the effectiveness of woman suffrage in Utah, published in Susan B. Anthony's *History of Woman Suffrage:* "One of the bugaboos of the opposition [to woman suffrage] was that women would be compelled to sit on juries. Not a single instance of the kind has happened in the State, for the reason that women are never summoned; the law simply exempts them, but does not exclude them."[138]

POLITICAL RIGHTS

The national suffrage movement, Utah's location in the more liberal West, Mormon interests, and federal authority all converged when the Utah's territorial legislature granted Utah women the right to vote in 1870. During the 1860s, Congress introduced several bills extending the franchise to women of the various territories, partly as an experiment in female suffrage, as an inducement to female migration to the West, and as a mean of eradicating polygamy in Utah. Since plural wives were particularly oppressed, it was reasoned, suffrage in Utah territory would help elevate them by giving them the political power to remove the source of their oppression.[139]

When Congressional attempts at woman suffrage legislation failed, Utah's delegate, William H. Hooper, embraced the idea of suffrage for Utah women as a means of countering the image of subjugated Mormon women while also enhancing Mormon political unity. There was little fear that women would use the vote as a tool to outlaw polygamy since they were as committed to the principle as LDS men. In fact, in a show of unity, a number of LDS women, responding to a particularly punitive anti-polygamy congressional proposal, planned a general woman's rally for January 1870. Declaring that it was time to "rise up . . . and speak for ourselves," they also drafted a resolution to "demand" from Acting Governor S. A. Mann "the right of franchise" and planned to send two women to Washington, D.C., to plead their case before lawmakers.[140] As matters turned out, it became unnecessary for them to act on either resolution. The territorial legislature granted them the right to vote just weeks later, and various business associations throughout the country decried the harsh economic restraints and political ramifications of the proposed bill.[141] The pressure of Hooper's recommendation, the favorable attitude toward woman suffrage of church leaders, positive articles in the *Deseret News,* and adoption of woman suffrage in nearby Wyoming a few weeks earlier all contributed to a favorable outcome in Utah. To cap these persuasive developments, Mormon women's bold initiative in mounting a rally in defense of plural marriage influenced the legislature to return a unanimous vote to enfranchise women. In the prolonged absence of the newly appointed governor, Mann reluctantly signed the act on February 12, 1870.[142] National suffragists were delighted, Congress surprised, and federal officials in Utah alarmed.

Although enfranchisement did not expressly confer the right to hold office, Mary Cook ran for Salt Lake County Superintendent of Common

Schools in 1874 and her sister Ida was elected Superintendent of Schools in Cache County in 1877. Both women, however, were ruled ineligible.[143] In 1878, women attended caucuses of the Mormon People's Party for the first time, and three women were elected delegates to the county convention. At that convention, Emmeline B. Wells, editor of the *Woman's Exponent,* was nominated for county treasurer. When it was again determined that the statute did not allow a woman to hold office, women began a two-year campaign to amend the law. The first attempt in 1878 failed. A second effort in 1880 passed the legislature but the federally appointed governor refused to sign the bill.[144] In commiserating with Utah women, Susan B. Anthony lamented the "utter hopelessness of making any changes. . . . Men have so long had absolute control," she continued, "that every activity of woman to shape matters in the primary meetings and nominating conventions is still deemed an intrusion on her part."[145] Emmeline B. Wells, a strong proponent of the bill, quickly retorted. In Utah, she said, "every office open to woman, she has been allowed to occupy," including membership on nominating committees. As delegates to county and territorial conventions, women have always "been most politely treated, invited to speak, and express opinion." Failure to amend the law to include the right to hold office, she wrote, cannot be laid at the feet of the Mormon legislature, but solely at the door of the federally appointed governor, who had "refused to extend the courtesy of his signature."[146] Women made no further attempts to achieve the right to hold elective office until statehood.

In 1878, almost simultaneously with the drive to extend women's political rights, a group of disaffected and non-Mormon women organized the Anti-Polygamy Society. One of the society's first acts was to draw up a memorial to President Rutherford B. Hayes denouncing polygamy and urging the repeal of woman suffrage in Utah. Mormon women countered with a second mass rally and their own memorial affirming their constitutional right to the free exercise of their religion.[147] The Anti-Polygamy Society, however, caught the interest of many national moral reform associations dedicated to stamping out immoral practices, among which they included polygamy, and proved to be a formidable national force in publicizing the practice and creating public opinion against it.

Local efforts to disfranchise Mormon women climaxed in 1880, when members of the non-Mormon Liberal party challenged the validity of the 1870 law giving women the vote. They filed suit for a writ of mandamus to compel the voting registrar in Salt Lake County to strike the names of all women from the registration list. Their challenge was based on the claim that the act was discriminatory because the 1859 act enfranchising male voters required them to be taxpayers while the 1870 act contained no such requirement for women. In addition, men were required to be citizens but women who were only wives or daughters of citizens (and not citizens themselves) were eligible to vote. The large number of immigrant converts to Mormonism made the provision particularly relevant. The defense argued that the court had no jurisdiction and that the complaint did not state a cause of action. The court affirmed its jurisdiction but denied the mandamus, ruling that this writ was capable only of compelling a person to do what the law as enacted required him to do, not to prevent a person from following the law or compel him to act contrary to the law.[148] Letters and telegrams of congratulations to the women of Utah poured in from suffragists throughout the country.

In *Lyman v. Martin,* decided the next year, the validity of the act granting women voting rights was again challenged on the same basis. In that case, a candidate sued to have election results publicly announced by officials who had refused to do so because they claimed the election law was void. Rather than voiding the statute giving women the vote, however, the court ruled that the taxpayer requirement for men should be stricken. It also held that the act *perhaps* permitted a female noncitizen to register and that other territorial statutes requiring voters to be citizens applied to women as well.[149] Several other unsuccessful local attempts to disfranchise Utah women followed, but suffrage was left intact.[150]

Where local court action was unable to rescind women's right to vote, federal legislation succeeded. The Edmunds Act of 1882 denied suffrage to all participants in plural marriage and empowered a federally appointed Utah Commission with control of elections. In *Murphy v. Ramsey,* the plaintiffs contested the constitutionality of a "test oath" requiring voters to declare whether they were then practicing or ever had practiced plural marriage. In 1885 the case reached the U.S. Supreme Court, which held that the retroactive sweep of the oath was beyond the commission's power but upheld the disfranchisement of those currently practicing polygamy. Two of the plaintiffs, both women and both married to polygamists, were thus allowed to vote, since the husband of one had died before passage of the Edmunds Act, and the other had separated from her husband since its passage. The court required that the prospective voter be evaluated on the basis of his or her status at the time of registration.[151] Thus non-Mormon and Mormon women who did not practice polygamy or no longer practiced it (widowed, divorced, separated, deserted) were still entitled to vote—but only temporarily. The Edmunds-Tucker Act, which Congress passed in 1887, the most sweeping of all anti-polygamy bills, disfranchised all Utah women. Thus, the 1870 gratuitous offering of suffrage to Utah women, which had met a pressing religious need, had now, like other laws associated with polygamy, also bowed to federal intervention. Many non-Mormon women living in Utah willingly relinquished the franchise, their aversion to polygamy being stronger than their appreciation of the vote.

The final chapter in the story of woman suffrage in Utah concerns the effort of Mormon women and a few other Utah suffragists to regain the vote. After Mormon Church president Wilford Woodruff issued his manifesto in 1890, counseling church members to obey the law of the land and withdrawing support for new plural marriages, the forty-year wait for statehood gradually drew to a close. Presidential pardons and a general amnesty in 1891 by outgoing President Benjamin Harrison restored some of the rights of citizenship cancelled by the Edmunds-Tucker Law. A second amnesty in 1893 by Grover Cleveland restored the franchise to polygamist males but not to women. Utah women had already organized to regain suffrage, however, in anticipation of statehood. They were therefore ready to mount an extensive grassroots effort to secure a commitment of support from both political parties when the Constitutional Convention met in March 1895.[152] Once the delegates were elected, however, and the Convention convened, the status of woman suffrage became uncertain.

An unexpected debate on the issue lasted twelve days, a fifth of the time allotted for the entire Convention. One prominent delegate, B. H. Roberts, a Democrat from Davis County and a member of the third-tier General Authorities (First Council of Seventy, just below the First Presidency and Quorum of the Twelve), persuasively argued first, that woman suffrage might elicit a negative reaction in Congress and jeopardize passage of the constitution, and second, that as voters or office holders, women lost their womanliness. Other delegates tended to agree with one or the other of these arguments. A compromise, to which many delegates agreed, was to submit the woman suffrage clause to the voters separately from the constitution. However, despite the numerous petitions favoring separate submission and the eloquent oratory of Roberts, pro-suffrage delegates Orson F. Whitney and Franklin S. Richards were more persuasive. The delegates finally passed the woman suffrage proposal, as did the voters at the ratification election, and Utah's women once again enjoyed the vote. Riding on its coattails was a broad affirmation of equality of rights for women: "The rights of the citizens of the State of Utah to vote and hold office shall not be denied or abridged on account of sex. Both male and female citizens of this State shall enjoy equally all civil, political and religious rights and privileges."[153]

A further twist in the history of woman suffrage in Utah occurred after the close of the Constitutional Convention. Ambiguity in the language of the Enabling Act, which permitted Utah to apply for statehood, raised the possibility that women might be eligible to vote at the ratification election in November 1895. Franklin S. Richards, a convention delegate, proposed that they do so but it was never brought before the assembly. Thus, the intent of the Enabling Act had to be judicially decided. Sarah E. Anderson of Ogden, Utah, agreed to be party to a test case. In July, two months after adjournment of the Constitutional Convention, Anderson attempted to register and was denied. She sued and was issued a writ of mandate against the registrar of voters, Charles Tyree, who appealed to the Utah Supreme Court.

While awaiting the court's decision, both Democrats and Republicans wooed women to their parties. The Republicans went so far as to put the names of three women on their ballot, holding to the assumption that they would

Sarah E. Anderson, Ogden,
Utah, agreed to be a test case
for the Enabling Act. In 1895
she attempted to register to
vote and was denied.

be legally entitled to hold office by the time they were installed in January of the following year. Though the District Court had ruled in favor of Sarah E. Anderson, the Utah Supreme Court ruled against her appeal. The qualifications designed by the Enabling Act (male, citizen, twenty-one or over), it ruled, were in force for the November election and the provision in the Utah Constitution making women qualified voters could have no effect until the constitution was ratified and Utah was a state.[154] Public pressure forced the women to withdraw at that point; but the next year, legally empowered to vote and hold office, Utah women helped to elect Martha Hughes Cannon as the first woman state senator in the United States, and two other women, Sarah E. Anderson of Ogden and Eurithe K. LaBarthe, as state representatives, along with several other women as county recorders.[155] And so, after a tumultuous half-century, the longest territorial period of any state in the United States, came to a close, and Utah entered the Union as the forty-third state and the third state to grant its women the right to vote.

With Wilford Woodruff's 1890 Manifesto against polygamy and the 1896 grant of statehood, the Mormon experiment in legislating support of what came to be an illegal practice became irrelevant. The umbrella of the Constitutional guarantee of freedom of religion, which Mormons had always claimed, failed to protect them from the storms of public outrage and federal prosecution. For nearly half a century the Mormon Church had held tenaciously to a religious practice at odds with the country's social norms, using the law to protect that practice. The resulting zigzag course of law-making in nineteenth-century Utah also reflected the looser gender boundaries resulting from the expanding women's rights movement and the freer Western social environment of which it was a part. In the process, it advanced a consciousness of women's need for a separate legal and political identity, moving Utah women into the forefront of the movement for equal rights. By the time of statehood, however, other Utah laws and its judicial system were generally harmonious with more traditional American jurisprudence. There were clear jurisdictional boundaries between the district and probate courts, and Mormon ecclesiastical courts heard fewer domestic and civil disputes, confining themselves to traditional ecclesiastical matters.

For nearly fifty years, territorial Utah served as a study of the interplay of law and the community of interests it serves. To achieve statehood, Utah had to acknowledge the broader community of which it was a reluctant part by eliminating the offending practice of plural marriage as well as those laws designed to protect it. Utah began the territorial period with a statutory disassociation from the common law and public disdain for the legal profession. Yet its dominant institution, the Mormon Church, found itself drawn ineluctably into a protracted legal battle with the federal government, ironically dependent on the legal profession to defend its interests. In that legal struggle, the women of Utah, both Mormon and non-Mormon, found their legal status constantly in flux. Plural wives were ultimately the losers. Following statehood, a time of enormous legal readjustment, they continued to face legal discrimination as they attempted to press mainly unsuccessful claims for legal protection. But Utah entered statehood bringing with it a number of legal and political entitlements to women, including the right to vote, hold elective office, practice law, serve on juries, and other advances still unavailable to women in the majority of states. The half-century struggle had its rewards. Perhaps the major legal insight culled from Utah's territorial experience is how the law can serve as an instrument of social innovation, even as it serves as a tool of social conformity.

NOTES

1. Joan Hoff [Wilson], *Law, Gender, and Injustice: A Legal History of U.S. Women* (New York: New York University Press, 1991), 89–90, 119–22.

2. William Blackstone, *Commentaries on the Law of England,* 4 vols. (1765–69; reprinted New York: W. E. Dean, 1853), 1:355. Many editions of this work were printed in the United States during the nineteenth century.

3. For more details on coverture and women's rights under common law, see Marylynn Salmon, *Women and the Law of Property in Early America* (Chapel Hill: University of North Carolina Press, 1986); Norma Basch, *In the Eyes of the Law: Women, Marriage, and Property in Nineteenth-Century New York* (Ithaca, N.Y.: Cornell University Press, 1982) and Basch, "Invisible Women: The Legal Fiction of Marital Unity in Nineteenth Century America," *Feminist Studies* 5 (Summer 1979): 346-66; Linda K.

Kerber, "From Declaration of Independence to the Declaration of Sentiments: The Legal Status of Women in the Early Republic 1776-1848," *Human Rights* 6 (1976-77), 115-24; John D. Johnston, "Sex and Property: The Common Law Tradition, The Law School Curriculum, and Developments Toward Equality," *New York University Law Review* 47 (1972): 1033-83. Several treatises published in America in the late nineteenth and early twentieth centuries summarized the common law and its effect on women, also outlining statutory and judicial modifications of it. See, for example, Joel Prentiss Bishop, *Law of Married Women* (Boston: Little, Brown, and Co., 1875); John C. Wells, *A Treatise on the Separate Property of Married Women* (Cincinnati, Ohio: Robert Clark and Co., 1879); C. H. Scribner, *A Treatise on the Law of Dower* (Philadelphia: T. and J. W. Johnson, 1883); George E. Harris, *A Treatise on the Law of Contracts by Married Women* (Albany, N.Y.: Banks and Bros., 1887); Charles Austin Enslow, *Law Concerning Women* (Seattle, Wash.: I. N. Davidson, 1928); Charles Garfield Vernier, *American Family Laws* (London: Oxford University Press, 1935).

4.   Basch, Kerber, and Johnston all address this legal concept. Early nineteenth-century feminists used Blackstone and the strictures of the common law in their unmodified form as a symbol of the inequalities that women experienced. The 1848 "Declaration of Sentiments" drafted at the first woman's rights convention in Seneca Falls, New York, included the inability of married women to hold property and control their wages as one of the grievances enumerated. See Susan B. Anthony, Elizabeth Cady Stanton, and Matilda Joslyn Gage, eds., *History of Woman Suffrage,* 3 vols. (New York: Towles and Wells, 1881), 1:70–71.

5.   Blackstone, *Commentaries on the Law of England,* 1:355. Johnston, "Sex and Property: The Common Law Tradition, the Law School Curriculum, and Developments Toward Equality," 1033–83, discusses four rationales for the common-law status of married women, none of which fully accounts for it: (1) the biblical ideal that husband and wife become one flesh may justify the merger of identities but does not justify women's subordinate status; (2) the theory of a husband's guardianship of his wife is invalid because the law is inconsistent in its treatment of women as the weaker sex, and single women do not fall under this rationale; (3) marriage as a contract does not hold, given the uniformity of results in each marriage arrangement and the lack of free bargaining power; (4) the practical need for final authority to resolve disputes does not necessarily require that the husband have all power. In business partnerships, management and decision-making powers are shared.

6.   Hoff, *Law, Gender and Injustice,* 120–128, 87–90. Initially, removal of legal disabilities dominated the arguments of the early feminists; and while twenty-nine states had passed some form of married women's property legislation by 1865, it was in many cases limited and narrowly interpreted. Legal historians have traced the continuity of traditional judicial attitudes in New York and elsewhere, especially in appellate decisions, despite the passage of married women's property acts.

7.   Hoff, *Law, Gender and Injustice,* 119–22; see also Nancy Cott, *Public Vows: A History of Marriage and the Nation* (Cambridge, Mass.: Harvard University Press, 2000), 52–55.

8. Joan Hoff [Wilson], "The Legal Status of Women in the Late Nineteenth and Early Twentieth Centuries, *Human Rights* 6 (1976–77): 126–27. This success in altering the law provided impetus for the political struggle for greater rights for women that followed.

9. The disappointing wording and legal construction of the Fourteenth (1866) and Fifteenth (1869) Amendments dashed the expectations of women suffragists who then began their long struggle for another amendment guaranteeing sex equality.

10. "Declaration of Sentiments and Resolutions," in Miriam Schneir, *Feminism: The Essential Historical Writings* (New York: Vintage Books, 1972), 76–82; also Anthony and Stanton, *History of Woman Suffrage,* 1:70–71.

11. Mari J. Matsuda, "The West and the Legal Status of Women: Explanations of Frontier Feminism," *Journal of the West* 24, no. 1 (January 1985): 47–56.

12. Brigham Young, June 22–29, 1865, *Journal of Discourses,* 26 vols. (London and Liverpool: LDS Booksellers Depot, 1855–86), 10:329. Young's discourse urged the blending the temporal and the spiritual.

13. A popular Mormon hymn, "O My Father," written by Eliza R. Snow, expresses the notion of a Heavenly Mother, a doctrine accepted and understood but seldom taught in Mormon theology. Linda P. Wilcox, "The Mormon Concept of a Mother in Heaven," in *Sisters in Spirit: Mormon Women in Historical and Cultural Perspective,* edited by Maureen Ursenbach Beecher and Lavina Fielding Anderson (Urbana: University of Illinois Press, 1987), 64–77; Cheryl B. Preston, "Feminism and Faith: Reflections on the Heavenly Mother," *Texas Journal of Women and Law* 2 (1993): 337.

14. Wilford Woodruff's Journal, July 25, 1847, quoted in B. H. Roberts, *A Comprehensive History of the Church of Jesus Christ of Latter-day Saints,* 6 vols. (1930; Provo, Utah: BYU Press, 1965), 3:269.

15. R. Collin Magrum, "Furthering the Cause of Zion: An Overview of the Mormon Ecclesiastical Court System in Early Utah," *Journal of Mormon History* 10 (1983): 79–90; Mangrum and Edwin B. Firmage, *Zion in the Courts: A Legal History of the Church of Jesus Christ of Latter-day Saints, 1830–1900* (Urbana: University of Illinois Press, 1988); Raymond Swenson, "Resolution of Civil Disputes by Mormon Ecclesiastical Courts," *Utah Law Review* 12 (1978): 573–95; and Stephen J. Sorensen, "Civil and Criminal Jurisdiction of LDS Bishops and High Council Courts, 1847–1852," *Task Papers in LDS History, No. 17* (Salt Lake City: LDS Church Archives, April 1977).

16. "An Act to Establish a Territorial Government for Utah," September 9, 1850, 9, *United States Statutes at Large,* 453. A study of that first bid for statehood is Dale L. Morgan, "The State of Deseret," *Utah Historical Quarterly* 8 (January 1940): 65–251. For the Deseret statutes re-passed by the Utah Territorial Legislature, see *1851 Utah Laws* 205. Though Mormons numerically dominated Utah during the territorial period, the laws enacted by its legislature were interpreted by a federally appointed Utah Supreme Court, which to a large extent represented the minority population of Utah. Paul A. Wright estimated the non-Mormon population at 7 percent in 1867, 17 percent in 1874, and 25 percent in 1887. Quoted in Elizabeth D. Gee,

"Justice for All or for the 'Elect'? Utah County Probate Court, 1855–1872," *Utah Historical Quarterly* 48 (Spring 1980): 129. The territorial legislature was even more imbalanced. Of the 381 men who served in the legislature between 1851 and 1894, 330 (86.6 percent) are known to be Mormon, 26 non-Mormon, and 25 of unknown religious affiliation. Through 1884 no known non-Mormons served, although ten men of unknown religion were members. Federal anti-polygamy legislation in 1882 disqualified polygamists as voters or office-holders. Non-Mormons serving in the legislature rose from one in 1886 to ten by 1894 with five of unknown religion also serving the latter year. Of the 330 known Mormons, 46 were General Authorities of the church, 132 had served or would serve in stake presidencies and high councils, and 125 were in bishoprics (ecclesiastical offices). Marital statistics of the 340 for whom information is available indicate that 55 percent were monogamous, 43 percent were polygamous, and 3 percent were single at election. Despite Brigham Young's antagonism toward lawyers, there were 37 in the legislature (most serving in the latter part of the territorial period), 24 or nearly two-thirds of whom were Mormon (Statistics were compiled from unpublished data collected by Davis Bitton and Gordon Irving. Used by their permission).

17. As quoted in Gustive O. Larson, *Outline History of Territorial Utah* (1958; reprinted, Provo, Utah: Brigham Young University Press, 1972), 85–86.

18. Federal law provided: "All laws passed by the Legislative Assembly and Governor of any Territory except in the Territories of Colorado, Dakota, Idaho, Montana and Wyoming, shall be submitted to Congress, and, if disapproved, shall be null and of no effect." Title 23, "The Territories," Section 1850, *1875 Revised Statutes of the United States,* 328.

19. Gordon M. Bakken, "Judicial Review in the Rocky Mountain Territorial Courts," *American Journal of Legal History* 15 (January 1971): 56–75; Everett L. Cooley, "Carpetbag Rule: Territorial Government in Utah," *Utah Historical Quarterly* 26 (April 1958): 107–29.

20. "An Act Providing for a Probate Court," Section 29, *1851–52 Laws of Utah,* 85, granted authority to Utah probate courts over a wide range of cases that traditionally could be tried only in courts of general jurisdiction—which, in Utah territory, were federal courts, administered by federally appointed judges.

21. James B. Allen, "The Unusual Jurisdiction of County Probate Courts in the Territory of Utah," *Utah Historical Quarterly* 36 (Spring 1968): 132–42. See also Jay E. Powell, "Fairness in the Salt Lake County Probate Court," *Utah Historical Quarterly* 38 (Summer 1970): 256–62; and Gee, "Justice for All or for the 'Elect'?"

22. Utah State Archives webpage, "Utah Court System, Territorial Period, 1850–1896," retrieved on February 13, 2004, from http://archives.utah.gov/Referenc/utcourts.htm.

23. Brigham Young, "Correspondence between His Excellency Governor Brigham Young and David Adams, M.D.," *Millennial Star* 14 (May 29, 1852): 215.

24. "An Act Concerning Provisions Applicable to the Laws of the Territory of Utah," Section 1, January 14, 1854, *1853-54 Laws of Utah,* 16. See also Shane Swindle, "The Struggle over the Adoption of Common Law in Utah," *Thetean,* May 1984, 76–97.

25. Quoted in Bakken in "Judicial Review," 61.

26. *Mormon Church v. U.S.,* 136 United States Reports 1 (1889). The Utah Statute disclaiming common law was challenged in *People v. Green,* 1 Utah Reports 11 (1855): operative pursuant to section 17 of the Organic Act; *Thomas v. Union Pacific Railway Co.,* 1 Utah Reports 232 (1875); *First National Bank v. Kinner,* 1 Utah Reports 100 (1876): The people "tacitly agreed" to the maxims of the common law, but these maxims awaited court recognition to become the territory's common law; *Hilton v. Thatcher,* 31 Utah Reports 360 (1906); *Hilton v. Stewart,* 31 Utah Reports 255 (1907); *Norton v. Tufts,* 19 Utah Reports 470 (1899).

27. For two recent accounts of the anti-polygamy crusade, see Sarah Barringer Gordon, *The Mormon Question: Polygamy and Constitutional Conflict in Nineteenth-Century America* (Chapel Hill: University of North Carolina Press, 2002); and Joan Smyth Iversen, *The Anti-Polygamy Controversy in U.S. Women's Movements, 1880–1925* (New York: Garland Publishing, 1997).

28. "Anti-Polygamy Act," An Act to Punish and Prevent the Practice of Polygamy in the Territories of the United States and other Places, and Disapproving and Annulling Certain Acts of the Legislative Assembly of the Territory of Utah, July 1, 1862, 12 *United States Statutes at Large,* 501 (1862); "The Poland Bill," An Act in Relation to Courts and Judicial Officers in the Territory of Utah, June 3, 1874, 18 *United States Statutes at Large,* 253 (1874); "The Edmunds Law," March 22, 1882, 22 *United States Statutes at Large,* 30 (1882); and "The Edmunds-Tucker Law," March 3, 1887, 24 United States Statutes at Large 635 (1887).

29. Carol Cornwall Madsen, "'At Their Peril': Utah Law and the Case of Plural Wives, 1850–1900," *Western Historical Quarterly* 20 (November 1990): 425–44.

30. "An Ordinance, incorporating the Church of Jesus Christ of Latter-day Saints," February 6, 1851, *Laws and Ordinances of the State of Deseret,* 66. The ordinance did not prohibit any other ecclesiastical or legal agency from performing marriages. "Legal Marriage," *Deseret Evening News,* May 3, 1876, 218, explains the accepted practice without specifying a law. "The Judges of the District or Probate Courts, Mayors and Aldermen of Incorporated Cities, Justices of the Peace and ministers of any religious denomination can officiate in the marriage ceremony, and in the eyes of the law the act is equally lawful performed by either as by the others. A priest or elder of the Church of Jesus Christ of Latter-day Saints has just as much lawful authority to solemnize a marriage as any minister of any other Church. And it makes no difference where that ceremony is performed." The article concludes, "The marriage of more than one woman to the same man, is, under certain conditions sanctioned by the law of God in the Church of Jesus Christ of Latter-day Saints and the marriage of the plural wife is just as binding, sacred and divine as that of the first wife. But it is not recognized by the law of the land."

31. Lyman D. Platt, "The History of Marriage in Utah, 1847–1905," *Genealogical Journal* 12 (Spring 1983): 32–33. A record of marriages compiled from various sources is the *Utah Territorial Vital Records Index, 1847–1905,* Family History Library, Family and Church History Department, Church of Jesus Christ of Latter-day Saints, Salt Lake City. This index also includes records of divorce, naturalization, and probate as well as other vital statistics.

32. Governors' Messages: December 10, 1862, Stephen S. Harding; January 9, 1872, George L. Woods; January 11, 1876, George W. Emery; January 13, 1874, George L. Woods; *1878 Journals of the Legislative Assembly of Utah.*

33. Cott, *Public Vows,* 74.

34. Edmunds-Tucker Law, Section 9, 24, *United States Statutes at Large* 635 (1887): "An Act Regulating Marriage," March 8, 1888, *1888 Laws of Utah,* 88.

35. In early America, divorces were rare, granted only by state or territorial legislatures. By the mid-nineteenth century, however, general divorce laws were passed in the vast majority of jurisdictions giving the judicial branch the power to dissolve marriages. Michael Grossberg, *Governing the Hearth: Law and the Family in Nineteenth-Century America* (Chapel Hill: University of North Carolina Press, 1985), 251.

36. Hendrik Hartog, *Man and Wife in America: A History* (Cambridge, Mass.: Harvard University Press, 2000), 264–67.

37. "An Act in Relation to Bills of Divorce," Sections 2 and 3, March 6, 1852, *1851-52 Laws of Utah,* 83. See Richard I. Aaron, "Mormon Divorce and the Statute of 1851: Questions for Divorce in 1980s," *Journal of Contemporary Law* 8 (1982): 5–46.

38. Indiana was the first (1824), followed by North Carolina (1827), Illinois (1832), Connecticut, Iowa, and Maine. Following Utah in adopting lenient divorce laws were Arizona, Louisiana, the Dakotas, and Washington. See also Cott, *Public Vows,* 50.

39. According to D. Kelly Weisberg, "'Under Great Temptations Heer': Women and Divorce in Puritan Massachusetts," *Feminist Studies* 2 (Summer 1975): 183–94, disharmony was a valid basis for the comparatively rare divorces of Puritan times.

40. Quoted in John D. Lee, *Mormonism Unveiled or the Life and Confessions of the Late Mormon Bishop, John D. Lee,* edited by W. W. Bishop (St. Louis, Mo.: Brand and Co., 1977), 146–47; see also Lawrence Foster, "A Little Known Defense of Polygamy," *Dialogue: A Journal of Mormon Thought* 9 (Winter 1974): 21–34.

41. Quoted in James Beck, "I Notebook, 1859–65," October 8, 1861, December 11, 1869, Special Collections, Marriott Library, University of Utah, Salt Lake City. See also "Few Words of Doctrine Given by President Brigham Young in the Tabernacle in Great Salt Lake City," reported by George Watt, October 8, 1861, LDS Church Archives. The case of Emma Mallory is illustrative. Emma desired a certificate of divorce, which Brigham Young granted on August 1, 1862 "because her husband [Alisha (sic) Mallory] . . . has been cut off from the Church of Jesus Christ of Latter-day Saints for apostasy and therefore forfeited his privileges and blessings." Office Files, Files Relating to Divorce and Family Difficulties, Brigham Young Papers, Box 65, fd. 21 (Reel 76), LDS Church Archives.

42. Brigham Young, June 28, 1874, *Journal of Discourses,* 17:118–19.

43. Eugene E. Campbell and Bruce L. Campbell, "Divorce among Mormon Polygamists: Extent and Explanations," *Utah Historical Quarterly* 4 (Winter 1978): 4–23. Brigham Young asserted that he never denied a woman who desired a divorce but seldom granted one to a man.

44. Contrasting approaches to divorce found public expression in a well-publicized 1860 national debate on divorce between Horace Greeley, who took the conservative

side, and Robert Dale Owen, who argued that easy divorce preserved the "purity of marriage." Greeley, *Recollections of a Busy Life* (New York: J. B. Ford, 1868). See William L. O'Neill, "Divorce as a Moral Issue: A Hundred Years of Controversy," in *Remember the Ladies: New Perspectives on Women in American History,* edited by Carol V. R. George (Syracuse, N.Y.: Syracuse University Press, 1975), 127–43.

45.   "Divorce," *Deseret News,* October 3, 1877, 532.

46.   Brigham Young, Letter to Frederick Kesler, April 12, 1873, Kesler Papers, Special Collections, Marriott Library, University of Utah; Young, Letter to Benjamin F. Johnson, March 20, 1865, Brigham Young Letterbooks 7:517, LDS Church Archives; Young, Letter to Bishop Philo T. Farnsworth, November 22, 1859, Ibid., 5:132. Linda P. Wilcox, "Brigham Young as a Domestic Counselor," n.d., unpublished paper in our possession courtesy of Wilcox.

47.   Carroll Wright, *Marriage and Divorce in the United States, 1867–1886* (1889; reprinted, New York: Arno Press, 1976), 203.

48.   *Hilton v. Roylance,* 25 Utah Reports, 129 (1902).

49.   Wright, *Marriage and Divorce in the United States,* 203–6, 414–17.

50.   "An Act Amending Sections 1151 and 1154 of the Compiled Laws of Utah," Section 1, February 29, 1878, *1878 Laws of Utah,* 1. See also *Journals of the Legislative Assembly of Utah,* January 11, 1876 and January 1878, and "Divorce," *Deseret News,* October 3, 1877, 532.

51.   The causal relationship between liberal divorce laws and increased divorce is disproved by the statistics of the latter half of the nineteenth century. Divorce laws became more stringent even as divorce began its precipitous rise. This phenomenon is explained by a change in attitude toward divorce, which was no longer considered morally or socially unacceptable except among conservative, usually religiously based groups. Mormons were an exception among most ecclesiastical groups in their views on divorce. Sarah Barringer Gordon, *The Mormon Question,* 175–77, explains that many anti-polygamists, rather than recognizing divorce as a safety valve for plural wives, felt that liberal divorce was an undesirable side effect of polygamy and just as antithetical to traditional family life. See also O'Neill, "Divorce as a Moral Issue"; and Nelson Manfred Blake, *The Road to Reno: A History of Divorce in the United States* (New York: Macmillan, 1962).

52.   Elizabeth Cady Stanton was an even stronger proponent of accessible divorce for women than for woman suffrage. See Ellen Carol DuBois, ed., *Elizabeth Cady Stanton and Susan B. Anthony: Correspondence, Writings, Speeches* (New York: Schocken Books, 1981), index s.v. "divorce."

53.   Michael Grossberg, "Who Gets The Child? Custody, Guardianship, and the Rise of a Judicial Patriarchy in Nineteenth-Century America," in *Reproduction, Sexuality, and the Family,* edited by Karen J. Maschke (New York: Garland Publishing, 1997), 1, 4; also Grossberg, *Governing the Hearth,* 235.

54.   "An Act in Relation to Guardians," Section 1, February 3, 1852, *1851–52 Laws of Utah,* 79.

55.   Norma Basch, *Framing American Divorce: From the Revolutionary Generation to the Victorians* (Berkeley: University of California Press, 1999), 115.

56.   "An Act in Relation to Bills of Divorce," Section 6, March 6, 1852, *1851–52 Laws of Utah,* 83–4.

57.   "An Act in Relation to Guardians," Sections 4, 5, February 3, 1852, *1851–52 Laws of Utah,* 79.

58.   Grossberg, "Who Gets the Child?," and his *Governing the Hearth.* A few states passed "tender years" statutes, a victory for women, granting mothers presumptive custody of infants, children with health ailments, children below the age of puberty, or, in some cases, all female children. Not until 1900 did ten jurisdictions lead the way by passing statutes giving mothers an equal right to guardianship.

59.   Martha Cragun Cox, Biographical Record, 1928, typescript copy in our possession; holograph in LDS Church Archives.

60.   Martha Sonntag Bradley, "Woman and Land Ownership, 1847," 1977, unpublished paper in our possession, used by permission. Bradley identifies the following plural wives who received title to property: Jane Baker, Nancy Baldwin, Margaret Henderson, Nancy Perkins, Patty Sessions, Jemima Young, and Susan Young. She also identifies several other female recipients of property who may have been plural wives: Laura Bess, Abigail Bradford, Ann Burland, Martha Burwell, Sarah Harris Gadbury, Cathrine Clawson, Lucy Gregory, Terissa Judd, Mary Moseley, Elizabeth Moss, Sally Murdock, Sarah Ogden, and Abigail W. Smith. The practice of land distribution to polygamists does not appear to have been consistent. Leonard J. Arrington, *Great Basin Kingdom: An Economic History of the Mormons* (Cambridge, Mass.: Harvard University Press, 1966), 52, states that polygamists were entitled to receive one lot for each family. In most cases, title appears to have been entered in the husband's name. This is one reason that many polygamists, e.g., Brigham Young, gained extensive real estate; yet some wives received title in their own name, including a few of Brigham Young's wives. It may be that, in the absence of federal land law in the territory, some formalities regarding land titles were ignored. Moreover, the right of married women to control property does not necessarily follow from the vesting of title to the property in them.

61.   Katherine Harris, "Homesteading in Northeastern Colorado, 1873–1920: Sex Roles and Women's Experience," in *The Women's West,* edited by Susan Armitage and Elizabeth Jameson (Norman: University of Oklahoma Press, 1987), 165–78.

62.   The Homestead Act was extended to Utah pursuant to "An Act to Create the Office of Surveyor-General in the Territory of Utah, and Establish a Land Office in Said Territory, and Extend the Homestead and Pre-emption Laws over the Same," July 16, 1868, 15 *United States Statutes at Large,* 91. See Arrington, *Great Basin Kingdom,* 249; and Lawrence Linford, "Establishing and Maintaining Land Ownership in Utah Prior to 1869," *Utah Historical Quarterly* 42 (Spring 1974): 126–43.

63.   "An Act for the Relief of the Inhabitants of Cities and Towns upon Public Lands," March 2, 1867, 14 *United States Statutes at Large,* 541; "An Act Prescribing Rules and Regulations for the Execution of the Trust Arising under an Act of Congress Entitled "An Act for the Relief of the Inhabitants of Cities and Towns upon the Public Lands,'" February 17, 1869, *1876 Compiled Laws of Utah,* 379; amended February 20, 1880, *1880 Laws of Utah,* 47; amended March 4, 1888, *1888 Laws of Utah,* 37.

64. *Pratt v. Young,* 1 Utah Reports, 347 (1876). Additional details of the case are in Breck England, *The Life and Thought of Orson Pratt* (Salt Lake City: University of Utah Press, 1985), 254.

65. Colfax, "The Mormon Defiance to the Nation: Suggestions as to How It Should be Met," *Deseret Evening News,* October 1, 1879, quoted in Jennie Anderson Froiseth, *The Women of Mormonism or the Story of Polygamy* (Detroit: C. G. G. Paine, 1882), 360–61.

66. While feminists petitioned for legal change as an expression of their individual rights as citizens, state legislatures were influenced more by economic pragmatism than a sense of equality in the law. Salmon, *Women and the Law of Property in Early America* and Basch, *In the Eyes of the Law.*

67. "An Act Concerning the Property Rights of Married Persons," Section 1, February 16, 1872, *1876 Compiled Laws of Utah,* 342.

68. Cott, *Public Vows,* 53.

69. *Utah Constitutional Convention, 1895, Official Report of the Proceedings and Debates,* 2 vols. (Salt Lake City: Star Printing, 1898), 2:1782–85.

70. "An Act Concerning the Property Rights of Married Persons," Section 1, February 16, 1872, *1876 Compiled Laws of Utah,* 342.

71. "An Act Relating to the Estates of Decedents," Section 3, February 18, 1876, *Journals of the Legislative Assembly of the Territory of Utah,* 76, 239–40.

72. "An Act Relating to the Estates of Decedents," Sections 5, 43, 18 February 1876, *1876 Compiled Laws of Utah,* 271, 277.

73. Cott, *Public Vows,* 55.

74. Third District Court, Salt Lake County, Wills, No. 911, November 15, 1881, Utah State Archives; emphasis ours. Utah State Archives, series #3578.

75. Ibid., Wills of Salt Lake County, No. 1353, February 9, 1889, Utah State Archives.

76. Ibid., Wills, No. 2175, December 31, 1860.

77. Ibid., Wills, No. 481, January 7, 1876.

78. Ibid., Wills, No. 755, August 15, 1881.

79. Ibid., Wills, No. 1526, April 28, 1890.

80. "An Act Concerning the Property Rights of Married Persons," Section 2, February 16, 1872, *1876 Compiled Laws of Utah,* 342.

81. "An Act Revising the Code of Civil Procedure of Utah Territory," Sections 227, 228, March 13, 1884, *1884 Laws of Utah,* 192.

82. *Oliphant v. Fox,* November 6, 1867, Salt Lake County Probate Records, Box 23, No. 1472, Utah State Archives.

83. *Thomas v. Union Pacific Railroad Co.,* 1 Utah Reports, 235 (1875): husband and wife filed suit for injuries caused to the wife and her child by the defendant (railroad company); *Eccles v. Union Pacific Railway Co.,* 7 Utah Reports, 335 (1891): husband and wife sued for injuries to wife including premature delivery of her child resulting from a train accident; *Thomas v. Springville City,* 9 Utah Reports, 426 (1894): suit for injuries to wife, including miscarriage due to accident on a bridge; *Tucker v. Salt Lake City,* 10 Utah Reports, 173 (1894): suit for injuries to wife from falling on a defective sidewalk.

84. "An Act Licensing and Regulating the Manufacturing and Sale of Intoxicating Liquors," Section 7, March 9, 1882, *1882 Laws of Utah,* 32.

85. "An Act to Regulate Proceedings in Civil Cases in the Courts of Justice of This Territory, and to Repeal Certain Acts and Parts of Acts," Section 11, February 17, 1870, *1876 Compiled Laws of Utah,* 402; *1888 Compiled Laws of Utah,* Vol. 2, Section 3178.

86. "An Act Revising the Code of Civil Procedure of Utah Territory," Section 232, March 13, 1884, *1884 Laws of Utah,* 193.

87. "State Homestead Exemption Laws," *Yale Law Journal* 46 (1937): 1023–41.

88. "An Act in Relation to Estates of Decedents," Section 1, 14, 2021, March 3, 1852, *1851–52 Laws of Utah,* 67, 69–70; "An Act in Relation to Estates of Decedents," Section 1, March 8, 1852, *1851–52 Laws of Utah,* 265.

89. "An Act in Relation to the Estates of Decedent," Section 1, 14, 2021, March 3, 1852, *1851–52 Laws of Utah,* 67, 69–70.

90. Ibid. *Dooly v. Stringham,* 4 Utah 107 (1885); *Rand v. Brain,* 5 Utah 197 (1887): holding that a widow had only a life interest. In 1884 the legislature made a confusing and short-lived attempt to make the homestead provisions reciprocal, available to either husband or wife, and engraft thereon a distinction between homesteads of common property and separate property origin, giving a fee simple interest to the survivor if from a common property origin, but not if from separate property of the decedent, which ultimately passed to the heirs of the decedent. See "An Act Relating to Procedure of Probate Courts in the Settlement of Estates and in Guardianship," Sections 1–8, March 12, 1884, *1884 Laws of Utah,* 406–9. These provisions were repealed in 1888.

91. *1888 Compiled Laws of Utah,* Vol. 2, Sections 5113-19.

92. Salt Lake County Probate Court Records, Salt Lake County Estates, Book A, 1859–65, August 20, 1862, 173, Family History Library, Salt Lake City.

93. Ibid., 205. See also Estate of H. Jessee Turpin, ibid., 43. The homestead allowance was only a lifetime interest and available to the widow and minor children only as long as they continued to occupy the property. Estate of Almon W. Babbitt, 124. Early Salt Lake County probate court records indicate that widows were often well provided for by the homestead allowance. In 1856, when Babbitt died, he left no will and an estate worth $15,2251.79. His widow, Julia Babbitt, was granted the homestead she and her family occupied, valued at $5,000, and property exempt from execution in the amount of $6,235. Salt Lake County Probate Court Records, Salt Lake County Estates, Book A, 1859–69, 107, LDS Family History Library, Salt Lake City. Similarly, in 1856 Thomas Tennant's widow was granted use of the house and lot which she occupied and $40 a month support. Ibid., 112. See also Estate of John M. McKay, October 1865, ibid., 220; and Estate of Simon Baker, March 1864, ibid., 196.

94. *Knudsen v. Hannberg,* 8 Utah Reports, 203 (1892).

95. "An Act in Relation to the Estates of Decedents," Section 24, March 3, 1852, *1876 Compiled Laws of Utah,* 268. It could be argued that the widow holds the child's

interest for her life or widowhood and/or if there is more than one wife, the estate is divided according to the number of children alive or deceased leaving heirs, each wife to hold her children's share for her life or widowhood. This does not appear to have been the construction given the statute, however. Although this provision is written in terms of the "wife," Section 28 states that the husband shall inherit the estate of a deceased wife in the same manner that a wife inherits the estate of a deceased husband. Adding to the ambiguity of the 1852 act is another provision which states that "in all cases where the deceased leaves a wife, the *inheritance* shall not pass therefrom, so long as the name of the dead shall be perpetuated thereon." "An Act in Relation to the Estates of Decedents," Section 26, March 3, 1852, *1876 Compiled Laws of Utah,* 269, emphasis ours. See *Dooly v. Stringham,* 4 Utah Reports, 107 (1885) which construes "inheritance" to mean "homestead."

96. *Cain Heirs v. Young,* 1 Utah Reports, 361 (1876). The court apparently did not apply the homestead provision, possibly because the widow's one-third interest exceeded that amount.

97. Mary Ann Weston Maughan, "Journal," in *Our Pioneer Heritage,* edited by Kate B. Carter, 20 vols. (Salt Lake City: Daughters of Utah Pioneers, 1959), 2:396.

98. *1851-2 Laws of Utah,* 71-72.

99. *Chapman v. Handley,* 7 Utah Reports, 49 (1890).

100. Ruth Victor, "Emma Jeffs Gunnell," and Louis Jeffs Gunnell, "Lewellyn (Louis) Jeffs Gunnell," typescript, 5-6, in our possession. Both wives became financial dependents of their children.

101. Anne W. G. Leischman, Oral History, interviewed by John Steward, 1973, typescript, 6, 37–38, Utah State University Voice Library Interview, microfilm copy in LDS Church Archives.

102. Governors' Messages, George W. Emery, January 11, 1876, *Journals of the Legislative Assembly,* 1876, 31.

103. *Cope v. Cope,* 137 United States Reports, 682 (1891), applying 1852 intestacy law, reversing *In re Estate of Cope,* 7 Utah Reports, 63 (1890). See also *In re Pratt's Estate:* same result applying intestacy law as amended in 1876, 7 Utah Reports, 278 (1891).

104. "The Edmunds Law," Section 7, 22 *United States Statutes at Large,* 30 (1882).

105. "The Edmunds-Tucker Law," Section 11, 24 *United States Statutes at Large,* 635 (1887).

106. Wills of Salt Lake County, No. 379, February 16, 1874, Utah State Archives.

107. Wills of Salt Lake County, No. 440, February 21, 1875, Utah State Archives.

108. Wills of Salt Lake County, No. 376, November 19, 1873, Utah State Archives.

109. "Woman's Right of Dower," editorial, *Woman's Exponent* 11 (December 1, 1882): 100.

110. George L. Woods, January 15, 1874, *Journals of the Legislative Assembly, 1874.* See also "An Act Concerning the Property Rights of Married Persons," Section 3, February 16, 1872, *1876 Compiled Laws of Utah,* 342. Authorities do not agree about whether Utah recognized the common law right of dower before 1872 when it was declared

statutorily invalid. No specific territorial statute recognized the right of dower. Thus, if it were in force, it would have been so because the common law generally was in force in Utah. As discussed earlier, this was disputed by Brigham Young and territorial legislative enactments, but it was asserted by the federal judiciary.

111. Schuyler Colfax, "The Mormon Defiance to the Nation: Suggestions As to How It Should be Met," *Chicago Advance,* December 22, 1881, reprinted in Froiseth, *The Women of Mormonism,* 360–61.

112. Edmunds-Tucker Law, 24 *United States Statutes at Large,* 635 (1887).

113. "An Act Prescribing the Procedure in the Matter of Dower," March 10, 1892, *1892 Laws of Utah,* 53; "An Act to Amend Section 4119 of the Compiled Laws of Utah, of 1888, and Enacting New Sections 4120, 4121, 4122, 4123, Relating to the Assignment of Dower," March 10, 1892, *1892 Laws of Utah,* 55.

114. *Kelsey v. Crowther,* 7 Utah Reports, 519 (1891) affirmed 162 U.S. 404 (1896) held that a wife could not be compelled to convey her dower interest. *Knudsen v. Hannberg,* 8 Utah Reports, 211 (1892) held that a widow's dower interest and intestacy interest were cumulative. *Norton v. Tufts,* 19 Utah Reports, 470 (1899) held that a wife did not forfeit her dower right if, while separated from her husband, she committed adultery.

115. *Beck v. Utah-Idaho Sugar Company,* 59 Utah Reports, 314, 322–23, 1921.

116. "An Act Defining and Providing for the Right of Dower," April 5, *1896, Laws of Utah, 1896,* 356.

117. Brigham Young, July 18, 1869, *Journal of Discourses,* 13:61.

118. Elizabeth Wood Kane, *Twelve Mormon Homes Visited in Succession on a Journey through Utah to Arizona* (Salt Lake City: Tanner Trust Fund/University of Utah Library, 1974), 5.

119. The women's Relief Society supported a number of women in their medical training as doctors, nurses, and midwives. Training women to become telegraphers and to learn the business of printing and typesetting was also a priority in early Utah.

120. "Lady Lawyers," *Woman's Exponent* 1 (October 1, 1872): 68. By encouraging women to study these trades and professions, especially the law, Brigham Young showed a marked reversal of his earlier attitude to lawyers. In 1852 he did not mince words in describing his feelings: "To observe such conduct as many lawyers are guilty of, stirring up strife among peaceable men, is an outrage upon the feelings of every honest, law abiding man. To sit among them is like sitting in the depths of hell, and their hearts are as black as the ace of spades. . . . They love sin, and roll it under their tongues as a sweet morsel, and will creep around like wolves in sheep's clothing, and fill their pockets with the fair earnings of their neighbors, and devise every artifice in their power to reach the property of the honest and that is what has caused these courts." Quoted in Andrew Love Neff, *History of Utah: 1847–1869* (Salt Lake City: Deseret News Press, 1940), 196.

121. "An Act for the Regulation of Attorneys," Sections 1, 2, February 18, 1852, *1851–52 Laws of Utah,* 55.

122. Martha Jane Knowlton Coray, Diary, April 17, 18, 20, 22 1874, L. Tom Perry Special Collections, Harold B. Lee Library, Brigham Young University, Provo, Utah.

123. Rule 21, Rules of the Supreme Court by the Territory of Utah, 1 Utah Reports, 6. Although the qualifications for admittance to the bar were not published until 1876, they had been in effect earlier.

124. "Ladies Admitted to the Utah Bar," *Deseret News,* September 25, 1872, 512.

125. *Bradwell v. Illinois,* 83 United States Reports [16 Wall], 1130 (1873). See also Albie Sachs and Joan Hoff Wilson, *Sexism and the Law: Male Beliefs and Legal Bias* (New York: Free Press, 1978), 97–100.

126. "Editorial Notes," *Woman's Exponent* 20 (June 1, 1892): 172. See also Carol Cornwall Madsen, "'Sisters at the Bar': Utah Women in Law," *Utah Historical Quarterly* 61 (Summer 1993): 208–32.

127. Linda K. Kerber, *No Constitutional Right to Be Ladies* (New York: Hill and Wang, 1998), 137.

128. "An Act Regulating the Mode of Procedure in Civil Cases in the Courts of the Territory of Utah," Section 11, December 30, 1852, *1852-53 Laws of Utah,* 8.

129. "An Act Regulating the Mode of Procedure in Criminal Cases," Section 9, January 21, 1853, *1852–53 Laws of Utah,* 8; emphasis ours.

130. "Home Affairs," *Woman's Exponent* 3 (September 15, 1874): 61.

131. "An Act Amending an Act Prescribing Certain Qualifications Necessary to Enable a Person to Be Eligible to Hold Office, Vote, or Serve as a Juror," Section 1, February 5, 1868, *1868 Laws of Utah,* 4.

132. *People vs. Hampton,* 4 Utah Reports, 262 (1886).

133. Alma Lutz, *Susan B. Anthony* (Boston: Beacon Press, 1959), 211–13. See also Ellen Carol DuBois, "Outgrowing the Compact of the Fathers: Equal Rights, Woman Suffrage, and the United States Constitution, 1820–1878," *Journal of American History* 74 (December 1987): 853.

134. Linda K. Kerber and Gretchen Ritter, "Jury Service and Women's Citizenship before and after the Nineteenth Amendment," *Law and History Review* 20 (Fall 2002): 479–515.

135. *Hoyt v. Florida,* 368 United States Reports 57 (1961).

136. Kerber, "No Constitutional Right to Be Ladies," 136.

137. Section 1299, *1898 Revised Statutes of Utah,* 349. This provision is similar to Wyoming law, in effect since territorial days. Suffragist Emmeline Wells makes mention of this aspect of the voting law in her diary, January 21, 1896, Perry Special Collections.

138. Susan B. Anthony and Ida Husted Harper, eds., *The History of Woman Suffrage,* 6 vols. (Rochester, N.Y.: Susan B. Anthony, 1902), 4:1089. Reprinted in Carol Cornwall Madsen, ed., *Battle for the Ballot: Essays on Woman Suffrage in Utah, 1870–1896* (Logan: Utah State University Press, 1997), 310.

139. T. A. Larson, "Woman Suffrage in Western America," *Utah Historical Quarterly* 38 (Winter 1970): 7–19; Thomas G. Alexander, "An Experiment in Progressive Legislation: The Granting of Woman Suffrage in Utah in 1870," ibid., 20–30;

"Woman Suffrage in Pioneer Days," lesson pamphlet for February 1977 (Salt Lake City: Daughters of Utah Pioneers); Beverly Beeton, *Women Vote in the West: The Woman Suffrage Movement, 1869–1896* (New York: Garland Publishing, 1986); Madsen, *Battle for the Ballot;* Lola Van Wagenen, *Sister-Wives and Suffragists: Polygamy and the Politics of Woman Suffrage, 1870–1896* (Ph.D. diss., New York University, 1994; printed Provo, Utah: Joseph Fielding Smith Institute for Latter-day Saint History and BYU Studies, Dissertations in LDS History Series, 2003).

140. Fifteenth Ward Relief Society, Minutes, 1868–73, January 6, 1870, LDS Church Archives.

141. The far-reaching effects of the economic provisions of the bill, named for its sponsor, Illinois Representative Shelby M. Cullom, elicited opposition from sources other than Utah. Members of Congress, newspaper editors, and other economic and political factions throughout the country registered objections to its economic restraints. Others thought it might provoke another civil war because it provided enforcement by federal troops. Larson, *Outline History of Territorial Utah,* 226–27. See also Orson F. Whitney, *History of Utah,* 4 vols. (Salt Lake City: George Q. Cannon and Sons, 1893), 2:405–39.

142. "An Act Conferring Upon Women the Franchise," February 12, 1870, *1876 Compiled Laws of Utah,* 88. Utah thus became the second territory to enact woman suffrage. Several other territories besides Wyoming, which passed a woman suffrage bill in December 1869, also debated woman suffrage but passed no legislation. Utah women were the first to vote because it held an election earlier than Wyoming after both territories passed suffrage bills. Seraph Young is credited as being the first woman in Utah to cast her ballot.

143. Jill Mulvay Derr, "Zion's Schoolmarms," in *Mormon Sisters: Women in Early Utah,* edited by Claudia L. Bushman (1976; reprinted with a new introduction by Anne Firor Scott, Logan: Utah State University Press, 1997), 67–88.

144. The "woman's bill" generated a great deal of debate among women, much of which was printed in the *Woman's Exponent.* See, for example, "Agitation Is Educational," 8 (February 1, 1880): 132; "Our Opinion," "A Woman on the Woman's Bill," and "Correspondence," 8 (February 15, 1880): 138; 139, 141; "Legislative Proceedings," "Another Woman's Opinion," and "Work and Wait," 8 (March 1, 1880): 145, 146, 148.

145. Untitled and undated 1881 newspaper clipping in Papers of Elizabeth Cady Stanton and Susan B. Anthony, Library of Congress, microfilm at Utah State Archives, reel 5, LC control #78011049.

146. "Woman Suffrage in Utah," undated clipping from unidentified newspaper, ibid.

147. Whitney, *History of Utah,* 3:60–63. For the conflict, see Robert Joseph Dwyer, *The Gentile Comes to Utah* (Salt Lake City: Western Epics, 1971).

148. "Woman Suffrage in Pioneer Days," 283–84; *Woman's Exponent:* "Woman's Right to Vote in Utah Contested," 9 (October 1, 1880): 68; and "The Decision of the Supreme Court in the Mandamus Case," 9 (October 15, 1880): 77–79. This case does not appear in Utah Reports.

149. Utah Reports, 136 (1881), 144–47, 153–57.

150. Whitney, *History of Utah,* 3:235.

151. *Murphy v. Ramsey,* 114 United States Reports, 15 (1885). An overview of the federal disfranchisement effort is Joseph H. Groberg, "The Mormon Disfranchisements, 1882–1892," *BYU Studies* 16 (Spring 1976): 399–408. See also Sarah Barringer Gordon, *The Mormon Question: Polygamy and Constitutional Conflict in Nineteenth-Century America* (Chapel Hill: University of North Carolina Press, 2002), 168–71.

152. Jean Bickmore White, "Woman's Place Is in the Constitution: The Struggle for Equal Rights in Utah in 1895," *Utah Historical Quarterly* 42 (Fall 1974): 344–69 and Madsen, *Battle for the Ballot,* 221–243. See also White, "Gentle Persuaders: Utah's First Women Legislators," *Utah Historical Quarterly* 38 (Winter 1970): 31–49; Madsen, *Battle for the Ballot,* 291–307. The Republican platform stated: "We favor the granting of equal suffrage to women." The Democratic platform was more generous: "Democrats of Utah are unequivocally in favor of women's suffrage, and the political rights and privileges of women equal with those of men, including eligibility to office, and we demand that such guarantees shall be provided in the Constitution of the State of Utah and will secure to the women of Utah these inestimable rights." Quoted in White, "Woman's Place Is in the Constitution," 347.

153. Utah Constitution, Article 14, Section 1 (1896).

154. *Anderson v. Tyree,* 12 Utah Reports, 129 (1895).

155. Madsen, "Schism in the Sisterhood: Mormon Women and Partisan Politics," in *Battle for the Ballot,* 245–72.

3

Conflict and Contributions

Women in Churches, 1847–1920

John Sillito

From the very beginning of its existence as a territory, Utah's political, social, and economic life has been characterized by division along religious lines. Both perceived wrongs and real injustices exacerbated tensions between Mormons and Gentiles. Throughout the nineteenth century, the fledgling Mormon Church was targeted by preachers in the pulpit and politicians on the platform for its "un-American and un-Christian" beliefs. While Mormon communalism and theocracy was at the root of the antipathy toward the Saints, the most determined, strident—and public—opposition focused on the doctrine of plural marriage, or polygamy.[1]

For women active in religious denominations, both Mormon and non-Mormon, polygamy was a difficult question that often seemed to pit woman against woman. Although Mormon women may have experienced private pain and doubt, the public position of most was that plural marriage was ordained of God; it was a religious commandment and a necessary step toward eternal exaltation. Their feelings are typified by the fervent "words of faith in the defense of my religion" of Helen Marr Clark Callister, the second wife of Thomas Callister, of Fillmore. As one of the first to enter plural marriage, and after living it for more than thirty years, Callister asserted in this draft of a public address that she knew the principle of plural marriage to be both a truth and a blessing:

> I have shared hunger, poverty, and toil with my husband's first wife whom I love as a dear sister; together we trod the trackless wilds to reach these then sterile valleys; together we battled the hardships of the "first year." The remembrance of those days are indelibly stamped upon my mind never to be erased. I have seen my husband stagger for want of food. I have heard my babies cry for bread and had nothing to give them; but with unceasing toil, and by the

blessings of God, our efforts were crowned with success. . . . Through these trying scenes, ties closer than those of sisterhood bound us together and the principle of plural marriage was firmly planted in our souls.[2]

For non-Mormon women, however, polygamy seemed foreign and repellent. As Jana Kathryn Riess observed, no other social practice "so distressed the American evangelical community in the late nineteenth century, when Mormonism had achieved a powerful foothold in the Rocky Mountains and was importing converts by the thousands."[3] Moreover, as Peggy Pascoe notes, "the very existence of polygamy," was seen as a threat to all women because Mormon women were "trapped in a marriage system that made a mockery of female authority and virtually enslaved wives." For these women, polygamy, constituted a "diabolical attempt to reduce the status of women by making women into sacrifices."[4]

Thus, while they criticized their Mormon sisters for living as plural wives, and often found an explanation for their behavior in gullibility, credulity, or even religious fanaticism, most Gentile women believed that plural wives were unwilling participants who, if given an opportunity, would reject polygamy. Of course turning their backs on plural marriage was a difficult challenge to Mormon women as even the *Salt Lake Tribune* realized when it editorialized: "Does the country expect that these people are going to plead guilty of the fact that they have for thirty years been wronging women and outraging civilization? Does it expect that the poor women who have been caught in these tolls [sic], and who if they break away have nothing but starvation before them, are going to come forward and unaided undertake to denounce this infamy?"[5]

Women's role in the debate over polygamy is problematic. In the nineteenth century, sizeable numbers of non-Mormon women provided moral and financial impetus for the crusade against this "relic of barbarism," while some served as foot soldiers in the battle itself as missionaries. Simultaneously, Mormon women fought for their right to practice their religious commitments. Today, many modern Mormon women consider their nineteenth-century foremothers heroines and even feminist role models.[6] Other historians, view nineteenth-century women, both Mormon and Gentile, as pawns of men with personal political and economic agendas, used willingly or unwillingly, wittingly or unwittingly, against their sisters.[7] In any event, the clash between Mormon and Gentile, particularly over polygamy, was the single most important feature of nineteenth-century Utah life.[8]

In assessing these questions, the work of Peggy Pascoe provides some important insights. In her study *Relations of Rescue: The Search for Female Moral Authority in the American West, 1874–1939,* Pascoe asserts that, in the 1870s, middle-class Protestant women "joined together" in an effort to establish "female moral authority." Influenced by the Victorian belief that women should be "pious moral guardians," they set out to "'rescue' female victims of male abuse." Clearly such impulses motivated the Gentile women who came to Utah seeking to save their Mormon sisters from the trap of polygamy. As we will see, these assumptions were also at the root of the efforts of Angie Newman and others to establish Salt Lake's Industrial Christian Home for Mormon women seeking shelter from plural marriages. Moreover, Pascoe argues that the concept of "female moral authority" provides a better lens from which to view the actions of nineteenth-century Protestant women than either the "timeworn" notion of "female moral superiority," or the assertion that women were simply the "civilizers" of the American West.[9]

Against this background of conflict, however, between 1847 and 1920, an impressive panorama of constructive activities, spearheaded and carried out by women of many denominations, contributed to the building of the state. Many of these contributions were traditionally those assigned to women: providing for the comfort of husbands and children, heading up charitable efforts, nursing the sick, and educating the unschooled. Their economic contribution, though seldom quantified, was significant: They gardened, harvested, preserved, and prepared food; they raised sheep and flax, manufactured cloth, and sewed clothing and bedding; their flocks of chickens, their milk cows, and their pigs were significant, not only for household consumption, but as items for barter. Charles S. Peterson attributes to women and their children the creation and maintenance of Utah's cheese industry during the nineteenth century.[10] In social life, they promoted art, culture, music, literature and theater. In religious life, Mormon women sustained the faith, accepted and defended plural marriage, supported husbands on missions, and simultaneously labored in church auxiliaries including the Relief Society for adult women, the Primary for children, and the Young Ladies Mutual Improvement Association for young women.[11]

Similarly, non-Mormon women worked as teachers, missionaries, nurses, and in other capacities as they built churches, pursued careers, raised families and supported spouses. Yet much less is known about, and little scholarly attention has been paid to, the activities of these women during this crucial period in Utah history. This chapter provides an overview of the contributions of women active in the Protestant, Catholic, Jewish, Unitarian, Christian Science, and other faiths. A good starting point, however, is an examination of the activities of LDS women.[12]

MORMON WOMEN AND THEIR ZION

When the Mormon pioneers entered the Salt Lake Valley in July 1847, nine women and two girls were among the company. Stanley B. Kimball has commented that the "unanticipated inclusion" of three women when the main camp left Winter Quarters "was occasioned by the insistence of Brigham [Young]'s younger brother Lorenzo that he be allowed to take his asthmatic wife, Harriet, and their two children," in hopes of improving her health. This decision necessitated taking "one or two other females along" to keep her company.[13]

Other women, traveling with a separate migration of Saints from Mississippi, joined this main party at Laramie, Wyoming. From the record, these women seem to have performed vital tasks on the way. While much of their time was spent on such traditional activities as cooking, sewing, and tending children, several women served as scribes and diary keepers. While Kimball implies that the men did not particularly welcome these women at first, the mood changed. Originally Brigham Young and Heber C. Kimball shared a wagon, thus foregoing their "conjugal rights." But by May 1847, a month after setting out, Heber Kimball had moved into another wagon with "Ellen Sanders, his strong young Norwegian wife," who gave birth eight months later to Samuel Chase Kimball, one of the "first white children" born in the valley.[14] By then, the female Mormon population in the Salt Lake Valley was roughly equal with that of men.[15]

Despite the last-minute inclusion of these women in the vanguard party of Mormon settlers, it is clear that the Saints, unlike some others in the broader national movement westward, intended for women and children to join them as soon as possible. The Mormons were intent on building a permanent settlement, and their families would be part of that development. Mormon women, drawing on their experiences during successive migrations from New York, Ohio, Missouri, and Illinois, arrived in the valley with a body of organizational skills and experiences that would be profitably employed in the initial settlement and later expansion along the Mormon Corridor.

As in other areas of the West, Utah had a moving frontier. Probably it is fair to say that each settlement went through a somewhat similar process of exploration, colonization, settlement, readjustment, and then development. After a decade or two of settlement and pioneering in Salt Lake City, for instance, Mormons had the money and spare time to begin developing their literary, cultural, and social interests, while Bear Lake in the north and St. George in the south were experiencing earlier stages of development, and the process had yet to begin for colonies in Arizona and Wyoming.

The LDS women's auxiliaries were either reestablished or first created in the late 1860s. The most important of these was the Relief Society, initially established in Nauvoo under the leadership of Emma Smith, wife of the Mormon prophet. The Relief Society had been another casualty of the events of 1844 which saw the martyrdom of Joseph Smith and his brother Hyrum, the succession crisis, and the eventual forced migration of the Mormons from Illinois. In 1867, Eliza R. Snow, who had served as secretary of the Nauvoo Relief Society, was selected to reestablish Relief Societies in each ward by Brigham Young.

Snow, a plural wife of both Joseph Smith and Brigham Young, was one of the most powerful and respected leaders of Mormon women in the nineteenth century. As "Prophetess" of the Relief Society, Snow was "president of woman's work of the Church in all the world," and a major leader of Mormon women's organizational activities in the years prior to statehood.[16]

The Relief Societies, organized one per ward, performed a variety of functions, perhaps most importantly helping the bishop in assisting the local poor. Women collected and disbursed money and commodities, and also performed such tasks as sewing, cleaning, gleaning, and manufacturing small items collectively. As a part of their efforts, Relief Societies in various wards purchased real estate, built their own meeting halls, and also erected granaries.[17]

Moreover, the Relief Society, at the direction of Brigham Young, began raising silkworms as early as 1855 and storing grain in 1876.[18] Though the silk industry proved to be only marginally successful, the grain storage program continued until World War I when, by action of the Presiding Bishop, the wheat was sold to the federal government for the war effort.[19]

Additionally, the Relief Society played an important part in providing social and cultural activities for Mormon women, reporting these activities through minutes and reports, and encouraging literary or journalistic work which was printed in the pages of the *Woman's Exponent,* an independent publication which began in 1872 and was subsumed in the newly created *Relief Society Magazine* in 1915.[20] Along with other nineteenth-century periodicals like the *Contributor, Juvenile Instructor, and the Young Woman's Journal,* the *Woman's Exponent,* according to Bruce L. Campbell and Eugene E. Campbell, "carried the principles and programs of purification into Mormon homes, and when the time for reconciliation with the world came, they were vehicles for that enterprise as well."[21]

The Relief Society aimed its efforts toward the mature women of the church—its mothers and grandmothers. In 1869, the same year that the railroad reached Utah, Brigham Young organized a Young Ladies Retrenchment Society for his daughters, encouraging them to eschew worldly fashions. With his encouragement, the movement spread throughout the state. Six years later, Junius F. Wells organized a parallel organization for young men. In January 1880, both organizations were systematized as the Young Ladies' Mutual Improvement Association with Elmina Shepherd Taylor as its first president, and the Young Men's Mutual Improvement Association led by Junius Wells, Heber J. Grant, and others.

In August 1878 in Kaysville, Aurelia Spencer Rogers organized the first local Primary Association, designed to provide instruction and recreation for Mormon children. In the same January 1880 meeting establishing the Mutual Improvement Associations, Louie B. Felt was named first president of the churchwide Primary program.[22]

In assessing the accomplishments of Mormon women in the late nineteenth and early twentieth century, Jill Mulvay Derr has observed:

"Extensive family ties as well as friendships emerging from shared feelings and experiences in the woman's sphere were the main components of Mormon sisterhood. Overlaid onto this network . . . was the churchwide organization of Mormon women into local Relief Society units that not only provided women with common goals and tasks but aroused the commitment to work publicly for the common good of women." Moreover, Derr realizes, the fact that "all of these elements of sisterhood" present in this period led to a "culmination of strength and union unique in the history of Mormon women." [23]

Protestant Women in the Mormon Stronghold

As historian Gary Topping has noted, few "mission fields challenged the zeal of American Protestantism as the Mormon stronghold in Utah." Indeed, many of Mormonism's theological, ecclesiastical, and behavioral tenets were viewed as "direct affronts to the . . . Protestantism of the East and the Midwest."[24] Protestant missionaries in Utah employed a wide range of tactics in confronting the nineteenth-century "Mormon menace," and women played an important, if occasionally overlooked or marginalized, part in this effort. During the late 1870s and early 1880s, a number of home missionary societies and women's missionary societies were organized in the Baptist, Congregational, and Methodist churches, which supported activities in Utah.[25] Most Protestant female activity in Utah centered around teaching, nursing, and, to a lesser degree, missionary work itself, although on a few occasions women also served as clergy.

By providing free education, and generally professional training, Protestant women teachers guaranteed an attractive alternative to the generally inadequate, Mormon-controlled, territorial schools which were woefully characterized even by the *Deseret News* in an 1855 editorial as having teachers who "had no other qualifications excepting they were out of employ,"[26] and also by overcrowding, inadequate facilities, and high tuition. Consequently, some Mormon parents were willing to risk the proselyting against their faith carried on in Protestant schools in exchange for the superior education they offered.[27]

An interesting assessment of this effort from a Mormon's viewpoint appears in local historian David F. Smith's memories of Centerville. Smith recalls that, when he was young, there were no publicly funded schools. Instead, parents paid monthly tuition to each teacher instructing a child. In addition to the local Mormon schools, parents had the option of sending children to a Presbyterian teacher named Abbey Benedict, who taught the "free sectarian school" in the community for a number of years. Her school was "maintained by sectarian church contributions from people in the eastern part of the United States," who believed that if "the Mormon boys and girls could be educated it would be a contribution to humanity. Further education would spell the end of the Mormon church, they argued."[28] Still, Smith recalls that Benedict was "highly respected," not only by the non-Mormon population of the community but by the Mormons as well.

Women like Abbey Benedict exhibited considerable devotion and unusual professionalism in their efforts. The twenty-fourth annual report (1901) of the Women's Baptist Home Mission Society, headquartered in Chicago, includes an illuminating account of the various responsibilities of Baptist missionary Emma Parsons, who taught sewing classes for girls and wood carving for boys in Salt Lake City's East Side Baptist Church. Her classes were large, and she was particularly concerned with making a "special effort to save the boys," whom she found "irreverent, immoral and profane." In addition to teaching, Parsons records that her duties

> varied with the season and the conditions of the church. I have taught in Sunday school, been church and Sunday school organist, or pianist, regularly or irregularly as the occasion demanded; served on committees in the Christian Endeavor Society, had charge of the Junior Christian Endeavor Society, assisted in the Ladies Aid and Missionary Society, served on committees and helped others to develop their talents, helped to prepare programs for special days and have written papers for special meetings. I am a delegate to the Young People's Christian Union and Chairman of one of its working committees; am superintendent of East Side's Home Department of the Sunday school and represent our church in the Home Founding Association of Utah.[29]

Combining sound curriculum and sound religious principles were, however, an indirect form of proselyting in Utah. By 1901 when Parsons wrote her report, the greatest battle between women in nineteenth-century Utah—the campaign to destroy polygamy—had been virtually ended by Wilford Woodruff's Manifesto, issued in September 1890 and voted on at the church's semi-annual general conference the next month, although skirmishes would continue in the first decade of the twentieth century. During the years after 1852, when the first public acknowledgment and defense of plural marriage was made, the practice of polygamy drew increasing attacks, gradually mobilizing the weight of the United States legislative, judicial, and executive branches of government to suppress it. It was a crusade that united almost all non-Mormons in the state, men and women alike, without regard to creed.

While it can be argued that both the defense of, and the opposition to, polygamy was largely directed by men, they actively enlisted large numbers of women on both sides of the question. Furthermore, the greatest impetus for the removal of polygamy came from women tied to religious denominations, who believed, in the words of historian Robert J. Dwyer, that they had "a holy mission to open the eyes" of deluded Mormon women and help them divest themselves of the "folly and indignity of their way of life." As Dwyer puts it, throughout the country these women

> gathered to discuss the salvation of their Mormon sisters. Sober, dignified and purposeful, they sat on horse-hair sofas around tables with green baize

and passed resolutions. But they did more. . . . From their capacious reticules came the dollars that made possible the maintenance of the sectarian missions schools in far-off Utah. It was they who sent out teachers and paid their salaries. And it was to them, as to a rock of refuge and strength that the Gentile women of Utah confidently turned for encouragement and support as they launched their campaign to strike the shackles from the women of Mormondom.[30]

In November 1878, a mass meeting at Salt Lake's Independence Hall—a bastion of Gentile influence located at Third South and Main streets—attracted over two hundred women, who drafted a resolution sent to Lucy Hayes, wife of President Rutherford B. Hayes. After detailing the growth of plural marriage in the territory, the resolution asserted that Congress had "entirely failed to enact efficient or enforce existing laws for the abolition of this great crime." Moreover, the petition charged that "more of these unlawful and unhallowed alliances have consummated the past year than ever before in the history of the Mormon church." Asserting that the Mormon-dominated territorial legislature had used "every possible legislative safeguard in their power," to prevent attacks on polygamy, the women called on Mrs. Hayes "to circulate and publish our appeal in order to arouse public sentiment against an abomination which peculiarly stigmatizes women."[31]

In the aftermath of that meeting, an Anti-Polygamy Society (APS) was organized, calling upon all Christian women in the country to join the effort to end plural marriage in Utah. The group sponsored lectures, published books and tracts, and sponsored a newspaper, the *Anti-Polygamy Standard* (1880–83). Its pages were filled with articles and editorials calling for an end to the remaining "relic of barbarism." Its articles linked the goals of the organization with those of the early abolitionists who had mobilized public opinion and eliminated slavery a generation before.

A conspicuous—and successful—effort of the women in the APS in the 1880s was a campaign to take suffrage away from Utah women who had voted since 1870. While such measures would disfranchise them as well, these women believed that Mormon women were "merely puppets of their much married husbands" and were not truly free to vote as they pleased.[31]

As Robert J. Dwyer noted, "pressure politics" by Utah Gentile women found attentive ears in the halls of Congress. Spurred on by the Anti-Polygamy Society, thousands of signatures from all over the country sought Congressional support to "deprive the women in Utah of their voting privilege. Thus, the Woman's Home Missionary Society of the Methodist Episcopal Church, meeting in Cleveland, Ohio, in October, 1884, heard a report of the committee entrusted with securing such signatures. Two hundred and fifty thousand names were stated to have been forwarded to Senator George Frisbie Hoar. . . . These efforts were brought to fruition when, on March 15, 1887 the Edmunds-Tucker bill became law."[33]

Simultaneously, however, during these polarized and contentious times, Mormon women also sought the support of Gentile women in organizing a branch of the Woman's Suffrage Association in Utah. Despite the feeling of many Gentile women that restoring suffrage was really a tool to "assure the political domination of [Utah] by the Mormon church," several prominent Gentile women—Emma J. McVicker, Isabelle E. Bennett, and Lillie R. Pardee among them—joined with Mormon women in the Utah Suffrage Association. Moreover, as Carol Cornwall Madsen suggests, "Whatever their own antipathy to polygamy, Eastern suffragists deplored this move to disfranchise such a large body of voting women and did not join the anti-polygamy movements."[34]

The state constitution accepted by Congress, which authorized statehood in 1896, granted woman suffrage and outlawed polygamy; but some Gentile women continued to see polygamy linked to Mormon political power. As part of their concern, the Women's Missionary Union of Salt Lake City joined with the Utah Ministerial Association to organize the "Gentile Information Bureau," which sought to educate the non-Mormon populace to "the extent to which the rightfulness of polygamy is taught and the offense of polygamous living is encouraged and practiced."[35] In 1906, Mrs. L. H. Ehlers, superintendent of the Methodist Sunday School in Mercur, Utah, wrote Senator Fred T. Dubois of Idaho, a leading congressional foe of Mormonism, congratulating him for his fight against the "blight of Mormonism." Noting that her own sister had been "stolen from her parents and taken into [the] awful clutch of polygamy," Ehlers asserted that many Gentile women saw Mormon women as being "under the thumb of Joe Smith" but were "tired of being aliens and under alien control and government."[36]

The campaign of Utah's Gentile women against polygamy and the national support for this crusade was important in pressuring the government to take a firmer stance toward the Mormons.[37] As noted, their political clout was partially responsible for the passage of the Edmunds-Tucker Act of 1887.

While women in Utah's various Protestant denominations, pursued many of the activities listed above, each denomination made distinctive contributions as well. A fuller understanding emerges by examining their efforts in more detail.

Baptist Women

Baptist missionary work in Utah began in 1871, when Reverend George W. Dodge, recently appointed Territorial Superintendent of Indian Affairs by President U. S. Grant, arrived in Salt Lake City. Dodge, along with Reverend Sewell Brown who had been appointed to labor in Utah by the American Home Baptist Missionary Society, organized a small Baptist congregation in Salt Lake City in the home of "one Mr. Palmer on third south street."[38] The congregation of twenty had dissolved by 1874 because Dodge left the territory and Brown neglected his missionary work. In 1881, the society appointed the more energetic Reverend Dwight Spencer to Utah. During his decade of service in the state, Spencer organized churches in a number of towns including Salt Lake City and Ogden. As one observer has noted, Baptist work was primarily undertaken in "the main centers of population, and the churches of these two cities represented the "foundation and backbone" of the denomination's efforts in Utah.[39]

In May 1881, the Women's American Baptist Home Mission Society (WABHMS) meeting in Indianapolis, Indiana, devoted much of its deliberations to the "Utah question." Stating that the Baptist church had a "two fold duty to the people of Utah"—to send them the gospel and the means of Christian education while simultaneously supporting the legal system in its efforts to "overthrow the monstrous system of polygamy"—those in attendance passed a resolution outlining their goals for Utah.[40] Focusing on Salt Lake City and Ogden, the delegates urged that special efforts should be made to "bring the children and youth of the Mormon population under the influence of the Gospel. It is within the knowledge of some . . . that the young people of many of the Mormon families in Utah are not in favor of polygamy, as they have seen it developed in their own early homes. The aim should be to reach the young people with the Gospel so as to lead them away from the paths of temptation before they are hardened in sin."[41]

In 1881, the WABHMS sent Lydia Paine, a Baptist missionary from Chicago, to Utah. She took over much of the denomination's proselytizing responsibility and gave valuable service both in Ogden and Salt Lake City by "visiting homes, helping in all phases of church work, and reaching children not otherwise touched in the industrial schools held on Saturday."[42]

Furthermore, local Baptist women were active in several other ways. A Ladies Aid Society was organized in Salt Lake City in 1884 to "assist the needy whenever found, and while ministering to the needs of the body, to also feed the hungry soul."[43] In 1890, a Utah chapter of the Woman's Missionary Society was formed to expand Baptist work. This group focused specifically on the "spiritual rather than the material body."[44] Additionally Baptist Sunday schools and Christian Endeavor societies were organized in Salt Lake City and Ogden, drawing upon women as teachers and leaders.

One member of the Baptist missionary society in Salt Lake City, Mrs. J. J. Corum, organized a Sunday School on the city's west side in 1892. Her work was so successful that the school soon enrolled over a hundred pupils, and she organized a women's aid society as well. Within a few years, Corum's missionary work led to the establishment of the Rio Grande Baptist Church.[45]

Baptist women also contributed energetically to education. The case of the previously mentioned Lydia Paine is probably typical of the activities of others. In September 1883, she organized the Baptist school of Salt Lake City with the financial support of WABHMS. Fannie Thompson served as principal and Mary Berkeley as her assistant. Before its close in 1889, the school employed five female teachers.[46] Baptist women made similar efforts at the Mound Fort and Wilson Lane Chapel schools in Ogden. In Provo, in 1890, a "small but efficient band of women," led by Emma F. Parsons and Mrs. H. W. Coffin, and sponsored by a second national Baptist group, the Women's Baptist Home Missionary Society, "conducted missionary meetings, and taught both a day and Sunday school," with eight grades and some 70 students.[47] Coffin and Parsons assisted Reverend H. B. Turner in organizing the Provo Baptist church in 1891.[48] Parsons not only directed the Baptist Sunday School in Provo but also conducted Bible study, gave temperance lectures, provided the school girls with a "regular course in sewing and fancy work," and functioned as secretary of the Utah Baptist Association's statewide Sunday School convention in the late 1880s.[49]

Between 1881 and 1920, scores of Baptist women, both Utah residents and outsiders, contributed untold hours as teachers and missionaries. The work was strengthened when the Women's Missionary Union of the Utah Baptist Association was created in September 1896.[50] Under its auspices, for example, Frieda A. Dressell, a graduate of the women's missionary society training school in Chicago, came to Provo in 1898 and worked in the state for more than four decades. Other female missionaries taught and proselytized among several ethnic communities. Because of Utah's large Scandinavian population, Anna E. Nillson and Caroline C. Larson came to Utah in 1885 to make an attempt "to reach their own people."[51] They undertook efforts among the Danish, Norwegian, Finnish, and Swedish communities. Nillson and Larson soon discovered that many of the women "were poor, especially those who had apostatized from the Mormon Church, and many of the children were unable to read but eager to learn. In their homes they often invited women who called to stay for a meal which was much appreciated."[52] After her marriage to August Olander, Caroline Larson maintained a small Swedish Sunday School in her home in Murray and later at the Burlington Baptist Church.[53]

Around 1900, Mina B. Maford, a worker sent by Salt Lake's East Side Baptist church, spent one day per week working among Salt Lake's small black community. Maford's efforts led to the creation of a black congregation of approximately fifty communicants under the leadership of Reverend J. W. Washington. Additionally, Lillian Blair and Lillian Plimpton organized a Loyal Temperance Union, as well as working in the usual Sunday School and missionary efforts.[54] In 1901 Blair served as a missionary in Thistle, Utah. Maude Dittmars was active in the fledgling Baptist efforts in Garfield.[55]

Congregational Women

Congregationalists first held regular services in Utah in 1865 with the arrival of Reverend Norman McLeod, who came to Utah under the auspices of the church's American Home Missionary Society. McLeod, who organized Salt Lake's First Congregational Church in February, 1865, has been described as "bitterly anti-Mormon" but such a "spell-binding, fire-and-brimstone orator" that even some Mormons came to his sermons.[56] He was the main force behind the construction of Independence Hall, which numerous Gentile groups used for a variety of purposes including civic and political rallies as well as religious meetings.[57] Ultimately, McLeod dropped his ministerial career in 1872 and pursued journalism as editor of the *Utah Grant Vedette,* a revival of the defunct *Union Vedette* which had been published at Camp Douglas (1864–67). One early twentieth-century observer, Francis Sherman, concluded that McLeod "made many mistakes that a conservative man would not have made. In his lectures he made many ranting assertions about the Mormons and their faith, [and] used little judgement in attacking it."[58]

McLeod's departure from the ministry did not hamper the Congregational Church's activities. By then it had established itself firmly in Salt Lake City and Ogden, and continued its efforts, including proselyting among the Mormons and working against polygamy. Congregational women were very much a part of this effort. In addition, Congregational women also established ladies' benevolent societies, sewing schools, and a Young Ladies Missionary Society. Typical was the Ladies Benevolent Society of Phillips Congregational Church in Salt Lake City. Organized in March 1887 "to relieve the wants of the poor and sick in the neighborhood," the society raised funds through weekly sewing projects, private donations, and fairs.[59]

In Salt Lake City in 1882, Edith McLeod, daughter of Reverend McLeod, opened the Burlington School in Salt Lake City which was primarily financed by the First Congregational Church of Burlington, Vermont. A year later Annie E. Chapman organized a Sunday and evening school for Chinese residents of Salt Lake. Originally located in a room over a Chinese store, the school expanded quickly and relocated to Independence Hall. By 1894, the group, now known as the Chinese Christian Association and Evening School, was meeting at the first Congregational Church every weekday evening to study English and Christianity. Anna Baker established a kindergarten at Salt Lake's Phillips Congregational church in 1895 with a charge of "a dollar a month" per pupil.

Ogden's First Congregational Church was organized in 1876 and two women—Jane Taylor and Aura Thompson—were among its initial ten members. After a difficult period of inactivity between 1877 and 1883, the church was reorganized in 1884 with twelve members. Two years later, Lydia Bailey, wife of Reverend A. J. Bailey "delivered appeals for funds in 12 states and raised $2550" for a new building. Dedicated in October 1887 at 2464 Adams Avenue, the building and lot cost $7,000. At that time the church had a membership of twenty-two which more than doubled to forty-eight in 1889 and gradually grew until it reached a high point of 225 in 1915. During those years, women were active in the growing congregation, especially in the Ladies Aid Society, which among other things, carried on missionary work on Ogden's notorious west Twenty-fifth Street in the 1890s.[60]

Teachers at the New West Education Commission Utah Annual Conference, 1890.

Other Congregational women were especially active in Provo as well. In 1883, Emily Clapp, a Mount Holyoake Female Seminary graduate from East Hampton, Massachusetts, opened a similar school in Provo. Clapp arrived in Provo on November 12, 1883, and found space in the Daniels home on Second East and Second South. She circulated a number of flyers and began school with six students, but very quickly "her little classroom could no longer accommodate all her students. In March 1884, . . . she moved her school into a larger hall above the Bee Harness and Saddle Shop on the South side of West Center Street." In addition to the school, Clapp was "expected to set up a Sunday School as well," which she did on December 9, 1883. Her initial group of thirteen soon doubled. Clapp left for health reasons in 1885, but Mary E. French took her place and, laying for the foundation for expansion, gained the support of Joseph O. Proctor of Gloucester, Massachusetts. She opened the Proctor Academy in September 1857.[61] Alice Isley, who came to Proctor as a teacher in 1895, kept the Congregational work alive during 1897–98 until the arrival of Reverend Samuel H. Goodwin in 1898, accompanied by his wife.[62]

Of all the educational endeavors sponsored by the Congregational Church in Utah, the most important were the activities of the New West Education Committee (NWEC), organized at a Congregational ministers' meeting in Chicago in 1879. The NWEC saw itself as a temporary agency to "provide free, high quality elementary and secondary education" for three different groups: Native American children, Mexican American children in New Mexico, and the young people of Utah, both Mormon and Gentile. NWEC leaders hoped that, once these schools were established, the Congregational Church itself would take over their operation.[63]

Ambitiously, the NWEC "built the largest educational system in Utah Territory, establishing twenty-six schools by the end of the 1880s, that educated nearly 2,500 children each year." In the fourteen years of its existence, the NWEC spent about half a millon dollars in its work, allotting some $60,000 annually, and educating more than 7,000 children, "three fourths of them of Mormon parentage."[64] As Gary Topping has noted, the goal of these schools was to "wean Mormon children away from their Church" and "topple the Latter-day Saints."[65] According to the commission's publication, the *New West Gleaner* for August and September 1887, thirty-seven of the forty-two Utah teachers were women. "It was thought that the highly educated Gentile women, most of them unmarried, standing on their own, would serve as worthy examples to Mormon women who allegedly suffered mightily from the horrors of polygamy."[66]

The NWEC showpiece in Utah was the Ogden Academy, a two-room brick building built in 1882. The school accommodated an initial class of thirteen pupils and two teachers, Hiram Waldo Ring and Virginia W. Ludden. Ludden, described as a "tireless worker" despite frail health, directed the elementary department. By 1889, a colleague reported that Ludden, who was the only teacher to serve the academy during the entire ten years of its existence, "had made a large place for herself in church and school and had the respect of the community."[67]

A third teacher joined Ludden and Ring in 1883: Beatrice Peaslie Ring, Hiram's bride. She took over some of her husband's teaching responsibilities and taught English, anatomy, and music while also taking charge of the intermediate grades. The music, recalled former student Ruth E. Prout Bullock, consisted of gospel hymns, "usually chosen by the students" that Mrs. Ring led and accompanied.[68]

The Ogden Academy continued to grow and moved to a larger, two-story building in 1887, when average attendance reached more than 200. By 1889–90, the school reached "its greatest size and greatest influence," when five more teachers—Alice B. Hamblin, Mary L. McClelland, Abbie P. Noyes, Florence Blanchard, and Marion S. Copeland—joined the faculty. According to Noyes's biographer, Gary Topping, her papers at the Utah State Historical Society provide an interesting view of a Protestant missionary teacher's daily life in pre-statehood Utah. Her letters record her views on parental and student apathy, her personal conflicts with Principal Ring, antagonism between fellow teachers, the difficulty of getting an "Eastern standard of system and order accepted & lived up to," and many other matters related to the academy.

Abbie Parish Noyes was a teacher with the New West Education Commission located in Ogden Academy, 1889–1890.

Increasingly Noyes was concerned with the fluctuations of enrollment: "School reopened today. Some of our pupils who came from outlying districts were not there and I presume will not be this term. And yet no cowboys or young ranch men have come in as they often do for the winter term. I rather wish they would to take the place of the half-dozen we have lost. I do not like to see vacant seats having seen all full."[69]

By 1890, the academy faced a serious financial crisis, in part stemming from the national economic downturn. The school managed to negotiate a $10,000 donation from Nathaniel Gordon of Exeter, New Hampshire, in 1892, and renamed itself the Gordon Academy in his honor. However, on-going financial difficulties forced the academy to lease its facilities to the Ogden school district, then relocate in Salt Lake City in 1896. At that point, the academy became a preparatory school. The NWEC also supervised schools in Hooper taught by H. M. Loomis and Abbey E. Parks; in Lynne taught by Stella F. Hutchins; and in South Weber with Miss M. D. Shute as teacher.[70]

By the end of the decade, the Congregational Church cut back on its educational and full-scale evangelical work in Utah, despite frequent pleas from local Congregational leaders for more financial support from the East.

This decision was predicated on a number of factors including the Woodruff Manifesto, statehood, the development of a national party system, creation of an independent school system, and the financial difficulties of the 1890s. Though their efforts to undermine and destroy Mormonism through the influence of the mission-schools failed, Utah Congregationalists "left Utah cultural life richer than they found it . . . [and] its challenge to education undoubtedly hastened the development of the public-school system and it brought to Utah's pioneer society schooling of a remarkably high quality."[71]

Methodist Women

Methodist missionary work in Utah began in a systematic way in May 1870 when Reverend Gustavus M. Pierce arrived with his wife, Lovina, and family in Salt Lake City. On May 22, Pierce preached to some forty listeners in Faust's Hall—a loft over a livery stable.[72] Within the next two years, Pierce organized churches and schools in Salt Lake City, Corinne, Tooele, Provo, and Beaver.[73] He also established the Rocky Mountain Seminary, a Methodist school in Salt Lake City, which boasted 200 students in 1872 and was in operation until 1893.

The denomination's activities expanded six years later when Dr. Thomas C. Iliff became presiding elder of the Utah Conference. During his quarter century of service in Utah, Iliff employed twenty-five women teachers and several women missionaries. Because the wives of Methodist pastors were considered their assistants in pastoral work, the actual total of Methodist women directly involved in furthering their church in Utah likely numbered around a hundred between 1876 and 1900.[74]

One of Utah Methodism's earliest teachers later played an important role in another religious tradition. Iliff recruited Alma White, then living in Montana in the summer of 1884, to teach in his seminary in Salt Lake City. White arrived in September 1884, accompanied by her sister Nora, who taught in a Methodist school in Tooele. A series of conflicts erupted between the southern-born White and Reverend S. J. Carroll, a New Jersey native and pastor of Salt Lake's First Methodist Church, who illustrated his sermons "mainly with incidents of the Civil War, which aroused prejudice unnecessarily in the hearts of his . . . congregation . . . composed largely of people from the South." This dynamic made White's stay in Utah difficult. Similarly, there were problems between White and the principal of the seminary, Mr. Garvin, and several of her fellow teachers. She left in June 1885, characterizing Mormonism as a "false religious system" which left its adherents "disappointed and sometimes robbed of all they possessed[,] . . . mangled and bleeding at the foot of the oppressor." Several years later, White became prominent as the founder and first bishop of the Pillar of Fire Church, headquartered first in New Jersey and later in Denver, Colorado.[75]

The Methodist Church's national Woman's Home Missionary Society, organized in 1880, took an active role in funding and operating Methodist schools in Utah. By 1882, it established a "Utah fund" and sought pledges of ten dollars from at least five hundred women to furnish the five thousand dollars deemed necessary to support both educational and missionary efforts.[75] This women's society continued to play a key role in building Utah Methodism in the next four decades. During this time the society "raised funds through public collections, cake sales, lectures, musicals and other schemes" to support missionary work.[77] Among its interests was Utah's large Scandinavian population. It supported a Scandinavian mission in Salt Lake City in 1882 and the next year sent Lisa M. Sangstad as its first missionary.[78]

The Methodist Ladies Aid society was also an important presence. Between 1880 and 1920, it employed deaconesses, who were social workers, teachers, and preachers. At the high point of Methodist missionary activity in Utah in the years prior to World War I, more than twenty deaconesses worked in nine cities in the state. The society sponsored two boarding houses for women known as Esther Houses, one in Salt Lake City and one in Ogden, and also established the Ogden Home for Girls.[79]

As one commentator has noted, between 1870 and 1894, Methodist education in Utah "thrived," establishing forty-two schools. Some were shortlived; but by 1890, the most successful year, more than two dozen schools were operating with 32 teachers and 1,467 pupils. These pupils included 544 Mormons, 673 former Mormons, and 250 Protestants." Moreover, most of the teachers were "young women representing the Women's Home Missionary Society."[80]

Although Methodist missionary and educational efforts were carried on throughout the state, the greatest activity occurred in Salt Lake City. At one point between 1888 and 1892, four separate ladies' charitable societies were operating in the Methodist churches in the territory's capital. All four groups undertook to help "any whom we find in need" regardless of creed or denomination. One of the four, the Ladies Aid Society of Liberty Park Methodist Church made constructing a chapel its highest priority and raised several hundred dollars from "membership fees and tea parties held at the homes of members."[81]

Utah Methodist women, under the direction of the energetic Anna M. Davis, were also active in promoting the Epworth League, a nondenominational organization for young people. During the 1890s, the league ran a successful chapter in Salt Lake City, helped organize and run a series of "gospel tent" revivals sponsored throughout the state in 1898, and joined women of other denominations to coordinate educational, charitable, and missionary efforts.

An ambitious, yet ultimately unsuccessful, effort led by Utah Methodist women began in 1881 when Angie F. Newman, described as "a reform-minded evangelistic Methodist," presented a plan to the Methodist Utah Mission Conference calling for the creation of a "house of refuge for discontented and abandoned plural wives and children."[82] The conference saw the proposal as a positive step toward ending polygamy and approved the plan. Because Utah

Methodists felt they lacked the ability to undertake this project by themselves, they called a mass meeting in Salt Lake City in November 1882 to organize an interdenominational effort. The next year, Newman persuaded the WHMS to support the project, "securing from it $660 in initial pledges and appointment as its bureau secretary for Mormon affairs."[83] As Peggy Pascoe has argued, this effort to assert female moral authority was led by Protestant women who "singled out the institution of Mormon polygamy as the most significant symbol of male control over community social order," in a western city "where male domination was actually celebrated."[84]

Between 1883 and 1886, however, support within the Methodist missionary society ebbed in part because Newman was recovering from an accident. In March 1886, the indefatigable Newman broadened her efforts, calling together a core group from the Anti-Polygamy Society to form the interdenominational Industrial Christian Home Association. The U.S. Congress underwrote the project with two appropriations of $40,000 and later $74,000. At the same time Congress, wary of turning financial control over to women, appointed an all-male board of control consisting of Utah's territorial governor, its supreme court justices, and the district attorney. Throughout the life of the project, there would be severe disagreement between the women of the association and the board. A $100,000 building, capable of housing approximately forty people was completed in 1887. Despite high hopes for its success, the project was a failure. In September 1887, the point of highest occupancy, the home sheltered only eleven women and twenty-two children. The failure of the home "exposed the fault lines between Protestant women and men in Salt Lake City." While 154 women and children had applied for admittance to the home, the board kept the number actually admitted low because it "favored a narrow interpretation of the language of the legislation which provided that entrance to the home be limited to 'women who renounce polygamy and [to] their children of tender age.'" The women of the association defined the legislation broadly, arguing that "almost every woman in Utah was a potential victim of polygamy."[85]

Although they had long since given up direct involvement in the project, Utah Methodist women, while recognizing their failure to dissuade polygamous wives, still termed the project as a success because it kept the issue of polygamy before the public at large.[86] The home ceased operations in June 1893 and was sold in 1899 for $22,500 at a public auction.[87]

PRESBYTERIAN WOMEN

Of all the Protestant denominations active in Utah probably the most significant in terms of education, missionary activities, and overall impact were the Presbyterians. Initial Presbyterian contacts in Utah apparently began when Reverend John Anderson arrived in Utah as a chaplain under Colonel Patrick Connor. Anderson had only a short stay in the territory, but he did conduct both non-denominational and Presbyterian services at Camp Douglas. Other early Presbyterian contacts included the visit of Dr. Henry Kendall, secretary of the denomination's Board of Home Missions, in 1864 while on his way to the Pacific Coast. Kendall spent "several days in Salt Lake City investigating the conditions of the city." His stay also included speaking at the Tabernacle at Brigham Young's invitation.[88]

Brigham Young told Kendall that he had no objection to the Presbyterians either establishing churches or sending missionaries. LDS attitudes toward outsiders in the 1860s when contacts were "infrequent and of short duration," changed dramatically after the coming of the railroad, when outsiders "came in increasing numbers."[89]

Permanent Presbyterian work began in Utah in June 1869 when Dr. Sheldon Jackson arrived in Corinne. Appointed by the board of missions to oversee the work in several western states and territories, Jackson brought in a minister to Corinne and supervised construction of the first permanent Presbyterian church building in Utah which opened in July 1870 "with a roster of nine members."[90]

In May 1873, Reverend J. P. Shell arrived in Alta, Utah, "fresh from seminary to organize a church reading room and school." He opened the Alta School, a day school with a Miss Mosby as the teacher. Five years later, the school building was destroyed by fire.

Presbyterian activities in Utah intensified in the 1870s. In response to the denomination's General Assembly call to organize women's societies, the Utah Presbytery meeting in Ogden in February 1877 called on the Board of Home Missions to "commission lady teachers and Bible readers" to be sent to Utah with the stipulation that these individuals must "be supported by money especially raised and designated for that purpose."[91]

As a result of these actions, educational work in Utah expanded rapidly. In 1877, Anna Noble opened a school in a "small one story adobe building with two rooms" in Springville. Noble, "standing in the low doorway and hardly able to stand upright," taught a class of thirty-eight. During the next three years, three other women came to assist Noble; Eugenia Munger replaced Noble when she was called to another field.[92] Similar activities took place in a variety of Utah communities during the late 1870s and early 1880s.

During this same period, Presbyterian schools with predominantly female faculty were organized in Manti, Mount Pleasant, Springville, Payson, Manti, Ogden, St. George, Parowan, Logan, Cedar City, Kaysville, Gunnison, Salina, and other places. In many cases, the teachers were the wives or daughters of the local Presbyterian minister. At the same time, these mission schools brought many single Presbyterian women to Utah Territory. At times life in Utah Territory could be dangerous. Late one October 1884, evening in Mendon in Cache Valley "two inebriated men, apparently intent on rape, broke into the residence of a lone female Presbyterian teacher. After being 'roughed up,' the woman escaped through a bedroom window clad only in her nightgown. Her cries roused Mormon neighbors who provided refuge and apprehended her attackers."[93]

The two men were turned over to local civil authorities for trial and punishment, and both men were also excommunicated by Mendon Ward leaders. Moreover, Bishop Henry Hughes of the Mendon Ward publicly condemned the incident, saying that it was a "shame" to think that "a young lady could come to reside in our midst" and be subjected to such "outrages by hoodlums." Hughes told his congregation that it was the "duty of the saints" to protect the right of all to "worship how, where or what they may." He further charged members of the priesthood to see to it that the woman "wants for nothing and that she is protected in her rights."[94]

Like other Protestant denominations, the Presbyterian Church relied on the activities and financial contributions of its church women to support the missionary effort in Utah. In 1875, the church's General Assembly, headquartered in Philadelphia, directed the Board of Home Missions to organize women's societies to facilitate communication between the church's governing board and its women. The outgrowth was the Women's Board of Home Missions which raised money for Utah missionary work, published tracts and books about Mormonism, emphasized the importance of hiring women teachers in Utah, and helped alter church practices to allow mission schools to be organized prior to establishing a church itself. The women of the home missions board believed that stable mission schools would lay the foundation for on-going ecclesiastical work.[95]

In addition to thirty-three day schools, a part of the Presbyterian work consisted of building academies, which often included all elementary grades and facilities for boarding students. In September 1878, Logan Academy, a Presbyterian day school for girls was organized by Reverend Calvin Parks and his wife. The school was renamed the New Jersey Academy in 1890 when women in that state contributed $11,000 for a new building. The principal at the time was Susan V. Parks.[96] In 1875, Reverend Josiah Welch of Salt Lake City's First Presbyterian Church approached John Coyner with an offer of "three rooms in his new [church] building for a mission school."[97] The Presbyterian Preparatory School, with kindergarten through grade twelve and twenty-seven, students opened in April 1875, with Mary Coyner, wife of the principal, as head of the primary department, and their daughter Emma directing the intermediate department. By the end of the first term, enrollment had reached sixty-three. The school continued to grow and, in August 1875, began its first full year of operation with 142 pupils and a new teacher, Jennie Dennison, who replaced Emma Coyner who was engaged to marry Reverend Welch. Two years later, the school had outgrown space in the church and plans were made to build a new school building. Coyner had "six young women in his advanced class" write three thousand letters to Presbyterian Sunday Schools around the country

Giovale Library, Westminster College, Salt Lake City.

A postcard photograph of a group of students and their instructors at the Presbyterian mission school of Panguitch, ca. 1920.

seeking funds. The letters netted $1,300 to match the $1,300 raised from local sources. The new school opened in August 1877. Among the early teachers were Sarah J. Irwin McNiece and Mary E. Moore.

In 1880 this school became known as the Salt Lake Collegiate Institute. That same year, the school rented additional space in a building known as the "Octagon," to house a girls' boarding school under the direction of Mrs. M. K. Parsons. By 1887 the school had seven departments—high school, grammar, two intermediate, two primary and a kindergarten—with 319 pupils in attendance.[98]

In addition, the school sponsored a Girl's Home under the direction of Mary E. Moore. Beginning with four girls, Moore was able to obtain private financial support to allow the girls to attend school. The home was eventually moved to the Octagon and was housing twenty girls by 1892. As Emil Nyman has observed, some of the girls

> were able to pay the small charge for board, while others were assisted by the Home Mission board and private individuals. The girls, with the assistance of one servant, did all of the work of the house while attending school. As the accommodations were limited, much care was used in the selection of the girls to be admitted, and consequently, these were the most earnest and promising pupils. Under the wise, faithful home training of Miss Moore, the girls made outstanding progress both academically and in domestic areas.[99]

As the public schools strengthened in the 1890s, demand for facilities for private kindergarten through high school facilities had decreased, and so did calls for creating a college. In 1895, Sheldon Jackson pledged $50,000 with a commitment to raise an additional $1,500 annually to organize a college. Space was rented from the Collegiate Institute, and the school was named Sheldon Jackson College. The college and the institute were combined in the 1890s and renamed Westminster College in 1902. The new college attracted eight to ten students per year through the first few years of the twentieth century. Despite periods of economic difficulties, it has remained an educational presence in the state until the present time.

Other Presbyterian academies included Hungerford Academy in Springville and Wasatch Academy in Mount Pleasant. Still in existence today, Wasatch Academy was organized by Reverend Duncan McMillan in April 1875. Beginning with 44 students, the enrollment grew to 109 by the end of the year. The first principal was Delia R. Snow. Preferring female teachers to men, McMillan hired a number of women educators including Alice C. Sowles, Mrs. C. J. Wilcox, Maria Fishback, and Clara Pierce in the early years. Primarily a grade school, Wasatch Academy came under the control of the Board of Home Missions in 1880. In 1887, the curriculum was expanded and the school became a true academy. A new two-story brick school was built in 1891 at a cost of $10,000 largely provided by the Ladies Missionary Society of New York. Growing steadily through the 1890s and early twentieth century, Wasatch Academy became a college preparatory school in 1912. It remains both a preparatory school and a Presbyterian administered school to the present time.[100]

In Ogden, the First Presbyterian Church maintained a school which was organized in 1878 by Mrs. G. W. Gallagher, wife of the pastor, as principal. She was succeeded in 1879 by a Miss Olmstead and, over the next several years, was succeeded in turn by "Misses Campbell, Scovel, Dickey and Vaughn." Classes were conducted in Peery's Hall on Twenty-Fourth Street until 1880 when it was moved to the corner of Twenty-Fourth and Lincoln. The school closed in 1890.[101]

In the first ten years of their existence (1880–90), the thirty-seven Presbyterian schools in Utah enrolled more than two thousand pupils and employed more than fifty teachers, most of them women.[102] These figures remained relatively constant until statehood. Approximately 75 percent of the students in Presbyterian schools were Mormon and, in the words of one Presbyterian writer, "many Mormon parents in spite of prohibitions from church leaders . . . persisted in sending their children to these schools."[103] By 1905, the same writer estimated that more than 30,000 young people had passed through Utah Presbyterian schools.

Shortly after Utah became a state in 1896, Presbyterian work in Utah declined, and many of the schools were closed. In part, this was a response to the creation of a public school system; but Presbyterian efforts were also affected by the economic dislocations of the 1890s in the United States.[104] At the same time, the denomination was also shifting its emphasis from the

West to the new immigrants in large eastern urban areas. Sherman H. Doyle, in a pamphlet entitled *Presbyterian Home Missions,* lobbied hard for their continuation, arguing that "hundreds of girls who have attended our schools have refused to be polygamous wives [and] a large number have had their faith shaken."[105]

At the same time, however, even grudging contacts between Mormons and Presbyterians increased their mutual respect. As R. Douglas Brackenridge has noted, letters from the missionaries themselves often present a "contrasting" view from those in denominational publications

> Women teachers frequently refer to Mormon kindness, generosity, and acceptance, and to friendships established both with children and adults. In 1880 Ada Kingsbury, missionary in American Fork, described how she held singing, sewing, and reading classes after regular school hours. . . . In the same year, Marcia A. Scovel wrote from Ogden, "In our calls upon Mormon families we are received with the utmost cordiality and they nearly always think to thank us for coming." Unprepared for such positive receptions, Scovel noted that Ogden must have been an exception "because all the Mormons with whom we have to deal treat us very kindly."[106]

Brackenridge chronicles similar experiences on the part of Presbyterian missionaries, even among those who had "firmly implanted negative impressions." One such missionary, Mary Agnes Craig, who came to Fillmore in 1881 "initially expressed revulsion at the primitive, immoral conditions" she encountered in Utah. "We are like lions among dogs," she wrote to her family in 1882, indicating that she did not plan to return when her two-year contract ended. Over time, however, Craig's extensive correspondence refers to pleasant social contacts with Mormons and their families. When Craig and a co-teacher needed boarding accommodations for the summer, she informed her family that "you would have thought everybody in town wanted us."[107]

Another important area of Presbyterian activity in Utah was organizing kindergartens. In 1883, the national Women's Executive Board sent Elizabeth Dickey to organize kindergartens in the mission schools. Dickey opened a kindergarten in the basement of Salt Lake's First Presbyterian Church with branches at Westminster College and in a local day nursery. Dickey also "trained a class of young ladies in kindergarten methods" to continue the work. In 1892, Mrs. E. H. Parsons, who had studied under Dickey, spearheaded the formation of the Salt Lake Kindergarten Association. The following January, the group lobbied the legislature who passed a bill giving territorial schools the legal authority to open kindergartens in the public schools themselves.[108]

Besides educational work, Utah Presbyterian women organized clubs and auxiliaries for a variety of purposes. A Home and Foreign Missionary Society, organized in 1878 at Salt Lake's First Presbyterian Church, met once a week except in the summer, listened to papers presented by members, and raised more than five hundred dollars for missionary work. A Young Ladies Missionary Society was organized in 1883 among the pupils of the Collegiate Institute. In 1882 a Woman's Aid Society was organized at First Presbyterian Church to spearhead benevolent and charitable work among its own members and the community at large and also assist their pastors in various ways. Similar societies were organized at Westminster Presbyterian Church in Salt Lake City and other congregations around the state.[109]

Other Denominational Activities in Utah

In addition to the work of these denominations, several other religious groups afforded Utah women an opportunity for service and leadership. Their story is illuminating as well.

Between 1882 and 1920, seven different Lutheran synods were represented in Utah. The most active was the Augustana (Swedish) Synod reflecting in part an evangelical response to the 10,000 Scandinavian Mormons living in the state. Lutheran clergy—hoping to return Mormon converts to their original religious roots as well as to serve Utah Lutherans themselves—first established Zion Swedish Lutheran Church in Salt Lake City in July 1882. Elim Lutheran Church was organized in Ogden in 1888. Prior to the church's organization, Lutherans met at the home of Hannah Lund in Five Points. By the decade's end, other Lutheran congregations opened in the largely Scandinavian area of Sanpete County, as well as in Provo, Spanish Fork, Eureka, and Park City. Most congregations were started "on the basis of nationality and language, [thus] worship services usually were conducted in the native language or at least alternated with services in English."[110]

Three women were among the five individuals who joined with Pastor John Telleen to organize Zion Swedish Lutheran Church. One, Maria Wahlquist, was a Mormon convert who came to Utah a decade earlier. Ultimately Maria and her husband August were excommunicated from the Mormon church, "he for refusing to take a second wife, and she for joining the Lutheran church."[111]

As Zion Lutheran grew, a Young Girl's Sewing Society was organized in 1885 as well as a Ladies Aid Society. In 1890 the two groups merged, remaining united until 1918, when the Martha Society was formed for young working women and those who could not attend the group's regular meetings on the last Thursday afternoon of the month. As Paul Mogren, author of a history of the church, has noted, it was "the women, through the bad times as well as the good, who carry out the many necessary functions of church life."[112]

In 1912, Lutheran services were held in the Erick Olson home in Riverton to provide a "Lutheran identity" to a group of Scandinavian farmers in the Sandy and Riverton area. Three years later, the Sandy-Riverton-Murray Ladies Aid Society was organized for women in the South Valley.[113]

In assessing the activities of Lutheran women, Ronnie L. Stillhorn, a historian of the group, has noted that, while most of the activities have been

Giovale Library, Westminster College, Salt Lake City.

Miss Sarah Louisa Conklin with school children in St. George, ca.1920.

directed to their congregations, at times assistance has been directed at non-Lutheran groups as well. "For instance in 1912, the Ladies Aid of St. John's Lutheran church in Salt Lake City, not only assisted the congregation, but helped the sick and needy. During World War I, the ladies of Elim Lutheran Church in Ogden organized themselves into a Red Cross chapter, rolled bandages, knit socks for the doughboys, and sent money for Belgian relief."[114]

Finally, as was the case with so many denominations, Lutheran women were also involved with education and teaching. In 1883 the congregation at Zion's first petitioned the Augustana synods mission board to send a teacher to Utah. The board responded in 1885 by sending Hilda Carlson, who established a school in the church basement. Known as Augustana Academy, the school had an enrollment of fifty with one full-time teacher and an assistant. Unable to attract sufficient numbers, the school closed in 1890, although Carlson remained in the area teaching in the public schools. The Norwegian Synod organized two separate schools in the Salt Lake Valley to "provide a parochial education for Norwegian Lutheran children." From 1897 to 1899, Miss G. Gomvich conducted a kindergarten in Sandy; it closed when the Congregationalists also moved their educational efforts into kindergarten.[115] Finally, St. John's Lutheran Church of the Missouri Synod established a parochial school in Salt Lake City which operated from 1909 to 1918. Women played an important role in all of these endeavors.[116]

During the 1890s, a small group of women assisted in the work of the Disciples of Christ (Christian) Church. Working both in Salt Lake City and Ogden, these women organized two groups: a "Christian work circle" to raise money to retire church debts and a Ladies Aid Society to raise funds for the church and "aid the pastor in his work of visiting the sick or in such other ways as he may suggest."[117] As historian, Leslie L. Zook has observed, "While it had social and spiritual aspects, its principal goals and accomplishments were financial. The 'Aid' was literally that, and worked to supplement the church budget. . . . Noonday meals were served to businessmen and banquets were prepared for fraternities and other organizations. Ice cream, strawberry, and watermelon socials were served in season. Much painting, cleaning and renovating took place, bringing no monetary return but saving the cost of hiring outside help."[118]

By 1896 the Salt Lake church had organized the Women's Missionary Society which averaged between 15 and 35 members. Its outreach work was largely funded by an annual Woman's Day service held in December where "special offerings were received."[119]

The roots of Calvary Baptist church—one of Salt Lake's first two black churches—can be traced to the organization of a women's Mutual Aid Society in 1898. The society met on West Temple between South Temple and First South until 1911 when the church relocated to 679 E. 300 South.[120]

A Progressive Society of Spiritualists was organized in Salt Lake City in January 1891 with a ladies' auxiliary following within the month to "help those women whom we found could not help themselves." The auxiliary, which met every Friday afternoon, raised its operating expenses "from dues, socials and entertainments."[121] By 1893 the church had a membership of 80.[122]

In addition, communicants of other churches made important contributions. Among these women were members of the Episcopal, Christian Science, Unitarian, Catholic, and Jewish faiths.

Episcopal Women

When two Episcopal ministers, George W. Foote and T. W. Haskins, arrived in Salt Lake City in May 1867, they attended the Sunday School directed by their Congregationalist colleague, Reverend Norman McLeod, in Independence Hall.[123] Eventually Foote assumed the leadership of this congregation of forty to sixty members. Three members of this congregation were Episcopalians, women identified only as Mrs. Hamilton, Mrs. Durrant, and Mrs. Tracy. From this small beginning has grown the substantial Episcopal congregation in Utah.

Utah's first Episcopal bishop, Daniel S. Tuttle, arrived in July 1867. Though he stayed less than two weeks, Tuttle was in Salt Lake City long enough to "approve heartily of Messers Foote and Haskins in deciding that a day school would be a most efficient instrumentality in doing good missionary work."[124] The trio promptly organized a school in a vacant bowling alley.[125] Beginning with sixteen students on July 1, 1867, the school grew to the point where it had to be relocated in Independence Hall three months later. The school's faculty consisted of two women, Sarah Foote and a Miss Wells, "an apostate Mormon who had come across the plains at the age of six." Wells taught the younger children, while Foote taught the older students rhetoric and composition.[126]

Continued growth, supported by scholarships funded by Eastern individuals and organizations, resulted in a third move to Nicholas Groesbeck's store on Main Street in 1869. By 1873, St. Mark's had a studentbody of 118, both a primary and a secondary department, and a building of its own comprising a large chapel, several classrooms, and a small library. The faculty, under the direction of a Miss Davenport, an experienced public school teacher from Brooklyn, New York, consisted of "the clergy and several women volunteers [working] in a free atmosphere that attracted students from the entire community." The $22,000 structure was primarily funded by contributions from Episcopalian congregations in the East, though $4,000 was raised locally.[127] Moreover, Harriet Tuttle, the bishop's wife, "worked along with her husband advising and helping. Often times she led the singing and played the organ."[128]

In 1873, J. H. Van Rensselaer became the first woman to teach at St. Mark's, serving as principal of its high school department. During 1873–74, seven women complete the normal course. All seven remained to teach classes of their own. Two other women, identified only as Mrs. Beauchamp and Mrs. Webster, also served as principals of the high school department, Webster "safely piloting the last class to graduation" in 1891.

After the completion of St. Mark's Cathedral in 1871, a day school for elementary-age girls was established in the church's basement and averaged more than fifty pupils per term. Its first director was Charlotte E. Hayden; and over the next decade, three women served as her successors.

In September 1881, the Bishop's School, named for its founder, Bishop Tuttle, began operations as a boarding school. At that time the day school at St. Mark's became the primary department. By 1883, there were "seventeen boarders and sixty pupils" on the rolls.[129] That same year the school was renamed Rowland Hall when Virginia L. Rowland, widow of Benjamin Rowland, along with her daughter Josephine, donated $5,000 toward the $8,000 needed to purchase a new building.

One boarder, Farnetta ("Nettie") Alexander of Bozeman, Montana, and thirteen day students received their tutelage from Lucia Mason Marsh and Isabella E. Douglas. By Christmas of the first year, Douglas later recalled, several new boarders had arrived and Bishop Tuttle hired two new teachers, Emma Chandler and Abby Marsh. An interesting reminiscence of these years comes from Theresa Godbe, whose father, William, led the Mormon schism that bears his name. She remembered that the school "grew rapidly," and included "Miss Fidelia Hamilton, vocal music, and Madame Fitzgerald, a Parisian married to an Irishman, [who taught] French." By 1882, there were "seventeen boarders and sixty pupils" on the rolls.[130]

The first principal was Lucia Marsh, succeeded by a Mrs. Beauchamp when ill health forced Marsh to move to California. After several years of direction from Beauchamp and Van Rensselaer, the principalship went to a third woman, Addie Coleman, in 1890. Four years later a fourth woman, Clara Colburne, became principal. She headed the school until well into the next decade.[131] In 1904, all of the school's faculty were women.[132]

In addition to the schools in Salt Lake City, the Episcopal Church organized schools in Ogden (1870), Logan (1873), and Plain City (1873). Bishop Tuttle estimated that, between 1870 and 1900, an average of a thousand students attended the Utah Episcopal schools annually.[133]

Besides educational activities, women's social and charitable work was promoted at an early date. In the 1870s, the Episcopal Church sponsored sewing classes. By 1880, the women organized a sewing guild with the two-fold goal of raising money for the poor and generating additional income for church work. Other Anglican organizations included the Guild of St. Agnes for single women, the Guild of the Good Shepherd for younger girls, and the Guild of St. Mary and St. Martha and the Altar Guild, both of which sought to involve young women in the pastoral work of the diocese. By the early twentieth century, the church had also organized a woman's auxiliary and a Girl's Friendly Society.

In 1870, Tuttle recruited Emily Pearsall of Bainbridge, New York, to come to Utah and "help in our pastoral work, especially among the sick and the poor and the children and the ignorant and the stranger." Pearsall worked in Utah for two years, then died in 1872. Tuttle paid tribute to Pearsall, remarking that "the efficiency of the pastoral work of a clergyman can be more than doubled by the aid of a devoted Christian woman of intelligence and refinement."[134] Over the next fifty years, a number of women served as Episcopal missionaries in Utah.[135]

Typical of this number was Sara Napper, a missionary in the first decade of the twentieth century. In quarterly reports kept between 1902 and 1905, Napper provides a glimpse of her activities in the Salt Lake City area. In December 1902, Napper recorded that, in the previous quarter, she had made 300 calls and taken charge of the Sunday School at St. Peter's Mission. Napper was particularly interested in working with girls and young women:

> In place of the former local sewing class I have organized a . . . class of the Girl's Friendly Society, and have 21 names in the roll. The GFS with its central rule of 'purity of life' seems especially suitable to the needs of St. Peter's mission— and its neighborhood as it is in the midst of a Mormon population. We have Mormon girls in each class who seem much interested in the society and its aims and rules, and sing with fervor the candidates hymn, and are learning to say the prayer and recite the creed at weekly meetings.[136]

Similar activities and concerns for the young Mormon women appear in Napper's reports for the next two years. By March 1904, she was "starting a sewing class in St. John's mission which, if successful, may lead to a branch being established there." Serving as secretary of the local board of missions, Napper "assisted the Dean [of St. Mark's] in answering the correspondence and sending out circular letters to the various missions."[137]

Most of her work tended to be routine—visiting "the sick and strangers," assisting with correspondence, and keeping mission records. Still Napper's efforts did not lack challenges: "About the middle of October," she reported, "I boarded a street car to go to the Girl's Friendly Society meeting at St. Peter's. When near the railway track, the brake refused to act and the car ran at full speed into a train. All the passengers were injured and I was taken to St. Mark's Hospital. I have been home for a time now and hope to be able to resume my work this week. I have kept in touch with the people and my sister has taken my place on several occasions."[138]

Another important effort of the Utah Episcopal community was the above-mentioned St. Mark's Hospital, which opened in a small adobe building on the corner of Fourth South and Fifth East in Salt Lake City in April 1872, moved three times, and then in 1890 found a more permanent home in the northwest part of the city. The hospital involved a number of women on its staff, first as matrons and later as nurses. A nursing training school was organized in 1894 when rapid hospital growth generated the need for trained professionals. Mary Edith Newitt, an 1893 graduate of St. Luke's School for Nurses in New York, was appointed superintendent by Bishop Abiel Leonard. The twenty-three-year-old Newitt found the hospital in poor shape when she arrived and spent the first few days cleaning and establishing sanitation standards. Eventually, Newitt reorganized the hospital staff, raising the necessary money to make needed improvements through a benefit performance.

As W. H. Behle, son and biographer of Dr. Augustus C. Behle, one of St. Mark's early surgeons, wrote: "The first thing done with the money was to have the windows screened since the flies were terrible in the daytime and the mosquitoes were bad at night. She also had the first instrument case made. The private rooms, she said, were nice, but the wards were deplorable, being crowded with miners and railroad patients. The nurses slept in the basement with no private quarters. . . . The outside of the hospital was forlorn. No trees or lawn had been planted yet and [Newitt] insisted that this be done."[139]

Newitt also improved procedures for sterilizing instruments, required physicians to wear masks (previously they had simply tied back their hair), and insisted they wear surgical gloves while operating.

Nursing training, originally a two-year program, was extended to three in 1898. Student nurses, known as probationers, spent their first year assisting in general cleaning, food preparation, and other tasks as well as nursing. Each nurse was assigned to a particular ward on regular rotations. Between 1896 and 1920, more than 200 nurses graduated from St. Mark's. Many married doctors and stayed on the Wasatch Front where they worked in hospitals, established

Giovale Library, Westminster College, Salt Lake City.

St. Mark's Hospital School of Nursing, Salt Lake City, Utah, ca. 1919.

the Utah Nurses Association, and developed public health nursing in the state. Episcopal women also organized auxiliary units like the St. Mark's Guild and the Nurses Alumnae Association, which sponsored charitable projects and helped raise money for the Bishop Leonard Memorial Nurses' home which was built in 1906. The home was enlarged and a new story added in 1916 and 1917.

CHRISTIAN SCIENCE WOMEN

In July 1891, eleven Christian Scientists—eight men and three women—met at the residence of Mary Ann Bagley to organize "a more systematic work as Christian Scientists" in Utah. Most of those present were newcomers to the state, but two women were closely tied to Utah and Mormon culture. One was Henrietta Young, the thirty-seven-year-old daughter of Joseph Young, one of the First Council of the Seventy and a brother of Brigham Young. The other, Lucretia Heywood Kimball, was daughter of Mormon bishop Joseph L. Heywood and the daughter-in-law of Sarah M. Kimball, a prominent Mormon suffrage worker and president of the Nineteenth Ward Relief Society.

Henrietta Young became a Christian Science practitioner in 1895, serving as librarian of the Salt Lake church and as a worker in the local reading room. Lucretia Kimball was a member of the board of directors and a worker in the reading room. In the mid-1890s, Kimball studied with Mary Baker Eddy in Boston and received a bachelor's degree from Massachusetts Metaphysical College, returning to Utah in 1896 where she worked as a practitioner and reader.

Both of these women from two important Mormon families "helped build a strong foundation for Christian Science work" not only in Salt Lake City but in Ogden, Provo, Vernal, and a number of other Utah cities from Logan to Green River.[140]

UNITARIAN WOMEN

Mormon roots are also found among the Utahns who helped found the Unitarian Church in the state.[141] November 30, 1890, Reverend Samuel Eliot, a Unitarian minister from Denver, preached in Salt Lake City on the need for a "broad, non-sectarian" People's Church. After his address, some 30 of those in attendance remained to discuss such an organization. In December 1890, another meeting was held to elect a seven-member organizing committee with two women members—Emily M. Almy and Leonora Trent. In February 1891, the First Unitarian society was established and the Reverend David Utter selected as the first minister. Though an all-male Board of Trustees was selected, among the 186 signers of the original charter, almost half—eighty-two—were women. Approximately one-fourth were single, and most of the rest were married to men also in the movement. These women played a key role in Utah Unitarianism, and it was largely through their efforts that "the society was able to survive financially through many difficult years."[142]

In September 1891, the Salt Lake City branch of the Ladies Unitarian Society, with Emily Almy as President and Rebecca Utter, the minister's wife, as vice president, was organized. These women sought not only to strengthen their local church but also to exchange ideas and discuss current events. The alliance met twice a month and sponsored dances, teas, dinner parties, and card parties to raise money for charitable relief. In addition, women were active as superintendents of religious education in the church.

Like most denominations, the Unitarians were adversely affected by the economic difficulties of the 1890s. To supplement his income, Utter took a job as principal of Sumner School. After the Salt Lake City Board of Education ruled that he could not hold the position while also serving as a minister, Utter resigned as minister in 1894, though his wife continued as president of the women's group which had been renamed Unity Circle. The next year he taught at West High before the couple moved to Denver.

The Unitarian Church in Utah was one of the few to have female clergy as regular ministers. In December 1897, Reverend R. A. Maynard and his wife, Mila Tupper Maynard, arrived in Salt Lake City to begin their dual ministry. Of the two, Mila was more experienced in pastoral duties. She had graduated from Cornell University in 1889 and served as the minister of the

First Unitarian Church of La Porte, Indiana. R. A. Maynard had practiced law from 1880 to 1893, the year they were married in Chicago, and turned to the ministry. They lived briefly in Hull House before establishing a joint pastorate in Reno, Nevada, and later in Santa Monica, California.

During their two-year ministry in Utah, the Maynards gave the sermons on alternate Sundays and worked to advance Unitarianism services in other areas of the state as well. Mila, a talented public speaker, was in great demand for lectures and club talks and was particularly active in the mining communities of Park City and Mercur.[143] They invigorated the local Unitarian congregation, saw church membership and attendance rise to its highest level up to that point, and sponsored the *Unitarian,* a four-page newspaper for the congregation funded through local advertising. The departure of the Maynards in 1899 to serve as ministers in Denver was "felt keenly" by local Unitarians.[144]

For two years, the Unitarian society was all but dormant. In 1901, however, it was reinvigorated with the arrival of a new minister. In May 1901, the Unity Circle was reestablished and the twenty women in attendance elected Estelle G. Cowan as president. During the next few years, the group was active in raising funds for needy widows and the local kindergarten association. It also solicited funds for victims of the 1906 San Francisco earthquake. In October of that year, the group was renamed the Lloyd Alliance, in honor of eighty-five-year-old Mary Lloyd, one of the society's original members.[145]

During the first fifteen years of troubled existence for the Salt Lake Unitarian community, it was women who "were able to raise the necessary funds to pay not only the debts but [who] . . . ultimately assumed all major [financial] needs of the church." As Linda Thatcher has pointed out, the "continued existence of the Unitarian church in Salt Lake City" was largely due to the efforts of its women.[146]

Between 1906 and 1920, the Unitarians expanded their presence in Salt Lake City, again with an important role played by women. This was particularly true during World War I when Unitarian women were active with "all day sewing sessions to provide funds for the Red Cross, soliciting canned fruit and jellies for convalescents at Fort Douglas and conducting rummage sales and dinners."[147]

Catholic Women

The Catholic Church has long been a part of the Utah experience. The first European explorers into Utah were led by two priests, Francisco Atanazio Dominquez and Silvestre Velez de Escalante. Their missionary efforts, particularly among the Ute Indians, was still evident when trappers and explorers began to enter Utah in the early nineteenth-century. Contacts during the first half of the century were sporadic. In the 1860s, however, the combination of mining and the railroads brought increasing numbers of Catholics and Catholic priests to Utah. Moved from one diocese to another, Utah was finally placed in the Diocese of San Francisco in 1870. Three years later, Archbishop Joseph S. Alemany appointed Father Lawrence Scanlan to oversee "the approximately 800 Catholics among Utah's 87,000 residents."[148] Scanlan, who arrived in August 1873, cemented the Catholic presence in the state, serving first as a priest and later as bishop (1873–1915). A commitment to education, health, and charitable service has characterized the activities of Catholic women in Utah for more than a hundred years.

In the spring of 1874, Scanlan wrote to the Sisters of the Holy Cross in Indiana, asking for their help in organizing a day school in Salt Lake City. Two sisters, M. Augusta Anderson and M. Raymond Sullivan, arrived in June 1875, toured the state in the summer, and raised funds for the school. Five other sisters of Holy Cross arrived from Notre Dame, Indiana, in August and established the first Catholic convent in Utah. Beginning with some ten sisters, the order had grown to forty by 1880 and sixty by 1890.

Local Catholic officials broke ground in June, and St. Mary's Academy opened that fall, even though the building was not completed. The school was located on Second West between First and Second South. In the last quarter of the nineteenth century, more than 2,600 day students and 1,500 boarding students attended St. Mary's. In addition to the academy, the sisters opened St. Joseph's School for Boys on the academy grounds in 1875, and it was in operation until 1903. An interesting view of St. Mary's Academy during the late 1890s is captured in a memoir by Ann Basset, a student whose father believed she should be educated in a convent: "I was met at the station by the Sisters (and later) tabulated and turned out among 400 girls of every age and size, from tots to twenties. . . . Our clothing was beautifully pressed and placed ready to wear. . . . And what thrilling sensations I experienced listening to those innumerable bells to ring! At the slightest symptoms of illness or fatigue we were gently whisked away to another part of this endless building, to the infirmary."[149]

The success of the Salt Lake school prompted Scanlan to organize Sacred Heart Academy in 1878 and a second St. Joseph's School for Boys in 1882, both in Ogden and both under the direction of the Sisters of Holy Cross. Other important Catholic schools established during this period included All Hallow's College in 1885 in Salt Lake City. Both a day and boarding school, it attracted more than 100 students. Maria Gorlinski taught at the school in 1887–88. The Marist Fathers assumed responsibility for it from 1889 to 1919, when it closed. In addition, parochial schools primarily staffed by women were established in several other Utah cities including Park City, Silver Reef, Eureka, and Price.

The sisters' talents soon expanded beyond education. In 1875, Bishop Scanlan and a group of prominent Utah Catholics asked the Sisters of Holy Cross to organize a hospital. Sister M. Holy Cross Walsh and Sister M. Bartholomew Darnell arrived in Salt Lake City in October and rented a building for $50 at 50 South Fifth East, close to the Catholic Cathedral of the Madeleine. Utah's

Courtesy of the Archives of the Catholic Diocese of Salt Lake City (Utah).

Holy Cross Sister at St. Mary's Academy founded at Salt Lake City, Utah in 1875.

hospital was the first that Sisters of Holy Cross founded in the United States. Originally housing only thirteen patients, the hospital, despite being damaged by a violent storm in 1877, thrived and moved to a new location on east First South in 1881 where it eventually had a staff of nineteen sisters and room for 200 patients. At one point, it served as the Salt Lake County Hospital. During its first twenty years, it provided medical services for more than fifteen thousand people.

Between 1875 and 1920, three women—Sisters M. Holy Cross Walsh, M. Lidwina Butler, and M. Beniti O'Connor—served as administrators. Three years after Holy Cross Hospital was organized, Bishop Scanlan opened another hospital in the mining community of Eureka, and still another in Ogden, also under the direction of the Sisters of Holy Cross.[150]

In 1901 the Holy Cross School of Nursing was established. Housed initially in the sisters' community room, the school was relocated to the basement of a newly created west wing in 1907 which also includes the nursing students' dormitories. An alumni association was organized in 1914 to support state and national efforts to promote nursing professionalism. In 1917, after the passage of a Utah law providing for registration of nurses, the school was accredited.[151]

The same year the nursing school was organized, Mary Judge, widow of John Judge, told Scanlan she wanted to fund a home for aged and infirm miners

Courtesy of the Archives of the Catholic Diocese of Salt Lake City (Utah).

Holy Cross Sisters with children at Kearns-St. Ann's Orphanage, Salt Lake City, Utah, ca. 1910.

with a hospital where they could receive proper medical treatment. Known as the Judge Mercy Hospital and Home and staffed by the Sisters of Mercy, the home—located on Eleventh East between Sixth and Seventh South—opened in 1909 and closed in 1916. In part its success was hindered by the existence of St. Mark's. During its years of operation, the Judge Mercy Hospital League was a woman's organization that helped secure additional funding for the home. In 1918, the Red Cross used the unoccupied building during the influenza epidemic. Two years later it became the home of a Catholic elementary school.[152]

The Sisters of Holy Cross also urged Scanlan to open a much-needed orphanage, and in October 1891, St. Ann's was opened on First South and Third East in Salt Lake. Scanlan obtained a large plot of land in the south part of the city, funded in large measure by a $55,000 donation from Thomas and Jennie Kearns.[153] The orphanage, with a staff of twelve sisters and room for 200 children was located on Twenty-first South and Fifth East where it still occupies a handsome red brick building. It provided care and education for both boys and girls and helped "graduates" find good jobs. "Special attention was given to teaching the girls to sew, cook and perform . . . household duties intelligently and skillfully." They also learned shorthand and typing.[154] Another important contribution was $76,000 from Patrick Phelan's estate in 1902.[155]

Catholic lay women organized a large number of social, business, and charitable groups. St. Ann's Sewing Society helped raise funds for the orphanage. The Catholic Business Women's organization, formed in 1917, assisted unmarried Catholic working women in their spiritual and social needs. It was renamed the Meynell Club in 1922. The better-known Catholic Woman's League was first organized in Salt Lake City in March 1916, with 382 original members. Other chapters followed in Ogden, Park City, and Eureka. Its purpose was both to do charity work and to "advance the culture [and] education" of Catholic women in the state on secular issues and in matters of faith. It also successfully promoted good fellowship within the state's Catholic community.[156]

The Young Ladies Sodality was an early Catholic youth association. It had its own meeting hall and library, sponsored socials, and organized an annual project to supply needy families on Salt Lake's west side with Christmas trees.[157]

By the 1920s, the large and diverse Catholic population of Utah had achieved a fair amount of acceptance. That success was at least partially the result of the Catholic women, both religious and laity, who had worked to meet the temporal and spiritual needs, not only of their denomination, but of the state as a whole.[158]

JEWISH WOMEN

Utah's first Jewish settlers arrived about 1849, only two years after the Mormon vanguard. As Hynda Rudd, a historian of the Utah Jewish experience, notes, Jewish settlement in the West was "mobile and fluid in nature" though two communities—Denver and Salt Lake City—"developed in the mid 19th century and have continued to remain stable."[159] Rudd suggests that because Salt Lake City was already an established community, it was attractive to Jewish settlers who preferred urban areas with a sense of commerce, culture, and relative sophistication. Moreover, Jews and Mormons had a unique relationship because both were "pariah groups" and because early Mormon leaders, particularly Joseph Smith, held Judaism in deep respect.[160]

By the 1860s, according to historian Leon L. Watters, there were "not more than fifty Jewish adults in Salt Lake City, with a few more in other parts of the state."[161] An undated letter from A. Kutner published in the *San Francisco Hebrew* reported that the Jewish residents of Salt Lake City "number about seventy, and are constantly increasing." Kutner also reported that several young Jewish men had married Mormon women, some of whom had embraced Judaism "and others are expected to follow."[162]

That same year, a Jewish Ladies Benevolent Society was organized in Salt Lake. For several years, the society was particularly active in charitable work, reaching across religious boundaries to supervise the annual Christmas charitable balls sponsored by the local Masonic Lodge.

Another organization, the Ladies Hebrew Benevolent Society, was organized in 1888. By 1893, membership had grown from twenty-one to fifty-three women. The society devoted its membership dues to charitable work and undertook many fund-raising events for the same purpose. Before statehood in 1896, this society assisted approximately thirty people per year with an annual budget of less than a thousand dollars.[163]

Additionally, Utah Jewish women took an active part in raising funds with which to operate and maintain the synagogues. In Congregation B'Nai Israel, for example, women not only raised the necessary funds for the building's stained-glass windows, but also "embroidered the curtains in Hebrew designs." In April 1895, Israel Kaiser established a sabbath Hebrew school attended by some sixty pupils and taught by several local Jewish women.

CONCLUSION

In the fifty years between the arrival of the Mormon pioneers in Salt Lake Valley and the granting of statehood, antagonism between the Latter-day Saints and their Gentile neighbors, particularly those who came to proselytize, was an important fact of life. Toward the end of the century, much of this antagonism diminished as the Mormon hierarchy made a conscious effort to make an accommodation with the outside world, principally by abandoning the practice of plural marriage, its cooperative economic institutions and attitudes, and its all-Mormon political party in favor of two-party politics. After 1900, it was much more likely for Mormons and Gentiles to work together in social, civic and political organizations, and various causes. As Jan Shipps has noted, in the years "after the demise of plural marriage and the Mormon political kingdom," Mormons and secular Gentiles were "far less concerned about Mormon religious beliefs than about the willingness of the Saints to permit Gentiles to participate fully in the creation of a modern society in the Intermountain West." Relations between Mormons and Gentiles in the first two decades of the twentieth century was thus not a story of "unending conflict" but rather one of "surprising cooperation" with "healthy rather than destructive challenges."[164]

For Utah women, both Mormon and Gentile alike, a similar softening of attitudes occurred. As part of the Utah observances of the World's Fair of 1893, Emmeline B. Wells conducted a survey of women's charitable work. She was assisted by several Mormon women, but also by several non-Mormons including Emma J. McVicker, who shared Wells's fervent suffrage convictions. Indeed McVicker seems to be a key player in the Mormon non-Mormon cooperation. Mormon and Gentile women were associated with the work of the Orphans Home and Day Nursery Association, and the Salt Lake Kindergarten Association. Similarly Mormon and non-Mormon women were involved with the non-sectarian Ladies General Aid Society and Young Ladies Aid Society organized in 1886. Social and service organizations like the Ladies Literary Club also brought women from various religious backgrounds together in support of mutual interests and causes. World War I seems to have been a watershed event, motivating women to put aside religious differences and unite behind the war effort. And yet, a measure of distance continued and remains today.

On balance, however, though there is a heritage of conflict between women active in the Mormon and non-Mormon faiths, there is also a record of joint activity and mutual respect which, combined with the accomplishments of individual denominations and other religious traditions, constitutes an important aspect of the Utah experience.

NOTES

1. For a good overview of this period, see James B. Allen and Glen M. Leonard, *The Story of the Latter-day Saints,* 2d ed. (Salt Lake City: Deseret Book, 1992), chaps. 12–13. See also chaps. 1 and 11, this volume. Through much of this period, Mormons referred to those of other faiths collectively as "Gentiles."

2. She further notes: "And now that peaceful homes and smiling plenty have succeeded those bitter hardships, these invaders come seeking to spread destruction through our fair Eden by sundering those sacred family ties and may God mete out to them even the measure they are seeking to mete out to us." Helen Marr Clark Callister, untitled draft of speech, ca. 1878, Thomas Callister Collection, Ms 5112, Box 1, fd. 12, Archives, Family and Church History Department, Church of Jesus Christ of Latter-day Saints, Salt Lake City (hereafter LDS Church Archives).

3. Jana Kathryn Riess, "'Heathen in Our Fair Land': Presbyterian Women Missionaries in Utah, 1870–90," *Journal of Mormon History* 26 (Spring 2000): 165.

4. Peggy Pascoe, *Relations of Rescue: The Search for Female Moral Authority in the American West, 1874–1939* (New York: Oxford University Press, 1990), 21. Another valuable resource is Joan Smyth Iversen, *The Anti-Polygamy Controversy in United States Women's Movements, 1880–1925* (New York: Garland, 1997).

5. "Polygamy," *Salt Lake Tribune,* January 4, 1884, 2.

6. See Maureen Ursenbach Beecher, "'The Leading Sisters': A Female Hierarchy in Nineteenth-Century Mormon Society," *Journal of Mormon History* 9 (1982): 25–39.

7. See Marilyn Warenski, *Patriarchs and Politics: The Plight of the Mormon Woman* (New York: McGraw-Hill, 1978), 179–80.

8. For a description of polygamy's place in Mormon theology and society of the nineteenth century, see Jessie L. Embry, *Mormon Polygamous Families: Life in the Principle* (Salt Lake City: University of Utah Press, 1987); Richard Van Wagoner, *Mormon Polygamy: A History* (Salt Lake City: Signature Books, 1989); B. Carmon Hardy, *Solemn Covenant: Mormonism's Polygamous Passage* (Urbana: University of Illinois Press, 1992); Kathryn M. Daynes, *More Wives than One: Transformation of the Mormon Marriage System, 1840–1910* (Urbana: University of Illinois Press, 2001); Jeffrey Nichols, *Prostitution, Polygamy, and Power: Salt Lake City, 1847–1918* (Urbana: University of Illinois Press, 2002); Sarah Barringer Gordon, *The Mormon Question: Polygamy and Constitutional Conflict in Nineteenth-Century America* (Chapel Hill: University of North Carolina Press, 2002). Davis Bitton's "Mormon Polygamy: A Review Article," *Journal of Mormon History* 4 (1977): 101–18 provides

a valuable historiographical overview. Another valuable perspective is contained in Jessie L. Embry and Martha Sonntag Bradley, "Mothers and Daughters in Polygamy," *Dialogue: A Journal of Mormon Thought* 18 (Fall 1985): 98–107.

9. Pascoe, *Relations of Rescue,* xvi-xxiii.

10. Charles S. Peterson, "New Mormon/New Western History," paper presented at the annual meeting of the Mormon History Association, May 1992, St. George, Utah; photocopy in my possession.

11. Although no full history of nineteenth-century Mormon women has yet been written, the following collections of essays provide both biography and analysis: Maureen Ursenbach Beecher, *Eliza and Her Sisters* (Salt Lake City: Aspen Books, 1991), Maureen Ursenbach Beecher and Lavina Fielding Anderson, eds., *Sisters in Spirit: Mormon Women in Historical and Cultural Perspective* (Urbana: University of Illinois Press, 1987); Vicky Burgess-Olson, ed., *Sister Saints* (Provo, Utah: Brigham Young University Press, 1978); and Claudia L. Bushman, ed., *Mormon Sisters: Women in Early Utah* (1976; reprinted with an introduction by Anne Firor Scott, Logan: Utah State University, 1997). Edited writings by nineteenth-century Mormon women appear in Kenneth W. Godfrey, Audrey M. Godfrey, and Jill Mulvay Derr, eds., *Women's Voices: An Untold History of the Latter-day Saints, 1830–1900* (Salt Lake City: Deseret Book, 1982). Two institutional histories are Jill Mulvay Derr, Janath Russell Cannon, and Maureen Ursenbach Beecher, *Women of Covenant: The Story of Relief Society* (Salt Lake City: Deseret Book, 1992) and Carol Cornwall Madsen and Susan Staker Oman, *Sisters and Little Saints: One Hundred Years of Primary* (Salt Lake City: Deseret Book, 1979).

12. I have chosen these dates because they encompass the period from the initial Mormon settlement through the end of World War I. While there is nothing magical about dates generally, or even these years specifically, most historians believe that the Utah of pre-1920 is considerably different than in the years since then. As Thomas G. Alexander has noted, the "most important characteristic of twentieth century Utah has been the decline of ecclesiastical domination of politics, society, and the economy," with a corresponding "integration into the national economic, political and social framework." Thomas G. Alexander, "Twentieth-Century Utah: Introduction," in *Utah's History,* edited by Richard D. Poll, Thomas G. Alexander, Eugene E. Campbell, and David E. Miller (Provo: Brigham Young University Press,1978), 405.

13. Stanley B. Kimball, *Heber C. Kimball: Mormon Patriarch and Pioneer* (Urbana: University of Illinois Press, 1981), 150.

14. Ibid.

15. Ann Vest Lobb and Jill Mulvay Derr, "Women in Early Utah," in Poll et al., *Utah's History,* 337.

16. A good overview of her life is found in Maureen Ursenbach Beecher, "Eliza Roxcy Snow," in *Utah History Encyclopedia,* edited by Allan Kent Powell (Salt Lake City: University of Utah Press, 1994), 509–10; and Beecher, ed., *The Personal Writings of Eliza Roxcy Snow* (Salt Lake City: University of Utah Press, 1995).

17.   Derr, Cannon, and Beecher, *Women of Covenant,* chap. 3. Another valuable perspective comes from Carol Cornwall Madsen, "Creating Female Community: Relief Society in Cache Valley, Utah, 1868–1900, *Journal of Mormon History* 21 (Fall 1995): 126–54.

18.   Derr, Cannon, and Beecher, *Women of Covenant,* 105. See also Jennifer Lynn Hyde, "Sericulture's Heroines in Utah Economics: Silk Production as a Home Industry, 1875–1902," paper presented at the annual meeting of the Mormon History Association, May 1992, St. George, Utah; photocopy in my possession.

19.   Money from the sale was kept in the Presiding Bishop's Office, earned interest and was used for a variety of projects including maternal and child health care during the 1920s and the construction of a commercial-style grain elevator for wheat storage as part of the church's welfare project during the 1940s. In 1978 the Relief Society general president turned over to the church president control of this fund, then amounting to more than $2 million dollars, as part of the correlation movement that greatly reduced the autonomy of all Mormon auxiliaries, including the Relief Society. Derr, Cannon, and Beecher, *Women of Covenant,* 103–4, 210–13, 231, 291, 355. See also Jessie L. Embry, "Relief Society Grain Storage Program, 1876–1940" (M.A. thesis, Brigham Young University, 1974); and Embry, "Grain Storage: The Balance of Power between Priesthood Authority and Relief Society Autonomy," *Dialogue: A Journal of Mormon Thought* 15 (Winter 1982): 59–66.

20.   Sherilyn Cox Bennion, *Equal to the Occasion: Women Editors of the Nineteenth-Century West* (Reno: University of Nevada Press, 1990), 75–77.

21.   Bruce L. Campbell and Eugene E. Campbell, "Early Culture and Intellectual Development," in Poll et al., *Utah's History,* 305–6.

22.   For a good overview of Mormon women's activities during this period, see Leonard J. Arrington and Davis Bitton, *The Mormon Experience: A History of the Latter-day Saints* (New York: Alfred A. Knopf, 1979), 220–42.

23.   Jill Mulvay Derr, "'Strength in Our Union': The Making of Mormon Sisterhood," in *Sisters in Spirit: Mormon Women in Historical and Cultural Perspective,* edited by Maureen Ursenbach Beecher and Lavina Fielding Anderson (Urbana: University of Illinois Press, 1992), 171, 180.

24.   Gary Topping, "The Ogden Academy: A Gentile Assault on Mormon Country," *Journal of the West* 24 (January 1984): 37.

25.   Joseph B. Clark, *Leavening the Nation: The Story of American Home Missions* (New York: Baker and Taylor, 1903), 309.

26.   "Education," *Deseret News,* December 26, 1855, 5.

27.   Ward Platt, *The Frontier* (Philadelphia: American Baptist Publication Society, 1908), 134. Platt quotes an unnamed but influential Mormon woman as saying that, while she disliked sending her children to a Protestant school, she did so "as that school was the best."

28.   David F. Smith, *My Native Village: A History of Centerville* (N.p.: privately published, 1943), 34–35. Smith asserts, but does not document, that in Centerville "those who attended these free schools did not carry on into higher education to the extent that

children from other schools did. The survey shows that few of the boys and girls who attended these free schools obtained a college education."

29. Women's Baptist Home Mission Society, *Twenty Fourth Annual Report of the Women's Baptist Home Mission Society* (New York: Women's Baptist Home Mission Society, 1902), 40.

30. Robert J. Dwyer, *The Gentile Comes to Utah* (Salt Lake City: Western Epics, 1971), 194–95.

31. Ibid.

32. Lobb and Derr, "Women in Early Utah," 351. See also Thomas G. Alexander, "An Experiment in Progressive Legislation: The Granting of Woman Suffrage in Utah in 1870," *Utah Historical Quarterly* 38 (Winter 1970): 20–30; Lola Van Wagenen, "In Their Own Behalf; The Politicization of Mormon Women and the 1870 Franchise," *Dialogue: A Journal of Mormon Thought* 24 (Winter 1991): 31–43; and Lola Van Wagenen, *Sister-Wives and Suffragists: Polygamy and the Politics of Woman Suffrage* (Ph. D. diss., New York University, 1994; printed, Provo, Utah: Joseph Fielding Smith Institute for Latter-day Saint History and BYU Studies, Dissertations in LDS History Series, 2003).

33. Dwyer, *The Gentile Comes to Utah,* 201–2.

34. Carol Cornwall Madsen, "Schism in the Sisterhood: Mormon Women and Partisan Politics, 1890–1900," in *New Views of Mormon History: A Collection of Essays in Honor of Leonard J. Arrington,* edited by Davis Bitton and Maureen Ursenbach Beecher (Salt Lake City: University of Utah Press, 1987), 213.

35. Photocopy of prospectus in my possession.

36. Mrs. L. H. Ehlers to Fred T. Dubois, June 27, 1906, Fred T. Dubois Papers, Oebler Library, Idaho State University, Pocatello, Idaho.

37. Madsen, "Schism in the Sisterhood," 213.

38. Herbert W. Reherd, "An Outline History of the Protestant Churches of Utah, in *Utah: A Centennial History,* edited by Wain Sutton (New York: Lewis Historical Publishing Company, 1949), 651. See also David L. Schirer, "Baptists in Utah," in *Utah History Encyclopedia,* edited by Allan Kent Powell (Salt Lake City: University of Utah Press, 1994), 31–32.

39. Reherd, "Outline History," 651.

40. R. Maude Dittmars, "A History of Baptist Missions in Utah, 1871–1931," (M.A. thesis, University of Colorado, 1931), 20.

41. Ibid.

42. Ibid., 44.

43. Mrs. M. R. Warner, "Report on Charities and Philanthropies of the Baptist Church," *Charities and Philanthropies: Woman's Work in Utah,* edited by Emmeline B. Wells for the World's Fair (Salt Lake City: George Q. Cannon and Sons, 1893), 39.

44. Ibid.

45. Florence Crosby Parsons, "The Baptist Church," in *World's Fair: Ecclesiastical History of Utah,* compiled by Representatives of the Religious Denominations (Salt Lake City: George Q. Cannon and Sons, 1893), 281.

46. Ibid., 282. The other women were Maggie Taylor, Mary Pearce, and Helen Mann.

47. Ibid., 287

48. David H. Streets, "American Baptist Church," in *Protestant and Catholic Churches of Provo: A Study of the Non-LDS Christian Congregations,* edited by David M. Walden (Provo, Utah: Brigham Young University, Center for Family and Community History, 1986), 46.

49. Parsons, "The Baptist Church," 287; WPA, Historical Records Survey, *Inventory of the Church Archives of Utah,* 3 vols. (Salt Lake City: Utah Historical Records Survey, 1940), 2:48.

50. Ibid., 25.

51. Dittmars, "A History of Baptist Missions," 53.

52. Ibid., 54.

53. Ibid.

54. Ibid., 55.

55. WPA, *Inventory of Church Archives,* 2:48.

56. Gordon K. Harrington, "The Lonely Pilgrim in Zion," *Bulletin of the Congregational Library* 30 (Winter 1970): 5. See also Gordon K. Harrington and Mary Paulson Harrington, "Congregationalism in Utah," in *Utah History Encyclopedia,* edited by Allan Kent Powell (Salt Lake City: University of Utah Press, 1993), 111–12. Originally organized as the First Church of Jesus Christ (Congregational), it was renamed First Congregational Church in 1893.

57. Mildred Stockman, an early member of the Congregational church described Independence Hall in some detail based on her childhood memories: "Independence Hall . . . was located between Main and West Temple, on the south side of Third South. Really not on the street, but about 20 rods south in the block, the space between the Hall and the street, being used for wagons and horses and buggies. There was a long board walk leading from Third South to the entrance of Independence Hall which was on the Northwest corner of the building. You entered a vestibule, where over-shoes and rubbers were often deposited. Then into the rear of the main hall where stood a great potbelly stove with quite a gathering space around it before you came to the benches or pews. The pulpit was on a platform at the east end of the hall, with the organ just below on the right and a door on the left leading to the Primary Department, then presided over by Mrs. Sprague, mother of our late Sale Lake City librarian. In this department there was a group called the Pansy Mission Society, which was led by Miss Alice Stevens, a New West teacher. This group saved their pennies in little earthen jugs with only one slit, and these were presented annually at the Christmas celebration." Mildred Stockman, "This I Remember," January 18, 1967, typescript, Utah State Historical Society, Salt Lake City.

58. Francis Sherman, "Chronological Development of Missions in Utah" (B.A. thesis, University of Utah, 1910), 10.

59. "Report of the Phillips Benevolent Society," in *Charities and Philanthropies,* edited by Emmeline B. Wells for the World's Fair (Salt Lake City: George Q. Cannon & Sons,

1803), 49. Despite the close resemblance of title, publisher, date and editor, this work should not be confused with that cited in note 45.

60. Hugh F. O'Neil, "Records Show A. W. Stafford First Pastor; Congregationalists Began Services in Ogden in Year of 1876," *(Ogden) Standard-Examiner,* January 22, 1939, A-10.

61. Streets, "American Baptist Church," 27–28.

62. Ibid.

63. In fact, it did in 1893 when the Congregational Educational Society was created. Harrington, *Lonely Pilgrim,* 10.

64. J. Duncan Brite, "Non-Mormon Schools and Churches," in *The History of a Valley: Cache Valley Utah-Idaho,* edited by Joel E. Ricks and Everett L. Cooley (Logan: Cache Valley Centennial Commission, 1956), 30. See also Milford Randall Rathjen, "The Distribution of Major Non-Mormon Denominations in Utah" (M.S. thesis, University of Utah, 1966), 24–53.

65. Topping, "The Ogden Academy," 38.

66. Ibid., 37–38.

67. Ibid., 39.

68. Ibid., 41.

69. Abbie P. Noyes to her father, 6 January 1890, quoted in Topping, "The Ogden Academy," 42.

70. Neil, "Records Show A. W. Stafford First Pastor," A-10.

71. Topping, "The Ogden Academy," 46.

72. Emory S. Burke, ed., *History of American Methodism* (New York: Abingdon Press, 1968), 442.

73. Henry P. Merkel, *History of Methodism in Utah* (Colorado Springs: Dentan Printing, 1938), 153.

74. Ibid., 73–74.

75. Alma White, *Looking Back from Beulah* (Zarephath, N.J.: Pillar of Fire Church, 1902), 74–94. See also Susie Cunningham Stanley, *Feminist Pillar of Fire: The Life of Alma White* (Cleveland, Ohio: Pilgrim Press, 1993), 15–16. A good biographical overview can be found in Edward T. James, Janet Wilson James, and Paul S. Boyer eds., *Notable American Women, 1607–1950,* 3 vols. (Cambridge, Mass: Harvard University Press, 1971), 3:581–83.

76. Merkel, *History of Methodism in Utah,* 198.

77. Thomas E. Lyon, "Evangelical Protestant Missionary Activities in Mormon Dominated Areas, 1865–1900" (Ph.D. diss., University of Utah, 1962), 161.

78. (no author), "The Methodist Episcopal Church," in *World's Fair: Ecclesiastical History of Utah,* 273.

79. Ibid., 199–202.

80. Connie Fife, "Methodists," in *Utah History Encyclopedia,* edited by Allan Kent Powell (Salt Lake City: University of Utah Press, 1994), 362.

81. Mrs. J. Post, "Methodist Episcopal," in *Charities and Philanthropies,* edited by Wells, 50.

82. For information on Newman, see Pascoe, *Relations of Rescue,* 23–24.

83. Ibid., 24.

84. Ibid., 21.

85. Ibid., 24–27.

86. Dwyer, *The Gentile Comes to Utah,* 214.

87. After its sale, the building was operated as the Fifth East Hotel, then the Ambassador Hotel. In 1945 it became the home of the recently organized Ambassador Athletic Club and maintained that identity until it was razed in 1986. See "History of a Utopian Failure," *Deseret News,* July 29, 1899, 9; and Twila Van Leer, "Ambassador Club's Next Big Ball May Be the Wrecker's," *Deseret News,* November 26, 1985, C-1.

88. Carl Wankier, "History of Presbyterian Schools in Utah" (M.S. thesis, University of Utah, 1968), 2. See also H. Jeffrey Silliman, "The Presbyterian Church in Utah," in *Utah History Encyclopedia,* edited by Allan Kent Powell (Salt Lake City: University of Utah Press, 1994), 442–43.

89. R. Douglas Brackenridge, "Mormons and 'Outsiders' in Utah, 1870–1890," paper delivered at the Sunstone Symposium, Salt Lake City, August 1995; photocopy in my possession.

90. Ibid., 3.

91. Wankier, "History of Presbyterian Schools," 19.

92. Ibid., 22. The other women were Mattie Voris, R. A. Wray, and Fannie Perley.

93. Brackenridge, "Mormons and 'Outsiders,'" 3–4, 12.

94. Ibid.

95. For a fuller discussion, see Riess, "'Heathen in Our Fair Land,'" 165–95. See also Sandra Dawn Brimhall and David A. Hales, "Frances R. Burke: Toquerville Presbyterian Missionary," *Utah Historical Quarterly* 72 (Spring 2004): 156–66; and R. Douglas Brackenridge, "Presbyterians and Latter-day Saints in Utah: A Century of Conflict and Compromise, 1830–1930," *Journal of Presbyterian History* 80 (Winter 2002): 205–24.

96. Brite, "Non-Mormon Schools," 312–13.

97. Emil Nyman, *A Short History of Westminster College* (Salt Lake City: Westminster College, 1975), 2. See also R. Douglas Brackenridge, *Westminster College of Salt Lake City: From Presbyterian Mission School to Independent College* (Logan: Utah State University Press, 1998).

98. Nyman, *A Short History of Westminster College,* 5.

99. Ibid., 6.

100. James B. Crosby, "Wasatch Academy," in *Utah History Encyclopedia,* edited by Allan Kent Powell (Salt Lake City: University of Utah Press, 1994), 618–19.

101. Milton R. Hunter, *Beneath Ben Lomond's Peak: A History of Weber County, 1840–1900* (Salt Lake City: Deseret News Press, 1944), 462–63, 552–53.

102. For a list of the schools, see Wankier, "Presbyterian Schools in Utah," 40. Another essential source for understanding the Presbyterian efforts in the West generally and Utah specifically is Mark T. Banker, *Presbyterian Missionaries and Cultural Interaction in the Far Southwest, 1850–1890* (Urbana: University of Illinois Press, 1993).

103. Sherman H. Doyle, *Presbyterian Home Missions* (New York: Board of Home Missions, 1905), 161.

104. The amount of money spent on school work in Utah by the denomination fluctuated considerably from 1895 through 1900. After declining from $44,000 in 1895 to $40,000 in 1900, expenditures rose again until 1911 when they began a marked decline. See Wankier, "Presbyterian Schools in Utah," 34.

105. Ibid., 164.

106. Brackenridge, "Mormons and Outsiders," 14.

107. Ibid., 15.

108. Ibid., 38.

109. Mrs. J. [Emma J.] McVicker, "Home and Foreign Missionary Society of the First Presbyterian Church of Salt Lake," in *Charities and Philanthropies: Woman's Work in Utah,* edited by Wells. McVicker's name is misspelled as "McVickor" on the committee list on the title page.

110. Mary Peach, "Lutherans in Utah," in *Utah History Encyclopedia,* edited by Allan Kent Powell (Salt Lake City: University of Utah Press, 1994), 339.

111. Paul A. Mogren, *Zion Lutheran Church, Salt Lake City: A Centennial History, 1882–1982* (Salt Lake City: Zion Lutheran Church, 1982), 4.

112. Ibid.

113. Ibid., 6.

114. Ronnie L. Stillhorn, "A History of the Lutheran Church in Utah" (M.S. thesis, Utah State University, 1975), 153.

115. In the nineteenth century, non-Mormon churches endorsed the principle of comity. Under this arrangement, "It was agreed that where a community had one or more churches a third would not enter; that a feeble church should be revived rather than a new one started; and that the preferences of the Protestants in the area should always be respected. In nineteen places in Utah, adjustment between the five denominations [Congregational, Episcopal, Methodist, Baptist, and Presbyterian] was agreed upon with the smaller churches consolidating with the stronger." Brite, "Non-Mormon Schools and Churches," 31.

116. Stillborn, "A History of the Lutheran Church in Utah," 155–57.

117. Ibid., 54.

118. Leslie L. Zook, *A History of Central Christian Church, Salt Lake City, 1890–1969* (Salt Lake City: Central Christian Church, 1970), 76.

119. Ibid., 77.

120. "Calvary Baptist Church Marks 86th Anniversary," *Salt Lake Tribune,* November 9, 1985, A-11. See also Rev. France Davis, *Light in the Midst of Zion: A History of Black Baptists in Utah, 1892-1996* (Salt Lake City: Empire Publishing, 1997), 13–15.

121. E. J. Peabody, "Spiritualists," in *Charities and Philanthropies,* edited by Wells, 57.

122. H. K. Carroll, *The Religious Forces of the United States* (New York: Christian Literature Co., 1896), 352.

123. A good overview can be found in Mary Peach and Kathryn L. Miller, "Episcopalians in Utah," in *Utah History Encyclopedia,* edited by Allan Kent Powell (Salt Lake City:

University of Utah Press, 1994), 171–74. See also Frederick Quinn, *Building the "Goodly Fellowship of Faith": A History of the Episcopal Church in Utah, 1867–1996* (Logan: Utah State University Press, 2004).

124. Daniel S. Tuttle, *Reminiscences of a Missionary Bishop* (New York: Thomas Whittaker, 1906), 363.

125. Tuttle was elected missionary bishop of the territories of Utah, Idaho, and Montana at a meeting of the House of Bishops in New York City in October 1866 and was consecrated in May 1867.

126. Mary R. Clark, "Rowland Hall-St. Mark's School: Alternative Education for More than a Century," *Utah Historical Quarterly* 48 (Summer 1980): 273.

127. Paul L. Martin, "A Historical Study of the Religious Education Programs of the Episcopal Church in Utah" (MRE thesis, Brigham Young University, 1967), 35.

128. Sherman, "Development of Missions," 20.

129. Daniel S. Tuttle, "History of the Missionary District of Utah and Idaho," Archives of the Episcopal Church, Austin, Texas; photocopy in my possession.

130. Quoted in Clark, "Rowland Hall-St. Mark's School," 281.

131. Colburne's obituary called her "widely known in local educational and social circles." "Pioneer of Rowland Hall Dies in East," *Deseret News,* September 6, 1933, 8.

132. They were Martha K. Humphrey, mathematics and science; Annie Starling, English; Katherine Russell, Latin and history; Henrietta English, languages; Sarah J. Simpson, preparatory departments, grades 1–4; Marian Starling, preparatory department, grades 5–7; and, Gratia Flanders, music and piano. See S. A. Kenner, *Utah As It Is* (Salt Lake City: Deseret News Press, 1904), 307–8.

133. Tuttle, *Reminiscences of a Missionary Bishop,* 377.

134. Ibid., 272.

135. Mary S. Donovan, "Women Missionaries in Utah," *Anglican and Episcopal History* 66 (June 1997): 154–74.

136. Sara Napper, Quarterly Report to the Domestic and Foreign Missionary Society, December 1, 1902, Record Group 52, Box 57, Episcopal Church Archives, Austin, Texas.

137. Ibid., March 1, 1904.

138. Ibid., December 1, 1903.

139. William Harroun Behle, *Biography of Augustus C. Behle, M.D., with an Account of the Early History of St. Mark's Hospital, Salt Lake City, Utah* (Ann Arbor, Mich.: Edwards Brothers, 1948), 34–36, quoted in Lottie Felkner, ed., *The St. Mark's Hospital School of Nursing Story* (Salt Lake City: St. Mark's Hospital Nurses Alumni Association, 1970), 9.

140. Jeffery O. Johnson, "The Kimballs and the Youngs in Utah's Early Christian Science Movement," paper presented at the annual meeting of the Utah Historical Society, August 1984, Salt Lake City.

141. The best source is Stan Larson and Lorille Miller, *Unitarianism in Utah: A Gentile Religion in Salt Lake City, 1891–1991* (Salt Lake City: Freethinker Press, 1991). Also important is Irma Watson Hance and Virginia Hendrickson Picht, *In Commemoration*

of the Seventy-Fifth Anniversary of the First Unitarian Church, Salt Lake City, Utah, 1891–1966 (n.p., 1966).

142. Linda Thatcher, "Women in the Early Unitarian Church in Salt Lake City," paper presented at the annual meeting of the Utah Historical Society, August 1984, Salt Lake City; photocopy in my possession.

143. For a representative sermon by Mila Tupper Maynard, see Larson and Miller, *Unitarianism in Utah,* 189–201.

144. Hance and Picht, *Commemoration,* 74.

145. Larson and Miller, *Unitarianism in Utah,* 68.

146. Thatcher, "Women in the Early Unitarian Church," 11.

147. Larson and Miller, *Unitarianism in Utah,* 84.

148. Bernice Maher Mooney, "The Catholic Church in Utah," in *Utah History Encyclopedia,* edited by Allan Kent Powell (Salt Lake City: University of Utah Press, 1994), 78.

149. Quoted in Bernice Maher Mooney, *Salt of the Earth: The History of the Catholic Diocese in Utah, 1776–1887* (Salt Lake City: Catholic Diocese of Salt Lake City, 1987), 67.

150. Mrs. W. S. [Hannah] McCornick, "Catholic Charities of Utah," in *Charities and Philanthropies,* edited by Wells, 30–35.

151. Mooney, *Salt of the Earth,* 86.

152. Ibid., 115.

153. Louis J. Fries, *One Hundred and Fifty Years of Catholicity in Utah* (Salt Lake City: Intermountain Catholic Press, 1926), 126.

154. Wells, *World's Fair History,* 34.

155. W. R. Harris, *The Catholic Church in Utah, 1776–1909* (Salt Lake City: Intermountain Catholic Press, 1909), 304.

156. Duane G. Hunt, "History of the Roman Catholic Church in Utah," in Sutton, *Utah: A Centennial History,* 736.

157. Fries, *History of Catholicity,* 139.

158. For an overview of Catholic women's activities in Utah, see Mooney, *Salt of the Earth.*

159. Hynda Rudd, "The Jews of the Mountain West: A Guide to Historical Sources" (M.A. thesis, University of Utah, 1979), 68.

160. Steven Epperson, *Mormons and Jews: Early Mormon Theologies of Israel* (Salt Lake City: Signature Books, 1992).

161. Leon L. Watters, *The Pioneer Jews of Utah* (New York: American Jewish Historical Society, 1952), 162.

162. Quoted in Juanita Brooks, *History of the Jews in Idaho and Utah* (Salt Lake City: Western Epics, 1973), 53.

163. Mrs. Louis Hyams, "Hebrew Benevolent Society," in *Charities and Philanthropies,* edited by Wells, 52.

164. Shipps, "Beyond the Stereotypes: Mormon and Non-Mormon Communities in Twentieth Century Mormondom," in Bitton and Beecher, *New Views in Mormon History,* 342–60.

4

Ethnic Women

1900–1940

Helen Z. Papanikolas

Forty years after the Mormons entered the Salt Lake Valley and many centuries after the Anasazi Indians left traces in Utah's varied terrain, immigrant women from the Mediterranean, the Balkans, and Asia began long fearful journeys that led them to Utah. They would not see Native Americans on far-off reservations, but perhaps they would pass an occasional African American woman on the streets. These newcomers were impelled forward by ancient needs to go beyond their current arduous existence in search of a brighter destiny. They were among a legion of women throughout the ages who left their homelands, willingly or unwillingly.[1]

American immigration has been divided into the "old immigrants" and "new immigrants." The old immigrants came to Utah in the latter part of the nineteenth century. Most immigrated from Britain, northern Europe, and Scandinavia, and came in family groups. They intended to stay and immediately accepted the United States as their adopted country.

After 1900, the new immigrants began arriving in Utah in increasing numbers from Mediterranean, Balkan, Asian, and Middle Eastern countries. These new immigrants were primarily men who expected that their sojourn would be short. Except for the Asians, they had come from countries that had recently freed themselves from foreign rule, and all were intensely nationalistic. They became the force that industrialized Utah.

When the new immigrants lengthened their stay in the United States and sent for brides, the women obediently followed. They had no other choice; in their impoverished countries, dowries were necessary for marriage. Isolated and unassimilated in the larger American-Mormon culture in Utah, they lived as ethnic women did in the East and Midwest—in neighborhoods where religious rituals were recited in old-country languages. As mothers they instilled the traditional ways in their children, hoping to return eventually to their people.

129

Like Native American and African American women, they experienced historical and social forces that both repressed them and, for many, fulfilled them. This paper gives a general view of the lives of Utah's ethnic women during the first four decades of the twentieth century.

ETHNIC GROUPS

Native Americans

For Utah's Native-American women, dispossession began even before the Homestead laws of 1862 brought more settlers to plow their lands, destroy the native seeds, and frighten away the small game that constituted an important part of their diet. On that land their mothers and grandmothers had gathered seeds, nuts, and berries; their men had hunted and returned with game for them to dry and preserve. On this sacred ground, they had danced and sung ancient invocations to their gods.

Starving, stealing to survive, Indians were forced onto federal reservations, most often on land the white man did not want.[2] There the old nomadic ways degenerated into weekly allotments from government agencies which included a small amount of meat, bulk lard, salt bacon, flour, beans, and soap. Men were restricted in their hunting and fishing, but women continued to work harder than husbands and sons. They gathered firewood, carried water, picked berries, dried meat, corn, and fruit, cooked meals, raised children, repaired tents, and as a symbol of wifely pride and acknowledgment, braided their husbands' hair.[3]

With the degradation of their people, Native American women suffered on the Uintah-Ouray Reservation and none rose to speak in council meetings as had Chipeta,[4] a leader in the 1860s when the days of following the migrations of elk, antelope, and deer were becoming memories. No woman would dare approach a white agent as his equal as Chief Tsau-wi-ats's wife ("of great influence, and . . . much revered") had faced John Wesley Powell.[5] Like Indian women throughout the country, Utah's Native American women valiantly kept their culture alive and mourned their people's history. The 1900 census listed only 1,270 Native American females in Utah, slightly fewer than the 1,353 males. (See appendix.)

In northern Utah, Western Shoshone women lived on the fringes of white hamlets, working at times as servants to settlers and becoming converts to Mormonism as a prelude to assimilation. In southwestern Utah, Paiute women struggled with poverty on the outskirts of towns and bartered work for food. Farther out in the desert, they slowly starved on reservation land, destitute, their race dying out.

Least affected by white settlers' incursions were the four bands of Gosiutes in western Utah. They lived in Deep Creek, Skull Valley, Snake Creek, and Trout Creek in *wickiups* of stacked sagebrush. Poorest of the tribes, they refused to leave their ancestral land for the Uintah Valley reservation in the

Navajos learned weaving from neighboring tribes and then surpassed them in skill. Monument Valley, 1941.

1860s, preferring extreme cold and hunger to government subjection. Each day was spent searching for seeds and small animals. There was no time for ceremonies. However, they continued the round dance to the beat of a drum—an invocation to make grass seeds grow. The women made capes from rabbit skins; the children wore nothing. Early explorers were surprised at these people, whom they viewed as savages. John Wesley Powell recorded brief vignettes: "the mother studiously careful of her little one, by causing it to nestle under her rabbit-skin mantle" and a very old, infirm woman portioning out her bread to children. Only after they were fed did she "take the small balance for herself."[6] In 1912 the Skull Valley and Deep Creek reservations were established. A young doctor who set up practice in the area wondered if the Gosiute women were being "wiser than I when they . . . let the unfit die? They were good mothers, kind and gentle with their children. Were they also kind in eliminating the weak that the tribe might be perpetuated by the strong?"[7]

Navajo women fared far better in their matriarchal society among the red monoliths of the Four Corners area in southern Utah. Many among them had made the Long Walk in 1864 when government troops under Kit Carson had forced 8,500 Navajos to walk through the desert to Bosque Redondo in New Mexico. After four years of suffering in this nineteenth-century concentration camp where they clung to their religion and didactic myths, they returned and began establishing themselves again, gradually increasing their sheep. The women wove rugs using both traditional designs and new patterns preferred by white easterners; the men worked in turquoise and silver.

By crossing spindly Merino ewes with Rambouillet rams, the Navajos produced strong sheep with thick wool. The sheep belonged to the women who herded and butchered them, and also carded, spun, dyed, and wove the wool. They brought the sheep and rugs to white traders in Oljato, Goulding's, Gap, Hatch's, Aneth, Bluff, and Blanding. Although they often received little for their sheep and handiwork, they increased their flocks. Their hogans were relatively comfortable. Their gardens of squash, beans, corn, and melons provided adequate food.

Native American women retained the rituals of the past into the twentieth century. The Navajo squaw dances, sings, the Kin-nahl-dah (puberty ceremonies for girls), were occasions of clan gatherings and feasting. In spring the Ute and Paiute women faced their men in the ancient ritual of the Bear Dance to the rhythm of drums and singing. They watched for four days and nights as their men danced the regenerating Sun Dance.

African Americans

Decades before Mormon settlement in Utah, several African American trappers and adventurers had traveled within the territory. Not until 1847, however, did the first African American women enter Utah, mainly as slaves of southern converts. The matriarch of the black community was a free woman, Jane Manning James,[8] who had converted to Mormonism in the early 1840s and had worked in Joseph Smith Jr.'s household until his death. Eliza Partridge Lyman, a plural wife of Apostle Amasa M. Lyman, wrote in her journal on April 8, 1849: "we baked the last of the flour today. . . . Jane James, the colored woman, let me have two pounds of flour, it being half of what she had."[9] Jane Manning James repeatedly asked Mormon church authorities to seal her to the Joseph Smith family. She held the millennial beliefs of the time and wanted temple ordinances to ensure her future salvation. She was unwilling to wait for church racial policies to change.

In 1852, the territorial legislature passed a law affirming the legality of slavery. Women as well as men were sold by their masters. One African American woman had tried to escape with other slaves while the wagon train was traveling through Kansas on its way to the Utah territory, but she "was not successful in that direction."[10] In later years not all felt discriminated against. Florence Legroan Lawrence recalled that her mother grew up in the Murray area:

> She came from rather a large family with brothers and sisters, and at that time she said there was not the prejudices you felt afterwards because, of course there was not the work either. And I guess it was a way of life that they just understood and that's the way they lived. But she said that they didn't have any problems in the schools for segregation or felt like they were different or anything like that. Of course, you know that's the way it is when you grow up but she seemed like they had a very good time and a nice life growing up.[11]

The women worked as domestics, the men as field hands, carpenters, and shoemakers. Almost all became farmers after a time. Following the Emancipation Proclamation, several former slaves left Utah. Those who remained continued to intermarry and congregated in three areas of Salt Lake County: Union, East Millcreek, and the Salt Lake City neighborhood later called Central City. When the Denver and Rio Grande Western and Union Pacific railroads recruited African Americans to work as porters and waiters, census figures showed a marked increase in the population, from 672 in 1900 (218 females) to 1,144 in 1910 (453 females). A community of African Americans grew around the Union Pacific railyards in Ogden at this time. (See appendix.)

African American women worked long hours in the houses of others, in their own homes, and in their small fields. Because of discrimination, more intense than that felt by any other ethnic group, they relied on each other for help and recreation. They did not readily seek medical help for themselves and their families; instead, they used folk cures handed down through centuries. Their communities were self-contained islands in which church services, fraternal organizations, visiting, and the sharing of limited resources gave cohesiveness to their lives. In Salt Lake City and in Ogden, the women found relief from work in clubs such as the Ladies Civic and Study Club, the Camelia Arts and Crafts Club, and the Nimble Thimble Club.[12] Lone women whose husbands worked in isolated railroad terminals and in mines had none of these social outlets; their existence was circumscribed by the walls of their homes.

African American churches were the nuclei of African American life. Some pioneer African Americans adopted the Latter-day Saint religion, but most African Americans formed their own churches. In Salt Lake City, the Trinity African Methodist Episcopal Church was established in the 1890s, followed by Cavalry Baptist Church soon afterwards. In Ogden, the Wall Street Baptist Church opened for services in the early 1900s.

The small African American population remained stable until World War I greatly accelerated railroad activity for transporting matériel, troops, coal, and steel. The Union Pacific and Southern Pacific railroads actively recruited African Americans from the South and, with the Denver and Rio Grande Western, became their principal employers.[13] This brought the African American population to 1,146 in 1920 of whom 612 were females. After the war, in 1919, a branch of the National Association for the Advancement of Colored People was founded in Salt Lake City; an Ogden branch was established during World War II. African American women were and are among the most dedicated workers in these organizations.

Discrimination, based on the color of their skin, was everywhere—in housing, employment, and whenever African Americans came in contact with whites. Several African American women worked closely with the YWCA, particularly Mignon Richmond who had graduated from Utah State Agricultural College (now Utah State University) in 1921 but was refused work

Widow and children of Archie Henderson, an African American family living in Castle Gate. Henderson was killed in the Castle Gate mine disaster. Left to right: Mrs. Henderson, Archie, Jr. (9), and Myrtle (12). Elizabeth (15) and Lewis (19) were absent when the picture was taken. Mrs. Henderson was expecting another child, 1924.

as a teacher. For decades she was the attendant in the women's restroom in the University of Utah's Kingsbury Hall. Richmond, whose grandmother had been an object of curiosity in Wellsville, vividly remembers shopping in Salt Lake City's Woolworth store. When her mother ordered hot dogs, they were not allowed to sit at the counter and instead ate them standing in a corner. In theaters ushers directed African Americans to the balcony.

Jews

Jews arrived in Utah during the first decade of Mormon migration. Two single men preceded the first couple, Julius Garson Brooks and his wife Isabell ("Fanny"), a milliner, who arrived in July 1854. Jewish merchants and freighters were supplying Camp Floyd by 1858; and until the Zion Cooperative Mercantile Institution (ZCMI) was established in 1868, the Auerbach brothers had no competition in general merchandising.[14]

By the beginning of the twentieth century, former Jewish peddlers and shop owners had become leading members of Utah's business community. They were German-Jews who began to be outnumbered by eastern European coreligionists escaping pogroms and other forms of virulent antisemitism. After weeks in steerage, the new arrivals came to Utah, often following a short, unproductive stay in the gray, man-made canyons of eastern slums. The Utah

Jews sheltered these newcomers and found work for them, usually in shops, the first step to future ownership. Although many of the Jews moved on, lamenting the lack of kosher food, soon the unmarried were paired up through ubiquitous matchmaking and new families began in Mormon Zion.[15] For the most part, Jewish families lived in the area of Ninth South between Main Street and West Temple. Until 1883 when their first synagogue was erected, they conducted services in private houses and assorted buildings.

Less fortunate were the 150 Jewish immigrants from New York and Philadelphia who arrived in Clarion, near Gunnison, in 1910 to establish an agricultural colony. The exodus to Utah was part of a dedicated effort of eastern Jewish philanthropists to transfer their people from city slums, where tuberculosis and other diseases were rampant, to rural areas in the East and West. Among these settlers were well-educated men, idealists who thought farming would be the answer to the rootlessness of Jews. However, the experiment failed after three years of freezing winters, miserably hot summers, ignorance about farming, and a fatal shortage of irrigation water.[16]

Nathan Ayerhoff, a member of the colony, recalled: "The women for instance they were objecting from the first day they came in. . . . I had to go 7 miles to Gunnison to bring some [drinking] water, by the time I brought the water it was all frozen. . . . Most of the children didn't see a cracker, a candy or anything like this."[17]

Of the few Clarion colonists who remained in Utah, two became the heads of successful enterprises: Benjamin Brown founded the Utah Poultry Cooperative Association, and Maurice Warshaw pioneered a chain of supermarket/department stores. The Auerbach, Bamberger, and Rosenblatt families had, by then, become business and community leaders in Salt Lake City.

Matriarchs of the founding Jewish families kept boardinghouses for employment-seeking sojourners, enhanced the family's financial condition by their creative frugality, and faithfully maintained their religious and cultural traditions. Friends and relatives converged from small towns and surrounding states for the Jewish High Holidays. These were the most important days of the year for the women. Faith, friendship, and food reaffirmed their Jewishness.

Within a generation of their arrival in Utah, women became prominent in the Jewish experience in Utah. More than any other ethnic group, they were businesswomen, working in family concerns. In 1903 they founded the local Hadassah to support Zionism and have been in the vanguard for promoting the arts in Utah.

During the last half of the twentieth century, Jewish-Mormon relationships eased through emphasis, from the Mormon side, that they are also of the "house of Israel," a theological concept related to Mormon belief in being a covenant people. This view countered the widespread animosity toward Jews that was based on their not accepting Christ as the Messiah and in the widespread stereotype that Jews had a stranglehold on business. In the early years of life in Utah, Jewish women struggled to keep a dignity that this prejudice denied them. Doris Neiditch Guss, who lived in Ogden as a young girl, remembered:

> I don't recall the name of the family, but he was what they call a *melamed,* a teacher. He felt sorry that I couldn't understand a word of Yiddish. Actually, I never wanted to speak Yiddish. I never wanted my mother to speak Yiddish in front of my friends. I was embarrassed by it. When I was a child, in Chicago, and we'd take the streetcar, whenever she took out the *Jewish Daily Forward* to read, I'd say, "Mama, please, put it down."
>
> She would tell me, "Doris, never be ashamed of who you are. Don't ever do that to yourself because you'll never be a happy person."[18]

Armenians

The Armenians are an ethnic people whose experience in Utah as new immigrants is unique. Like the Jews, the Armenians also fled persecution; but in their case, they were persecuted because they were Christians under Muslim authority. Their ancestral land between the Black and Caspian seas had been ruled ruthlessly by the Turks since the early 1500s. Beginning in 1897, a handful of Armenian families—fewer than fifty individuals all told—began arriving in Utah thanks to the efforts of Mormon missionary H. H. Hintze, who chose to serve a mission in Constantinople in 1888 rather than face punishment for practicing polygamy. Hagop Thomas (Tumas) Gagosian, one of Hintze's converts, records his wife's fear of this new American religion that had replaced his ancient Armenian faith: "My wife would cry and plead with me to quit this new religion and come back to my old fold. My old friends and neighbors did not help either because they would take my wife's part and tell her I was lost."[19]

Gagosian and his family tried to farm in both Utah and Nevada but he ended up working at the smelter in Midvale. Other Armenians worked for the Denver Fire and Clay Company in Salt Lake City. Between 1910 and 1920, the employment records of Utah Copper Company (later Kennecott) lists 150 Armenians. Wherever they lived, the mothers attempted to maintain some of the old traditions while those who had become Mormon converts practiced their adopted religion faithfully. Several Armenian and Lebanese women sold notions and Middle Eastern bedspreads and tablecloths door to door with better success than their men, who were looked upon with suspicion.

The transition to Mormonism and Americanism was often difficult. "In the ward," a daughter of converts who had settled in Murray, said, "people looked at us as if we were intruders. I was conscious of being darker than the rest of the congregation. I felt I didn't belong."[20] A few children of immigrants married out of their group into the encompassing Mormon community,

Armenian family store located in Salt Lake City, ca. 1910. (Notice the American patriotic décor on the background pole and balcony.)

but "Mormon Armenian immigrants have married among themselves to an intense degree—especially so among the children and grandchildren of the first settlers."[21]

The Turkish program of Christian genocide in 1915 and 1921 was especially devastating to the Armenians, and the two World Wars brought other Armenians to Utah who were not Mormon converts. They were mainly affiliated with the Gregorian, or Apostolic church; a few were Eastern Orthodox. These Armenians followed the experience of the new immigrants except they did not come with the belief that they were sojourners in America; they came to stay.

New Immigrants

The immigrants who came to Utah in the greatest numbers between 1900 and 1930 were not fleeing persecution nor had they converted to Mormonism. Rather, the poverty in their homelands pushed them, while the promise of a better economic life in America pulled them. They came from the Balkans, Middle East, and Mediterranean countries, from Japan,[22] and later, from Mexico. A few of the earliest arrivals from each ethnic group became labor agents for the mine, mill, smelter, and railroad companies that were industrializing the agrarian West. These agents, the *"padrones,"*[23] provided management with an unending supply of laborers who were willing to work for lower wages than

Americans. In Utah, the importation of industrial workers was unconsciously aided even more because of the strong emphasis within Mormonism of working on the land.

The early immigrants, almost all men, moved from one mining camp or railroad gang to another. Management seldom provided adequate housing, and the men lived in abysmal conditions. Few boardinghouses were available. Workers sheltered themselves in tents; others rented old houses and set up housekeeping under an elected leader.

The men had left their native countries expecting to return after having provided sisters with dowries and support for aging parents, hoping to save enough for themselves to open a shop or become money lenders. When the steady work that America offered kept them longer in the country than they had intended, they began to think of marrying; women would provide the amenities they had known in their native countries.

So few women of their national heritage were available that competition for them became intense. Girls as young as fourteen eloped. Mainlander Greeks who ran off with Cretan women had to be protected by their friends against the ire of their bride's parents and the Cretan community as a whole that vehemently opposed such unions. Although less fanatical, north and south Italians also discouraged marriage between their groups. Among the South Slavs (Yugoslavs), "frequent resorts to violence were made by males and many murders arose from the inflamed passions which developed."[24] Asians tolerated marriage with women from other ethnic groups or Americans, but they far preferred to import brides from their own villages.

When the prospective husbands could afford to return home to court and marry, they were desirable bridegrooms with their new clothes, their money, and their wealth of information about America. After ancient wedding festivities that gave zest to the toil of village life, these brides left for America as properly married wives under the protection of husbands. Often the men brought several other women along to become brides of their friends and relatives.

Most immigrant men, though, could not leave their work to find wives, spending weeks on trains and ships that depleted their savings and deprived them of earnings. Sending for "picture brides" was one solution to finding a wife from their native countries. Such arrangements were risky but also promised hope. In the villages of their homeland, girls began working in the fields from the time they could walk. They lived in one- and two-room huts with earthen or rough-planked floors. They slept on mats, sheep pelts, or hand-woven blankets, crowded among their sisters. In good weather, animals were penned beneath the houses, in winter often at one end of the room, separated from the family by a partition. Only in provincial towns did a few parents send their daughters to school for a smattering of reading and writing.

Educated or not, married or not, women lived under the rule of husbands, fathers, brothers, and village elders. The slightest breach of conduct

Wedding of Mr. and Mrs. Angelo Heleotes, Magna, at the First Greek Church in Salt Lake City, located on 400 South between 300 and 400 West. The church was dedicated October 29, 1905, and served the Greek, Serbian, and Russian communities until the present Greek Orthodox Church located at 300 South and 300 West was constructed.

stigmatized them and their children. Mothers, grandmothers, and mothers-in-law were on their guard so that no aspersions could be cast upon their own respectability, and they exercised strict control over their daughters so that impeccable reputations could claim the most desirable marriages—those that would strengthen the clan.

But economic realities forced different choices on them. The bride's wishes were of no concern. Sorrowing but hopeful, mothers acquiesced in their husbands' decisions to send their daughters to America where people had enough to eat and where even a dowryless girl could be married. A Greek folksong of the 1910 decade pleads: "Don't send me, Mother, to Ameriki / I'll wither there and die."

Sometimes several picture brides would travel together, apprehensive of what awaited them in the new country, but drawing comfort from each other. Many others came alone, demoralized and fearful at leaving their homes to enter a land of strange people, language, and customs, clutching pictures of the strangers who would meet and marry them. Sewed to their coat lapels were tags on which were written their destination and their future husbands' names. The discomfort of their journey—crammed into steerage quarters in the bowels of pitching steamship, overwhelmed by fear and confusion for a few days in New

York ghettoes, and then exhausted by the cross-continental train trip—was often comparable to the days of sail and wagon.[25]

They were further oppressed by their ancient cultures' dictum that respectable women did not travel without male relatives. My mother, Emily Zeese, used her dowry to secretly purchase passage to America, traveling on the ship with a Jewish family:

> [She] talked to no one so that nothing would be known about her. One day the [Greek] woman approached her and asked where she was going. "To New York, Kyria."
>
> "Is someone meeting you or are you going on?"
>
> Emily thought she should lie so that the woman would not consider her immoral for traveling without a male relative, yet impelled to tell the truth, she answered, "I am with a Jewish family. The father will meet us."[26]

Jun Kuramada recalled in an interview the family stories of his mother's intense reluctance to accept a marriage that had been arranged through family connections:

> The family in Japan had induced my mother to come over here. And like this one conversation with my uncle says that well we practically had to carry her, screaming and hollering that she didn't want to go. And they finally got her on the boat. And—I guess she cried all the way over. And, whether she actually knew my father except just by name, and, I guess it was just the case where— many of the cases at that time where—the men who would send photographs back and they might—ah—might send a photo of a very handsome friend of theirs, not themselves. And so those things going on—but—ah— But my father actually was a very handsome man. He really was. So I'm sure she wasn't all that disappointed when she got here.[27]

A few of these brides were well-educated women who became teachers in Greek and Asian schools for children of immigrants. Haruko Terasawa Moriyasu recalls: "My mother, Kuniko Muramatsu Terasawa, was the first girl in her family to leave for Tokyo and school. She asked her parents to use her dowry money for schooling. She taught for two years when my father, who had gone to Utah in 1906, returned to Japan for a wife. This was in 1922. My father had intended to make money in America and return to Japan to enter politics. [Instead] in 1914 he began publishing the *Utah Nippo* and my mother became the business manager."[28]

Besides the illiterate picture brides and the small group of educated women were an even smaller handful of women who had defied the mores of their people, married beneath their class or chosen men of whom their families disapproved, and left for America to avoid ostracism. Other difficulties awaited them in Utah. Filomena Bonacci, whose husband Frank, a hereditary laborer in Italy, became the foremost United Mine Workers organizer in Utah from

1920 to 1950, found herself shunned in Carbon County because of his labor activities.[29] Jinzaburo Matsumiya, a section foreman near Jericho in Juab County, returned to Japan where he married a wife who proved herself adaptable and hard-working: "In the desert she cared for her children, raised three hundred chickens at a time, ripped the seams of her husband's clothes to make patterns for new ones that she sewed on a treadle machine, and was one of the shearers herself when the sheep were driven to the water tank."[30]

Some women were frankly exploited for their labor. Italian Margaret B. Bertolina came to America under the protection of her brother, who promised to find a husband for her. Instead, he put her to work in his hotel in Helper. "From the basement to the top floor, four floors, all day long, I carried heavy buckets, mops, made beds, all day long," she recalled.[31]

For Thelma Siouris, a Greek woman, the loneliness of her new home at Soldier Summit in Carbon County where her husband was a railroad gang foreman become almost unbearable. "There were no Greek women there. I could not speak English. I was so lonely that I baked sweets and waited for the children to pass my house after school. I had them sit down and eat the cookies. Then I sat down and looked at them."[32]

Other women experienced similar isolation from nearly all human contact: Chinese mothers lamenting the children that federal laws forced them to leave behind; wives of Asian railroad gang foremen living in railroad houses next to water stops; young Greek mothers, a great distance from each other, homesteading with their husbands on the Uintah-Ouray Reservation opened to white settlers; Italian women on farms far out on sagebrush plains; Jewish women, alone in Mormon communities. The lives of these women recall Mari Sandoz's Midwestern homesteaders in *Old Jules* (Boston: Little, Brown and Co., 1935) and Beret in Ole Edvart Rolvaag's *Giants in the Earth* (New York: Harper and Brothers, 1927).

Most brides, however, were met by cheering countrymen. In coal mining towns, uniformed Italian musicians played arias at the depots. Men left their mine, smelter, and mill shifts, eager to bath and shave, put on their Sunday suits, and get a glimpse of the women. A Yugoslavian from Midvale remembered when the first Yugoslavian woman arrived: "Gus Murphy's father run a bakery there. They had the saloon there and some Serb used to run a saloon there. First woman come there, his wife come, the Erol. God, well, you know we crazy. See here, first woman come from Yugoslavia. We give her $800 that night. . . . Because they hadn't seen a woman for a long time?"[33]

These earliest arrivals became the matriarchs of each ethnic community. They were remembered with respect by the young men who ate the foods of their native lands in their houses and who brought their brides to live with them until their wedding days.

As Balkan, Mediterranean, and Asian women continued to arrive, Congress passed the Cable Act of 1922. Women could no longer automatically

Widow and children of Joe Talarico. Joe Talarico was killed in the Castle Gate Mine disaster, 1924. The Italian family from left to right: Mrs. Talarico, Marck (6 mos.), Frances (15), Mary (12), John (9), Sam (8), Amelia (6), Catherine (3). Nick (14) was absent when the photograph was taken. He was salvaging the coat his father wore in the mine.

become citizens through their husbands; and American-born women of Asian ancestry married to *Issei* (Asian immigrants) had their citizenship revoked. Most important were the immigration restrictions of 1921 and 1924, with the lowest quotas assigned to southern and eastern European countries. To circumvent the law, immigrant men traveled to Mexico, Cuba, and Canada to marry picture brides who could then enter the United States legally. The Exclusion Act of 1924 prohibited all Asian immigration; the Chinese Exclusion act had been passed in 1882.

DAILY LIFE IN ETHNIC COMMUNITIES

If the women were lucky, they would be living in neighborhoods already formed by each ethnic group—collections of homes, shops, coffeehouses, cafes, and bakeries. Americans referred to them patronizingly as "Greek Town," "Wop Town," "Little Italy," "Lebanese Town," "Jap Town," etc. Company houses owned by the mining companies, despite cheapness and shoddy workmanship, were often better than the women's ancestral homes. Their wooden floors were sometimes covered with linoleum. Fuel was cheap, and the houses, no matter how poor, all had large black coal stoves. Nails pounded into the doors and walls held the familiy's clothing. In America even the poor had beds, a luxury available only to the middle and upper classes in the homelands.

In their "towns" the mothers planted gardens and watered them with Utah's plentiful irrigation water. They learned quickly about water turns, the dictates of water masters, and how to outwit "water hogs." This seeming drudgery, added to washing by hand, chopping wood, and baking bread in outdoor earth ovens, resembling beehive-shaped Navajo ovens, could often be almost restful. One daughter remembers her mother "coming in from tending the garden with her face smoothed out, a look of peace on it."[34] Almost all ethnic women in rural and industrial areas raised animals and fowls: sheep, pigs, a cow or two, chickens, pigeons, and rabbits. They could afford the cost of feed in Utah that was prohibitive in their homelands.

Many brides discovered that their first task was to take in boarders, either male relatives or some of their countrymen. It was not only out of economic necessity but also out of respect for the traditional demands of hospitality. Hospitality was an aspect of "Old World" cultures to which the mothers were bound. The mothers taught by proverbs, cooked the special foods associated with religious observances, and insisted on the native language being spoken in their homes. All immigrants had centuries-old means to strengthen the family, mainly by extending kinship ties to include sponsors at weddings and godparents. In the "towns," the women, deprived of female kin, rushed to help each other with births, illnesses, and deaths. Men were not expected to help. A girl of six, however, was considered old enough to tend her younger brothers and sisters.

Folk-healers were in demand: the workers feared company doctors, and women preferred the old village remedies. In the "towns," brides of every nationality would find at least one welcoming midwife. One of them, Magerou, a Greek midwife and folk-healer in the Salt Lake County area, set bones and used numerous cures that were touted as more effective than the company doctors' academic ones.[35]

Food was a strong bond with the homeland. Even before women arrived in Utah, Jewish, Greek, Italian, and Asian stores sold imported foods distinctive to each culture: olive oil, octopi, salted cod, Turkish paste, many varieties of olives, cheeses, matzo flour, prosciutto (cured peppered ham), pastas, and Jordan almonds. Soon Greeks and Italians became owners of goat ranches on the outskirts of every mine, mill, and smelter town, providing housewives and boardinghouses with various hard and soft cheeses.

Food was important to ethnic people—not only for sustenance and well being; it was synonymous with necessary, elaborate hospitality. Families were judged by their adherence to these ancient rites. Informality or indifference to them branded a family as one without breeding. Rocco C. Siciliano wrote in his autobiography: "The other symbol of well-being was plentiful food. Uppermost in my parents' minds was to make sure that we ate well. They remembered life in Italy, where they had so little. Dad would bring food home from the restaurant kitchen, and that gave us a sense of surplus that made us feel better off than others, especially during the hard survival days of the Depression."[36]

Mothers toiled by day over hot stoves, washtubs, and ironing boards, yet they were squeezed out the time to prepare pastries and sweets for both expected and unexpected visitors. At weddings, baptisms, bar mitzvas, confirmations, and communal picnics, women brought out their specialties while men turned lambs or pigs on spits over hot coals; and men and children danced to the music of instruments brought over the ocean. The Asians often watched sumo wrestlers at their gatherings.

Churches, synagogues, and Buddhist temples were the center of ethnic life. They served as an adjustment in America and as continuity with the homelands. Men built and administered the religious structures, but women sustained and maintained them. Frequently in these buildings, mainly for Greeks, Jews, and Asians, schoolmasters taught the native country's history and language, the most important element in culture. Many Asian also sent their children to grandparents in Japan to learn the culture of their people.

Within their communities, women were the center of their homes, as their proverbs clearly attest. Men's domain was the work world. The two were separate spheres. Mothers bonded with their daughters and deferred to their sons, particularly the oldest. Fathers were feared and honored, but mothers managed the households, took complete care of the children, and instilled their people's vales. Even the strongly patriarchal Mexican society "offer[ed] the wife an unchallenged monopoly over domestic life."[37] Family members who failed to uphold the ethnic code of honor lost their relatives' respect, although they still had a place within the group. Asians, however, were stricter and frequently ostracized deviants.

PERCEPTIONS OF OUTSIDERS

Ethnic people regarded Mormons and other Americans as inhospitable. The lack of ritual ceremony towards visitors meant to immigrants that they were living among a cold people with peculiar attitudes toward food: forcing children to eat everything on their plates; sending children to bed without food as punishment; using sweets as rewards or discipline. Further, American children waited in misery until fathers came home from work to punish them. Immigrant mothers punished at the moment of wrongdoing; fathers were involved when they witnessed misbehavior. The mothers heard, too, that Mormon wives asked permission from their husbands about household matters. This was strange to the immigrant women who were responsible for properly run households without the interference of men.

The young mothers observed other odd characteristics among the American families who lived within their "towns" or on the peripheries. Over chicken-wire fences they talked about these parents who allowed young men to take out their daughters. In their native countries, girls and women did not speak to boys and men; even when meeting male relatives in full public view, they only nodded or bowed to acknowledge them, eyes downcast. The mothers were shocked that American women stopped on the street to speak with men, addressed them by their given names, got on trains and stages alone, even occasionally smoked, and shockingly, could divorce without being isolated from the community.

American religion seemed to them as bland as American food. Italian mothers lamented the lack of rituals for their provincial saints, ignored by American and Irish priests. The color and ancient rites of Jewish High Holy Days, the bar mitzvahs celebrating thirteen-year-old boys' readiness to assume moral and religious duties; the Christian saint-day feasts when open houses were held for fathers, husbands, and sons named for biblical and canonized figures—all were eagerly anticipated events in which the immigrants' faiths and histories converged with great emotion. Easter, not Christmas, was the high point of the year for Christian immigrants who saw gifts and Christmas trees as an American superficiality. Nothing was as shocking, though, as the American celebration of Easter. Proceeded by a forty-day fast, church services followed Christ's journey to the cross and culminated in the joyous resurrection. Mothers saw Americans marrying during Holy Week ("While Christ hangs on the cross!") and going to dances on Good Friday as monumental sacrilege. They were particularly offended by the Mormons who, they believed, had replaced Christ with Joseph Smith.

Each group followed ancient rituals of mourning and were shocked by Americans' simple funeral customs. Where was the extravagant grief merited by the departed?[38] Each ethnic group lamented deaths. Native Americans chanted spirits to the other world; African Americans sang spirituals; Hispanics spent the night reciting the rosary and singing *alabados* or hymns. Balkan and Mediterranean immigrants keened dirges at the side of open caskets. All draped black cloth over mirrors and photographs, wore black clothing for long periods (widows until death), and held memorial services at designated times. Jews remembered their dead by reciting the Kaddish in morning prayers.

Some immigrants also feared Americans. Anti-immigrant campaigns escalated during the first World War, in Utah as across the nation. The Ku Klux Klan organized in the first half of the 1920s in Utah. Klan marches and cross burnings occurred in Salt Lake City, Bingham, Magna, and Helper.[39] The immigrant "towns" trembled. Mothers stood on porches looking down dirt roads for tardy sons. They sent their daughters, always restricted, on errands only within their neighborhoods. Wives of Basque, French, and Greek sheepmen, whose husbands were away for the summer grazing or on winter grounds, were alone and felt most vulnerable. "When my dad was away at sheep," recalls a daughter, "my mother pushed a chest and trunk against the door. We knew it was because she was afraid of the Americans."[40]

The separate male and female spheres merged, ironically enough, in labor wars, with male immigrants accepting and praising female involvement. Men were regularly killed by falls of coal or ore, by electrocution, by defective machinery, by explosions; their cases fill the pages of the Utah Coal Mine Inspectors' yearly report.[41] The foreign-language press editorialized against industrial deaths and maimings, little or no compensation to dependents, and poor working and living conditions.

In the Carbon County Strike of 1903, Italian women joined their husbands in tent colonies after mine managers evicted them from company houses. The women marched down dusty and muddy roads to support the strike while Americans lined the streets to stare. One of the women, Caterina Bottino, successfully hid Mother Jones, the great labor leader, from authorities. Strikers stopped for shelter at her house, called "Halfway House" because it was half way between Helper and Castle Gate.[42]

Italian and South Slav women championed their men in subsequent strikes in 1922 and 1933. Asian culture, like the Greek, would not permit women to display themselves in public activities. The Italian and Yugoslav women who marched for unionization had their husbands' approval; otherwise they would not have dared take on a role alien to their cultures' dictates.[43]

In the 1933 Carbon County strike, Yugoslav women became leaders.[44] In that bleak Depression year, women marched against deputies, taunted and harassed them, threw pepper in their eyes, and brought food and blankets to their men imprisoned in jail and fairground buildings. They rallied strikers in union meetings, and many kept up a vociferous campaign after the strike was lost.

The Next Generation

By the 1920s, immigrant families had become established and had prospered along with the rest of the country. During the decade, many families moved out of their "towns" into more affluent neighborhoods. Some took advantage of Prohibition and, like a number of enterprising Americans, shared in the enormous profits of bootlegging.[45] Their children were still in school, studying to meet their parents' expectations but not yet rebelling strenuously against their immigrant cultures. The restrictive immigration laws of 1921 and 1924 brought relief to women who ran boarding houses.

By the 1930s, however, children were young adults. Pulled in opposite directions by their parents' and American cultures, they wanted to be free from the restrictions of patriarchal bonds. With a freedom denied their sisters, young men began to marry American girls. "They still go for the honey blondes," a Chicana respondent wryly noted in the 1970s.[46]

Most demeaning to ethnic women was the assumption of their inferiority. Family resources gave priority to educating the sons. Sisters often worked to provide college educations for their brothers. "Italians of the immigrant generation [believed that] to give a daughter more education than required by law was an extravagant waste of money."[47] Deprived of further education and moving in social circles restricted by Old World mores, many daughters never married and became typists and sales clerks.

During the Depression decade of 1930-40, immigrant women helped each other, expanded their gardens, and raised more chickens and rabbits. African American women had a harder time; white women had turned to domestic service and black men were the first to be laid off work. Mexicans, some naturalized citizens, were deported to Mexico.[48] All Native Americans suffered. The Navajos had known a period of relative prosperity; but by the 1930s, their flocks were overgrazing the red earth. In that decade the federal government gave the Navajos the choice of selling some of their cherished sheep for as little as two dollars a head or living on rations.[49] The Indian Reorganization Act of 1934, however, provided for decreased federal control of tribes, an increase in self-determination, and other reforms.

World War II coincided with the end of the immigrant era. Many sons and a small number of daughters served in the armed forces and their loyalties were with the United States. Although still highly concerned about their native homelands, parents by then recognized America as their true country. The war brought a mobility unknown previously; ethnics ventured into the world beyond their neighborhoods. The parental hold on daughters loosened. Intermarriage with other groups became common. Funeral customs also changed. The custom of bringing the dead to homes had to be discontinued during the war emergency. Keening for the dead dwindled under the discouragement of grown American-born children. Except for the Hispanics, folk-healing was replaced by conventional medicine.[50]

After the war, many immigrants returned to their native countries for visits. Jun Kuramada's mother was one who eagerly returned, but "seeing the changes—all the tremendous changes that had taken place, she much preferred to come back here."[51]

The war deeply affected life for Native American, African American, and Hispanic women. Activist organizations began determined campaigns to gain rights for their people. Ironically, the war also had a salutary effect on second-generation Japanese-American women who had been incarcerated in relocation camps. Until then, they had been subservient to fathers and brothers. In the camps they were often paid as much as males, sixteen dollars a month. This equality gave them the confidence to seek college educations and careers for themselves as teachers, nurses, social workers, and attorneys.[52] Seeing these improvements in the economic and social lives of their grandchildren comforted the women who had ventured into the unknown as frightened but hopeful immigrants. "Yes, we pined for our country and talked about it all the time," confessed Emily Zeese, "but we didn't go back as we said we would. Where else could our children become educated and be free of other people deciding their lives?"[53]

These immigrants' daughters thought themselves successful if they did not have to work outside the home. Their granddaughters consider themselves successful if they have a career. Daughters of immigrants seldom married outside their ethnic group, but grandchildren marry "out" in ever increasing

Lucero Ward Relief Society members, ca. 1938.

numbers. For all the energy ethnic groups spent on attempts to preserve the native languages, they were lost by the third generation. Only the Hispanics continue to speak their language in their homes and organizations. However, customs connected with religious observances and secular holidays endure and are celebrated with communal and family feasting.

Appendix

U.S. Census figures for 1900, 1910, 1920, 1930 and 1940 show the fraction of Utah population belonging to the indigenous inhabitants and the immigrant generations. When country of origin did not denote ethnicity, mother-tongue designation was used. Beginning in 1920, women were counted separately (shown in parentheses). The categories are riddled with questions: Russian-Jews may have been counted as Russians, rather than Jews; Basques as either Spanish or French; Serbs, Croats, and Slovenes as Austrians but, after 1928, as Yugoslavs.[54]

1900 Census

Population of Utah: 276,749

Ethnic Group	Total Utah Population: M/F	Total Utah Population: Female
Indians	2,623	1,270
Blacks	672	218
Chinese	572	21

Japanese	417	11
Italians	1,062	—
Austrians (Includes Slovenes, Serbs, Croats)	272	—
Russians	119	—
Mexicans	41	—
Greeks	3	—

1910 Census

Population of Utah: 373,351

Ethnic Group	Total Utah Population: M/F	Total Utah Population: Female
Indians	3,123	1,450
Blacks	1,114	453
Chinese	371	26
Japanese	2,110	89
Austrians (Includes Slovenes, Serbs, Croats)	2,628	—
Serbs	275	—
Greeks	4,062	—
Italians	3,172	—
Finns	1,535	—
Mexicans	273	—
French	550	—
Syrians	215	—
Yiddish (sic)	198	—
Arabic	118	—
Armenian	35	—

1920 Census

Population of Utah: 449,396

Ethnic Group	Total Utah Population: M/F	Total Utah Population: Female
Indians	2,711	1,269
Blacks	1,146	612
Chinese	342	28
Japanese	2,936	762
Mexicans	1,083	154
Slovens, Serbs, Croats	993	164
Greeks	3,033	299
Italians	3,261	1,008
Yiddish (sic)	404	169
Finns	779	—
French	626	281
Spanish	365	70
Arabic (sic)	162	61
Armenians	80	24

1930 Census

Population of Utah: 507,847

Ethnic Group	Total Utah Population: M/F	Total Utah Population: Female
Indians	2,869	1,353
Blacks	1,108	499
Chinese	342	60
Japanese	3,269	1,213
Italians	2,814	1,012
Greeks	2,197	414
Yugoslavs	934	281
Finns	507	201
Mexicans	2,386	610
Russians	342	116
French	484	219
Spanish	277	67
Yiddish (sic)	280	114
Arabic (sic)	144	59
Armenians	41	15

1940 Census

Population of Utah: 550,310

Ethnic Group	Total Utah Population: M/F	Total Utah Population: Female
Indians	3,611	1,778
Chinese	228	52
Japanese	2,210	655
Blacks	1,235	552
Mexicans	1,069	228
Italians	2,189	839
Greeks	1,882	402
Yugoslavs	661	228
Finns	309	164
Russians	286	105
French	184	87
Syrians	137	57
Spanish	131	40

Notes

1.   For a comprehensive overview of ethnic groups in Utah, see Helen Z. Papanikolas, *The Peoples of Utah* (Salt Lake City: Utah State Historical Society, 1976).

2.   Gregory Coyne Thompson, *Southern Ute Lands, 1848–1899: The Creation of a Reservation,* Occasional Papers of the Center of Southwest Studies, No. 1 (Durango, Colo.: Fort Lewis College, 1972).

3.   Y. T. Witherspoon, ed., *Conversations with Connor Chapoose, A Leader of the Ute Tribe of the Uintah and Ouray Reservation Recorded in 1960,* University of Oregon Anthropological Papers No. 47 (Eugene, Ore.: Department of Anthropology and Oregon State Museum of Anthropology, University of Oregon, 1993), 12–13.

4.   Susan Lyman-Whitney, "Chipeta (1843–1924): She Didn't Want to Come to Utah," in *Worth Their Salt: Notable but Often Unnoted Women of Utah,* edited by Colleen Whitley (Logan: Utah State University Press, 1996), 76–87.

5.   John Wesley Powell, *Report of J. W. Powell: Exploration of the Colorado River of the West and Its Tributaries* (Washington, D.C: Government Printing Office, 1875), 42.

6.   Ibid., 42.

7.   Joseph H. Peck, *What Next, Doctor Peck?* (Englewood Cliffs, N.J.: Prentice-Hall, 1959), 170.

8.   Henry J. Wolfinger, "Jane Manning James (ca. 1820–1908): A Test of Faith," in *Worth Their Salt: Notable but Often Unnoted Women of Utah,* edited by Colleen Whitley (Logan: Utah State University Press, 1996), 14–30.

9.   Ibid., 19.

10. Ronald G. Coleman, "Blacks in Utah History: An Unknown Legacy," in *The Peoples of Utah,* 115–40, quotation from p. 122.

11. Florence Legroan Lawrence, interviewed by Leslie Kellen, September 30, 1983, Salt Lake City, 3; Interviews with Blacks in Utah (1889–1988), Ms 453, Box 5, fds. 7–8, Manuscript Division, J. Willard Marriott Library, University of Utah, Salt Lake City, 3. Hereafter cited as Marriott Library.

12. Coleman, "Blacks in Utah History," 135.

13. Ibid., 132–33.

14. Juanita Brooks, *History of Jews in Utah and Idaho* (Salt Lake City: Western Epics, 1973); Eileen Hallet Stone, *A Homeland in the West: Utah Jews Remember* (Salt Lake City, Utah: University of Utah Press, 2001).

15. Jack Goodman, "Jews in Zion," in *Peoples of Utah,* 187–220, esp. 194–96.

16. Robert Alan Goldberg, *Back to the Soil: The Jewish Farmers of Clarion, Utah, and Their World* (Salt Lake City: University of Utah Press, 1986).

17. Ibid., 13 note 29.

18. Doris Neiditch Guss, "Farm Life and the *Jewish Daily Forward*," quoted in Stone, *A Homeland in the West,* 186.

19. Viola Woodbury Kelsey, "Diary of Hagop Thomas (Tumas) Gagosian," 5, translated by F. H. Gagosian, Price, Utah, 1961, photocopy of typescript in my possession. See also Papanikolas, *Peoples of Utah,* 406.

20. Isabel Gagon, Letter to Helen Papanikolas, 1939, Salt Lake City.

21. Robert F. Zeidner, "From Babylon to Babylon: Immigration from the Middle East," in *Peoples of Utah,* 403.

22. Yuji Ichioka, *The Issei: The World of the First Generation Japanese Immigrants, 1885–1924* (New York: Free Press, 1988); Ted Nagata, ed., *Japanese Americans in Utah* (Salt Lake City: JA Centennial Committee, 1996).

23. Gunther Peck, *Reinventing Free Labor: Padrones and Immigrant Workers in the North American West, 1880–1930* (Cambridge, Eng.: Cambridge University Press, 2000).

24. Joseph Stipanovitch, *The South Slavs in Utah: A Social History* (San Francisco: R and E Research Associates, 1975), 75.

25. Goodman, "Jews in Zion," 212.

26. Helen Zeese Papanikolas, *Emily—George* (Salt Lake City: University of Utah Press, 1987), 194.

27. Jun Kuramada, interviewed by Helen Papanikolas, August 24, 1984, Salt Lake City, 14–15 in Interviews with Japanese in Utah, Accn 1209, Box 2, fd. 5, Marriott Library.

28. Haruko Terasawa Moriyasu, interviewed by Helen Papanikolas, 1984, Salt Lake City; see also Haruko T. Moriyasu, "Kuniko Muramatsu Terasawa (1896–1991): Typesetter, Journalist, Publisher," in *Worth Their Salt,* 203–17.

29. Margaret Bertolina, interviewed by Phil Notarianni, July 12, 1974, Salt Lake City, 20, Utah Minorities Series, Ms 580, Box 1, fd. 4, Manuscripts Division, Marriott Library.

30. Helen Z. Papanikolas and Alice Kasai, "Japanese Life in Utah," in *Peoples of Utah,* 340.

31. Margaret B. Bertolina, interviewed by Helen Papanikolas, 1942, Salt Lake City.

32. Thelma Siouris, interviewed by Helen Papanikolas, 1983, Salt Lake City.

33. Joe Mikich, interviewed by Joe Stipanovich, January 27, 1973, Midvale, Utah, 32–33; South Slavs Oral History Project, Accn 1502, Box 2, fd. 2, Marriott Library.

34. Mary Papas Lines, interviewed by Helen Papanikolas, 1984, Salt Lake City.

35. Helen Z. Papanikolas, "Magerou: The Greek Midwife," *Utah Historical Quarterly* 38 (Winter 1970): 50–70; Helen Z. Papanikolas, "Georgia Lathouris Mageras (1867–1950): Magerou, the Greek Midwife," in *Worth Their Salt,* 159.

36. Rocco C. Siciliano with Drew M. Ross, *Walking on Sand: The Story of an Immigrant Son and the Forgotten Art of Public Service* (Salt Lake City: University of Utah Press, 2004), 32.

37. Linda Keller Brown and Kay Mussell, *Ethnic and Regional Foodways in the United States: The Performance of Group Identity* (Knoxville: University of Tennessee Press, 1984), 123.

38. William H. Gonzales and Genaro M. Padilla, "Monticello: The Hispanic Cultural Gateway to Utah," *Utah Historical Quarterly* 52 (Summer 1984): 9–28; Helen Z. Papanikolas, "Wrestling with Death: Greek Immigrant Funeral Customs in Utah," *Utah Historical Quarterly* 52 (Winter 1984): 29–49.

39. Larry B. Gerlach, *Blazing Crosses in Zion: The Ku Klux Klan in Utah* (Logan: Utah State University Press, 1982).

40. Mary Pappas Lines, interviewed by Helen Papanikolas, 1984, Salt Lake City.

41. James W. Dilley, *History of the Scofield Mine Disaster* (Provo, Utah: n.pub., 1900); Michael Katsanevas Jr. "The Emerging Social Worker and the Castle Gate Coal Mine Disaster," *Utah Historical Quarterly* 50 (Summer 1982): 241–54; Janeen Arnold Costa, "A Struggle for Survival and Identity: Families in the Aftermath of the Castle Gate Mine Disaster," *Utah Historical Quarterly* 56 (Summer 1988): 279–92; Allan

Kent Powell, "Tragedy at Scofield," *Utah Historical Quarterly* 41, no. 2 (Spring 1973): 182–94.

42. Philip F. Notarianni, "Utah's Ellis Island: The Difficult Americanization of Carbon County," *Utah Historical Quarterly* 47 (Spring 1979): 788–93; Nancy J. Taniguchi, *Castle Valley America: Hard Land, Hard-Won Home* (Logan: Utah State University Press, 2004), 118–20.

43. For more on Italian immigration, see Janet E. Worrall, Carol Bonomo Albright, and Elvira G. Di Fabio, eds., *Italian Immigrants Go West: The Impact of Locale on Ethnicity* (Cambridge, Mass.: Italian American Historical Association, 2003).

44. Helen Z. Papanikolas. "Unionism, Communism, and the Great Depression: The Carbon County Strike of 1933," *Utah Historical Quarterly* 41 (Summer 1973): 254–300; Allan Kent Powell, *The Next Time We Strike: Labor in Utah's Coal Fields, 1900–1933* (Logan: Utah State University Press, 1985).

45. Helen Z. Papanikolas, "Bootlegging in Zion: Making and Selling the Good Stuff," *Utah Historical Quarterly* 48 (Fall 1980): 374–89.

46. Lucy Valerio, Letter to Helen Papanikolas, 1976.

47. Cecyle S. Neidle, ed., *America's Immigrant Women* (Boston: Twayne, 1975), 90.

48. Vicente V. Mayer, "After Escalante: The Spanish-Speaking People of Utah," in *Peoples of Utah,* 461.

49. Kay Bennett, *Kaibah: Recollection of a Navajo Girlhood* (Los Angeles: Westernlore Press, 1964), 249–53.

50. Ferol E. Benavides, "The Saints among the Saints: A Study of Curandisimo in Utah," *Utah Historical Quarterly* 41 (Fal! 1973): 373–92.

51. Kuramada, interview, 45–46.

52. Valerie Matsumoto, "Japanese American Women During World War II," paper delivered to the Women's West 1984 Symposium, Park City, Utah, July 14, 1984, typescript, Marriott Library.

53. Emily Zeese, interviewed by Helen Papanikolas.

54. See also Pamela S. Perlich, *Utah Minorities: The Story Told by 150 Years of Census Data* (Salt Lake City: Bureau of Economic and Business Research, David S. Eccles School of Business, University of Utah, 2002).

5

The Professionalization of Farm Women

1890–1940

Cynthia Sturgis

"Household manager, cook, laundress, seamstress, dressmaker, nurse and teacher, to say nothing of the sacred duties of wife and mother: are these duties not sufficiently varied and important to require special preparation for their performance? In what other profession would an individual be allowed to practice without experience, without training or knowledge?"[1]

The eighty-five farm women who heard Dalinda Cotey speak those words at the Farmers' Institute held December 12, 1905, in Mount Pleasant, Sanpete County, no doubt appreciated this formal recognition of their many responsibilities as homemakers. It would be interesting to know their response to the rest of the statement, however. For Mrs. Cotey, a faculty member at the Utah Agricultural College in Logan, was expressing a new but increasingly powerful philosophy: that the role of the farm wife was changing, and must change, in response to the needs and values of modern industrial society. Her query was both a challenge and a threat. Under the new order, women would find their work elevated to the status of profession; but, increasingly, they must defer to outside experts who alone could instruct them in the proper way to keep a home. Decreasing autonomy was the price of a higher life-style.

Farm women in Utah, like those elsewhere in the nation, experienced an important shift in their role during the early years of the twentieth century. Their function changed from the predominantly productive one which rural women had traditionally exercised to a more diversified, consumption-oriented, though still complementary position often defined as that of "household manager." Significantly, this role paralleled that of urban women, who were becoming the models farm wives would be exhorted to copy. Farm wives, along with their husbands, needed to adopt more "modern" and scientific techniques, to use new technology, and to rely upon the advice of trained specialists. The goal, then, was not merely a revolution in behavior but also

154

in values; farm wives must not change not only their activities but also their self-definition.

This change was promoted by a rising class of experts in governmental and private agencies which proliferated in the first decades of the twentieth century. The increasing respect accorded business and science was reflected in the stress reformers placed on managerial techniques, record-keeping, and experimentation. The growing influence of large-scale organizations such as the interlocking governmental programs for agricultural education and the burgeoning network of electric utility companies and retail merchandisers provided a major shaping force. But the call for modernization also addressed real and deeply felt needs in the agricultural sector. Despite a so-called "Golden Age" just prior to the First World War, American farmers in the early twentieth century experienced both a relative and absolute decline in prestige, power, and standard of living, particularly in comparison with the rising urban population. The result was a widely recognized "flight from the farm" which had drawn the attention of reformers in and out of government since the presidency of Theodore Roosevelt.[2] Indeed, agencies established by the federal government would provide much of the personnel and energy for the campaign to reshape the roles of farmers and their wives.

While Utah reflected these national trends, certain characteristics unique to the state affected farmers in significant ways. In Utah, perhaps to a greater degree than most other areas, the organizations promoting change were tightly interrelated and were centered in the Utah Agricultural College at Logan, later Utah State University. The ideas emanating from the UAC, as it was often called, therefore reached the state's inhabitants through a variety of public and even private bodies, thus providing significant reinforcement of a coherent set of policies and proposals. The relatively homogeneous culture and prevalent influence of the Church of Jesus Christ of Latter-day Saints (Mormons) may also have allowed new practices and principles to spread widely and rapidly. And finally, the residential plan of the Mormon village, which located a substantial proportion of farmers' homes in the village rather than in the country, meant that access to electricity and its benefits came earlier to Utah's farm wives than to those elsewhere in the nation.[3] All of these factors would be critical in reshaping the lives of farm women in Utah in the twentieth century.

The federal-state impetus for change had begun as early as the 1862 passage of the Morrill Land Grant College Act, which provided federal support for the establishment of agricultural and mechanical colleges in the western states. The 1887 Hatch Act created an affiliated network of experiment stations. The Utah Agricultural College was founded in Logan in 1890, primarily to train young men for farming, engineering, or other related careers. It also offered a domestic arts program as one of its four "distinctive lines of instruction." Women students took the same basic two-year course of study as the men (excluding shop, farm labor, or horticulture) and with the substitution

First faculty of the Utah Agricultural College (Utah State University) located in Logan. Right to left; standing: E. S. Richman, J. M. Sholl, Abby L. Marlatt, Mrs. C. I. Goodwin, H. L. Everett, A. A. Mills. Sitting: W. P. Cutter, President J. W. Sanborn, and J. T. Caine, Jr., 1890.

of French for German in the language division. Special studies for women included cooking, sewing, music and painting, "belles-lettres" (literature and elocution), hygiene, and dairying.[4] This curriculum reflected the educators' vision of the farm wife's proper role. In addition to her traditional responsibility for feeding and clothing the family, tending poultry, and managing the dairy, the modern woman should be sensitive to scientific standards of cleanliness and provide a rich cultural atmosphere for her family. Only one of the college's eight original instructors was a woman; and Miss Abby L. Marlatt constituted the entire domestic arts faculty, presiding over the thirty-three women who enrolled with their 136 male counterparts in Utah Agricultural College's first class.[5] The year 1903 saw the formal establishment of a school of home economics.[6] By 1911, six faculty members were teaching domestic science, and enrollment had risen to over a hundred.[7] The Branch Normal School located in Cedar City in southwestern Utah became an adjunct of the Utah Agricultural College in 1913.[8] Eventually both regular four-year college courses and a shorter two-year vocational program became available at the Logan campus. Course offerings also grew more diverse. The 1914–15 catalog lists four possible majors in the School of Home Economics: food and dietetics, domestic arts, home sanitation and construction, and art.[9] Enrollment in these areas had risen to 115 of the 467 students attending the college during 1913–14, up from ninety-four out of 456 the previous term.[10]

Domestic arts received another boost with the opening of a Home Economics Practice House in 1917.[11] The expanding role of the department was represented by its sixteen faculty members (some on leave) in the 1919–20 catalog, several with B.S. degrees.[12] A new Home Economics Cottage on the college grounds replaced the rented Practice House by 1926–27 and represented the "expression of the institution's home ideal," allowing students to polish their skills in a simulated domestic atmosphere.[13] Despite such innovations, the number of faculty had fallen to five by 1928–29, and only 128 students out of the 1,222–member student body were enrolled in home economics classes.[14] The available majors were restructured to three: food and dietetics, textiles and clothing, and household administration.[15] This apparent decline in the department's activities may be related to economic hard times; but it might also be due to the expansion of related activities beyond the campus itself.

The curriculum offered at the Utah Agricultural College clearly could reach only a fraction of the state's rural women directly. Indeed, the overwhelming majority of graduating home economics students cited Logan as their home. The same concern held true for the more prominent men's program as well. To address this problem, the Utah State Legislature had passed a law some twenty years earlier on March 28, 1896, which established annual "farmers' institute" meetings to widen the influence of the college among the state's agricultural population.[16]

Utah thus joined a national trend in the late 1800s and early 1900s toward simultaneous sociability and education for farmers.[17] While most of the sessions were directed toward farmers, women's topics were presented in special meetings or joint sessions. A U.S. Department of Agriculture report published that year on "Farmers' Institutes, 1903" notes that they were currently being held in all but three states and three territories, but that "in no two of the states are institutes organized in the same manner or conducted by the same methods. . . . This diversity is due to the fact that the work is new."[18] Nationwide attendance in that year was estimated at over 900,000.[19] The first decade of the new century seems to have been the peak for the institute movement. Marilyn Irvin Holt, citing a federal study, argues that the program began to decline by 1914. That study reported 5,651 institutes in 1910, with sessions "exclusively for women" offered at 444 of the sessions in 16 states.[20]

Utah's land-grant colleges, like others in the nation, provided most of the speakers for the regional meetings, which attracted substantial numbers. According to Utah institute records, some 6,441 men and women attended the sessions held between December of 1905 and March of 1906; the next year roughly 19,000 people turned out, and over 26,000 came to the traveling shows and institutes presented during the 1907–08 season.[21] Attendance varied,

Courtesy Special Collections and Archives, Merrill Library, Utah State University.

Farmers' encampment, looking west through a row of tents toward Old Main, Utah State University, located in Logan, November 13, 1923.

influenced perhaps by such factors as location, weather, and program; but the format proved successful, and by the mid-teens a typical "Farmers' Roundup and Housekeepers' Conference" might last more than a week.[22] Better roads and increased automobile ownership allowed more farmers to attend such meetings, generally held at a different site in each county every year. Improved mobility also prompted the first state-wide Farmers' Encampment meeting held at the Utah Agricultural College in Logan in 1921, with nearly a thousand of the state's farmers in attendance.[23] These encampments continued through the twenties, supplemented by smaller county sessions. In addition, special railroad cars carrying exhibits prepared at the college occasionally traveled across the region.[24] And in 1924 the Utah Agricultural College instituted a National Summer School to spread new agricultural techniques; 1,163 individuals from twenty-four states and five foreign countries journeyed to Logan to participate.[25]

Farming simultaneously received national promotion. The federal government entered the process again in 1914, with the passage of the Smith-Lever Act, formally establishing the Agricultural Extension Service. In many parts of the country, especially the South, activities of county agents predated the bill.[26] L. M. Windsor, who served as agent in Uintah County in 1911, may have been the first such official active in the northern and western states. The next year, Dr. Elmer G. Peterson became extension director in Utah and Gertrude McCheyne the "first woman specialist in charge of improvement of the associations."[27] Both were UAC faculty members. Amy Lyman, later the wife of M. C. Merrill, journeyed to Sanpete County as the state's first home demonstration agent in 1913, possibly one of the first in the northern and western states.[28]

The 1914 law formalized and promoted this statewide outreach program. Under the bill's provisions, extension agents would serve under a director affiliated with the State Agricultural College. These individuals were assigned to various counties in the state to provide farmers with the latest information about agricultural machinery and practices, teaching by persuasion and example. To aid rural women, the act also authorized the employment of female counterparts known as "home demonstration agents." While initially many areas received only county agents, the ultimate goal was to have both male and female representatives in each county. These teams, which in at least some cases might be husband and wife, required the sponsorship of a county agricultural organization.[29]

In Utah, as in many other states, the group which came to support extension work was the Farm Bureau.[30] Local (precinct-level) and then county farm bureau units had formed in many areas prior to the establishment of a statewide body in 1916; the Utah Farm Bureau Federation officially came into being in 1920.[31] The next year, the state was one of several joining together to form the American Farm Bureau Federation. By 1923, thirty-five states nationwide had Farm Bureaus; in Utah, over three thousand "locals" existed in fifteen counties.[32] The county organizations, representing several local bodies, sponsored the extension and home demonstration agents.

At all levels of its organization, the Farm Bureau formally recognized the complementary roles of men and women in agriculture. The constitutions of local chapters generally granted membership on a family basis, which recognized the economic realities of farm life and implied an equal role for women. In practice, female activity tended to center in the "Home and Community" sections of the groups, for which the home demonstration agent, when present, provided leadership and direction.[33] Women do not seem to have acted as officials of local farm bureaus or to have shaped county or state policy in a significant way outside of these particular bodies. And, as often occurs, the domestic concerns subsumed under the "home and community" heading were defined as peculiarly feminine interests and were generally left solely to the women.

The state and national bodies made some attempts to modify this segregation. A promotional publication for the Utah Farm Bureau Federation in the mid-1920s argued that "although the leadership of the Home and Community section has thus far been found among the women members of the Farm Bureau, yet it is not to be thought of as a section in which only women are interested and concerned, but as one phase of Farm Bureau work in which cooperation of men and women members is particularly desirable." The booklet added that the American Farm Bureau Federation, the parent group, had recently adopted a policy stating: "We recommend a full development of the home and community program and urge that county, state and national organizations place women on their governing board so that the whole program, social, economic, legislative, and marketing, may be worked out by men and women together."[34] Despite such rhetoric, the separation of functions remained.

In fact, women's involvement in both extension-related and other Farm Bureau work continued to be seen as auxiliary to and less central than that of men. Home demonstrators were not present in every county served by male extension personnel. As late as 1939, for example, the state had twenty-nine agricultural agents but only eight home demonstration agents.[35] In such cases, the county agent coordinated the activities of the women in the local Farm Bureau chapter. These members might form their own groups to focus on sewing, canning, civic beautification, or other "appropriate" concerns. Whether or not a female agent was actually present in a given county, however, the Farm Bureau-Extension Service tie created another important avenue through which the educators at the Agricultural College could reach their targeted audience.

The farm press in Utah also allied itself with the Farm Bureau, the Extension Service, and the Utah Agricultural College. The statewide agricultural journal, originally titled the *Deseret Farmer* and, after 1912, the *Utah Farmer,* announced itself as the "official organ of the Utah Agricultural College Extension Division" throughout the 'teens and 'twenties. In 1918, the paper became officially affiliated with the Farm Bureau and acted as its formal sponsor after 1921.[36] The *Utah Farmer* regularly reported on the activities of the state, local, and national branches of the American Farm Bureau Federation, particularly during its most active period of expansion in the early 1920s. And from its inception, the journal provided regular columns of advice to women, often in addition to a recurring "Home" or "Home and Community" section. Faculty from the Utah Agricultural College domestic arts program contributed many of these essays. Through its news and editorial copy, then, the state's farm press actively promoted reforms proposed by the Utah Agricultural College, the related Extension Service, and the Utah Farm Bureau Federation.

The advertising in such journals, as well as advertisements in community daily or weekly papers, also constituted a powerful educational force. Advertising, still a young art in the 'teen's and 'twenties, began to move away from the fairly simple task of informing readers of the price, description, and availability of goods to the more aggressive and didactic role of arguing the necessity and explaining the function of the burgeoning number of new and unfamiliar products on the market.[37] Advertising copy generally upheld and reinforced the messages expressed in editorials and feature articles. This close connection grew even more obvious in journals such as the *Utah Farmer,* directed as it was toward a narrowly defined audience.

These private agencies—the Farm Bureau, the state's farm press, and advertisers in such journals—supplemented the campaign for "modernization" of housekeeping methods which was spreading throughout the state's lower schools as well. In an attempt to mold future generations and, it was hoped, to encourage their elders to profit by their example, the Utah Agricultural

College began promoting home economics clubs in the public schools as early as 1915, inviting high school groups to share in programs offered at the college's two campuses.[38] During the 1918–19 school year, for example, 112 students engaged in such "Junior Extension" work at Logan and fourteen at Cedar City locations; attendance was evenly divided between boys and girls.[39] Obviously, the program could reach only a fraction of the state's youth directly. They, however, would return to their own communities to serve as leaders for extension-affiliated agricultural and homemaking clubs.

Again the federal government encouraged the dissemination of modern agricultural and homemaking with the passage of the Smith-Hughes Act of 1917. This bill, given formal approval and support by the Utah State Legislature in 1919, promoted public school courses in agriculture, vocational training, and home economics by funding teachers for these subjects.[40] By 1920, the Utah Agricultural College catalog included extensive descriptions of course work required for such "Smith-Hughes" teachers, signaling its key role in the training of these educators.[41] "Domestic arts and science" classes, some begun prior to the passage of the act, spread throughout the high schools and even down to the elementary level. Home economics students in the upper divisions were often referred to as "Smith-Hughes girls" in the Sevier County School Board records of the period.

Related club work formed a major part of this educational experience. Groups connected with the schools became the precursors of the Future Farmers of America and Future Homemakers of America, and those affiliated with the Farm Bureau and Extension Service became the nucleus of the 4–H organization. The college at Logan provided training for adult club leaders as well. In 1917, J. C. Hogenson founded the state's first 4–H group, located on the Utah Agricultural College main campus. In 1919, the first 4–H Club Leaders' training school for adult volunteers took place there also.[42]

And the institution affected club members even more directly: In 1921, the college announced the start of an annual Junior Extension Service, whose purpose was to train high-school students to become project leaders in their local groups.[43] That first year, nine girls and five boys attended.[44] The program grew steadily, and in 1928, thirty-nine boys joined sixty-three girls at club leaders training school; forty-one women also traveled to the Logan campus to learn how to supervise the girls' organizations.[45] The interrelationship between the Extension service and the Farm Bureau at the adult level was echoed here, since county agents and home demonstrators often acted as club leaders too. In the words of the Agricultural College's catalog, "County Club agents are maintained for the purpose of organizing junior units of the farm bureaus and supervising and assisting the boys and girls in carrying out definite projects of the bureaus. Under this plan, the primary purpose is to develop leadership and train boys and girls in better methods of farm and home practice."[46] The county club presidents were seen as the Farm Bureau leaders of tomorrow.

Courtesy Special Collections and Archives, Merrill Library, Utah State University.

4–H Club girls and their leader, Mrs. M. K. Jacobs at their canning, sewing and baking exhibit, Riverdale, 1918.

These structural innovations carried considerable significance for the changing roles and responsibilities of farm women in particular. Basic tasks such as cooking, sewing, laundering, and even table setting, which had previously been taught in the home through example and one-to-one contact between mother and daughter, became the province of professional educators. By making such courses a part of the curriculum, and by providing public support for after-school club work, the state tacitly promoted a shift in women's authority and influence. Responsibility for instruction in the most traditional of female tasks—the proper running of a household—had been removed from the home and placed in the hands of trained specialists, some of whom were not even married. And the revolution went even deeper: The explicit goal of such educators was for these youngsters, either directly or by example, to convert their backward parents to more modern forms of behavior. As the *Utah Farmer* noted in a 1925 discussion of the 4–H movement, "There's an old saying that it is hard to teach old dogs new tricks, but fathers and mothers are quick to adopt the gospel and methods of better agriculture when they see their sons and daughters giving practical demonstrations of its worth."[47] Where once the parent had trained the child, now the child was to instruct the parent.

The pacing as well as the content of education changed. Traditional practice tended to be conservative. Formal education, combining as it did the experience of several generations and individuals, could innovate at less risk, thereby accelerating the rate of change. In a few decades, the efforts of this new class of experts could affect entire generations of homemakers. It would be erroneous to suggest that all those exposed to the new agenda adopted it immediately or wholeheartedly. But patterns of behavior which in a less centralized or literate society could take several generations to reshape might now change in a lifetime.

The values and practices promoted by these interrelated authorities posed a direct challenge to traditional assumptions. By comparing farm life with that in the city, reformers sought to focus rural discontent in favor of modernization. In their definition, homemaking became "household management"; and like any other skilled professional, the farm wife was advised to seek formal training. This urban, business-oriented model which stressed efficiency and planning naturally promoted the role of experts such as educators and scientists—outside authorities who would now direct the farm wife in the proper management of her sphere. As a result, the standard by which the housewife would be judged became stricter, and the emotional content of her work increased.

The use of an urban model to stimulate change in the agricultural sector had its roots in the declining prestige accorded rural life in the early twentieth century. Critics of farm living often pointed to its isolation, lack of cultural opportunities, poor level of health and sanitation, and absence of modern conveniences. These conditions, noted by Country Life Reformers in the early 1900s, only worsened after the onset of a nationwide agricultural depression in 1921.[48] Such handicaps were blamed for the much-discussed "flight from the farm" taking place during the 'teens and 'twenties.

The lure of the city and its special appeal to women seemed critical to many observers. As William Peterson, director of the Utah Agricultural College Experiment Station, noted in 1925, "It has been said by some that the movement from the country to the city is a women's movement, and the reason for this is to avoid the hardships associated with the home in a country life."[49] Advertisers of home improvements even used the contrast to promote their wares. Promising that the "CONVENIENCES OF THE CITY—the comforts of life—can be had on the farm," one maker of electric pumping equipment noted, "City women live longer than women of the country. Why? Chiefly because of a difference in the home arrangement—a lack in the country of the conveniences that would make the day's work a delight."[50]

Rural beautification and improvement became standard remedies proposed to stem the outward flow of the farm population. As the *Utah Farmer* pointed out in a 1921 front-page article headed "The Home Is the Heart of the Farm": "There are plenty of good reasons why everyone should aim to make the home attractive. Among them are the following: (1) It makes the family contented, and encourages the boy and the girl to stay on the farm. (2) It provides refreshing recreation for the family after the work of the day. (3) It increases the value of the farm. (4) It promotes health and happiness."[51]

Extension and home demonstration agents joined with local Farm Bureaus to wage "Clean Home—Clean Town" campaigns throughout the teens and twenties. Although all members of the community were urged to support efforts at civic beautification, much of the direction continued to come from Extension Service representatives and the "home and community" sections of the Farm Bureaus, organized and run by the women. The seeming appropriateness of this association of women and home improvement resulted in a strong identification of the movement with that gender. As the *Utah Magazine* confidently stated in its 1941 "Beautification Issue," "Ladies seem to be especially adapt [sic] at getting things done in this respect."[52]

The goal of such activity was to make the rural home as much like its urban counterpart as possible. To this end, farm families should plant lawns and flowers, rural villages should put in sidewalks and streetlights, and dwellings should be equipped with the latest in household conveniences. As one supporter put it:

> The farm home should be made so convenient and inviting that the wife and mother would not exchange it for a city residence. The sense of isolation so often complained of in country homes is more often the result of out-of-date equipment rather than lack of near neighbors. . . . But labor-saving devices for the wife are necessities—just as much so as up-to-date plows and drills are necessities for the farmer. . . . A country home thus provided with modern conveniences would not readily be deserted for a home in the village, nor would wife and children voluntarily make the exchange.[53]

However, an additional difficulty in keeping girls "down on the farm" grew from the lack of outside job opportunities available there. As late as 1930, the U.S. Census listed most Utah women (nearly 95 percent) in rural-farm areas as "not gainfully employed." The rural-non-farm, or village, count was slightly lower at almost 93 percent, as compared with the roughly 87 percent figure for urban areas. But the most striking differences appear in the comparison of those women who were classified as employed. Just over half of the rural-farm women worked at home, the overwhelming majority (82 percent) in agricultural occupations. In contrast, over 90 percent of the gainfully employed urban women worked away from home, as did the bulk (85 percent) of the rural-non-farm (village) women. Urban workers were most likely to be servants or waitresses, office workers, or professional or industrial workers. While some of the rural-farm women found work as waitresses and servants and others in professional jobs, nearly one-third fell into the category defined as "other," probably meaning part-time seasonal, agriculture-related work. Rural-non-farm women, on the other hand, had their strongest representation in the servant/waitress category and the next highest percentage in the professional class, with an additional component working as saleswomen and office workers. Such a job profile reflects the role of rural villages as service centers for the agricultural hinterland and demonstrates the superior job opportunities for young women off the farm. Clearly, as late as 1930, farm women were the least likely to work outside the home, and those who did either worked in agriculture or were concentrated in the lowest-paying occupations.[54]

In an effort to elevate the status of homemaking and make it more desirable, representatives of the Extension Service and the Utah Agricultural College repeatedly stressed its professional nature. Indeed, articles with titles such as "Housekeeping as a Profession" began to appear in the farm press during the 'teens, usually promoting education in the domestic arts.[55] It is significant, too, that the women's sessions held during farmers' institutes took the title "Housekeepers' Conference." The use of a business model by educators and reformers was pervasive. A writer in the *Utah Farmer* in 1921 presaged a later trend by querying "What Should [a] Housewife's Salary Be?" and providing a dollars and cents answer: $4,000 per year.[56] Then as now, such estimates were made less for practical purposes than to demonstrate more dramatically the importance of a housewife's contribution to the family economy. The intended message could not be missed: Housekeeping was a highly skilled pursuit, one in which a woman could engage with pride. The author of one Extension Service Bulletin insisted: "The attitude of contempt hitherto assumed by society towards domestic duties indicates ignorance alike to their variety, their call for skill and their responsibility. It is even now giving place to the realization that these familiar duties are infinitely more varied and demand a far higher degree of intelligence than do the callings of stenographer, clerk, or factory-hand, which appeal so strongly to the young women today."[57]

Granting formal job titles to different facets of women's work reflected the business orientation that educators favored for the modern home. Dalinda Cotey noted that housewives should view themselves as nurses, teachers, and household managers, among a number of other positions. Rose H. Widtsoe, a member of the Utah Agricultural College Home Economics faculty, relied upon similar professional imagery in her 1920 *Utah Farmer* articles discussing "Efficient Household Purchasing." As she put it, "Women spend nine-tenths of the money earned. If a sepcially [sic] trained purchasing agent is necessary to the success of a business enterprise, how much more necessary a well-trained purchasing agent is for the home." Like all good business managers, farm wives should plan carefully, follow budgets, and promote efficiency wherever possible. Widtsoe, confident of the superiority of the scientific method, promised, "Every housekeeper may become an efficient household purchasing agent by continuous trying, by experimenting, and by study."[58]

Increasingly, housewifery meant knowing how to shop wisely—that is, becoming an informed consumer. When authorities like Widtsoe stated that women "must be trained to buy commercially made products," they spoke quite seriously. The list of required new knowledge was impressively complex and deserves quoting at length. Aside from the rudiments of choosing and cooking food, an efficient purchasing agent should know the merits of various kinds of distribution methods, [such] as parcel post, mail order, co-operative buying and public market. She should realize the importance of knowing city, state and national laws governing the standards of various articles such as food, clothing and equipment and also the methods of handling raw and manufactured goods. She will search out the markets that are sanitary and well ordered, avoiding markets where food is exposed to flies and dust. She will learn the standard weaves of cotton, linen, and woolen materials and the points of judgment is [sic] determining household equipment. She will in fact learn the values of everything that comes into the house. . . . Another important qualification is to be able to detect food adulterations and malpractice among dealers, and to know the various trade labels and the most economical sizes of cans and other containers. In fact to be a good purchasing agent, the mother in the home must know her business. If she is to get the best returns for her money she must know values.[59]

But diligence and good intentions alone could not take the place of professional training in enlightened consumerism. The elevation of formal education in homemaking promoted the role of the expert. As a columnist for the "Home" section of the *Deseret Farmer* noted in 1911, "Isn't it passing strange when we realize what an important profession housekeeping is—what it means to the home and community . . . that we expect a girl to grow up and without any special training become a first class homemaker?"[60] The staff of the Utah Agricultural College stood ready to fill that need. Advertisements for farmers' institutes and articles describing course offerings at the school repeatedly identified the faculty as "experts" or "leading authorities" in their fields.[61] Such rhetoric, repeated by the Extension Service, the Farm Bureau, and the agricultural press, as well as the educational bureaucracy stimulated by the Smith-Hughes program, made it clear that no woman could adequately keep house without rigorous training by the proper authorities.

The primacy of the expert reflected the school's curriculum, which stressed the importance of scientific instruction for the housewife. Utah Agricultural College's initial catalog noted that "the chemistry or science, and the art of cooking will be taught."[62] This tone continued. By 1916, the School of Home Economics offered, in addition to "Elementary Cooking" (prerequisite Chemistry 1), "Preparation of Foods and Food Study," involving the "study of the composition of foods and the fundamental principles of nutrition"; a separate course on "Dietetics and Nutrition"; "Pathological Nutrition," which dealt with preparing special diets for the "sick and convalescent"; and "Care and Feeding of Children." A class on "Food Economics" ambitiously covered "The function and nutritive values of food, the cost of food in relation to the family budget . . . [and] practical results of the 'pure food' laws [plus] the preparation of meals combining foods according to dietetic, aesthetic, and economic standards."[63]

Branch Agricultural College (BAC) in Cedar City (Southern Utah University) home economics class showing co-eds learning how to make pies, ca. 1920.

Training extended beyond such traditional female chores as food preparation. That same year, in the "Home Construction and Sanitation Department," students who had mastered Bacteriology 2 might learn "scientific principles and practices conducive to the maintenance of healthful conditions and their expression in house and environment" in a course entitled "Sanitation." Practice in "Home Care of the Sick" supplemented discussions of "Home Laundering," which included a "study of equipment for the home laundry" and "laundering processes." The prerequisites for this class were Chemistry 2 and Bacteriology 1. And girls might round out their knowledge with "Household Administration," which dealt with "the meaning of homemaking and home activities" and "their relation to the industrial world and to society at large"; it also included consideration of "standards of living, income and expenditures, savings, service and management."[64]

One of the main thrusts of professional training was the need to acquire and understand modern household technology. College catalogs boasted that "special mention should be made of the well equipped home nursing laboratory, . . . additions and changes in the dietetics laboratory course," and "the Home Economics cottage, serving primarily as a laboratory for the household management course . . . [which] makes it possible for senior students to apply and correlate the principles of home management, food engineering, household accounting, home planning and interior decoration, etc." Although the catalog went on to state that "considerable emphasis is placed also on the spiritual side of home-making in order that students may have an opportunity of studying its relative importance in family life," science and technology clearly carried more weight.[65]

Both the Home Economics Cottage and its predecessor, the Practice House, introduced students to the latest in household equipment. For example, the earlier establishment featured both a coal range and one of the "up-to-date ranges [which] economizes fuel," complete with the "Fireless Cooker." As the promotional material for the project commented, "The students study the convenience and economy of electricity" on equipment "donated to the Practice House by the Utah Power and Light Company."[66] The farm press also promoted modern household conveniences. Articles like "The Electrified Farm House" presented a litany of home improvements powered by electricity, ranging from room heaters and lights through "feed mixers and grinder[s] of all kind[s], bone cutters, electrical ranges, electrical fireless cooker, electric iron, toaster, coffee percolator, samavor [sic], table stove, chafing dish and curling iron," plus "every task which could be done with motive power, including running the sewing machine." While acknowledging that "comparatively few women will have homes as completely electrified as this," the author insisted: "There are few homes where some electrification is not possible" and painted a glowing picture of how applying electrical power to the major tasks of washing, ironing, churning, sewing, and cooking would shift the bulk of a farm wife's chores into the "light housekeeping class."[67]

The *Utah Farmer* continued to print periodic articles extolling "Modern Light and Power for the Home" and discussing the important relationship of "Electricity and Farm Life" throughout the 'teens and 'twenties.[68] Writers pointed out the safety features as well as the labor-saving benefits connected with the use of such new technology versus old-fashioned oil lamps and candles. In the words of one convert to the new ways, "Electric lights about the farm house are just as delightful, from the standpoint of comfort and convenience, as they are in any city home. The relief from the care of the smoky, unsafe, kerosene lamps appeals to the housewife and she saves considerable time over the old way when she can light her home with electricity."[69]

Not surprisingly, accompanying advertising reinforced these editorial messages. The Utah Power and Light Company sponsored frequent ads for electrical service and also sold appliances requiring it. A typical example is a January 1925 message proclaiming:

> Your resolution for 1925 Should Be—
>
> To take the drudgery out of housekeeping in your home. Put modern electric servants to do the work. They mean health and happiness for women— and a cleaner, brighter and more delightful home for the whole family.

Electric Ranges
Electric Washers
Electric Ironers
Electric Vacuum Cleaners
Electric Irons.[70]

Dealers like the W. K. Lovering Company of Salt Lake City advised *Utah Farmer* readers in 1920 to "Keep the Home Lights Burning and the Fresh Water Running" by installing a Paul Electric Water system and Universal Lighting Plant.[71] Advertisers repeatedly emphasized the indispensability of their products. Modern conveniences had a greater social role to play than was immediately obvious. Alamo Electricity explained "Why *You* Should Install Electric Light and Power" with the argument that "Four things are of vital importance to every farmer in these days of stress. Workers must be attracted to the farm. Time and labor must be saved in every possible way. Boys and girls must be kept at home. The burden on farm women must be relieved. Electric light and power will solve these problems as nothing else can." Although that message was particularly applicable in the war year of 1918, it would be repeated over the years. The crusading spirit remained uppermost; few merchandisers would disagree with the confident statement, "Dealers who handle these lighting plants could be real missionaries to the farmers," and to their wives as well.[72]

Although electricity was the prerequisite for many home improvements, advertisers and educators alike stressed that it need not be the *sine qua non*. The Maytag company boasted that "even if you had Electricity—you could have no better Washer Service" than that provided by their model with its own built-in gas engine.[73] And the Perfection Oil Cook Stove promised that it "Drives out Drudgery" (an oft-repeated term) by eliminating the "heavy coal scuttles; dirty ash cans; [and] sooty pots and pans" which characterized traditional cooking methods.[74]

But even these devices could, if necessary, be foregone if the woman of the house demonstrated sufficient ingenuity and profited from expert advice. The Utah Agricultural College Extension Service published a discussion of "Labor-Saving Devices in the Household" in the early 'teens, which noted many inexpensive improvements that could ease the work of the average farm wife. Suggestions included using a high stool to avoid long periods of standing while ironing or washing dishes, buying china and glassware with simple, easy-to-clean shapes, using dishes which could go from oven to table, wearing low-heeled shoes to save the feet, and adding long handles to brooms and brushes to end stooping. Under the heading "Labor-Saving Devices of a Mechanical Nature," Alice Ravenhill mentioned the steam pressure cooker, bread and cake mixers, tea wagons or wheeled trays, and mangles to limit the need for ironing. Finally, the homemaker should develop a "Household Record File," containing handy references to household hints, recipes, family clothing sizes, repair information, financial information, and a general inventory of household supplies.[75] It was a far cry from the way Mother used to keep house.

While emphasizing the need for formal training in homemaking, educators were also expanding the definition of the term itself. Ironically, the role of the home was elevated just as, increasingly, the ultimate authority for family concerns was removed from it. The 1920–21 Utah Agricultural College catalog offered this explanation: "The steady growth of Home Economics courses in leading colleges and universities indicates the ever increasing realization that the well conducted home is the most important factor in the development of healthful and capable citizenship. But the multiplying complexities of modern life demand further that those in charge of the family understand much that is beyond the exact limits of the home. Hence the stress laid on the study of childhood and adolescence, the cause underlying the high cost of living, and the problems of social, industrial, and civic life."[76] The proliferation of course offerings at the Utah Agricultural College demonstrated this shift in authority, as did the gradual inclusion of courses on child care and development and, by the 1930s and '40s, the elimination of earlier classes on home sanitation. Successful modernization of rural residences had made the latter obsolete; intensified focus on the emotional needs of the family made the former seem imperative.

As the subject matter became more inclusive, the responsibility of the wife and mother for all aspects of the home expanded. Women needed to be trained to buy consumer goods wisely and economically; they must learn to operate and choose among the new labor-saving devices on the market; they must feed their families balanced and nourishing as well as filling meals; and they must care of their children's spirits as well as bodies. Although the ostensible goal of formal training in homemaking was to ease the housewife's burden, the introduction of new household technology actually raised standards. The stress on efficient, scientific, sanitary procedures not only made traditional methods outmoded, but also established an ever-receding pinnacle of perfection for the housewife to seek. For example, a 1916 *Utah Farmer* article recommended daily vacuuming and house inspection (in contrast to the usual practice of twice-yearly cleanings), adding, "To keep a thoroughly sanitary home we must understand sanitary conditions within the house as well as out."[77]

The emotional component was also escalated. As early as the 'teens, a Utah Agricultural College domestic arts specialist would tell women that it was no longer enough to get adequate meals on the table; they should ask themselves if their families were emotionally nourished as well.[78] By 1939, an expert on vocational homemaking education in the state could assert, "The homemakers [sic] job then becomes twofold: (1) The management of the material resources of the family in order to provide for the physical, emotional and psychological needs of the family members, and (2) the maintenance of desirable relationships among the family members and with people outside the family."[79] On the mother's shoulders now lay the responsibility for the family's emotional and social well-being.

Guilt, a natural accompaniment to this new job description, could also be used to move products. A 1936 "Farm Electrification Manual" sponsored jointly by Utah Power and Light Company, the Western Colorado Power Company, and Bountiful Power and Light Company, offers a classic example. After asking the reader "DO YOUR GUESTS SECRETLY FEEL SORRY FOR YOU? Must you apologize for your home?" the text described a hypothetical visit of a city couple to a home without indoor plumbing or piped-in water. Clearly, rural dwellers who lived in unimproved housing would be politely despised for failing to meet urban standards.[80] By making farm people sensitive to such comparisons, both advertisers and educators hoped to shame them into improvement.

Even family disunity might be traced to a failure to modernize. In the words of one Extension worker, "The breaking up of more than one family may be traced to disharmonies among its members, consequent upon discomforts which need never have existed, had the woman in the home been less weary from her unceasing labors on their behalf, and better equipped for the duties devolving upon her."[81] Another advocate of home economics training mused in print, "I wonder just how many divorces are really caused by the women not being prepared to perform intelligently and happily their part as homemakers?"[82] Such statements provided powerful ammunition in the battle over modernization.

Perhaps these tactics seemed necessary to overcome initial resistance to what was admittedly a revolutionary program of change. The faculty members at the A.C. repeatedly complained about their difficulties in getting farm women to respond to their advice. As noted, female enrollment at the college remained a fraction of the total, averaging about 25 percent over time; and women's attendance at farmers' institute meetings also trailed that of men. For example, during the December 1905–March 1906 season, according to institute figures, 5,093 men and 1,348 women attended sessions. In 1908–09, female attendance was 4,962 versus 11,828 for males. And in 1908–09, only one-third as many women as men turned out.[83] In part these disparities reflected the year-round nature of women's work, which made it more difficult for them to leave the farm; but other factors may also have contributed.

One obstacle was traditional resistance to educating women. Supporters of home economics countered by assuring the public that their proposals actually supported the role of wife and mother. If anything, female education had the greater importance. As the *Deseret Farmer* noted in 1910, "girls were to be the mothers and chief inspirers of unborn men, and they needed the trained mind and satisfied life just as much, nay more, than if they were to be mere breadwinners."[84] The strongest argument seemed to be that "the best education for women is the one that makes her [sic] the most womanly."[85] Utah

Agricultural College spokesman Leah D. Widtsoe accused women themselves of "lack[ing] that certain progressiveness which enables men constantly to use their brains in thinking out devices for saving energy. If the men would be the housekeepers for a few years," she believed, "we would have as fine dishwashing machines and cookers, as we have hay derricks and harvesters. . . . Women's very conservatism and content is often her [sic] worst enemy."[86] Ellen Huntington, speaking to women at farmers' institutes in 1910, had agreed. "Housekeepers are too apt to make slaves of themselves," she concluded. "It seems to me that while we are living in this aeroplane age, our housekeeping is in the street car age."[87]

But farm wives alone were not to blame for failures to modernize. Leah Widtsoe conceded, "In one respect, that of money, woman cannot help herself, because in most cases the man holds the purse strings. Most farm women make their living out of their chickens and dairy, and ready cash is a thing they seldom see. Any help or labor saving device that costs money, is for that reason forbidden. Now this is the case, not because men as a class are stingy, nor because they do not want to help their wives, but because they do not think about it, and the women do not make them think."[88] Hers was an unusually generous view. Frequently, the woman's enforced economic dependence, as much as her tendency towards self-sacrifice, were responsible for her continued drudgery.

Educators decried the reluctance of some farmers to provide for their wives the kinds of amenities they insisted upon for their own work as false economy. It was common wisdom that electricity frequently reached the barn before the house. Reformers challenged this behavior by, first, noting the significant economic contribution of the farm wife and, second, by extolling the emotional benefits from home improvement. After all, as one such spokesman asked:

> What good is a large bank account to any man if he has the consciousness of a worn-out, ill-tempered wife and a cheerless home to greet him when his day's work is done? And no woman whose energy is taxed to the breaking point by the ceaseless daily, and often nightly grind of toil, can be cheerful and companionable for any length of time. Is there a money equivalent for the cheerful smile and life companionship of the woman who was once the best on earth? . . . The farmer who understands that there are things in life worth infinitely more than dollars and cents, will use every spark of intelligence and some hard cash as well, in making the most perfect possible home.[89]

The new ideal of the companionate marriage thus merged with the movement to upgrade the housewife's working conditions.

A final difficulty may have been the domestic ideal itself. Industrialization removed many tasks to the factory, where mass production, economies of scale, standardization, and managerial skill created greater efficiency in production. Farmers, too, banded together to purchase and use large-scale harvesting equipment and cooperative buying feed and seed. Only in homemaking were tasks still individualized and dispersed. Leah D. Widtsoe echoed the ideas of feminists like Charlotte P. Gilman in calling for the establishment of community laundries and bakeries and the joint ownership of expensive equipment such as vacuum cleaners.[90] Although practical, this solution perhaps seemed too direct a challenge to the entrenched notions about woman's special sphere to succeed.

Despite such resistance, circumstances unique to Utah promoted adoption of the new definition and practice of homemaking. The powerful network of authorities and agencies centered around the Utah Agricultural College certainly played a decisive role. The village patterns in rural Utah—which had farm families living in town and going out to work on surrounding farms—allowed earlier and wider access to electricity. And the predominant influence of the Church of Jesus Christ of Latter-day Saints may also have resulted in a more rapid dissemination and reinforcement of new attitudes and behavior.

The U.S. Census Bureau defines as "urban" all settlements over 2,500 in population, a figure which effectively describes a large village or county seat in the late nineteenth and early twentieth centuries. In 1880, roughly three-fourths of Utah's population resided in rural areas or communities smaller than 2,500, a proportion typical for the mountain region as a whole and only slightly higher than the national average. By 1900, however, the rural population stood at 61.9 percent for Utah, again close to the national average of 60 percent but lower than the regional average of 67.7 percent. More significantly, only sixteen states were more highly "urbanized" than Utah in 1900, almost all of which were located in the northeastern United States. In 1920 Utah's "urban-farm" population stood at 8,377 and the rural-farm count was 131,872. By 1930 the urban-farm count had risen to 9,046 and the rural farm had dropped to 106,667. Although the total farm population declined absolutely (from 140,249 to 115,713) and relatively (from 31.2 percent of the total population to 22.8 percent), the number of farms actually rose from 25,662 in 1920 to 27,159 (52.4 percent) in 1930, much higher than the regional average of 39.5 percent. And Utah continued to lead thirty-one other states in the percentage of its population dwelling in urban centers.[91]

However, such figures can be misleading. Utahns on the whole were not leaving the country for the city; rather, the rural villages in which many of them lived had simply grown beyond the 2,500 mark. The 1930 census puts these figures into better perspective. In that year, Utah boasted only one city with a population over 100,000 (Salt Lake City, with 140,267). In addition, the state had only one city in the 25,000–100,000 range, one in the 10,000–25,000 range, and four in the category of 5,000–10,000. Over 28 percent of the state's people lived in towns with fewer than 5,000 inhabitants, and an additional 28 percent lived in unincorporated, or strictly rural, areas. Well over half the state's population, thus, lived either in small agricultural villages or in the country.[92]

This pattern mitigated the isolation so often complained of by rural dwellers; it also had a dramatic impact on the rate of physical improvement.

Since electric power became available in urban areas much earlier than in the countryside, many Utah farm families, as village-dwellers, had access to this powerful force for modernization much earlier than rural inhabitants in other regions. Utility companies such as Utah Power and Light boasted that the state was a leader in rural electrification. That company, which served much of Utah and part of Idaho, cited the dramatic expansion of its own system in a mere decade. Between 1912 and 1922, the miles of transmission line roughly doubled, the number of communities served rose from 130 to 205, and the number of customers increased from 39,700 to 83,074, up 110 percent. The utility claimed it could reach 95 percent of the homes in its territory by 1922, while at the same time keeping rates constant or lowering them. Indeed, Utah Power and Light asserted that its rates were lower than the national average and among the lowest in the continental United States.[93] Furthermore, connecting lines to such concerns as Telluride Power Company serving southern Utah created a truly statewide system.[94]

U.S. Census figures also demonstrate the pace of electrification in the state. Some 11,125 farm dwellings had electric power in 1920, growing to 15,778 in 1930 and 18,285 in 1945.[95] Utah ranked well above most states on this score. One 1930 study pointed out that only California and Massachusetts had more farms equipped with electricity than Utah. The state also fared well regarding water piped into rural homes; only ten of the other forty-seven states (and only two Western states, California and Oregon) exceeded its 38.9 percent total.[96] The 6,179 farm dwellings with running water in 1920 rose to 10,561 in 1930 and 15,936 in 1945. By 1954, 20,808 had indoor water, nearly equal to the number electrified.[97]

After electricity came labor-saving appliances. As early as 1922, Utah Power and Light estimated the presence in its service area of 4,300 electric ranges, 19,000 washing machines, 70,000 electric irons (more than one for each home), 14,000 grills and toasters, 7,500 vacuum cleaners, and 10,000 "miscellaneous" devices.[98] Radios and telephones, although not necessarily dependent upon electric power, tended to accompany it. Although only 386 of the over 27,000 farm homes in the state had radios in 1925, by 1930 over 17,000 had acquired them, and by 1945 the overwhelming majority enjoyed this convenience.[99] In fact, Utah ranked slightly above the national average in radio ownership. In 1930 40.3 percent of all U.S. homes had sets, compared with 41.1 percent in Utah. But among farm dwellers, Utah exceeded the national average even more impressively—31.8 percent versus 21.0 percent.[100] Telephones were somewhat less common; 6,295 rural homes were on the line in 1920, 7,416 in 1930, and 8,479 in 1945, after a downward dip to 4,998 in 1940.[101]

Farm families who obtained one modern convenience often reported others as well, with running water and electricity heading the list in popularity.

In 1945, 85.4 percent of the state's farm homes were electrified, 74.4 percent had running water, and 72.5 percent had both. Those rural residents who could get electric power usually did; 77.5 percent of the state's farmers lived within one-quarter mile of an electric distribution line, and only 2.82 percent of them lacked electricity. Over a third (37.4%) of farm homes were equipped with telephones, and most of these also had electricity, radios, and automobiles.[102] By the end of World War II, it can be argued, the technological revolution had taken firm hold.

One final cultural characteristic, harder to measure in absolute terms, which may have supported the spread of modernization ideology was the statewide influence of the Church of Jesus Christ of Latter-day Saints (Mormons), especially in rural areas. The various agencies extending outward from the Utah Agricultural College, be they women's branches of the Farm Bureau, 4–H clubs, or home economics groups, overlaid a well-established social network created by the church itself. Intentionally or otherwise, it may have profited from that cohesion. In discussing the formation of twenty home economics groups in 1913, Utah Agricultural College literature noted that such improvement associations "generally operated through the existing women's organizations of the state of a religious, literary, or civic nature."[103] Frequently, those functions overlapped to a great degree, and LDS Relief Societies may have acted as an important conduit for the doctrine of scientific housekeeping.

Young people also mixed in church-based social bodies, even more frequently than in secular organizations. Indeed, most of the social activity available for farm youth centered around the LDS Church. A 1938 study of rural women ages sixteen to twenty-five found that 95 percent were members of the Mormon Church, 85 percent had attended services during the last year, and 84 percent attended Sunday School. Young Women's Mutual Improvement Association (YWMIA) activities through the church attracted 83 percent: Beehive for girls twelve to sixteen, plus Junior Gleaners (fourteen to sixteen) and Gleaners (ages sixteen on up). Many also served as teachers or officers in Primary, the organization for children.[104] Among those girls still in high school, church-related activities outdrew other group attractions. Over 91 percent of these individuals belonged to MIA, while only 17.5 percent were currently active in Home Economics clubs sponsored by the school, and a mere 9.6 percent were involved in 4–H. It should be noted, however, that fully 77.1 percent of the girls currently in school and 67.4 percent of all girls surveyed had some 4–H experience.[105] It is reasonable to assume that the students carried at least some of the ideas and experiences from the homemaking organizations over into their discussions at church social gatherings.

The various programs intended to teach women to become modern homemakers reached a substantial portion of the state's farm population by the 1930s and '40s. Over 90 percent of the girls in that 1938 survey had taken courses in home economics, averaging 2.6 years of study apiece.[106] Another official study indicated that fifty-one of the state's seventy-five high schools offered such training with the support of either state or federal funds.[107] In 1941, the current membership in 4–H, male and female, was estimated at over 5,600.[108] And by 1947, the Extension service provided twenty-four home demonstration agents to counties throughout the state.[109]

Farm women had adopted ideology as well as technology. They had, for example, become consumers. A 1929 survey of farm family habits indicated an acceptance of brand-name products such as Crisco; more tellingly, it indicated that more items were being purchased and fewer produced. Farm families still demonstrated a self-sufficiency not possible in the city, but reliance on outside producers was on the rise. A random survey of eleven western Utah counties found rural dwellers growing 70 percent of their food on the farm, notably milk, honey, and vegetables.[110] A sampling done in Summit County the next year estimated that the farms were providing only about half of the total value of the food consumed. Again, home production of eggs and dairy products remained high, but half the poultry and meat came from off the farm, as did three-fourths of the fruits and vegetables and nearly all of the flour and cereal.[111] Such studies are not conclusive, but they seem to indicate a trend away from a more absolute self-reliance; farm women, slowly and incompletely, were growing more like their city counterparts.

While changes in behavior can be measured with at least some accuracy, shifts in attitude prove harder to delineate. If various federally sponsored "County Agricultural Plans" are an accurate barometer, farm women by the late 1930s and early 1940s had apparently absorbed the value system that agricultural educators had promoted, with its reliance on urban images, reverence for science and technology, and use of businesslike managerial techniques. The goals outlined in such documents include rural beautification, home improvement, better sanitary conditions in home and community, and efficient and economical home management. The means include formal planning, reliance on outside authorities, and informed consumerism. The Utah County women who entitled one section of their 1937 report "Happiness—the Result of Planned Family Living," drew up a highly revealing list of actions leading to success in the "business of life":

1. Planned home activity.
2. Study better buymanship—know how to shop. Recognize values.
3. A spending plan made by all family members. Rewards come as a result of planned spending.
4. Be immune to installment buying.[112]

A few years later, farm women in Iron County similarly advised, "Record keeping is absolutely essential to the efficient management of any business, whether it be a range livestock unit, a farm, or a home. The proper keeping of an adequate record will point the way to proper management and

Courtesy Special Collections and Archives, Merrill Library, Utah State University.

Utah Agricultural College (now Utah State University) Extension Service meeting with Ute women, Uintah Basin Industrial convention, Uintah County, 1927.

the intelligent adjustments of any business. Record keeping will encourage careful systematic planning for production and consumption."[113] Statements like these, made by farm women in significant positions of leadership, indicate a firm acceptance of the values introduced only decades before. Ellen A. Huntington, in her 1910 address to farmers' institute audiences entitled "Woman's Life on the Farm," had stated: "In this twentieth century, housekeeping on the farm is not essentially different from that in the city."[114] It had been less an observation than a hope. Three decades later, it was fact. The farm wife had become a "household manager," a consumer, and a believer in planning and education. It seems only just to leave the last word to one of those many experts who had brought her to this point. Angelyn Warnick, examining vocational homemaking education in Utah in 1939, summed up the dramatic changes of the recent decades thus: "In the past when life was simpler and each generation lived in basically the same manner as the preceding, customs and traditions, hand[ed] down from mother to daughter and father to son, dictated the solution to family problems. . . . Now daughters spend their days in school or in industry and the school must supplement the home in preparing them for homemaking responsibilities. The home, formerly a producing center, has become a consuming unit and the problem is less that of construction and more that of management of all of the resources of the family. Modern families are more influenced by outside factors. Transportation and radio brings [sic] the world to the door of every home."[115]

Notes

1. Utah State Farmers' Institutes, *Annual Report,* No. 9 (Logan: Utah Agricultural College, 1906), 50.

2. See the 1909 "Report of the Country Life Commission," sponsored and signed by President Theodore Roosevelt, in Wayne D. Rasmussen, ed., *Agriculture in the United States: A Documentary History, Vol. 2: 1860–1906* (New York: Random House, 1975), 1860–1906. The report notes the impact of the lack of labor-saving devices on farm women (pp. 1890, 1892).

3. Many farmers had to wait until creation of the Rural Electrification Administration (REA) during the New Deal to have access to electricity. See Audra J. Wolfe, "'How Not to Electrocute the Farmer': Assessing Attitudes Toward Electrification on American Farms, 1920–1940," *Agricultural History* 74 (2000): 515–29, for a useful examination of responses to rural electrification efforts. Mary Ann Beecher, "Building for 'Mrs. Farmer': Published Farmhouse Designs and the Role of the Rural Female Consumer, 1900–1930," *Agricultural History* 73 (1999): 253, estimates that "only 10 to 25 percent of all farmhouses were equipped with electricity and running water" in the early twentieth century, with only 27 percent enjoying electricity by 1926.

4. Utah Agricultural College, *The Organization and Course of Instruction of the Agricultural College of Utah, 1890–1891* (Logan: Utah Agricultural College, 1890), 21–22; hereafter cited as Utah Agricultural College, *Catalog,* by relevant year.

5. Joel Edward Ricks, *The Utah Agricultural College: A History of Fifty Years* (Salt Lake City: Deseret News Press, 1938), 26, 32.

6. Utah Agricultural College, *Catalog,* 1928–29, 31.

7. Ibid., 1911–12, 5–10.

8. Ibid., 1928–29, 31.

9. Ibid., 1914–15, 45.

10. Ibid., 175.

11. Utah State Agricultural College, Home Economics Practice House, *Extension Service Bulletin,* 18, no. 1 (Logan: Utah Agricultural College, 1918).

12. Utah Agricultural College, *Catalog,* 1919–20, 10–14, 20.

13. Ibid., 1928–29, 31.

14. Ibid., 221, 246.

15. Ibid., 64.

16. The law authorizing the institute movement was printed as the frontispiece to the yearly publication of papers presented. For a typical example, see Utah State Farmers' Institute, *Annual Report* No. 9 (Logan: Utah Agricultural College, 1906), not paginated.

17. Roy V. Scott, *The Reluctant Farmer: The Rise of Agricultural Extension to 1914* (Urbana: University of Illinois Press, 1970), 87, 64–103.

18. Rasmussen, *Agriculture in the United States,* 1312.

19. Ibid., 1314.

20. Marilyn Irvin Holt, *Linoleum, Better Babies, and the Modern Farm Woman, 1890–1930* (Albuquerque: University of New Mexico Press, 1995), 45.

21. Utah State Farm Institute, *Annual Report*, 1906, 6–7; 1907, 5; 1908, 6.

22. One of the many notices for such gatherings appears in the *Utah Farmer*, February 5, 1916, 10.

23. Ibid., January 19, 1921, 1.

24. Utah State Farm Institute, *Annual Report*, No. 13, 1910, 8–9.

25. Utah Agricultural College, *Catalog*, 1925–26, 78–79.

26. See especially Scott, *The Reluctant Farmer*, 206–37, for a discussion of early extension work in the southern United States.

27. Utah Agricultural College, *Twenty-Five Years of Extension*, Extension Circular No. 104 (Logan: Utah Agricultural College, 1939), 3–4.

28. Ibid., 6.

29. Holt, *Linoleum, Better Babies, and the Modern Farm Woman*, 56–57 discusses the background of some early agents. While their role is still understudied, a useful contribution is Kathleen R. Babbitt, "The Productive Farm Woman and the Extension Home Economist in New York State, 1920–1940," *Agricultural History* 67 (1993): 83–101.

30. William J. Block, *The Separation of the Farm Bureau and the Extension Service: Political Issue in a Federal System* (Urbana: University of Illinois Press, 1960), offers a detailed discussion of the involvement between this federal agency and the farmers' organization. A more recent examination, which includes a helpful discussion of women's roles, is Nancy K. Berlage, "Organizing the Farm Bureau: Farm, Community, and Professionals, 1914–1928," *Agricultural History* 75 (2001): 438–69.

31. V. Allen Olsen, *As Farmers Forward Go: A History of the Utah Farm Bureau Federation* (Salt Lake City: Utah Farm Bureau Federation, 1975) is the official history of the state body.

32. Utah State Farm Bureau Federation, *The Utah Farm Bureau Federation and Its Activities: You and Your Neighbor—That's All It Is* (n.p., 1923), 11.

33. Utah Agricultural College, *Catalog*, 1920–21, 53.

34. Utah Farm Bureau Federation, *You and Your Neighbor*, 20.

35. Utah Agricultural College, *Twenty-five Years*, 13.

36. Olsen, *As Farmers Forward Go*, 11.

37. An excellent discussion of this process is Stuart Ewen, *Captains of Consciousness: Advertising and the Social Roots of the Consumer Culture* (New York: McGraw-Hill Book, 1976).

38. *Utah Farmer*, September 11, 1915, 13; August 7, 1915, 10.

39. Utah Agricultural College, *Catalog*, 1919–20, 228.

40. Ibid., 1925–26, 228.

41. Ibid., 1920–21, 68–69.

42. Utah Agricultural College, *Twenty-five Years*, 10. See Holt, *Linoleum, Better Babies, and the Modern Farm Woman*, 165–66, for examples beyond Utah.

43. *1941 Annual Cooperative Service Report: Sevier County, Utah* (Logan: University Extension Service, 1921), 25.

44. Utah Agricultural College, *Catalog,* 1920–21, 20.

45. Ibid., 1928–29, 246.

46. Ibid., 1920–21, 53.

47. *Utah Farmer,* May 9, 1925, 2.

48. An effective discussion of the Country Life Reform Movement and the farm experience can be found in David B. Danbom, *The Resisted Revolution: Urban America and the Industrialization of Agriculture, 1900–1930* (Ames: Iowa State University Press, 1979).

49. William Peterson, "Women Play Major Part in Rural Advancement," *Utah Farmer,* February 14, 1925, 23.

50. Advertisement, ibid., August 23, 1919, 7.

51. "The Home Is the Heart of the Farm," ibid., May 14, 1921, 1.

52. "Improving Rural Landscapes," *Utah Magazine,* April 1941, 37.

53. *Utah Farmer,* August 30, 1919, 9.

54. U.S. Bureau of the Census, *Fifteenth Census of the United States, 1930: Population,* 6:1340.

55. *Utah Farmer,* July 1, 1916, 10; *Deseret Farmer,* July 22, 1911, 4.

56. "What Should [a] Housewife's Salary Be?" *Utah Farmer,* April 9, 1921, 8.

57. Alice Ravenhill, *Labor-Saving Devices in the Household,* Utah Agricultural College Experiment Station Circular No. 6 (Logan: Utah Agricultural College Extension Service, 1912), 3–4.

58. Rose H. Widtsoe, "Efficient Household Purchasing," *Utah Farmer,* February 28, 1920, 15.

59. Ibid., March 6, 1920, 6.

60. *Deseret Farmer,* July 22, 1911, 4.

61. For example, Professor Alice Ravenhill was described as "an international authority on nutrition and child study" in an advertisement for the Utah Agricultural College Summer School which appeared in the *Utah Farmer,* May 18, 1918, 9. See also ibid., January 24, 1925, 3.

62. Utah Agricultural College, *Catalog,* 1890–91, 21.

63. Ibid., 1916–17, 95–96.

64. Ibid., 99–100.

65. Ibid., 1925–26, 71–72.

66. Utah Agricultural College, *Practice House,* 5.

67. "The Electrified Farm House," *Utah Farmer,* December 11, 1915, 16.

68. Ibid., July 20, 1918, 16.

69. Ibid., 5.

70. Advertisement, ibid., January 10, 1925, 9.

71. Advertisement, ibid., April 3, 1920, 11.

72. Advertisement, ibid., July 20, 1918, 5.

73. Advertisement, ibid., June 13, 1925, 15.

74. Advertisement, ibid., June 6, 1925, 11.

75. Ravenhill, *Labor-Saving Devices in the Household,* 13–23, 45.

76. Utah Agricultural College, *Catalog,* 1920–21, 57.

77. *Utah Farmer,* June 24, 1916, 10.

78. Utah State Farm Institute, *Annual Report,* No. 13 (1910): 106–7.

79. Angelyn Warnick, *A Survey of the Need for Vocational Homemaking Education in Utah* (N.p., 1939), 7.

80. Utah Power and Light Company, the Western Colorado Power Company, Bountiful Light and Power Company, *Farm Electrification Manual* (n.p., 1936), not paginated.

81. Ravenhill, *Labor-Saving Devices in the Household,* 3, 6.

82. *Deseret Farmer,* August 27, 1910, 13.

83. Utah State Farm Institute, *Annual Report,* No. 9, 1906, 6–7; No. 11, 1908, 6; No. 12, 1909, 22. This disparity between male and female attendance was typical nationwide; see Scott, *The Reluctant Farmer,* 120–21.

84. *Deseret Farmer,* August 27, 1910, 5.

85. Ibid., December 3, 1910, 4.

86. Leah D. Widtsoe, *Labor-Saving Devices for the Farm Home,* Experiment Station Circular, No. 6 (Logan: Utah Agricultural College, 1912), 42.

87. Utah State Farm Institute, *Annual Report,* No. 13, 1910, 108.

88. Widtsoe, *Labor-Saving Devices for the Farm Home,* 42.

89. Ibid., 43.

90. Widtsoe hoped that passage of a bill proposed by Utah Senator Reed Smoot allocating additional funds for home economics research would be directed toward such reforms. Widstoe, *Labor-Saving Devices for the Farm Home,* 76.

91. U.S. Bureau of the Census, *Fifteenth Census of the United States, 1930: Population,* 2:13–15.

92. U.S. Bureau of the Census, *Fifteenth Census of the United States, 1930: Population,* 1:16–17. Isolation and distance from major population centers was a key concern for many farm families well into the twentieth century. Utahns were an important exception, however. According to the 1930 census, the largest percentage of the state's farms (roughly 67 percent) were located in six counties: Utah (18.3 percent), Salt Lake (14.1 percent), Davis (8.9 percent), Weber (8.9 percent), Cache (8.7 percent), and Box Elder (7.8 percent). Yet these were not predominantly agricultural counties. Therefore, the bulk of the state's farmers lived relatively close to urban centers. Ibid., 6:1343.

93. Utah Power and Light Company, *Electrifying the Wheels of Progress, 1912–1922* (N.p., 1922), 12–14, 21.

94. Utah Power and Light Company, *A Prophecy Fulfilled* (N.p., 1949). Its map, located between pages 16–17, shows areas of Utah served in 1922.

95. U.S. Department of Commerce, Bureau of the Census, *Census of Agriculture, 1954,* vol. 1, pt. 31, p. 3.

96. Joseph A. Geddes, *Farm Versus Village Living in Utah: Plain City—Type "A" Village,* Extension Bulletin No. 249 (Logan: Utah Agricultural College, 1934), 62.

97.   Ibid., 12.

98.   Utah Power and Light Company, *Electrifying the Wheels*, 21.

99.   U.S. Department of Commerce, Bureau of the Census, *Fifteenth Census, 1930: Population*, 6:1345; U.S. Department of Commerce, Bureau of the Census, *Census of Agriculture, 1954*, vol. 1, pt. 31, p. 3.

100.   U.S. Department of Commerce, Bureau of the Census, *Fifteenth Census, 1930: Population*, 6:33, 53.

101.   U.S. Department of Commerce, Bureau of the Census, *Census of Agriculture, 1954*, vol. 1, pt. 31, p. 3.

102.   Ibid.

103.   Utah Agricultural College, *Catalog*, 1913–14, 42.

104.   Bernard D. Joy and D. P. Murray, *Situations, Problems, and Interests of Unmarried Rural Young People 16–25 Years of Age—Utah*, Extension Circular No. 282 (Logan: Utah Agricultural Extension Service, 1938), 23–24.

105.   Ibid.

106.   Ibid., 12.

107.   Warnick, *A Survey of the Need*, 4.

108.   Wilford D. Porter, "Building Better Farms," *Utah Magazine* August 1941, 33.

109.   Utah Agricultural College, *Catalog*, 1947–48, 28–29.

110.   Almeda Perry Brown, *Food Habits of Utah Farm Families*, Extension Bulletin 213 (Logan: Utah Agricultural Extension Service, 1929), 8.

111.   Edith Hayball and W. Preston Thomas, *Family Living Expenditures, Summit County, Utah*, Extension Bulletin No. 232 (Logan: Utah Agricultural Extension Sevier County, 1930), 5, 21.

112.   Utah State University, *County Agricultural Planning Activities in Utah, 1937* (Logan: Utah Agricultural Extension Service, 1937), 2. The page cited is from Utah County.

113.   Utah State University, *County Agricultural Planning Activities in Utah, 1941* (Logan: Utah Agricultural Extension Service, 1937), 156. The page cited is from Iron County.

114.   Utah State Farm Institute, *Annual Report*, No. 13, 1910, 104.

115.   Warnick, *A Survey of the Need*, 7.

6

Gainfully Employed Women

1896–1950

Miriam B. Murphy

In the seventeenth century, women wage earners were primarily domestic servants. Following European traditions, American women did not usually hold land or have access to apprenticeships that could have provided skills leading to economic independence. Nevertheless, the idea of a man supporting his wife was not commonly accepted, for "husband and wife were . . . mutually dependent and together supported the children." The colonial wife used her physical stamina to produce "household necessities and ply . . . her crafts and her plow beside a yeoman husband."[1]

In the change from an agrarian economy to a balance of farming and manufacturing in the Revolutionary War period, the work of women became critical. Women from all levels of society labored in support of this war as they would in subsequent wars involving U.S. troops. Following the war for independence, urban poor women and surplus farm women were sought as factory workers. However, confusing messages produced confusing role perceptions. Home and family were to remain the centerpieces of their lives. Yet America's lack of an adequate supply of workers and ongoing need for cheap labor required that women become the first industrial proletariat.[2]

With the development of factories and mills, men like Alexander Hamilton saw mercantilism as the helpmeet to agriculture, with industry providing jobs for farm wives and children. Factories would also absorb the idle and dependent, making them productive members of society. With the decline in home manufacture of many items, farm women had the time to accept either "given out" work (clothes to be sewed at home from cutout patterns, for example) or to spend their days at nearby mills or factories.

The large number of women working in factories and mills challenged basic assumptions about the role of women in society and led, among other things, to the beginning of class differences between women who had to work for their own or their family's survival and those who did not, paternalism, and public reaction against women who organized or went out on strike to better working conditions and wages.

With increasing urbanization and higher factory productivity, upper-class women—most often native-born whites—no longer needed to contribute their wage labor to ensure the financial security of home and family; but poorer women—especially widows, free blacks, immigrants, and rural women who moved to the cities in search of jobs—had no choice. Female wage earners, "whether they worked inside or outside their homes . . . fulfilled the hopes of the most ardent Hamiltonians. They constituted the essential core of industrial development."[3] By 1840 some 65 percent of the industrial workers in New England were women, while in the less industrialized South, 10 percent of free white women worked in industry. Despite the regional disparity, half of all workers employed in manufacturing in America were women.

As industrialization moved ahead, fueled in large measure by female labor, something else was affecting women's lives in the first half of the nineteenth century. Social mores were changing, and a new domestic code embracing the old Puritan ethic and laissez-faire economics was becoming a powerful force. While this new outlook encouraged men to develop competitive, individualistic attitudes and to look for greater economic success, it offered women very constricted roles. Pious, nurturing, submissive creatures, they were to provide males with emotional support, make the home a refuge, and guard society's moral values. Homemaking came to be viewed as a profession requiring training, and women became almost the sole supervisors of children with men gone from home for long hours trying to climb the economic ladder.

Although the domestic code could mean little to new immigrants, blacks, and other women for whom work was a necessity, society's "sympathetic perceptions of women wage earners sacrificing for the sake of their families gave way to charges of selfishness and family neglect." Women workers were very adversely affected. They did not stop working—most of them could not afford to—but "the belief that women belonged at home permitted employers to pay wages that were merely supplemental," justified men in discriminating against their female co-workers, increased job stereotyping, and thwarted the efforts of women to unionize for their mutual benefit.[4]

Middle-class, non-wage-earning women failed to understand or support their working sisters. Myths arose: The workplace was more dangerous for women than men and would harm future mothers and their unborn children. Women would find it difficult to overcome the temptation to sin. Marriage would solve all or most of the problems of women. Governments often collaborated in such myths by passing legislation that restricted the roles of women at work, thereby confining them to the lowest rungs on the economic ladder.

Nevertheless, after 1880 married women began entering the work force in greater numbers for several reasons: smaller households, lower birthrates, and technology that displaced domestic help. As a by-product of the new technology, married women became more isolated in their homes, and the more affluent of them became bored. Young unmarried women began looking for work and aspired to new goals. Professions like medicine and anthropology attracted women, and education at the college level became more accessible. Despite these changes, at the end of the nineteenth century, notions of woman's place in the home and the temporary nature of female employment were solidly entrenched. Such ideas channeled most women into a few slots in the work force and, instead of providing them with the safe, clean jobs talked of in state legislatures and union halls, reduced them to working under some of the worst conditions of any wage earners.

Necessarily brief, this overview provides at least some context for examining the economic role of women in Utah.

From the beginning of permanent white settlement in the mid-1800s to the turn of the century, Utah experienced a gradual shift from a frontier economy based primarily on agriculture to the mixed economy of a developing agricultural-commercial-industrial state. The role of women in that transformation resembled that of women in other parts of westering America.[5]

In the first stage of settlement in Utah the individual family formed the basic economic unit of most towns. Husband, wife, and children worked together to build the family dwelling, raise food, and make or barter for as many of the other necessities of life as possible. Some Mormon women assumed larger roles in the home economic unit when polygamy required them to share a husband or when missionary work took him from home for prolonged periods. Polygamy and evangelism aside, the frontier farm home as the center of economic activity was essentially the same in Salt Lake City, Cache Valley, and Parowan as it had been in colonial New England; however, transformation occurred much more rapidly in Utah.[6]

Almost as soon as a new settlement was firmly rooted, it began to change. Individuals with special skills—dressmaking and teaching, tinsmithing, and bricklaying, for instance—found outlets for their talents and began altering the character of the town. Structures to house fledgling businesses and industries were erected along dozens of Main Streets from Kamas to Kanab. As these businesses became increasingly important, the economic life of most towns no longer rested entirely on more or less self-sufficient (although interdependent) farm families.

Once begun, the breakdown of the family economic unit continued apace. As commercialization and urbanization increased, the family and its activities became divided. Some women participated in the shifting economy by opening millinery and dress shops or running boardinghouses and small hotels. A few entered the professions. Some continued to work alongside their husbands by becoming active partners in a family business. Young unmarried women became clerks, telegraph operators, and office workers, while other women and girls—especially the foreign-born and black—entered domestic service and worked in factories and laundries. The number of women working outside the home increased each decade from 1850 to 1900, with economic necessity as the principal factor propelling them toward gainful employment. Yet society consistently undervalued the contribution of women to the economic development of cities and towns. Furthermore, no matter how vital her wages were to the survival of her family, the female domestic or factory worker of the late nineteenth century never enjoyed the status of the sturdy farm wife of frontier fame.

By the turn of the century, the pattern of most working women's lives in Utah was largely set by national events and trends. War and peace, depression and prosperity dictated the circumstances of daily life, while social theorists and the arbiters of social convention defined the proper role of women whether they lived in Buffalo, Memphis, or Ogden. The dynamic interplay of national forces with the particular conditions found in urban and rural Utah has affected working women from 1900 to the present. This chapter focuses on the contributions of gainfully employed women in Utah, the conditions of their employment, and their place in the larger regional and national context. Special attention is paid to women in business and industry during the first half of the twentieth century, with other female workers mentioned in passing to show the total employment picture.

Change and Opportunity, 1896–1920

The quarter-century from statehood in 1896 through the first two decades of the twentieth century may have produced more dramatic changes and opportunities for women than any comparable period in Utah history. The events leading up to statehood brought at least to an official end the practice of polygamy, and the state constitution restored women's right to vote and guaranteed other equal rights. Laws enacted in 1911 and 1913 set maximum hours (fifty-four per week) and minimum wages ($1.25 per day). A workmen's compensation law was finally passed in 1917.

In addition, technology dramatically altered women's lives, especially in urban areas. Electric service, indoor plumbing, central heating, and the small power motor revolutionized homemaking. The growth of commercial laundries and expanding factory production of clothing, processed foods, and other household items relieved women of many tasks and created hundreds of jobs for them outside the home. Although agriculture and mining dominated the economic life of the state, manufacturing, retail and wholesale trade, banking, and services were growing rapidly. The success of many of these ventures depended on women.

Utah was not a major manufacturing state, but it boasted a larger and more diverse list of manufacturers than most of the Mountain West. During these years, Ogden, for example, became a center for the canning industry, and

Interior of the shipping room, J.G. McDonald Chocolate Company, Salt Lake City, July 6, 1911.

by 1914 Utah ranked fifth among the states in canning. World War I stimulated further growth of this industry when twenty-two Ogden canneries secured government contracts.[7] The development of the canning industry hinged on the availability of female workers. Many were young unmarried women, but the seasonal nature of canning operations also attracted married women who could join the work force for a while without permanently altering their domestic arrangements. A majority of these women were apparently not recorded as workers by the census. The Utah Manufacturers Association (UMA) reported 1,715 employees in thirty-five canneries in August 1913, but the 1910 census showed only fifty-eight cannery workers in the state, thirty-six of them male; the 1920 census fell far short of the UMA figures, too. The UMA defined canning as "light" work that could be "done as well by women and children as by men." Tomatoes topped the list of canned items. Jets of hot steam followed by a cold spray loosened the skins so that a girl could peel fourteen to sixteen bushels a day. "Girls" helped to produce over 600,000 cases of Utah canned foods in 1913.[8]

 Candy was a logical by-product of Utah's booming sugarbeet industry. By 1916 Utah ranked third in the nation in sugar production, and Utah's candies were being exported to such distant places as Tokyo. The number of women working in candy factories more than doubled between 1910 and 1920, rising from 178 to 459, according to the census. However, these figures

Millinery store in Moab run by "Cap's" mother who was a member of the Taylor family. She is on the right of Philander Maxwell, Sr., ca. 1910.

are probably low since, like canning, candy making has seasonal peaks that require part-time or temporary workers—most likely women—who may have eluded the census net. The J. G. McDonald Candy Company in Salt Lake City employed some 400 workers in 1914 in a new factory that featured a roof garden where employees took breaks. McDonald's was one of the twenty-one wholesale and manufacturing confectioners along the Wasatch Front. At least one of these firms, the Miriam Brooks Candy Company, had a woman in top management.[9]

Textile mills and clothing factories continued to be major employers of women in the United States until outsourcing sent many such jobs to Third World countries later in the twentieth century. Historically, thousands of women

Whitaker & Dallas Cigar Factory (located in Salt Lake City) interior showing cigars being made, May 24,1905.

contracted to do piece work at home or were self-employed as dressmakers, seamstresses, tailoresses, and milliners. The self-employed sometimes parlayed their talents into business careers, opening small retail clothing shops in almost every city or town. In 1900 female dressmakers and seamstresses working outside of factories totaled 1,533 in Utah, while milliners and millinery dealers totaled 277. These numbers rose in 1910 but by 1920 had dropped to 759 and 219 respectively. However, as further evidence of Utah's continuing industrialization, the number of women working in textile mills and clothing factories rose from a reported 278 in 1900 to 553 in 1920. Underwear and work clothes were among the finished goods that found a market out of state, especially in mining towns.[10]

The ZCMI clothing factory, which shipped its overalls, jumpers, and other heavy cotton wear throughout the West and into Canada and Mexico, was managed by Annie H. Bywater, probably the most important woman in Utah manufacturing. Trained in the industrial center of Manchester, England, she was associated with ZCMI for many years and was described by the UMA as "a remarkably shrewd woman, with exceptional executive ability." She supervised a production line of 100 power-driven sewing machines, bought all the material used by the factory, and personally directed the filling of all the wholesale orders.[11]

Whether Bywater received compensation comparable to male manufacturing executives is not known, but most female factory workers did

Telephone operators, Mountain States Telephone and Telegraph Company, Salt Lake City, February 3, 1945.

not. The Utah Manufacturers Association, in an article on the knitting industry, noted that in 1915 Utah had thirteen knitting factories employing nearly 300 workers—mostly young women who earned an average of $9.00 for a six-day week, $1.50 above the legal minimum for women. Men employed in the same factories earned an average of $17.00 a week, according to the UMA, which did not comment on the disparity.[12]

By 1920 the variety of products women were helping to make in factories included, among others, chemicals, soap, cigars, crackers and other baked goods, and sugar. Women also continued to be an important factor in the printing and publishing business where one out of every seven workers was a woman in 1920. Females had begun working as compositors as early as the 1880s when the *Salt Lake Herald* employed Sadie Asper. Asper and another woman, Mrs. E. E. Sylvester, served for a time as officers in the Salt Lake Typographical Union, Local 115.[13]

In all, the number of women engaged in manufacturing and mechanical pursuits in Utah rose less than 10 percent between 1900 when 2,440 such workers were counted and 1920 when the census enumerated 2,667. However, the most significant fact concerning these women is not their number but the nature of their work and the work place. The individual dressmaker working out of her home was disappearing. Almost 800 abandoned this occupation, most of them in the 1910–20 decade. Nevertheless, the number of women in manufacturing grew. The growth of factory work for women was so rapid in the early twentieth century that it easily absorbed the loss of dressmakers. Fully a thousand new jobs were created for women in manufacturing and mechanical industries located primarily along the Wasatch Front.[14] Additionally, some one thousand female workers may have gone uncounted by the census because of the seasonal or part-time employment already discussed. Except in agriculture, gainful employment for women at home was rapidly diminishing in importance.

It is difficult to appraise the role of women in agriculture. The number of female farmers and farm laborers in Utah declined from 1,013 to 887 between 1900 and 1920, but these census figures do not reflect the actual contribution of women to agriculture. The census reveals only how many women owned or operated farms or were paid laborers in farming. Although most farms were run by families and required the daily work of each family member, only the farm husband and hired hands were likely to be listed as gainfully employed by the census. The farm wife—who may have raised poultry and garden crops, made and sold dairy products, and kept the farm accounts in addition to managing the household, rearing the children, and assisting with seasonal farm chores— was seldom listed as employed by the census. Yet it seems obvious that her labor included an economic component lacking in the tasks of many urban housewives.

Rural farm women were among the last to benefit from electric service and improved household technology. As a result, their lifestyles changed more slowly than those of urban and rural nonfarm women. Because their work was essential to the success of the total farm operation, they seldom looked for employment elsewhere, although many of their daughters did. The census notwithstanding, agriculture was no doubt the principal occupation of Utah women in the first two decades of the twentieth century, just as it had been during the last of the nineteenth.[15]

Although a majority of Utahns still lived in rural areas in 1920, the margin was dwindling. Urbanization was proceeding at a steady pace. At the turn of the century 61.9 percent of the population was rural. A dramatic shift in the first decade of the twentieth century dropped the rural percentage to 53.7. This movement slowed in the 1910s, but by 1920 Utah's urban areas had attracted 48 percent of the population and, in the next decade, would take the lead. Nowhere was urban growth more visible than in downtown Salt Lake City where more than fifty major office buildings, warehouses, hotels and apartments, and other business and civic buildings were erected between 1900 and 1920. While hundreds of women found work in Utah's new factories, many more found employment in communications, retail stores, and hotels in developing cities and towns throughout the state.[16]

Women's role in communications began in the 1860s when young single women as well as young men were trained as telegraph operators at the suggestion of Brigham Young. The telegraph remained an important link in the communications network in Utah in 1910 with 32 female and 215 male operators, numbers that had increased to 127 females and 250 males by 1920. But the telephone was gaining preference for many personal messages and was indispensable in intracity business transactions. From the beginning, women predominated as telephone operators. Only 23 males were Utah telephone operators in 1910 and 29 in 1920, while women operators in the state increased from 427 to 745 in the same period. Yet despite their early and persistent work in this field, few women advanced beyond the lowest supervisory positions.[17]

The jobs created for women by the expanding telephone system were among the 2,590 new positions women found in trade and transportation between 1900 and 1920. Job opportunities for women in these fields tripled in the first two decades of the twentieth century and doubled for men. That women found increased employment in retail stores is hardly surprising. By 1920 Utah's population stood at 449,396, having grown almost 60 percent since 1900. Immigration, especially of southern Europeans who came to work in mines and smelters and for the railroad, plus the highest birthrate since 1880, fueled the population growth. Growth, in turn created a demand for additional goods and services. By 1920 women filled 2,059 sales positions and 580 jobs as store clerks. They also found work in insurance, banking, and real estate. In addition, at least 223 women owned or managed retail businesses, a figure that may not include women who were co-owners of family enterprises.[18]

In the professions, the number of women more than doubled between the turn of the century and 1910 and increased by another 26 percent by 1920. Most of these women were concentrated in the fields of teaching and nursing. However, several hundred pursued careers in the visual, literary, and performing arts. The number of female physicians and surgeons dropped from a high of 55 in 1910 to 22 in 1920, while male physicians dropped from 481 to 439. Stricter professional standards may have prevented some practitioners from hanging out their shingles; but in the case of women, conditions that had encouraged them, especially in the developing West of the nineteenth century, had changed. Additionally, women's medical colleges had closed and coeducational institutions had begun limiting the percentage of female applicants accepted for medical school.[19]

Of the almost 2,900 new positions women found in professional fields during the first two decades of the twentieth century, more than 60 percent were as schoolteachers. That figure is not surprising in light of a school enrollment that had grown 140 percent in twenty years. With women averaging only five years in teaching, replacements were needed for one-fifth of the women teachers every year, a challenge the state's colleges and the normal school at Cedar City were hard pressed to meet. Low salaries and the failure of local school boards to implement an 1896 state law mandating equal pay for female and male public schoolteachers accounted for much of the turnover. Rather than fight for their turf, women abandoned it. Many, according to the Utah Education Association, found greater financial rewards in office employment.[20]

Whether they were former teachers looking for better pay or high school graduates who had taken classes in typing, shorthand, and bookkeeping, office workers were usually young, single, native-born white women. Office work appealed to them for very good reasons: "It was cleaner and less strenuous than factory work, and socially much more acceptable. Workers were paid a weekly salary rather than hourly wages, and work tended to be regular, layoffs less frequent." Equally important, no doubt, it put young women into legitimate contact with men, including potential husbands. Although some women encountered unfavorable working conditions—long hours, low pay, and sexual harassment—most did not.[21]

By 1900 women had gained a solid foothold in business offices, although 40 percent of the stenographers and typists were still men in 1900, and men outnumbered women as bookkeepers, accountants, and clerks. Women filled only 518 positions in these five job categories in Utah in 1900, but twenty years later their numbers had increased eightfold to 4,168. Utah enjoyed "unprecedented prosperity" until the end of World War I, and the heightened business and commercial activity of those years is reflected in the phenomenal growth of office jobs for women. No matter that most of these positions offered little opportunity for advancement, for few women thought of competing with men for promotion in the office hierarchy. The office, more than most other work places, mirrored for many employees a pattern of socialization (the patriarchal family) that they accepted with little question, then and for many years to come.[22]

About a fourth of all gainfully employed women in Utah in 1920 found work in domestic and personal service. Although this category had increased from 4,519 female workers in 1900 to 5,458 by 1920, it could not keep pace with the growth of other occupational fields for women. During this twenty-year span, the number of servants declined by 600. Young women were refusing to enter such a low-paying, low-status occupation. Instead, they harkened to the whistles of commercial laundries or the clatter of dishes in the fast-growing cafe and restaurant business. The dozen new hotels in Salt Lake City gave hundreds of women jobs making beds and cleaning rooms. Although the tasks were similar to those performed in private homes by domestic servants, the pay was generally better for hotel workers and they were not on call twenty-four hours a day. Service workers outside of private homes also found greatly increased opportunities for socializing, even in the physically demanding environment of a steam laundry. They also encountered union activity.[23]

During the first decades of the twentieth century "strong union organization and a high degree of job control . . . were . . . major features of skilled occupations in Salt Lake City and Ogden."[24] Union activity was especially intense in the 1910–20 decade. In April 1911 an estimated two thousand people paraded in Salt Lake City in support of the laundry workers' drive to achieve union recognition. Almost one-fourth of the seven hundred laundry workers went out on strike. The Crystal Laundry signed a closed-shop agreement with the union, and in May the remaining laundries agreed not to discriminate against union members.[25]

Other unions had a more difficult time establishing themselves. On January 15, 1910, female employees of the McDonald Candy Company, claimed they were "underpaid considering the high price of living" and petitioned management for higher wages. When the company denied their request, the women returned to work; but when a foreman insulted them, they walked off the job and, with the help of union official J. G. Wilks and others, organized the Chocolate Dippers Union of Utah #1 with Sarah Rindfleish as president. The women wanted a flat $10 wage per week for eight-hour work days. However, while the chocolate workers were organizing, helpers at the McDonald's factory, typically girls age twelve to fifteen, replaced the strikers. The Utah State Federation of Labor and the Salt Lake Federation of Labor raised funds to help the chocolate dippers and asked all union members to refrain from buying McDonald products. There is no evidence that a boycott actually occurred or that the company policy was changed.[26]

The most significant union activity involving women occurred after World War I when the Culinary Alliance succeeded in closing most of the restaurants in Salt Lake City as union members walked off the job at 6:00 P.M. on May 1, 1919. The union demanded "straight eight-hour shifts" with a twenty-minute break for a meal instead of the split shifts they typically worked. Dishwashers, vegetable peelers, and other miscellaneous male restaurant workers wanted a wage of $2.50 per shift, and the union asked "that female waitresses be granted a minimum scale of $2.25 per shift." According to the *Salt Lake Tribune*, employers were willing to accede to the $2.25 wage for waitresses but countered the other demands with offers of their own. As the strike dragged on—because of "the union's insistence on a closed-shop agreement"—the publicity ended up helping Utah Associated Industries, an employers' organization, in its effort to promote the American Plan (open shop) as the standard in Utah.[27]

Unfortunately for union workers, 1919 was a watershed year in Utah. Radical elements appeared to be taking over the labor movement, triggering a backlash that effectively destroyed all that labor had gained in several decades of organizing efforts. The long-range effect of this collapse on the Utah work environment is difficult to assess.

As women became more visible in the work force, they became a subject for editorial comment. Locally, a Mormon periodical, the *Young*

Woman's Journal (1889–1929) displayed ambivalent attitudes toward women's roles in society during this period. A series of articles in 1891–92 discussed in rather heady language the opportunities for young LDS women in such fields as dentistry ("there is no good reason . . . why our girls should not crowd out the men from this easy, lucrative and fairly clean business") and law. Stenography and typewriting were seen as "sedentary" occupations for girls who wanted to "dress up and look always 'sweet' and now-a-days that is a great thing." As for merchandising, girls were advised to set their sights above a small millinery or candy shop and plan to own a general merchandise store. However, this series, "Professions and Business Opportunities for Women," cannot be considered typical of LDS thought. The avowed purpose was to solve a perceived "surplus women problem" since polygamy had officially ended. The editorial page more accurately reflected Mormon values: God intended girls to become homemakers. Their math studies should prepare them for keeping domestic rather than commercial accounts. If misfortune kept a woman from marriage and motherhood there would be "time enough then to study the occult sciences [chemistry!] and dabble in stocks and real estate."[28]

Later articles in the *Young Woman's Journal* focused more realistically on women in industry and business rather than professions like dentistry and law. Girls were told how to prepare themselves for office work and how to conduct themselves on the job. Home and family remained "the big job" for young women to prepare themselves for, but office work could be a training ground of sorts for the responsibilities of marriage and something to fall back on should a woman need to earn a living later in life.[29]

The Mormon attitude toward women who chose a career over marriage—or worse, perhaps, tried to combine them—fit right in the midstream of American thinking on this volatile topic. Nationally, even reformers like Florence Kelley worked to block "any programs that might have encouraged the employment of married women, such as day nurseries, charitably run kindergartens, or cash relief payments contingent upon women's accepting any available work."[30] The working wife and mother might be decried from the pulpit and lecture platform and have many obstacles placed in her path, but she was part of a "long range shift in the female work force from young, single women to older, married women workers."[31]

When the working mother could define her job as a matter of survival, rather than a social or political statement, she sometimes found allies. That was the case in 1894 when Emma McVicker, a prominent educator and state school superintendent during 1900–01, and other women leaders organized the Free Kindergarten Association that evolved into the Neighborhood House serving the west side of Salt Lake City. In addition to the kindergarten, Neighborhood House offered a day nursery, a library, sewing and other domestic classes, and club activities for girls, boys, and mothers. The program won support from all segments of society and even received a small yearly grant from the state.[32]

Over the years, Neighborhood House outgrew its facility several times. It clearly filled a need in the lives of some working women, as its history notes: "During 1915–1916, the day nursery department . . . had a remarkable increase. Mothers engaged in work, were coming to appreciate the privilege of leaving their infants in the care of competent nurses. A charge of ten cents a day for each child was asked by the association if the mother could afford it, if not, the child was cared for regardless of circumstances."[33]

Neighborhood House was "strained to the utmost" during World War I to meet the demands placed on it, but individuals came forward with donations of time and money so that services could continue to grow.[34] The broad support that Neighborhood House found in Salt Lake City did not, of course, signal a change in society's attitude toward working mothers. Rather, the community recognized a specific need in a specific place and responded appropriately.

The twenty-five-year span that began with statehood and the equal rights section in the Utah State Constitution and ended with ratification of the Nineteenth Amendment to the U.S. Constitution brought many dramatic changes to women's lives. Technology altered both the home and the work place. Urbanization and industrialization encouraged many rural dwellers, especially single women, to seek new lifestyles in cities and towns where automobiles, bobbed hair, and the fox-trot seemed to be ushering in a new age. More women found work outside the home, and more of them continued their education beyond high school. Although it is tempting to label these changes revolutionary, they were, in the main, evolutionary. Many changes had arrived on the wings of a healthy economy, but those wings were about to be clipped.

GAINS AND LOSSES IN THE 1920S

Economic growth in agriculture, mining, and manufacturing could not be sustained after the end of World War I, and Utah suffered a depression in the early 1920s. The immediate effect on the economy was "in some ways . . . worse than that of the crash of the early 1930s, although the optimistic 'boosterism' of business and governmental spokesmen camouflaged the earlier hard times to a degree. The aggregate current liability of Utah businesses that failed during the four years from 1921 to 1924 was actually greater than the liability of failures from 1931 to 1934. Retail sales during 1921 and 1922 were actually below the 1935–39 average."[35]

The postwar economic distress in farming lasted throughout the 1920s and 1930s and affected entire families. Manufacturing, especially food processing, slumped without wartime contracts; and when the federal government dumped cases of stockpiled canned goods on the market, the industry was further undercut. The number of manufacturing firms in Utah dropped from a thousand in 1919 to 645 in 1921. The best women could do in manufacturing and mechanical pursuits was to remain in 1930 about where they had been in 1920, gaining only two dozen jobs in this category.[36]

The kinds of jobs women held in manufacturing shifted during the decade. The number of dressmakers not working in factories and the number of milliners and millinery dealers continued to decline, following a trend that had begun in 1910. Offsetting these losses were notable gains in clothing factories and textile mills where women increased their number by more than 60 percent between 1920 and 1930 as 343 new jobs were created for them. Women also made gains in the furniture industry and as forewomen, managers, and manufacturers.[37]

After 1922 the economic picture brightened. Growth in transportation, communications, construction, and tourism helped to spark the recovery.[38] A quick run-down of census figures in four important job categories for women shows that the number of female telephone operators increased by more than a third between 1920 and 1930. Women picked up 963 jobs in trade with two-thirds of the new positions found in sales. The number of office jobs for women continued to rise, up from 4,268 to 5,835 in 1930.

In the professional category, women gained 1,652 positions, most of them as teachers and trained nurses. None of these increases is surprising, for each carried on a trend established in earlier decades. What *is* surprising during the 1920s is the leap in the number of jobs for women in domestic and personal service. Service occupations rose from 5,458 in 1920 to 8,123 in 1930. Gains and losses within in this category reflect changing lifestyles. For example, the 1920 census counted only 84 hairdressers; ten years later there were 569. The first permanent waves had been given by London hairdressers in 1909, and bobbed hair had swept the fashion world in 1917. Utah women in the 1920s were obviously willing to pay hairdressers to arrange their locks in the latest styles.

More Utahns must have been dining out as well, for women gained 661 new jobs as cooks and waitresses, and about one in four eating establishments was operated by a woman. There were more elevator operators, dry-cleaning workers, and commercial laundry employees in 1930 than in 1920, while the number of home laundresses, midwives, and untrained nurses declined. These shifts in employment document an increasingly urban society's demand for a variety of services and the willingness of women to supply those services.

In 1930 the number of persons age ten or older in Utah stood at 386,347, 44 percent of whom were employed. When the census described these

Table 1

Gainfully Employed Utahns Age Ten or Older, 1930

Ethnic Group	Males Employed	Females Employed
Native-born whites	68.7%	15.6%
Foreign-born whites	86.4%	14.1%
Negroes	82.9%	29.0%
Other races	83.6%	10.7%

Sources: U.S. Bureau of Census, *Fifteenth Census . . . 1930: Occupations, Utah*, Table 6. p. 11.

people in terms of their nativity, race, and gender, significant data were revealed. (See Table 1.)

Immediately noticeable are the high employment rate of foreign-born males, followed by other races and blacks, and the quite different rankings among females. It is reasonable to suppose that native white males were in a better position than other males to extend their educational years and join the ranks of the employed at a later age than immigrants and racial minorities. As for the high employment rate of black women, it does not necessarily validate the stereotypical image of large numbers of black households headed by women. The typical black household in Utah in the early twentieth century consisted of a husband, wife, and children. However, since "racial discrimination and the lack of educational skills generally limited black Utahns to employment opportunities in the servant or laborer categories," it seems likely that some black women ensured the family's economic survival by providing a second income.[39]

The lower employment rate of women of other races (Native Americans and Asians) and foreign-born white women may have been due to cultural factors, in some instances. First-generation Greek women, for example, would have been most unlikely to seek work outside the home.[40] Language barriers and prejudice undoubtedly kept non-English-speaking women and non-white women out of burgeoning female fields such as teacher, trained nurse, telephone operator, sales, office work, and perhaps waitress and hairdresser as well. (See Table 2.)

More than 90 percent of the employed black women were in domestic and personal service. Although most were listed as servants, five were restaurant, cafe, or lunch-room keepers, three were waitresses, and six were boarding and lodging housekeepers. Two black women were trained nurses and one was a retail dealer. Women of other races enjoyed a wider variety of occupations. About 40 percent worked in manufacturing, the highest percentage of any group. Most of these were textile workers and may, in fact, have been Navajo women self-employed as weavers. Some owned or operated farms, retail stores, hotels, and restaurants. A few were nurses and schoolteachers, waitresses and saleswomen. Along with blacks, no Native Americans worked in candy factories, other food industries, or clothing manufacturing plants. None were telephone or telegraph operators or employed in public service. Fewer than 20 percent of them worked in Salt Lake City.[41]

Almost half of the foreign-born women were employed in domestic and personal service, many as servants. But they also worked in commercial laundries, kept boardinghouses, and ran hotels.[42] They filled many more jobs in factories, offices, trade, and communications than non-white workers; and more were professionals—teachers, trained nurses, and librarians. Although native-born white women made up the bulk of the female work force in Utah, other foreign-born whites and women of other races made important contributions in proportion to their numbers in the population.

Table 2

Nativity and Race of Females Ten or Older in Major Census Employment Categories in Utah, 1930

Employment Sector	Total	Native White	Foreign White	Negro	Other Races
All categories	28,984	25,688	2,910	122	284
Agriculture	963	760	156	1	46
Extraction of Minerals	8	8	—	—	—
Manufacturing/ Mechanical	2,701	2,139	450	4	108
Transportation/ Communication	1,294	1,240	53	—	1
Trade	3,978	3,654	314	1	9
Public service	105	100	5	—	—
Professional service	5,977	5,726	235	5	11
Domestic/ personal service	8,123	6,442	1,441	110	86
Clerical	5,835	5,576	255	1	1

Source: Bureau of the Census, Fifteenth Census . . . 1930: Occupational Statistics, Utah, Table 11, p. 16.

In 1929 married women made up 17.4 percent of the female work force in Utah. Ten years later they accounted for 23.9 percent. As noted earlier, this was part of a long-term, nationwide trend. Some social critics in the twenties saw this pattern as the end of the family and of society itself. Deep levels of class and racial anxiety are revealed in some of the criticism directed toward middle-class white women who were accused, among other things, of committing "race suicide" by allowing the birthrate to decline.[43] Middle-class mores and fears obscured very real problems in the work place for wives and mothers who had to work: adequate wages, child care, health, etc. For lower-class women, many immigrants, and non-whites, working was not a feminist issue, a challenge to the social order, or a way to pay for luxuries or a child's college education. Work meant bread on the table. Unfortunately, when women earned the bread, it was most often only half a loaf.

As one might expect, census statistics also show a gradual aging of the female work force. Compulsory education through high school is largely a twentieth-century phenomenon in the United States. In 1905, there were only 181 high school graduates in Utah. But as notions of education evolved and reaction against child labor mounted, the time was ripe for change. Utah's compulsory education law was passed in 1919.[44] By 1930 there were 20 percent fewer girls between ages ten and seventeen at work in Utah than in 1920. All other age categories posted increases. The number of women ages twenty to twenty-four who were working grew by 37 percent; and among women twenty-five to forty-four, the growth rate was 47 percent. Women ages twenty to forty-four made up over 73 percent of the female work force in 1930. In 1920 they had accounted for 63 percent of the working women.[45]

By 1930 slightly more than one out of every six workers in Utah was a woman, and in Salt Lake City more than one-fourth of the work force was female. These women were older and more were married than ever before.[46] Overwhelmingly white, they formed, despite obstacles and objections, the essential core of workers in communications, education, hospitals, laundries, libraries, lodging and restaurant businesses, most offices, domestic service, and the manufacturing of textiles, clothing, and several food products. They also made significant contributions in retail trade, the printing industry, real estate, recreation, cleaning and dyeing, hair care, and the visual, performing, and literary arts. Although the Great Depression would subject these working women to new trials and criticism in the 1930s, they were sometimes in a better position than working men to retain their jobs unless they were married.

Despite the development of certain industries and services, the Utah economy grew at a slower rate than the national economy during the first three decades of the twentieth century. As a result, "jobs had not opened up fast enough to absorb those who wanted to work"; and unlike other western states, Utah had experienced a net yearly out-migration since 1910. The sluggish economy affected wages as well, and per capita income slid from 90.1 of the national average in 1900 to 79.5 percent in 1929. When the stock market crashed in 1929, the shock waves were immediately and severely felt in Utah. High freight rates further distressed agriculture and mining, while "weak labor organizations, a high birthrate, and a severe drought in 1931" compounded the economic woes. When the depression hit bottom, 35.8 percent of Utah's workers were unemployed, and more than 20 percent of the population was on relief.[47]

The unemployed organized and protested, and the Socialist and Communist parties gained adherents, but the government at first did little. The 1931 state legislature could only recommend the "dismissal of working wives, no overtime work, and the saving of leftover food." These simplistic ideas did not pass muster at the local level, and every county in Utah had some relief plan for the unemployed in place by 1931. The following year, Reconstruction Finance Corporation funds began to trickle in, the beginning of a monumental federal relief program for Utah that would eventually provide thousands of women with jobs.[48]

THE CHALLENGES OF THE 1930S

Women found work under the programs of the Civil Works Administration in 1933–34, the Federal Emergency Relief Administration in 1934–35, and most important, under the Works Progress Administration from 1935 to 1943. After the scattershot projects of the CWA gave way to the FERA and WPA programs, a clear division became discernible between works or building projects (they employed mostly men and left the state with many visible improvements such as roads, reservoirs, and school buildings) and service projects (that employed many women and left few, if any, tangible remains).

The Services projects under both the FERA and the WPA fell into several broad categories: the manufacturing of clothing and household items, canning and other food programs, the arts, adult education, recreation, health, school lunches and other programs geared to children, and miscellaneous programs.[49]

The Services Division of the WPA, under the direction of Ruby S. Garrett, was "set up . . . to provide projects for women, and create employment for artists, writers, musicians, clerical workers, teachers, and others who were not involved in . . . construction." The WPA aimed "to include more professional people [than the earlier programs] and also recognize the problems of unemployed women who were heads of households." The program promised improved working conditions for women and nondiscriminatory wages.[50]

The manufacturing of clothing, first aid supplies, and household items employed 500 women. Many of those who were certified as eligible for WPA employment "began working here, as it was a 'buffer project' or labor pool." Manufacturers who had at first objected to the project came to realize that clothing made for those on relief did not compete with their goods. During World War II, factory owners found that women trained by the WPA had become skilled workers who could make everything from uniforms to parachutes.[51]

Under the WPA the extensive canning projects of the earlier FERA program that had employed 100 women in Salt Lake City alone were abandoned, and food was preserved primarily for the school lunch program sponsored by the Utah State Board of Education, local boards, and other organizations.[52]

From its inception during the 1935–36 school year, when 405 persons were employed, the WPA school lunch program grew each year until 1941–42 when it employed 858 persons in all twenty-nine Utah counties and served an average of 32,039 children every school day.[53] Mildred Younker, the school lunch supervisor in Cache County, described how her program worked:

In 1938 the food in Cache County was prepared in cooks' homes and carried to the school; often WPA men or NYA men were assigned to this task of transporting the food. The women were paid $5.00 per month for using their kitchens. However, as the program progressed, many kitchens were added to the schools. . . .

When school terminated in the spring, the cooks became seamstresses and made their own uniforms, with the state furnishing the patterns and material. During the summer many of the school lunch workers canned peas, corn, and fruits, and after the tomatoes were canned in October, the school lunch program began.[54]

The WPA adult education programs involved 1,700 as teachers of a range of subjects from citizenship, art, and agriculture to health and vocational training. Nursery schools in fourteen Utah communities employed

Women workers canning produce in Salt Lake City, ca.1930s.

needy professionals, assisted preschool children and parents from low-income families, and trained potential nursery school workers. During World War II, some of these nursery schools provided day care for the children of women working in war industries. WPA recreational programs that served thousands of Utahns grew out of earlier CWA and FERA efforts that had trained leaders and stimulated community interest. Both Salt Lake City and Ogden offered separate recreational programs for "colored" children and adults.[55]

It is impossible to detail here all of the federal programs of the 1930s and early 1940s that employed women, but clearly their cumulative effect was enormous. Both professional women and skilled workers found employment in the arts and as nurses, teachers, administrators, social workers, cooks, factory workers, recreational supervisors, and clerical workers. In addition, on-the-job training enhanced future employment opportunities for some women.

Although the 1940 census showed many women still employed on WPA projects, a majority of working women had jobs in the private sector. The female labor force totaled 33,888, of whom 28,777 were either at work or had jobs, while 2,078 were engaged in public emergency work (WPA) and 3,033 were looking for work. The job seekers included 2,195 experienced workers and 838 new workers hoping to find employment. The unemployment rate for experienced females was only two-thirds that of experienced males, one indication that working women may have fared better during the Great Depression than men.[56]

The poor economic performance of agriculture, mining, and heavy industry put many skilled males out of work, while layoffs for women tended to be more sporadic. Over a third of the women at work were in office or sales positions like stenographer or department store clerk. Professional work, primarily as teachers and nurses, and various service occupations such as domestic servant, waitress, and hairdresser accounted for almost half of the jobs women held. The highly sex-segregated nature of most women's jobs belied the criticism often heard during the depression that working women were taking jobs away from men. An unemployed steel worker could not serve as an operating room nurse or style hair no matter how desperate his situation. Although sex stereotyping protected some women from layoffs during the depression, in the long run it reinforced trends that concentrated women in a few occupational categories at the low end of the pay scale.[57]

Nevertheless, the popular belief that a woman at work kept a man in the unemployment line affected women in Utah and elsewhere. A spate of bills introduced in twenty-six state legislatures across the country sought to curtail the employment of married women. When the Utah House of Representatives passed its version of this discriminatory legislation, women rallied against it. The Salt Lake Council of Women, representing forty-two women's clubs, passed a resolution condemning H.B. 67 "and demanding that a public hearing on the bill be held." Judge Reva Beck Bosone, a former state legislator and future U.S. congresswoman, compared the abuse of women's rights to what was "going on in Germany and Italy" under fascism and pointed out to rural legislators that, under H.B. 67, their wives might be prohibited from selling butter and eggs while their husbands worked for the state.[58]

Businesswomen and housewives joined in denouncing the measure which made it "unlawful for the state or any of its political subdivisions to employ a person whose husband or wife is regularly employed in private industry" and earning $800 or more a year. Backers of the legislation claimed it was "aimed at one of the vultures that is tearing away at the very purse strings of economic recovery" and declared that the bill's intent was to place "a bread-winner in every household." Bosone countered that a similar measure in Washington,

D.C., had failed to distribute jobs more equitably and was later repealed. In the end, "only the lower houses of Ohio and Utah passed discriminatory bills." However, the legislature issued a joint resolution requesting political units in the state not to hire persons who had an employed spouse or other family member living with them. The defeat of these bills nationally was an important victory for women who had learned from experience that it is easier to defeat legislation than to repeal it.[59]

Despite the defeat of H.B. 67 in Utah, married women did lose jobs. Public schoolteachers were especially vulnerable because local school districts often "fired women teachers who married. Some women deeply resented this . . . and kept their marriage a secret as long as they could in order to keep working." Female office workers in state government, the WPA, and private business sometimes lost their jobs upon marriage as well. As one might expect, women doing drudge work as domestic servants, migrant farmers, or laundresses did not offend society when they married and continued working.[60]

The depression challenged women who were already in business or self-employed and tempted others to launch new businesses on the uncertain economic waters. The 1940 census shows 221 female farmers and farm managers and 1,587 other proprietors, managers, and officials. Another 2,503 women are listed elsewhere as employers or "own-account workers." The latter figure certainly overlaps the other two, but, even so, the woman business owner or self-employed woman accounted for at least 8 percent of the employed females in Utah.[61]

Women had ventured into business from the earliest days of white settlement in Utah. The small millinery or dress shop and the boarding house were among the first businesses in almost every town. State and city directories provide yearly lists of women operating a variety of small businesses, and detailed community histories have preserved the names of many businesswomen.[62]

Women in the small town of Gunnison in southwestern Sanpete County, for example, have owned or managed an impressive number of businesses over the years. Many businesses were jointly run with another family member—usually a husband, but there were also two mother-son operations and one business that teamed a daughter with her father. The enterprises included specialty stores, restaurants, motels, a theater, an insurance agency, a builders supply house, and a sawmill. Surprisingly, several of these ventures were founded during the depression: Iva Christensen opened a bonnet shop in Gunnison in 1931 and later expanded into infants' and children's wear and formal and wedding attire. Several motels built in the 1930s were owned by women or wife-husband teams. A sawmill established in 1930 and later operated by a woman and her son produced a half-million board feet of lumber in later years. Finally, in 1941, the last lean year before the war, Mr. and Mrs. Vance B. Peterson opened Valley Builders Supply that in less than two decades boasted branch stores in five other central Utah towns.[63]

Gunnison was by no means unique in offering women entrepreneurial opportunities. The histories of Midvale, Payson, Richfield, and Murray—to name only a few—tell similar stories of women involved in private enterprise.[64] Metaphorically at least, these pioneering entrepreneurs can be called foremothers of such late twentieth-century business giants as Debbie Fields (chocolate chip cookies) and June Morris (Southwest Airlines), nationally and even internationally known in the food and travel industries.

Nevertheless, the historical role of women in business remains dimly perceived at best. Census data may not accurately reflect the number of women actively engaged in business as partners if the partner was also the husband. Furthermore, without business records and interviews with those involved it would be difficult to gauge what each partner contributed to the running of a business. It is fair to say, however, that women as sole proprietors, partners, and corporate officers have carved a sizeable niche for themselves in the Utah business community and that a number of them chose to begin during the depression.

While some women were opening stores and restaurants or seeing them foreclosed, other women, employees of the Utah State Industrial Commission, were monitoring the wages, hours, and working conditions of women throughout the state. When the first hours and wage laws affecting women were passed in 1911 and 1913, the State Bureau of Immigration, Labor, and Statistics was assigned the task of overseeing compliance. The reports of this bureau and, after 1917, of the Industrial Commission indicate that women investigators visited almost every city and town in Utah, examined payrolls and time sheets, and talked with employers and employees.[65]

After some initial hostility most employers welcomed the investigators and attempted to comply with the laws. Relatively few violators were turned over to county attorneys for prosecution, for employers were usually ready to pay back wages to employees who had been underpaid or to adjust hours or improve restroom facilities rather than go to court; but in other instances, employees who refused to testify against employers for fear of losing their jobs forestalled court action.[66]

One theme running through these reports is the inadequacy of the minimum wage: "The Utah female wage scale provides for a smaller wage than that fixed by any wage scale commission in any other State." When the depression hit, some women took 5 to 30 percent wage cuts. The Industrial Commission report issued in 1932 noted that "in some cases women and girls were hardly able to eke out an existence and hundreds are without employment at all." Even some employers joined with employees in requesting "a reasonable minimum wage for women." After the minimum wage was repealed in 1929, some employees were paid as little as $2 a week including meals. From mid-1933 to October 1936 the Women's Division of the State Industrial Commission had no funds for inspection, and many employers failed to abide by the eight-hour law.[67]

Under legislation enacted in 1911, the Industrial Commission adopted standards governing the welfare of women and minors in industry and made time and wage reports mandatory under an order that became effective on June 1, 1937. Wage boards were set up to recommend wages in retail trade, manufacturing, laundries, cleaning and dyeing establishments, restaurants, beauty shops, and canning and poultry packing. The U.S. Supreme Court had established the constitutionality of minimum wage laws for women and minors in March 1937, but the Utah law was challenged in the Utah Supreme Court by 125 retailers. In December 1938 the court ruled that the law was constitutional but that the wage order of the Industrial Commission had been implemented without following proper procedures.[68]

To comply with the Utah Supreme Court order, a group of experts conducted a cost-of-living survey, completed in July 1939, and determined that working women needed a wage of $19.42 a week "to protect health and morals and provide a standard of living essential to . . . well being." As had happened in other states where minimum wage surveys were made, Utah responded to the report by setting a minimum wage considerably below the one recommended— $10 to $14 a week in different "zones" throughout the state.[69]

While the mandatory wage orders were being formulated, the Industrial Commission surveyed retail stores, bakeries, hotels, cafes, beauty parlors, dry cleaners, laundries, offices, and hospitals in central and southern Utah in 1939. Its report, published as *Bulletin No. 5* in 1940, gives payroll data on 428 working women. The commission found hotel employees to be among the lowest paid and office workers the highest. At one hotel, investigators found "a girl who was on duty practically all the time for $2 per week with board and room." However, "the worst example of low pay for skilled work" was found in a drugstore where "a girl, working full time and being acquainted with the stock to such a degree that the owner could leave her alone in charge of the store for several hours" received only $5 a week.[70]

Most of the women surveyed worked eight-hour days and forty-eight hour weeks—the legal maximum for most jobs. However, many cafes worked their employees seven days a week at an average wage of $7 plus meals. When restaurant owners cut weekly hours to comply with the law, most of the employees would lose a day's pay, the investigator reported.[71]

Wage surveys in Salt Lake City and Ogden showed that urban wages were slightly higher than wages in rural nonfarm areas of the state. The weekly wage in Salt Lake City ranged from $4 to $22.50 with 50 percent of the women surveyed receiving between $12 and $14 a week. The very few women earning $16 to $22.50 had "extra" responsibilities.[72]

WORLD WAR II'S NEW JOB OPPORTUNITIES

The problems of the depression were not fully solved until World War II primed the economic pump. Women who had lost jobs, endured pay cuts, enrolled in WPA projects, fought for the right to work, and struggled to launch new businesses or keep old ones solvent were ready to face the challenges of the greatest mobilization effort in American history. Gender, marital status, age, and experience would mean very little to employers during World War II, for Utah would have "a higher concentration of war workers than any other state in the Union" and would have to enlist many marginal workers to meet the demand.[73]

Wartime need sent women into the work force in unprecedented numbers and opened many job categories to them. "Rosie the Riveter" became a symbol of women filling nontraditional jobs while men served in the armed forces, but society's attitude toward Rosie and her female co-workers was ambivalent. On the one hand, government and industry actively courted women workers, sometimes providing day care and wage parity as incentives; on the other hand, women were sometimes harassed or ridiculed, given only minimal training, denied equal pay, and quickly dismissed after the war. Despite women's varied experiences during World War II, "the evidence offers little support to those who suggest that the war was either a turning point or a milestone."[74] The work force generally resumed the sex-segregated configuration of the prewar years in the late 1940s, and many "Rosies" returned home—where society told them they belonged—married G.I. Joes, and contributed to the postwar baby boom, suburban sprawl, and consumer demand for goods and services.

Almost 50,000 new jobs were created in Utah during World War II as military installations were built or expanded and war-related industries boomed. Operations at Hill Field, for example, required 15,000 civilian workers, and the Remington Small Arms Plant in Salt Lake City employed 10,000. Besides these new jobs, the war found many established businesses and industries looking for workers to replace employees who enlisted or were drafted. By the end of 1942, the worker shortage was acute.[75]

The canning industry and the public schools—traditional employers of women—reported staffing problems in September 1942. Gus P. Backman, vice-chairman of the Utah Council of Defense, urged school boards and other community organizations to respond to the canning plant emergency in northern Utah where 450 workers were needed to process tomatoes before the crop spoiled. The problem arose because "some students, mothers and teachers quit jobs at the factories" when the new school year started. The Salt Lake City School District reported a shortage of schoolteachers and clerical workers as government and industry attracted school personnel with high wartime wages. Students replaced clerical workers in some school offices.[76]

The increased wartime need for processed foods created a demand for women workers at other factories in Utah. One young Mexican American widow with a child to support began working for the Purity Biscuit Company during World War II. With overtime and double shifts, she sometimes earned as much as $100 a week, which enabled her to help her family make the down payment on a home in Salt Lake City. Although she later remarried, this energetic woman

Women working in the parachute factory located in Manti, during World War II.

continued to contribute to her family's income by working as a candy dipper, making—with the help of her children—as many as 100 dozen tortillas a week for local Mexican restaurants, quilting, and doing other needlework.[77]

Classified advertising reflected the new labor needs by soliciting both men and women for traditional male jobs like drill press operator and bus driver. From the number of newspaper advertisements for female laundry workers, chocolate dippers, and waitresses, it seems apparent that many women left those low-paying jobs to work in defense plants.[78]

The job market changed dramatically for women in 1942. One nineteen-year-old woman who had spent many months looking for work and felt lucky when she found a half-day job in a department store tea room suddenly found Salt Lake City full of job opportunities. When Remington began taking applications, she tried for a position and was hired. The lure, of course, was full-time work and much higher pay. She worked rotating shifts as a final inspector of small cartridges for about $30 a week. All her co-workers were women, except for the supervisors and machine repairmen. The work called for good hand-eye coordination in machine-checking cartridges for quality control. The routine sounds monotonous and the rotating shifts were hard on one's biological clock, but this young woman enjoyed the work and was able to widen her circle of acquaintances because the plant attracted workers from

Courtesy of Kennecott Utah Copper.

Women workers at the Kennecott Mine/Smelter during World War II.

many outlying towns. She and her co-workers enjoyed the new freedom of stopping for a late evening meal at a downtown Chinese restaurant when they worked the swing shift and sharing a variety of social activities such as dancing at Saltair on their days off.[79]

This young Remington worker was one among thousands who contributed to the "marked increase in the number of women workers in private industry between January 15 and October 15, 1942." During this nine-month period, the number of women in manufacturing rose by almost 7,000, while wholesale and retail trade posted a gain of 1,000; transportation, communications, and utilities 700; and construction 500. Most of the women in Utah's booming construction business held clerical or secretarial positions. Although the new jobs were concentrated in the Wasatch Front counties of Salt Lake, Weber, Utah, and Davis, most outlying counties noted some gains. The number of women in manufacturing in Sanpete County, for example, almost tripled when a parachute factory opened. Tooele women gained 125 new jobs in construction; and spurred by the building of Bushnell Hospital near Brigham City, several hundred women in Box Elder County found work in construction, manufacturing, and trade. Only Uintah, Summit, and Rich counties showed losses in jobs for women during this period.[80]

Employment prospects were brighter than they had ever been for women in Utah; but the job market fluctuated, reflecting seasonal employment in food processing and retail trade and, in 1943, heavy losses in manufacturing as Remington phased out its Salt Lake City operation. However, some industrial occupations barred to women were so shorthanded in late 1943 and early 1944 that "legal barriers were set aside" and over a thousand women "worked in these occupations during the last two years of the war." A special order permitting women to work in what were considered hazardous jobs enabled steel plants and rolling mills to hire 669 women, copper mines to place 452 women "in jobs ordinarily held by men," and copper and lead smelters to engage 87 women.[81]

The Utah Department of Employment Security estimated total female employment during the wartime peak at 64,510 in June 1943 and 66,334 in September 1943. By December 1946 the number of employed women had dropped to an estimated 50,852 and three months later to 45,972.[82]

New jobs poured money into the economy. The 1942 payroll for business and industry in Utah eclipsed by $100 million the largest payroll of the late 1920s and by $80 million the record payroll of 1941. These figures do not include the payrolls of federal, state, and local governments, farms, or domestic service.[83]

Some households that had struggled through the 1930s on less than one full-time worker's paycheck sent father, mother, and older children off to jobs in the 1940s. Large installations like the Clearfield Naval Supply Depot encouraged the employment of several members of one family by opening a nursery for employees' children in May 1944. Higher family income, changing family lifestyles, and some boomtown conditions brought prosperity and opportunity to many homes, but some suffered the consequences of divorce, juvenile delinquency, and other social problems.[84]

Some companies like Remington paid workers in Utah less than their workers received in other parts of the country; nevertheless, local manufacturers protested, apparently fruitlessly, that wages were still above the level they were used to paying. Women with typing and shorthand skills found themselves in a seller's market. Local businesses that complained about the salaries paid office workers by the military and defense industries were told the pay was civil service standard.[85]

Although the Remington plant filled its urgent wartime mission in less than two years and closed, some historians feel it exercised a "powerful effect on the labor market and industrial potential of Utah" by training thousands of workers in assembly-line procedures and other mechanical, industrial, and technological skills.[86] No doubt the training programs at Remington, Hill Field, and other installations offered Utah workers, especially women, unusual opportunities to train for industrial jobs; and the postwar growth of Utah's manufacturing sector enabled some women to transfer their wartime skills to other jobs.

If World War II led women to new work opportunities, it also exposed them to familiar types of harassment and condescension. At the Ogden Arsenal, for example, employees were chastised for jeopardiz[ing] "the safety of their fellow employees by indulging in playful pranks that are definitely childish in nature and extremely dangerous." Women were the victims and men the perpetrators of all the "pranks" cited, which ranged from threatening a woman with a dead snake to taking a "playful swing" at a woman. Three of the incidents required hospitalization, and two appear to have had sexual overtones. On a more positive note, the arsenal newsletter, the *Bombshell,* featured stories on outstanding women workers. One forelady was commended for her success in conducting a blood drive, and three "girls" who cleaned gun barrels were praised for performing a dirty job well. The writer nevertheless felt obliged to assure readers that however "dirty" the women gun cleaners looked in the accompanying photograph, they were all "pretty" after they washed up.[87]

During World War II, long-term trends in the number, age, and marital status of working women in Utah were greatly accelerated. While the population of females age fourteen and over increased 22 percent between 1940 and 1950, the number of employed females over age fourteen rose by 68 percent. In 1940 women ages twenty to twenty-four accounted for one in every four female workers. By 1950, the swing to older women that had begun earlier found those ages thirty-five to forty-four dominating the work force. With the shift to an older work force, it is not surprising that the census found that more than half of the women employed in Utah in 1950 were married and living with their husbands.[88]

White females made up the vast majority of Utah working women, with only 277 black women and 845 women of other races listed as employed in the 1950 census. These numbers reflect the general population of Utah, still overwhelmingly Caucasian in 1950. Black working women were clustered in the service occupations. Only twelve were clerical workers—the largest single female job category in Utah—and one suspects that most of them were employed in black-owned businesses. There were actually more black women managers, officials, and proprietors (twenty) than black clerical workers, and only twenty-one held jobs in industry, including manufacturing. Women of other races found jobs primarily in industry, service occupations, offices, and as farm workers in that order. The role of Mexican women in migrant farm workers' families in Utah has been largely ignored. It is an area ripe for historical research.[89]

THE POSTWAR RETURN TO TYPE

When the war ended, women could take pride in the many contributions they had made toward winning the war. Their willingness to fill a wide variety of job assignments was as essential to the successful prosecution of the war as the enlistment of men in the armed forces. But pride and patriotism were not enough to sustain women and men who found themselves out of work at the end of World War II. The Department of Employment Security handled thousands of applications for unemployment benefits beginning in late 1945. In January 1946, a record 10,566 claims for unemployment insurance were filed in Utah. Many of the unemployed quickly found new jobs. However, some workers insisted on jobs identical to ones they had lost, even when the prospective availability of such jobs was almost nil. Workers unprepared to face the new realities of the postwar economy, including lower wages, were often disqualified from receiving unemployment benefits. Those denied benefits included, for example, a former female platen press operator who refused other work in a print shop and an unskilled female war industry employee who refused unskilled work in a candy factory. This unskilled woman was one of thousands of "marginal workers" who found employment during the war because of the high demand for workers of any kind.[90]

By 1950 the Utah economy had attained "a measure of stability" with its basic sectors of mining, manufacturing, and agriculture providing diversity in employment. Interstate transportation, communications, utilities, finance, trade, tourism, government, and nonprofit organizations added strength to the basic triad.[91] Although many female workers left the ranks of the gainfully employed after World War II, many did not. The number of Utah women in the work force in 1950 stood at 57,294, with 54,018 actually employed and 3,239 looking for work. Only 82 of the unemployed were new workers.[92] Census data show the kinds of jobs women held after the war boom, compared with 1940 statistics. (See Table 3.)

The tremendous rise in the number of clerical workers—the only category other than private household workers that women rather than men dominated numerically—demonstrates more graphically than any other statistic that World War II did not create major changes in the job patterns of women. After the war, most working women still filled jobs typically associated with females: stenographer, typist, waitress, laundress, nurse, teacher, food processor, and textile or clothing factory worker.

The number of women at work in 1950 represents an astonishing leap of more than 87 percent over the 1940 figure. But the 1940 economy was still depressed; only 17.6 percent of the women age fourteen or older were employed, the same percentage as in 1930. Had the economy posted even a modest growth rate in the thirties, more jobs would have been created, and the 1950 employment figure would not look so impressive.

Except for the depression and other lesser setbacks, Utah's economy generally grew and diversified during the fifty-five years following statehood. As a result, the female work force grew and diversified, for women have almost always accepted whatever jobs and economic opportunities were available. World War II refueled a stagnant economy and increased job diversity, but the major trends for working women ran as deep as wagon ruts on an old trail. The war diverted attention from the main path that women were traveling to such passing sights as women cleaning gun barrels or helping to roll steel. Women proved they could do it, but the necessity of their doing it was short-lived. Women who held typically male jobs during the war did not attempt in any significant number to breach other male bastions after the war or remain

Table 3

Major Occupation Groups of Employed Women in Utah, 1950 and 1940

Employment Sector	1950	1940
Total employed	54,018	28,077
Professional, technical, and kindred workers	8,043	5,500
Farmers and farm managers	277	221
Managers, officials, proprietors except farm	2,673	1,454
Clerical and kindred workers	17,812	7,858
Sales workers	5,864	3,077
Craftsmen, foremen, and kindred workers	787	280
Operatives and kindred workers	5,307	2,803
Private household workers	2,671	2,628
Service workers except private householders	8,522	4,193
Farm laborers, unpaid workers	505	99
Farm laborers, except unpaid and foreman	267	44
Laborers except farm and mine	324	146
Occupation not reported	966	474

Source: Bureau of the Census, Census of Population: 1950 . . . Utah, Table 29, pp. 33–44.

in the steel mills.[93] Rather, they kept by and large to their well-worn trail until the civil rights and feminist movements of later decades led them to challenge, among other things, professional school enrollment policies, career ladders that advanced only males, and unequal pay.

Over the years, women worked in many occupational categories, but by far the greatest number were employed in sex-stereotyped jobs that offered few opportunities for advancement. Some lived out their working years as poorly paid domestic servants; other were physicians and artists, and some ran their own businesses. Most worked on farms or in offices, factories, hotels, hospitals, schools, restaurants, and stores. They entered and left the work force primarily out of economic necessity but also to fill other personal, family, or career goals. Education, marriage, the birth of children, the growing up of children, divorce, widowhood, spinsterhood, race and ethnicity, patriotism, and probably even boredom affected their need to work or their choice to do so.

The number of women at work grew from 11.2 percent of the females age ten and older in 1900 to 24.4 percent of the females age fourteen and older in 1950. By 1950 almost one out of every four workers in Utah was a woman, and in Salt Lake City 30 percent of the work force was female. But for some these women remained as mysteriously unseen as if they were in purdah. An economist and bank vice-president writing a 1956 textbook would note "the extremely small percentage of women who are gainfully employed" in Utah.[94] Men ran the working world and that was the important and visible thing. That they could never have run it without the labor of women did not occur to most men or women in the 1950s.

Postscript: Fast Forward to a New Century

The civil rights and feminist movements, as well as changing national and world economic conditions, affected women workers and the workplace environment in many ways during the second half of the twentieth century and into the twenty-first. These changes lie beyond the scope of this essay; nevertheless, noting a few trends and changes may help to place the working women discussed in this article in a broader historical context.

It is important to note that data currently available show that certain long-term trends in the employment of women are expected to continue. According to a Utah Department of Employment Security forecast issued in 1987, some 62 percent of women over age sixteen would be employed by the year 2000.[95] This prediction proved fairly accurate. Census data compiled by the state in July 2003 indicate that 60.9 percent of Utah females were employed, compared to 68.7 percent of males.[96] These data from the 2000 census show that, at the beginning of the new millennium, gainful employment had become almost as important to Utah women as to men.

The state's largest employers now include local, state, and federal government agencies, including Hill Air Force Base; educational institutions both public and private (e.g., Brigham Young University), Intermountain Health Care, Wal-Mart Associates, Convergys, and Kroger Group. Mining, once a keystone of the Utah economy and a male-dominated industry, now employs fewer than 7,000 workers, while fields associated with women as well as men—education and health—produced more than 22,000 jobs between 1998 and 2002. Utah's population, close to 2.5 million in 2002, requires such steady job growth.[97]

Perhaps the most significant population figure in the new millennium will prove to be the continuing rise in the number of non-white residents. One in ten Utahns is now identified as of "Hispanic" ancestry, and the number of Utahns with Asian or Pacific Island ancestry has grown in recent decades.

Two other trends, both significant to women, are wage parity and entrepreneurship. According to the AFL-CIO, "working women in Utah are not as far along the road to equal pay as women in most states," earning only 71.1 percent as much per hour as men. Nationwide the figure is 77.6 percent. In fact, Utah ranks dead last among the fifty states in equal pay. "At the current rate of change, working women in Utah—as well as . . . nationwide—won't have equal pay until after 2050."[98] For minority women the road will most likely be even longer.

The issue of equal pay for equal or similar work is not the same as actual wages paid. Statistics compiled by the prestigious Institute for Women's Policy Research show that Utah ranked thirty-fifth among the states in women's median annual earnings in 1997. Other significant findings in this report show that Utah women ranked fifteenth in labor force participation in 1998.[99] This ranking corrects the popular stereotype that Utah (i.e., Mormon) women are not as likely to work outside the home as other women. Without attempting to challenge that stereotype, one might assert that the number of Utah women at work may also demonstrate the changing nature of gainful employment. In the twenty-first century (as during World War II) employers appear willing to make work schedules for women and men more flexible and accommodating for working parents and to make commuting easier. Moreover, changing technology has made the home itself a potential work site for many workers, including women, both nationally and in Utah.

Finally, one should acknowledge that in 2004 Utah was ranked number one nationwide in the growth of female-owned businesses. Utah had 102,194 such businesses employing 217,260 workers, with sales of almost $22.8 million.[100] "Female-owned" is defined as owning 50 percent or more of a business. These female entrepreneurs have followed in the pioneering footsteps of the industrious Utah women who opened every kind of business from millinery shops, to motels and restaurants, to building supply stores in the early decades of the twentieth century. It is possible that entrepreneurship may prove to be one of the hallmarks of Utah women. That's for future historians to decide.

Notes

1. Alice Kessler-Harris, *Out to Work: A History of Wage-Earning Women in the United States* (New York: Oxford University Press, 1982), 7, 5. This is an excellent general history of working women in the United States. Other useful works include Barbara Mayer Wertheimer, *We Were There: The Story of Working Women in America* (New York: Pantheon Books 1977) and Joseph A. Hill, *Women in Gainful Occupations, 1870 to 1920: A Study of the Trend of Recent Changes in the Numbers Occupational Distribution and Family Relationship of Women Reported in the Census as Following a Gainful Occupation* (1929; reprinted, Westport, Conn.: Greenwood Press, 1978). My introductory historical summary is based primarily on Kessler-Harris.

2. Kessler-Harris, *Out to Work,* 22.

3. Ibid.

4. Ibid., 53, 59.

5. Although Mormon leaders orchestrated the settlement of Utah and introduced cooperative and communal institutions that flavored both economic and social life, census data show that the unique features of life in Utah did not affect income-earning women to any degree. The variety and number of jobs held in Utah, the West, and the United States as a whole ultimately depended on local resources and needs. The development of manufacturing and trade almost inevitably led to the employment of more women, whereas mining and heavy industry did not. Utah's first large factory, the Provo Woolen Mills, opened in 1872 and employed many women, especially immigrants who had obtained their skills in the textile mills of England and Scotland. See article describing the "young lady operators" in "Provo Woolen Mills," *Deseret News,* July 24, 1897, 23.

6. Mining and railroad towns developed along different lines. Many, like Corinne, existed for only a few years and had fewer female than male residents. Others endured and offered women a mix of business opportunities in lodging, food service, retailing, etc., early on in their development. See, for example, Aird G. Merkley, ed., *Monuments to Courage: A History of Beaver County* (Milford, Utah: Beaver County Daughters of the Utah Pioneers, 1948), 216–17, 242–46, 267–71, 272, 312–14, for notations on dozens of working women and female business owners in the mining and railroad towns of Beaver County. Ann Vest Lobb and Jill Mulvay Derr, "Women in Early Utah," in *Utah's History,* edited by Richard D. Poll, Thomas G. Alexander, Eugene E. Campbell, and David E. Miller (Provo, Utah: Brigham Young University Press, 1978), esp. 338–46, provide a good overview of women during the early settlement period and their economic roles.

7. Leonard J. Arrington and Thomas G. Alexander, *A Dependent Commonwealth: Utah's Economy from Statehood to the Great Depression,* Charles Redd Monographs in Western History, No. 4. (Provo, Utah: Brigham Young University, 1974), 41.

8. "Canning Factories in Utah," *Payroll Builder* (publication of the Utah Manufacturers Association) 1 (August 1913): 6–8; U.S. Bureau of the Census, *Thirteenth Census of the United States . . . 1910,* Vol. 4, *Population 1910: Occupation Statistics* (Washington, D.C.: Government Printing Office, 1914), occupational tables beginning on p. 138 (note: cannery workers are divided between laborers and semiskilled operatives); U.S. Bureau of the Census, *Fourteenth Census of the United States. State Compendium: Utah* (Washington, D.C.: Government Printing Office, 1924), 38.

9. U.S. Bureau of the Census, *Population 1910: Occupational Statistics,* Table 2, beginning p. 138; U.S. Bureau of the Census, *Fourteenth Census of the United States . . . 1920,* Vol. 4, *Population 1920: Occupations* (Washington, D.C.: Government Printing Office, 1923), Table 15 beginning on p. 116; Arrington and Alexander, *A Dependent Commonwealth,* 39, 42; R W. Eardley, "James G. McDonald," *Payroll Builder* 3 (June 1915): 16–20. City directories for Salt Lake City, Ogden, Provo, and Logan list candy manufacturers.

10. U.S. Bureau of the Census, *Twelfth Census of the United States . . . 1900,* Vol. 2, *Population, Part 2* (Washington, D.C.: U.S. Census Office, 1902), Table 93, pp. 540–59; U.S. Bureau of the Census, *Population 1910: Occupation Statistics,* Table II beginning on p. 138; U.S. Bureau of the Census, *Population 1920: Occupations,* Table 15 beginning on p. 116 (it is necessary to add several job categories together to arrive at totals); Arrington and Alexander, *A Dependent Commonwealth,* 41–42.

11. "The Overalls Industry," *Payroll Builder* 5 (November 1917): 45.

12. "Industries of Utah: The Knitting Industry," *Payroll Builder,* May 1915, 8.

13. U.S. Bureau of the Census, *Population 1920: Occupations,* Table 15, beginning on p. 116 (including laborers, semiskilled operatives, apprentices, linotype operators, engravers, editors, reporters); Miriam B. Murphy, "The Working Women of Salt Lake City: A Review of the *Utah Gazetteer,* 1892–93," *Utah Historical Quarterly* 46 (Spring 1978): 135; J. Kenneth Davies, *Deseret's Sons of Toil: A History of the Worker Movement in Territorial Utah* (Salt Lake City: Olympus Publishing, 1977), 168–69, 174–75.

14. See census tables previously cited. The census categorized the individual dressmaker, seamstress, tailoress, and milliner as manufacturing workers. Hundreds of women left these independent occupations; however, the *total* number of women in manufacturing rose anyway because more women were at work in factories of various kinds.

15. Arrington and Alexander, *A Dependent Commonwealth,* 35–38, describe the 1910–20 agricultural economy. In 1920 there were 25,700 farms in Utah. If only one woman per farm contributed to the farm's production, that number (25,700) would exceed by almost 4,000 the total number of employed women in all occupations in Utah (21,783).

16. Ibid., Table 2.1, p. 49. John S. McCormick, *The Historic Buildings of Downtown Salt Lake City* (Salt Lake City: Utah State Historical Society, 1983) lists building dates for most of the structures in the downtown area. My count is based on buildings included in this book.

17. Miriam B. Murphy, "The Telegraph Comes to Utah," *Beehive History* 8 (1982): 29–31. See also tables previously cited.

18. See census tables previously cited; Poll et al., *Utah's History,* Table D, 688; and Helen Z. Papanikolas, "The New Immigrants," ibid., 447–49.

19. Kessler-Harris, *Out of Work,* 114, 116–17.

20. John Clifton Moffitt, *A Century of Service, 1860–1960: A History of the Utah Education Association* (Salt Lake City: Utah Education Association, 1960), 455–64.

21. Wertheimer, *We Were There,* 233. Some fifty women who worked in Utah responded to a two-page questionnaire on the conditions of their employment. These questionnaires are in my possession. For a summary of their responses pertaining to office employment, see Miriam B. Murphy, "Women in the Utah Work Force from Statehood to World War II," *Utah Historical Quarterly* 50 (Spring 1982): 152–54.

22. See census tables previously cited. Arrington and Alexander, *A Dependent Commonwealth,* 54, 57–60; Lois Scharf, *To Work and to Wed: Female Employment, Feminism, and the Great Depression* (Westport, Conn.: Greenwood Press, 1980), 13.

23. See census tables previously cited. Considered a step above domestic servants, women laundry, hotel, and restaurant workers performed their tasks under some of the most grueling conditions of any laborers. See Kessler-Harris, *Out to Work,* 236; Wertheimer, *We Were There,* 214–17.

24. Arrington and Alexander, *A Dependent Commonwealth,* 84.

25. Karl Alwin Elling, "The History of Organized Labor in Utah (1900–1920)" (M.S. thesis, University of Utah, 1962), 98–99. In addition to the laundry workers and other workers cited below, Elling notes that Bessie S. Seabolt organized the Utah Association of Public Multigraph Operators in February 1914 (81). The organizing of telegraphers in April 1918 cost seven women their jobs (87–88). The union activities of women in industry contrast sharply with organizations like the Capitol Girls Club, founded in 1921 to provide social activity for women employed in various state offices. See Capitol Girls Club Records, 1937–44, Utah State Historical Society Library, Salt Lake City.

26. Ibid., 95–96; "Chocolate Girls Organize Union," *Salt Lake Tribune,* January 23, 1910, 32.

27. Elling, "The History of Organized Labor," 105–6; *Salt Lake Tribune,* May 2, 1919; Thomas G. Alexander, "From War to Depression," in Poll et al., *Utah's History,* 471.

28. Dr. Caroline Hedger, "Making Good on the Job," *Young Woman's Journal* 33 (March 1922): 163–67.

29. "Her Business Life," Lesson 7 of Latter-day Saint Women, Senior Course of Study, *Young Woman's Journal* 33 (October 1922): 623–26.

30. Quoted in Scharf, *To Work and to Wed,* 17. Scharf calls combining a career and marriage "the dominant feminist issue of the 1920s" (20).

31. Susan Ware, *Holding Their Own: American Women of the 1930s* (Boston: Twayne Publisher, 1982), 199.

32. Lela Horn Richards, *The Growth of Neighborhood House* (Salt Lake City: Neighborhood House, 1929).

33. Ibid., 10–11.

34. Ibid., 12. Almost 24,000 women volunteered to aid the war effort doing thirty-five different kinds of work. In addition to volunteering, women also took paid employment. A committee chaired by Mrs. E. F. Morris "helped many patriotic girls and women to secure and hold places made vacant by the enlistment of men for military service." Noble Warrum, *Utah in the First World War* (Salt Lake City: Utah State Council of Defense, 1924), 122–23. It is difficult to document women's wartime work. The best guess is that Utah's booming factories provided many more jobs for women in food processing and the manufacturing of clothing. See 1917–18 issues of *Payroll Builder.* World War I may also have allowed women to increase their number in office jobs, an area that had been feminizing rapidly since the turn of the century.

35. Alexander, "From War to Depression," 469.

36. Ibid., 467. Arrington and Alexander, *A Dependent Commonwealth,* 71.

37. U.S. Bureau of the Census, *Fifteenth Census of the United States: 1930; Occupational Statistics, Utah* (Washington, D.C.: Government Printing Office, 1931), Table 4, beginning p. 6. U.S. Bureau of the Census, *Population 1920: Occupations,* Table 15 beginning p. 116. All data cited for 1920 and 1930 hereinafter are drawn from these two tables unless otherwise noted.

38. Alexander, "From War to Depression," 469–71.

39. Ronald G. Coleman, "A History of Blacks in Utah, 1825–1910" (Ph.D. diss., University of Utah of Utah, 1980), 70, 80. Black Latter-day Saints, for example, typically lived in "family units." See ibid., App. B, pp. 226–28, for a listing of black workers from 1870 to 1910. For a thought-provoking comment on the stereotyping of black women, see Ware, *Holding Their Own,* 13. Black women were often employed at the bottom of the pay scale or in service jobs but not necessarily because they lacked education or skills. Mignon Richmond, who graduated from Utah State Agricultural College in 1921, failed "to find work as a teacher and for many years worked as a laboratory technician and school lunch supervisor." Ronald G. Coleman, "Blacks in Utah History: An Unknown Legacy," in *The Peoples of Utah,* edited by Helen Z. Papanikolas (Salt Lake City: Utah State Historical Society, 1976), 139.

40.   Helen Z. Papanikolas, conversation with Miriam B. Murphy, May 1979.

41.   Helen Z. Papanikolas and Alice Kasai, "Japanese Life in Utah," in *The Peoples of Utah,* describe a boardinghouse run by Suga Iwanoto in Latuda, Utah, and women's involvement in farming (338–39). Don C. Conley, "The Pioneer Chinese of Utah," ibid., 268, notes a Chinese enterprise, the King Doll Hospital. One of the King daughters, Ruth M., became a physician.

42.   Joseph Stipanovich, *The Southern Slavs in Utah: A Social History* (San Francisco: R. and E. Research Associates, 1975) 80, describes boardinghouses kept by Slavic women in Utah. These small operations may not have been tabulated in the census. Some Italian women also kept boardinghouses and worked as clerks in family-owned businesses like the Double Rock Store in Helper, Utah. Philip F. Notarianni, conversation with Miriam B. Murphy, May 1979.

43.   Kessler-Harris, *Out of Work,* 252.

44.   John Clifton Moffitt, *The History of Public Education in Utah* (Provo, Utah: Deseret News Press, 1946), 190–91.

45.   U.S. Bureau of Census, *Population 1920: Census Occupations,* Table 16, 442–43; U.S. Bureau of Census, *Fifteenth Census . . . 1930; Occupational Statistics,* Table 11, 16.

46.   U.S. Bureau of Census, *Fifteenth Census . . . 1930: Occupation Statistics, Utah,* Table 3, p. 5, Tables 13, 14, p. 20.

47.   John F. Bluth and Wayne K. Hinton, "The Great Depression," in Poll et al., eds., *Utah's History,* 481–83.

48.   Ibid., 484–85.

49.   FERA projects involving women are described in some detail in Federal Writer's Project, "Utah's Program of Work Relief under the Federal Emergency Relief Administration, April 1, 1934 to July 1 1935," typescript, Utah State Historical Society Library: clothing, 24–25; canning, 25–28; household domestic goods, 28–29; public health, 31; recreation, 31–32; nursery schools and school lunch programs, 32–35. Ella B. Heim was director of the women's department and Mrs. V. M. Parmelee of social service. Larry H. Malmgren, "A History of the WPA in Utah" (M.S. thesis, Utah State University, 1965). See also LaVon B. Carroll, "Melba Judge Lehner and Child Care in the State of Utah," *Utah Historical Quarterly* 61 (Winter 1993): 40–62, for a detailed look at the WPA and Lanham Act nursery schools and the women involved in them.

50.   Malmgren, "A History of the WPA in Utah," 81–82.

51.   Ibid., 42–67.

52.   Ibid., 104.

53.   Ibid., 106.

54.   Ibid., 107–8.

55.   Ibid., 97, 98–100, 108–9.

56.   U.S. Bureau of the Census, *Population, Second Series: Characteristics of the Population, Utah* (Washington, D.C.: Government Printing Office, 1941), Table 16, p. 28. Women seem to have been less vulnerable psychologically to the problems created by the depression, especially job loss. See Scharf, *To Work and to Wed,* 140–41, and

John S. McCormick, "Women in Utah during the Great Depression," Utah Women's History Association Lecture in Midvale, January 24, 1984; photocopy of typescript in my possession, courtesy of McCormick.

57. Ware, *Holding Their Own,* 35.

58. Scharf, *To Work and to Wed,* 55; O. N. Malmquist, "Utah House Head for Bills Record," *Salt Lake Tribune,* February 6, 1939, 1, 6.

59. "Utah's Houses Resume Duties Today," *Salt Lake Tribune,* February 14, 1939, 7; "Working Wives Ban Doubtful," *Deseret News,* February 16, 1939, 6; Scharf, *To Work and to Wed,* 56, 58; State of Utah, *Senate Journal* (Salt Lake City: State of Utah, 1939), 597.

60. Murphy, "Women in the Work Force," 146, 153; G. A. Done, Letter to Gov. Henry H. Blood, March 29, 1933, and Blood, Letter to Done, May 2, 1933, in Henry H. Blood, General Correspondence collection, Utah State Archives, Salt Lake City. Done complained about a married woman who worked for the state while her husband was employed in private business. The woman was probably fired, since she is not listed as employed in subsequent city directories. See also Scharf, *To Work and to Wed,* 104–5. Vicente V. Mayer, "After Escalante: The Spanish-Speaking People of Utah," in Papanikolas, ed., *The Peoples of Utah,* 447, describes the "harsh realities of migrant life."

61. U.S. Bureau of Census, *Population, Second Series . . . Utah,* Table 18, p. 31, Table 16, p. 28.

62. In city directories, look especially under listings of grocers, hotels, etc.

63. Centennial Committee, eds., *Memory Book to Commemorate Gunnison Valley's Centennial, 1859–1959* (n.p., [ca. 1959]), 186–95.

64. Maurine C. Jensen, ed., *Midvale History, 1851–1979* (Midvale, Utah: Midvale Historical Society, 1979), 129–59: Edna Irving, a milliner, built her own shop in 1910 (129); Sabrina Goff opened a mortuary in 1935 with two men (132); Mrs. Sherman Johnson Sr., with her son opened Utah Bit and Steel in 1930 (158). Madoline Edward Dixon, *Peteetneet Town: A History of Payson, Utah* (Payson, Utah: Author, 1974), mentions a millinery establishment with sixteen employees and branch sales (132–33), and a flower shop and greenhouse (207–14). Pearl F. Jacobsen, ed., *Golden Sheaves from a Rich Field: A Centennial History of Richfield, Utah 1864–1964* (Richfield, Utah: Richfield Centennial Committee, 1964), 239–77, notes bakeries opened by a Dutch immigrant couple (290); an all-girl orchestra organized in 1929 (299); and store owner Lucy Sorensen Stucki (314).

65. State of Utah, *Second Report of the State Bureau of Immigration, Labor, and Statistics . . . 1913–1914* (Salt Lake City: Arrow Press/Tribune Reporter Co., 1915), 10. These reports contain some of the best information available on employment conditions for women.

66. State of Utah, *First Report of the State Bureau of Immigration, Labor and Statistics . . . 1911–1912* (Salt Lake City: State of Utah, 1913), 27.

67. State of Utah, *Second Report . . . 1913–1914,* 13; State of Utah, *Bulletin of the Industrial Commission of Utah, July 1, 1930 to June 30, 1932,* 164–65; State of Utah, *Bulletin No. 5 of the Industrial Commission of Utah, July 1, 1926 to June 30, 1938,* 6.

68. State of Utah, *Bulletin No. 5 . . . 1938,* 7–9; State of Utah, *Bulletin No. 5 of the Industrial Commission of Utah, July 1, 1938 to June 30, 1940,* 6.

69. Ibid., 8–9.

70. Ibid., 16–17.

71. Ibid., 16–18.

72. Ibid., 20.

73. "Utah Benefits Far below National Average," *Utah Employment Security Digest,* May 12, 1948, 6.

74. Kessler-Harris, *Out to Work,* 295–99.

75. John E. Christensen, "The Impact of World War II," in Poll et al., eds. *Utah's History,* 498, 500–501.

76. "School Head to Seek Aid in Coast Meet," *Deseret News,* September 10, 1942; "S. L. Schools Lack Teachers," ibid., October 27, 1942, 13.

77. See Rebecca Phillips Guevara, "Guadalupe Otanez Guevara," MSS A-4316, Utah State Historical Society Library, Salt Lake City. In an unusual look at the working environment of women, Guevara states that for Lupe, employment was "a pleasant social experience as well as a means for an income. . . . She . . . traded stories while working with the other employees and through the years they watched . . . each other's children grow."

78. "Help Wanted—Women," *Deseret News,* September 11, 1942, 19; "Help Wanted—Women," ibid., November 10, 1942, 15.

79. Laura Byrne, conversation with Miriam B. Murphy, July 1984. Laura is my sister.

80. *Utah Employment Security Digest,* October 1942, 1–4.

81. Ibid., June 15, 1947, 1, 3.

82. Ibid., 3. These figures are all undoubtedly low because the number of women in industries not covered by unemployment insurance is projected as a constant based on the 1940 census figure. Taken as is, the figures could mean that women had to find 11,000 new jobs between March 1947 and 1950 to achieve the figure of 57,294 employed shown in the 1950 census.

83. Ibid., March 15, 1943, 1.

84. "Mrs. Noorda Takes Seagull Spotlight as 'Featured' Civilian," *Seagull* (publication of the Clearfield Naval Supply Depot), March 18, 1944, 3, for example, has an article by Mrs. Alice Noorda, a job interviewer, whose husband and daughter also worked at the depot. Mrs. Noorda had left a job at Purity Biscuit Company for what was probably higher pay at Clearfield. "Nursery Opens at Anchorage," *Seagull,* May 2, 1944, 1, announced the nursery opening. For a study of social problems during the war, see Thomas G. Alexander, "Utah War Industry during World War II: A Human Impact Analysis," *Utah Historical Quarterly* 51 (Winter 1983): 72–92.

85. Thomas G. Alexander and Leonard J. Arrington, "Utah's Small Arms Ammunition Plant during World War II," *Pacific Historical Review* 34 (1965): 189–90.

86. Ibid., 189.

87. "The Safety Hazard of the Month—Horseplay," *Bombshell* (publication of the Ogden Arsenal), January 20, 1945, 4; "Here's the Latest Dirt," ibid., February 25, 1945, 12, 13.

88.   I computed these percentages from figures in U.S. Bureau of the Census, *Census of Population: 1950,* Vol. 2, *Characteristics of the Population,* Part 44: *Utah* (Washington, D.C.: Government Printing Office, 1952), Table 26, pp. 44–31. The work force's age is detailed in Table 69, pp. 44–95. The number of women ages thirty-five to forty-four and forty-five to fifty-four who were working had more than doubled in ten years. The marital status of the employed is in Table 70, pp. 44–96, which shows 30,305 married women employed out of the 57,145 total. Information in the following paragraph comes from Table 77, pp. 44–119.

89.   See, for example, Magdalena Mora and Adelaida Del Castillo, eds., *Mexican Women in the United States: Struggles Past and Present* (Los Angeles: Chicano Studies Research Center Publications, University of California, 1980).

90.   "January Job Insurance Claims Break Records," *Utah Employment Security Digest,* February 15, 1946, 1; "Problems of Suitability," ibid., December 29, 1945, 1–2.

91.   "Unemployment Insurance and the Utah Economy," ibid., January 15, 1951, 6.

92.   U.S. Bureau of the Census, *Census of Population: 1950 . . . Utah,* Table 25, pp. 44–30. The sum of those employed and those looking for work do not total 57,294. Evidently 37 female military personnel stationed in Utah were included in the total work force but not with employed civilians.

93.   Ibid., Table 74, pp. 44–106, shows seven women still employed as operatives in steel mills and a total of forty-three in all metal manufacturing industries.

94.   El Roy Nelson, *Utah's Economic Patterns* (Salt Lake City: University of Utah Press, 1956), 13.

95.   Leicia L. Parks, ed., *The Next Millennium—Utah Workforce 2000* (Salt Lake City: Utah Department of Employment Security, 1987), 23. This remarkably well-written bulletin contains a wealth of information on the state's workers, with special emphasis on changing demographics in relation to employment.

96.   Mark Knold, Utah Department of Workforce Services fact sheets, July 1, 2003, retrieved July 2004 from mknold@utah.gov and jobs.utah.gov/wi.

97.   Ibid.

98.   Rachna Choudhry, "The Long and Winding Road to Equal Pay," retrieved in July 2004 from rchoudhr@aflcio.org. See also www.aflcio.org/women.

99.   Institute for Women's Policy Research, "The Status of Women in Utah: Highlights," retrieved in July 2004 from www.iwpr.org.

100. Jennifer K. Nii, "Women's Firms Booming in Utah," *Deseret Morning News,* April 29, 2004.

7

From Schoolmarm to State Superintendent

The Changing Role of Women in Education, 1847–2004

Mary R. Clark and Patricia Lyn Scott

"Come children, come. We will begin now." With these words, tradition holds, sixteen-year-old Mary Jane Dilworth opened Utah's first school with nine pupils on October 24, 1847, three months to the day after the first Mormon pioneers entered the valley of the Great Salt Lake. This event and the public exhortations of church leaders have been used to illustrate Mormon commitment to education. While Mormons valued education, territorial schools were not necessarily the "firm foundation upon which is built the present day system of education" in Utah.[1] Educational historian Frederick Buchanan found that Utah's present public school system "cannot be explained by simply claiming it developed out of Utah's inspired, prophetic pioneer heritage."[2] Ideology was less important than practical considerations as political leaders shaped the Mormon educational perspective.[3] Like other western territories, education was spurred and retarded sporadically by the political, economic, and social realities of frontier life. In Utah, Mormon idealogy simply became a fourth element.

Three distinct kinds of schools developed in early Utah. First were the ward schools, infrequently supported by taxes and most commonly funded through tuition. Second were the private or "select" schools operated and funded privately. Third were non-Mormon schools operated and funded by missionary boards from Protestant denominations in the East. All three types of schools played a role in the development of public education in Utah and women participated significantly in each.[4]

Mormon desecularization became a major element in the prolonged struggle for Utah statehood, not achieved until 1896.[5] The schools were an early battleground to end Mormon control of daily life in Utah. During the twentieth century, educational practices and policies, while still strongly reflecting Mormon values, were primarily influenced by national trends and standards. What has been the role of women, individually and collectively, in the development of education from 1847 to the end of the twentieth century?

Background

Historical accounts, personal documents, and public records reveal patterns of employment and compensation, occupational status, academic preparation, and standards of professionalism in Utah schools since the days of early settlement, especially in the broader context of other Western states and the nation as a whole. As late as 1966, a report on women in Utah found: "The social transition resulting in part from the influences outside the religious subculture today presents many Utah men, women, employers, educators, and families with conflicts in values and attitudes about the appropriate role of women in relationship to their families; women have been affected to a greater extent than almost any other segment of the population."[6]

In the eighteenth and early nineteenth centuries, teaching was considered an acceptable extension of the female domestic sphere, an occupation suited to women because of their "natural" ability to nurture and train children.[7] In 1822, Catherine Beecher noted that "generally speaking there seems to be no very extensive sphere of usefulness for a single woman but that which can be found in the limits of the school-room."[8] She and Horace Mann, among others, campaigned for women as elementary school teachers, especially in the West, Beecher estimated that 90,000 were needed and argued: "It is chimerical to hope that men would become teachers when there are multitudes of other employment that will . . . lead to wealth." Thus, "it is woman who is fitted by disposition and habits and circumstances, for such duties, who to a very wide extent must aid in educating the children and youth of the nation." Further, "moral and religious education must be the foundation of national instruction," and energetic and benevolent women" must be its mainstay.[9] Thus, the stereotype of the young schoolmarm bringing civilization and culture to rough frontier towns is actually how many school teachers saw themselves.[10]

Pioneer Schools

Utah's territorial schools paralleled those in other western territories with some notable exceptions. Public meetinghouses were often the first buildings erected—places in which to worship and, as the need was felt, to hold school on weekdays. Local ward bishops collected school taxes and hired teachers until a local board of school trustees took over the responsibility. In addition, the first legislative assembly in 1851 established a legal framework for schools based on the system used for the university at Nauvoo, Illinois, with schools in each ward, supervised by three wardens. In 1851, the office of territorial school superintendent was also created. The Regents of the University of Deseret (renamed the University of Utah in 1894) appointed the superintendent, who made annual reports to them. Between 1865 and 1896, the superintendent's appointment varied according to political control of the territorial government. The territorial legislature mandated the creation of local school districts in 1852. The lack of territorial funds left the burden of school support on the districts themselves, which, in those days were usually comprised of only one school.[11] By 1854, about 13,000 students were enrolled in 226 schools in the Utah Territory.

In the 1860s the office of county superintendent of schools was created, promoting centralized school policy and curriculum, at least in theory. Early school laws were generally ineffective or unenforced at the local level. By 1864, there were 144 school districts and only 120 schools. Two years later, the trend shifted so that there were more schools than districts, but even then these districts averaged fewer than seventy students apiece.[12]

Utah, like other western territories, had no true public school system until the last decade of its territorial period. Whether organized by local LDS wards or by private individuals, most early school were open only to children whose parents could afford to pay the required tuition.

In early Utah, men and women entrepreneurial teachers opened private schools to fill the gap in public education by offering schooling for tuition ranging from 50 cents to $4 per pupil for a ten-week term. The *Deseret News* records the opening of many such schools. For example, Lydia Knight arrived in Salt Lake City in 1850, noted the shortage of schools, and opened a school in her home. In October 1858, newly widowed Sarah Ann Cooke began advertising a "select" school for girls at her home in Salt Lake's Fourteenth Ward. She offered instruction in primary and advanced English and lessons on the melodeon for $12 a quarter, plus a $3 fee for use of books and instruments.[13] By 1855, 125 students were enrolled in four private schools in Utah County.[14]

While school trustees had the "power to assess and collect a tax upon all taxable property" in the district and the "power to dispose of personal property and real estate," many communities supported their schools through tuition and not taxes.[15] When taxes were collected, they often went for construction and maintenance of school buildings. Teacher salaries and textbooks had to be financed through tuition. Since cash was in short supply, families often paid tuition with crops and/or labor. From 1860 to the 1880s, LDS leaders spoke often against public education. Brigham Young did not support free schools and publicly declared his opposition "to taking from one man and giving it to another."[16] He believed that every child ought to have the opportunity of receiving an education but not as financed by taxation: "I do not believe in allowing my charities to go through the hands of a set of robbers who pockets nine-tenths themselves, and give one-tenth to the poor."[17] Free public schools did not become a part of Utah's history until the Free Public School Act of 1890.[18]

School was conducted for a few months during the winter and then for only a few hours a day. Most schools in the first decades were taught by

Fourteenth District School First Reader class, taken on the front steps of the old Fourteenth Ward Assembly Hall, Salt Lake City, September 1890.

"interested or needy persons simply volunteering to teach as much as they knew."[19] Courses of study were elementary, and textbooks rare. There were no compulsory education attendance laws, no standards for teacher certification, and no legally defined length for a school year. The superintendent of territorial schools had no supervisory authority, but only power to recommend and report.[20]

Mormon ward bishops who "generally supplied both the civic and religious leadership in the local districts" were responsible for establishing and maintaining local schools.[21] Hence, standards for the quality and effectiveness of the schools varied with the tenure of the ward authorities and also varied from ward to ward. Although schooling was in the temporal control of male school church leaders, few wards could find qualified men who had either the time or the inclination to teach school. For most, "education was not the most important thing in the lives of early settlers. Making a living for one's family came first," as one historian put it.[22] Thus Brigham Young encouraged women in July 1869 to "develop the powers [with] which they are endowed . . . [and] to enlarge their sphere of usefulness for the benefit of society at large."[23] His reference to women's sphere echoed nineteenth-century America's doctrine of domesticity which kept a distinct boundary around the home sphere and limited women's participation in work and public life. This separate-spheres concept "help explain[s] . . . the configurations of opportunity and exclusion in employment of women."[24]

Mormon women often had greater responsibilities than other pioneer women. Their husbands were often away from home on missions or dividing their time with other plural families. Mormon women felt economic pressures to become self-sufficient by bartering goods and services, or finding employment. Many plural wives set up home schools to teach basic skills to the family's children, for Brigham Young had preached in 1852: "The duty of the mother is to watch over children, and give them their early education. . . . Let education commence at this point, you mothers! and then with brother [Orson] Spencer and the [B]oard of Regents" of the University of Deseret.[25]

For example, Lucy Meserve Smith, a plural wife of Apostle George A. Smith, taught school in Provo, accepting food as tuition. During the early 1850s, she "would come home at noon and go back to my school without a bit of dinner til[l] some one threshed, then I would get wheat on schoolbill."[26]

In St. George, Martha Cragun Cox's pay was twenty dollars worth of produce a month, which she had to collect herself, going from house to house. Josephine Miles, another St. George teacher, wrote, "Many couldn't pay anything. Those who could, paid the teacher in produce which they could spare; whether or not it was useful for the teacher mattered little."[27]

One unidentified resourceful teacher in St. George, collected a quart of milk from each student every week for tuition. From the milk she made cheese. At the end of the twelve-week term, she loaded her carefully wrapped cheeses into a wagon and drove to Salt Lake City to sell them.[28] Less fortunate was another unnamed teacher who, after teaching for three months, received three red ruffled petticoats for her salary. She wasn't able to sell them or to trade them for either produce or tithing scrip.[29]

While some teachers lived at home, out-of-towners boarded with their students. Eighteen-year-old Lena Mortensen in Elsinore lived and taught in the house of the family of one of her ten students for about a week, then moved on to the next.[30]

A romantic aura surrounds the accounts of early women teachers in Utah. No doubt they accomplished much good, but they cannot be said to have shaped Utah's educational policies. Teaching was often a temporary task undertaken to supplement family income or to meet a community need for young children. Like sixteen-year-old Mary Jane Dilworth, they were often very young and had no professional training beyond elementary school. Their schools usually dissolved when they married, moved away, or were replaced with male teachers.[31] While these women provided an important service, they were not professional teachers. As Frederick Buchanan notes: "The romantic portrait of dedicated individuals committing themselves to the children of the pioneers has sometimes obscured the fact that the achievement of a teaching profession in Utah was not a result of spontaneous growth and 'natural' development, but came only after years of struggle against lack of resources . . . parochial self interests, community apathy and lack of adequate facilities for teacher preparation."[32]

In 1862, forty-three men and fifty-nine women were teaching in the territory. Two years later, only four more women were teaching while the number of male teachers had increased to eighty-eight. As more teachers were needed, more women were hired, although men continued to hold the majority of teaching positions. In 1868, 55 percent of all teachers were men. By 1871, the total teaching force had increased to 358, but the gender ratio remained the same.[33]

In 1870, when national statistics became available for the first time, about 60 percent of the teachers nationwide were female.[34] The percentage of woman teachers in Utah slowly increased to almost 64 percent at the turn of the century, but the state still had a significantly higher proportion of men teachers compared to the nation. Numbers, however, do not tell the whole story. Far outnumbering women employed as teachers in any given year were those who had been teachers at some time in their lives. They saw teaching as an acceptable, though temporary, occupation for their daughters. In addition, women teachers served as role models for young girls, giving them the desire to continue their education and perhaps to become teachers themselves.[35]

Nor does this ratio reflect an official church policy. In 1869, Brigham Young suggested: "We have sisters here, who, if they had the privilege of studying, would make just as good mathematicians or accountants, as any man; and we think they ought to have the privilege to study. . . . We have as good teachers as can be found on the face of the earth, if our bishops would only employ and pay them, but they will not."[36] In 1873, he berated ward bishops "who can not have anybody but a stranger for a school teacher."[37] In fact, Utah Territory needed trained women who would teach for low wages. In Utah, as in eastern states thirty years earlier, "teaching became the legitimation for women's entry into higher education."[38]

Training Teachers

A significant number of the first women students enrolled at the University of Deseret were daughters of territorial officials.[39] Territorial Superintendent Robert L. Campbell, in his 1870 report, congratulated the territorial assembly on the "establishment of the University" and expressed his hope that the new "normal department" would soon provide the territory with a supply of competent schoolteachers. He recommended legislation to provide full scholarships for a limited number of students from each county. That he expected many to be women is evident in his recommendation that school trustees should choose the most talented women for teachers. Where no women were sufficiently qualified, each district should send eligible women to the normal department.[40] He also deplored the sex discrimination of local districts:

> In the minds of some Trustees there is a prejudice against female teachers, but the experience of the Superintendent proves to him that the female teacher, if she be as intelligent and educated, is equal in capacity and ability to instruct and govern youth, and so far as regards the primary scholars, the female

teacher will sometimes excel in patience and forbearance; and wherever there is a healthy influence exerted by Trustees and parents, the government in a school taught by a dignified female, will not be lacking. The presence of a lady imparts an inspiration of respect, awe and reverence even to the rude of the other sex, which none but the vicious and barbarous can ignore.[41]

The 1876 legislature appropriated five thousand dollars for "normal training" at the University of Deseret "on condition that forty pupils annually be instructed free of charge, for tuition, books or apparatus, for one year in the normal department of said university."[42] Scholarship students were obliged to teach one year in their districts for each year of aid received. An early recipient was seventeen-year-old Ellen Langton from Smithfield who had taught eighty children in all grades the previous year. Ellen described her year at the university as "wonderful" and felt that, "after that year . . . she could really teach.[43]

Shauna Adix, who studied the differential treatment of men and women educators in Utah, found that "the early inclusion of women in the student body of the University of Deseret was generally ahead of such developments for women in other parts of the country, . . . [but] this inclusion had a pragmatic base, did not give women equal access to university resources, and was not rooted in basic commitment to . . . equal education for both men and women." Furthermore, educational patterns and goals for each sex differed: Men were encouraged to enter all professions; women were to be educated for their roles as wives, mothers, and teachers."[44] About the same period, liberal Mormon women advocated the cause of higher education for women in the pages of the *Woman's Exponent.* Yet, with few exceptions, women were limited to teacher training or domestic science programs.

In 1878, the faculty of Brigham Young Academy consisted of Karl Maeser, principal, Milton Hardy, head of the Intermediate Department, and Zina Presendia Young Williams, head of the Primary Department and Ladies Work Department. Hardy was paid $800, Williams $240.[45] Through the 1890s women comprised one-fourth to one-third of the University of Utah and Brigham Young Academy faculties. At the turn of the century, the few women faculty members were primarily found in domestic science and teacher training, where women students were concentrated. Not until 1904 was Maud May Babcock promoted to professor of elocution at the University of Utah, making her the first woman in the state to achieve the rank of full professor.[46]

As university teaching became more professional, it began to require an education beyond that considered "proper" for women. Normal schools provided an acceptable entry point. Alice Louise Reynolds graduated from Brigham Young's normal school in 1890. She was teaching at the Juab Stake Academy in Nephi when Benjamin Cluff, Brigham Young Academy's new president, proposed that she enroll at the University of Michigan for an advanced degree in literature. She completed her class work in Ann Arbor and, at age

Special Collections, Sherratt Library, Southern Utah University.

First graduating class at the Branch Normal School (Southern Utah University) located in Cedar City, 1900. Pictured are: Emma Gardner, Alice Redd, Amelia Dalley, Ella Berry, Joseph T. Wilkinson, Jr., and J. S. Dalley.

twenty-one, began her forty-four year career in Brigham Young Academy's English Department. During that time, she did further work at seven other universities including Chicago, Cornell, and Berkeley and became the second woman in Utah to achieve the rank of full professor.[47]

More typical of how women faculty fared in rank and teaching was Emma Kees, a graduate of the Pennsylvania State Normal School and Cook County Training School in Illinois. The University of Utah's Normal School hired her in 1891 as supervisor of primary work (elementary school) teacher training and as the first principal of its "model school," where student teaching was done.[48] She was not invited to attend a faculty meeting until April 1896, when she was given the rank of "instructor in the Theory of Teaching."[49]

The number of students in the Normal School grew steadily. During 1874–75, the average enrollment of men at the University of Deseret was sixty-five while that of women was thirty-nine. A decade later the average enrollment of men had doubled, but they outnumbered women only by 18 percent. Prior to the 1882–83 school year, total enrollment in the Normal Department was consistently below or equal to the forty scholarships provided annually by the state. In that year, however, enrollment doubled, partly because of an increasing demand for better teachers but mainly because the university gave tuition scholarships to forty normal students in addition to the legislature's forty and extended the course to two years.[50] Despite this encouragement of trained teachers, however, between 1882 and 1890 the legislative assembly consistently opposed efforts to make school attendance mandatory or to provide free, tax-supported schools.

DENOMINATIONAL SCHOOLS

An important development in Utah's education was high-quality schools operated by missionaries from other religious denominations. In 1915, Utah's Superintendent D. H. Christensen noted the high standards established by denominational schools: "With this [mission] school . . . music and art soon became daily exercises, nature study was introduced into the primary grades, and the study of Latin, of algebra and geometry pupils in seventh and eighth grades under trained teachers was not uncommon."[51] By 1875, Presbyterians, Episcopalians, and Baptists had established denominational schools in Utah Territory. For the next twenty years, these mission schools received consistent support from their various denominations and showed healthy enrollments of Utah students. They had two main goals: to educate and to convert.

In 1866, Congregationalist and Presbyterian minister Rev. Norman McLeod had become the first to propose that the best way to Christianize the Mormons "would be through the operation of free schools conducted by the mission board of the churches, in which to educate the young people of the LDS faith."[52] With the exception of the University of Deseret's preparatory division, there were no public high schools in the territory. The various Protestant missionary churches thus met a genuine need in establishing denominational academies (high schools).[53]

The mission schools, with their eastern funding, offered better and well equipped school buildings, a nine-month school year, and certified teachers who had college degrees. In most cases, the schools were tuition free, particularly to Mormon children. Unquestionably, the education received in these schools was almost always superior to that in Mormon ward schools.

The New West Education Commission, an independent arm of the Congregational Church headquartered in Chicago, drew many of its early teachers from the exemplary Cook County Normal School. One of the first to accept an appointment to Utah was Lydia Tichener, a teacher with several years of public school experience. She opened a school in Hooper in 1880 with seventeen pupils ranging in age from six to eighteen. By the end of the year, enrollment had quintupled and "even the Mormon bishop acknowledged . . . that the influence of her school was good."[54]

Members of the New West Commission traveled throughout the East fund raising and recruiting. Having broken her engagement to be married, twenty-one-year-old Gertrude Samson of West Medford, Massachusetts, ignored her family's opposition and came to Utah in 1883 to teach first in Sandy in Salt Lake County and then in Trenton, in Cache County. Her students recall her as "about 5' 6" tall with sparkling brown eyes and rosey [sic] complexion. She was very pretty, slim and the athletic type. She could play baseball with her students or put on a bathing suit and dive off an eight foot bank into the river . . . That made the boys envious as they didn't dare dive that far."[55]

While "most of the young single women stayed in Utah for only a few years and then returned East, . . . [some] remained in small Utah communities and made teaching a life-long career."[56] For example, Presbyterian missionary Frances R. Burke arrived in Toquerville in September 1881 and remained there until her death in 1927. She taught in the mission school until it was closed in the 1890s, then continued her missionary efforts until her health failed.[57]

Laura McCurdy Clark, went to a Presbyterian school in Gunnison. The teachers, Martha M. Green and her daughter Alice, believed that "the life of a child ought to be a process of adventure, experience, and practice of fine thinking and living."[58] Clark also recalled:

> We were taught etiquette, politeness, cleanliness of body and soul along with literature, music history, and mathematics. At the age of ten I was doing cube roots, algebra, and rhetoric. I had finished Reed and Kellogg's Grammar (usually the course of the eighth grade). I could diagram a sentence from Browning or Carlyle . . . and we gathered flowers, plants and bugs—to sketch and classify, "mount" and "cure" for specimen study.
>
> We were told to go afield and do things or find something of interest, and we did it.[59]

For the last two decades of the nineteenth century, denominational schools set new standards for Utah education for both boys and girls. Since Protestant mission schools provided better educational opportunities than the Mormon-controlled, poorly financed district schools, many Mormon parents put concern for their children above denominational loyalty. By 1885, more than 1,900 students, about two-thirds from Mormon backgrounds, were enrolled in twenty-eight New West Schools; and about nine hundred, "75 percent of them [with] Mormon parentage," attended thirty-one Presbyterian day schools with fifty-three teachers. The territory also had thirteen Methodist schools with 865 enrolled, five Episcopal schools with 795 students, four Catholic schools with 610 students, and two Baptist schools with 205 scholars.[60]

In 1890, over 67 percent of high-school students attended non-Mormon schools.[61] About 28 percent attended the preparatory school at the University of Utah or the new public Salt Lake High School. From the beginning, college preparatory schools like St. Mark's in Salt Lake City were staffed by experienced non-Utah teachers teaching Latin, Greek, higher mathematics, composition, and rhetoric. While some St. Mark's girls went on to college, many trained to be teachers and held positions in both public and denominational schools. In 1888, the headmaster of St. Mark's reported that thirty-nine of its graduates were teachers.[62] One, Anna Youngberg taught in the Fourteenth Ward school, was active in teacher organizations and institutes, and studied under Colonel Francis Parker of the Cook County, Illinois Normal School. In 1895, she became a highly regarded critic teacher at William M. Stewart's "model school" at the University of Utah, supervised all instruction in history and geography, and wrote several pamphlets for teachers of those subjects.[63]

Boarding and day schools like St. Mary's Academy and Rowland Hall, both in Salt Lake City, established a reputation for excellence in educating women and produced many of the state's early schoolteachers. Also notable was the instruction provided for young women by the Salt Lake Collegiate Institute supported by the Presbyterian Woman's Board of Home Missions. Jeannette Ferry, wife of a wealthy miner, helped fund the institution that became Westminster College in Salt Lake City. In 1902, she and her husband donated the land for the college under several conditions, one of which stipulated: "A portion of campus not exceeding five acres was to be set apart as a site for a woman's college building, to be erected by women . . . [with] a board of five women managers named by [Ferry] and approved by the [B]oard of Trustees." All classes were to be opened to female students and they were to enjoy all the advantages afforded to their male counterparts.[64] The women's building was completed in 1911 and was named Ferry Hall.

While the passage of the Edmunds-Tucker Act in 1887 ended the Mormon Church's control of Utah public schools, it also crippled church-sponsored schools. The territorial government assumed responsibility for public education and supervising all mission schools.[65]

Mormon Converts as Teachers

Reinforcing the denominational contribution were the activities of a group of professional educators who came to Utah after joining the Mormon Church in other states and Europe. According to Utah historian Charles S. Peterson, these teachers and administrators "emerged as a distinct and specialized community within Mormon society in the decades preceding the 1890s. Actively sponsored by Mormon leaders, . . . [they] adapted national and educational trends and principles to the Utah situation."[66]

Notable among them were Mary and Ida Cook, educated in Eastern normal schools. In about 1870, they came to Utah where they became Mormons the next year. They established grade schools, trained teachers, and upgraded the professional skills of in-service teachers through summer normal institutes and early teacher associations. Mary became principal of a model school for the University of Deseret's Normal Department in 1871. She also presided over the fledgling university during 1872 in the absence of President John R. Park. Ida was also employed for a time at the university, but established a high school in Logan, then was appointed principal of Brigham Young College where she also taught educational methods classes.

Maypole Dance at Rowland Hall, Salt Lake City, ca. 1920.

Ida Cook's students remember her as a hard task-mistress. One student, initially scared, came to "adore" Miss Cook.[67] Another student, Margaret Winifred Thomson Merril, was reduced to tears when Miss Cook, trying to teach her to speak louder, made her read a passage over five times, then continued the lesson after school, "until both were worn out." Nevertheless, "Margaret learned to love her as the best teacher she ever had."[68]

Each of the Cook sisters was nominated as superintendent of schools in different counties; but by law, women could not hold that office. In Salt Lake County, Mary's name was removed from the 1874 ballot.[69] Peterson summarizes "They were extraordinary women, but they were women, and therein lay limitations."[70]

Camilla Cobb had a similar career pattern. Born in Saxony, Germany, the youngest daughter of the principal of a "progressive" school for young children, she came to Utah with her more famous brother-in-law, Karl G. Maeser in 1860. In New Jersey, she studied the child-centered methods of Friedrich Wilhelm Froebel (1782–1852), a German educator and founder of the kindergarten system. Although she was the mother of seven, she devoted much of her life to educational activities, opened Utah's first kindergarten in 1875, and was instrumental in introducing progressive methods to Utah teachers.[71]

SALARY AND STATUS EQUALITY

An important break-through came when the first legislature after statehood in 1896 required that women public school teachers "shall in all cases receive the same compensation as is allowed to male teachers, for like services, when holding the same grade of certificate."[72] Still most local school boards did not comply with the law, and subsequent state school reports neither condemn this noncompliance nor cite the legislation. In 1906, for example, the average monthly salary of male teachers was $86.40, while that of female teachers was $55.41. In 1907, men teachers in Millard County made 85 percent more than women. In 1919, compulsory attendance laws required most students to stay in school through high school. To cover the increased cost of additional teachers, local school boards tried to economize by hiring teachers at lower salaries, bargaining with teachers individually.[73] They also hired teachers who did not hold state certificates. Despite an 1897 law requiring specifying certification, a minimum age of twenty years, and "requisite scholarship and culture,"[74] women under twenty still taught in the primary grades of county schools by passing an examination, often oral, conducted by the county board of examiners. Nineteen-year-old Dora Snow, for example, began teaching at an Ogden grade school in 1899, receiving a state grammar grade certificate five years later.[75]

In 1906, a law providing for uniform examinations under the State Board of Education eliminated so many teachers that the state board "found it necessary to issue a considerable number of permits or temporary certificates in order that the schools in several districts might not be forced to discontinue work."[76] Evidently many of the teachers retained in this manner were men.

State Superintendent A. C. Nelson was especially concerned about retaining male teachers: "There is a formative period in a child's life when he should not fail to come in touch with the strong and sturdy influence and personality of the progressive male teacher. Keep the salaries too low to admit our strong men remaining in the teaching corps, and you will cripple the system which every thoughtful citizen is so eager to raise to the highest possible standards."[77]

Still, the percentage of women teachers continued to increase as men moved into higher paying supervisory positions or sought better-paying jobs outside the classroom. While the number of teachers during 1905–06 had increased by 174, only 14 were male. Salt Lake City had 297 elementary teachers in 1906, eight men. Male teachers constituted only a third of the high school teachers, though both high school principals were men, as were 73 percent of the elementary school principals.

Men vastly outnumbered women as county school superintendents. Although women held these positions in Garfield, Piute, San Juan, and Wayne school districts, some for two or more years, they probably served because no

Emma J. McVicker (1849–1916) was the only woman to serve as Utah's State Superintendent until 2004. After her predecessor's death, she was appointed in 1900, to fill the remaining three months of his unexpired term. This photograph appeared in the *Church Review,* December 29, 1895, while she was an instructor at the Salt Lake Collegiate Institute.

Courtesy of the Giovale Library, Westminster College.

men were willing to work for the low salaries. In 1904, Garfield paid $250, Piute and Wayne paid $150, and San Juan paid $100 to their chief school officers. Marinda Halliday, superintendent of Kane County, received only $75! In addition to her supervisory duties, she probably taught, a common practice where salaries were so low.[78] Helen M. Knight was Grand County superintendent of schools from World War II until 1961. From 1952 to 1961, she was the only woman listed in the roster of district and city superintendents, and was replaced by a man in 1961.[79]

By 1922, women were serving as state superintendents in nine western states.[80] In 1900, Utah's governor had appointed Emma J. McVicker to fill the unexpired term of her male predecessor. An instructor at the Presbyterian Salt Lake Collegiate Institute and first president of the Children's Service Society of Utah in Salt Lake City, she was the first woman appointed as a University of Utah regent (1896) and the first woman to be elected president of the Utah Teachers' Association (1901), almost a decade before a woman was chosen to lead the national organization. In 1895, the Republican Party nominated Mrs. McVicker as state school superintendent, but the courts ruled that, since women could not vote, they were ineligible to run for office. John R. Park's name replaced hers on the ballot. When he died in 1900, she was appointed to fill the remaining three months of his unexpired term.[81] No woman held that position in Utah until June 2004 when the Utah Board of Education unanimously chose Patti Harrington. (See below).

In her 1900 report to the state legislature Mrs. McVicker observed: "As a whole the teachers were found to be faithful and to some degree efficient although there were marked exceptions, principally among the men teachers."[82]

As late as 1925, the Utah Education Association asserted that, in several districts, salaries were "not based on training, experience and merit."[83] Women educators moved to "professionalize" teaching by playing an active role in teachers' associations, first organized during the 1860s and 1870s.[84] They pressed for changes in policy, sometimes by legislation, that would require districts to hire, promote, and pay teachers by uniform standards. But Utah's economy was severely depressed until World War II brought federal defense contracts to the state.

Furthermore, until World War II, the average female teacher in America saw her job as temporary. If she married, she usually retired, either voluntarily or because the local school board would not rehire her. A pregnant teacher in the classroom was considered particularly unseemly. This policy was simply "understood" between the teacher and local school trustees, but about 1928 it became part of district contracts.[85] Historian Miriam B. Murphy reported: "Some women deeply resented this [practice], and some women kept their marriage a secret as long as they could in order to continue working."[86] As late as 1925, only 18 percent of women school teachers nationally were married.[87]

During the thirties and the Great Depression, married men were given preference over equally qualified single women throughout the nation, and Utah was not an exception. Men who taught older children were paid more than women who taught younger children, a policy which had been in force much earlier and which lasted into the 1950s. Men were paid for extra work during the summer as well as during the school year and were given preference for "merit" raises and promotions into higher paying supervisory positions. They were also eligible to receive additional compensation based on the number of dependents they could claim.[88] In 1932, Utah had 1,656 teachers; 1,023 of them were women (62 percent), but only 11.5 percent were married, while 85 percent of male teachers were married. Many of the married women were allowed to teach only because their husbands were physically unable to work.[89]

The depressed economy also reduced the number of teachers at a time when the school population continued to increase. The Utah Education Association (UEA) made repeated efforts to have all school boards adopt salary schedules; and the Utah chapter of Delta Kappa Gamma, in one of its few instances of overt political action, presented a documented study of preferential salaries to the Salt Lake City Board of Education in 1940, successfully forestalling a "differential wage scale for men educators in Salt Lake City Schools . . . which prevented the inauguration of disastrous discriminating measures against Salt Lake City women teachers."[90]

World War II created a need for more teachers as men were called into the armed services or took better-paying jobs that opened up in other occupations. New defense projects also created a higher-paying market for the women's employment. Between September 1941 and June 1942, "972 Utah teachers left the profession" and others did not sign contracts in the fall. As a result, "175 permits [were] issued . . . to teachers who could not meet certification requirements . . . despite the fact that there are approximately 6,500 qualified and certified persons . . . who cannot be induced to return to the school room because Utah school districts cannot pay salaries comparable to those paid in other fields."[91]

Eventually, the districts were forced to pay higher wages and recruit married women, some of whom quit again after the war but some of whom decided to continue teaching.[92] In 1949, 1,194 of Utah's 4,037 professional employees (teachers and administrators) (29.6 percent) were women: 47 percent married, 39 percent single, and 14 percent widowed or divorced. Of the male majority, 95 percent were married, 4 percent single, and 1 percent widowed or divorced.[93]

Although the number of male teachers increased markedly in Utah's elementary and secondary schools, as it did nationally, the overall ratio of men to women was higher in Utah than nationally. The percentage of men remained at 43 percent in 1952 and 1965, increased slightly to 45 percent in 1972, and then steadily decreased—to 35 percent in 1987 and to 33 percent in 1993. This figure remained slightly higher than the comparable national averages: 31 percent in 1961, 33 percent in 1976, 31 percent in 1986, and 28 percent in 1991.[94]

Furthermore, while the proportion of men in rural schools decreased nationally, the number of men in Utah's school districts increased steadily after 1930 and more than doubled between 1945 and 1952. Men outnumbered women teachers in twenty-four of the thirty-two school districts outside the Wasatch Front as late as 1978.[95]

The national increase in men teachers can be attributed partially to the G.I. Bill's educational benefits, but some Utah school district also paid returning veterans a "bonus" over base salaries, counted years of military service as years of teaching experience, and had dependency clauses. At least two districts in 1952 still made "special allowances for teachers having dependents," while the Utah Foundation, a conservative nonprofit research organization, argued for pay discrimination because "many occupations are competing with the teaching field for college-trained men, while relatively few occupations are competing with teaching for college-trained women."[96] Discriminatory pay was finally discontinued in 1973 as a result of legal action taken against the Davis County School District.

The tale of Lucile Roper reflects the lives of many women teachers during the mid-twentieth century. She graduated from Snow College in 1931 with a two-year certificate, taught school in Oak City and Deseret for a few years, attended summer school at Brigham Young University, and then taught for two years in Carbon County. She was forced to resign after she married

Patti Harrington, Utah State
Superintendent of Public
Instruction, ca. 2004.

Courtesy of Patti Harrington and Russ Robinson Photography, Salt Lake City (Utah).

Albert Hales in 1940. In 1947, she was asked to return to teaching and taught for a year. After raising her children, Mrs. Hales returned to teaching in 1960, responding to an acute teacher shortage. She updated her credentials through attending summer school and correspondence schools, but was forced to retire in 1974 after reaching the mandatory retirement age of sixty-five.[97]

As part of the same trend, the percentage of women principals dropped from 24 percent in 1945 to 13 percent in 1952. In 1966, the Governor's Committee on the Status of Women reported: "There is only one woman high school principal, . . . no junior high principal, and only 50 out 393 elementary principals are women."[98] By 1980, "Utah had the fewest women principals of any state in the country, a scant one percent compared to a 17 percent nationally.[99] By the 1990s, however, this percentage in Utah had increased dramatically to 26 percent, compared to 30 percent nationally. By 2001, 36 percent of Utah principals were women, compared to 44 percent nationally.[100]

For more than twenty-five years in Utah, the position of school district superintendent was filled by men in all forty school districts. Change began slowly with the Park City School District's appointment in July 1989 of Nancy M. Moore, a principal of Altara Elementary School in the Jordan School District as its first women superintendent.[101] By 2001, six women were serving as district superintendents: Nancy Deford (Park City), Patti Harrington (Provo), Christine Kearl (Rich County), Darline Robles (Salt Lake City), Patricia Rowse

(Tintic), and Kolene Granger (Washington County). As of this writing (spring 2005), only two districts have women superintendents: Catherine Ortega in Ogden and Jessie Pace in Wayne County.[102]

During the fifteen years between 1989 and 2004, eight districts (20 percent) of Utah's forty school districts had a woman superintendent. They represented four of Utah's seven urban school districts (Ogden, Park City, Provo, and Salt Lake City), two fast-growing districts with large populations from outside of Utah (Park City and Washington County), and three small rural districts (Rich County, Tintic, and Wayne County). Park City had two women superintendents during this period.[103]

For more than a century, no woman served as state school superintendent. Then in June 2004 the Utah Board of Education unanimously chose Patti Harrington over three male finalists. Her twenty-six years of educational experience ranged from acting as a substitute teacher and working as a school bus driver to serving as the Provo School District superintendent and finally to her position as associate state superintendent for student achievement and school success. In 1997, she was named Utah's Secondary School Principal of the Year for her work at Provo High School.[104] She greeted her new appointment as an opportunity "to represent education" and "looked forward to bridge building with the community and to working toward innovative solutions to perplexing issues in Utah's education."[105]

Women's status in higher education was also improving. In 1930, women faculty held 30 percent of faculty positions in Utah public universities; in 1960, that figure had fallen to 22 percent.[106] A 1969 study of eighteen leading universities nationally found that women constituted 10 percent of the faculties and less than 4 percent of the full professors. Women at the University of Utah constituted 15 percent of the faculty but only 8.6 percent of the associate professors and 2.7 percent of the full professors.[107] Since 1984, this trend has continued to improve. Women faculty increased from 20.4 to 27.1 percent in 1991, to 31.3 in 1998, and to 31.5 percent in 2000.[108] Despite these consistent gradual increases in the percentage of faculty women in public universities, it still lags slightly behind the national percentages in most ranks.

Utah was the only state where no woman had served as a college president when, in 1995, Westminster College appointed Dr. Peggy Stock as its fifteenth president. She had previously served for nine years as the first woman president of Colby-Sawyer College in New Hampshire. She described herself as having "been born under a blessed star because she served as the first woman president at two highly respected colleges."[109] Just a year later, the Utah State Board of Regents named Dr. Grace Sawyer Jones as president of the College of Eastern Utah. She was the school's first woman president, the first woman president of a public college, and the state's the first black president in the nine-campus Utah System of Higher education. Both women served longer than the average three year tenure of college presidents.[110] President Jones left in 2001 while President Stock resigned in 2002. Within months Utah's third woman president was named. On August 23, 2002, F. Ann Millner was named president of Weber State University, the first woman to be promoted from within Utah's System of Higher Education to a presidential post. She had served as an educator and administrator at the university since 1982, and as vice-president of university relations from 1993.[111]

Despite the feminist movement and national concerns for equal employment opportunities for women, men have continued to dominate Utah's most prestigious educational positions as they do in the nation. Many Utah women give priority to their families, especially to caring for young children. Furthermore, many women apparently prefer classroom teaching, do not want supervisory or administrative jobs, and assume other leadership roles in their schools or in professional organizations. In 1942, Hazel Bowen became the second woman to serve as UEA president. Fourteen women have held the position since: Maude Hardman, 1947; Afton Forsgren, 1952; Dorothy Zimmerman, 1956; Louise Bennett, 1963; Irene Hoyt, 1966; Marjean Ballard, 1973; Lucille Taylor, 1976; Kay Chatterton, 1977; Donna Peterson, 1980; Bettie Condie, 1981 and 1984; Beth Q. Beck, 1990; Lilia Eskelsen, 1990 and 1993, Phyllis Sorensen, 1996 and 2000, and Patricia Rusk, 2002.[112]

Women have contributed enormously to the development of education in Utah since the turn of the century by serving as trustees of private schools and colleges, as members of the Board of Regents, on the State Textbook Commission, on the State Course of Study Committee, and on the State Board of Education. They have provided untold numbers of hours of service in other uncompensated positions at district and local levels. Women gave notable service as members of the State Board of Education during the last forty years.

CONCLUSION

In summary, women have been represented at all levels of the educational system in Utah's history but have only recently been accorded the dignity, distinction, and compensation given to men. Women teachers were, in many ways, victims of accepted sex-role differentiation that adversely affected their employment, compensation, and professional advancement. Their collective activities created bonds of sisterhood and professional interests but did little to raise their status. Although few have achieved national distinction or enjoyed a status comparable to that of male educators in the state, some have been genuine leaders in the profession. Unfortunately, they stand out because they have been rarities.

NOTES

1.   Henry A. Smith, "The Church and Education," *Improvement Era* 38 (April 1935): 222; see also Joyce Kinkead, ed., *A Schoolmarm All My Life: Personal Narratives from Frontier Utah* (Salt Lake City: Signature Books, 1996), xxiii.

2.   Frederick S. Buchanan, *Education Among the Mormons: Brigham Young and the Schools of Utah.* University of Utah Graduate School of Education Report Series, No. 1,

1984 (Salt Lake City: Graduate School of Education, 1984): 14; see also Frederick S. Buchanan, "Education in Utah," *Utah History Encyclopedia,* edited by Allan Kent Powell (Salt Lake City: University of Utah Press, 1995), 153–55.

3.   Charles S. Peterson, "The Limits of Learning in Pioneer Utah," *Journal of Mormon History* 10 (1983): 65–78; Charles S. Peterson, "A New Community: Mormon Teachers and the Separation of Church and State in Utah's Territorial Schools," *Utah Historical Quarterly* 48 (Summer 1980): 293–312.

4.   Kinkead, *A Schoolmarm All My Life,* xxi.

5.   Gustive O. Larson, *The "Americanization" of Utah for Statehood* (San Marino, Calif.: Huntington Library, 1971); Stanley S. Ivins, "Free Schools Come to Utah," *Utah Historical Quarterly* 22 (October 1954); James R. Clark, "Church and State Relationships in Education in Utah" (Ed.D. diss., Utah State University, 1958); T. Edgar Lyon, "Evangelical Protestant Missionary Activities in Mormon Dominated Areas, 1865–1900" (Ph.D. diss., University of Utah, 1962); C. Merrill Hough, "Two School Systems in Conflict, 1867–1890," *Utah Historical Quarterly* 28 (April 1960), 113–28.

6.   Governor's Committee on the Status of Women in Utah, *Utah Women: Opportunities, Responsibilities: A Report of the Governor's Committee on the Status of Women in Utah, June 15, 1966* (Salt Lake City: Committee, 1966).

7.   Nancy Hoffman, *Women's "True" Profession: Voices from the History of Teaching,* 2d ed. (Westbury, N.Y.: Harvard Education Books, 2003).

8.   Quoted in Kathryn Kish Sklar, *Catherine Beecher: A Study in American Domesticity* (New Haven, Conn.: Yale University Press, 1973), 52.

9.   Ibid., 114; Glenda Riley, *A Place to Grow: Women in the American West* (Arlington Heights, Ill.: Harlan Davidson, 1992), 170; Courtney Ann Vaughn-Robertson, "Having a Purpose in Life: Western Women Teachers in the Twentieth Century," *Great Plains Quarterly* 5 (Spring 1985): 109.

10. Elliott West, *Growing Up with the Country: Childhood on the Far Western Frontier* (Albuquerque: University of New Mexico Press, 1989), 198.

11. Buchanan, "Education in Utah," 154.

12. Ibid.; Utah State Board of Education, *Historical Perspective on Major Educational Changes in Utah, 1847–1966* (Salt Lake City: Utah State Board of Education, 1966), 2.

13. Kinkead, *A Schoolmarm All My Life,* xxiii; Patricia Lyn Scott, "Sarah Ann Cooke: "The Respected Mrs. Cooke," in *Worth Their Salt, Too: More Notable but Often Unnoted Women of Utah,* edited by Colleen Whitley (Logan: Utah State University, 2000), 12.

14. Kinkead, *A Schoolmarm All My Life,* xxiv.

15. "An Act in Relation to Common Schools," *Acts, Resolutions, and Memorials Passed by the First Annual and Special Session of the Legislative Assembly of the Territory of Utah* (Salt Lake City: Brigham Young Printer, 1852), 98.

16. Quoted in Kinkead, *A Schoolmarm All My Life,* xxii.

17. Quoted in John D. Monnett, "The Mormon Church and Its Private School System in Utah: The Emergence of the Academies, 1880–1892" (Ph.D. diss., University of Utah, 1984), 22.

18. Ibid., 20.

19.   Ann West Lobb and Jill Mulvay Derr, "Women in Early Utah," in *Utah's History,* edited by Richard D. Poll, Thomas G. Alexander, Eugene E. Campbell, and David E. Miller (Provo, Utah: Brigham Young University Press, 1978), 346.

20.   T. Edgar Lyon, "Religious Activities and Development in Utah, 1947–1910," *Utah Historical Quarterly* 35 (Fall 1967): 295.

21.   John Clifton Moffitt, *The History of Public Education in Utah* (Salt Lake City: Deseret News Press, 1946): 32.

22.   Raymond Wiscombe, "One Hundred Years of Education in the Morgan County School District" (M.A. thesis, University of Utah, 1966), 48.

23.   Brigham Young, July 18, 1869, *Journal of Discourses,* 26 vols. (London and Liverpool: LDS Booksellers Depot, 1855–86), 13:61.

24.   David B. Tyack and Myra H. Strober, "Jobs and Gender: A History of the Structuring of Educational Employment by Sex," in *Educational Policy and Management: Sex Differentials,* edited by Patricia A. Schmuck et al. (New York: Academic Press, 1981), 132; see also Sklar, *Catherine Beecher;* Nancy F. Cott, *The Bonds of Womanhood: Women's Sphere in New England, 1780–1835* (New Haven, Conn.: Yale University Press, 1969); B. J. Harris, *Beyond Her Sphere: Women and the Professions in American History* (Westport, Conn.: Greenwood Press, 1978).

25.   Brigham Young, April 8, 1852, *Journal of Discourses,* 1:66, 68.

26.   Quoted in Kenneth W. Godfrey, Audrey M. Godfrey, and Jill Mulvay Derr, eds., *Women's Voices: An Untold History of the Latter-day Saints 1830–1900* (Salt Lake City: Deseret Book, 1982), 266.

27.   Quoted in Lorraine T. Washburn, "Culture in Dixie," *Utah Historical Quarterly* 29 (July 1961): 256.

28.   Ibid.

29.   Faye Jensen Buttle, *Utah Grows: Past and Present* (Provo, Utah: Brigham Young University Press, 1971), 201–2.

30.   James B. Allen, "Everyday Life in Utah's Elementary Schools, 1847–1870," in *Nearly Everything Imaginable: The Everyday Life of Utah's Mormon Pioneers,* edited by Ronald W. Walker and Doris R. Dant (Provo, Utah: Brigham Young University Press, 1999), 374.

31.   Ogden's first school teacher, Charilla Abbott, taught a few years, then married David Browning in 1853. Mae Browning Williams, "Charilla Abbott Browning: Ogden's First School Teacher," n.d., Delta Kappa Gamma Papers, Special Collections, Marriott Library, University of Utah Library, Salt Lake City. In the 1850s, when Sarah Kimball was replaced by a male teacher in Salt Lake City's Fourteenth Ward school, she opened a private school "convinced of the need of changed conditions for women engaged in work that came in competition with men." Jill Mulvay Derr, "Sarah Melissa Granger Kimball: The Liberal Shall Be Blessed," in *Sister Saints,* edited by Vicky Burgess-Olson (Provo, Utah: Brigham Young University Press, 1978), 29.

32.   Frederick Buchanan, "Gender in Utah Education," n.d., photocopy of typescript in our possession.

33. Unless otherwise noted, we have extrapolated all Utah statistics from tables published in *Reports of the Territorial Superintendent/Commissioner of Common Schools* and *Reports of the Superintendent of Public Instruction of the State of Utah* for the biennial period cited in the text.

34. Tyack and Strober, "Jobs and Gender," 133.

35. Utah chapters of Delta Kappa Gamma, an international society of outstanding women educators, collected biographical material on some of early Utah's notable women teachers. Many incidents support these findings. Several of the subjects recalled "playing teacher" as children, while others remember being impressed by their teachers and encouraged by their mothers. Most took every opportunity to further their own education, even after they were employed in schools. Delta Kappa Gamma Papers, Special Collections, Marriott Library.

36. Brigham Young, July 18, 1869, *Journal of Discourses,* 13:60–61.

37. Young, April 7, 1873, *Journal of Discourses,* 16:17–18.

38. Patricia Sexton, *Women in Education* (Bloomington, Ind.: Phi Delta Kappa Education Foundation, 1976), 46.

39. Shauna McLatchy Adix, "Differential Treatment of Women at the University of Utah from 1850" (Ph.D. diss., University of Utah, 1977), 46.

40. Robert L. Campbell, "Report of the Superintendent of Common Schools," *Journal of the Legislative Assembly of the Territory of Utah, Nineteenth Annual Session for the Year 1870* (Salt Lake City: Deseret News Book, 1870), 191–93.

41. Ibid., 193.

42. Moffitt, *The History of Public Education in Utah,* 286.

43. Elaine Norr, "A Pioneer in Education," n.d., typescript, not paginated, Delta Kappa Gamma Papers, Special Collections, Marriott Library.

44. Adix, "Differential Treatment of Women," 175–76; see also Kathleen Underwood, "The Pace of Their Own Lives: Teacher Training and the Life Course of Western Women," *Pacific Historical Review* 55 (November 1986): 513–30.

45. *Biennial Report of the Superintendent of District Schools for the Territory of Utah for the School Years 1878 and 1879* (Salt Lake City: Deseret News Steam Printing, 1880), 24; hereafter cited as *Territorial Report* by year.

46. David G. Pace, "Maud May Babcock: Speak Clearly and Carry a Big Umbrella," in *Worth Their Salt: Notable But Often Unnoted Women in Utah,* edited by Colleen Whitley (Logan: Utah State University, 1996), 151.

47. Ann Clark Bergendorff, "Life of Alice Louise Reynolds," n.d., typescript, not paginated, Delta Kappa Gamma Papers, Special Collections, Marriott Library; see also Amy Brown Lyman, *A Lighter of Lamps: The Life of Alice Louise Reynolds* (Provo, Utah: Alice Louise Reynolds Club, 1947).

48. Frances Gilroy Davis, "A History of the William M. Stewart School, 1891–1940" (M.A. thesis, University of Utah, 1940), 13.

49. Adix, "Differential Treatment of Women," 53.

50. *Territorial Report 1882–83,* 10.

51. D. H. Christensen, "Mission Schools in Utah," *Utah Educational Review,* January 1915, 13.

52. Quoted in David L. Bigler, *Forgotten Kingdom: The Mormon Theocracy in the American West, 1847–1896* (Logan: Utah State University, 1998). 272.

53. Monnett, "The Mormon Church and Its Private School System," 20.

54. Jennie Anderson Froiseth, *The Women of Mormonism* (Detroit, Mich.: C. G. G. Paine, 1882), 375–76.

55. "New West Schools," n.d., unsigned typescript, not paginated, Delta Kappa Gamma Papers, Special Collections, Marriott Library.

56. Jessie L. Embry, "Separate and Unequal: Schoolmarms of Utah 1900–1950," in *From Cottage to Market: The Professionalism of Women's Sphere,* edited by John R. Sillito (Salt Lake City: Utah Women's History Association, 1983), 63.

57. Sandra Dawn Brimhall and David A. Hales, "Frances R. Burke: Toquerville Presbyterian Missionary," *Utah Historical Quarterly* 72 (Spring 2004): 158.

58. Laura McCurdy Clark, *Others: An Enduring Symbol of Pioneer Vision* (N.p.: privately published, 1950), 24–25.

59. Ibid.

60. Bigler, *Forgotten Kingdom,* 275.

61. Clyde Wayne Hansen, "A History of the Development of Non-Mormon Denominational Schools in Utah" (M.A. thesis, University of Utah, 1953), 3.

62. G.D.D. Miller, "To the Friends of St. Mark's School," September 1886, St. Mark's School Manuscript Collection, Utah State Historical Society Library, Salt Lake City.

63. "Anna Youngberg," n.d., unsigned typescript, Delta Kappa Gamma Papers, Special Collections, Marriott Library.

64. Carl Wankier, "History of Presbyterian Schools in Utah" (M.A. thesis, University of Utah, 1968), 62–63. Named as managers in addition to Mrs. Ferry and her two daughters (Mary M. F. Allen and Kate Hancock) were Carrie (Mrs. Hal) Brown, Eunice (Mrs. F. S.) Gordon, Emma (Mrs. H. G.) McMillan, Sara (Mrs. Robert G.) McNiece, and Elizabeth (Mrs. Sam) Williamson, all from Utah, and Lillian E. (Mrs. John) Emerson from Pennsylvania, Frances B. (Mrs. T. S.) Hamline from Washington, D.C., Mary E. James (Mrs. Darwin R.) from Brooklyn, and Miss S. F. Lincoln from New York City. Women's Board of Westminster College, Minutes, Book 1, 6–7, Westminster College Archives, Giovale Library, Salt Lake City. The women's building was designed to provide housing for forty students and six teachers as well as to provide classrooms for female art and music students. R. Douglas Brackenridge, *Westminster College of Salt Lake City: From Presbyterian Mission School to Independent College* (Logan: Utah State University Press, 1998), 111–13. Ferry Hall was condemned and razed in 1987.

65. Jana Kathryn Reiss, "'Heathen in Our Fair Land:' Presbyterian Women Missionaries in Utah, 1870–1890," *Journal of Mormon History* 26 (Spring 2000): 193.

66. Peterson, "A New Community," 298. Occupying a narrow niche between Mormonism and denominations in direct competition were a few non-Mormon women teachers who had nonreligious reasons for coming to Utah. Josephine Hirst, for example, had been a pioneer teacher in the Midwest before she married a Union Pacific Railroad agent who was transferred to Utah. After his death, she taught for many years in Ogden's public schools. Florence Hirst Newcomb, "A Tribute to a Pioneer Teacher,"

n.d., unsigned typescript, Delta Kappa Gamma Papers, Special Collections, Marriott Library.

67. Jill Mulvay, "The Two Miss Cooks: Pioneer Professionals for Utah Schools," *Utah Historical Quarterly* 43 (Fall 1975): 405.

68. Ibid.

69. "Mrs. Margaret Winifred Thomson Merrill," ca. 1966, typescript, Delta Kappa Gamma Papers, Special Collections, Marriott Library.

70. Ida Ione Cook is listed as superintendent of Cache County in the Biennial Report, 1876–77, 19; see also Mulvay, "The Two Miss Cooks," 406.

71. Peterson, "A New Community," 305.

72. Catherine Britsch Frantz, "Camilla Clara Meith Cobb: Founders of the Utah Kindergarten," in *Worth Their Salt, Too,* 41–60.

73. Quoted in Moffitt, *History of Public Education,* 322.

74. John Clifton Moffitt, *A Century of Service, 1860–1960: A History of the Utah Education Association* (Salt Lake City: Utah Education Association, 1960), 464–72.

75. *Third Report of the Superintendent of Public Instruction of the State of Utah* (Salt Lake City: Arrow Press, 1901), 103; hereafter cited as *Utah School Report.*

76. "Dora Snow," n.d., unsigned typescript, Delta Kappa Gamma Papers, Special Collections, Marriott Library.

77. *Utah School Report, 1906,* 18.

78. Ibid., 19.

79. *Utah School Report, 1904,* 39–40.

80. David Tyack and Elizabeth Hansot, *Managers of Virtue: Public School Leadership in America, 1820–1980* (New York: Basic Books, 1986), 187. The nine states were probably Washington, Oregon, California, Idaho, Montana, Wyoming, Colorado, Nevada, and Arizona.

81. Carol Ann Lubomudrov, "A Woman State School Superintendent: Whatever Happened to Mrs. McVicker?" *Utah Historical Quarterly* 49 (Summer 1981): 254–61.

82. *Utah School Report, 1900,* 20.

83. "Notes from the House of Delegates," *Utah Educational Review* 19 (November 1925): 92–93.

84. In October 1870, sixteen educators (nine were women) met and organized the Salt Lake Teachers Association for the "improvement in the science of teaching, the diffusing of information upon the system of common school education among the people and to promote harmony of feeling and action and the greatest possible advancement in literary, scientific and general information." The nine women were Eleanor J. Pratt, Hannah King, Mary Morgan, Mildred C. Randall, Seraph C. Young, Josephine Taylor, Libbie Pratt, Mary E. Cook, and Ida Jane Cook. "Salt Lake Teachers Association Minutes, 1871–1873," Utah State Archives, series 1852, Salt Lake City.

85. Patricia A. Carter, *"Everybody's Paid But the Teacher": The Teaching Profession and the Women's Movement* (New York: Teachers College, Columbia University, 2002), 98, 111. By 1931, 77 percent of all U.S. school districts had instituted bans on married women teachers.

86. Miriam B. Murphy, "Women in the Work Force from Statehood to World War II," *Utah Historical Quarterly* 50 (Spring 1982): 146.

87. Carl N. Degler, *At Odds: Women and the Family in America from the Revolution to the Present* (New York: Oxford University Press, 1980), 412.

88. An examination of the Utah School Reports from 1930 to 1940 clearly shows the salary differences. See specifically *Utah School Reports, 1936,* 170–72.

89. Embry, "Separate and Unequal," 101.

90. Delta Kappa Gamma Society International, *Utah Heritage: Alpha Theta State* (N.p.: Alpha Theta State, 1980), 41; Irvin S. Noall, "Personal Factors Affecting Teachers' Salaries in Utah," *Utah Educational Review* 35 (May 1932): 439.

91. Alan M. West. "Can We Keep Teachers in Our Schools?" *Utah Educational Review* 35 (November 1942): 76, 80; Utah State Board of Education, *Report of 1941–42 Salary Equalization* (Salt Lake City: Utah State Department of Public Instruction, 1942), 8–9, 60.

92. Embry, "Separate and Unequal," 72–73.

93. Utah Foundation, "Salaries and Qualifications of Professional Public School Employees in Utah," *Report, No. 52* (Salt Lake City: 1949), Tables 3, 4.

94. Tyack and Strober, "Jobs and Gender," 147; Office of the State Superintendent of Public Instruction, *Status of Teacher Personnel in Utah, 1965–66, 1972–73, 1987–88, 1993–94* (Salt Lake City: Office of the State Superintendent of Public Instruction, 1979), Table 26, p. 31; National Center for Education Statistics, *Digest of Education Statistics, 1994* (Washington, D.C.: U.S. Department of Education, Office of Educational Research and Improvement, 1994), 79.

95. Office of the State Superintendent of Public Instruction, *Status of Teacher Personnel in Utah, 1977–78* (Salt Lake City: 1979), Table 26, p. 31.

96. Utah Foundation, "Financing Public Schools in Utah," *Report No. 74* (Salt Lake City: Author, 1952), 20.

97. David A. Hales, "School Days and Schoolmarms," *Utah Historical Quarterly* 67 (Spring 1999): 100–110.

98. Governor's Committee on the Status of Women, "Utah Women," 22.

99. *Status of Teacher Personnel 1993–94,* 4; "Room at the Top," *NEA Newsletter* 13 (November 1994): 14.

100. Jennifer Toomer-Cook and Jeffrey P. Haney, "Utah Women Lag in Top School Posts," *Deseret News,* August 19, 2001, A-1; Marie Byrd-Blake, "Female Perspectives on Career Advancement," *Advancing in Leadership Journal,* Spring 2004, 1, retrieved in spring 2004 from http://222.advancingwomenlaw/.

101. "3 Educators fill Top Posts in Districts," *Deseret News,* July 1, 1989, B-6; Brooke Adams, "Park City Superintendent Loves Her Job—Challenges and All," *Deseret News,* February 1, 1990, B-4.

102. Toomer-Cook and Haney, "Utah Women Lag in Top School Posts." Analysis of the *Utah Public School Directory,* 1989–2004, identifies superintendents during this period.

103. Analysis of the *Utah Public School Directory,* 1989–2004, identifies superintendents during this period.

104. Jennifer Toomer-Cook, "State Schools Chief Is Chosen," *Deseret News,* June 2, 2004, A-1.

105. Toomer-Cook and Haney, "Utah Women Lag in Top School Posts."

106. University of Utah Committee on Women's Education, *Final Report of the University of Utah Committee on Women's Education, February 1, 1970* (Salt Lake City: University of Utah, 1970), 33.

107. Ibid., 35.

108. The Salt Lake Community College has the largest percentage of women faculty: 46.4 percent in 1999–2000, increased from 41 percent in 1999. Snow College has the smallest: 24 percent in 1999–2000, decreased from 24.7 percent in 1991. Utah Board of Regents, "1999–2000 Annual Report on Women and Minorities in Faculty and Administrative Positions in the Utah System of Higher Education," retrieved on February 4, 2005, from http://www.utahbr.edu/reports.html.

109. Carli Dixon, "Dr. Peggy Stock Accepts Position as New Westminster President," *Westminster Review,* Summer 1995, 4–5.

110. Joe Costanzo, "Regents Pick N.Y. Educator as New President at CEU," *Deseret News,* July 16, 1996, B-1.

111. Maria Titze, "CEU President Set to Leave Her Trailblazing Post," *Deseret News,* August 15, 2000, B-5; Kristen Stewart, "Surprise Choice for WSU," *Salt Lake Tribune,* August 29, 2002, C-1. On May 23, 2005, Dr. Cynthia A. Bioteau of North Carolina was named the seventh president of Salt Lake Community College, the largest Utah campus to be headed by a woman. See, "Search Finally Up, SLCC Picks Chief," *Salt Lake Tribune,* May 24, 2005, A-1.

112. Telephone conversation with Kristie Rasmussen, UEA administrative assistant, November 19, 2004. In 2003, Lily Eskelsen was elected National Education Association (NEA) secretary-treasurer.

8

Scholarship, Service, and Sisterhood

Women's Clubs and Associations, 1877–1977

Jill Mulvay Derr

In a Different Voice, Carol Giligan's landmark study of psychological theory and women's development, concludes that male voices typically speak "of the role of separation as it defines and empowers the self," while female voices speak "of the ongoing process of attachment that creates and sustains the human community."[1] Certainly the Utah community has been shaped in part by the networks women have built and maintained. Clubs and associations have enabled women to assume an important role in public life, at the same time providing them a means to educate and sustain each other. Surveying a century of Utah women's formal connections, this chapter samples rather than lists the variety of organizations in which women have invested.

The hundred-year period defined by the 1877 founding of the Ladies Literary Club and the 1977 International Women's Year is broad enough to show how the nature and programs of women's associations changed in response to state and national developments. The chapter groups these changes into three periods: (1) 1877–1917, when women began establishing a new network of clubs and associations; (2) 1917–45, when both new and well-established organizations for women addressed the challenges of war, depression, and peace; and (3) 1945–77, an age of discontent and discovery informed by the twentieth-century women's movement. The choice of a hundred-year span precludes dealing with a single association or club in depth or across the full duration of its existence. Fortunately, women's groups have kept good records and a number of informative studies have been completed or are underway. Associations connected to Utah churches are not examined in depth here because of the separate chapter on women in religion. (See chap. 3.) Often these associations have been involved in activities parallel to, if not connected with, those of women's secular associations. Information regarding women's political, professional, and labor associations is likewise to be found elsewhere. (See chaps. 6, 7, and 11.)

The history of Utah women's clubs and associations is best understood within the context of the ongoing national discussion about woman's role in the public sphere. During the mid-nineteenth century, as industrialization spread in the United States, the question of appropriate roles of women emerged as a burning topic. In many of the nation's homes, woman's direct contribution to the family income decreased and she assumed more exclusive responsibility for the "domestic sphere," as nurturer, homemaker, and moral guardian. Karen Blair, historian of the woman's club movement in the United States, explained that the growing apart of "man's public and woman's domestic spheres" resulted in the "virtual banishment of women from the public sphere."[2] The nineteenth-century suffrage movement, the women's club movement, and the twentieth-century women's liberation movement represent approaches women have taken to gain access to the public sphere. Since women themselves have disagreed about the best means of entering into the public sphere, the "woman question" has been a controversial political question. Thus, even though this discussion focuses on aspects of women's connection and attachment, tension and disagreement are important counterpoints.

THE AGE OF ASSOCIATION, 1877–1917

American women began organizing benevolent societies before 1800, and by 1840 the organizations numbered well into the thousands. Mormon, or Latter-day Saint women, whose Female Relief Society had been organized in Nauvoo, Illinois, in 1842, reestablished the organization in Utah in each local ward or congregation, beginning in 1867. By 1880, more than three hundred branches of the society were carrying forward traditional benevolent work and such significant economic ventures as silk raising, cooperative merchandising, and grain storage. Mormon women established and staffed a woman's newspaper and a hospital, as well as organizations for young women (the Young Ladies' Mutual Improvement Association, founded in 1870) and for children (the Primary Association, founded in 1878). They were vocal defenders of their practice of polygamy or plural marriage and active advocates for woman suffrage.[3] Protestant women in Utah territory opposed polygamy, established schools and youth associations, and also organized for benevolent purposes. For example, Methodist women inaugurated a Ladies Aid society (1880), Presbyterian women a Woman's Aid Society (1882), and Congregational women a Ladies Benevolent Society (1887). Jewish women, a significant minority in Utah's early population, founded their Ladies Hebrew Benevolent Society around 1874.[4] Like their counterparts throughout the United States, these benevolent, relief, and aid organizations had a religious base and administered to the sick and the poor but also taught their members important lessons about women's capability for autonomy and sisterhood.

The founding of Sorosis in New York in 1868 and of the New England Women's Club in Boston in 1870 signaled the beginning of a nationwide change in women's networks. "It was the appearance of women's clubs all over the country," wrote Sophonisba Preston Breckinridge in 1933, "which represented the general unspecialized leisure time activity of women, for which no prerequisite in the way of education, belief, or male relationship was required." According to Breckinridge, women's clubs "marked the emergence of the middle-aged and middle class woman from her kitchen and her home."[5]

Unquestionably modern conveniences facilitated the development of clubs. Domestic plumbing, gas lighting, improved stoves, and sewing machines partially released women from the grinding physical labor of keeping a house and feeding and clothing their families. However, club women were not merely women with time on their hands. They advocated women's education and public involvement, but they differentiated themselves from Elizabeth Cady Stanton, Susan B. Anthony, and other suffragists who were widely criticized for resisting male authority and supporting such controversial measures as birth control. Generally club women were committed to traditional religious and family values. Some scholars have termed their ideology "domestic feminism" because their strategy was "winning a place outside the home using domestic credentials . . . not by breaking out of their prescribed roles but by stretching and circumventing them when necessary."[6] By thus appropriating, rather than denying, the ladylike ideal, club women hoped to improve the status of women, encourage self-improvement, and bring new respect to women in the public sphere.

The Ladies Literary Club

By the time the "woman question" was being seriously discussed in Utah, lines between Mormons and non-Mormons had already been clearly drawn. When Utah's Territorial Legislature, predominantly Mormon, passed an 1870 law enfranchising women, many Latter-day Saint women enthusiastically aligned themselves with the suffrage cause and argued that their enfranchisement was proof that the practice of polygamy or plural marriage did not subjugate women. National Woman Suffrage Association leaders Elizabeth Cady Stanton and Susan B. Anthony visited Utah a few months after the vote was granted; and beginning in 1879, some Mormon delegates traveled east to attend NWSA conventions. Mormon women and men spoke in support of female suffrage, and Anthony and the NWSA lobbied against proposed federal anti-polygamy legislation disfranchising women. In contrast, Utah's "Gentile" (non-Mormon) women supported anti-polygamy legislation and opposed woman suffrage on the grounds that it would increase the Mormons' political power.[7] Their stance simultaneously differentiated them from Mormons and from radical suffragists, placing them firmly with women in the American mainstream. In addressing the question of woman's role in the public sphere, these Utah women, mostly Protestants, followed the pattern established by their "domestic feminist" sisters in the East and began forming clubs.

Utah's first culture club appeared in 1875 when Jennie Anderson Froiseth gathered a group of friends in the parlor of her Rose Cottage in Salt Lake City. Mrs. Froiseth, a personal friend of Julia Ward Howe, who was president of the New England Women's Club, presided over the Anti-Polygamy Society of Utah, founded in 1878, and edited Salt Lake City's *Anti-Polygamy Standard.* Her attack on polygamy as a threat to the nation's morality and home life, "a curse to children and destructive to the sacred relations of the family," is illustrative of American women's broader concern with guarding the moral values of home life.[8]

The group of non-Mormon women who gathered at Mrs. Froiseth's home in 1875 organized the Blue Tea "to promote mental culture" and "literary research."[9] The club was to be limited to twenty-five women. After meeting for a few months, some of the members expressed their desire for a "nonexclusive women's club," that is, a group "not only for the literary elite, but also for women who were just learners."[10] Some members resigned in 1877 and formed the Ladies' Literary Club, a more democratic organization, which, according to its devotees, "holds the distinction of being the first woman's club west of the Mississippi River."[11] Jennie Froiseth, among others, became a member.

According to Eliza Kirtley Royle, founder and first president, the Ladies' Literary Club professed an "open-door" policy and its constitution excluded no one. Yet, as historian Patricia Lyn Scott observes, it was "a common understanding" that "Gentile women, a tiny minority in the entire territory of Utah, felt a need to form a sisterly enclave."[12] Apparently, it was a number of years before Mormon and Jewish women were accepted as readily as Methodist and Unitarian applicants. In 1927, club historian Katherine B. Parsons looked at the positive results of the increasingly open membership policy, explaining that the club had "been a factor in breaking down prejudices here in Utah, and in promoting a Christian tolerance and a more united citizenry, by bringing together women of all creeds and of no creed, on the common ground of desire to grow intellectually and to be helpful."[13]

Most of the club's early members were young mothers, the wives of ministers and government officials who had arrived in Utah fairly recently. Eventually club rolls would include almost all of the wives of Utah governors. Eager not to leave culture too far behind them, these women met on Friday mornings for two hours, generally discussing history or art. In 1882, when the club incorporated, its membership numbered twenty-eight. By 1897, that number had grown to 110, and different sections were established: art, current events and literature, entertainment, history, library, music, Shakespeare, and "tourist."[14] In 1912, the club built its own clubhouse, planned by the Salt Lake architectural firm of Ware & Treganza, which still stands at 850 East South Temple in Salt Lake City.[15]

The Ladies' Literary Club, still in operation in 2005, was clearly the vanguard of Utah's clubs, the vast majority of which were organized after 1890.

Only known photograph of an actual meeting of the Ladies Literary Club held in their original location, 20 South 300 East, Salt Lake City, ca. 1910.

By then the Church of Jesus Christ of Latter-day Saints had issued its Manifesto signaling the beginning of its withdrawal from plural marriage and Mormon women intensified their outreach to other women in Utah and the United States. By then, too, the culture club movement had spread to "almost every city, town, and village in the country."[16] Utah was no exception. Before the turn of the century, the number of women's clubs in Salt Lake City, Ogden, and Provo had multiplied significantly, and clubs had been established in a number of smaller communities: Pleasant Grove (Sorosis, 1894); Bountiful (American History and Literary Club, 1895); Springville (Woman's Club, 1893, and Inquirer's Club, 1896); Coalville S.B.L. (1896); and Park City (Woman's Athenaeum, ca. 1897).[17] Not all of Utah's culture clubs would be so large or so long-lived as the Ladies Literary Club, but they all offered women a means of expanding their interests and their roles within the community.

Utah's early women's clubs followed the national pattern: they were secular organizations in which women linked themselves to each other according to special interests. In Salt Lake City, the Women's Club (1892) studied American government and statesmen, Cleofan (1892) studied the history of London and famous epics of the Middle Ages, and the Reviewers Club (1896) studied "current literature." In Ogden, Aglaia[18] (1893) pursued the history of drama while La Coterie (1896) took up "history and allied studies." Provo's

Nineteenth Century Club (1891) sought something more esoteric—meeting to study Italian history and art and parliamentary law. Another Provo club, Utah Sorosis (1897) "formed as a study club" but quickly branched out, raising funds to sponsor a public library.[19]

Clubs typically chose colors, symbols (often flowers), and mottos to represent and describe their ends. The name of the Reapers Club, formed in 1892 in Salt Lake City, spoke for itself. Its objective of "social and intellectual development" was once phrased with studied eloquence as "to grasp the sickle of industry and enter the fields of science and knowledge to reap and bind into sheaves, golden truths, with which to store the granaries of the intellect as food for thought and action in a daily progressive life, in all that is helpful and uplifting to the human race."[20]

Sometimes disparagingly referred to as "middle-aged women's universities," clubs in fact "served the cause of cultural enlightenment for masses of women." Historian Karen Blair observed that, within these clubs, middle-aged women whose "primary efforts had been put into family life . . . sought an education that would not demand too much of them."[21] Club women had their own reading programs, and club work often initiated them into public speaking. Sometimes they listened to guest lecturers, but they also took pride in researching and writing papers to deliver to one another. In fact, the effort to find books for their research prompted their interest in founding and supporting libraries.

Mary Ann Freeze, defending clubs in the 1892 Mormon *Woman's Exponent,* argued that while "the duties of home come first of all . . . aside from that there is much [woman] can do to bless herself and humanity at large. Through going abroad and mingling with her sisters, she will learn . . . important truths not to be learned in seclusion from society, hence I think we are not apt to appreciate too highly this important factor in the higher education of women."[22] One requirement of the Utah Women's Press Club, organized in 1891 in Salt Lake City for women writers, was that each woman had to produce original papers. Ruth May Fox, a young mother and emerging writer who affiliated with the club, testified that her "association with the well-educated women of the Press Club" had encouraged her toward greater education and helped build a foundation "for whatever success in public life I have achieved."[23]

The clubs' educational emphasis had such appeal that other women's groups integrated similar study programs into their organizational work. The Unity Circle, for example, grew out of the Ladies' Unitarian Society founded in Salt Lake City in 1891 "to promote the welfare of the church, good fellowship, charitable and intellectual endeavors."[24] The weekly afternoon meetings of the circle in 1897 included time for charity sewing, for the orphans' home, for example, followed on alternate weeks of the month by lessons in literature, music, and current events, or a social. Similarly, the LDS Relief Society continued

Utah Women's Press Club luncheon given by Susa Young Gates upon the occasion of the club being dissolved. (Left to Right) Front row: Louise Y. Robison, Julia B. Nibley, Augusta W. Grant, Alice R. Richards, Susa Young Gates, Louisa ("Lula") Greene Richards, Annie Wells Cannon, Zina Young Card, Emily S. Richards, Jane W. Skolfield, Ellen Lee Sanders. Back row: Emma Lucy Gates Bowen, Mable Young Sanborn, Hattie C. Jensen, Margaret Fisher, Elizabeth S. Wilcox, Emma H. Jenson, Mary F. K. Pye, Florence S. Critchlow, Aimee Shiller, Ellis S. Musser, Lilian W. Robins, Marian Kerr, Clarissa Beesley, and Flora B. Horne, December 6, 1928.

its charitable work but added an educational component in 1902 when local units began sponsoring lessons for mothers. These "mothers' classes" gradually expanded to include such topics as biography, literature, and art, and proved so popular that the society's central board began a standardized educational program in 1914.[25]

Clubs not only helped educate women but also provided a setting in which women could share their lives and support each other in difficulties. For many women, clubs replaced old support networks, particularly the institution of house-to-house visiting so prevalent earlier in the nineteenth century.[26] Club meetings, while more formal than visits, were generally scheduled so they did not conflict with members' home responsibilities. Whether members met in one another's homes, in rented rooms, or in their own club house, clubs "inevitably had the effect of cultivating in women an appreciation of each other."[27] By-laws of the Edina Literary and Debating Society specified that members should have "due consideration for the opinions and feelings of others."[28] Beyond courtesies, formalities, and the parliamentary procedure often employed, "the ongoing process of attachment" described by Carol Giligan was, for many women, at the core of club life.[29] An original composition presented by Dr. Ellis Reynolds Shipp to the Utah Woman's Press Club expressed this sentiment. After examining women's right to worldly resources, the ballot, wifehood, and motherhood, Shipp concluded with a celebration of women's right to sisterhood, to

> Engage in social converse, enjoy a sweet communion,
> Let heart come close to heart, and angels join our union.[30]

Feminist author and leader Charlotte Perkins Gilman put it in so many words: "Club women learn more than to improve the mind; they learn to love each other." It must be acknowledged, however, that some clubs spawned a sense of smug exclusivity rather than sisterhood. Indeed, "pettiness, social climbing, and cliquishness were unattractive elements that at times were evident in club life."[31]

The General Federation of Women's Clubs

By the time Utah became a state in 1896, women across the nation were reaching out to connect in ever-broader circles. Maria Owen, founder of the Women's Club in Springfield, Massachusetts, appraised the movement that was affecting both men and women: "Association is the watchword of the age—associations for labor, for trade, for instruction, for entertainment, for advance of all kinds. Women naturally feel the impulse and are banding together for work."[32]

Women's proclivity to gather reached beyond clubs, in the strict sense of that term. Many women affiliated with organizations that never carried the "club" appellation and were different in purpose. The Young Women's Christian Association began in Boston in 1866, the Woman's Christian Temperance Union in 1874, the Jewish Women's Congress in 1893, the National Association of Colored Women in 1896, the National Congress of Mothers (later the PTA) in 1897, the National Consumers' League in 1899, the National Woman's Trade Union League in 1903, and the American Home Economics Association in 1908.

Club women, too, reached beyond their own small circles to join larger state and national networks. In 1893, in a significant step, Utah's many culture clubs in various cities and towns formed a state federation of women's clubs—thus becoming the second such federation in the United States.[33] Two years later, many Utah clubs affiliated with the General Federation of Women's Clubs, resolving in 1896:

> That the women of Utah take the heartiest interest in all organizations tending to ameliorate the condition of women throughout the world.
>   That they recognize the great educational work of the Federation of Clubs, and will as far as they are able, cooperate with them.[34]

In 1898 when *The History of the Woman's Club Movement in America* was written by Jane Cunningham Croly, founder of both Sorosis and the Woman's Press Club in New York and the single most important figure in the movement, she commented on the federation's unifying function: "No line is drawn in the Utah Federation. Mormons and Gentiles enter on an equal footing, and the work is doing much to break down the walls of ancient prejudice."[35] At that time, seventeen Utah clubs representing about 520 members were affiliated with the General Federation of Women's Clubs.

At the third annual convention of the state federation in 1896, Romania B. Pratt described the levels of association, proclaiming the Reapers Club to be "a small streamlet, singing a glad song of pride and thankfulness as it glides into the larger stream of the State Federation, and with it sweeps into the General Federation of Women's Clubs, helping to create a mighty force of woman's power which will raise the standard of morals in the world and spiritualize and refine the material and physical in man and thus hasten the era of peace on earth and good will to all men."[36]

The December 1940 issue of the *Utah Clubwoman,* official organ of the Utah Federation of Women's Clubs, carried news from seven districts and listed state federation officers from twenty-eight separate communities, including such outposts as Marysvale, Monroe, and Moroni. The December 1939 issue of the magazine quoted a past president as saying: "Hand in hand we reach around the world; single handed we can hold only so much of the world's crust." The article emphasized that "the federation stands for every good thing," that its ideals were "Christian, endeavoring to bring more love, joy, and beauty into the Home and Community Life," and that individual club women could derive "both material and spiritual" benefits through Club involvement.[37]

Though Croly observed in 1898 that Utah clubs "have been rather slow in doing practical work," local clubs that moved into the GFWC followed the national trend toward greater community involvement. As already noted, Utah's women's clubs were instrumental in getting the signatures required for Salt Lake City to receive state funding for its first public library.[38] The Ladies Literary Club energetically promoted the public good. For instance, it supported the Masonic Library during its first year, 1893, by raising the princely sum of $3,100. It also worked for the passage of a library bill in 1897, thus ensuring the opening of a free public library in the Salt Lake City and County Building in 1898, established a traveling library, established free kindergartens, placed art in local schools, sponsored early closing hours for department stores, encouraged high school art and music contests, created Girls' State scholarships and a scholarship fund at the University of Utah, and gave early support to establish the Community Chest (now United Way).[39]

The Authors' Club followed a typical pattern of first organizing to represent largely personal interests, then gradually integrating social concerns into its cultural program. Although the club, still meeting regularly in 2005, never veered significantly from its study of literature and history, from the late 1890s through the 1930s it allotted ten minutes weekly for discussion of questions like these: "Can women eliminate personality from public affairs?" "Can anything be done to raise the moral tone of our Show Houses?" "How far should an able instructor go in teaching sex hygiene to high school students?" "Should not the wages of our policemen be made higher in the protection of their families in case of death . . . ?" and "What shall we do with the tramps that come to our door?" There was also a surge of activity in what its secretary called "philanthropies" after the club's affiliation with the Utah Federation of Women's Clubs in 1896. Members made contributions to a traveling library, contributed money to sufferers from the Scofield Mine disaster, raised money for the free kindergartens, contested public entertainments that "in any way have a tendency toward immorality or coarseness" and expressed concern with health, sanitation, and the preservation of historic sites. A member in one meeting suggested doing something "to prohibit men from taking cigars or cigarettes in street cars" and another observed that "in many of restraurents [sic], the napkins used by the people at the table were afterwards used to wipe the dishes."[40]

In 1899 the Utah Federation worked to improve public educational facilities and to establish kindergarten classes within the schools. Both the state and general federations had a strong record of public service, structuring almost all of their departments and programs around social concerns. The 1940 listing of departments and divisions within the Utah Federation of Women's Clubs was extensive: American citizenship, the American home, education, fine arts, international relations, employment and industries, juniors, legislation, press and publicity, and public welfare. Five of these departments had more than five standing subcommittees.[41]

During this era of federation, the LDS Relief Society and Young Ladies Mutual Improvement Association became charter members of an international alliance for women—the International Council of Women (1888)—and its United States affiliate, the National Council of Women (1891). Their purpose was to foster "better understanding among organized women of varying interests and beliefs."[42] The Mormon organizations maintained membership in the two councils until 1987.[43]

As they assembled in clubs, societies, and organizations, and affiliated with state and national councils and federations, Utah women bridged differences and strengthened connections. "During the last decade of the nineteenth century Latter-day Saint and gentile women blurred their former hostilities over polygamy and joined their common community interests in collective civic action," observed historian Carol Cornwall Madsen.[44]

The "Daughters" Associations

As the U.S. population increased and industrialization made life increasingly complex, clubs and associations provided women with a sense of identity and connection. The last decade of the nineteenth century, which coincided with a great influx of European immigrants, spurred a developing interest in genealogy, historical societies, and ancestry, which prompted men's and women's associations in lineage groups. The National Society of the Daughters of the American Revolution was formed in 1890, originally to protest against the exclusion of women from the Sons of the American Revolution. The Daughters of the Revolution became a break-off group the next year. The Colonial Dames of America and the National Society of U.S. Daughters of 1812 were also founded in 1891, followed by the United Daughters of the Confederacy in 1894.

Utah women affiliated with a variety of these groups, most of which banded together to teach lessons in patriotism and good citizenship. The Woman's Relief Corp of the Grand Army of the Republic, founded in Utah in 1885, included the wives, sisters, daughters, granddaughters, and cousins of Union soldiers in the Civil War. Although its activity dwindled during the decade after its establishment, it revived significantly in 1896 and continued into the 1930s, raising money through socials to aid veterans and their families in need. By 1898, there was also a camp in Ogden. This interesting group was largely founded by non-Mormon women. When B. H. Roberts was elected to Congress in 1898, they sponsored a series of anti-Mormon seminars and passed a resolution in February 1899 protesting his scheduled seating since he was a polygamist. Expressing their belief that "the home, where one wife is its guardian, is the true foundation of the government of a free people," they resisted "the seating of this open defier of the law."[45] Their objections were similar to those formally stated by women's associations throughout the United States. He was not seated.

More frequently than political activities, the GAR sponsored educational and social activities and engaged in relief work. An 1898 program featured stereopticon views of Civil War battles. Accounts for a fund-raising card party in 1904 show that total expenditures were $6.75 ($2 for twenty sets of tables, 40 cents for cream and milk, 60 cents for coffee, $1 for cards, $2 for prizes, and 75 cents for dishwashing). They sold $20.50 worth of tickets and received a 50 cent contribution, making their profit $14.25, which went to the families of servicemen. In 1901, they spent $1.37 on food for a certain Mrs. Walton, reporting that she was "still feeble but able to care for herself."[46] Minutes indicate that the group provided support for several men and women.

A Utah chapter of the Daughters of the American Revolution was organized in Utah in 1897, the year after statehood. In 1990, the national DAR centennial year, there were seven Utah chapters and approximately 350 members who carried forward such educational and service programs as providing awards for good citizenship among Utah youth. About 1915, an early unwritten policy of excluding Mormon women apparently became a formal resolution to exclude from membership "descendants of polygamous marriage." It was later rescinded.[47] In December 1897, a group of Mormon women countered their exclusion from the DAR by meeting under the direction of Susa Young Gates to propose forming a state chapter of the Daughters of the Revolution; by November 1898, they had the required twenty members and were chartered as the Wasatch Chapter by the national association.[48]

Utah women also affiliated with Daughters of Veterans, United Daughters of the Confederacy, and Daughters of the American Colonists. Like the Ladies of the Grand Army of the Republic, these patriotic societies sought to make the American heritage more readily and tangibly available to Utah's citizens. The Daughters of the Revolution, for example, donated facsimiles of the Declaration of Independence to the University of Utah and to various Salt Lake high schools, presented a hand-sewn American flag of Utah silk to the governor, and assisted with research at the Utah Genealogical Society library. Membership in the group peaked in the 1920s and declined in the 1970s; the Utah chapter closed in 1977 and the national organization disbanded in 1984.[49]

Of particular significance to Utah was the founding of the Daughters of Utah Pioneers. In April 1901 a group of fifty-four women met in Salt Lake City and formed an organization to "perpetuate the names and achievements of the men, women and children who were the pioneers in founding this commonwealth."[50] Like other national lineage societies, the Daughters of Utah Pioneers was organized as a nonpolitical and nonsectarian organization with membership open to any woman whose ancestors had reached Utah before the completion of the transcontinental railroad in 1869. Its membership is primarily but not exclusively Mormon.

A national federation of local units incorporated in 1925, the International Society of Daughters of Utah Pioneers, particularly during the decades of leadership provided by its indomitable president, Kate B. Carter (1941–76) worked energetically and effectively to conserve historical sites and landmarks, to collect relics, manuscripts, and photographs, and to educate its members at monthly meetings through presentations by individual members of local and personal history. A thriving organization with an on-going publications program, by its centennial year in 2001, the DUP had published more than fifty volumes of monthly history lessons, cookbooks, pamphlets, children's book (such as the popular *Pioneer Tales to Tell),* and a four-volume collection of biographical sketches, *Pioneer Women of Faith and Fortitude* (1998). In 2001, its international membership numbered more than 19,000.[51] It maintained numerous "relic halls" throughout the West, including eighty-six in Utah, with an extensive and invaluable collection in its Salt Lake City museum.

The Daughters of the Utah Handcart Pioneers was organized in 1910; and the remarks of its second president, Isabella Siddoway Armstrong, are innocently revealing about the thirst for association. The wife of Salt Lake's mayor and the mother of eleven children, she noted apologetically in her autobiography: "Having had such a large family my time has been so taken up rearing them that I have been unable to do as much church and public work as I would like to have done." She characterized her presidency as "one of the greatest pleasures of my life to help in a small way to build up an organization which will band together and perpetuate the names of some of the most courageous people the world has ever known."[52]

The membership of the Daughters of the Utah Handcart Pioneers undoubtedly overlapped that of the DUP to some degree. A listing of the activities of early DUP members indicates that each member also belonged to other clubs and associations. Clearly, none of these groups demanded exclusive loyalty. Multiple memberships were popular, and it was not unusual for a woman to be affiliated with four or five or more women's organizations.

Mothers' Clubs and Domestic Science

Most clubs and associations appealed to "mature" women whose children were grown, but mothers' clubs often targeted younger women. Early meetings for mothers were held in connection with kindergartens which emphasized the importance of teaching mothers about children and how they learn. Camilla S. Cobb opened Utah's first kindergarten in the fall of 1874 in the vestry of Brigham Young's schoolhouse and employed the ideas of kindergarten founder Friedrich Froebel, who emphasized the development of the child's body, mind, and spirit. In the fall of 1875, through the columns of the *Woman's Exponent,* Cobb explained her ideas about child's play and kindergarten to Mormon mothers.[53] The Presbyterian Women's Executive Board of Commissioners sponsored a kindergarten in 1883 and support grew steadily for a broader movement.

Since the question of control of Utah schools divided Mormons and non-Mormons at this time, for a while each group pushed forward independently. The Salt Lake Kindergarten Association, organized in 1893 by Mary A. Parsons and interested mothers, imported Elizabeth Dickey from Philadelphia to set up a kindergarten and commence teacher training.[54] In order to forward its agenda to establish kindergartens in the public schools, the association solicited support from women's organizations; and in 1894, the more broadly based Free Kindergarten Association was founded at a meeting of the Ladies Literary Club, with educator Emma McVicker as president. The association employed as a teacher trainer Alice Chapin, who had studied in Boston under Elizabeth Peabody, founder of the first American kindergarten. The Woman's Christian Temperance Union, one of many groups who lent support to the Free Kindergarten Association, sponsored lectures by Chapin, inaugurated monthly meetings for interested mothers, and helped establish kindergartens. In 1894, Emma McVicker founded a WCTU kindergarten in Salt Lake City which served as a charitable day nursery for the children of working mothers; incorporated as Neighborhood House in 1911, it continued to provide services for children into the twenty-first century.[55]

Latter-day Saint women organized the Utah Kindergarten Association in 1895 and installed Camilla Cobb as a teacher of mother's classes. Louie B. Felt and May Anderson, leaders of the Mormon organization for children, the Primary Association, attended Alice Chapin's class and then established their own private kindergarten. They gradually implemented the new educational methods in the Primary Association's teaching program and encouraged the creation of mothers' classes in local wards and stakes. It was the adoption of mothers' classes by the Relief Society in 1902, however, which effectively spread mother education among Latter-day Saints.[56] That movement followed the establishment of the Utah State Kindergarten Association, in which Mormon, Protestant, and other women and men combined their efforts and, in 1898, pushed successfully for legislation mandating the establishment of local kindergartens and a state kindergarten training school.[57]

In 1897 the National Congress of Mothers provided national affiliation for mothers' clubs all over the United States. Established in Utah the following year was the Utah State Mothers Congress, which encouraged the kindergarten movement and sought to break down the barriers between home and school. It continued until 1914 when the Utah State Parent Teachers Association began functioning as a section of the National Education Association and, after 1925, as part of the National Congress of Parents and Teachers, which had emerged from the original National Congress of Mothers.[58]

Kindergartens were successfully integrated into Utah's public schools; and mothers' classes and clubs continued in various forms, providing instruction, camaraderie, and support for mothers of all ages. The Utah Young Mothers Council, for example, in an effort to strengthen the moral and spiritual foundation in the home, provided study and enrichment materials for use in informal neighborhood groups. The Utah Mother's Association underscored the importance of mothering by annually nominating a candidate for "Mother of the Year." Both groups affiliated with the American Mothers Committee.[59] Many other mothers clubs, such as the University of Utah's Mothers' Club or the Mother of Twins Club, have been geared to more specific populations.

Just as twentieth-century educational precepts informed women of possibilities for better parenting, so the new century's domestic science encouraged them to be more efficient housekeepers and homemakers. "Devices and 'contraptions' for the lessening of work in the home, arrangements to save steps, to lessen the friction everywhere in the domestic machinery . . . are the order of the day," declared Susa Young Gates in 1916.[60] Gates had established a Home Economics Department at Brigham Young University in Provo in 1894. Two years later, James E. Talmage established a similar department at the University of Utah, and Dalinda Cotey effected such a department at Utah Agricultural College (Utah State University) in Logan in 1903.[61] In February 1910 several home economics teachers from around the state gathered at the Agricultural College in Logan to form a Utah branch of the National Association for Home Economics. The Utah State Home Economics Association worked to develop a uniform course of study for the state's high schools, proposing a curriculum that included sewing, sanitation, cooking, household arts, laundry, and "housekeepers as consumers." Through USU's extension division, which truly turned domestic arts into a science, homemakers all over the state received extensive aid on household, gardening, food preparation, and food preservation. (See chap. 5.) The association also succeeded in establishing a state standard for teacher competency and for pure milk. Still a vigorous organization in 1954–55, it advocated "education in home economics for individuals of all ages and both sexes for more effective living and competent leadership."[62]

Student and Youth Associations

Student clubs and associations developed concurrently with those of older women. Nineteen members of the Edina Literary and Debating Society first met in Salt Lake City in October 1884, determining that they would meet weekly on Wednesday afternoons and open membership to "any Ladie [sic] student of the University of Deseret" with the approving vote of two-thirds of the other members. Before the end of the year, intent upon "enlarging our fund of General Intelligence," the members had debated whether a woman were capable of being president of the United States, whether the steam engine or the printing press had "done more service to mankind," whether education was "more essential to men than to women" (they decided it was more essential to women), and whether it was more important to study botany than civil government (they decided it was). Although student organizations are notoriously ephemeral, minute books survive from as late as 1894, chronicling the activities of the society's forty-seven members. By then they had added book discussion, recitations, and spelling matches to their fare.[63]

About the same time the first Greek women's sororities were founded at the University of Utah, beginning with Gamma Phi in 1897 (later Pi Beta Phi), Theta Upsilon in 1905 (later Chi Omega), and Delta Epsilon in 1911 (later Delta Delta Delta). Shortly after affiliating with the National Panhellenic Association in 1912, all three groups became chapters of national sororities.[64] Utah State University's Sorosis, founded as a literary society and as that school's first sorority in 1898, became a national chapter of Alpha Chi Omega in 1934 and officially disbanded. However, the original members continued to meet. In 1981, about forty members were still active, and the disbanded sorority was named grand marshal of the USU homecoming parade that year. "Since we take in no new members, our fate is eventual dissolution," said Sorosis president Ruth Layton Harrison. "However, we will continue to meet as long as two of us are left."[65]

The story is indicative of the strong ties women forged during their college years. Many Greek sorority alumnae groups function as their own women's organizations, supporting and advising active student chapters and pursuing philanthropic projects. Another indication that college alumnae wanted continuing association with other college-educated women was the May 1917 establishment of a Utah chapter of the American Association of University Women. This continuing organization, which requires a college baccalaureate for membership, unites alumnae of different institutions to promote "equity for all women and girls, lifelong learning, and positive societal change."[66]

The urge for association was felt by a generation still younger than college students. Some religious associations for younger women were well underway by the turn of the century. The LDS Young Ladies Mutual Improvement Association, for example, had operated local units in Utah since 1870. The Young Women's Christian Association was established in Salt Lake City in 1906. In a secular vein, the 1911 Polk's Directory for Salt Lake City listed a Home Economics Society at LDS High School and a High School Athletic Girls Association, suggesting the important role that clubs and associations would come to play in the lives of high school girls.

Volunteers in Ogden, Utah founded the first Girl Scout unit in 1920. The local and regional councils affiliated into a statewide council in 1961; and the 2005 membership stood at 9,000 girls between the ages of five and seventeen led by some 3,500 adult volunteers.[67]

Women's Organizations and the Progressive Movement, 1890–1915

Clubs and associations had effectively moved women into the public sphere where, in fact, they had to be to address many concerns related to home life. By the end of the nineteenth century, much of the food preparation and clothing manufacture previously performed by individual women in their own homes had become social enterprises; and "the historic sphere of woman was more and more influenced by political life, as governments passed laws concerning food, water, the production of clothing, and education."[68] Building upon their traditional home concerns and their responsibility as moral guardians, women united to become, in effect, "social housekeepers." In the midst of the national Progressive Movement (ca. 1890 to 1915), women's organizations waged campaigns for peace, purity, prohibition, pure food and drugs, municipal improvement, and educational reform, affirming that "the very intensity of our feeling for home, husband, and children gives us a power of loving and working outside of our homes, to redeem the world as love and work only can."[69]

Prominent among causes espoused by these women were movements to promote world peace. From 1899 when women from eighteen nations of the world had held a Universal Peace Demonstration preceding an International Peace Conference at The Hague, Utah women's organizations, like their American counterparts, sponsored annual community peace meetings. In July 1901, May Wright Sewall, president of the International Council of Women, visited Utah where she reestablished her contacts with leading Mormon women, whose Relief Society and Young Ladies Mutual Improvement Association were council members. She urged them to organize demonstrations for peace in May 1902, the anniversary of the opening of the Court of International Arbitration at The Hague. The general presidencies of the Relief Society, Young Ladies Mutual Improvement Association, and Primary Association responded energetically, and also enlisted prominent Catholic, Protestant, and Jewish women throughout the state.[70] In May 1902, for example, women in Huntington, Utah, discussed "The Costs of War and Its Effects Morally."

Following the lead of national women's organizations, that same May several Utah gatherings resolved to "repudiate war as a means of settling international difficulties," promote "the universal brotherhood of man," and "rejoice that women throughout the world are beginning to feel their responsibility for human conditions outside of the home, as well as within its sacred walls."[71] Annual demonstrations continued to draw thousands of enthusiastic and determined supporters. A state Peace Society was formed in 1907 under the direction of Utah Governor John Cutler and continued various activities until the outbreak of World War I. In 1917, when the United States joined the conflict, civic leaders and religious leaders, including Mormons, swung the efforts of the women toward patriotic support. Revivals of pro-peace activities in the 1930s, as historian Leonard J. Arrington points out, sadly, "proved to be only harbingers of another war of destruction."[72]

The founding of the Young Women's Christian Association in Salt Lake City in 1906 was indicative of the growing interest in social justice. Concerned with the welfare of wage-earning women, the "Y" established an employment bureau, lunch rooms, restrooms, and recreational facilities. Its building on Third South in Salt Lake City, designed by Julia Morgan, was erected in 1919 and provided housing and meeting rooms for YWCA-sponsored classes, workshops, and conferences. The association has served an important role in bringing together women from different racial, religious, social, and economic backgrounds.[73]

Utah women, who had exercised the franchise from 1896 when the state's constitution went into effect, not only lobbied for Progressive Era reforms but also helped select the candidates who would enact them. In 1912, the Salt Lake City Association of Clubs sent a pointed list of questions to candidates for various offices:

1. Are you in favor of and will you support legislation—social and industrial—looking to the protection of women, children and the home?
2. Are you in favor of a minimum wage scale for both men and women and will you support such a bill?
3. Are you in favor of a workmen's compensation and employers' liability act, in the interests of men and women workers?
4. Are you in favor of the present nine-hour law for women; also a better child labor law?

5. Are you in favor of and will you support an amendment to the present marriage law, which will require a certificate of health from a reputable physician showing the applicant to be free from transmissible or communicable diseases?

6. Are you in favor of and will you support the appointment of women on all state and local boards—industrial, educational, [and] charitable?[74]

In 1912–13, a Legislative and Industrial Committee of the General Federation of Women's Clubs was organized and declared itself in favor of a minimum wage law for women, a Woman Deputy Commissioner of Labor, and a mother's pension act, among other proposals.[75] Following the national lead, in 1913 the UFWC spearheaded an attempt to pass a minimum wage law for women, presenting testimony and arguing further for a commission with the power to investigate conditions and regulate wages. After a struggle, the Utah Legislature passed a minimum wage for the state.[76] Such victories reflected the conviction of Utah's voting women, expressed by the masthead of the *Woman's Exponent* from 1897 to 1913, that "The Ballot in the Hands of the Women of Utah Should Be a Power to Better the Home, the State, and the Nation."

WOMEN'S NETWORKS IN WAR AND PEACE: 1917–45

The Impact of World War I

After the United States declared war on Germany on April 6, 1917, most American women's groups directed their energies toward supporting the war, but not without a continuing commitment to principles of peace. Writing from Salt Lake City, the Relief Society general presidency advised members in Utah and elsewhere

> to keep the even tenor to their ways, making homes clean, comfortable and peaceful; administer in the spirit of love and patience to your husbands and to your children; guard the little ones; do not permit them to imbibe the spirit of intolerance or hatred to any nation or to any people; keep firearms out of their hands; do not allow them to play at war nor to find amusement in imitating death in battle; inculcate the spirit of loyalty to country and flag, but help them to feel that they are soldiers of the Cross and that if they must needs take up arms in the defense of liberty, of country and homes they shall do so without rancor or bitterness.[77]

Working through their various clubs, associations, and organizations, Utah women thrust themselves into the war effort, becoming part of what President Woodrow Wilson called the "great civilian army without whose backing mere fighting would be useless."[78] This army of women took its orders from two sources: the American Red Cross and the Council of National Defense,

Young Women's Christian Association (Y.W.C.A.) truck and group during World War I, Salt Lake City, ca. 1916.

created in August 1916 to survey U.S. military resources and to increase farm and factory production for civilian and military needs.

Through its Women's Division, the Utah State Council of Defense, organized April 26, 1917, served as the clearinghouse for the "patriotic activities of the women of Utah."[79] It had four main tasks: conservation, recreation, sanitation [health], and "Americanization." As head of the new Federal Food Administration, Herbert C. Hoover was responsible for coordinating national efforts to curb waste and stimulate food production and conservation. If Americans could be educated to use substitutes for conventional materials, the armed forces could have first claim on certain commodities. Hoover's first official move was an appeal to housewives and other food preparers to "Win the War by Giving Your Own Daily Service." It encouraged wheatless meals, meatless meals, and the thrifty use of milk, fats, sugar, and perishable foods: "Preach the 'Gospel of the Clean Plate.' Don't eat a fourth meal. Don't limit the plain food of growing children. . . . Full garbage pails in America mean empty dinner pails in America and Europe," Hoover advised.[80] In response, Utah women's organizations distributed Hoover pledge cards and held "Hoover luncheons," published government recipes, and sponsored contests for raising and preserving fruits and vegetables. Federal food administrators in Idaho and Utah requested that the LDS Church sell the government the two hundred thousand tons of grains that local Relief Societies had been storing as an independent project since 1876. The Presiding Bishop and Relief Society officers and members complied in 1918.[81]

Women responded with energy to the call to help U.S. servicemen. The Utah Federation of Women's Clubs, among others, had canteen services on call to provide traveling soldiers with sandwiches and coffee. The Ladies Literary Club in Salt Lake City collected 3,500 phonograph records and some phonographs which found their way through the Red Cross and YMCA to American and allied soldiers at embarkation camps in the United States and France and also in the Near East and Russia.[82]

The Utah State Council of Defense also promulgated programs to ensure sanitation and health for home defense. For example, it designated April 1918–April 1919 as "Children's Year," with the goal of saving the lives of 100,000 American children through preventive health measures. The Child Welfare Department of the National Council of Defense, in connection with its state counterparts and the U.S. Children's Bureau, carried the campaign into communities nationwide by working through local women's groups. Utah women's clubs, societies, and associations emphasized the importance of proper nourishment for children, set up and manned milk depots to provide fresh milk, educated women in prenatal care, and weighed and measured Utah children under five years of age. Wrote Clarissa S. Williams, chairman of Utah Woman's Council and first counselor in the Relief Society general presidency: "While this terrible conflict is depopulating the world, every patriotic citizen—man or woman—will consider it a duty to lend every effort toward prolonging the life, and promoting the health and happiness of the rising generation."[83]

The council's fourth task was "Americanization," which included "educational work for the purpose of giving enlightenment and encouragement to the alien population." Helping the immigrant work toward naturalization and "winning his love for our institutions and ideals" involved a cooperative effort among various men's and women's organizations, Utah's public school system and universities, churches, and industrial institutions. Americanization meant enlightening native-born Americans, as well, with an aim toward turning "every knocker into a booster for freedom."[84]

Unquestionably, Utah's women's associations were active boosters. Almost all groups, even very small ones, purchased the government's Liberty Bonds, which helped to finance the war. For example, each member of the Jolly Stitcher Club in Delta, Utah, donated "one fat hen," and the club used the proceeds of the poultry sale to buy a fifty-dollar bond. The Utah Woman's Liberty Loan Committee, comprised of representatives from various organizations, coordinated women's efforts in the five Liberty Loan drives, all of which were oversubscribed in Utah. Some organizations "adopted" French orphans or sent money to allow children to stay with their parents, or contributed to the American Women's Hospitals in Europe organized by the Medical Women's National Association.[85]

Women's Red Cross Auxiliaries

The American Red Cross carried out its work within individual states through county chapters. Auxiliaries to each chapter were temporary local organizations that could be formed wherever there were "ten paid-up [Red Cross] members including a chairman, secretary and treasurer."[86]

Auxiliaries did military support work such as knitting clothes for soldiers and refugees, making surgical dressings and other hospital supplies, and similar activities. Many church-based groups like the Catholic Women's League and Episcopal Women became individual Red Cross auxiliaries.[87] When women had their own buildings or rooms, the Red Cross helped furnish the locations with necessary supplies. For example, the Ladies' Literary Club Red Cross Auxiliary set up sewing machines at its clubhouse and turned out clothing for hospital patients and Belgian servicemen. Red Cross chapter offices provided work rooms for auxiliaries who wanted to schedule time to use them.

Minutes of the Oliver O. Howard Post of the Women's Relief Corps of the Grand Army of the Republic show that between August 1917 and March 1918, its members had worked 126.5 hours in the "gauze room." In the "cutting room," they had prepared 167 garments, 438 compresses, and 30 sponges. They had also made 17 bed sheets, 15 convalescent capes, 30 operating sheets, 40 pairs of bed socks, 48 pairs of ether socks, 35 abdominal bandages, and 56 towels. Knitted articles included 22 sweaters, 10 mufflers, 11 pairs of wristlets, and 9 pairs of socks.[89] These numbers are impressive, but when multiplied by the number of auxiliaries across the state and in the Mountain Division (Utah, New Mexico, Wyoming, and Colorado), the magnitude of women's volunteer contributions becomes even more significant. In January 1918, women in the Mountain Division of the Red Cross contributed 567,684 articles of the type listed above. By March 1918, Clarissa S. Williams reported, the division's "record-breaking" production had "practically doubled," reaching 992,169 articles that would "be of great assistance in keeping old General Von Suffering from advancing his forces into allied territory."[89]

Women's organizations had a significant impact on the war effort; and the war effort, in turn, expanded their opportunities to work and serve within the public sphere. Three postwar developments have particular relevance to this study. First, World War I generated new patriotic organizations for women whose continuing emphasis on "Americanization" would be felt in Utah for the next six decades. Second, postwar passage of the Nineteenth Amendment in 1920 enabled women to continue their prewar and wartime social welfare and reform work as voting citizens. Finally, the war expanded the number of women in the work force and likewise increased the number of women who united to forward professional and career interests, a trend that would continue in the wake of World War II.

Patriotic Organizations

After the United States entered the war in 1917, groups of female relatives of servicemen began organizing to help their "boys" overseas, and to keep up their own morale. The War Mothers of America, incorporated in 1918, joined with seven similar groups to form the Service Star Legion, where the initials of "Serve" were assigned the meanings of sisterhood, education, relief, vigilance, and remembrance. In April 1920, the Salt Lake County Chapter of the Service Star Legion asked the City Commission for part of City Creek Canyon and planted 300 small trees there a month later. The resultant twenty-acre Memory Grove was dedicated in 1924, and the legion's Memorial House was erected there.[90]

Utah's Service Star Legion established an education loan fund for the sons and daughters of ex-servicemen, welcomed newly naturalized citizens, and honored Gold Star Mothers—women whose sons had been killed in the line of duty. The national organization attempted cooperation with a similar organization for men. The local history notes: "At the American Legion's first convention [1919], we offered our services as a sister organization, but were told they 'did not want any women.'" Two years later, however, the American Legion's own Auxiliary Department was officially organized. Utah's Service Star Legion remained intact, but, its historian observed, the group lost "some to the many different organizations that followed." Through the 1940s and '50s, it supported better education of children, campaigned to keep American classrooms and libraries free of Communist materials, and sought to improve the attractiveness of careers in the armed services.[91]

In 1922 Nephi, Utah, had the honor of registering Unit #1 of the American Legion Auxiliary Department of Utah. In the wake of World War I, the auxiliary, working "for God and Country," carried out through many local units the program of the American Legion, finding numerous ways to promote Americanism and train and strengthen citizens. It addressed the needs of veterans and aided their families with direct cash assistance. Units built up welfare funds in part from the sale of poppies in commemoration of World War I during the week before Memorial Day. When the homes of three veterans were "destroyed by fire, members through rummage sales and donations furnished food, clothing, and necessities."[92] The auxiliary also worked for the rehabilitation of disabled veterans.

Auxiliary units supported patriotic education, including the commemoration of American involvement in the two world wars. For example, following the completion of a new football stadium at Brigham Young University in 1928, Provo Post No. 13 and its auxiliary sponsored a Fourth of July program there commemorating the "Second Battle of the Marne." Units presented patriotic musical programs and awarded flags to schools. Citizenship training for girls through Girls State began in 1937 and for Girls Nation in 1947.

Committed to "active Americanism," auxiliary units urged voter participation and involved themselves in community service, often helping sponsor troops of Brownie Scouts, Girl Scouts, and Campfire Girls. Some units sponsored projects for children with cerebral palsy, polio, rheumatic fever, and other handicaps. Others contributed money, scrapbooks, games, and dolls to the Shriners' Children's Hospital, the Primary Children's Hospital, and the State Training School.

The American Legion Auxiliary, like the American Legion itself, upheld and defended the U.S. Constitution and supported U.S. military action. A 1951 auxiliary report quoted the comments of Mrs. Harry D. Ferrington, president of the Department of Utah, at the end of the Korean War's first year: "We in America, have been, and are fighting subversive activities, Communism, black market, and those who would undermine our American Democracy and our Way of Life."[93] At that point, ninety-two units were active in Utah, and a new district had been formed including units in Kamas, Heber City, Jensen, Vernal, Roosevelt, Myton, Altona, Duchesne, Coalville, and Park City. As of January 1986, women eligible for membership in the auxiliary included women in the service and the wives, daughters, sisters, granddaughters of American Legion members and the same women relatives of men who served during World War I, World War II, the Korean War, and the Vietnam War. That year, there were eighty-seven units throughout the state and a membership of 5,000.

Organizations for Women as Citizens

Over time, many American women who maintained a strong commitment to traditional home and family values resolved to become voting citizens. These "domestic feminists" believed the franchise would enable them to more effectively carry out their "social housekeeping," or social reforms. J. Stanley Lemons described their effective blending of feminism and social concerns, observing that "as they worked for progressive reform, they advanced the status of American women. And as they fought for women's rights, they pushed progressivism along in a decade of waning reformist impact."[94]

Passage of the Nineteenth Amendment in 1920 marked the culmination of the united work of numerous and diverse women's organizations. In Utah, Governor Simon Bamberger called the legislature into special session in the summer of 1919 to ratify the amendment and signed it into law in October.[95] The next month, November 1919, Carrie Chapman Catt, president of the National American Woman Suffrage Association, visited Utah to celebrate this local continuing victory and to organize a Utah unit of the National League of Women Voters, the designated successor of the NAWSA. Utah's "Suffrage Council was drafted almost in its entirety into the Utah League of Women Voters." Susa Young Gates represented Utah at the National League's first convention held in Chicago the following February upon the centennial of the birth of Susan B. Anthony, when ratification of the Nineteenth Amendment was virtually assured. Before adopting a plan of educational work centered on child welfare, public health, and social improvement, the league honored living pioneer suffragists from each state, including Emmeline B. Wells, Emily S. Richards, and Gates herself from Utah.[96]

Neither the Utah League of Women Voters nor the National League drew the full participation of those who had worked for suffrage. In 1925, the membership of the Utah League was still small, only forty-three. After a decade of active service, it went into a period of decline until it was revived in 1952. Since that time, it has remained a significant part of social awareness in Utah. Catt had been adamant that women join the national parties rather than forming a separate women's party, and the league from its beginning focused on issues and candidates rather than lobbying for a separate women's platform. In recent times, it has undertaken such projects as measures "to improve budgetary procedures in the State of Utah," and "to promote comprehensive regional and river basin planning," and it has explored such issues as year-round schools, migrant housing, allegations of religious and racial discrimination at federal facilities, and proposed community renewal programs.[97]

Civic Contributions of Women's Organizations

The fact that women did not rally again for a single issue as they had rallied for suffrage was not an indication that their interest in public issues or in exercising the franchise had declined. Quite the contrary. "Long before masses of women were deeply concerned with suffrage," Lemons explains, "they were working to make their communities more 'homelike.' When the great diversion—the suffrage crusade—ended, social feminism tended to resume its previous interests and multiple purposes. . . . Success would have to be measured by hundreds and thousands of little items from 1920 onward."[98]

Women's successes were "little" because they were primarily local. Close cooperation between volunteer organizations and local governments reached a high point during the 1920s and 1930s before the severity of the Great Depression expanded the role of state and federal governments in local welfare, health, and education concerns. Small town and rural women's clubs, particularly, show the important role of women's volunteer organizations in community betterment. The main impetus in 1916 for forming the Magna Woman's Club was to "take an active interest in the civil welfare . . . and social betterment" of the community. Projects included a public playground with a trained supervisor, a library, a pre-school child clinic, and clean-up campaigns. Modestly but tellingly, its historian concluded, "As our town is unincorporated we have no city official to appeal to for help in our work, and as we are the only organization doing civic work we have many calls for help. Many of us would like to take up a line of study but as the great need of the town is for civic work we feel justified in sacrificing our desires for the good of the community."[99]

In 1928, the Women's Civic Club of Bingham Canyon, reported that "a complete list of the pies in which we have had our fingers would be too long for this article," but the partial list included a better class of movies in the community, a public library, relief for miners out of work, a school cafeteria, clean-up campaigns, swat-the-fly campaigns, and fund-raising for "many objects, ranging from [the]

Photograph taken on the twenty-second anniversary of the Jolly Stitcher Club, Delta, July 1934.

University of Utah scholarship fund to milk for undernourished children." It is possible, reading between the lines, to see impressive leadership. The women would spearhead a project, then involve the male businessmen and civic leaders to stabilize and perpetuate the project: They "gained the cooperation of the picture producers . . . so that the Club has never felt the need of taking up the work again. . . . About this time the men of the town took hold of the matter. . . . With the assistance of the local doctors . . . . We persuaded the school board," etc.[100]

In the little town of Union, the Unity Club was organized in 1914 with seven members "to bring sociability, good literature and good music into the lives of the country women." In addition to studying Longfellow, Lowell, and music, its fifteen members had, by 1927, provided solid community service as well, including buying school furniture, entertaining the teachers at an annual luncheon, purchasing playground equipment, landscaping the school ground, contributing a hundred books to its school library, and loaning it almost a hundred more. One of its members served as a member of the Women's State Legislative Committee.[101] This group of representatives from various women's associations met at the capitol while the legislature was in session and engaged in "legitimate lobbying," encouraging bills "which they consider worthy," particularly those "affecting education and the welfare of women and children." In 1927, for example, the committee succeeded in repealing a horse-racing act.[102]

The historian of the Jolly Stitcher Club of Delta, formed in August 1913, summarized the importance of her small club's work over a fifteen-year period: "Our members have come from all over the United States, from Delaware to California, from Michigan to Arizona, and from Scotland and Wales. Although we have done much valuable charitable and social work, yet the main value of our club has been its broadening influence on the community life."[103]

A common concern around which many Utah women united during the 1920s was maternal and child health. Women's groups had been sponsoring milk stations, school health programs, and well-baby clinics for several years before the Congress passed the 1921 Sheppard-Towner Maternity and Infancy Protection Act. After the U.S. Children's Bureau had revealed high maternal and infant death rates, women's groups had lobbied strongly for the legislation. States and individuals were free to reject the proffered aid; but through the efforts of Amy Brown Lyman (a state representative and future general Relief Society president) and others, Utah passed enabling legislation and authorized the required matching funds. Various women's associations took up the important work, sponsoring child health consultation centers, child-care conferences, and instruction in the hygiene of maternity and infancy through public health nurses. The act expired in 1929, when even women's organizations became divided over the political question of the extent to which states should receive federal funds.[104]

The LDS Primary Association undertook another major project for children's health during this period. The LDS Children's Convalescent Hospital was opened May 11, 1922, in a home on North Temple in Salt Lake City. After thirty years of providing medical treatment for children of all races and creeds, expansion was long overdue and the Primary Children's Hospital was completed in 1952. It and its successor, the Primary Children's Medical Center at the University of Utah, have received support and contributions from many women's groups, secular as well as religious.[105]

Between the wars, the depression took its toll of women's associations, particularly larger clubs whose dues proved too high for women in straitened financial situations. Many clubs reported a drop of membership or, in the case of state associations, a decrease in units during this time period. For instance, in 1931–32, 135 members of the Utah Federation of Business and Professional Women's Clubs disaffiliated, and three clubs dropped their federation membership.[106]

For many affiliated women who remained active during this period, concern with state and national issues continued. In April 1935, at its annual district convention held at Cedar City's LDS First Ward meetinghouse, the Utah Federation of Women's Clubs discussed such topics as birth control, old age pensions, unemployment insurance, sterilization of criminals and the mentally unfit, narcotics, cancer, baby registrations, and statewide safety movements. At the convention, UFWC president Mrs. Weston Vernon, summarized achievements of the past three years, citing "cooperation with the attorney general in abolishing

Women workers associated with the Church of Jesus Christ of Latter-day Saints Victory Gardens project preparing beans, August 8, 1943: Mrs. E. E. Ericksen, Mrs. A. M. Woodbury, Mrs. LeRoy E. Cowles, Mrs. I. Daniel Stewart, Mrs. C. L. Walker, Mrs. J. J. Orme, Mrs. L. H. O. Stobbe, Mrs. Alexander Schreiner, Mrs. A. LeRoy Taylor, Mrs. William H. Bennett, Mrs. J. Albert Peterson. The gardens were scattered over hundreds of miles of the intermountain region and were tended by church members of all ages and their produce canned by women workers.

slot machines and preventing their reappearance, protest against a proposed merger of the juvenile court with district courts, an active stand on the Senate munitions investigation, and a memorial to Congress in support of pure food and drug legislation."[107] In October 1935, fighting the overwhelming tide of unemployment, Salt Lake City's six thousand club women sent hostesses to the State Fair to cooperate with the Utah Manufacturers' Association in impressing "upon Utah women that employment can be improved by purchasing Utah-made goods."[108] The December 1940 issue of the *Utah Clubwoman* included an extensive listing of departments and divisions within the UFWC, many of which (American citizenship, the American home, education, fine arts, international relations, employment and industries, legislation, and public welfare) reflected a continuing interest in social concerns.[109]

Those concerns became more urgent as the United States mobilized military and civilian resources for the Second World War. Utah clubs and associations supported the war effort; those in Salt Lake City often worked in close collaboration with the Woman's Board of the Conservation Division of the War Production Board, later known as the Salt Lake City Minute Women. Repeatedly, women set other interests aside and "organized waste paper drives and collected tin cans, nylon and silk hosiery, scrap metal, rubber and other needed items." The goal was to involve everyone in the salvage effort, and the widespread campaign was highly successful. To "illustrate the enormity of the Minute Women's salvage efforts of household fats," for example, in Utah, "2,262,538 pounds of fats were collected between 1942 and 1945," which could have been "translated into any one of the following uses: alkyd resin paint for 45,600 medium tanks; or 1,140,000 pounds of dynamite; or, 9,120,000 anti-aircraft shells; or annual pharmaceutical supplies for 76,000 hospital beds."[110] Women's clubs and associations, through war and depression, plainly manifested their durability and usefulness.

Content, Discontent, and Discovery, 1945–77

In July 1946, addressing the women's Society of Christian Service assembled at Park City's First Congregational Church, a Reverend Gravenor opined: "A generation ago women worked only for equality. That equality has not made the world better." He affirmed that "men and women together must be trustees of the future," emphasizing "the importance of women being good mothers and keeping a Christian home. Woman's duty," he concluded, "is to preserve the goodness in the world by raising God-fearing children."[111]

The minister's statement typifies the emphasis on women's traditional role as wife and mother that characterized popular culture in the United States during the period after World War II. For many women, the years that followed war, depression, and war again, seemed a blessed return to normalcy when peace and prosperity allowed home and family values to be firmly established rather than merely longed for. It was an era when Americans prized "togetherness," when, as *McCall's Magazine* observed in 1954, "men, women and children are achieving together . . . not as women alone, or as men alone, isolated from one another, but as a family, sharing a common experience."[112]

A different type of women's organization reflected this commitment to achieving together: wives' auxiliaries. These groups, determined by a husband's occupation rather than by the wife's interests, provided women with a means of associating with other women who faced similar challenges in supporting their husbands' work. For example, women who joined the University of Utah Medical Students' Wives could commiserate over their husbands' grueling schedules or their de facto single parenthood while engaging in their own educational activities or service such as the March of Dimes or the Festival of Trees.

Other groups forwarded the work of their husbands. The Utah Dental Association Women's Auxiliary assisted the Utah Dental Society in public dental health efforts; the Utah State Bar Auxiliary supported Utah State Bar activities and goals; the Salt Lake Jaycees Women's Organization supported the Jaycees' community projects; and the Consulting Engineers Council of Utah, Women's Auxiliary, worked to support council projects and promote "whatever may contribute to the welfare of the community."[113]

At the same time that wives' associations and auxiliaries were multiplying, the trend toward professionalization for women was also intensifying. During the wartime labor shortage, women had moved into positions in trades, industries, and professions, which previously had been reserved for men. Leaving behind their domestic service, or restaurant or laundry work, women were quickly trained to operate linotypes, lathes, and elevators, and to work as typesetters, electrical linemen, blacksmiths, mechanics, and bricklayers. Women lawyers were asked to serve on exemption boards and legal advisory committees. The percentage of women in the civil service more than doubled during World War I, reaching 20 percent.[114] In many cases, women held on to their positions after the war ended. The same trend was magnified in the wake of World War II. An estimated 24,000 Utah women joined the work force, nearly 30 percent of them in war industries.[115] Unlike post-World War I, World War II working women tended to remain at their jobs; by 1950, one-fourth of Utah's women "held remunerative jobs."[116]

As the percentage of women working increased, so did the interest in organizations for working women. The Business and Professional Women in Utah had organized in 1913 with the stipulation that 75 percent of its membership be actively engaged in business and professions. During the 1920s, the BPW maintained representation on the Utah Women's Legislative Council, lobbying for legislation to advance educational and professional opportunities for women. It marshaled its forces to eliminate policies that discriminated against hiring married women, provided scholarships and professional guidance for young people, and made community service an important component of local BPW club work. In 1937, its Beaver club was raising money for city recreational facilities. In Bingham Canyon, it bought equipment for a community house. In Ogden, the group had a project to help children with disabilities. The Brigham City club bought a piano and flower boxes for Bushnell Hospital. In Cedar City, the BPW sponsored scholarships. In Coalville, it supported a public library, a safe skating pond, and an eye clinic.

"The projects in which they were involved developed ingenuity, team spirit, interest, civic pride, and a sense of accomplishment for the clubs as a group and the members individually in addition to the visible community improvements," wrote Olive Davis Fagg in her 1979 study of the organization. "These organizations and their work lent courage and guidance to other groups with like aspirations."[117]

A healthy organization, the BPW continued to thrive throughout the 1970s and 1980s. In December 1977, it numbered thirty-three active units in the state with 1,132 members, including clubs in towns as large as Salt Lake City and as small as Lakeview.[118]

Many other organizations for professional women likewise emphasized the importance of service. In November 1923, twelve Salt Lake City women formed the Altrusa Club to foster "vocational training." Both the Salt Lake

City club and its sister club in Ogden were offshoots of Altrusa International, organized nationally in 1917 to "help girls and women adjust to the demands of the business and professional world." Starting with an initial loan fund of $400, by 1935 Altrusa of Salt Lake City was offering fifty-dollar scholarships to young women interested in social services graduate work. It also sponsored job clinics for older women but its main purpose has been to involve business and professional women in addressing "civic and social welfare problems in the community." Similarly, Utah chapters of Zonta and Soroptimist provide business and professional women opportunities for community service.[119]

Given the plenitude of service-oriented groups, some women's organizations focused more expressly on helping women forward their professional careers. A 1981 partial listing of Utah women's organizations and chapters suggested the number of associations developed to support women in specific professions, including: American Society of Women Accountants, Credit Women International, Executive Women International, National Association of Women in Construction, Insurance Women of Salt Lake City, Utah Women's History Association, Women in Social Work, Women's Architectural League, Women Entrepreneurs Association, and Women's Law Caucus.[120]

Appealing to women in a range of careers, the Wasatch Chapter of the American Business Women's Association, was chartered in 1968, an affiliate of the national organization founded in 1949 to "promote the professional, educational, cultural, and social advancement of women." In 1984, a Utah woman, Lois Yoakam, was elected national first vice president.[121] At that time, through its seminars, monthly meetings, and fund-raising to sponsor scholarships (which nationally provided more than $2.5 million annually), the group offered women "the opportunity to exchange information and ideas with other working women in a variety of professions, to build self-confidence, and to advance their education in both their business and personal lives."

The organizations for business and professional women that proliferated in the wake of both World Wars helped heighten awareness of women's continuing economic and legal disabilities, problems not resolved by the amendment granting suffrage. Many women's groups began campaigning for equal pay for equal work and equal opportunities for women in jobs, promotion, and training. Organizations for professional women were among the first to support the efforts of the National Woman's Party to work toward complete equality by "amending specific laws, blanket equality bills in all the states, and an amendment to the Constitution guaranteeing equal rights."[122]

In 1923, the Utah Federation of Business and Professional Women's Clubs indicated a keen awareness of the need for equal rights for women in employment, in wages, and in legal treatment. The national federation of Business and Professional Women's Clubs would not endorse the proposed Equal Rights Amendment until 1937. Though it had allowed state federations to act as they pleased in the matter, for a sixteen-year period it had remained neutral, siding neither with those who favored equal rights for women nor with those who favored protective legislation for women. For, as Stanley Lemons explains, "The feminist movement divided into warring factions on the question of how best to continue women's progress after winning the vote. Given the particular climate of legal opinion, labor legislation generally meant laws for women to protect them from abuse in the industrial system. Social feminists preferred to pursue this line; however, the national Women's Party wanted a constitutional amendment guaranteeing equality even though the amendment would destroy labor laws for women."[123] Both sides took strong stands and both sides could argue intelligently and persuasively on behalf of women, making it difficult for women's organizations to unilaterally endorse either position. The general Federation of Women's Clubs, for example, opposed the amendment in 1921 but endorsed it in 1944. There was clearly no consensus about "how best to continue women's progress"; and though the years following World War II brought prosperity and provided women's organizations with the opportunity to channel their energies into less controversial issues, the question of women's progress remained and opposing viewpoints and warring factions were destined to reemerge.

Since the majority of women's clubs and associations had their roots in nineteenth-century domestic feminism, they had long fostered rather than opposed traditional home and family values and did not find themselves out of step with post-war emphasis on the nuclear family and woman's mother-housewife role. Affiliated women had an advantage in having learned that homemakers did not need to be isolated, that on-going connections with other women could complement rather than damage family life. Most of these organizations had lost their fervor for social housekeeping some time between the failure of the child labor amendment in 1925 and passage of the Social Security Act in 1935, which included provisions for child and maternity welfare; but they did not discontinue community service. There were still immunization campaigns to be waged, youth groups to be financed, trees to be planted, legislators to be lobbied, historic sites to be marked, hospitals to be supported, arts to be sponsored, schools to be supplied with books and equipment, and dozens of drives for health research to be staffed by volunteers. And Utah's affiliated women accomplished this. For the most part, their work was neither controversial nor highly visible. They blended, perhaps too unselfconsciously, into the background.

For example, in 1962, Salt Lake City hosted the golden jubilee conference of the central Pacific Coast Region of Hadassah, the women's Zionist organization. Coverage of the event brought the organization and its local chapter momentarily into the limelight and revealed the purpose and complexity of a women's organization whose work was probably unknown to large numbers of Utahns. The group, established in 1912, "to raise health standards in what was then Palestine," had grown to include some 318,000 women in thirteen hundred chapters. Over a fifty-year period, the Hadassah program had "expanded to include an intricate system of healing, teaching and medical research, child rescue work, vocational education, social welfare and land redemntpion [sic]." In addition, Hadassah sought to "protect democratic ideas at home," its chapters "disseminating information on civic and political issues, economic projects, and welfare programs."[124]

The New Feminism

Hadassah was unique but it was not alone among women's organizations in its substantiality. Issue-oriented and community-conscious women continued associating, learning, and serving during the 1950s and early 1960s, but these interests were out of harmony with the era's popular interests. "By the time I started writing for women's magazines, in the fifties," wrote Betty Friedan, "it was simply taken for granted by editors, and accepted as an immutable fact of life by writers, that women were not interested in politics, life outside the United States, national issues, art, science, ideas, adventure, education, or even their own communities, except where they could be sold through their emotions as wives and mothers."[125] Attacking the past decade's glorification of women's occupation as housewives, Friedan's 1963 bestseller, *The Feminine Mystique,* lamented the shattering of "the image of the American woman as a changing, growing individual in a changing world" and called upon women to turn from an immaturity that has been called enmity to full human identity."[126] In 1965, she joined others in founding the National Organization for Women (NOW) to "take *action* to bring women into full participation in the mainstream of American society now, exercising all the privileges and responsibilities thereof, in truly equal partnership with men."[127] The emerging women's liberation movement, like the contemporary civil rights movement and student protest movement, challenged the values of "the establishment" and demanded revolutionary societal change.

At first, the new movement distanced itself from the long-standing women's networks, clubs, and associations which had upheld traditional roles for women as homemakers and volunteers, criticizing them, much as earlier radical feminists had criticized clubs for upholding the ideals of "ladydom."[128] A growing number of women sought self-understanding in lieu of social betterment. They wanted the economic power that came with university degrees and jobs, not literary club scholarship or community service. They developed alternative women's organizations: consciousness-raising groups, health centers, political caucuses, and educational groups.

Other institutions, too, were addressing women's concerns. The President's Commission on the Status of Women, established in 1961 by President John F. Kennedy, explored "education; home and community services; private employment, in particular that under federal contracts; employment in the federal government; labor standards; federal social insurance and taxes as they affect women; and the legal treatment of women in respect to civil and political rights."[129] The commission's 1963 report detailed the discriminatory wages and salaries women were earning (about three-fifths the average for men), and the declining ratio of women in professional and executive jobs. The commission recommended, among other measures, that women be counseled to use their abilities in society, that they receive equal opportunity in hiring, training, and promotion, and that child care centers and other services be available to women at all economic levels.[130]

Utah's own Governor's Commission on the Status of Women, established as an informal committee in 1964, was permanently established by executive order in 1968 by Governor Calvin G. Rampton.[131] In addition to several reports on the challenges of "employment opportunity, threats to the family, housing, and gender and minority discrimination,"[132] it also sponsored a groundbreaking study on adolescent pregnancy in the state and, in 1986, published a resource handbook, *Utah Women and the Law,* which had been in preparation since 1979. In 1989, this group's name was changed to the "Governor's Commission for Women and Families."

State universities likewise sought to address women's issues, including the concerns of middle-aged women, many of whom were returning as "nontraditional" students to pursue undergraduate and graduate degrees. At the University of Utah in 1971, a new Women's Resource Center was established to help break down sex-role stereotypes and provide a flexible forum for addressing education, counseling, and personal needs for women.[133] Utah State University established a women's Center for Life-Long Learning in 1974. Within a few years, both schools also initiated new programs in women's studies.

The International Women's Year

The insistence of new feminists that women reopen the discussion of their rights, particularly biological and economic rights, revealed the disparity of women's opinions on those issues. Neither the ratification of the Equal Rights Amendment nor the legalization of abortion was an exclusively legal question. Both were discussed in terms of their ramifications for women's lives in the private sphere as well as in the public sphere, and rarely was that discussion successfully separated from the perennial question: What is woman's role?

Profound disagreement surrounding that question emotionally charged the atmosphere in which women discussed their concerns and developed support networks. A radical anti-male faction of the movement successfully disrupted conferences, won publicity, and polarized positions. Traditionalists recoiled, sometimes overreacting. One bizarre manifestation was the name selected by some Utah women who united in opposition to the passage of the Equal Rights Amendment: Humanitarians Opposed to Degrading Our Girls (HOTDOG).[134] As concern became widespread, the viewpoints became more polarized and organizations sprang up on both sides of the issues.

If consensus seemed unlikely, dialogue seemed imperative. The concerns of Utah women reflected worldwide debate and discussion. The United Nations created a commission on the status of the women of the world in 1972 and proclaimed 1975 the "International Women's Year." That year, from June 19 to July 2, the International Women's Year Conference and Tribune—1,300 official U.N. delegates from 133 nations—assembled in Mexico City. An additional 7,000 unofficial observers, including 41 Utah women, also attended. The conference officially urged governments "to dedicate themselves to the creation of a just society where women, men and children can live in dignity, freedom, justice and prosperity."[135]

In the United States, a National Commission on the Observance of the International Women's Year was created by executive order in January 1975, with a mandate "to spread the word about IWY as widely as possible throughout the United States and to stimulate appropriate activities by nongovernmental women's organizations."[136] The commission scheduled a national IWY conference to convene in Houston in 1977, to be preceded by state meetings. The national and state meetings were to explore a variety of women's issues and to consider recommendations proposed by the commission.

Utah was allotted fourteen delegates to the Houston meeting, but the selection of those delegates and the discussion of proposed recommendations brought tensions and tempers to the eruption point and strained the state's sisterhood to its limits. Utah's IWY Coordinating Committee, charged with organizing the state conference, was purposefully drawn to represent a variety of political, social, ethnic, religious, and geographical backgrounds. It hoped "to capitalize upon that diversity so that we might better address ourselves to the variety of interests, needs, and concerns unique to Utah. . . . As a committee we are determined to be an example to the rest of the women in the state, showing that diversity doesn't have to divide people."[137]

Members of the coordinating committee, who had hoped to have two thousand women attend, were not prepared for the nearly fourteen thousand women who ultimately registered at the Salt Palace in Salt Lake City to attend "The Voice of Womankind: Utah's First State-Wide Women's Meeting on 24–25 June." The convention was the largest in the nation with more than twice the attendance at any of the other state meetings. And it was one of the most contentious, split largely along religious lines. "In states that had not yet ratified the ERA, the IWY conferences were poisoned by emotional and impassioned confrontations and turned into forums for continuing the battle," observed historian Martha Sonntag Bradley.[138] Ratification of the Equal Rights Amendment, state by state, had been pending since its approval by the U.S. Senate in March 1972. The Utah Legislature defeated the amendment in February 1975, two months before the National Commission on the Observance of IWY met for the first time and "chose ratification of the Equal Rights Amendment as its top priority issue."[139]

Utah delegation to the National Women's Conference, November 18-21, 1977 held in Houston, Texas.

However, the commission intended much more than a popular referendum on the ERA. State meetings were to vote on twenty-six national recommendations, addressing issues categorized under the headings of Arts and Humanities, Child Care, Credit, Education, Female Offenders, Legal Status of Homemakers, International Interdependence, Mass Media, Equal Rights Amendment, Older Women, Rape, Teenage Pregnancy, and Women in Elective Appointive Office.[140] As in other states, Utah's coordinating committee set up task forces to discuss the national recommendations and draft local recommendations.[141]

Though Utah's population had grown in numbers and diversity during the twentieth century, the majority of Utah women were still LDS or Mormon and, since 1971, all Latter-day Saint women were automatically enrolled as Relief Society members. The LDS Relief Society, like all other known women's organizations in the state, received information about the conference and an invitation to have its women participate. With encouragement from the IWY coordinating committee, Relief Society general officers, led by President Barbara Bradshaw Smith, encouraged their members in Utah to attend IWY's preliminary mass meetings, slated as opportunities to present information about the meetings and discuss varying opinions, but the turn-out was disappointing.[142] Subsequently, a letter sent through male ecclesiastical channels suggested that ten women from each ward unit attend the IWY meeting. Although church officials denied any conscious effort to "overwhelm" the convention, certainly its official letter brought forth the throngs who attended.[143] "The LDS Church unwittingly provided large numbers of sheep, and some opportunistic shepherds stepped in to manipulate the women toward one side of the issue before the conference," observed one dismayed LDS participant.[144]

The church's positions opposing the Equal Rights Amendment and abortion were already well known to its members.[145] These positions coincided with the private political agendas of such non-church groups as the Eagle Forum and the Conservative Caucus who, during the two weeks preceding Utah's IWY meeting, set up their own "informational" mass meetings directed at Latter-day Saint women in Kearns, Provo, Logan, Bountiful, and Salt Lake City. Implying official church sponsorship, playing on fears that "the national IWY was staging the conferences to pass a national agenda, including the ERA and pro-abortion laws," and warning of increased federal interference, political organizers passed out lists of "approved" delegates and instructed the women "to vote no on all recommendations on the ballot."[146] Consequently, most delegates did not come to the June 24–25 IWY meeting prepared to discuss issues or work together toward a common agenda. They had decided a priori to vote against proposals put forward by IWY organizers. "The acrimony that prevailed at the convention overrode nearly every attempt at a thoughtful discussion of women's issues," observed a *New York Times* reporter.[147] Utah's IWY convention came to epitomize the polarization its organizers had hoped to reverse.

Sixteen organizations picketed the convention, protesting that "right-wing and Mormon viewpoints were the only ones that the convention tolerated. They also accused the Church of Jesus Christ of Latter-day Saints and specifically . . . the Relief Society of interfering with the conference."[148] These organizations included the National Organization for Women, the Equal Rights Coalition of Utah, Order of Women Legislators, Utah Women's Political Caucus of Price and Salt Lake City, League of Women Voters, Women's Democratic Club, Parents for Good Day Care, Women Aware, Women's International League for Peace and Freedom, ACLU, Equal Rights Legal Fund, National Abortion and Reproductive Rights Action League (NARAL), YWCA, Women Entrepreneurs, the Phoenix Center, and Utah Welfare Rights Organization.

Utah's IWY convention rejected "by overwhelming majorities resolutions favoring the equal rights amendment, abortion on demand, and more than a score of other women's rights proposals put forward by the I.W.Y. organizers."[149] Other resolutions that they voted down were sex education in public schools, welfare, day care, and bilingual and cultural school programs. Several of the workshops moved that there be no discussion of the resolutions and went on to bring up other agendas. When the final count was in, the convention had rejected all of the national recommendations put before them, usually by at least seven thousand votes.[150] The fourteen delegates elected to attend the national convention in Houston represented these majority views.[151] Eight other women, who had "spoke[n] for the minority" at the Utah meeting, attended the Houston convention at their own expense as Utah delegates at large.[152]

The political polarization in the state created or gave new energy to several political organizations, many of them single-interest groups and many of them also including men. These groups included Right to Life of Utah, Minority Women's Coalition, Equal Rights Coalition of Utah, Women Aware (which worked to improve the status of gay women), and the Utah Association of Women (which opposed the Equal Rights Amendment but more generally promoted the exchange of ideas and fostered research on political issues).

Another organization formed in the aftermath of the IWY was the Women's Information Network. According to Pam Wilson-Pace, a member of the group's steering committee, "Our major goal is to coordinate women's groups to let everybody know what everybody else is doing. After IWY, we were all aware of the lack of unity in the women's movement."[153] *Network,* a thriving tabloid-sized monthly newspaper (1978–89), spoke to and for women in the business community, and took strong editorial stands on legislation and social issues affecting women.[154]

Conclusion

Perhaps it is precisely because women value "the ongoing process of attachment" that a lack of unity is disappointing and painful. It is ironic that a century of women's association in Utah, which began with a sharp division between Mormon and non-Mormon women, should close the same way; but the intervening history is instructive. The differences so apparent in 1877 confronted women with a challenge that their clubs and associations helped them meet. Over time, the Ladies Literary Club, originally exclusively non-Mormon, succeeded in bringing "strongly diverse elements together." Likewise, before the end of the nineteenth century, the work of the Utah Federation of Women's Clubs "did much to break down the walls of ancient prejudice."[155]

Still, though Utah women united in movements for peace and social reform, wartime support, and postwar community service, their common goals never dissolved significant differences, however much prevailing cultural images might have obscured them. "If ever a culture set up a grindstone, it is in Utah," acknowledged Mormon Emma Lou Thayne, poet and essayist, five months after Utah's IWY convention. "And paradoxically, if there were a place where living the many-faceted-life was encouraged, it is also here . . . . Is it possible to let the grindstone polish, not flatten, and the shaping of facets enrich and not fragment? Is it possible simply to fit?—and retain difference comfortably?"[156]

Both connectedness and identity are essential. "Unity and Diversity" is the longtime motto of the Utah Federation of Women's Clubs. It is an ideal but elusive combination, a challenge that continues to beckon Utah women of varying races, classes, and religious and political persuasions, to find commonalities during a second century of association.

Notes

1. Carol Giligan, *In a Different Voice: Psychological Theory and Women's Development* (Cambridge, Mass.: Harvard University Press, 1982), 156.

2. Karen Blair, *The Clubwoman as Feminist: True Womanhood Redefined, 1868–1914* (New York: Holmes and Meier Publishers, 1980), 3. Feminist historians have questioned the reality of "separate spheres." See, for example, Linda K. Kerber, "Separate Spheres, Female World, Woman's Place: The Rhetoric of Women's History," in *Toward an Intellectual History of Women: Essays by Linda K. Kerber* (Chapel Hill: University of North Carolina Press, 1997), 1959–99.

3. Jill Mulvay Derr, Janath Russell Cannon, and Maureen Ursenbach Beecher, *Women of Covenant: The Story of Relief Society* (Salt Lake City: Deseret Book, 1992), 23–126.

4. See John Sillito, "Conflict and Contributions: Women in Utah Churches, 1847–1920," chap. 3 in this volume; see also Leon Laizer Watters, *The Pioneer Jews of Utah* (New York: American Jewish Historical Society, 1952), 98–99.

5. Sophonisba Preston Breckinridge, *Women in the Twentieth Century: A Study of Their Political, Social, and Economical Activities* (New York: McGraw-Hill Book Company, 1933), 17.

6. Blair, *Clubwoman as Feminist,* 10, 12.

7. The conflict has been discussed by numerous scholars, many of whom are represented in Carol Cornwall Madsen, *Battle for the Ballot: Essays on Woman Suffrage in Utah, 1870–1896* (Logan: Utah State University Press, 1997).

8. Peggy Pascoe, *Relations of Rescue: The Search for Female Moral Authority in the American West, 1874–1939* (New York: Oxford University Press, 1990); Robert Joseph Dwyer, *The Gentile Comes to Utah: A Study in Religious and Social Conflict, 1862–1890,* rev. ed. (Salt Lake City: Western Epics, 1971), 194. Another women's organization created in opposition to the Mormon's "peculiar institution" was the Industrial Christian Home Association of Utah, organized in 1886 to maintain a capacious refuge and rehabilitation center for plural wives seeking to escape their husbands. Three years later, it housed only three women and six children; and despite ardent lobbying, it closed its doors in 1893. Pascoe, *Relations of Rescue,* 20–31, 87–90; Dwyer, *Gentile Comes to Utah,* 209–11; see also Gustive O. Larson, "An Industrial Home for Polygamous Wives," *Utah Historical Quarterly* 38 (Summer 1970): 263–75.

9. "The Minutes of the Blue Tea," September 14, 1876 to May 2, 1883, September 14, 1876, and September 28, 1878, Special Collections, Marriott Library, University of Utah, Salt Lake City, as quoted in Patricia Lyn Scott, "Jennie Anderson Froiseth and the Blue Tea," *Utah Historical Quarterly* 71, no. 1 (Winter 2003): 24, 28.

10. Katherine Barrette Parsons, *History of Fifty Years [of the] Ladies' Literary Club, Salt Lake City, Utah, 1877–1927* (Salt Lake City: Arrow Press, 1927), 24.

11. Hazel S. Parkinson, "Ladies Literary Club Notes 100 Years of Tradition" *Salt Lake Tribune,* February 20, 1977, W-1.

12. Patricia Lyn Scott, "Eliza Kirtley Royle: Beloved Club Mother," in *Worth Their Salt: Notable But Often Unnoted Women of Utah,* edited by Colleen Whitley (Logan: Utah State University Press, 1996), 51.

13.   Parsons, *History of Fifty Years,* 153.

14.   Jane Cunningham Croly, *The History of the Woman's Club Movement in America* (New York: Henry G. Allen & Co., ca. 1898), 1109.

15.   Parsons, *History of Fifty Years,* 104.

16.   Blair, *Clubwoman as Feminist,* 62.

17.   Croly, *History of the Woman's Club Movement,* 1109–11.

18.   In 1940, the first Junior Club in Ogden—an organization of young women that the district federation strongly encouraged—again chose Aglaia as its group name, apparently not realizing that an older namesake had preceded it. Mrs. W. H. Peck, "Achievements," *Utah Clubwoman* 4 (February 1940): 17.

19.   Croly, *History of the Woman's Club Movement,* 1109–11. Another club, also named Sorosis, was a social and literary club, organized in Pleasant Grove in 1894, to study the pronunciation of words, U.S. history, and popular authors. Grace Mayhen, "Woman's Social and Literary Club," *Woman's Exponent* 23 (July 15, 1894): 163.

20.   "Utah Federation of Women's Clubs, Reapers' Club," *Woman's Exponent* 25 (June 1896): 2. See Sharon Snow Carver, "Salt Lake City's Reapers' Club," *Utah Historical Quarterly* 64 (Spring 1996): 108–20.

21.   Blair, *Clubwoman as Feminist,* 58.

22.   "Benefits of the Club," *Woman's Exponent* 20 (April 15, 1892): 150.

23.   Ruth May Fox, "My Story," typescript, 24, Special Collections, Marriott Library, University of Utah, Salt Lake City. See Linda Thatcher and John R. Sillito, "'Sisterhood and Sociability': The Utah Women's Press Club, 1891–1928," *Utah Historical Quarterly* 53 (Spring 1985): 144–56.

24.   Unity Circle, First Unitarian Society of Utah, Minutes, September 10, 1891, 18–19, Utah State Historical Society. The group was known by various names including Ladies Unitarian Society, Unity Circle, Lloyd Alliance, Alliance of Unitarian and Other Liberal Christian Women. Irma Watson Hance and Virginia Hendrickson Picht, *In Commemoration of Seventy-Fifth Anniversary of the Founding of the First Unitarian Church, Salt Lake City, Utah, 1891–1966* ([Salt Lake City: First Unitarian Church], 1966), 163.

25.   Derr, Cannon, and Beecher, *Women of Covenant,* 157–61, 188–89.

26.   Carroll Smith-Rosenberg, "The Female World of Love and Ritual: Relations between Women in Nineteenth-Century America, *Signs: Journal of Women in Culture and Society* 1 (Autumn 1975): 9–11; see also Jill Mulvay Derr, "Strength in Our Union: The Making of Mormon Sisterhood," in *Sisters in Spirit: Mormon Women in Historical and Cultural Perspective,* edited by Maureen Ursenbach Beecher and Lavina Fielding Anderson (Urbana: University of Illinois Press, 1987), 155–57, 169–70.

27.   Annette K. Baxter, quoted in Blair, *Clubwoman as Feminist,* xiii.

28.   "Constitution and By Laws of the Edina Society," October 15, 1884, Edina Literary and Debating Society, Minute Book and Attendance Record, 1884–85, 1890–94, Special Collections, Marriott Library.

29.   Giligan, *In a Different Voice,* 156.

30.   Ellis R. Shipp, "Sphere of Woman," *Woman's Exponent* 22, no. 4 (September 1, 1893): 27.

31. Charlotte Perkins Gilman, quoted in Blair, *Clubwoman as Feminist,* 69, 71.

32. Ibid., 61.

33. Croly, *History of the Woman's Club Movement,* 1112.

34. "Woman's Day at Saltair, Final Resolution," *Woman's Exponent* 25 (September 1, 1896): 38.

35. Croly, *History of the Woman's Club Movement,* 1117. See also Carol Cornwall Madsen, "Decade of Détente: The Mormon-Gentile Female Relationship in Nineteenth-century Utah," *Utah Historical Quarterly* 63 (Fall 1995): 298–319.

36. "Utah Federation of Women's Clubs, Reapers' Club," *Woman's Exponent* 25 (June 1896): 1.

37. Mrs. Ernest Urien, "What Federation Means to Us," *Utah Clubwoman* 5 (December 1939): 10, 17.

38. Croly, *History of the Woman's Club Movement,* 1116.

39. Parkinson, "Ladies' Literary Club Notes," W-1. For more on the civic work of Utah's early clubs, see Sharon Snow Carver, "Club Women of the Three Intermountain Cities of Denver, Boise and Salt Lake City between 1893 and 1929" (Ph.D. diss., Brigham Young University, 2000).

40. Authors Club Papers, Special Collections, Marriott Library, quoted in Donna T. Smart, "Sage Green and Paintbrush Red: Symbols for the Authors Club, Established in 1893," ca. 1986, 6, 11. Used by permission.

41. "UFWC Directory," *Utah Clubwoman* 4 (February 1940): 18–19.

42. Derr, Cannon, and Beecher, *Women of Covenant,* 137–38. The Relief Society was incorporated as the National Woman's Relief Society in 1892 and maintained the name until 1945, when it again identified itself as Relief Society. It enrolled members and, from 1898 until 1971, charged dues. All Latter-day Saint women of eighteen years and older automatically became Relief Society members in 1971 and dues were eliminated. Ibid., 144–46, 345.

43. Carol Cornwall Madsen, "'The Power of Combination': Emmeline B. Wells and the National and International Councils of Women," *BYU Studies* 33, no. 4 (1993): 646–73; Rebekah J. Ryan, "In the World: Latter-day Saints in the National Council of Women, 1888–1987," in *Latter-day Saint Women in the Twentieth Century: Summer Fellows' Papers, 2003* (Provo, Utah: BYU Joseph Fielding Smith Institute for Latter-day Saint History, 2004), 131–48.

44. Madsen, "Decade of Détente," 299.

45. Grand Army of the Republic and Women's Relief Corps (Department of Utah Records, 1885–1931), Minutes, December 1894–March 1901, February 8, 1899, Utah State Historical Society.

46. Ibid., February 24, 1904.

47. The National DAR's committee for Welfare of Women and Children reported in 1915: "In view of the grave importance to the society of all questions relative to pure marriages and lawful genealogy . . . the committee in its report to the Continental Congress recommended the adoption of a resolution indorsing [sic] legislative, judicial, and moral remedies for the great American social problem of the instability

of the family." *Eighteenth Report of the National Society of the Daughters of the American Revolution, October 11, 1914, to October 11, 1915* (Washington, D.C.: Government Printing Office, 1916), 136–37. A decade earlier, the Utah DAR's Spirit of Liberty Chapter reported: "In March 1905, the chapter joined the National League, agreeing to support its efforts to protect the country against treasonable practices and to maintain the Christian idea of marriage." *Eighth Report of the National Society of the Daughters of the American Revolution, October 11, 1904, to October 11, 1905* (Washington, D.C.: Government Printing Office, 1906), 178.

48. "Report of Utah Society Daughters of the Revolution" and "History of the Utah State Society Daughters of the Revolution, Daughters of the Revolution, Scrapbook, 1898–1967, Special Collections, Marriott Library; *History of the Organization and Work of the National Society Daughters of the Revolution* [1891–1930], compiled by Mrs. Henry T. Kent et. al. (New York: n.pub., 1930), 109–12.

49. "Report of Utah Society of Daughters of the Revolution" and "Register of Utah State Society Daughters of the Revolution," 4, Special Collections, Marriott Library.

50. "The Daughters of Utah Pioneers," *Heart Throbs of the West,* compiled by Kate B. Carter, 12 vols. (Salt Lake City: Daughters of Utah Pioneers, 1939–51), 11:329–428.

51. Carma Wadley, "100 Years of Protecting the Past: Daughters of Utah Pioneers Celebrates Its Centennial This Month," *Deseret News,* April 5, 2001, A-25; also information at www.dupinternational.org, accessed April 27, 2005.

52. "Sketch of Life of Isabella Siddoway Armstrong," in Emma Louise Armstrong Notebook, 1917–50, holograph, LDS Church Archives.

53. Catherine Britsch Frantz, "Camilla Clara Mieth Cobb: Founder of the Utah Kindergarten," in *Worth Their Salt, Too: More Notable But Often Unnoted Women of Utah,* edited by Colleen Whitley (Logan: Utah State University Press, 2000), 45–47.

54. Mary A. Parson, "Reminiscences of the Beginning of Kindergartens in Salt Lake City, Utah," typescript, Anne Marie Felt Fox Papers, Special Collections, Marriott Library.

55. Ibid.; Lela Horn Richards, *The Growth of the Neighborhood House* (Salt Lake City: Arrow Press, 1929); Susan Lyman-Whitney, "Neighborhood House: 100 Years of Gentle Care," *Deseret News,* June 12, 1994, S1–S2.

56. Carol Cornwall Madsen and Susan Staker Oman, *Sisters and Little Saints: One Hundred Years of Primary* (Salt Lake City: Deseret Book, 1979), 41–43. See also Derr, Cannon, and Beecher, *Women of Covenant,* 157–60.

57. Madsen, "Decade of Détente," 306.

58. Breckinridge, *Women in the Twentieth Century,* 24.

59. Index cards, Salt Lake Public Library Information File, accessed in October 1981, with last update indicated: Utah Young Mothers Council, October 23, 1980; Utah Mother's Association, June 12, 1981. Photocopies in my possession.

60. Susa Young Gates, "Efficiency," *Relief Society Magazine* 3 (February 1916): 109–10.

61. Kim M. Gruenwald, comp., *Our Living Legacy: Improving the Quality of Family Life* (Logan: Utah State University, 1988), 7.

62. Utah State Home Economics Association, "Tentative History of the Utah State Home Economics Association, 1909–1955," 18, n.d., Utah State Historical Society.

63. Edina Literary and Debating Society, Minute Book and Attendance Record, 1884–85, 1890–94.

64. Ralph V. Chamberlin, *The University of Utah: A History of Its First Hundred Years, 1850–1950* (Salt Lake City: University of Utah Press, 1960), 310.

65. "Disbanded Sorority to Lead Parade," *Salt Lake Tribune,* October 4, 1981, B-12.

66. Salt Lake City Branch Yearbook of American Association of University Women, August 1989, retrieved on April 27, 2005 from www.aauwutah.org.

67. "Profile," Girl Scouts of America (Murray, Utah: Girl Scout Council, 1990), in my possession; telephone update on April 27, 2005, from Girl Scouts of Utah, Salt Lake City, 84107–3101.

68. Aileen S. Kraditor, *The Ideas of the Woman Suffrage Movement 1890–1920* (New York: Columbia University Press, 1967), 67–68.

69. Julia Ward Howe, AAW, Fourteenth Congress of Women, 1886, quoted in Blair, *Clubwoman as Feminist,* 48.

70. Leonard J. Arrington, "Modern Lysistratas: Mormon Women in the International Peace Movement, 1899–1939," *Journal of Mormon History* 15 (1989): 91–93.

71. "An Appeal to the Citizens of Utah," *Woman's Exponent* 30 (May 1902): 97.

72. Arrington, "Modern Lysistratas," 102–3.

73. Register of Young Women's Christian Association, Salt Lake City Chapter, Records, 1918–1977, Special Collections, Marriott Library, University of Utah.

74. "Honor Role," *Salt Lake Tribune,* November 5, 1912, 14.

75. Utah Federation, *Yearbook 1918–20,* 32.

76. Juanita Merrill Larsen, "Women in Industry with Special Reference to Utah" (M.A. thesis, University of Utah, 1933), 263.

77. Emmeline B. Wells, Clarissa S. Williams, and Julina L. Smith, "Epistle to the Relief Society Concerning these War Times," *Relief Society Magazine* 4 (July 1917): 64.

78. Woodrow Wilson, quoted in Noble Warrum, *Utah in the World War* (Salt Lake City: Utah State Council of Defense, 1924), 84.

79. "Women of Utah Respond: Records Show over 23,926 Engaged in War Work," *Salt Lake Herald,* July 13, 1919, under date in Journal History of the Church of Jesus Christ of Latter-day Saints (chronology of typed entries and newspaper clippings, 1830-present), LDS Church Archives.

80. Herbert Hoover, quoted in Warrum, *Utah in the World War,* 133–34.

81. Jessie L. Embry, "Grain Storage: The Balance of Power between Priesthood Authority and Relief Society Autonomy," *Dialogue: A Journal of Mormon Thought* 15 (Winter 1982): 63; Derr, Cannon, and Beecher, *Women of Covenant,* 210–14; James B. Allen and Glen M. Leonard, *The Story of the Latter-day Saints,* 2d ed. rev. (Salt Lake City: Deseret Book, 1992), 494.

82. Parkinson, "Ladies Literary Club," W-1.

83. Clarissa S. Williams, "Patriotic Department: Red Cross," *Relief Society Magazine* 5 (June 1918): 349.

84. "Women of Utah Respond," *Salt Lake Herald,* July 13, 1919; Utah Federation, *Yearbook 1918–20,* 38.

85. Jolly Stitcher Club, Delta, Utah, Minutes and Roll Book, 1913–1963, Utah State Historical Society; Warrum, *Utah in the World War,* 32–35, 121–24.

86. Amy Brown Lyman, "Notes from the Field: The Red Cross Plan," *Relief Society Magazine* 4 (September 1917): 510.

87. Antonette Chambers, "The Catholic Women's League of Salt Lake City: The First Ten Years (1916–1926)," ca. 1986, photocopy in my possession. Used by permission.

88. Grand Army of the Republic and Women's Relief Corps (Department of Utah Records, 1985–1931), Minutes, January 1917–February 1999, March 13, 1918, Utah State Historical Society.

89. Williams, "Patriotic Department," 346.

90. *The Story of Memorial House,* pamphlet (Salt Lake City: Service Star Legion, Salt Lake County Chapter, Inc., n.d.), Service Star Legion Papers, Special Collections, Marriott Library.

91. "The Story of the Service Star Legion," Service Star Legion Papers, Special Collections, Marriott Library.

92. American Legion Auxiliary Department of Utah, "Report of Child Welfare Committee," American Legion Auxiliary History Department of Utah, 1950–51, Utah State Capitol, Salt Lake City.

93. Mrs. Harry D. Ferrington, quoted in "American Legion Auxiliary History."

94. J. Stanley Lemons, *The Woman Citizen: Social Feminism in the 1920s* (Urbana: University of Illinois Press, 1973), vii-viii.

95. "Governor Bamberger Urges Legislation for Fallen Women," *Deseret Evening News,* October 4, 1919, 10.

96. Gwen Hovey, "Historian's Report to the Board, League of Women Voters of Utah," Exhibit 1, "The League of Women Voters in Utah," April 19, 1983, 1–2, League of Women Voters (Utah) Records, 1919–81, Utah State Historical Society.

97. Utah League of Women Voters, State Convention Minutes, 1955, 1961, and 1969, League of Women Voters (Utah) Records, 1919–81, Utah State Historical Society.

98. Lemons, *Woman Citizen,* 234.

99. Mrs. Lontenstock, "Origin, Purpose, and Growth of the Magna Woman's Club," in *The Utah Payroll Builder: The Utah Manufacturer's Association* (publication of the Utah Federation of Women's Clubs, Utah Shippers Traffic Association, and Service Star Legion) 17 (April 1928), n.p.

100. A. C. Cole, "The Women's Civic Club of Bingham Canyon, Utah," *The Utah Payroll Builder: The Utah Manufacturers Association* 17 (April 1928): n.p.

101. "History of the Unity Club of Union," *The Utah Payroll Builder: The Utah Manufacturers Association* 17 (April 1928), n.p.

102. Parsons, *History of Fifty Years,* 122.

103. Mrs. Martin, "A Short Account of the Jolly Stitcher Club [of Delta, Utah]," *The Utah Payroll Builder: The Utah Manufacturers Association* 17 (April 1928): n.p.

104. Loretta L. Hefner, "The National Woman's Relief Society and U.S. Sheppard-Towner Act," *Utah Historical Quarterly* 50 (Summer 1982): 255–67; Lemons, *Woman Citizen,* 153–80.

105. Madsen and Oman, *Sisters and Little Saints.*

106. Olive Davis Fagg, "A Survey of National and Utah Federations of Business and Professional Women's Clubs" (M.A. thesis, University of Utah, 1979), 34.

107. "Club Women Urged to Act for Society," Elks' Ladies Club Scrapbook, 1922–41, Elks Ladies Club Papers, Special Collections, Marriott Library.

108. Ibid.

109. *Utah Clubwoman,* 18–19.

110. Katie Clark Blakesly, "'Save 'em, Wash 'em, Clean 'em, Squash 'em': The Story of the Salt Lake City Minute Women," *Utah Historical Quarterly* 71 (Winter 2003): 37, 49.

111. "The Women's Society of Christian Service Reports," July 1, 1946, 3–4, Park City's First Congregational Church, Utah State Historical Society, Salt Lake City.

112. Betty Friedan, *The Feminine Mystique* (1963; reprinted, New York: Dell, 1974), 42.

113. Index cards, Salt Lake Public Library Information File, accessed in October 1981, with last update indicated: University of Utah Medical Students' Wives, June 8, 1981; Utah State Bar Auxiliary, October 14, 1981; Utah Dental Association Women's Auxiliary, February 12, 1981; Salt Lake Jaycee Women's Organization, September 16, 1981; Consulting Engineers Council of Utah Women's Auxiliary, October 25, 1980; other wives' groups or women's auxiliaries in this file include: Utah State Medical Association Auxiliary, Salt Lake County Medical Society Auxiliary, Homebuilders of Greater Salt Lake Auxiliary, Utah Pharmaceutical Association Women's Auxiliary, American Institute of Mining, Metallurgical Engineers Women's Auxiliary.

114. Lemons, *Woman Citizen,* 18–22.

115. Antonette Chambers Noble, "Utah's Rosies: Women in the Utah War Industries during World War II," *Utah Historical Quarterly* 59 (Spring 1991): 123–45.

116. Ibid., 140–41; see also Maureen Ursenbach Beecher and Kathryn L. MacKay, "Women in Twentieth-Century Utah," in *Utah's History,* edited by Richard D. Poll, Thomas G. Alexander, Eugene E. Campbell, and David E. Miller (Provo, Utah: Brigham Young University Press, 1978), 582.

117. Fagg, "Survey of National and Utah Federations," 270.

118. Ibid., 256.

119. Altrusa or Altrusia Club Collection, 1938– , Utah State Historical Society; index cards, Salt Lake Public Library Information File, accessed in October 1981, with last update indicated: Altrusa, April 6, 1981; Soroptimist, September 2, 1981; Zonta, August 1, 1981.

120. Index cards, Salt Lake Public Library Information File, accessed in October 1981, with last update indicated: American Society of Women Accountants, April 7, 1981; Credit Women International, January 12, 1981; Executive Women International, January 3, 1981; National Association of Women in Construction, August 1, 1981; Insurance Women of Salt Lake City, November [1981]; Utah Women's History Association,

June 23, 1981; Women in Social Work, July 2, 1981; Women's Architectural League, June 8, 1981; Women Entrepreneurs Association, June 20, 1981; Women's Law Caucus, June 23, 1981.

121. Sue Thurman, "ABWA Enjoys Increasingly Viable Status," *Deseret News,* September 10–11, 1984, C-3.

122. Lemons, *Woman Citizen,* 184.

123. Ibid., 204.

124. "Golden Jubilee Meeting," *Salt Lake Tribune,* May 19, 1962; "A Half Century of Benign Service," *Deseret News,* May 22, 1962, A-16.

125. Friedan, *Feminine Mystique,* 44.

126. Ibid., 38, 72.

127. Ibid., 370.

128. Blair, *Clubwoman as Feminist,* 1–5.

129. *American Women: The Report of the President's Commission on the Status of Women and Other Publications of the Commission,* edited by Margaret Mead and Frances Balgley Kaplan (New York: Charles Scribner's Sons, 1965), 9.

131. "Governor's Commission on the Status of Women: Agency History," compiled by G. Glen Fairclough Jr., 1990, typescript, Administrative Histories binder, Utah State Archives.

132. Beecher and McKay, "Women in Twentieth-Century Utah," 583.

133. Shauna Adix, Oral History Project, 1975, 116, Special Collections, Marriott Library, University of Utah.

134. Index cards, Salt Lake Public Library Information File, accessed in October 1981, with last update indicated: HOTDOG (Humanitarians Opposed to Degrading Our Girls), October 18, 1978.

135. *Report of the World Conference of the International Women's Year* (New York: United Nations, 1976), 58, as quoted in Martha Sonntag Bradley, "The Mormon Relief Society and the International Women's Year," *Journal of Mormon History* 21, no. 1 (Spring 1995): 110.

136. Ibid.

137. "Utah Coordinating Committee for the State Wide Meeting on the Observance of the Decade of the Woman," March 24, 1977, Press Release, 3–4. Photocopy of typescript in my possession.

138. This quotation and preceding information in the paragraph drawn from Bradley, "Relief Society and the International Women's Year," 114.

139. "Report of Equal Rights Amendment Committee," *". . . To Form a More Perfect Union . . ." Justice for American Women: Report of the National Commission on the Observance of International Women's Year* (Washington, D.C.: National Commission, 1976), 219.

140. "Appendix B: Utah IWY Conference Votes on the Twenty-Six National Recommendations," in Bradley, "Relief Society and the International Women's Year," 156–61.

141. "Appendix C: Summary of Recommendations Drafted by Pre-Conference Task Forces, Discussed in Workshops and Voted on in Plenary Session at Utah's IWY Conference,

June 24–25, 1977," in Bradley, "Relief Society and the International Women's Year," 161–67.

142. Derr, Cannon, and Beecher, *Women of Covenant,* 370–72.

143. Ibid.; Bradley, "Relief Society and the International Women's Year," 126–28.

144. Reba Keele and other BYU women, "Report on the Utah International Women's Year Meeting," July 1, 1977, 2. Photocopy of transcript in my possession.

145. Not all Latter-day Saint women supported their church's position on the Equal Rights Amendment. See, for example, Mormons for the ERA, *The Equal Rights Amendment Is Not a Moral Issue* ([Salt Lake City]: Mormons for the ERA, 1979).

146. Bradley, "Relief Society and the International Women's Year," 133–35.

147. John M. Crewdson, "Mormon Turnout Overwhelms Women's Conference in Utah," *New York Times,* July 25, 1977, 26.

148. "Protesters Picket IWY Meet," *Salt Lake Tribune,* June 26, 1977, 1.

149. Angelyn Nelson, "Women's Convention Hostility Mounts," *Salt Lake Tribune,* June 26, 1977, 1.

150. "Majority at Women's Meeting Disagrees with All National Recommendations," *Salt Lake Tribune,* June 26, 1977, 1.

151. The delegates were Belva Ashton, Delores Bennett, Elaine Cannon, Margaret Cassun, Jennie Duran, Ruth Funk, Carol Garbet, Dixie Nelson, Stella Oaks, Jaynann Payne, Georgia Peterson, Lois Pickett, Belle S. Spafford, and Naomi Udall. Alternates were Gloria Firmage, Florence Jacobsen, Ann Leavitt, Amy Y. Valentine, and Dona Wayment. Ashton was a member of the LDS Relief Society General Board and Spafford was its past general president; Jacobsen, Funk, and Cannon were respectively past, present, and future general presidents of the LDS Young Women, formerly the Young Women's Mutual Improvement Association.

152. Nelson, "Women's Convention Hostility Mounts," 1–2. The at-large delegates included Esther Landa, Jan Tyler, and Kathleen Flake, all of whom had been among the conference organizers. Lynne Van Dam, Alberta Almada, Joan Draper, Eloise McQuown, Reba Keele, and Sandra Haggerty were also at-large delegates but had not been conference organizers.

153. Robbie B. Snow, "Two Groups Aid Utah Women in the 'Ole Girl' Network," *Salt Lake Tribune,* October 9, 1977, W-1.

154. *Network* Magazine Records, 1978–89, Special Collections, Marriott Library.

155. Croly, *History of the Woman's Club Movement,* 113, 117.

156. Emma Lou Thayne, "Ashtrays and Gumwrappers: Women in Utah Mormon Culture," *Task Papers in LDS History, No. 19* (Salt Lake City: LDS Family and Church History Department, November 1977), 3; copy in LDS Historical Department Library.

9

Women of Letters

A Unique Literary Tradition

Gary Topping

All writers, no matter how imaginative their work, are affected to some degree by their environment; but defining those effects, positive or negative, creative or destructive, is always difficult and often impossible. Environmental effects can be paradoxical. Readily available patronage, for example, may result only in the proliferation of mediocrity, while thoroughly oppressive circumstances can produce a Dostoevski or a Dickens. Thus, while Utah's unique cultural circumstances have produced a unique literary tradition, it is possible to define that gestative process only partially and dimly.[1]

The harshness of frontier life, though poignantly present in early Utah, seems to have been generally less of a factor in inhibiting cultural development than elsewhere. An important factor was Mormonism's characteristic gregariousness. Mormon migration and colonization were movements of an entire society rather than a diffusion of individuals. Thus, while the poet behind the plow and the historian in the haymow were to be found on the Utah frontier as elsewhere, Mormon society from the beginning sought a degree of specialization that potentially included the arts, sciences, and letters. Occupying their own sphere within Mormonism's solidly patriarchal society, Mormon women organized an impressive array of clubs and organizations and participated in many with both male and female membership that supplemented the officially directed auxiliaries. Official or not, these groups became in major ways, culture bearers of Mormonism. Rare indeed was the community, even in the farthest-flung corners of Mormondom, that could not boast of a ladies' literary or debating club as well as a branch of the ubiquitous women's Relief Society by 1900. And of course the preponderance of women schoolteachers in Utah as elsewhere in nineteenth-century America gave Utah women, Mormon and Gentile alike, a vitally important role in the cultural life of the territory.

Emmeline B. Wells (1828–1921) was a women's rights advocate and active in the women's suffrage movement, editor of the *Woman's Exponent,* and Relief Society general president for the Church of Jesus Christ of Latter-day Saints, n.d.

Other institutions also encouraged cultural development. The difficulty of transportation made books highly prized commodities during the pioneer period, though the Territorial Library assembled by John R. Bernhisel and the libraries of certain individuals were impressive collections. Libraries began to proliferate more rapidly after the arrival of the transcontinental railroad in 1869, although it was not until statehood in 1896 that Salt Lake City undertook, as a government responsibility, the support of a public library.

Educational institutions were ambiguous in their encouragement of culture. Throughout most of the nineteenth century, the Mormon-dominated school system was notoriously poor, though many Protestant mission schools with well-trained teachers were available even in remote communities by the 1870s. By the turn of the century, the Mormon Church was running several academies of higher learning, though with little distinction, while the University of Deseret, founded in 1850, had been mired in mediocrity until John R. Park, had assumed the presidency in 1869, and had begun to attract faculty members of merit.

The ready availability of publishing outlets for writers of all abilities was a conspicuous characteristic of Utah culture during the nineteenth century. While established eastern publishing houses seem to have been little interested in native Utah talent except for exploitative exposés by apostate Mormons, prominent Utah women like Eliza R. Snow and Susa Young Gates were occasionally published in the East. Much more important, though, were the local outlets—the *Young Woman's Journal,* the *Woman's Exponent,* the *Relief Society Magazine,* and the local newspapers—often capably edited by women like Gates, Louisa ("Lula") Greene Richards, and Emmeline B. Wells, who were constantly seeking publishable material in all genres.[2]

These cultural institutions and opportunities, while encouraging, did not produce a great flowering of literature in nineteenth-century Utah. The tight-knit community that allowed easy organization for group life also insured that group values would be those most often promulgated by its institutions and publications. The pious, the sentimental, and the conventional thrived at the expense of the original, the critical, and the creative. Also, many of the literary clubs and organizations were "literary" in name only, existing primarily to meet social needs. For example, the venerable Ladies' Literary Club of Salt Lake City, founded in 1877 by wealthy non-Mormon women, held a particularly memorable meeting during the club's early years. Mrs. Eliza Kirtley Royle, the club's first president, said she could

> think of no time when we made such advance in systematic and improved methods of literary work as we did that year. . . . It was there that three of our members gave us, one afternoon, a most delightful object lesson. Tea, coffee, and chocolate were the miscellaneous topics for discussion. Interesting and instructive papers were read by Mrs. Hamilton, Mrs. G. Y. Wallace, and Mrs. Tuttle. We felt we had a feast of reason, when in came at the rear door, the flow of tea, coffee, and chocolate, served in the daintiest china and with most delicious cake.[3]

The "Arts and Crafts Section" of the club, founded in 1922, devoted its attention to making such things as lamp shades and lace work, while its historian reported in 1927 that its members "frequently indulge in the 'cup that cheers.'" The club also "fostered creative talent," sponsoring programs of original works and offering prizes to recognize local talent.[4]

The Utah Women's Press Club, which lasted from 1891 to 1928, offered more promise as a vehicle for the improvement and encouragement of women writers. Primarily, though not exclusively Mormon in its membership, it was founded by Emmeline B. Wells to serve the needs of "women engaged in active journalistic or newspaper work." Though none of its members became major literary figures, some of them—Wells, Susa Young Gates, Ellis Reynolds Shipp, and Ruth May Fox—were persons of solid intellectual ability and writers and editors of at least middling talent. Moreover, the agenda of the meetings included opportunities for criticism of each other's work, and the nature of the membership provided contact between editors and those wishing to publish.[5]

Eliza Roxcy Snow (1804–87),
Relief Society general president,
writer (books, poetry, church
hymns), and acknowledged
leader of Mormon pioneer
women of the nineteenth
century, n.d.

During the last decade of her life, Susa Young Gates (1856–1933) worked on an ambitious history of women in Utah. Although she left it unfinished, her chapter on women writers is illuminating. "In purely literary ventures," she states, "women have certainly dominated the race for self-expression. There are less than a half-dozen men who have published books of verse or fiction. There are many such women authors." She lists and critiques sixteen women writers in addition to herself who, to her mind, constituted the feminine literary heritage of Utah: Eliza Roxcy Snow, Hannah Tapfield King, Emily B. Spencer, Mary Jane Mount Tanner, Hannah Carnaby, Augusta Joyce Crocheron, Lula Greene Richards, Ellis R. Shipp, Reba Beebe Pratt, Emmeline B. Wells, Alice Merrill Horne, Nancy Norvell, Helen Mar Whitney, Aurelia Spencer Rogers, Lydia D. Alder, and Ruth May Fox.

From a late twentieth-century perspective, most of these women are minor lights. No more than three or four of the seventeen are read at all today. Some of them are more of historical than literary interest. The group is heavily weighted with poets (all but Gates, Norvell, Whitney, and Rogers); but none of the poetry is memorable, and surviving names are remembered for something else: Tanner for her fine autobiography, Horne for her sponsorship of fine art, Rogers as founder of the Primary, Shipp for her medical career and memoirs, Wells as editor of the *Woman's Exponent,* and Fox as a suffragist and long-time general president of the Young Ladies Mutual Improvement Association.

Although Gates was as positive about the group's achievement as possible, she obliquely admitted that the achievement was not beyond improvement, charitably blaming most of the shortcomings on external circumstances such as the frontier environment and heavy domestic obligations. Even the poems of the awesome Eliza R. Snow, "Zion's Poetess," whose piety and didactic purposes would seem to have paralleled Gates's own values most closely, required guarded apologies: "Uneven in poetic merit, they still bear the stamp of genius held down, at times, to rigid standards, or mayhap, forced into personal or practical channels to please friends and especially to convey abstract principles in verse to the youthful studious mind."[6]

The name of one female poet is missing from the list, no doubt because she married Gentile Jonathan M. Williamson, post doctor at Fort Douglas, and thus, perhaps, to the daughter of Brigham Young, was no longer a genuine Utah woman. The omission is most unfortunate, for unless some unknown literary genius comes to light, Sarah Elizabeth ("Lizzie") Carmichael (1838–1901) was by far the best Utah poet of the nineteenth century and perhaps the only one, by rigorous literary standards, authentically to deserve the designation of poet.[7]

Carmichael's parents were double cousins, a genetic heritage that caused some emotional instability. (A sister, Mary, was mentally retarded.) According to Miriam B. Murphy, Carmichael's biographer, she "went into a severe mental decline about a year after her marriage" and was seen in the 1890s at the state mental hospital in Provo.[8] Eliza R. Snow generously used her formidable powers to introduce her younger colleague to Brigham Young and boosted her along the road to publication. Carmichael's work survives mainly through sporadic appearances in the *Deseret News* and in a collection, *Poems* (San Francisco: Towne and Bacon, 1866), published in a limited edition "for private circulation" at her husband's insistence. Carmichael prefaces the book with a modest protest:

> Ephemeral thing! Unwisely sought!
> Who dares to win a woman's thought?

The poems themselves deal with fairly conventional themes and are sometimes burdened with sentimental devices of Victorian poetry, but even her tributes to Brigham Young and the Mormon pioneers are free of the formal piety of Eliza R. Snow, and one would have to reach almost as far as Walt Whitman to find more moving lines on Lincoln's death and the Civil War:

Sarah Elizabeth ("Lizzie") Carmichael (1838–1901) was a nineteenth-century poet who wrote on regional themes and nature as well as conventional topics. Sarah has been called the "best Utah poet of the nineteenth century."

> Tears were frozen in their sources,
> Blushes burned themselves away;
> Language bled through broken heart-threads,
> Lips had nothing left to say.

Regional and nature themes, too, played a major role in her poetry, in such haunting lines as:

> Lake Tahoe, sweetest lake of lakes!
> The crescent moon oft overtakes
> And tramples on the soft white feet
> Of day . . . . [9]

Susa Young Gates dominated the literary world of turn-of-the century Utah through her energetic personality, her influential editorial positions, and her prolific pen. Her place in Utah's literary history is assured as author of the first novel on a Mormon subject written by a Mormon, *John Steven's Courtship: A Story of the Echo Canyon War* (Salt Lake City: Deseret News, 1909). Her works are largely unread today; they are sadly dated, sentimental, and unremittingly didactic. Critic Paul Cracroft argues for the literary merit of her posthumous novel, co-authored with her daughter Leah Eudora Dunford Widtsoe, *The Prince of Ur* (Salt Lake City: Bookcraft, 1945), claiming that her didactic intensity called forth her greatest literary power in her essays and editorials.[10]

As Utah moved into the twentieth century, new cultural influences helped to create a literature of much greater maturity. After the demise of polygamy (1890–1911) and the achievement of statehood in 1896, Utah moved toward the mainstream of American life. While permanently retaining many uniquely Mormon institutions and folkways, Utah strongly and patriotically embraced middle-class American culture. For Utah writers this meant that the Mormon Church was no longer their dominant literary seedbed even though it would always have its own form of "home literature" in its own magazines. Instead more critical rigor developed a willingness to look at the culture of Mormonism rather than the faith as a source for literary exploration and also produced greater sophistication in literary techniques.

The development of higher education undoubtedly influenced literary development. At the University of Utah, for example, the presidency of Dr. John R. Park (1869–92) marked the beginning of independence from church domination and solid commitment to high academic standards.[11] Bernard DeVoto, on one end of the spectrum, found that commitment less than perfectly realized, while Wallace Stegner, in contrast, characterized himself during his student years in Utah as "happy as shrimp in cocktail sauce."[12] By the time of the Great Depression and World War II, the University of Utah's English faculty included Vardis Fisher and Stegner. They have been followed in the last half of the twentieth century by such nationally important scholars, writers, and teachers as Brewster Ghiselin, Clarice Short, David Kranes, and even national Poet Laureate Mark Strand. Similar qualitative improvements have characterized Utah's other institutions of higher learning.

Women writers sprang forth in abundance during the 1940s, almost certainly because of the disruptive effects of the Great Depression and World War II on traditional gender roles. Maurine Whipple, Blanche Cannon, Virginia Sorensen, Fawn Brodie, and Juanita Brooks, among others, emerged during that decade—a development scarcely paralleled in the male realm. These women's writings document a cultural phenomenon of major proportions.

For example Blanche Cannon's *Nothing Ever Happens Sunday Morning* (New York: G. P. Putnam's Sons, 1948) shows a degree of detachment in interpreting Mormon culture that would probably have been impossible for an earlier generation. The thesis implicit in the title is that even trivial events have deep historical antecedents, and Cannon uses extensive flashbacks in the minds of the major characters. The story takes place during fast Sunday morning (the first Sunday of the month when, instead of regular assigned sermons, the time is spent in spontaneous "testimony-bearing") in a typical Mormon town named Lakeview in 1900. These flashbacks reveal a tyrannical and hypocritical father, Bishop Eben Benson, his oppressed wife and children, and the frustration and yearnings of two of those children for independence and exposure to a wider world.

Benson treats his wife, Matilda, as a servant; she has no life apart from the responsibilities of home and family and suffers unremitting humiliation in support of his business and church ambitions. Unable to find even enough of a chink in his cold personality to announce her first pregnancy, she bears her child while Eben is in England on a mission and endures the blow of receiving Eben's pretty second wife who travels home ahead of him. She learns only later of their relationship.

As a father, Benson tries to eradicate the individualism of his children, driving each to find a way to retain his or her own dignity. The two younger sons, "had little to do with him. They obeyed him without question, and although they seemed to feel no fear of him, they never played when he was in the room." A younger daughter, Elspeth, "never seemed to be naughty but she never seemed to be obeying the rules either. She went her own way, according to some law of her own."[13]

But it is the two older children, Jasper and Margaret, upon whom the story focuses. Both have yearnings for a fuller life beyond Lakeview and the Mormon Church. Margaret becomes infatuated with a vagabond hired man whom we know simply as "Jonathan," a free-thinking radical with a knapsack full of poetry and atheism. She tries to get him to remain with her in Lakeview, unwittingly revealing her perception of the shallowness of her father's religion: "Can't you see, Jonathan, if you'll go to church a few times, it won't matter what books you read, or even what you think in your own mind? They wouldn't understand about those things, anyway. But if they saw you at church they'd forget what they believed about you, and soon they'd think you were just like everybody else."[14] Jonathan agrees to meet her in church on that fateful fast day but instead leaves in the middle of the night, devastating her hopes.

Jasper's lot is more tragic than a broken heart. His contact with the outside world is Dr. Robinson, a Gentile professor at Brigham Young University which he attends for a year. Robinson, impressed with Jasper's intellectual abilities, offers to help get him into Harvard if he can get his father's permission and assistance. Jasper puts in a dutiful year in Eben's hardware store earning his tuition, but falls in love with Ellie Dickerson, daughter of the town drunk. She becomes pregnant. The biggest "happening" on that Sunday morning when "nothing happens" is Ellie's forced confession of her sin in front of the entire community and a visiting apostle; but she refuses to name her child's father, and Jasper lacks the backbone to proffer his own confession. Thus Eben Benson is ultimately triumphant: Jasper is so submerged by his father's personality that he cannot make a moral choice, to admit his love for the disgraced Ellie Dickerson, and find his own way to Harvard.

Nothing Ever Happens Sunday Morning is strongly reminiscent of Edith Wharton, whose works Blanche Cannon taught while a faculty member at the University of Utah. Even more, though, it is rooted in Cannon's own experience and knowledge of small-town Mormon culture. The story originated, she says, as a short story including only the church confession episode. After seeing a polygamist house like the one described in the novel, she began to fill out the social and emotional elements, adding the character of Jasper from the experiences of one of her mother's brothers, and the character of Eben from that of her own grandfather.[15] Richard Scowcroft, reviewing the book, said he almost regretted, for Cannon's sake, that she had chosen to use Mormon culture as the milieu for such a fine story, fearing that readers would be distracted from seeing her expert handling of larger human themes by her critique of that culture.[16] Actually, one could no more remove the Mormonism from her novel than one could remove the New England from Edith Warton's *Ethan Frome* (New York: Scribner, 1911). Only an unsophisticate would regard either work as of only regional significance.

Nothing Ever Happens Sunday Morning is Cannon's only published novel. Her publisher rejected a second manuscript "Twentieth Century Gothic," and "she ran out of enthusiasm" for it, both for literary and personal reasons. She confesses that she "dislikes the tiresome chores" of seeing a book through the publication process, particularly a novel, which takes "second place to drama" in her interests. When her husband's health suggested a move to a gentler climate, Cannon took early retirement from the university and has written little since.[17]

Blanche Cannon's career almost begs for comparison with that of Maurine Whipple, if only because both began writing at about the same time and each produced only one novel, each published by a national publisher. Beyond those facts, though, the similarities rapidly decrease both in number and significance. Whipple's fine novel, *The Giant Joshua* (Boston: Houghton-Mifflin Company, 1941) is a very different book from *Nothing Ever Happens Sunday Morning;* it is much longer, and much less tightly focused on a single type of conflict. Like *Nothing Ever Happens, The Giant Joshua* deals centrally with the theme of the oppression of women and free spirits under Mormonism's patriarchal, polygamous society, but it is historical, while Cannon's was contemporary in setting, and has a sentimental and optimistic conclusion, in contract to Cannon's tragic and pessimistic ending.

The Giant Joshua is the story of the founding and early development of St. George, where Maurine Whipple was born in 1904 and where she spent virtually her entire life. Her family, by her account, could offer little in financial support or encouragement, and she was forced to take sporadic and low-paying jobs as a housekeeper and dance instructor while writing in off hours. During a period of recuperation from illness, she wrote a thirty-thousand-word novella, "Beaver Dam Wash," which attracted the attention of Ford Madox Ford at a writers' conference. Ford put her in touch with editor Ferris Greenslet of Houghton Mifflin, who encouraged her to submit samples from a more ambitious work in application for the 1938 Houghton Mifflin Fellowship. Her outline and sample chapters from *The Giant Joshua* won the fellowship of $1,500, which supported her meagerly until she could finish the book.

The Giant Joshua was widely and favorably reviewed and remains to this day a classic novel of the Mormons. Though it has never been out of print and has appeared in paperback and foreign editions, Miss Whipple claims not to have experienced much financial success. Her 1945 picture book, *This Is the Place, Utah* (New York: Alfred A. Knopf, 1945) and appearances in slick magazines like *Collier's* and *Saturday Evening Post* were likewise not sufficiently remunerative to sustain a more productive literary career. Whipple promised two more novels to form a trilogy with *The Giant Joshua,* but the promise was unfulfilled.[18]

The Giant Joshua's point of view character is Clorinda McIntyre, the youngest of three plural wives of Abijah McIntyre, a thoroughly orthodox and insensitive tyrant cut from the same mold as Blanche Cannon's Eben Benson. Polygamy produces little more happiness for Clorinda McIntyre than for Matilda Benson; as the last of McIntyre's wives, she is also last in line for the meager creature comforts and emotional rewards that McIntyre and frontier St. George can afford. The arrogant and superstitious Bathsheba, McIntyre's first and therefore senior wife, and surely one of the most memorable harpies in all literature, is Clory's leading tormentor.

The density of historical detail effectively brought to fictional life and integrated with the plot is perhaps the novel's strongest contribution. The settlement of the lower Virgin River valley by the "Cotton Mission" is one of Mormondom's most successful and best documented colonization enterprises. That consciousness of historical importance and that abundance of documentation has produced some of Utah's finest historians—e.g., Nels Anderson, Juanita Brooks, and Andrew Karl Larson. Maurine Whipple, as author of arguably the finest novel based on Utah local history, is their literary counterpart. Historical characters, particularly Erastus Snow, are well developed both imaginatively and historically, and the frustrating and exhausting attempts of the community to cope with both the treacherous Virgin River and the seemingly insensitive expectations of the Mormon leaders from Salt Lake City are portrayed with both suspense and sympathy.

If *The Giant Joshua* has a flaw, it is perhaps in the central character, Clory McIntyre. Like Jasper and Margaret in *Nothing Ever Happens Sunday Morning,* Clory is a youthful free spirit who yearns for escape to a less stifling existence outside small-town Utah. She falls in love briefly with her husband's oldest son (symbolically named "Free"), who is also chafing against Abijah's tyranny, but their possibility of escape is dashed by his death during a skirmish with Indians. She tries to escape on her own but repeatedly finds ways to reconcile herself to her lot and remain. It is her grounds for reconciliation that seem unconvincing. On one occasion, for example, she has actually made a successful getaway when she is arrested by the overwhelming beauty of a field of wildflowers near her home and decides that she wants to remain in that pleasing environment. Whipple renders Clory's personal sufferings at the hands of Abijah and Bathsheba and her sharing in the collective sufferings of the community too poignantly to allow the reader to accept such a momentary emotion as a sufficient motive for returning.

In the end, then, *The Giant Joshua* is sentimental. Historically, it was the solid Mormon faith of the St. George pioneers that enabled them to make a success out of the most unpromising prospects. Clory is not devoid of faith; and for various reasons, her faith grows during the course of the novel, but Whipple has made the reasons for Clory's dissatisfaction so much more concrete than her reasons for reconciliation that her eventual acceptance of the community and her role in it seem artificial.

Of all the Utah women novelists who matured during the 1940s, Virginia Sorensen was certainly the most prolific. She strikes one as being in many ways the best writer of the group, although this is partly because she wrote enough to develop and display her impressive talent like none of the others.[19] With nine adult books and seven children's stories to her credit, one has ample opportunity to assess her abilities and to measure her contribution to Utah culture.

Sorensen's biography offers numerous clues for understanding her development as a writer.[20] Her ancestors included Danish Mormon handcart pioneers who settled in central Utah, although her family, as she remembered it, was loosely rooted there. Her father was a railroad man who was transferred from one station to another several times during her youth, so she had an opportunity to experience rather more variety in life than many other Mormon children who were rooted in one rural settlement. As a small-town Mormon girl who grew up and traveled the world, Sorensen knew Stanford as well as Brigham Young University, Tangiers as well as Provo, Utah. Such exposure gave her writing a cosmopolitan perspective. Though she considered herself a serious novelist, there is a distance between her and the church of her upbringing that introduces an objectivity, rather a skepticism, that is refreshing in the context of Mormon literature.

Sorensen's themes include the problems of Danish immigrants adapting to an alien culture, the ways in which daily realities temper religious idealism, the tensions between small-town complacency and the yearning for a wider world, and the achievement of maturity out of adolescence. She develops these themes in her novels with an occasional poignant lyricism, an expert narrative skill, a solid grasp of history, and considerable psychological insight.

A Little Lower Than the Angels (New York: Alfred A. Knopf, 1942), her first novel, reveals many of these skills already highly developed. It is the story of a Mormon couple, Simon and Mercy Baker, in Nauvoo, Illinois, in the months spanning the assassination of Mormon prophet Joseph Smith. The historical background is sketched in considerable detail but well integrated with the plot.

One learns about the shaky land titles, the city's geography, the personalities of Joseph Smith, John F. Bennett, Eliza R. Snow, and other historical figures, and especially the domestic and political tensions caused by the institution of polygamy. Into the character of Mercy Baker, the harried, exploited, and poorly appreciated Mormon wife, Sorensen poured much of the frustration, deeply felt but rarely expressed, in the souls of Mormon women. Simon's conversion to Mormonism is much more enthusiastic than Mercy's; in fact, she delays her baptism until pressure from the redoubtable Eliza R. Snow makes up her mind. Even so, Mercy's reasons for accepting baptism are anything but religious, and the scene where it occurs is remarkable for its absence of religious phraseology: "She tried to catch hold of the idea, the depth of idea that declared a man was purified and dedicated by the holy water upon his flesh. But this muddy water with a fish-smell in it sullied the idea and it escaped her while she struggled to hold it."[21]

Mercy's love for Simon leads her to accept his religion. It also leads to repeated pregnancies that take a heavy toll on her frail constitution and eventually lead to complete physical breakdown and death. As Mercy becomes increasingly worn out, Simon comes under pressure to make the ultimate commitment to Mormonism by taking another wife. But polygamy represents the ultimate humiliation for Mercy, who fights back with pathetic little acts of defiance, before yielding to the wishes of Simon and his church.

The characters of Eliza R. Snow and Joseph Smith, as well as their polygamous entanglement, are memorably developed. Sorensen makes a surprisingly good defense of Eliza's poetry: "Iambics as crisp as a pair of starched shams, and rhythms so sure and obvious there'd be no changing them in this world or another. Popey couplets, careful as egg-walking." And the departure of Joseph Smith, the empire builder, from Nauvoo the Beautiful, the city of his creation, is one of the unforgettable passages in Mormon literature: "Once he almost turned his head, as though he would have liked to look back yet again, but deliberately he held his face forward. With great effort he kept his back toward Nauvoo, because Nauvoo could make him soft and make him remember days that were better forgotten. Nauvoo had given him the power and the glory, she had almost given him the kingdom."[22] When Smith returns to Nauvoo at the beginning of the next chapter, he is in a coffin.

Sorensen's *Where Nothing Is Long Ago: Memories of a Mormon Childhood* (New York: Harcourt, Brace & World, 1963) is one of the truly delightful pieces of small-town Americana to emerge from Utah. It is a collection of stories based on her Manti girlhood. The stories are tied together by two threads: the varied aspects of rural Mormon village life and personality types, and the gradual emergence of the author from childhood to adolescence. One story deals with the theme, hardly comprehensible outside of arid Utah, of the murder of a man who cheated on his turn at the irrigation water, a murder that was ruled justifiable homicide. Others deal with the imperfect adaptation of the Danish

Mormon converts to the ways of Mormon culture, particularly their aversion to the Mormon "Word of Wisdom"—the prohibition of alcoholic drinks and the Danes' beloved coffee. "Polygamy and the Word of Wisdom," one character retorts, "—we Danes didn't take to either one." What they could not change, they simply ignored: "Over their cups, Utah Danes had a gentler rejoinder to those unfortunate orthodox who sniffed unappreciative noses: 'Brother Joseph never meant that Word of Wisdom for the Danes!'"[23]

Sorensen's heroes and heroines live on the fringe of Mormonism, the frontier between orthodox complacency and overt heresy, between placid acceptance of the established order and open rebellion. Chel Bowen, heroine of *On This Star* (New York: Reynal & Hitchcock, 1946), is caught between the stable, mundane life of her Mormon fiancé and the exciting life of his half-brother (their mothers were plural wives of the same man), a concert pianist and comfortable denizen of the eastern cultural scene. Kate Jackson, of *The Evening and the Morning* (New York: Harcourt Brace & Co., 1949), is an apostate who forces her granddaughter to come to grips with her Mormon past with a tongue-in-cheek defense of polygamy ("polygyny," she calls it, giving it its correct term).[24] It is the place where the greatest tensions exist and the greatest human dramas in Mormondom are possible, and Sorensen knows every crack and crevice intimately. She knows the ambiguous legacy of Mormon history, and she knows the multitude of revisions and compromises necessary in living its principles in the heartland of the church—rural Utah.

The works of Cannon, Whipple, and Sorensen all reveal the supreme importance of history in Mormon culture and literature. Mormonism is a historical religion in a way that even traditional Christianity cannot claim, historical though it is. Though the earliest records of Christianity claim to be historical, they are much more clouded in myth and dogma than the early records of the Mormon Church. The life of Joseph Smith took place fully in the bright light of history, and the rest of the course of church history is equally well documented. Mormons define themselves through their history perhaps more than traditional Christians, and it is through historical works that some of the most searching explorations of Mormonism have been accomplished.

Probably the most controversial historian to come out of Utah has been Fawn McKay Brodie (1915–81). An important pioneer in the field of "psychobiography," Brodie wrote much-admired, much-maligned, and especially much-read books on Joseph Smith, Thaddeus Stevens, Richard Burton, Thomas Jefferson, and Richard Nixon. Several are available in paperback editions and have been widely discussed, not only among historians, but among members of other professional disciplines and the general reading public.

Psychobiography is the application of psychoanalytic techniques to historical evidence in an attempt to delineate more elaborate motivational forces than can be discovered merely through a study of external behavior and rational statement. Sigmund Freud himself, in studies of Woodrow Wilson

Fawn M. Brodie (1915–81), author of the controversial *No Man Knows My History* and *Richard Nixon: The Shaping of his Character*. She was a professor in the history department at the University of California at Los Angeles, n.d.

and Leonardo Da Vinci, was an early practitioner of the method, which in subsequent years has been more commonly applied to European historical figures than American; Erik Erikson's studies of Luther and Gandhi, and the works of Philippe Aries are well known examples. In the field of American psychobiography, the works of Fawn Brodie are perhaps most prominent.

Psychobiography requires a highly developed sensitivity to the pregnant nuance in the available evidence, a sensitivity that must be honed through deep reading in psychoanalytical literature and an extraordinary maturity of judgment in interpreting such evidence in order not to make too much nor too little of it in delineating the full personality of the subject. Since psychobiographers characteristically utilize minute scraps of evidence previously overlooked or dismissed by traditional historians, critics tend to see them as imbalanced and given to overemphasizing trivial facts. Brodie's work has been a lightning rod for such criticism, and she has been careful to acknowledge, in the face of her scanty evidence, the lack of finality in her conclusions. In the preface to the revised edition of her biography of Joseph Smith, for example, she reminds her readers that the book "is not intended to be a comprehensive clinical portrait, which would have to be the work of a professional based on much more intimate knowledge of the man than is presently available."[25]

Brodie was a member of one of the first families of Mormondom; her uncle, David O. McKay, became president of the Church of Jesus Christ of Latter-day Saints. Born in the town of Huntsville, she received a fairly conventional Mormon upbringing, but exposure to a wider world of ideas and experience at the University of Utah led to a reexamination of her Mormon faith and background. That reexamination heightened after her marriage to Bernard Brodie, a non-Mormon Ph.D. candidate at the University of Chicago. The existence in the university library of a substantial collection of Mormon literature and New York state historical material helped her to focus her investigation on the obvious locus of Mormonism, its founder and prophet, Joseph Smith. The appearance in 1945 of her biography of Smith, *No Man Knows My History*, brought her fame within the historical profession and infamy among her family and fellow Mormons, eventually leading to her excommunication.[26]

The controversy over *No Man Knows My History* will never be resolved because, as Brodie observed in a 1975 interview, it hinges on a fundamental disagreement between Mormon and non-Mormon historians on what constitutes a fact.[27] Mormon historians, of course, are willing to accept Smith's evaluation of himself and his experiences at more or less face value, while Brodie prefers to read them as rationalizations of a quite different reality. Brodie's thesis is that Smith evolved from a highly intelligent, impressionable, and imaginative boy into a personality type known to psychoanalysts as "The Imposter"— specifically, that he began his career as something of a prank, but the impressive acceptance his ideas gained gradually deluded him into believing, quite sincerely, his own pronouncements. His success as a prophet was a result of his great personal magnetism combined with an impressive ability to sense cultural anxieties and aspirations and to codify them into a more or less consistent worldview and ecclesiastical structure. It is a fully secular interpretation of Smith's life, and one need not wonder that it so exasperated and enraged faithful Mormon readers.

Brodie subsequently made several minor contributions to Mormon and Utah history, but *No Man Knows My History* is her only major work in those fields. In later years, as a faculty member at the University of California at Los Angeles, she published psychobiographical studies of Thomas Jefferson and Richard Nixon that brought her wider national recognition than she had previously known, but consideration of Brodie as a Utah writer must be confined mainly to her Smith biography. Its effect on Utah and Mormon scholars was mighty, and perhaps best summarized in a posthumous tribute by Sterling McMurrin:

> Because of *No Man Knows My History*, Mormon history produced by Mormon scholars has moved toward more openness, objectivity, and honesty. For the past half century Mormon religious thought has been in decline, but since the

forties the Mormon treatment of Church history has greatly improved . . . because among the historians there has been more honesty, a more genuine commitment to the pursuit of truth, and greater courage in facing criticism or even condemnation. Numerous factors determine such things, but quite surely in this case the honesty and courage of Mrs. Brodie have been among the most important.[28]

Brodie and her friend and contemporary, Juanita Brooks, represent equal competence, though opposite poles of fame and influence. Of all the women historians of Utah, Brooks's career was far more typical in its concentration on local records and themes and in its basic support of the Mormon Church. Brooks was the epitome of the local Utah historiographic tradition, though she far surpassed, in mastery of sources and of critical sophistication, the vast majority of her colleagues.

Juanita Leavitt Pulsipher Brooks was born in Bunkerville, Nevada, in 1898. She was the granddaughter of Dudley Leavitt, one of the first pioneers of Utah's "Dixie," the region encompassed by the Mormon "Cotton" and "Muddy" Missions in southern Utah and Nevada, and she was related by blood or marriage to many other families who settled that region. Her early interest in the history of her family and the region in which they lived developed and expanded to become her life's work. She is still considered the foremost authority on the history of southern Utah.

Although Brooks made her reputation as a historian, most of her formal education was in the field of English language and literature. After graduating from Virgin Valley High School in Bunkerville in 1916, she attended Dixie Junior College in St. George, then Brigham Young University, from which she graduated with a bachelor's degree in 1925. She returned to Dixie to teach English and serve as its dean of women from 1925 to 1933. She took leave during the 1928–29 school year to complete her master's degree at Columbia University.

Her first marriage ended in 1920, a year after it began, when her husband, Ernest Pulsipher, died of throat cancer, leaving her with a baby son. She determinedly completed her college and graduate work as a widowed mother. The experience demanded a high degree of discipline, a discipline that made possible her later career as a historian, for she wrote most of her later outpouring of books, articles, and edited documents while caring for a large family by her second marriage. In 1933 she retired from teaching at Dixie to marry the local sheriff, William Brooks. Brooks had four sons from a previous marriage, and together they had four more children.[29] Rising well before daylight, she wrote for several hours before preparing breakfast for her family, then crowded in whatever writing time she could during busy days as a housekeeper and active church woman.

It was during these years, 1933–50, however, that Juanita Brooks's career as a historian developed, beginning with her project of collecting and

The University of Utah awarded Juanita Brooks (1898–1989) an honorary doctorate of humane letters, June 2, 1973.

transcribing manuscript diaries and other sources in southern Utah and culminating with the publication of her classic study *The Mountain Meadows Massacre* (Stanford, Calif.: Stanford University Press, 1950; rev. ed., Norman: University of Oklahoma Press, 1962.). The manuscript collecting project grew out of her earlier interest in the history of her region but began in earnest when sociologist Nels Anderson, who lived at the time across the street from her in St. George, suggested that federal funds from New Deal relief programs might be available. With grants first from the Federal Emergency Relief Administration and later from the Works Progress Administration's Historical Records Survey, Brooks hired several local women as typists who worked in her spare bedroom. Will Brooks's position as the man who knew everyone in Washington County opened many doors for Juanita on her manuscript collecting forays. Before long the quantity and quality of the work done on her project began to attract wider attention. One of the most fruitful results of Brooks's reputation during the project was a deep and long-lasting friendship with Dale L. Morgan, then director of the WPA Federal Writers' Project in Utah. He was beginning to attract national attention as a first-rate historian with a consuming zeal for accuracy, an appetite for hard work, and a graceful literary style—all qualities that came to characterize Brooks's work as well.[30]

During the 1930s, an almost constant stream flowed from her typewriter, practically all of which demonstrated an unparalleled depth of acquaintance with the sources for southern Utah history and an equally unparalleled objectivity and maturity of interpretation. But it was the appearance in 1950 of *The Mountain Meadows Massacre* that established her reputation. Her interest in that dark episode dated from her girlhood acquaintance with Nephi Johnson, one of the central participants, and his terrifying death when he deliriously recalled that day. During the intervening years, she quietly began to collect notes and sources relating to the massacre, and her book, particularly in its revised version (1962) remains the definitive account.

The book blames the heightened passions of the Mormon Reformation, the Utah War, and the overreaction of the stake leadership at Cedar City for the massacre—rather than Brigham Young (as skeptical Gentiles had always suspected) or John D. Lee (whom the Mormon Church singled out as the sole scapegoat to avoid further investigation). It seems a moderate, reasonable interpretation. For southern Utah Mormons, though, who had avoided all discussion of the event for almost a century, the book pricked sensitive folk and family memories; and Brooks, even though she was a loyal and active Mormon before and after, suffered considerable ostracism in her community.

A great deal of her research for *The Mountain Meadows Massacre* took place during a long association with the Henry E. Huntington Library as a manuscript collector and later as a researcher. Her acquaintance with the John D. Lee sources at that institution and with the Lee family led her to follow her Mountain Meadows Massacre book with a biography of *John Doyle Lee: Zealot—Pioneer Builder—Scapegoat* (Glendale, Calif.: Arthur H. Clark, 1961). She has also edited for publication the diaries of Lee, Thomas D. Brown, Hosea Stout, and other important pioneers of southern Utah.

During the 1950s Brooks returned to teaching at Dixie College while still devoting a large part of her time to the numerous requests to speak at academic functions and meetings of historical societies. During the 1960s she held a staff position at the Utah State Historical Society while she edited the

Helen Z. Papanikolas (1917–2004) was the daughter of Greek immigrants. She was the editor of the University of Utah's literary magazine, *Pen,* and did pioneering work on ethnic history and folklore, which broadened Utah history to include a fuller understanding of Utah's industrial development and the contributions of ethnic communities.

Hosea Stout diary. After her retirement in St. George, she continued to publish, but the books of her retirement years were manuscripts written many years previously and published with the editorial assistance of others, such as her biography of Jacob Hamblin and her autobiography, *Quicksand and Cactus: A Memoir of the Southern Mormon Frontier* (Salt Lake City: Howe Brothers, 1982). Brooks died in 1989.

Helen Zeese Papanikolas (1917–2004) is another important Utah historian.[31] A daughter of a self-made Greek grocer in Carbon County, she moved to Salt Lake City with her family as a teenager and was educated at East High School and the University of Utah. Motivated initially by a desire to serve her community as a medical doctor, she took an undergraduate degree in bacteriology, but her literary gift was discovered by English professor Sidney W. Angleman, and she worked for a time as associate editor of *Pen,* the University of Utah's literary magazine. Marriage to businessman Nick E. Papanikolas in 1941 and subsequent parenthood did not diminish her desire to write. Although she published an excerpt from a novel manuscript in an early issue of *Utah Humanities Review,* she delayed writing fiction in favor of recording and interpreting the experience of Utah's ethnic minorities. Blessed with a graceful writing style and a penetrating intellect, Papanikolas has enriched Utah historiography by bringing the viewpoints of women, non-Mormons, and ethnic minorities to prominence—none of which had conspicuously characterized the state's historical literature before her participation.

As creator and patron of the Peoples of Utah Institute at the University of Utah, she has been in the forefront of collecting and preserving records and reminiscences of Utah ethnic minorities. She also served long terms on the Board of State History. Much of her best work has been published by the Utah State Historical Society in the form of articles in the *Utah Historical Quarterly* and what is perhaps her crowning achievement as a historian, the Bicentennial collection of essays on *Peoples of Utah* (Salt Lake City: Utah State Historical Society, 1976).[32] In her later years, she returned to her first love, fiction, publishing *Small Bird Tell Me: Stories of Greek Immigrants in Utah* (Athens: Swallow Press/Ohio University Press, 1993); *The Apple Falls from the Apple Tree: Stories* (Athens: Swallow Press/Ohio University Press, 1996) and *The Time of the Little Black Bird* (Athens: Swallow Press/Ohio University Press, 2000).

Compared to fiction and historiography, poetry has been neglected to a large degree until recently among Utah writers. Kate Thomas, early in the century, gained some fame through her appearances in Mormon women's magazines and may be considered to have followed the tradition of Eliza Snow as a popular and pietistic poet. Though Thomas never developed into a major talent, her skill as a poet is clearly revealed in her famous works and matured in the nature and love poems in her unpublished notebooks.[33] Few other women poets of any significance emerged until the literary awakening among Utah women during World War II, and even then, only slowly.

One can hardly avoid being struck by two prominent themes among the poets who have matured since that time: a relative distaste for conventional piety and a profound interest in the land, both the cultivated soil and the virgin back country. The religious element is especially interesting. Among those poets for whom conventional religion has no vital appeal, religious themes are dealt with in a secular and skeptical manner, but few Utah women writers have found it possible to ignore them altogether. Even those whose affiliation with the Mormon Church is still close choose, it seems, to emphasize those elements in Mormon dogma that stress the finitude of God and the element of free moral choice—themes that are most in keeping with modern secular values.

Though fully within the bounds of Mormon doctrine, there is an emphasis in such poetry that one would likely not have found in Eliza R. Snow: the idea that intellectual freedom could lead to heresy as well as to orthodoxy, and the idea that a finite God, one of the central points of Mormon doctrine, might lead not only to the hope that man could himself become God, but also to meaningless tragedy, indeed, to despair.

One gets even less religious certitude in the poems of May Swenson (1913–89), a Logan-reared poet who became a highly respected figure in the New York literary scene.[34] After graduating from Utah State Agricultural College in 1934, Swenson worked for the *Deseret News* for a year, then went to New York City to seek her literary fortune. While working as an editor at

New Directions, she published a long string of poems in the *New Yorker,* most of which were eventually collected in her eleven volumes of poetry. Although she received awards from many sources, including the Guggenheim, Ford, and Rockefeller Foundations, her greatest honor perhaps was the MacArthur Foundation fellowship of $375,000 which she received in 1987. A poet of joy rather than of tragedy, Swenson couched her religious skepticism in witty and lighthearted verse. Since 1997 Utah State University has honored Swenson with the annual "May Swenson Poetry Award."

Religious poetry by Utah women outside the Mormon tradition achieved its highest mark in the work of Sister Mary Madeleva Wolff, principal of Sacred Heart Academy in Ogden and founder of St. Mary of the Wasatch in Salt Lake City. Born in a Wisconsin lumber town in 1887, Sister Madeleva was a precocious, though rebellious, girl who was translating Latin poets and Goethe while a high school senior.[35] As a student at the University of Wisconsin, she became attracted to the religious life, joined the Holy Cross order, and completed an M.A. from the University of Notre Dame in 1919. That same year she was sent to Ogden to teach English and act as principal of Sacred Heart Academy. Eventually she earned a Ph.D. at the University of California, Berkeley, and even studied with C. S. Lewis during a sabbatical at Oxford in 1933. While most of Sister Madeleva's poetry expresses her fervent Catholic faith, some of her verses reveal a love for the Utah outdoors acquired on long hikes with her students, and expressed in sensual language.

Phyllis McGinley (1905–78) was the daughter of a peripatetic land speculator, but she settled in Ogden at age twelve when her father died, studied at Sacred Heart Academy, Ogden High School, and graduated from the University of Utah.[36] After selling some early poems, she moved to New York City, where she married in 1937 and wrote for numerous magazines, including the *New Yorker.* Her early reputation rested upon her light verse. One of her twenty volumes of poetry, *Times Three: Selected Verse from Three Decades with Seventy New Poems* (New York: Viking Press, 1960), won a Pulitzer Prize.

However, McGinley perhaps attracted her greatest notoriety as a spokesperson for a conservative role for women during the feminist movement in the 1960s. *Sixpence in Her Shoe* (1964) was a response to Betty Friedan's *The Feminine Mystique* (New York: W. W. Norton, 1963), which claimed that a college-educated woman could never hope to find fulfillment in a domestic setting. As "a kind of autobiography," McGinley's best-selling *Sixpence* demonstrated that keeping house for a husband and two daughters was by no means inconsistent with her writing career. "By temperament I am a nest builder," she asserted, ". . . to keep a house is my native vocation and I consider it an honorable estate."[37]

Turning to the contemporary scene, Utah can boast of such an outpouring of literary talent that one can attempt no more than a discussion of a few rather arbitrarily chosen representatives and hope for the emergence

Miriam B. Murphy (1977) served as associate editor of the *Utah Historical Quarterly* for many years. She also authored books, poems, and articles on Utah history.

of a literary historian with more space at his or her disposal than this chapter. Salt Lake City remains Utah's cultural as well as its political capital, and writers like contemporary Mormon poet Emma Lou Thayne still live and write here.[38] So does Miriam B. Murphy, an enormously talented poet, editor, and historian whose excessive modesty alone has kept her from a reputation outside Utah's literary *cognoscenti*. During a quarter century as associate editor of *Utah Historical Quarterly*, Murphy has helped dozens of young historians, male and female alike, to find an outlet and a style for their writing, while contributing many pieces of her own, both prose and poetry, to that and other publications. Besides authoring numerous articles for the *Quarterly* and *Beehive History*, Murphy is the author of *A History of Wayne County* (Salt Lake City: Utah State Historical Society/Wayne County Commission, 1999); *That Green Light That Lingers: Poems* (Salt Lake City: City Art, 2001), and the epic poem "Keenings and Intermezzi on a Crystallization of Time: The Mine Disaster at Castle Gate, Utah, March 8, 1924," included in Thomas Lyon and Terry Tempest Williams, eds., *Great and Peculiar Beauty: A Utah Reader* (Salt Lake City: Gibbs Smith Publisher, 1995), 474–91.

New women writers continue to emerge as well and are active in Utah's literary scene, ranging from naturalist Terry Tempest Williams and the multi-talented Linda Sillitoe to Salt Lake Community College professors Nicole

Stansbury, whose short stories have appeared in a variety of publications and poet Lisa Orme Bickmore, whose first book, *Haste: Poems* (Salt Lake City: Signature Books) appeared in 1994.

Public and private endowments in recent years have been a positive force in encouraging women writers and providing outlets for publication. The Utah State Poetry Society is perhaps most prominent among organizations supporting poetry. The society was organized in 1950; and since 1965, it has published one volume of poetry per year with money from the Nicholas G. Morgan-Paul Pehrson Fund. Many of Utah's best women poets have been published by the society. In fact, the prize-winning annual publication has regularly been awarded to women poets.[39] The society also collaborated with the Utah State Institute of Fine Arts and the League of Utah Writers in 1975 to produce the *Utah Literary Arts Magazine,* which unfortunately was funded for only one issue. Many leading women poets were included in the issue, which also featured critical essays delivered as honor lectures at Utah State University by Veneta Nielson and at the University of Utah by Clarice Short. *Silver Vain,* a poetry periodical published in Park City, and *Quarterly West,* published at the University of Utah, have provided outlets in recent years. Other publishing outlets included *Utah Holiday* magazine, now defunct, which featured regular columns and investigative reporting by women writers, and the journals *BYU Studies, Sunstone, Dialogue: A Journal of Mormon Thought, Exponent II,* and *Salt Lake Magazine.* Programs funded by such agencies as the Utah Humanities Council and the Association of Mormon Letters are known for their receptivity to women's projects.

Limited mainly to a local reputation because her work focuses mostly on Mormon and Utah culture, Linda Sillitoe is a strong contender for the most talented young Utah woman writer. Like Phyllis McGinley, Sillitoe has forged a dual career as writer and parent. Twice nominated for the Pulitzer Prize for her work as a feature writer for the *Deseret News,* Sillitoe's investigative talents and writing style expanded as a writer for *Utah Holiday* magazine during the 1980s. Sillitoe's talent is diverse, ranging from investigative reporting through novels, stories, poetry, and history. Perhaps her best-known work is *Salamander: The Story of the Mormon Forgery Murders* (Salt Lake City: Signature Books, 1988), a history of the notorious Mark Hofmann forgeries and murders which she coauthored with Allen D. Roberts.[40] Most recently, Sillitoe is the author of *A History of Salt Lake County* (Salt Lake City: Utah State Historical Society/ Salt Lake County Commission, 1996) one of the Centennial Series of county histories sponsored by the Utah State Historical Society.

Joyce Eliason is another multi-talented writer still in mid-career. Born and educated in Manti and later at the University of Utah, Eliason's early writings explore the no-man's-land of small-town kids who seek careers in a big city. No longer content with the slow pace and frequent backwardness of rural life, yet yearning for the innocence and simplicity she once knew there, Eliason poured her frustration into her first novel, *Fresh Meat/Warm Weather.* "I can shut my eyes and see red cliffs and blue mountains and the green coming out and it is something I want to know again and knowing I can't," she laments, in one of the book's unforgettable outbursts: "Goddamn those hills and little faraway Mormon Utah towns with names like Moroni, Lehi, Nephi. Goddamn those towns that protected me, formed me, buried me in one single motion. Goddamn the red of them and the blue of them . . . . Goddamn it all because I can never get away from it. And I can never ever in any goddamn way get back to it."[41]

At the University of Utah, Eliason turned to acting, which led to a career in screen writing and a long list of credits in adapting Western themes and works for both the big and small screen. "Child Bride of Short Creek," for example, was a television film about the Arizona polygamy raids in the 1950s, and in 1994 she adapted Allan Gurganus's *Oldest Living Confederate Widow Tells All* (New York: Alfred A. Knopf, 1989) for a television miniseries.[42]

Judith Freeman, a Weber County expatriate to Los Angeles, has made her mark as chronicler of the "off center" world of the Mormon working class in which she grew up. After a collection of short stories, *Family Attractions: Stories* (New York: Penguin Books, 1989), Freeman wrote three novels: *The Chinchilla Farm: A Novel* (New York: Norton, 1989), *Set for Life* (New York: Norton, 1991), and *A Desert of Pure Feeling* (New York: Pantheon Books, 1996). Freeman's books are risky, high-wire balancing acts in which she succeeds in making believable some quite bizarre people and improbable encounters, although one wonders what readers outside Utah make of her unexplained references to Mormon garments, sacrament meetings, and other mysteries. In 2002 Freeman won the Utah Book Award for *Red Water* (New York: Pantheon Books, 2002), a historical novel based on the 1857 Mountain Meadows Massacre.

Terry Tempest Williams once held the title "Naturalist in Residence" at the Utah Museum of Natural History at the University of Utah. It is an old-fashioned designation—naturalist—that calls to mind the scientific generalists who accompanied many great Western exploratory parties in the days before academic specialization. But the title has been revitalized through the careers of writers like Lorin Eisley, Lewis Thomas, Stephen Jay Gould, and Carl Sagan—sophisticated specialists in various scientific disciplines who are able to see the aesthetics and the metaphysics of their professions and to reveal them to the educated general reader. Whatever Williams's scientific credentials, it is her attempt to see beyond mere data in a quest for spiritual meaning in the natural world that has earned her a large audience.[43]

Pieces of White Shell: A Journey to Navajoland, which won the 1984 Southwest Book Award, established William's reputation as a spiritual seeker through science, this time in anthropology. The book, she said in her preface, was "a journey into one culture, Navajo, and back out again to my own, Mormon," focusing on such commonalities as their recent arrival in the

Southwest, their strong sense of place, their spirituality, and the tension of being caught between the modern and the traditional.[44] In her next book, *Refuge: An Unnatural History of Family and Place* (New York: Pantheon Books, 1991), the science is ornithology. The extraordinary 1983 rise in the level of the Great Salt Lake in 1983 threatened the population of the Bear River Migratory Bird Refuge at the same time her own family was threatened by her mother's ovarian cancer. The book is the parallel story of the unfolding of those two "unnatural" disasters in the natural world. Other books by Williams include *An Unspoken Hunger: Stories from the Field* (New York: Vintage Books, 1994); *Leap* (New York: Pantheon Books, 2000); *Red: Passion and Patience in the Desert* (New York: Pantheon Books, 2001); and *The Open Space of Democracy* (Barrington, MA: Orion Society, 2004).

Other environment-oriented writers include Ann Zwinger, born in Muncie, Indiana, in 1925. She spent most of her youth along Indiana's White River. In 1946 Zwinger graduated from Wellesey College with a degree in art history and later completed a master's in art history at Indiana University in 1950. She married Herman Zwinger in 1952 and, after traveling widely, including in Utah, they settled in Colorado Springs, Colorado, where she wrote her first naturalist book. Since then, Zwinger has authored over a dozen books and contributed to numerous anthologies on natural history. Zwinger is currently a professor at Colorado College. Her works include: *Run, River, Run* (Tucson: University of Arizona Press, 1975); *Downcanyon: A Naturalist Explores the Colorado River Through Grand Canyon* (Tucson: University of Arizona Press, 1995), which won the prestigious Burroughs Award; *Wind in the Rock: The Canyonlands of Southeastern Utah* (Tucson: University of Arizona Press, 1986); and *The Near Sighted Naturalist* (Tucson: University of Arizona Press, 1998).

Ellen Meloy is another noted naturalist, artist, and writer. Born in California in 1946, she studied art at Goucher College and environmental science at the University of Montana after working as an illustrator and gallery curator. Enchanted by Utah, she and her husband Mark lived in Bluff, Utah, where she wrote three books on the Colorado Plateau: *Raven's Exile: A Season on the Green River* (Tucson: University of Arizona Press, 1994); *The Last Cheater's Waltz: Beauty and Violence in the Desert Southwest* (Tucson: University of Arizona Press, 2001) and *The Anthropology of Turquoise: Meditations on Landscape, Art, and Spirit* (New York: Pantheon Books, 2002), which won a Utah Book Award and was nominated for the Pulitzer Prize in nonfiction in 2003. Meloy died in 2004 at age fifty-eight after completing a new book manuscript, "Eating Stone."[45]

These writers, as previously indicated, by no means exhaust the list even of major women literary figures who are emerging in our day. It completely overlooks numerous women who specialize in children's and young adult writing. While some Utah writers are known only locally, many writers who were either born in Utah or influenced by their experiences in Utah, are known and respected at a national level, receiving prestigious awards and recognition. Utah women are finding a new voice, a mature voice, and there seems to be increasing support, an increasing number of outlets, and a growing audience for what they have to say.

NOTES

1. Cynthia James, "Literary Expression of 19th Century Utah Women," Mss A 2448 Utah State Historical Society, Utah History Research Center, Salt Lake City, offers a stimulating discussion of forces that helped shape women's writing.

2. Louisa Lula Greene Richards, "The Pioneer Women Editor of the Church," *Relief Society Magazine,* July 1925, 338–34; Leonard J. Arrington, "Louisa Lula Greene Richards: Woman Journalist of the Early West," *Improvement Era,* May 1969, 28–31; Sherilyn Cox Bennion, "The *Woman's Exponent:* Forty-Two Years of Speaking for Women," *Utah Historical Quarterly* 44 (Summer 1976): 222–39.

3. Katherine Barrette Parsons, *History of Fifty Years: Ladies' Literary Club, Salt Lake City, Utah, 1877–1927* ([Salt Lake City]: Arrow Press, 1927), 37.

4. Ibid., 68, 70. For the club's literary activities, see 70–78.

5. Linda Thatcher and John R. Sillito, "'Sisterhood and Sociability': The Utah Women's Press Club, 1891–1928," *Utah Historical Quarterly* 53 (Spring 1985): 144–56; Carol Cornwall Madsen, "A Bluestocking in Zion: The Literary Life of Emmeline B. Wells," *Dialogue: A Journal of Mormon Thought* 16 (Spring 1983): 126–40.

6. Susa Young Gates, "Books and Authors," Gates Papers, Mss B 95, Utah State Historical Society.

7. Miriam B. Murphy, "Sarah Elizabeth Carmichael: Poetic Genius of Pioneer Utah," *Utah Historical Quarterly* 43 (Winter 1975): 52–66; Lydia D. Alder, "Sarah E. Carmichael," *Woman's Exponent* 27 (January 15, 1899): 9.

8. Murphy, "Sarah Elizabeth Carmichael," 65–66.

9. Sarah E. Carmichael, *Poems* (San Francisco: Towne and Bacon, 1866), vi, 12.

10. R. Paul Cracroft, "Susa Young Gates: Her Life and Literary Work" (M.A. thesis, University of Utah, 1951), 61, 75.

11. Ralph Vary Chamberlin, *The University of Utah: A History of Its First Hundred Years, 1850 to 1950* (Salt Lake City: University of Utah Press, 1960).

12. Wallace Stegner, *The Uneasy Chair: A Biography of Bernard DeVoto* (Garden City, N.Y.: Doubleday & Co., 1974), 11–14; Elizabeth Haglund, ed., *Remembering the University of Utah* (Salt Lake City: University of Utah Press, 1981), 114.

13. Blanche Cannon, *Nothing Ever Happens Sunday Morning* (New York: G. P. Putnam's Sons, 1948), 239.

14. Ibid., 84.

15. Blanche Cannon, letter to Gary Topping, July 1984.

16. Richard Scowcroft, Review, *Utah Humanities Review* 2 (July 1848): 285–86.

17. Cannon, Letter to Topping.

18. Allene Jensen, "Utah Writers of the Twentieth Century: A Reference Tool" (M.A. thesis, University of Utah, 1957), 150; Maryruth Bracy and Linda Lambert, "Maurine

Whipple's Story of *The Giant Joshua*," *Dialogue: A Journal of Mormon Thought* 6 (Autumn-Winter 1971): 55–62.

19. Sorensen won the Newbery Medal in 1957 for her children's book *Miracles on Maple Hill* (New York: Harcourt, Brace, 1956).

20. L. L. Lee and Sylvia B. Lee, *Virginia Sorensen,* Boise State University Western Writers Series, No. 31 (Boise: Boise State University Press, 1978). See also a special issue of *Dialogue: A Journal of Mormon Thought* 13 (Fall 1980); Mary Lythgoe Bradford, "Virginia Eggertsen Sorensen Waugh (1912–1991): Utah's First Lady of Letters," in *Worth Their Salt, Too: More Notable But Often Unnoted Women of Utah,* edited by Colleen Whitley (Logan: Utah State University Press, 2000), 191–200.

21. Virginia Sorensen, *A Little Lower Than the Angels* (New York: Alfred A. Knopf, 1942), 59.

22. Ibid., 16, 238.

23. Virginia Sorensen, *Where Nothing Is Long Ago: Memories of a Mormon Childhood* (New York: Harcourt, Brace & World, 1963), 162.

24. Virginia Sorensen, *The Evening and the Morning* (New York: Harcourt, Brace & Co., 1949), 256.

25. Fawn Brodie, *No Man Knows My History: The Life of Joseph Smith,* (1945; 2d ed., New York: Alfred A. Knopf, 1971), xi.

26. Haglund, *Remembering the University of Utah,* 85–95; Shirley E. Stephenson, "Fawn McKay Brodie: An Oral History Interview," *Dialogue: A Journal of Mormon Thought* 14 (Summer 1981): 99–116. See also Gary Topping, *Utah Historians and the Reconstruction of Western History* (Norman: University of Oklahoma Press, 2003), 282–330; Newell G. Bringhurst, "Fawn McKay Brodie: Dissident Historian and Quintessential Critic of Mormondom," in *Differing Visions: Dissenters in Mormon History,* edited by Roger D. Launius and Linda Thatcher (Urbana: University of Illinois Press, 1994), 279–300.

27. Stephenson, "Fawn McKay Brodie," 111. There is a large literature on Brodie and her books. Hugh Nibley led the Mormon attack. Four reviews of the book, including his critical essay, "No Ma'am, That's Not History," were collected by him into a pamphlet available at the Utah State Historical Society Utah History Research Center under the title "F. M. Brodie's Reliability as a Witness to the Character and Accomplishments of Joseph Smith." "No Man Knows My History" in *Dialogue: A Journal of Mormon Thought* 7 (Winter 1972): 72–85 is well worth reading. The second edition of *No Man Knows My History* was reviewed by Marvin S. Hill, "Brodie Revisited: A Reappraisal," *Dialogue: A Journal of Mormon Thought* 7 (Winter 1972): 72–85.

28. Sterling M. McMurrin, "A New Climate of Liberation: A Tribute to Fawn McKay Brodie, 1915–1981," *Dialogue: A Journal of Mormon Thought* 14 (Spring 1981): 75.

29. For biographical information, see the Juanita Brooks Papers, Mss B 103, the Utah State Historical Society; unsigned entry on Brooks, *The Reader's Encyclopedia of the American West,* edited by Howard R. Lamar (New York: Thomas Y. Crowell, 1978), 128–29; Levi S. Peterson, *Juanita Brooks: Mormon Woman Historian* (Salt Lake City: University of Utah Press, 1988); Newell G. Bringhurst, "Juanita Brooks as a

Mormon Dissenter," *Mormon Mavericks: Essays on Dissenters,* edited by John R. Sillito and Susan Staker (Salt Lake City: Signature Books, 2002), chap. 9; Topping, *Utah Historians and the Reconstruction of Western History,* chap. 3.

30. Juanita Brooks, "Just a Copyin'–Word f'r Word," *Utah Historical Quarterly* 37 (Fall 1969): 375–95.

31. See Miriam B. Murphy, "Helen Zeese Papanikolas: A Unique Voice in America," in *Worth Their Salt: Notable But Often Unnoted Women of Utah,* edited by Colleen Whitley (Logan: Utah State University Press, 1996), chap. 18; *Journal of Hellenic Diaspora* 29, no. 2 (2003), a special issue of "Homage to Helen Papanikolas."

32. Articles included in the *Utah Historical Quarterly* include: "The Greeks of Carbon County," 22 (April 1954): 143–64; "Life and Labor among the Immigrants of Bingham Canyon," 33 (Fall 1965): 289–315; and "Toil and Rage in a New Land: The Greek Immigrants in Utah," 38 (Spring 1970): 97–206 (actually a book-length publication occupying an entire issue of the *Quarterly*). The index to the *Quarterly* lists other Papanikolas articles.

33. Kate Thomas Papers, Mss B 88, Utah State Historical Society.

34. "May Swenson, Poet and Former Utahn, Dies at 76," *Deseret News,* December 6, 1989, B-4. For biographical information, see R. R. Knudson and Suzzanne Bigelow, with a foreword by Richard Wilbur, *May Swenson: A Poet's Life in Photos* (Logan: Utah State University Press, 1996).

35. Gail Porter Mandell, *Madeleva: One Woman's Life* (New York: Paulist Press, 1994); John Sillito, "A Transplanted Utah Beehiver: Sister Madeleva Wolff," in *The Word from Weber,* edited by Bob Sawatzki (Ogden, Utah: Friends of the Weber County Library, 1996), 185–200.

36. [Linda Thatcher], "Phyllis McGinley," *Beehive History* 17 (1991): 21–22; "The Telltale Hearth," *Time,* June 18, 1965, 74–77; Linda Welshimer Wagner, *Phyllis McGinley* (New York: Twayne Publishers, 1971).

37. Phyllis McGinley, *Sixpence in Her Shoe* (New York: Macmillan, 1964), 1–2.

38. Cynthia Lampropoulos, "Emma Lou Warner Thayne (1924–): On the Side of Life," *Worth Their Salt, Too: More Notable But Often Unnoted Women of Utah,* edited by Colleen Whitley (Logan: Utah State University Press, 2000), chap. 16.

39. Helen Mar Cook, in a letter to Topping July 16, 1984, gives information on the Utah State Poetry Society and its prizes. The volumes published by the society since 1965 include the following authored by women: Vesta P. Crawford, *Short Grass Woman* (1965); Lael W. Hill, *A Legacy of Years* (1966); Berta W. Christensen, *Walk the Proud Morning* (1967); Betty W. Madsen, *The Amaranth* (1968); Alice Morrey Bailey, *Eden from an Appleseed* (1971); Maxine R. Jennings, *A Lamp to Shine* (1972); Geraldine R. Pratt, *Bell on the Wind* (1973); Helen Mar Cook, *Shape of Flight* (1975); Caroline Eyring Miner, *Lasso the Sunrise* (1976); Pearle M. Olsen, *Frame the Laced Moments* (1978); Laverde Morgan Clayson, *Furrows of Renewal* (1980); LaVon B. Carroll, *The Shrouded Carousel* (1982); Bonnie Howe Behunin, *Wake the Unicorn* (1983); Joyce Ellen Davis, *In Willy's House* (1984); Patricia S. Grimm, *Timepiece* (1985); Dorothy Logan, *Child in a Sculptured Bowl* (1986); Kathryn Clement, *Riddlestone* (1987);

Maryan Paxton, *Downwind Toward Night* (1989); Elaine Christensen, *At the Edges* (1990); Margaret Pettis, *Chokecherry Rain* (1993); Muriel Heal Bywater, *Stretching toward Wild Swans* (1994); Elaine L. Ipson, *Where Ghosts Are Garrisoned* (1995); Nancy Baird, *The Shell in Silk* (1996); Marilyn Darley Williams, *The Red Rooster Café* (1997); Marilyn Bushman-Carlton, *Cheat Grass* (1999); Kolette Montague, *Easing into Light* (2000); Rita Bowles, *God in Assorted Boxes* (2001); Evelyn Hughes, *Furnace of Affliction* (2002); Judy Johns, *If I Could Speak in Silk* (2003); Maureen Haltiner, *A Season and a Time* (2004).

40. Sillitoe and Roberts, *Salamander: The Story of the Mormon Forgery Murders* (Salt Lake City: Signature Books, 1988), with an essay by forensic investigator George J. Throckmorton; she explores the same theme from a fictional perspective in *Secrets Keep: A Novel* (Salt Lake City: Signature Books, 1995). She has also published a novel, *Sideways to the Sun* (Salt Lake City: Signature Books, 1987), a collection of short stories, *Windows on the Sea and Other Stories* (Salt Lake City: Signature Books, 1989), and poems, *Crazy for Living: Poems* (Salt Lake City: Signature Books, 1993).

41. Joyce Eliason, *Fresh Meat/Warm Weather* (New York: Harper & Row, 1974), 3–4. Her second novel is *Laid Out* (New York: Harper & Row, 1976).

42. Harold Schindler, "New Take on the Old West: Former Utahn's Screenplay Tells the Stroy of Blacks. Writer Puts New Spin on Old West," *Salt Lake Tribune,* February 24, 1995, D-1.

43. Katherine R. Chandler and Melissa A. Goldthwaithe, eds., *Surveying the Literary Landscapes of Terry Tempest Williams: New Critical Essays* (Salt Lake City: University of Utah Press, 2003).

44. Terry Tempest Williams, *Pieces of White Shell: A Journey to Navajoland* (New York: Charles Scribner, 1984), 2.

45. "Author Ellen Meloy Dies at Her Bluff Home," *Salt Lake Tribune,* November 9, 2004; Dennis Lythgoe, "Mourning the Loss of Naturalist Writer," *Deseret News,* November 14, 2004; "Ellen Meloy," in *At Home on This Earth: Two Centuries of U.S. Women's Nature Writing,* edited by Lorraine Anderson and Thomas S. Edwards (Hanover, N.H.: University Press of New England, 2002), 322–32.

10

Women in the Arts

Evolving Roles and Diverse Expressions

Martha Sonntag Bradley-Evans

A healthy artistic climate does not depend solely on the work of a handful of supremely gifted individuals. It demands the cultivation of talent and ability at all levels. It demands that everyday work, run-of-the-mill work, esoteric and unpopular work should be given a chance; not so much in the hope that genius may one day spring from it, but because, for those who make the arts their life and work, even modest accomplishment is an end in itself and a value worth encouraging. The pursuit of excellence is a proper goal, but it is not the race itself.

—Gough Whitlam, Prime Minister of Australia, 1973–74[1]

While it has been true that Utah women have created art throughout the region's history, the value that society has placed on their work has ranged dramatically. Navajo women fashioned some of Utah's earliest and most beautiful blankets and baskets. During the nineteenth century, this work was conducted privately, away from the "public" world of commerce; and the work women produced in the private sphere of the home was not considered "real" work but part of a woman's calling or role. Society considered artistic expression an appropriate female pursuit, in part because it enriched family life.

In the twentieth century, more and more women created art for pay, either as educators, as performers, or as fine artists who showed their art and sold their art in public venues. By then art was considered "real" work, or labor required for survival, a source of financial support for many women artists. The obstacles keeping women from producing art once it became "work" were enormous and included religious and societal prejudices, familial and personal responsibilities, and cultural assumptions.

Yet women drawn to the arts, like their male counterparts, were seldom impelled only by economic motives. They felt compelled to communicate intangibles to those around them and to use their art as a way of engaging in the world. Many of them could not imagine doing anything else. It required a sometimes formidable exercise of personal power, opposing the societal forces worked against them. The indomitable human spirit helped many of them succeed.

FEMINIST THOUGHT AND WOMEN ARTISTS

Beginning in the 1960s, feminist studies produced new theoretical angles which help access the contribution and experience of women artists, including Utah women artists. These approaches included the recognition by art historians of the traditions of domestic and utilitarian production by women that had conventionally been represented in negative ways in relation to both creativity and high culture. A desire to acknowledge the contribution of women, as well as centering women artists in the past two centuries' cultural production, emerged from the decade of the 1960s. This analysis questioned traditional categories of art and definitions of artists structured within past art history which privileged the work of men. Art Historian Whitney Chadwick suggests, "Originating in the description and classification of objects, and the identifying of a class of individuals known as 'artist,' art history has emphasized style, attribution, dating, authenticity, and the rediscovery of forgotten artists. Revering the individual artist as hero, it has maintained a conception of art as individual expression or as a reflection of preexistent social realities, often divorced from history and from the social conditions of production and circulation."[2]

As a whole, new scholarship produced during the past three decades during the last quarter of the twentieth century establishes that, while the experience of women artists is a gendered one, a single-image "woman artist" does not exist but instead is a myth and a stereotype that ignores reality. Germaine Greer's *The Obstacle Race* suggests that women artists were not "a string of over-rated individuals but members of a group having much in common, tormented by the same conflicts of motivation and the same practical difficulties, the obstacles both external and surmountable, internal and insurmountable of the race for achievement."[3] The experience of women artists was extraordinarily diverse, characterized by distinctive connections among class, race, historical context, and opportunity. Many women artists have worked in surprising isolation, while others served as apprentices to their husbands, fathers, or relatives. As a group, women have scaled daunting barriers to the production of their art and the recognition of their contribution in the official annals of art history and in society more generally. This is due in part because of art history's traditional identification of art "with the wealth, power, and privilege of the individuals and groups who commissioned or purchased it, and the men who wrote about it and identified with it."[4]

Scholarship on women's art history has drifted from historical categories of "art" and "artist" to broader, more pervasive ideologies such as gender, sexuality, power, and representation. This shift is supported by a "reexamination of the woman artist's relationship to dominant modes of production and representation in the light of a growing literature concerned with the production and intersection of gender, class, race, and representation."[5] The result is a more holistic vision of the contribution of women as well as a stronger theoretical analysis.

This chapter presents a general overview of the history of women's involvement in the arts in first the Territory and then the State of Utah. By focusing on women who have worked professionally in the visual arts, sculpture, dance, music, and theater, and on the ideologies which have shaped production and representation for women, this survey identifies major issues and summarizes the work which has been done to date. It also considers the discourses that have impacted women's choices about producing art and the way that art was accepted by society.

THE "PROPER ROLE" OF WOMEN

The history of Utah women and art is influenced by a strong sense of the proper role of women, gender, and the complication of the domestic sphere. In 1906, John Stuart Mill acknowledged the fundamental differences between men and women and the meaning of those differences in a way that accurately captures attitudes prevalent in nineteenth-century Utah:

> The love of fame in men is encouraged by education and opinion: to "scorn delights and live laborious days" for its sake is accounted the part of "noble minds" even if spoken of as their "last infirmity," and is stimulated by the access which fame gives to all the objects of ambition, including even the favour of women; while to women themselves all these objects are closed, and the desire of fame itself considered daring and unfeminine. Besides, how could it be that a woman's interests should not be all concentrated upon the impression made on those who come into her daily life, when society has ordained that all her duties should be to them, and has contrived that all her comforts should depend on them?[6]

Barbara Welter's pathbreaking work on what she called the "cult of true womanhood" described the complex discourse that defined the appropriate role women played in the nineteenth-century American world as perpetuated in women's journals, seminaries, and popular literature. Women were expected, Welter writes, to be pious, pure, domestic and submissive. "Put them all together and they spelled mother, daughter, sister, wife—woman. Without them, no matter whether there was fame, achievement, or wealth, all was ashes. With them she was promised happiness and power."[7] Education threatened a woman's marketability as a wife, and might even jeopardize her spirituality. Women's seminaries sought to instill and enforce religious values and to produce an "accomplished" woman.[8] Debates waged over the nature of female education centered on these values and questioned whether such subjects and history or literature would cause more danger to a woman than good, "whether a 'finished' education detracted from the practice of housewifely arts. Again it proved to be a case of semantics, for a true woman's education was never 'finished' until she was instructed in the gentle science of homemaking."[9]

The women of Utah Territory enthusiastically embraced this view, accepting the tenets of true womanhood despite the vast contradictions in their frontier lives which instead required considerable independence, aggressiveness, and ingenuity. In these debates, the arts—such as music, water-color painting, and poetry—escaped condemnation but instead seemed to be appropriate female pursuits. As long as women engaged in art as "hobbies" and "refinement," but without hoping to earn a living by their production, women's creative pursuits were tolerated and, on some level, encouraged.

Welter's discussion is significant to this discussion about the contribution of female artists to Utah's art history because gender identity is a social construction, reflecting the values of the world from which it emerged. In fact, "gender identities act as cognitive filtering devices, guiding people to attend to and learn gender role behaviors appropriate to their statuses. Learning to behave in accordance with one's gender identity is a lifelong process."[10] Family and society both reinforce and construct ideas about womanhood. As we move through our lives, society demands different gender performances from us and rewards, tolerates, or punishes us differently for conformity to, or digression from, social norms. As children and, later, as adults learn the rules of membership in society, they come to see themselves in terms they have learned from the people around them.[11] Such messages are difficult to challenge, and they imprint girls and women's minds with what is possible and desirable for their lives.

A persistent theme explored by feminist historians after the 1960s explaining the differences between the experience of men and women was the separation of sexual spheres in structuring the social order. In this schema, "appropriate" women inhabited the domestic sphere while the political or economic activities of the world outside the home belonged to men. A simplistic dichotomy, this division failed to recognize the role that even the most reserved women played in the public arena—visiting sick friends or neighbors, working in charitable organizations, or participating in church services and auxiliaries.[12]

The division makes sense if society is construed as a double culture governed by different norms or values. The aggressiveness, intelligence, and self-interested search for power that characterized business or politics was foreign to the refuge provided by home and characterized by nurturing, feelings, and caring. As historian Barbara Welter suggests, the "cult of motherhood" perpetuated these divisions and placed responsibility for the character development of children on women's shoulders. "The purpose of women's vocation was to stabilize society by generating and regenerating moral character," comments historian Nancy Cott. "This goal reflected an awareness, also apparent in other social commentary and reform efforts of the time, that the impersonal world of money-making lacked institutions to effect moral restraint."[13] Although such activities were important, "an emphasis on women's activity in certain areas, such as child-rearing could coexist with a conception of women as idle."[14]

Anthropologist Michelle Zimbalist Rosaldo claims that women's lives are shaped largely by the perceptions of others: "Woman's place in human social life is not in any direct sense a product of the things she does (or even less a function of what biologically she is) but of the meaning her activities acquire through concrete social interactions."[15] In other words, Rosaldo questions the universal domestic/public separation because it obscures the diverse causes and content of gender roles, and is a discourse that is socially constructed.

Also important during the last decades of the nineteenth century was a shift from the family as a vital unit *of* production to a haven *from* production, a restriction of the family's role in the past. As a result, the difference between private and public worlds became less distinct and a nondomestic sphere emerged for women. Linda Nicholson suggests that this "non-domestic sphere must be related to another social change: the increasing individualization of social relationships *within* the family. In the course of the modern period, the family, again most strikingly in its white, middle-class version, has increasingly come to be viewed as consisting of autonomous individuals whose relations with each other are of the nature of a contract."[16]

The concepts of domestic spheres and gender roles are significant in understanding the role women played as artists during the nineteenth century in Utah because they help define the limitations and parameters of the world in which they produced their art. A woman who could sing or play an instrument, paint a lovely watercolor, or act a convincing scene was considered an adornment of her home, an amenity to her community. She would have made the lives around her better, more cultured, and filled with entertainment. Women artists in Utah during the nineteenth century were seldom revolutionaries who challenged the patriarchal, religious worldview of the communities they lived in. They expressed their femininity in culturally acceptable ways. Art was not only permitted but was considered an appropriate expression of the feminine nature. The ways of being an artist would expand as women sought formal education and professional status.

COMMUNITY BUILDING AND THE ARTS

In Utah Territory, the arts were part of community building from the first, and thus Utah women artists were easily granted a place, though a restricted one. After the first pioneer company reached the Salt Lake Valley, some group members turned back to greet members of the next. Apostle John Taylor led this second party and met members of the first company at the Sweetwater River, four hundred miles east of the Great Salt Lake. That night, the pioneer encampment celebrated that nearing end of the journey: "Preparations were made for dancing; and soon was added to the sweet confusion of laughter and cheerful conversation the merry strains of the violin, and the strong clear voice of the prompter directing the dancers through the mazes of quadrilles, Scotch-reels, French-fours and other figures of nameless dances." At the end, Taylor said, they felt "mutually edified and blessed."[17]

Dancing, music, and theatricals were arts valued by the pioneer settlers of this region who saw them as contributing a richness, not a threat, to their righteousness. Many pioneer women brought with them hand organs, fiddles, accordions, or flutes carefully packed beneath linens, clothing, or other family treasures, although it was more often men than women who took the role of public performers. The arts helped build community, made it possible for the settlers to forget the difficulties of their lives building homes and communities, swept them away to imaginary places, and stimulated memories and emotions long buried by the challenges of life.[18]

Within a few years, virtually every town had its own dancing school. In 1853 in Brigham City, John Bynon directed a dancing school where young girls learned "Money Musk," "Twin Sisters" and other older, traditional dances accompanied by the accordion.[19] Former Mormon John Hyde carped, "In the winter of 1854–1855, there were dancing schools in almost every one of the nineteen school houses [in Salt Lake City]. . . . Necessarily so much more attention to dancing involved so much less attention to study. Just so much less education and just so much more injury."[20] Despite the fact that the pioneers came as a group to settle Utah territory, they came from diverse backgrounds—from the East and the South, from Great Britain and Scandinavia. Dance and music brought diverse people together in a common community activity.

Five decades after settlement, art patron and state legislator Alice Merrill Horne reflected on the important role art played in creating a city that was more than a frontier outpost in the West:

> If art reigns in the home there will grow out of it beautiful parks, streets, thoroughfares and cities. If art reigns in the home it will be surrounded and filled with influence of Honesty, Purpose, Work, Simplicity, Sentiment, Peace, Unity and Harmony, while banished must be Coarseness, Vulgarity, Deceit, Slothfulness, Shallowness, Gaudiness, Discord and Unrest. Life in the influence of art trains the soul to respond to the God-like in man and nature, to feel the beautiful and to cherish and follow higher ideals. Soul greatness is the ultimate end and aim of all effort. When this life is done I believe men will be judged more by what they think and feel and love and know than for the deeds done in the flesh.[21]

Although Mrs. Horne tellingly says "*men* will be judged," Utah's women contributed their share to the arts in Utah. And the most important contribution of her statement is that it captures so succinctly the nineteenth-century perception that the arts contributed to community building and were, in fact, essential to the good life. Women's contribution to community was valued and considered appropriate in Utah. Brigham Young's daughters danced on the Salt Lake Theater stage, for instance. One of his daughters, Zina Presendia Young Williams, sold her wax flower arrangements at local galleries to help support herself and her two sons after her husband's death.[22] What's more, the state has also given prodigious public support for arts organizations, made available numerous opportunities for education and training, developed several important professional companies, and encouraged widespread participation in cultural activities.

Perhaps because social isolation exacerbated the natural solitariness of arts, Utah art associations have flourished in the state. Both the 1863 Deseret Academy of Fine Arts and the 1881 Deseret Art Union welcomed male and female members. In 1873, the first powerful art organization in the state for artists, the Society of Utah Artists, excluded women, possibly in reaction to the Salt Lake Polysophical Society's policy of offering drawing classes for "ladies only." The Department of Fine Arts at the University of Utah was created in 1889, and periodically had women on its faculty. For instance, in the early twentieth-century, Myra Sawyer and Florence Ware were instructors and conducted careers as professional painters.[23]

DRAMATICS

Only three years after the founding of Salt Lake City, Brigham Young organized the Deseret Dramatic Association in 1850 out of the earlier Deseret Musical and Dramatic Society, which in turn was formed from the Nauvoo Brass Band. The group performed in the old bowery, an open-air building with a roof of branches laid over vertical poles, the forerunner of the first tabernacle. The first play performed there was *Robert Macaire* with three women in the cast—Mrs. Oran, Margaret Judd, and Miss May Badlam.[24] The Saints also gathered for group singing, oratory, and worship in the bowery.

Only two years later in 1852, at the top of State Street near South Temple the Social Hall, replaced the bowery as the principal amusement center of Salt Lake City. Here dances, theatricals, and socials were held on a regular basis. At the Social Hall amateur casts and crews performed then-popular musicals and farces. This modest forty by eighty foot building had a gabled roof and basement level perfect for dances, theatricals, and other social events. The year it first opened, Brigham Young announced: "I want it distinctly understood that fiddling and dancing are no part of our worship. The question may be asked, What are they for, then? I answer, that my body may keep pace with my mind. My mind labors like a man logging, all the time; and this is the reason why I am fond of these pastimes—they give me a privilege to throw everything off, and shake myself, that my body may exercise, and my mind rest. What for? To get strength, and be renewed and quickened, and enlivened, and animated, so that my mind may not wear out."[25] Leading actors and actresses performed at the Salt Lake Theatre alongside local talent who worked in virtually every capacity—as actors, as costumers, and set designers.

Within a decade, the Social Hall was too small for the crowds who came.[26] A British visitor to Salt Lake City, Sir Richard Burton, described a party that continued for thirteen hours in the Social Hall with Brigham Young leading the first cotillion. "Dancing seems to be considered an edifying exercise. The Prophet dances, the Apostles dance, the Bishops dance. . . . The dance is not in the languid, done-up style that polite Europe affects; as in the days of our grandparents, positions are maintained, steps are elaborately executed, and a somewhat severe muscular exercise is the result."[27] The first plays performed in the Social Hall were *Pizarro, The Lady of Lyons,* and a farce called *The Irish Lion* in 1853. Young, who began by prohibiting tragedies and non-Mormon actors, favored light-hearted farces.

In 1862 with the construction of the Salt Lake Theatre, more elaborate costumes, scenery, props, music, and dancing enhanced theatrical presentations. More than 1,500 persons attended the March 6, 1862, dedication of the new theater, which was featuring *Pride of the Market,* a farce. George Goddard recorded in his journal: "The new theater was dedicated, after which a new play was performed; Elisa and Mary Goddard took part as French peasant girls."[28]

The Salt Lake Theatre also created a great impetus for theater dancing— a performance dance that was a natural outgrowth of pioneer square dances as a universal form of entertainment for both children and adults in every ward. Brigham Young had called for dance numbers in performances in the late 1850s, because he had noticed that many of the young women in the valley, including his own daughters, were becoming "round shouldered."[29] Theater dancing was usually ballet pantomime, specialty dances, or some sort of after piece. Sara Alexander, Charlotte Clive, favorite local dancers, or one of their students usually danced in the background or played characters who danced.

At the opening of the theater, Brigham praised its potential effect on the city:

> There are many of our aged brethren and sisters, who, through the traditions of their fathers and the requirements of a false religion, were never inside a ball-room or a theater until they became Latter-day Saints, and now they seem more anxious for this kind of amusement than are our children. This arises from the fact they have been starved for many years for that amusement which is designed to buoy up their spirits and make their bodies vigorous and strong, and tens of thousands have sunk into untimely graves for want of such exercises to the body and mind. They require mutual nourishment to make them sound and healthy. Every faculty and power of both body and mind is a gift from God. Never say that means used to create and continue healthy action of body and mind are from hell.[30]

The Salt Lake Theatre was dedicated in 1862 and was known as a center for drama and music. Photo taken May 3, 1910.

In the 1870s, Salt Lake Theatre manager Hyrum B. Clawson formed a calisthenics class in which local girls (including several of Brigham Young's daughters) danced, did vocal drills, and exercised with wooden swords and wands. Clarissa Young Spencer, a daughter of Brigham Young, remembered these classes: "We [Brigham's daughters] had regular teachers to instruct us in gymnastics, fencing, and solo dancing. It was probably because of our training in dancing that the girls of our family were in such demand for fairy or ballet dances."[29]

"Fairy dancing" was a type of romantic dancing popular across the country. Sara Alexander, a comic actress, and a leading dancer of the Deseret Dramatic Association, taught a group of local girls how to do it and often choreographed dances to accompany theatrical works. Sara sometimes lived with the Youngs in the Lion House as a guest.[32] Young put his own daughters on the stage to set an example for others. Hepworth Dixon, writer for *New America,* a magazine, visited the Salt Lake Theater in the 1860s and described it for national readers: "Young understands that the true work of reform in a playhouse must begin behind the scenes; that you must elevate the actor before you can purify the stage. To this end, he not only builds dressingrooms and a private box for the ladies who have to act, but he places his daughters on the stage as an example and encouragement to the others. Three of these young girls, Alice, Emily, and Zina, are on the stage."[33] Dixon had seen Zina Presendia, then a teenager in the role of Mrs. Musket in a farce, *My Husband's Ghost.* He described her critically as "a ladylike girl, tall, full in figure, moon-faced (as the Orientals say), not much of an artist."[34]

In her own touring company, she played leading roles in *The Little Minister,*

One Utah actress, Maude Adams, began her career in the Salt Lake Theatre as she literally rocked in her cradle, oblivious to the audience who admired the realistic touch of an actual baby in a domestic scene. In 1878 her mother, Annie Adams Kiskadden, took the precocious five-year-old actress to San Francisco where Maude would perform for the rest of her life. Adams was renowned across the nation for her interpretation of Peter Pan. Salt Lake City was a regular stop on her national tours, and her appearance on her home stage predictably inspired lively publicity and fanfare. "La Petite Maude" played leading roles in numerous national but now forgotten productions in San Francisco including *La Belle Russe, Across the Continent, Barney's Courtship, Fritz,* and others. She acted with Charles Frohman's stock company in *All the Comforts of Home, Men and Women, Lost Paradise, My Geraldine,* and *Diplomacy.* In her own touring company, she played leading roles in *The Little Minister, Romeo and Juliet, Quality Street,* and *Peter Pan.*[36]

In addition to Maude Adams, nineteenth-century Utah actresses like Sara Alexander and others, showed up repeatedly on the programs of local performances and successfully made their careers outside the state as actresses. Although there was enthusiastic support for the theater in Utah, it was not economically possible to sustain a professional career outside of the national theater centers in New York, Chicago, and San Francisco. Traveling troupes presented the classics, serious dramas, or comedies; but more often audiences saw melodramas, minstrel shows, and musicals. Farces, like *State Secrets,* were local favorites.[36] The life of an American actress in the nineteenth century required constant touring under rigorous conditions and a wide and demanding repertoire of roles. These circumstances made it virtually impossible for the actress to have a family or normal home life. Few Utah women were willing to do this or had the national contacts to give them the option but instead contented themselves with amateur theatricals in their home towns.[37]

The Salt Lake Theater established the popularity of local theater, and the Salt Lake Amateur Dramatic Company performed what seems to have been their first play in Cache Valley in November 1879. The title has not survived, but admission was 25 cents, the *Logan Leader* reported.[38] The following summer, *Foiled, or A Struggle for Life and Liberty* (apparently a melodrama) featured several Cache Valley actresses. Charlotte Evans was very effective in her role, according to the *Logan Leader,* and "Miss Neal as 'Becky' showed talent and self-possession."[39] Only two weeks later, the Logan Dramatic Club presented the "nautical" drama, *Ben Bolt.*[40] Right after Christmas, a "Mrs. Tout" gave

Maude Adams and Ida May Savage, good friends and actresses, n.d. Maude Adams (1872–1953) was one of the premiere actresses of the early twentieth century. She was famous for her interpretation of James M. Barrie's "Peter Pan."

a recitation called *The Maniac Wife,* which the *Leader* considered "one of the best features of the entertainment." It continued, "The lady possesses a fine voice and good delivery, and displayed both to advantage in this piece. The audience generally speaking, observed good order. All went off pleasantly and the performance may be considered a success."[41]

Similar companies formed in Provo, Springville, Ogden, Brigham City, and St. George; but after 1869 and the coming of the railroad, home players in the major cities lost the stage to professional traveling companies. By the end of the nineteenth century, fewer amateurs acted or danced with professionals as more traveling stock companies brought their entire production, including sets and actors, into town for a few nights.

During the nineteenth century, neither the theater nor popular music was seen as a threat to morality but rather as signs of civilization and gentility as the territory's cities grew in size and sophistication. This attitude was due in part, according to historian Howard R. Lamar, to the perception that the arts were "educational as well as entertaining."[42] Brigham Young spelled out what he saw as the ideal relationship between entertainment and instruction in the theater: "Upon the stage of a theater can be represented in character, evil and its consequences, good and its happy results and rewards; the weakness and the follies of man, the magnanimity of virtue and the greatness of truth. The stage can be made to aid the pulpit in impressing upon the minds of a community an enlightened sense of a virtuous life, also a proper horror of the enormity of sin and a just dread of its consequences. The path of sin with its thorns and its pitfalls, its gins and snares can be revealed, and how to shun it."[43] Moreover, while in some states, actresses were considered to be "loose" women, most Utahns did not share that censorious view. Utah actor John Lindsay, wrote in his memoirs in 1905 "Woman had long since demonstrated her equality with man in the arena of dramatic art," and this equality included social standing and reputation as well as ability.[44] The widespread popularity of amateur theatricals meant that there was a pronounced community feeling for drama, enhanced by the fact that the plays selected for performance seldom had themes that offended public taste.

In the second decade of the twentieth century, Utah theater became linked to its universities. (See especially the discussion of Maud May Babcock's sponsorship of theater at the University of Utah in the section below on "Dance.") At the beginning of the twentieth century, the Salt Lake Theater was still attracting both nationally known players and the crowds to support them. However, when competition from motion picture studios began in the 1920s, attendance dropped to such a low point that, in 1928, the Salt Lake Theater was sold and razed.[45]

As early as in 1915, the Theater Guild admitted women to membership. The Federal Theater Project of 1935 was created to provide relief for both unemployed men and women. At the same time, it expanded the national theater movement.

Theater in Utah from that point forward was almost exclusively based in the universities and colleges. In the 1980s, the Theater Department of the University of Utah was again headed by a woman—Marilyn Holt—a former Miss Utah and Phi Beta Kappa besides being a fine actress. She balanced both administrative duties and performances as an actress in her years at the University. Like more than fifteen professional theaters nationally associated with universities, Pioneer Memorial Theater was located on campus, and featured a mixed annual season which included plays, classics, and Broadway musicals.

In terms of local theater, the Salt Lake Acting Company operated out of a renovated historic LDS meetinghouse in Salt Lake City's Marmalade district. Distinguished by the edginess of its performances, SLAC was the sixth largest performing arts company in the state, routinely featuring the original work of Aden Ross, former Utahn Wendy Hammond, and Nancy Borgenicht.

Music

Women have always written and performed music; but the local social climate, while encouraging such proficiency as a "polite" or genteel achievement, conversely discouraged professionalism or public performance as unsuitable for a lady. By the mid-nineteenth century, many families had pianos in their homes, and girls learned to play along with embroidery and flower arrangement. The occasional recital was acceptable, but not concertizing. Sarah Ann Cooke played the piano at the Salt Lake Theater professionally enough to support her family until she broke her arm.

Consequently, it is as teachers of music that Utah women were most visible. Music courses were first offered at universities in the 1860s.[46] Of the 38,799 women who lived in Utah in 1880, only a handful were professional musicians. Women rarely played in the orchestra at the Salt Lake Theater or in the popular brass bands that many communities supported in territorial Utah. Female musicians in the nineteenth century were primarily vocalists and amateurs.

After the turn of the century when artists like Emma Lucy Gates Bowen (a granddaughter of Brigham Young) and Lydia White Boothby left the state to study in Europe, the number of women musicians increased substantially; but according to one study, the state can boast no more than six hundred important women Utah musicians since 1900—a group still overwhelmingly amateur in its composition.[47]

The most prominent exception was Emma Lucy Gates Bowen, (1880–1957) a woman whom many consider the finest woman singer to emerge in Utah before World War II. Lucy's career began at fourteen in 1894 when she won the Welsh Eisteddfod competition held in the Salt Lake Tabernacle, performing Gottshak's "Last Hope" on the piano. When she was eighteen, she went to Germany with her half-sister, Leah D. Widtsoe, and her brother-in-law, John A. Widtsoe, to study piano, but was encouraged by her professor to study voice instead.[48]

Gates drew notice from the international press not only for her talent but also for her relationship to the notorious Brigham Young. After studying at the Berlin Royal Conservatory of Music under Blanche Corelli, she sang for Caruso in 1908 at the Royal Opera House in Berlin. During her career, she performed over fifty different roles as prima coloratura.[49] The threat of World War I dramatically curtailed Gates's career, and she returned to Utah in 1915. There, she and her brother, B. Cecil Gates, organized the Lucy Gates Opera Company. In 1916, she married LDS Apostle Albert E. Bowen and had a family but remained committed to fostering music in Utah—improving both the quality and the quantity of musical performance. From all reports, she was a charismatic woman who dominated Utah's vocal music scene for many years.[50]

As members of choruses and vocal groups, Utah women have always been extremely active and, in numbers impossible to document, thousands of Utah women musicians contributed to amateur of semi-professional choruses and performing groups.

Teaching was considered an appropriate extension of the woman's traditional role and consequently attracted many women musicians. One male critic wrote:

Emma Lucy Gates Bowen (1882–1951), daughter of Jacob F. and Susa Young Gates, was a renowned opera singer, known for her beauty, stage presence and theatrical ability. The photograph depicts her in "The Jolly Musketeer," n.d.

When we come to the regular music-lessons of the children we see that it is nearly all done by women, and rightly so, because this is a woman's spere. Probably if parents were asked why they engaged a lady teacher in preference to a man, the general answer would be that it was cheaper. Unfortunately, this is true, but it is not just. Work of equal merit should receive equal compensation, regardless of sex. But, in truth, pay is not the determining factor in this case. Women teach children because they are better fitted for the work than men.... They are in closer touch with childhood, and can therefore work along the line of child's sympathies.[51]

Beginning in the late nineteenth century, Utah successfully supported music education from both universities and private schools through the period. The high-minded objectives of one academy, the McCune School of Music and Art, were expressed in its handbook: "Its aim is to encourage the serious and fundamental study of music, and to establish such ideals, and to provide such courses as will establish such ideals, and to provide such courses as will insure its students becoming alike proficient in performance, sound in knowledge, and ethical in conduct."[52] Music training at the school, which was also affiliated with the LDS University from 1917 to 1919, was both theoretical and technical, designed to make artists out of gifted students, to train teachers, and to "disseminate music education among the masses."[53] The course listing offered a variety of classes from voice culture, sight-reading, orchestra, and harmony to history and art appreciation.

It has been through universities, schools, academies, and private classes that Utah women have had a significant impact on music in Utah in the twentieth century. In the first half of the twentieth century, three prominent women juggled successful careers in both teaching and music performance. Edna Evans Johnson, who headed the vocal department at the University of Utah, began as a soloist with the Tabernacle Choir. After earning a master's degree at the University of Utah, she joined the faculty to teach many students—including her three daughters, who all became professional musicians.[54] Helen Budge Folland, a pianist, was the first Mormon woman to earn a Ph.D. in music from Columbia in 1942. She was also one of the first women in the United States to become a full professor on a university music faculty and one of an ever smaller group of women who taught music theory.[55] There has always been a pecking order in the universities which has unofficially held that women were acceptable instructors of voice or piano, but that men should handle the classes in conducting, composition, harmony, and theory.[56]

During the nineteenth century, female instrumentalists were excluded from conventional orchestras. Official discrimination ended in 1903 when the Musicians Union, in order to join the American Federation of Labor, admitted its first female members. Between 1925 and 1945, several women's orchestras worked either as professionals accompanying musical theater or as unpaid amateurs. Only since the 1960s, have women surfaced in permanent positions in professional orchestras.

Florence Jepperson Madsen was a versatile contralto soloist, conductor, composer, and music educator. Her husband, Franklyn Madsen, headed BYU's music department during the 1920s and '30s. What is even more remarkable, considering the times, was that Florence Madsen was a conductor. After making her debut with the New York Symphony Orchestra, Madsen studied at the New England Conservatory of Music. During her career more than a hundred of her compositions were published. One was performed by the full Boston Symphony with a women's chorus of 165.[57] Mrs. Madsen, who was also a member of the Relief Society General Board, conducted women's choruses in the Salt Lake Tabernacle, as well as orchestras and choruses around the nation, including a memorable one in southern California in 1929 when President Calvin Coolidge was in the audience and a Tour of Great Britain in the 1960s by combined British-American "Singing Mothers" recruited from the Relief Societies of both countries.[58]

Children in a class at the McCune School of Music, July 19, 1944.

Florence Madsen was the only important Utah female conductor until the rise of Barbara Scowcroft in the 1980s. Scowcroft conducted the Utah Symphony occasionally as well as the Nova Chamber Music Series. After leading the group for eighteen successful seasons, in 1982 Scowcroft left the group in the hands of Corbin Johnston. Scowcroft assumed her position with the series in 1985 after the exit of Russell Harlow, Utah Symphony clarinetist (who had founded the group in 1978). Longtime member of the Utah Symphony's first-violin section, Scowcroft also conducted the Utah Youth Symphony after 1986.[59]

During the 1920s and 1930s, there were many female musicians who did not affiliate with the universities. During the 1910s the three Tout sisters left Utah to have successful national careers. Margaret Tout Browning was an opera singer who sang with the Metropolitan Opera Company. Grace and Hazel performed in light opera; Hazel Tout Dawn was known as the "Pink Lady" at the Ziegfield Follies.

One contemporary musician who balanced a professional career with life as a full-time mother in the second half of the twentieth century was JoAnn Ottley, whose beautiful soprano voice highlighted performances with the Utah Symphony, the Utah Opera Company, and the Mormon Tabernacle Choir, which her husband, Jerold Ottley, conducted. JoAnn Ottley studied voice under Josef Metternich while on a Fulbright in Cologne, Germany, and was known locally for her performances as Queen of the Night, Violetta, and Lucia. Moreover, as vocal coach of the Tabernacle Choir, JoAnn Ottley trained many other voices. The Mormon Tabernacle Choir, the official choir of the Church of Jesus Christ of Latter-day Saints since the 1860s, has, since 1929, presented a weekly broadcast on CBS. In addition, it has produced numerous recordings and maintained a vigorous international and national touring schedule. The choir consists of 400 voices—nearly half women—and is an important performing group in the state's history.

In 1940, a second major musical performing group was formed in Utah: the Utah Symphony. Under Maurice Abravanel's vigorous leadership, the symphony strengthened its repertoire and, in the 1970s, was recognized as one of the top twelve major symphony orchestras in the nation. Women have always been part of the Utah Symphony; and by the end of the twentieth century, there were many more women in musical professions and more opportunities to work locally on a professional basis.

Opera was first performed at the Salt Lake Theater. After 1947, Maurice Abravanel and the Utah Symphony performed opera each summer for twelve years in the university stadium under the night sky (1948–60). Under the leadership of Ardean Watts, the Opera Workshop (later named the University of Utah Opera Company), produced two or three operas yearly. The Utah Opera, directed by Glade Peterson, emerged from this company and presented between three and five operas yearly. After Peterson's death in 1990, the company hired Anne Ewers. Ewers was well known nationally as a stage director of opera in both Canada and the United States. She came to Utah after directing the Boston Lyric Opera. Conscious of the importance of educating the public about opera as well as building a repertoire, Utah Opera sponsors a young artists program, grooming a handful of young singers twice a year for professional voice work.

Another group of musicians might be best labeled pop artists, reflecting the unique periods that they worked in rather than the state of the art. In the 1940s, the King Sisters, a quartet of Utah Mormon women, sang nationally in the "bop" style of the Andrew Sisters. In the mid-1960s the King Sisters, their husbands, and children joined forces in a television variety show called *The King Family.*

Marie Osmond was only three years old when her brothers performed on the Andy Williams show in 1962 as a one-shot event. The boys were so popular they were invited back on a semi-regular basis, bringing with them both Marie and their younger brother Jimmy. In the 1970s when the Osmond Brothers were recording numerous gold records, Marie jumped into the act and recorded her own hit singles—"Painted Roses" and "I'm a Little Bit Country." Marie proved to be a remarkable phenomenon in her own right and starred for four years in her late teens, along with her brother Donny, on the *Donny and Marie Show.* At twenty-one, she branched out on her own and hosted her own variety show, *Marie,* on NBC. At the same time, she maintained a vigorous recording schedule, performing in Las Vegas, before heads of state—including Queen Elizabeth and Ronald Reagan—and in other concerts around the world. Marie also starred in movies produced by Osmond Studios like *Going Coconuts* and *The Gift of the Magi,* followed by *The Sound of Music* in 1994–95. An outspoken advocate of the traditional values of home and family, she seemed to personify Mormon morals and values.[60]

A locally popular LDS woman songwriter was Luacine Clark Fox, daughter of Mormon leader J. Reuben Clark. Fox composed Mormon musicals and dramas such as *Her Husband's Religion,* and *Hallowed Journey.* Her popular "As I Have Loved You" (1914), initially a song for LDS Church Primary children, was incorporated into the 1985 edition of the hymnal. During the 1940s and 1950s, she was also an actress, director, and playwright who worked on the daily KSL children's program, *Storytelling Time,* as "Miss Anna."

The Visual Arts

During the nineteenth century, the art of women most often graced the walls of their own homes. Paintings were exhibited and judged alongside prize sheep and turnips through the Deseret Agricultural and Manufacturing Society, organized in 1856. The general lack of formal exhibition space forced artists to show their work in shops, hotels, and recreation halls, which ultimately affected sales.

It was virtually impossible for a young woman to get a rigorous art education between 1800 and 1870 anywhere in the United States because she would have been officially excluded from professional art academies while ladies' seminaries or private drawing classes gave only limited instruction. Many artists were the daughters of painters who were taught at home. Women were excluded from most professional art classes, particularly figure drawing classes that used nude models. Drawing, like music, was considered a polite accomplishment not a serious professional pursuit.

In light of these handicaps, which were built into nineteenth-century society, the success of women artists in pioneer Utah was all the more remarkable. In the nineteenth century, only a few female visual artists were active. These women, like Bathsheba Wilson Bigler Smith, had an interest in painting as an avocation, rather than as a profession.

However, during the late nineteenth century, hundreds of American artists traveled abroad to study at the prestigious art schools of Paris. The École des Beaux Arts did not admit women until 1896; but during the 1890s, the less prestigious academies, Julian and Colarossi, opened their doors to female students. In what art historian Robert C. Olpin called the "pioneer in reverse" syndrome," Mary Teasdel studied with Utah pioneer artist J. T. Harwood in 1891, studied at the National Academy of Art in New York City in 1897, and then in 1898 went to Paris with Maye Jennings Farlow, another Utah artist, following the example of Utah artists John Hafen, John B. Fairbanks, and Lorus Pratt.[61]

Art patroness Alice Merrill Horne visited the women in Paris and described the school to Utah readers: "Have you a rosy picture of student life in Paris and of the art studios there? The studios are dirty and barren. No furniture embellishes them. There are plain bare stools from six inches to three feet high and a platform for the model—that is all. . . . The studios for women are a counterpart of those for men, but for women the tuition is double. The proprietors claim that the extra money is for keeping women's studios cleaner, but the fact remains they are just as dirty."[62]

Teasdel was the first Utah woman and the second Utah artist to exhibit at the French Salon. When she returned to Utah, she opened a private studio and taught painting at West High School, influencing other artists in the tradition of academic purity that she learned at the Academie Julian, where draftsmanship and a strict adherence to form were emphasized. Governor Heber M. Wells appointed her to the board of the newly created Utah Art Institute, where she eventually served as its president. In 1908 two other Utah women went to the Academie Julian—Rose Hartwell and Myra Sawyer. Both of them, like Teasdel, spent the summers painting in Normandy countryside.[63]

The strength of these women artists is that, in subjects, techniques, and achievement, they matched their male counterparts, thus making providing decisive evidence that women artists were "as good" as male artists. At the same time, however, because of this very strength, they did not make a unique or distinctive contribution as "female" artists. Although they walked through doors that were only reluctantly opened to them and worked as equals in the spaces beyond, at the same time, their work cannot be called radical, revolutionary, or purely original. The art world was not changed because they joined it. As Germaine Greer suggests, such women "seldom expressed their own creativity: they imitated the modes of self-expression first forged by integrated, self-regulating (male) genius, most often when they were already weakened by eclecticism and imitation."[64] Nevertheless, they were pioneering in their effort.

Seeking to stimulate the arts in general and women artists in particular, Alice Merrill Horne became a state legislator and sponsored a bill in 1899 to create the Utah Art Institute. The bill called for an annual art exhibit, an official state collection, a series of public lectures on art, and an annual purchase prize of $300 for the best painting of the exhibition. Although the creation of the Utah Art Institute was related to the vigor of the suffrage movement in Utah and to the woman's rights movement generally, its direct and proximate cause was the energy and skill of Alice Merrill Horne.[64]

Alice Merrill Horne was one of an elite group of American middle-class women driven by a vision of the potential for progress in their home states. Because it was still considered unsuitable for these women to earn money, they were very active volunteers in the cultural lives of their communities. They formed clubs, built schools, and founded museums. The Springville Art Museum, the Bertha Eccles Art Center in Ogden, and the Salt Lake Art Center

Mary Teasdel (1863–1937) was one of the first Utah women to go abroad (Paris) to study. A subtle colorist, she was proficient in several mediums (oils, watercolors and pastels), n.d.

(the Art Barn) were founded and sustained by women whose voluntary services made such success possible.[64]

Alice Merrill Horne served in the state legislature in 1898–99, openly pushing legislation that would help artists. Even after state support of what had become known as the "Alice Art Collection" was withdrawn in the 1920s, Mrs. Horne found other ways to keep alive her goal of making art accessible to all the communities of Utah. Her vigorous patronage of the arts, her voluminous writing on art topics, and her personal support of artists pushed the visual arts to the forefront of Utah culture. She devoted all her resources—financial, emotional, and intellectual—to the cause of art in Utah. Mrs. Horne told about her first years of work in the Utah Art Movement at the International Frauen (Women) Congress in Berlin in 1904. Among her many honors were the Medal of Honor from the Academy of Western Culture and election to the Utah Hall of Fame, nominated by the Utah Federation of Women's Clubs.[67]

A twentieth-century example of this same phenomenon is the story of the Salt Lake Art Center, founded in 1931 as the first public art gallery in Utah. Alta Rawlins Jensen led the movement to create an official home for the visual arts in Salt Lake City. Working with a group of fifteen women friends, Mrs. Jensen held several fund-raising events, organized a literary association known as Barnacles, and held an annual Beaux Arts Ball. Jensen worked tirelessly during the cash-strapped days of the Depression to provide a "gathering place for poets, writers, musicians and artists of all mediums."[68] In 1961, the Junior League of Utah took over partial responsibility for running the center—again on a volunteer basis.

The first significant generation of female artists born and raised in the state worked in the 1920s and '30s. Like their pioneer foremothers, they dealt primarily with figurative subject matter. Florals or landscapes were typical themes. For the first time, however, strong individuals emerged, often with eccentric personalities. Florence Truelson's work was less typically reflective and female in vision and more the expression of a unique personal aesthetic.

Relative compensation for art produced by women lagged behind rates paid to men. Most important, women failed to receive important commissions, public work that would have brought them more work and a measure of fame. The Federal Art Project administered under the auspices of the Works Projects Administration in the 1930s addressed this issue, and was in fact the first federal bill to include an equal opportunity clause. The FAP gave an unprecedented number of women artists the chance to work in their profession because of a stipulation embedded in the language of the legislation itself. These women created easel paintings, taught classes in community art centers, and painted a few large-scale murals for public buildings.

Despite the favorable atmosphere created by the New Deal WPA projects, however, few women actually worked as artists—perhaps fewer than eighty in a total female population of 161,750.[69] Still, approximately 40 percent of all artists on relief under the WPA were women.

The Utah co-chair of the Federal Arts Project in Utah was Helen Sheets, who assigned ten different artists to separate projects. The only woman of the ten Utah artists hired through the fund, Florence Ware, created a pictorial map of the early Salt Lake Valley and painted the double murals in the main chamber of Kingsbury Hall at the University of Utah. Still, thanks to the programs of the New Deal, the 1930s were a watershed for the arts in Utah. During that decade, new professional arts organizations provided unprecedented opportunities for artists to remain in the state rather than leaving to study and perform in the East.

Women artists required incredible independence and drive to defy societal attitudes and make their way in the largely male-dominated world of art. Florence Ware and her contemporary, Caroline Parry, were students of Utah artist Edwin Evans at the University of Utah in the 1910s and some of the first female artists to receive major commissions. In the twenties, Ware studied at the University of California at Berkeley, at Columbia University, with Mahonri Young at the American School of Sculpture, at the Art Students League, and at Cooper Union in 1927 on a scholarship. Ware mastered a variety of artistic media through this diverse combination of art instruction. Ware and Parry became educators and taught a new generation of artists. At the same time, they created a body of work that was both impressive in its scope and which reflected considerable talent.

Mabel Frazier's influence was felt at the University of Utah from 1921 to 1953. She taught as an assistant professor for forty-two quarters before being promoted to the rank of associate professor. Frazer was a versatile teacher who taught painting, anatomy, art history, sculpture, and ceramics. Active off campus as well as on, Frazier was a vocal member of the local art scene and produced a number of works of exceptional strength, including one important work—*The Furrow* (1935).[70]

She also secured major commissions, including refurbishing the murals in the Salt Lake Temple and painting murals in Salt Lake City's Thirty-third Ward Chapel. Unconventional and spirited, she said, "An artist must have something to say. Art is just another language and the would-be painter should at least learn the rudiments of that language—color, composing, drawing, etc." To George Dibble, Frazier was a demanding teacher who challenged her students to stretch beyond their limits. "She had a kind of easy, free watercolor approach, and encouraged this. . . . [She also] decried anybody's compulsion to hold to rigorous detail." Frazier continued to exhibit into her nineties.[71]

The flourishing of art during the Depression under the Federal Arts Project proved to be a false start. During the 1940s and 1950s, women exhibited in relatively few important shows across the country. Although at mid-century, some adventuresome Utah women began to paint in modernist styles that showed an awareness of national trends and avant-garde movements, as the American Art movement increased in strength and vigor, opportunities for women artists shrank. Abstract artists, both men and women, have always struggled for recognition in the conservative and traditional local art scene. It was not until the 1970s that new forms and images of women mirrored the changes in the social fabric of American society.

Lee Deffebach's (1928–present) talent, unique vision, and persistence brought her the respect of her peers and a loyal following. A peer of the second generation of the New York School (such figures as Kenneth Noland, Morris Louis, and Helen Frankenthaler), Deffebach found her voice as a painter by staining her canvases with thin washes, "glowing tones that melted and mingled with each other to create lyrical improvisations that evidenced her distinctively Western American aesthetic."[72] In a June 1993 retrospective of her work, according to Mary Francey, Deffebach demonstrated her path from abstract expressionism to "strong visual statements that emerge from episodes and experiences in her life."[73]

Anna Campbell Bliss studied mathematics and art at Wellesley College before deciding to attend architecture school at Yale. "Mathematics is pervasive,"

Artist Florence Ware (1891–1971) at the Neighborhood House, December 11,1962. Ware was known as a fine teacher, painter, and interior designer.

she said. "It's part of our structure of thinking, and not something you isolate."[74] This rich and diverse background is evident in work from every stage of her development. Bliss combined screen-print techniques with computer-generated designs, bringing her work "into the new scientific world of dynamical systems and fractals," according to art historian Mary Francey. Bliss saw each new artist production as an experiment, a process she valued and learned from.[75] Much of this exploration was through color and the effect of colors on each other. She tried, according to one author, to "overcome 'cliches of color'"—the idea that "red must always jump out and blue always recedes. 'You can make color do anything,'" she said at a 2004 retrospective of her work at the Utah Museum of Fine Arts at the University of Utah.[76]

Responding to the nation's bicentennial, the Springville Art Museum staged a woman's exhibit and commissioned a catalogue—"Out of the Land: Utah Women Then and Now" to document this historical event. Challenging local religious and moral values and perceptions, the exhibit included work produced by women, representing Utah's women's issues, contemporary concerns, attitudes, and range of experiences. Like exhibits from states throughout the nation, Utah's exhibit traveled to Washington, D.C., where it was shown at the National Museum for Women in the Arts.[77]

An art professor at the University of Utah, Maureen O'Hara-Ure continues the strong practitioner/educator tradition of Florence Ware and Mabel Frazier, educating a new generation of female artists in the twentieth-first century. According to Mary Francey, O'Hara-Ure "translates ideas into complex constructions that defy classification but are rooted more strongly in cultural ethos than a singular aesthetic."[78]

Dorothy Bearnson founded the University of Utah's ceramics program in 1948 and organized the Utah Designer Craftsman in 1960. Known as an innovator in her pottery techniques as well as in her teaching, Bearnson was active in national organizations including the American Crafts Council and National Council of Education in the Ceramic Arts. In April 1991, the NCECA awarded Bearnson an honorary membership, its most prestigious honor.[79]

A long-time faculty member in the Graduate School of Architecture, photographer Barbara Richards taught a whole generation of young architects the art of photographic seeing. More important, Richards's own work, whether in soft, quiet landscapes composed with black and white film, or color explorations made possible by the computer, is bold and vibrant, sensitive and intuitive.

No single artist has dominated twentieth-century art in Utah in the same way that painter Mary Teasdel or singer Emma Lucy Gates Bowen did, although many more women work as full-time artists today. The departments of fine arts at the universities and colleges in the state have significant numbers of talented, dedicated female students. The rosters of faculty at the state's colleges and universities demonstrate that increasing numbers of women are teaching at the university level in art departments. More important, Utah women are showing their work in virtually every local gallery and museum in the state, and nationally as well.

It is, however, ironic that the best-known piece of public art in the state was produced by an outsider. Nancy Holt's *Sun Tunnels* in the northwestern desert, ten miles from Wendover, draws visitors from across the country and beyond who come to welcome the sunrise at the time of the solstices or equinoxes.

DANCE

Dance, as discussed above, was largely associated with dramatics in the nineteenth century; but it was becoming a cultural art in its own right as the twentieth century neared. A major incentive for dance in Utah came when Maud May Babcock arrived in 1892. Babcock had graduated from the Philadelphia National School of Oratory in 1886 and in 1890 from the Academy of Dramatic Arts. The summer before her arrival, Susa Young Gates, a daughter of Brigham Young, attended Babcock's physical culture class at Harvard University summer school. She invited Babcock; and Babcock, for a "salary" of $500 a year, became the first woman to hold professorial rank at the University of Utah.[80] For almost four decades, she dominated theater and dance in Utah as an instructor of elocution in the Department of Speech and Drama. Her Delsarte training, credentials, and eloquent advocacy of the moral benefits of physical fitness shaped the public's acceptance of and participation in dance in Salt Lake City and Provo.

In 1893 Babcock organized the first university theater in the nation. The first performance was a demonstration of drills with dumb-bells, wands, Indian clubs, dances, and dramatic picturization that illustrated the combination of drama and dance movement that was central to both Babcock's philosophy and her method. Four years later, a group of students under her leadership formed the University Dramatic Club, again the first of its kind in the United States.[81] In 1893, the group performed at the Salt Lake Theater—an exhibition of "fancy steps, attitudizing muscular poses, drills, dances, Swedish movement, and Indian club and dumbbell performances." Two years later, more than one hundred of her students acted in the first play produced at a university in the United States: *Eleusinia,* which included "living statues of toga-ed figures in statuesque groups inspired by the Greek legends of Demeter and Persephone."[81]

Babcock estimated that she directed over 800 plays involving thousands of students in her years at the university. She introduced such new curriculum as classes in oratory, speech, and physical education. Although she failed to establish a professional theater in Utah, she played a significant role in the national Little Theater movement and directed the first university Little Theater west of the Mississippi in the 1920s. Above all else, by precept and example, she openly encouraged young women to choose careers, enter public life, and develop their talents. A colleague who taught in the Communications Department at the University of Utah remembered that "this woman could frighten you to pieces; a woman of great dignity, [who] could also be the sweetest."[83]

At Brigham Young University in Provo, Algie Eggertsen Ballif included dance drama as part of her physical culture classes in the 1920s. In bare feet, considered an innovation during the time, girls and women expressed in dance themes from Greek mythology. Under Ballif's direction, the physical education department's uniform changed from wool serge gym suits to gingham dresses. Eleanor Roosevelt asked Algie to serve on the Education Subcommittee of the U.S. Commission on the Status of Women.[84] Throughout the 1920s, women's dance classes—as opposed to physical culture that included dancing—were offered at both universities and exhibited a movement towards the new aesthetic dancing of Isadora Duncan.

Dance classes were also taught at the McCune Mansion at the beginning of the twentieth century. "Esthetic Dancing" classes were offered for $4 a term for children ages five to seven and on up to adults. This type of "expressive" movement was backed by a philosophy about the relationship between the mind and the body. "In this course the aim is to make the body the obedient and graceful servant of the mind. The student is led to see that a training which consists merely of freeing exercises results in lawlessness, leaving the body as free to do the wrong thing as the right. It is only when thought controls this freedom that the body becomes a truly expressive agent—a picture of a mind activity."[85]

A national ballet tradition had begun in such centers as New York City before the end of the nineteenth century which paved the way for this new type

Art class at the University of Utah, ca. 1920.

of dancing. During the early years of the twentieth century, it established itself as the center of avant garde art. Ballet joined other dance forms such as jazz dancing, tap dancing, and finally, at the turn of the century, modern dance for professionals. Isadora Duncan (1878–1927), whose concerts nationally shocked and revolutionized traditional norms of respectability, felt that dance should break through traditional boundaries and dignified dance as a career. In the early twentieth century, Ruth St. Denis (1879–1968), Martha Graham (1894–1991), Mary Wigman (1886–1973), and Doris Humphrey (1895–1958) popularized modern dance, expanded its meaning and repertoire of movements, and turned it into a legitimate and serious form of art. Lagging behind by several decades, Utah dancers would not move toward modern dance until after World War II.

In the early 1940s, dancer Virginia Tanner was faced with the decision of staying in Utah to teach or leaving to dance professionally in New York City. She chose Utah and began teaching children in the ballroom of the McCune School of Music and Art at the same time she was choreographing theater productions at the University of Utah and performing in them. Her student performing group became known as the Children's Dance Theater. For the next several decades, Tanner made a career out of teaching and training children. Before her death in 1979, CDT became a local institution and gained respect for creative dance throughout the state.

In 1953, the Children's Dance Theater was invited to perform at Ted Shawn's famous Jacob's Pillow in Massachusetts, the Connecticut College School of Dance, and New York University's summer camp. *Life* magazine praised the visit of the Utah children's troupe in glowing terms: "From the first, there was beauty. The children were wonderfully disciplined yet gloriously free. They danced as if they had faith in themselves, had a love those of us who were seeing them, actively believed in their God and rejoiced in all of these."[86] Since that time the group has danced from Washington, D.C., to Hawaii. Simultaneously, Tanner was helping to develop a national program for dance education through the National Endowment Arts Program titled "Arts Impact," publishing textbooks on the arts for children, and training teachers on a national level.

Jose Limon described Virginia Tanner as the "world's greatest and foremost teacher of dance," and *Life* magazine's arts critic Walter Terry called Tanner a "philosopher of children." Limon added, "In the world of children's dance, she has been an explorer, an interpreter, a great explainer. Implicit in everything she does in children's dance is her awareness of the historical, social, psychological, and yes, moral forces, that along with aesthetics and techniques, go into a child's pure dance expression."[87] After Tanner's death, Mary Ann Lee headed CDT, building on Virginia's vision: "Roots and Wings." Each year as many as 800 children between the ages of three and eighteen take classes in creative dance at the University of Utah and are trained to get in "touch with their own creativity."[88]

In 1966 with a $370,000 grant, Virginia Tanner, the Rockefeller Foundation, and the University of Utah modern dance faculty and administration organized a repertory dance company, first known as the University of Utah Repertory Dance Theater. The idea of a full-time professional modern dance company outside of New York City was a bold idea. For the most part, modern dance was still unfamiliar in the West.

The idea worked so well that, forty years later, the Repertory Dance Theater had a comfortable national reputation, a performing repertoire of over 165 master works spanning the full range of American dance history, and performance experience in more than 300 cities and towns located in forty-one states and Canada. Perhaps the greatest significance of the RDT was that it was a company where Utah dancers could find continuing training and employment so that more could stay in-state for their professional careers. Under the leadership of Linda C. Smith, herself a former dancer for the company, RDT maintains a modern dance repertory of more than 200 works choreographed by more than 100 modern dancers, including the complete works of Doris Humphrey.

In 1954, another dance troupe formed through the partnership of Shirley Russon Ririe and Joan Jones Woodbury: the Ririe-Woodbury Dance Company. Under their leadership, five choreodancers joined together to perform and choreograph at the University of Utah. In the early years of the company when there was no budget, no consistent predicable rehearsal space, and no salaries—just a modest touring schedule—the group persisted because of their dedication to the concept of a teaching-performing organization. This combination helped establish the group's reputation as a distinguished company of movement specialists with "choreographies off the beaten track and into the future by the co-directors and prominent guest choreographers."[89] Ririe-Woodbury performed in schools and communities in and outside of Utah. In fact, in one six-year period, over one-third of all Artists-in-the-Schools residencies in the entire United States were done by Ririe-Woodbury.[90] A publication for the 1979–80 season promoted the range of programs the company featured: "Extensive touring has built an enviable record—keeping us on the go and demanding that we give a great deal of attention to packing for a variety of performances. Our performances range from narrated concerts for uninitiated audiences to multi-media concerts for sophisticated dance tastes."[91]

Certainly the 1950s were years that witnessed a great flowering of dance in Utah. Along with the creation of Children's Dance Theater and Ririe-Woodbury, the first university ballet training school was created at the University of Utah by Willam Christensen, who also helped organize the Utah Civic Ballet in 1963. In 1968 the Federation of Rocky Mountain States made the Utah Civic Ballet its official regional company under the name of Ballet West.

Each year since 1955, Utah audiences have flocked to *The Nutcracker,* choreographed by Willam Christensen after he came to the University of Utah to start the first ballet department in the nation in a fine arts college. Known originally as the University Ballet, then Utah Civic Ballet, the company became Ballet West in 1966. Bolstered by the support of Glenn Walker Wallace, Ballet West moved into the Capitol Theater in 1978. Starting in the 1960s, Ballet West made several European tours and performed in New York City and at the John F. Kennedy Center in Washington D.C., receiving national and international recognition as a significant regional ballet company.

Ballet education at the University of Utah flourished under "Mr. C." as Christensen was known to local dancers, and eventually became a nationally respected and ranked department. In the late twentieth century, the Ballet West Conservatory, headed by John Hart and Sharee Lane, trained advanced students sent to the university from private studios throughout the area. Utah Ballet, is the university's own scholarship ballet group directed by Attila Ficzere in the 1990s who came to Utah from the San Francisco Ballet. In Utah County, Jacqueline Colledge directed the Utah Regional Ballet, which included *The Nutcracker* in its own repertoire.

In 1976 Bruce Marks joined Ballet West, and his wife, Toni Landers Marks, became its principal teacher. Landers had been a principal dancer with the Royal Danish Ballet for a few years and was renowned for her expertise in the Bournonville, a distinctive dance technique that combines mime with more traditional choreography. Other women worked in the administration of the Ballet Company, including former dancer Sondra Sugai, who since 1980 has been associate artistic director, and Helen Douglas, who was resident choreographer in the 1980s.

What Alice Merrill Horne did for art in early twentieth century, Glenn Walker Wallace did for dance and music. Her personal vision and dedication to the arts made steady contributions to Utah from the 1920s to the 1970s. Best remembered for her part in the founding of the Utah Civic Ballet in 1963, she served as president of its board until her retirement in 1971. Mrs. Wallace was also involved in the organization of the Salt Lake Symphony Orchestra in 1924, the Civic Music Association in 1930, and the Utah Symphony Orchestra in 1939.

Other Utah universities and dance academies offered a range of dance training and performance opportunities. At the end of the twentieth century, co-directors Caroline Prohosky and Marilyn Berritt produced inventive programs and showcased the talents of local dancers in Utah County. At Utah State University, Dance West summer school's director, Maggi Moar, recruited visiting faculty to supplement the teaching already available at the university and in Logan itself for its students. Southwest Dance Theater led by Candy Fowler continues the traditions Virginia Tanner established to the north of Salt Lake Valley in Davis County.

ARTS AND CRAFTS

The Arts and Crafts movement at the turn of the century, as preached by William Morris and John Ruskin, was another international movement in art that impacted the work of Utah women. A reaction against the ugliness and misery of newly industrialized society in both America and Great Britain, the proponents of Arts and Crafts advocated a return to an earlier era of handicrafts and in handmade products like furniture, wallpaper, and textiles. Many Utah women, for whom hand-crafted goods held a special significance, enthusiastically responded to the ideas of the Arts and Crafts movement.

Just fifty years after the settlement of Salt Lake City, pioneer virtues were already celebrated and "remembered," most prominently at the Jubilee celebrations and exhibitions and at the Women's Pavilion at the Chicago Exposition in 1893 where Utah women displayed dresses made from home-produced silk. The traditional and artful pioneer needlecrafts of their grandmothers were raised to the level of "craft," as fewer women produced the cloth used by their families for clothing. Spinning, weaving, knitting, crocheting, tatting, and embroidery were rapidly replaced by mass-produced goods available in stores.

Nevertheless, the abundance of female production displayed in the Daughters of the Utah Pioneers Museum in Salt Lake City, indicate that crafts continued to be popular folk art forms, functioning as tangible physical links with the traditions of their ancestors down to the present. Periodic quilt exhibits in the Springville Art Museum and the Museum of (LDS) Church History and

Art always draw large crowds, as do the American West Heritage Center's Festival of the American West and displays by the Utah Quilters Guild. More important, craftwork perpetuates the values of home manufacturing and craftsmanship, heightening the value of personally produced goods for one's family and friends. Much of this work is still produced in domestic environments, does not require that women leave their children for work, and is a highly personal expression of self, exhibiting both what a woman can do and who she is.

The original curriculum of Brigham Young Academy in the 1880s and '90s included such "female arts" as watercolors, setting an elegant table, and crocheting.[92] This line-up of classes, which included other housekeeping skills, reveals a sense of what constituted appropriate education, purpose in female education, and a discourse about women's proper role in society and in the Mormon church.

As the twentieth century began, Utah's high school curricula included classes in decorative and applied arts and crafts under the direction of Emma Francis Daft, Ruth Harwood (daughter of J. T. Harwood), and Margaret Merrill Fisher (sister of Alice Merrill Horne). Classes included jewelry, metallography, leather crafts, and lace making. Fisher taught students at West High School how to make the lace designs handed down to her from her mother, Bathsheba Smith Merrill, whose mother, Bathsheba Wilson Bigler Smith, had taken prizes in Nauvoo for her original lace designs and drawings for execution in hand-woven wool, linen, and cotton fabrics. Such a genealogy of traditional arts connects women through generations, perpetuates values and beliefs about women's roles, and produces a sense of competency and self-worth in the process.

One weaver who received national prominence for her work, Mary Meigs Atwater, moved to Utah at the end of the nineteenth century with her husband. Atwater was attracted to the tenets of the formal crafts movement and had attended the Chicago Art Institute and the Academie Julian in Paris at the same time as Rose Hartwell. Atwater authored several texts on weaving including *The Shuttle Craft Book of American Hand Weaving* that became nationally known.[93]

In the twentieth century, like the Native American women who are this area's original inhabitants, Utah women express their personal truths through folk art which is both domestic and work related, made to decorate their homes or yards or to give as gifts to others. "Like their pioneer forebears, contemporary folk artists have learned to create beauty in their everyday lives by pairing group-held values and personal ingenuity with the materials and tools at hand."[94]

Contemporary Utah women's folk art is characterized by a new diversity and variety in both subject matter and technique including weaving, fiber art, photography, and sculpture as well as painting. For example, Sharon Alderman's weavings reflect sensitivity to both materiality and texture. Her wall hangings, meticulously composed with cotton thread, create color compositions as subtle as the shifting light that moves across the valley at the end of the day.[95]

CONCLUSION

Barbara Welter sees forces at work at the end of the nineteenth century that spelled the demise of "true womanhood" and, hence, of the romanticized version of the appropriate woman. Progressivism and its attitude toward social reform depended in large measure on the quasi-professionalized work of a new generation of educated women. Industrialism, urbanization, and even the expanded political role of the United States in the world arena all impacted the place of women in society and at home. These circumstances, Welter writes

> called forth responses from women which differed from those she was trained to believe were hers by nature and divine decree. The very perfection of True Womanhood, moreover, carried within itself the seeds of its own destruction. For if woman was so very little less than the angels, she should surely take a more active part in running the world, especially since men were making such a hash of things. Real women often felt they did not live up to the ideal of True Womanhood: some of them blamed themselves, some challenged the standards, some tried to keep the virtues and enlarge the scope of womanhood.[96]

In the nineteenth century, women were firmly tied to the home, whether the home was a productive unit or not, and regardless of its degree of separation from the public sphere. Women in the twentieth century moved increasingly into participation in the paid labor force and public world. This movement resulted in a growing contradiction between the daily reality of women's lives and the dominant cultural ideologies that attached specific gender codes to each sphere and impacted women's ability to succeed in their new life.

According to Linda J. Nicholson, "Beyond the practical contradictions generated by old expectations being added to new responsibilities, the participation of women outside the home meant the development, particularly for professional women, of a new sense of self." She continues, "Such personality characteristics as being nurturant, self-sacrificing, and nonassertive were incompatible with at least a certain kind of nondomestic activity. Women's activity outside the home both generated conflicts with traditionally assigned tasks and traits within the family and provided alternatives to that family." [97]

An equivalent shift reduced the family's importance in material and economic production but assigned to women the role of guardians of the "inner life." The domain of emotions thus became equivalent with the female sphere.[98] At the same time, there was decisive evidence of female creative power as women spoke these interior truths with the language of their arts.

The image of the artist in the nineteenth century is that of an exceptional individual who, at great personal sacrifice and risk, nearly always left the state for both professional training and a portion of her professional career. Little was available in the way of either education or cultural opportunities in the state. Even now, artists still leave in large numbers for training at superior academies of music or art outside of the state but many choose to stay for instruction in the programs offered at every university. Art education in Utah has trained hundreds of teachers, helped promote art appreciation, and raised the level of local performances. Perhaps this is because art has always relied on an unique combination of talent, vision, and good fortune which cannot be produced by some academic formula. The same pattern holds true for dance, theater, and singing.

Although artistic creation suggests both individuality and interconnectedness, it is perhaps inevitable that issues of the "proper" role of women, the role of art in the life of the community, and the relationship between art and politics, economics, and family life continue to surface. The same problems that discouraged women from pursuing careers in art-related fields in the nineteenth century plague the contemporary artist—economic prohibitions, societal prejudices against women working in certain areas, and the problems of balancing a career with a family.

The LDS Church has encouraged cultural life through its auxiliary programs. For example, large numbers of women have participated in such activities as the LDS Church dance festivals, which began in the 1920s and ended in the 1960s, and the local ward road shows. Such experiences helped to create interest in those art forms. However, the church's emphasis on mass participation over individual achievement has diffused interest in solo or professional careers. The heavy assignments to LDS women to fill executive and teaching positions in its auxiliary organizations serving women and children become an obstacle, leaving little room for work outside of the official church programs.

According to the 2000 U.S. census,[99] since the 1960s more women identify themselves as artists than ever before in the state's history. This increase in numbers promises a great future for the arts in Utah as these women continued to work. As Utah's population becomes more cosmopolitan and places a higher value on cultural activities, art will be supported on a grander scale—which will in turn encourage more women to pursue careers as professional artists. Through programs like the Salt Lake City Arts Council's Percent for the Art, that sets aside 1 percent of the total cost of new public construction projects for art contributes to the quality of life in the community. Artists communicate essential human truths, interpret societal values and issues, and express the essence of culture. The diversity of women's art enriches local culture, builds community, and expands the possibilities women consider as they live their lives in Utah.

Notes

1. Gough Whitlam, quoted in Germaine Greer, *The Obstacle Race* (New York: Secher and Warburg, 1979), i.
2. Whitney Chadwick, *Women, Art and Society* (London: Thames and Hudson, 1990), 9.

3.   Greer, *The Obstacle Race,* 6.

4.   Chadwick, *Women, Art and Society,* 10.

5.   Ibid., 13.

6.   John Stuart Mill, *On the Subjection of Women* (1906) quoted in Greer, *Obstacle Course,* 12.

7.   Barbara Welter, "The Cult of True Womanhood: 1820–1860," in *The American Family in Social and Historical Perspective,* edited by Michael Gordon (New York: St. Martin's Press, 1983), 313.

8.   Ibid., 314.

9.   Ibid., 322.

10. Holly Devor, "Becoming Members of Society: Learning the Social Meanings of Gender," in *Gender Images: Readings for Composition,* edited by Melita Schaum and Connie Flanagan (New York: Houghton Mifflin, 1992), 23.

11. Ibid., 23.

12. Carroll Smith-Rosenberg, "The Female World of Love and Ritual: Relations between Women in 19th Century America," in *The American Family in Social and Historical Perspective,* edited in Michael Gordon (New York: St. Martin's Press, 1983).

13. Nancy Cott, *The Bonds of Womanhood: Woman's Sphere in New England, 1780–1835* (New Haven: Yale University Press, 1977), 97.

14. Linda J. Nicholson, *Gender and History: The Limits of Social Theory in the Age of the Family* (New York: Columbia University Press, 1986), 46.

15. Michelle Zimbalist Rosaldo, "The Use and Abuse of Anthropology: Reflections on Feminism and Cross-Cultural Understanding," *Signs* 5, no. 3 (1980): 389–417.

16. Nicholson, *Gender and History,* 52.

17. Brigham H. Roberts, *The Life of John Taylor* (Salt Lake City: George Q. Cannon & Sons, 1892), 192.

18. Clarissa Young Spencer, *One Who Was Valiant* (Caldwell, Ida.: Caxton Printers, 1940), 162; Howard Stansbury, *Exploration and Survey of the Valley of the Great Salt Lake of Utah* (Philadelphia: Lippincott, Grambo & Co., 1852), 138.

19. Levi Edgar Young, *The Founding of Utah* (New York: Scribners and Sons, 1923), 329. See also Milton R. Hunter, *Utah in Her Western Setting* (Salt Lake City: Deseret News Press, 1943), 207–9.

20. Quoted in Andrew Love Neff, *History of Utah, 1847 to 1869* (New York: Deseret News Press, 1940), 599.

21. Alice Merrill Horne, "Home and Ideals," *Woman's Exponent* 18 (February 15/March 1, 1901): 1.

22. Martha Sonntag Bradley and Mary Brown Firmage Woodward, *The Four Zinas: Mothers and Daughters on the Mormon Frontier* (Salt Lake City: Signature Books, 2000), 251.

23. Vern G. Swanson, Robert Olpin, and William C. Seifrit, *Utah Art* (Salt Lake City: Peregrine Smith, 1991).

24. Howard R. Lamar, *The Theater in Mormon Life and Culture,* Leonard J. Arrington Mormon History Lecture Series, No. 4 (Logan: Utah State University, December 1, 1998, 5.

25. John A. Widtsoe, ed., *Discourses of Brigham Young* (Salt Lake City: Deseret Book, 1925), 373–74.

26. Edward W. Tullidge, *The History of Salt Lake City* (Salt Lake City: Edward W. Tullidge, 1886), 737–38.

27. Richard F. Burton, *The City of the Saints* (New York: Harper and Brothers, 1862), 230–31.

28. Quoted in Horace G. Whitney, "The Salt Lake Theater," *The Drama in Utah* (Salt Lake City: Deseret News, 1915), 514.

29. Spencer, *One Who Was Valiant,* 29.

30. Widstoe, *Discourses of Brigham Young,* 373.

31. Spencer, *One Who Was Valiant,* 29.

32. Ibid., 29.

33. William Hepworth Dixon, *New America* (Philadelphia: J. B. Lippincott, 1867), 200–201.

34. Ibid.

35. Rachelle Pace Castor, "Maude Adams (1872–1953): No Other Actress Can Take Her Place," in *Worth Their Salt: Notable But Often Unnoted Women of Utah,* edited by Colleen Whitley (Logan: Utah State University Press, 1996, 189–202.

36. Edward W. Tullidge, *History of Utah* (Salt Lake City: Star Printing, 1886), 745.

37. Ila Fisher Maughan, *Pioneer Theatre in the Desert* (Salt Lake City: Deseret Book, 1961); Myrtle E. Henderson, *A History of the Theatre in Salt Lake City, 1850–1870* (Evanston, Ill.: n. pub., 1934); and Courtney H. Brewer, "A History of Drama in Logan, Utah and Neighboring Communities to 1925" (Ph.D. diss., Brigham Young University, 1972).

38. *Logan Leader,* November 22, 1879.

39. *Logan Leader,* August 6, 1880.

40. *Logan Leader,* August 18, 1880.

41. *Logan Leader,* December 27, 1880.

42. Lamar, *The Theater in Mormon Life and Culture,* 14.

43. Widtsoe, *Discourses of Brigham Young,* 375–76.

44. John Lindsay, *The History of Theatricals in Utah; with Reminiscences and Comments, Humorous and Critical* (Salt Lake City: n.pub., 1905), 77.

45. Martha Sonntag Bradley, *A Guide to Utah Architecture* (Layton, Utah: Gibbs Smith Publishers, forthcoming in 2006).

46. Lowell Durham, interviewed by Martha Sonntag Bradley, transcript, November 14, 1985.

47. Ibid.

48. John Louis Coray, "Emma Lucy Gates (Bowen), Soprano: Her Accomplishments in Opera and Concert" (M.A. thesis, Brigham Young University, 1956), 11.

49. Durham, interview.

50. Retrieved on March 25, 2005 from http://www.outlawwomen.com/EmmaLucy GatesBowen.htm.

51. Daniel Batchellor, quoted in Christine Ammer, *Unsung: A History of Women in American Music* (Westport, Conn.: Greenwood Press, 1980), 43.

52.	"McCune School of Music and Art," 4, n.d., pamphlet, Archives, Family and Church History Department, Church of Jesus Christ of Latter-day Saints, Salt Lake City (hereafter LDS Church Archives).

53.	Ibid.

54.	Durham, interview.

55.	Ibid.

56.	Ibid.

57.	Ibid.

58.	Ibid.

59.	Catherine Reese Newton, "After Nurturing Nova for 18 Seasons, Scowcroft Is Ready for New Adventures," *Salt Lake Tribune,* May 16, 2004, D3.

60.	Marie Osmond biographical information, retrieved on April 11, 2005, from http://www.osmond.con/donnyandmarie/.

61.	Robert Olpin, *Dictionary of Utah Art* (Salt Lake City: Salt Lake Art Center, 1980), 26.

62.	Alice Merrill Horne, *Devotees and Their Shrines: A Handbook of Utah Art* (Salt Lake City: Deseret News, 1914), 60.

63.	Martha S. Bradley, "Mary Teasdel (1863–1937): Yet Another American in Paris," in *Worth Their Salt,* 131–47.

64.	Greer, *The Obstacle Race,* 13.

65.	Harriet Horne Arrington, "Alice Merrill Horne (1968–1948): Art Promoter and Early Utah Legislator," in *Worth Their Salt,* 171–88.

66.	Ibid.

67.	Ibid.

68.	"History of Salt Lake Art Center," retrieved in April 2004 from http://www.slartcenter.org/history.html.

69.	U.S. Bureau of the Census, *Census Statistical Abstracts, 1920.*

70.	*The Furrow* is located in the Museum of (LDS) Church History and Art, Salt Lake City.

71.	Robert S. Olpin, *Utah Art* (Layton, Utah: Peregrine Smith Books, 1991), 120.

72.	Mary Francey, "Utah Art: Toward a New Century," in *Utah State of the Arts,* edited by Trudy McMurrin (Ogden, Utah: Meridian International, 1993), 19.

73.	Ibid.

74.	Christy Karras, "Painting by Numbers," *Salt Lake Tribune,* May 30, 2004, D3.

75.	Ibid.

76.	Ibid.

77.	*Utah Women Artist's Exhibition, 1987* (Springville, Utah: The Museum, 1987).

78.	Francey, "Utah Art: Toward a New Century," 33.

79.	"NCECA," retrieved on March 30, 2005, from http://www.nceca.net/resources/membership.html.

80.	David G. Pace, "Maud May Babcock (1867–1954): Speak Clearly and Carry a Big Umbrella," in *Worth Their Salt,* 148–58.

81. Interview with Ethel Baker Callas, Babcock's former student, quoted in Raye Price, "Utah's Leading Ladies of the Arts," *Utah Historical Quarterly* 38 (Winter 1970): 79.

82. Pace, "Maud May Babcock," 151–52.

83. Quoted in Lamar, *The Theater in Mormon Life and Culture,* 17.

84. "Algie Eggertsen Ballif, 1918," Women's Services and Resources, retrieved March 15, 2005, from http://www.campuslife.byu.edu/wst/women/rm2.htm.

85. "McCune School of Music and Art," 4, n.d., pamphlet, LDS Church Archives.

86. Walter Terry, quoted in *A Tribute to Virginia Tanner, Repertory Dance Theater Program* (Salt Lake City: Utah Holiday Publishing, 1978), 1.

87. José Limon and Walter Terry, quoted in ibid., 1.

88. Dorothy Stowe, "State of the Dance in a Dancing State," *Utah State of the Arts,* 63.

89. Ibid., 62.

90. Ibid.

91. "Ririe-Woodbury Dance Company," pamphlet, n.d., Utah Historical Society, Salt Lake City.

92. Bradley and Woodward, *The Four Zinas.*

93. Mary Meigs Atwater, *The Shuttle Craft Book of American Hand Weaving* (New York: Macmillan, 1941); and her *Weaving a Life: The Story of Mary Meigs Atwater,* compiled by Mary Jo Reiter (New York: International Press, 1992).

94. Carol Edison, "Indian Baskets, Pioneer Quilts & Hispanic Music," *Utah State of the Arts,* 136.

95. Carol Biddle, "A Legacy of Tradition and a Search for New Forms," *Utah State of the Arts,* 84.

96. Welter, "The Cult of True Womanhood," 328.

97. Nicholson, *Gender and History,* 59.

98. Ibid., 60.

99. U.S. Bureau of the Census, *Statistical Report, 2000.*

11

Women in Politics

Power in the Public Sphere

Kathryn L. MacKay

In November 2003, Olene Walker, Utah's first woman lieutenant governor, made history again by becoming Utah's first woman governor. She took over that position after Governor Michael Leavitt left the job to head the Environmental Protection Agency in the George W. Bush administration. Very popular with Utah voters, Walker intended to run for the position of the state's chief executive in 2004, but she was ousted from the race by Republican delegates at their state convention—this after more than twenty years of public service.

Walker, like many women, entered politics through leading PTAs and women's community organizations and through joining in on the "political housekeeping" within her (Republican) political party. Unlike most women officeholders, however, Walker's public life extended over several years. She was elected to four terms in the Utah State House and would probably have become that House's first female speaker had she not been defeated in her bid for reelection in 1988. She worked briefly for then-governor Norman Bangerter as his director of community development. In 1992 she intended to run for Congress in the Second Congressional District but jumped out to join Leavitt's bid for the state's top office. In that so-called "Year of the Woman," each of the three major male candidates for governor had women as their lieutenant governor running mates: Leavitt with Walker, Democrat Stuart Hansen with Paula Julander, and Independent Merrill Cook with Frances Hatch Merrill.

All three women had served in the state legislature. However, these women were among the very few to do so. In the years since the Center for American Women and Politics began collecting and analyzing women's political participation (1971), Utah has consistently ranked lowest in the West for percentage of women in elective office.[1] Utah politics is marked by the political power of the Church of Jesus Christ of Latter-day Saints whose members comprise about 70 percent of the state's population. Whatever social and political

Courtesy Utah State Archives.

Olene Walker is sworn in November 5, 2003, as Utah's first woman governor by Christine Durham, the first woman to serve as a Utah Supreme Court justice and later chief justice. Olene's husband, Myron, is in the center.

roles LDS leaders assign and promote for women—and men, the faithful will work to fulfill. The major roles for women are care-giver and companion which are more often expressed in private settings than in public.[2] And women are less likely than men to translate their church leadership experiences into political leadership. The percentage of active Mormons in the state legislature is far higher than that of the statewide population, but they are overwhelmingly males. The Utah legislature is an anomaly in the West.

The West led the nation in granting suffrage and in electing women to legislative positions. Soon after suffrage was extended to women throughout the nation (1919), however, the North caught up. From 1933 until 1987, the North had the highest percentage of women legislators of the four regions of the country. In 1987, the West once again surpassed the North and continues to be the region with highest percentage of women legislators.[3] Several studies suggest that female legislators are much more likely than male legislators to be concerned about issues relevant to the lives of women and their families, including violence against women, child support, employment, welfare, and reproductive rights.[4]

Utah women are more likely to work outside their homes than other American women. The gender gap in median income is larger in Utah than in the United States as a whole. The Utah birth rate remains more than 30 percent higher than the national birth rate. Utahns also marry and divorce more often

" WHEW! THAT WAS ENOUGH 'DIVERSITY' TO LAST ME FOR A WHILE."

Courtesy of Salt Lake Tribune *and Pat Bagley.*

Pat Bagley's cartoon appeared in the December 23, 2004, *Salt Lake Tribune.*

than other Americans.[5] Utah women might be better served by a state legislature in which they were more represented. However, the majority of women in Utah are members of the LDS Church. That religion supports male authority and a division of labor between men and women. LDS women play essential roles in grassroots community and church activities, but their participation in more formal ways through, for example, professional careers and elected offices, is discouraged both by the direct exhortation of church leaders and by more subtle sanctions against deviance from the church-approved ideal that women should be defined by and satisfied with roles as wives and mothers.[6] Governor Walker, a wife for more than fifty years and the mother of seven, is one LDS woman who negotiated the boundaries of her faith to become not only trained for public life but engaged in that life.

Such negotiations have, perhaps, become more challenging for LDS women since the 1960s, when church authorities took measures to give greater power to men through centralizing church auxiliaries and ending the financial autonomy of the women's auxiliary, the Relief Society, eliminating its monthly magazine, and formalizing instructions to women in mothering and wifely duties. Earlier in the century, church authorities had restricted women's spiritual expressions in healings and blessings, a hallmark of the nineteenth-century Relief Society. Several scholars have argued that the roles of LDS women have become much more diminished in the twentieth century by comparison with their activities in the nineteenth.[7] Perhaps the shift was that the pragmatic demands of involving all members of the society, including women, in whatever was needed to build the "kingdom of God" in the American West finally gave way to the luxury of more sharply defined gender roles. Perhaps it was loyalty fostered through strategies such as polygamy and cooperatives which offered some women relative autonomy and economic security that gave way to loyalty fostered through kinship ties and corporate structures in which males had greater authority.[8] Certainly the support that church leaders offered to Mormon women working to achieve suffrage in the nineteenth century was replaced in the twentieth century by intense support for women working to defeat the Equal Rights Amendment.[9]

The two major struggles which challenged the gendered structures of American political and social life were woman suffrage (1840s-1910s) and the Equal Rights Amendment (1960s-80s). In both movements, women organized to institutionalize their greater participation in the public sphere, their equal citizenship and legal status with men, and their autonomy and independence from men. Women also mobilized to oppose both these efforts. In these battles, women in Utah impacted the national as well as the regional outcomes. And in both battles, the political power of the LDS Church was an issue.

Even before the first settlements in Utah (1847), LDS women participated in congregational voting, a practice begun in LDS Church meetings in 1831. If politics is defined as being involved in the selection of rulers and in the formulation of public policy, then their participation was limited. They voted, not their choice of alternatives, but whether to sustain the acts of their leaders. Those leaders attempted to establish a theocracy. Public policy was both civil and theological. Government officials were both ecclesiastically ordained and democratically elected. Women were allowed to vote in public church meetings, but the persons and policies were already determined in private meetings of the clergy at which women were not allowed.

Mormonism, as the descendent of American Puritanism, with its communitarianism, militant faith, and providential interpretation of history and the Bible, defined the role of women as helpmeets to male priestly authority (authority vested in all adult males, but exercised hierarchically), not as equal partners and not as autonomous individuals.[10] Nineteenth-century Mormonism embraced the Puritan principle of women's subject status, but tempered the principle with the reality of the intervening centuries in which the private sphere of the family had been democratized and in which the participation of women in almost every arena of the public sphere except that ending at the polling place had increased.[11]

In 1807 the New Jersey legislature rewrote its state constitution, disfranchising women. This action marked a process of democratization which shifted the right to vote in the person rather than property. No women, even those with control of property (the previous requirement for voting) were thereafter allowed to vote. Power was redistributed so that all white males became voters;

all females became subjects. From that time until 1838 when women (white widows with children in school) voted in Kentucky school elections and 1870 when Utah women voted in Utah municipal elections, no woman in the United States was legally enfranchised.

That enfranchisement of women in Utah resulted from women willing to extend their congregational work into political work. And woman suffrage in Utah resulted from the need in a frontier society to utilize all resources, including women, in order to function and prosper. Because Mormonism needed all hands to "build the kingdom," LDS women's productive value expanded their social and economic functions and, consequently, their political participation. The enfranchisement of women in Utah was also part of a national debate about citizenship in relation to slavery and the civil rights of all Americans.

Efforts by Mormons to establish a theocracy in the West was a challenge to American ideals of democracy and the consent of the governed. In establishing the first Anglo-American government in Utah, the Mormons simply elaborated their ecclesiastical machinery into a political government. Early in 1849 LDS leaders created the State of Deseret. The constitution of the proposed state, adopted in March 1849, restricted suffrage to white male residents.[12] The first election was held March 12, 1849, with 655 votes polled. This election was not democratic even for male residents. Men for office were selected not by parties but by the Council of Fifty, the secret organization which attended to the church's efforts to establish a political kingdom of God. The names were then submitted to the electors for approval.[13] Public elections were not held in Utah until 1870, after the transcontinental railroad (1869) had opened the territory to greater numbers of non-Mormons.

The U.S. Congress rejected Utah's application for statehood and established it as a territory in the Compromise of 1850. Congress had plenary power over territories, with the U.S. president appointing governors, some judges, and law enforcement officials. President Millard Fillmore appointed church President Brigham Young as Utah's first governor. Young ordered the first territorial election to be held August 4, 1851. All the candidates for the first Legislative Assembly of the Territory, save one were unanimously elected. The candidates had been selected by the Council of Fifty.[14]

The scrutiny of church leaders on voting for the "right" candidates was further facilitated by the ballots being numbered as provided by a territorial law passed in 1853. Not until 1878 was the marked ballot abolished.[15] With such scrutiny and accustomed to unanimity in convention, Mormons were apathetic about elections. Newspaper editorials chiding the populace for their low voter turnout were numerous in the 1860s, although some of the abstention may also be considered the one way of "casting" votes in opposition.

Mormon women were excluded from participation in the male priesthood groups making religious and political decisions. The women did have their own organizations, but these were also subject to male control.

Mormon women had organized an auxiliary in Nauvoo, Illinois, in 1842, just twelve years after the church was founded. The group of eighteen women elected their officers, choosing Emma Smith, the wife of church founder Joseph Smith, as president. One of the group, Eliza Roxcy Snow, wrote a constitution and by-laws. However, Joseph Smith rejected the constitution and reorganized the Relief Society, as the women's auxiliary came to be called, under the male priesthood. From then until the present day, officers of the society are appointed by male church leaders, not elected by their female co-workers. However, the Relief Society was, and continues to be, a conduit by which LDS women could make public their religious concerns. LDS women took part in their first united political action when, as members of the Nauvoo Relief Society, they drafted a petition seeking protection for the community of Nauvoo and delivered it to the Illinois governor.[16]

The Relief Society was reorganized in Utah in 1867 to carry out relief and "for the accomplishment of every good and noble work." It again became, like other women's organizations around the country, both religious and secular, a vehicle for women's participation in the community and in politics. Through the society, Mormon women organized to take political action on many issues, including both support for and against women's rights. Much of this action has been encouraged and directed not by the women themselves, but by church leaders.

The Relief Society was one of the many women's organizations which proliferated on an immense scale in the nineteenth century. It claims to be the oldest as well as the largest active women's organization in the United States. (All Mormon women are automatically enrolled as members at age eighteen.) The Relief Society was a charter member of the International Council of Women (1888) and of the National Council of Women (1891); however, since the 1980s, that membership has not been maintained. These organizations served to integrate women into the political culture by providing functional representation for women's concerns. Many, including the Relief Society, had politically oriented civic programs. These organizations attempted to shape opinion on many issues and mediated between women and the public sphere.[17]

Three major issues activated women in the political sphere in the nineteenth century—the abolition of slavery, temperance, and woman suffrage. The first two were not issues in Utah. Governor Young accepted slavery as a biblically sanctioned institution. Utah Territorial law allowed the practice of slavery, although black slaves were few in number. Indentured servitude, on the other hand, proliferated, particularly in southern Utah as the Territorial Assembly acted in 1852 to control the trade in Indian servants which had been established under Mexican law. (Slavery and indentured servitude ended in Utah, as in the rest of the nation, in 1865 with the Thirteenth Amendment to the Constitution.) Nor was temperance an issue. Mormons were bound by their health code, the Word of Wisdom, to shun not only alcoholic beverages but also tobacco, coffee, and tea. Utah women were not, therefore, politicized by participation in these two issues of public policy.

Woman suffrage was, however, a major issue in Utah. It was an issue entangled with the "Mormon Question"—whether a theocracy would be tolerated in the midst of a democracy. Utah woman suffrage became symbolic, not just of women's liberation from subject status, but also of the political control of the LDS Church. That political control became focused in the national imagination on the practice of polygamy in Mormon country which, in turn, created a constitutional conflict over the meaning and scope of liberty and democracy in the United States. Both Mormon theorists and their critics appropriated woman suffrage to explain woman's nature and woman's rights.[18]

Even as the Mormons were establishing their theocracy in Utah, in which a few white males governed other males and all women, certain women in the United States were demanding equal rights with men. At the Women's Rights Convention held in Seneca Falls, New York, in July 1848, more than a hundred men and women signed a Declaration of Sentiments and Resolutions, including the resolution calling it "the duty of women of this country to secure to themselves the decreed right to the elective franchise." Those who signed the document pledged themselves to the principles that men and women were created equal and that men had no intrinsic right to exercise authority over women except with their consent. This declaration struck at the very heart of patriarchy.

Even without the vote, Northern women organized in church-related and reform-related societies to further the cause to abolition slavery.[19] During the Civil War, women on the Union side were effectively mobilized to support war efforts, and afterwards women campaigned for the dominant Republican Party, establishing habits of volunteerism which continue to mark women's work in political parties. During the eleventh National Women's Rights Convention in May 1866, participants created the American Equal Rights Association to influence Congressional debates on the Fourteenth Amendment to the Constitution, which came to include language giving all persons having "equal protection of law." In 1867 the Kansas ballot included referenda on Negro suffrage and woman suffrage. Both lost by wide margins, though woman suffrage did better than Negro suffrage.

Members of the New England Woman Suffrage Association (organized 1868) proposed a strategy for women suffrage. They suggested a gradual process to enfranchise women in the District of Columbia and the territories, to be followed by a Constitutional amendment at some unspecified time in the future. More radical suffragists led by Susan B. Anthony and Elizabeth Cady Stanton lobbied for an amendment that defined suffrage as a right of citizenship and enfranchised women as well as black men.

In 1869 the Equal Rights Association split in two. The American Woman Suffrage Association, which was descended from the New England

Association, agreed to withdraw opposition to the Fourteenth Amendment and to work within the Republican Party. The National Suffrage Association, led by Anthony and Stanton, limited its membership to women and followed a program of more aggressive tactics, including bringing cases to test in court the constitutionality of denying voting rights to women.[20]

It was during this period of Reconstruction that woman suffrage in Utah was proposed. In 1867–69, New York suffragist Hamilton Wilcox, a leading member of the Universal Franchise Association, proposed experimenting with woman suffrage in the territories, particularly in Utah. He reasoned that the experiment could be made in a territory where there was a large female population. As a fringe benefit, the Mormon marriage system of multiple wives might be eliminated. Utah could be "reconstructed" by enfranchising women, who would thereby be enabled to cast off the bonds of polygamy in the same way that enfranchised African Americans in the South were casting off the bonds of that other "relic of barbarism"—slavery.

The *New York Times* popularized this proposal. An editorial in January 1868 declared: "Female suffrage might perhaps be tried with novel effect in the territory of Utah—the State of Deseret. There the 'better half' of humanity is in such a strong numerical majority that even if all the other half should vote the other way, they would carry the election. Perhaps it would result in casting out polygamy and Mormonism in general. . . . Here would be a capital field for women suffrage to make a start, and we presume nobody would object to the experiment."[21]

In December 1868, George W. Julian of Indiana, one of the "radical Republicans" of Reconstruction, sponsored legislation to enfranchise the women of the western territories (H. R. 1531). When it stalled in Congress, Julian introduced a second bill which proposed suffrage for women in Utah only, with the justification that women there would use the ballot to stop plural marriage. Representatives of Wilcox's group spoke in support of the bill, explaining that women should be given the same rights that were extended to the "ignorant freedmen of the South."[22] If the project succeeded in Utah, it could be extended elsewhere. If not, only Mormons would suffer.

The bill was supported by Utah's Congressional delegate William Henry Hooper. When asked by Julian if he spoke for the leading men of Utah, Hooper allowed that he did not, but he said he knew of no reason why they "would not also approve it."[23] The bill, however, and that proposed by Senator Samuel C. Pomeroy, Republican from Kansas, to amend the Constitution granting franchise on the basis of citizenship only, died in committee.

During 1869, the issue of woman suffrage was much discussed in the Utah press. The *Deseret News,* edited by LDS Church authorities George Q. Cannon and Charles W. Penrose, endorsed the "experiment": "The plan of giving our ladies the right of suffrage is, in our opinion, a most excellent one. Utah is giving examples to the world in many points. . . . Our ladies can prove to the world that in a society where the men are worthy of the name, women can be enfranchised without running wild or becoming unsexed.[24]

Franklin D. Richards, editor of the *Ogden Junction,* supported woman suffrage. His wife, Jane Snyder Richards, and his daughter-in-law, Emily S. Richards, worked tirelessly for the cause. The *Utah Magazine,* a weekly literary journal published by E.L.T. Harrison and William S. Godbe, maintained that "women should be eligible for everything," although the editor reassured readers that "all that women want is the *right* to vote. . . . Practical turmoil will have no charms for the mass of women."[25]

The Godbe family was the center of women's rights activities in Utah at this time. William and three of his four wives—Annie Thompson, Mary Hampton, and Charlotte Ives Cobb—were all involved. They made the initial contacts with eastern suffrage leaders and convened the first meeting in Utah Territory dealing with woman suffrage. One of the Mrs. Godbes (first name not recorded) was among the distinguished guests at the twentieth anniversary celebration of the inauguration of the women's rights movement held in New York City in 1870. The Godbes were involved in a newly organized reform movement within the Mormon community—the "New Movement" which hoped to make polygamy a personal choice, not a religious tenet. National suffragists hoped that Godbe women's political activism gave credibility to the claims of the "curative power" of the vote.[26]

However, most Mormon women embraced suffrage not as a way to throw off their "bonds," but rather to publicly defend polygamy. Mormon women became politicized to support the very institution many others hoped their suffrage would destroy. During the first week of January 1870, the women of the Fifteenth Ward in Salt Lake City met to express their opposition to a bill proposed in Congress by Illinois Representative Shelby M. Cullom, designed to enforce the anti-polygamy law of 1862. With Sarah M. Kimball presiding, the women unanimously supported resolutions protesting the bill. Mormon writer and organizer Eliza Roxcy Snow suggested that similar meetings be held throughout the territory.

On January 13, 1870, a "great indignation meeting" was held at the old tabernacle on Temple Square. Despite the inclement weather, nearly 6,000 women of all ages rallied to object to the Cullom Bill. For the next six weeks, mass meetings of women were convened throughout the territory to sustain resolutions protesting the proposed legislation. The *Deseret News* explained that these "women's rights meetings" were to "assert the dearest of all women's prerogatives, mainly her right to choose a husband. . . . Viewed in this light we think the indignation meetings of the ladies of Utah are deserving of consideration by all."[27]

These indignation meetings were called and presided over by the so-called "leading sisters," the elite, most powerful women in Mormon society.[28] They commanded the supporting sisters who were officers of the local Relief

Societies and who, in turn, could call for support from thousands of the female rank and file. Mormon women used this religious network to mobilize quickly in particular causes or projects and to provide supportive friendships so important in women's political action.

In the midst of this mass action by Mormon women, the Utah Legislative Assembly considered the propriety of granting the suffrage to women. On January 27, 1870, the Committee on Elections was asked to consider the matter. After two weeks of discussion, members of both houses passed by unanimous vote a bill enfranchising women.[29] Brigham Young and other Mormon leaders—both men and women—had decided it would be helpful if the Utah legislature should pass an act granting woman suffrage. William Clayton, Utah's delegate to Congress explained: "To convince the country how utterly without foundation the popular assertions were concerning the women of the Territory, some members of the Legislative Assembly were in favor of passing the law; . . . others favored it, convinced of its propriety by the arguments of the friends of the great political reform."[30]

That some legislators were convinced of the rightness of woman suffrage on its own merits is possible. The use of woman suffrage to change public opinion negative to LDS women and their support of polygamy seems the more dominant motivation. LDS male leaders were not persuaded to woman suffrage by the rhetoric or actions of women; they had every confidence that the enfranchised Mormon women would vote as they were instructed. As William Clayton observed: "There are not many women here but will sustain all the measures of the authorities better than some of the men do."[31]

On February 12, 1870, Territorial Secretary and Acting Governor S. A. Mann signed into law the act conferring suffrage upon women twenty-one years of age or older who had resided in the territory six months, were born or naturalized in the United States, or were wives, widows, or daughters of native-born or naturalized citizens. Women were still ineligible to hold high judicial, legislative, or executive offices, though they might be allowed to hold minor positions.[32]

The act enfranchised about 43,500 women. Two days after the act was signed into law, municipal elections were held in Salt Lake City. Twenty-five women exercised their newly gained right to vote. Brigham Young's grand-nice Seraph Young was reportedly the first woman to cast her ballot. Six months later Utah women went to the polls to cast their ballots in territorial elections. About two thousand women entered the polling places through the separate women's entrances and cast their vote.[33] Many of these women had participated in civics classes sponsored by the Relief Society under the direction of Sarah M. Kimball.

In these elections of 1870 in which women voted, political parties emerged in Utah. Elections in Utah, thereafter, became livelier. Previously with candidates selected by LDS authorities and run without opposition, there was no campaigning. There was a lot of voter apathy. Voters knew the chosen candidates would be elected whether they voted or not. However, in 1870 the Liberal Party was organized to oppose the church's candidates. William S. Godbe, Edward H. Tullidge, T. B. H. Stenhouse, and others of the New Movement, who had been expelled from the church, formed the nucleus of the party. Their *Utah Magazine* became the *Salt Lake Tribune,* the vehicle for non-Mormon sentiments. After the paper was sold to outsiders in 1873, its editorial stance shifted away from suffrage. Agitator Cornelia Paddock was allowed even more latitude to use its pages to attack polygamy; she also attacked woman suffrage, as used by Mormon women, as meaningless.[34]

The LDS Church countered by organizing the People's Party. Both parties held conventions and mass rallies at which women participated. Women served on the governing state committee of the People's Party. (Women who served on the committee in the next decades included leading sisters: Mary Isabella Horne, Sarah M. Kimball, Emmeline B. Wells, and Emily S. Richards.)[35] Mormon women were much more involved in People's Party activities than non-Mormon women were in Liberal Party activities.

In fact, as LDS women continued to support their religious leaders by voting for church-approved candidates and by defending polygamy on public platforms and in memorials to Congress, non-Mormons increasingly opposed Utah woman suffrage. Those opponents noted that voting requirements for women were less strict than those for men in Utah. Women who were themselves not citizens could vote if they were married to citizens. The several wives of male citizens could all vote, even if they were not citizens. And the church was converting thousands of women in Europe and bringing them to Utah.[36]

National suffrage leaders carefully watched the Utah experiment. The suffrage movement had been split over several issues: the support for the Fourteenth Amendment, the association with feminist Victoria Woodhull, whose views on marriage were vigorously attacked, and the question of strategy: whether to focus on a national suffrage amendment or to concentrate on the states. Underlying these issues were, however, two different philosophies.

The fearful reactions to the rapid demographic and economic changes affected middle class social arrangements. Those having to do with family produced an ideology of "a woman's place" which adamantly asserted the sacredness of home and motherhood. The American Woman Suffrage Association was supported and directed by people who were attracted to that ideology, the National Woman Suffrage Association by those willing to attack it.

Others supportive of the cultural ideal of "true womanhood" vehemently opposed woman suffrage altogether. The cult of true womanhood defined a sphere secluded from public life where women could demonstrate their moral superiority and power over men. Turning submission into a noble virtue and self-sacrifice into a patriotic duty, the canon of domesticity was by the 1870s generating a large market for magazines and manuals that taught women proper feminine conduct by emphasizing gender differences. Using the most popular of these publications, *Godey's Lady's Book and Magazine,* a group of nineteen women noted for their social prominence and marriages to politically powerful men published, in May 1871, a petition to the U.S. Congress remonstrating against votes for women. This marks the "official" beginnings of women's anti-suffrage mobilization.[37]

It was a mobilization which, ironically, contradicted their argument against the vote since they petitioned legislators and produced propaganda for mass consumption—tactics not unlike those of the suffragists whose behavior they scorned. The elite, wealthy women who led the anti-suffrage campaign were very engaged in public affairs—often enjoying prestige as volunteers in various projects. They perceived no need of the ballot for themselves and regarded a mass electorate as a threat to their social position and political power. Their efforts help explain why 480 legislative campaigns in the first forty years of suffrage agitation yielded only four suffrage victories, all in the western states.

The suffrage fight in Utah was imbued with the language of "true womanhood." The Mormon system of multiple wives was considered an affront to Victorian sensibilities. Ironically Mormon women defended the system with rhetoric supportive of the idealogy of "woman's place." And certainly after the church became more "respectable," its leaders promoted this ideology in opposition to the women's rights movement. However, during these early years, it was the more radical NWSA which supported Utah woman suffrage and the conservative AWSA which was reluctant. LDS Church leaders accepted the NWSA support as helpful in their fights against anti-polygamy legislation and for statehood. As George Q. Cannon explained: "The extension of suffrage to our women was a most excellent measure. It brought to our aid the friends of women suffrage."[38]

In June 1871, while touring the western United States on behalf of woman suffrage, Elizabeth Cady Stanton and Susan B. Anthony, visited Salt Lake City and met with both New Movement and LDS women. They were invited to address the public from the Salt Lake Tabernacle; one meeting lasted five hours. Stanton, the mother of seven, included advice about limiting the number of children a woman should have. Subsequently, she was barred from Mormon podiums, but not from Mormon audiences. Stanton and Anthony continued to support suffrage for women in Utah, although even the NWSA did not admit Utah women as delegates until 1879, when Emmeline B. Wells and Zina Young Williams Card were chosen to attend the suffrage conference in Washington, D.C.[39]

For Stanton and Anthony, no marital arrangement was ideal for women. The Mormon arrangement was not offensive enough to the two feminists to prevent them from supporting woman suffrage in Utah.[40] For other suffragists, however, it seemed so outrageous that they demanded that women in Utah be disenfranchised. Suffrage had obviously not inspired Mormon women to act against the system of plural marriage nor against the political power of the Mormon Church. As Pauline W. Davis, the organizer of the 1870 celebration which Mrs. Godbe attended, explained: "In Utah it [woman suffrage] is of less account because the women are more under a hierarchy than elsewhere, and as yet vote only as directed."[41] It was the political power of the Mormon theocracy which many feared, and Mormon women voters only strengthened that power.

But Mormon women themselves felt powerful. They did not want to be rescued from polygamy. They treated polygamy as a feminist cause, as an institution which had the capacity to liberate women and help them develop independence. And in the *Woman's Exponent,* started in 1872 by Edward L. Sloan of the *Salt Lake Herald,* but from its inception edited by and for women, all of the themes in women's rights which circulated nationally were discussed: dress reform, health, equal pay with men, access to higher education, and rights to speak in public. Its longtime editor Emmeline B. Wells used its pages to keep Utah women in touch with the women's movement in the rest of the country. By 1881 Utah writer Edward Tullidge could declare that the *Exponent* "wields more real power in politics than all of the newspapers in Utah put together."[42]

The defense of polygamy continued to involve many rank and file LDS women in public action. They attended mass meetings and signed petitions opposing the several anti-polygamy bills which were considered in the U.S. Congress. In February 1873, the so-called Utah Bill was introduced by Senator Frederick Freelinghuyser of New Jersey. He called for the annulment of women suffrage and the extension throughout Utah of the "common law of England." Woman suffrage associations in Boston, New York, Indianapolis, St. Louis, and Santa Clara, California, were among the many associations which lobbied against its passage.[43]

It should be noted that attempts to repeal woman suffrage were also made in Wyoming. In January 1872, Governor John A. Campbell vetoed the repeal act passed by the Wyoming Territorial Legislature, saying: "No legislator has a right to disfranchise his own constituency." He pointed out that women as voters and jurors had conducted themselves with as much good sense as men.[44] These efforts to repeal woman suffrage were indicative of the growing opposition and the changing political climate. Never again would woman suffrage be gained so easily as it had in Wyoming and Utah. The move for woman suffrage in Idaho had already died in 1871 with a tie vote in the territorial legislature. (Idaho's state constitution was amended in 1896 to allow woman suffrage.)

In the general national political chaos of 1872, the Republican Party emerged victorious but devoid of reform pretensions. Reestablishing national stability replaced Reconstruction radicalism as America's political goal. Opportunities for winning women the vote were at an end, at least for the time being. Women suffrage failed in Colorado in 1877 by a vote of 16,000 against and 6,666 in favor. (Colorado had entered the Union in 1876 with the provision that women could vote in school elections. Not until 1893 did a Populist-supported woman suffrage referendum pass the Colorado voters.)

In January 1876, with other anti-polygamy legislation being considered in Congress, Mormon women again held mass meetings. They petitioned for repeal of the anti-polygamy laws of 1862 (the Morrill Act) and 1874 (the Poland Act). They also asked that each married woman in Utah be granted the right to homestead land in her own name.[45] The delegation of Mormon women which went to Washington to carry the petition visited woman suffrage leaders. Belva A. Lockwood, the first woman lawyer to be permitted to practice before the Supreme Court, was one of those appointed by the NWSA to denounce any congressional action to disfranchise the women of Utah.[46]

However, other women were politicized in support of anti-polygamy efforts. In 1878 more than 200 women attended a mass rally chaired by Sarah Ann Cooke, a disaffected Mormon.[47] Utah anti-polygamists prepared letters to the women of the nation and to national clergy denouncing polygamy and also drafted a memorial to Congress asking that Utah statehood be delayed. More than 250,000 signatures from across the country accompanied the petition to Congress. In November of that year, a group of women launched the "Ladies Anti-Polygamy Society," with former Mormon Sarah Ann Cooke as its first president, Gentile Jennie Anderson Froiseth as vice president, and Cornelia Paddock as secretary. Froiseth became the editor (April 1, 1880, to March 1883) of its *Anti-Polygamy Standard*.[48]

Froiseth is an example of a woman who gained confidence and skills through work in clubs. She helped found in 1875, the Blue Tea, Utah's first women's literary club. That network of non-Mormons became the organizational basis for the anti-polygamy movement in Utah. Froiseth took her campaign "to fight to the death that system which so enslaves and degrades our sex," to the national arena as she went on speaking tours of churches in New York and New England.[49]

In 1880 Liberal Party members brought a case testing woman suffrage by seeking a writ of mandamus requiring Robert T. Burton, the Salt Lake City Registrar, to strike from the list of voters the names of Emmeline B. Wells, Cornelia Paddock, and Maria M. Blythe, and the names of all other women before a certain date. The Territorial Supreme Court ruled that Burton had performed his duty in registering the women. In 1882 another test case was brought before the Third District Court. A registrar of Salt Lake City refused to place the names of women on the list of voters. Justice James A. Hunter sustained the Legislative Act of 1870 under which women voted.[50]

That same year Congress passed the Edmunds Act which disfranchised all polygamous men and all women cohabiting with polygamous men. Of the approximately 67,000 voters in the Territory, including 16,750 women, over 25,000 were disfranchised. The Utah Commission was set up to administer an oath before persons were allowed to vote. In the meantime, another, the fifth, statehood petition was sent to Congress. Three of the seventy-two delegates who had been elected to the convention to prepare the state constitution were women: Emmeline B. Wells, Sarah M. Kimball, and Elizabeth Howard. Women actively supported this statehood petition. It was refused.

Illinois Senator John A. Logan had introduced in Congress in February 1882 an amendment to repeal woman suffrage in Utah. That provision was included in the 1887 Edmunds-Tucker Act, which included other anti-polygamy measures. Thus, the only vote on woman suffrage taken by the full Congress in the nineteenth century was negative.[51] Mormon women had protested its eminent passage in mass meetings and through petitions. National suffrage leaders had rallied to their cause. However, woman suffrage in Utah was tied to the "Mormon Question." The act denied political rights to all women, even those who did not practice polygamy. Suffrage was being treated, not as a fundamental right for women citizens but as a weapon in the fight against the power of the LDS Church.[52]

In 1888 Emily S. Richards and Charlotte E. Brown (a non-Mormon) were appointed to represent Utah at the National Suffrage Convention in Washington, D.C., and there were authorized to form a Utah suffrage association. After several preliminary meetings of LDS women leaders in the office of the *Woman's Exponent,* a public call was made for a meeting in the Assembly Hall on January 10, 1889, to organize a Territorial Suffrage Association. Margaret Nightingale Caine, wife of John T. Caine, Utah's delegate to Congress, was elected president.[53] One hundred women were enrolled.

The national association appointed Emily S. Richards and Jennie A. Froiseth as state organizers. Froiseth refused to serve. Richards organized auxiliary societies in fourteen counties. By 1890 there were 300 paid members. For the next several years, annual meetings were held in Salt Lake City and delegates were sent to the national meetings. In 1890 the Utah Association held a large picnic celebrating Wyoming's statehood, whose constitution included woman suffrage. In 1892 a large rally celebrated Susan B. Anthony's birthday. By then the National American Suffrage Association had been formed (1890) from the two factions of the woman suffrage movement. The NAWSA concentrated its energies in the next decades on winning suffrage, but not equal rights, for women.

In September 1890, the Manifesto which withdrew public support for new plural marriages, was issued by LDS Church President Wilford Woodruff, after the Edmunds-Tucker Act had been declared constitutional by the U.S. Supreme Court in May 1890. This accommodation to national norms allowed the church to survive and prosper. By 1892 the Republican and Democratic parties had replaced the People's (Mormon) and Liberal (non-Mormon) parties. This division of Mormons and non-Mormons into a new configuration of political localities divided Mormon women on partisan issues, but not on suffrage.

In 1894 Congress passed the Enabling Act for Utah statehood. Susan B. Anthony wrote to the members of the Woman Suffrage Association of Utah urging them to fight to include their suffrage in the state's new constitution. The first evidence of the women's intention to do so appears in the platforms of the political parties which were ratified in conventions in September 1894. The eighteenth of the Republican Party platform's twenty-one planks was: "We favor the granting of equal suffrage to women." The Democratic platform was more emphatic: "The Democrats of Utah are unequivocally in favor of woman suffrage and the political rights and privileges of women equal with that of men, including eligibility to office."[54]

After the election was held in November, the president of the WSA of Salt Lake City, Dr. Ellen B. Ferguson, urged members to visit the newly elected delegates to the constitutional convention to see if they intended to put woman suffrage in the constitution. That women did their work is evident in the *Tribune's* report that "a strong sentiment in favor of giving women the right to vote is manifest by the delegates."[55]

On March 11, eight of the fifteen members of the committee on elections and suffrage met to consider approving a passage taken from the Wyoming constitution: "The rights of citizens of the State of Utah to vote and hold office shall not be denied or abridged on account of sex. Both male and female citizens of the State shall enjoy equally all civil, political and religious rights and privileges." Fred J. Kiesel, a non-Mormon businessman from Ogden, cast the one dissenting vote.

On March 18 both the Salt Lake and Utah Suffrage Associations presented memorials to the convention summarizing the reasons Utah women should have political equality with men. Seventy-five women crowded into the convention hall to present the memorials. For the next month the issue of woman suffrage was discussed in conventions, in the local press, in public debates, in church meetings, and in private conferences.

Many non-Mormons opposed the inclusion of woman suffrage in the constitution, concerned that the addition of some thirty thousand women to the voting rolls, four-fifths of them Mormons, would concentrate power in the hands of Mormon leaders. In April non-Mormons called a meeting in Ogden; they advised that the question of granting woman suffrage beyond participation in school elections would be postponed until a special election could be called by the first legislature.[56]

Mormon male leaders were divided on the matter. Brigham H. Roberts, a Democrat elected from Davis County and one of the Seven Presidents of the First Council of Seventy (the third tier of Mormon General Authorities after the First Presidency and Twelve), argued that the suffrage measure would hurt chances for statehood. He warned further that participation in the political arena would drag women from their high pinnacle. Orson F. Whitney, a Mormon bishop and future apostle, countered with the theory that women would help

Martha Hughes Cannon
(1857–1932), noted physician
and the first elected woman
state senator in the United
States, n.d.

purge away all that was unclean in politics. The woman suffrage section passed
by a vote of 75 to 14, with 12 absent and 5 excused. This action was upheld
April 18 in another vote (69 to 32) to reconsider the suffrage article.[57]

Susan B. Anthony and Dr. Anna Howard Shaw arrived in Utah May
12 and participated in a Rocky Mountain suffrage conference, held in the hall
where the constitutional convention had adjourned a few days before. For
two days the suffrage leaders spoke in meetings and were feted at receptions.
Mormon women leaders, such as Wells, Jane S. Richards, and Zina D. H. Young,
were prominent at these events, as were non-Mormon women like Corinne M.
Allen, whose husband, Clarence, had voted in favor of suffrage as a member of
the constitutional convention and was elected to Congress in 1895.

On November 5, 1895, the new constitution, with the woman suffrage
article, was put to male voters. Women were not allowed to vote. Sarah E.
Nelson Anderson had gone to court after a registrar refused to put her name
on the voting list. The Territorial Supreme Court had ruled two to one (the

dissenting opinion was given by the Mormon justice, William H. King) that women had not been enfranchised by the Enabling Act. Out of a total vote of 38,992, 7,687 or about one-fifth of the male voters opposed the adoption of the constitution.[58] The largest percentage of the "no" votes came from counties where there was a substantial non-Mormon vote. When Utah became a state January 4, 1896, it became the fourth to have woman suffrage.

A few women had been placed on the tickets in 1895—Emma McVicker, a non-Mormon educator, for Superintendent of Public Instruction, Lillie Pardee for the state senate (she was later appointed clerk of the Senate), and Emmeline B. Wells for the state house. They withdrew after the negative Supreme Court ruling on women enfranchisement. However, in the 1896 election women voted and ran for office—Dr. Martha Hughes Cannon, Emmeline B. Wells, and Lucy A. Clark for the state senate; Sarah E. Nelson Anderson, Eurithe K. LaBarthe, Martha Campbell, and Mrs. F. E. Stewart for the House.

Some concern was expressed prior to the November election about the low number of women registered to vote. An editorial in the *Deseret News* complained that "many of the women of Salt Lake City and county have neglected to register, either through indifference or opposition to the idea." The article further exhorted women to register as a civic duty, using their influence to purify and elevate local politics.[59] Women did register to vote in numbers only slightly fewer than men. In Salt Lake City 9,085 men and 8,596 women registered; in the county 3,937 men and 3,196 women registered.[60]

It was a year of victory for the Democratic-Populist tickets. The women running as Republicans lost. Dr. Cannon became the first woman state senator in the United States—in a contest in which her friend and woman suffrage co-worker Wells and her husband, Angus M. Cannon, lost. Anderson and LaBarthe, both non-Mormon Democrats, won their contests, and eleven women were elected throughout the state to positions of county recorder. However, all of the women legislative candidates ran behind their tickets.[61] In all subsequent elections, except those of 1900 and 1910, women have run for political offices in Utah.

The shift from local to national parties was challenging for Utah women. The local People's-Liberal struggle had emphasized the division between Mormon and non-Mormon. Adopting the national two-party system resulted in a new political alignment that often pitted Mormon women leaders against each other in different parties and united Mormons and non-Mormons in the same party.[62]

As a result of the prolonged Republican campaign to crush polygamy, Mormons were inclined toward the Democratic Party. However, as they worked to stabilize and expand the church's business interests, many Mormon leaders supported the Republican Party with its protective tariffs and pro-business stance. Most members of the Liberal Party, upon its dissolution, moved into the Republican ranks. Some Mormon women leaders like Wells joined male leaders in the Republican Party. And some non-Mormon women like Anderson and LaBarthe swelled the ranks of the Democratic Party.

The Socialist Party, organized nationally and in Utah in 1901, also brought together Mormons, non-Mormons, and non-religious people, 10 percent of whom were women.[63] Socialism was a popular cause in the West, and socialist women in Utah were mostly married housewives, a significant percentage of them active Mormons. Until 1912 the Socialist Party was the only national political organization unequivocally supporting full voting rights for women.

Women were also drawn to the Progressive Party which supported Theodore Roosevelt when he bolted the Republican Party in the 1912 election. That was a banner year for women candidates. Ten women, four Republicans, two Democrats, three Progressives, and one Socialist ran for the state legislature; and Margaret Zane Cherdion was selected as the first woman in the United States to the electoral college.[64]

Also 1912 saw the election in Kanab, Utah, of an all-women board, with Mary E. Woolley Chamberlain as chair and mayor. Chamberlain (serving under the name Howard to make less public her status as one of the six wives of Thomas Chamberlain who had spent 1888–89 in the state penitentiary for unlawful cohabitation), in reviewing her two years of service, downplayed her election as a "joke" but evaluated the all-women board as having done "more for the town than all the male Boards they have ever had."[65]

The fight for national woman suffrage continued through these years. In 1899 Carrie Chapman Catt, chair of the National Suffrage Association, visited Utah. A meeting was called and steps taken to form a Utah Council of Women to assist the suffrage effort in other states. (The Council of Women developed into the League of Women Voters.) The officers included women active in Utah woman suffrage efforts and other politics: Emily S. Richards (who wrote *The Republican Catechism Criticized and Amended for the Benefit of the Women of Utah* to convince women to join the Democratic Party) was president; Elizabeth A. Pugmire Hayward (elected in 1914 to the state House of Representatives and in 1918 to the Senate), Mrs. Ira D. Wines, Dr. Jane Wilkin Manning Skolfield (elected in 1912 to the state House), and Mrs. B. T. Pyper as vice-presidents; Elizabeth M. Cohen (elected in 1900 as delegate to the Democratic National Convention, the first woman delegate in the nation) secretary; Anna Thomas Piercy (elected in 1918 to the state House) as assistant secretary; and Hannah S. Lapish as treasurer.[66]

However, in the fourteen years following the triumphs of 1896, the woman suffrage movement met only a succession of defeats. In fact, some scholars suggest that victories in Wyoming, Colorado, Utah, and Idaho actually hampered the cause. Anti-suffragists were able to raise fears about the links of suffrage to populism and socialism, political movements which held "outsider" status in the nation as a whole. Even in the West, woman suffrage stalled. Suffrage

Kanab Ladies Town Board, 1912–14. The woman in the center is Mary E. Woolley Howard (Chamberlain),when she was chairman of the board and mayor of Kanab.

supporters were not able to translate into a widespread political movement the particular circumstances which had supported woman suffrage. In Wyoming it was about the hopes that suffrage would attract more Euro-American women to the region. In Utah it was about protecting the rights of a religious minority. In Colorado and Idaho woman suffrage was linked to supposed threats by national fiscal conservatives on the mining economy of the Rockies.[67]

During these years, the Utah Council met monthly to raise some money and write letters and petitions to aid the national cause. Then, between 1910 and 1914, seven more western states—Washington, California, Oregon, Arizona, Kansas, Nevada, and Montana—embraced woman suffrage. These successes were due to a shift in the arguments used by women's rights leaders and to the association of woman suffrage with Progressivism, a reform movement which sought the purification of society, a movement particularly successful politically in the West but which gained widespread national support.

People like Carrie Chapman Catt replaced the earlier feminists who had died or retired by the turn of the century. Catt and the new leaders evolved a set of tactics and a low level of rhetoric designed to minimize controversy. Historian Aileen Kraditor has called it a shift from the "argument from justice" which emphasized the inalienable rights of women as individuals, to an "argument from expediency," which emphasized the ballot as an agent for reforming society.[68] The new leaders deemphasized the principle that men and women had identical rights to engage in public activities and exploited instead the traditional assumptions about woman's separate sphere—a sphere which complemented man's and from which women could elevate the moral level of government, cope with human problems, and protect the family if only they could acquire the vote.

Progressivism represented an effort to clean up corruption, disease, and poverty. In this period of general commitment to "reform" (meaning, to extend democracy and eliminate social injustice), the suffragists were able to identify their own cause as being part of the Progressive coalition. The cause thus achieved legitimacy and broad-based support. When the national amendment for woman suffrage was ratified by the Utah Legislature in 1919, it was state senator Elizabeth Pugmire Hayward, long identified with populist and progressive politics activities, who introduced the measure.[69]

And just as woman suffrage became respectable, middle class, and middle-of-the-road, so too did Mormonism. Woman suffrage leaders tempered those ideas most likely to offend public sensibilities to secure the vote. By 1919, LDS leaders, bloodied in the 1904–07 Senate hearings over whether monogamous apostle and senator Reed Smoot should keep his seat, had strenuously disavowed the rhetoric of theocracy and embraced the rhetoric of mainstream democracy.[70]

Smoot's election had represented to some the continued power of the LDS Church in Utah politics, and they questioned whether his loyalty would be to church rather than country. Utah women were also drawn into the prolonged controversy. Corinne Allen used her positions as president of the Utah Mother's Congress (founded in 1898) and leader of the Municipal League (1897), which fought against prostitution, to influence the national congress, which formed an anti-Smoot coalition. Prominent non-Mormons launched the American Party to "free people from apostolic rule." Elizabeth Cohen, former president of the Women's Democratic Club, led the Women's American Club in attacks on senators who supported Smoot. Mormon women organized to accuse Cohen of lies and women's groups of being "the blind tools of certain political conspirators engaged in a relentless persecution of the Church of Jesus Christ of Latter-day Saints . . . to degrade American womanhood."[71] The outcome was that Smoot retained his seat and went on to create a Republican Party machine that dominated Utah politics until 1932.

The practice of polygamy went underground, clung to by those fundamentalists who would not accept the change in policy. It continued as the trait most identified in the public mind with Mormonism, but was publicly ignored by the church and, until recently, privately treated as a skeleton of history. The legacy of polygamy haunts Mormon women, continuing for many as the symbol of women's basic inequality in the church.

This basic inequality was not challenged by the Mormon women leaders as they became involved in politics. They politicked in support of their church and to protect its place and privilege. Most LDS women who became involved in politics did so, not to overthrow patriarchy, but to extend their domestic sphere into "municipal housekeeping," political purification, and protective social reform. Mormon women also became involved to show themselves capable, intelligent, and independent in countering the image as sluts or slaves.[72]

There were feminists who challenged male privilege, such as Charlotte Ives Cobb Godbe, who worked for woman suffrage because it was morally right for women to participate in their government. Utah populist and socialist Kate S. Hilliard lectured against Mormon "priesthood sexism" and all organized religion as hindrances to women's rights. But even these women were not misfits or malcontents on the periphery of society. They worked within established systems and with other women—Godbe was treasurer of the Territorial Suffrage Association in 1889; Hilliard was a state organizer for the Utah Federation of Women's Clubs in 1902.

Respectable women were involved in the Utah woman suffrage effort—married, mothers, active in church and community work. Respectable women ran for office and worked in the political parties. Many of the women who ran for office during the first decades after statehood had been involved in the suffrage effort: Cannon, Wells, Clark, Anderson, Coulter, Hayward, and Wolstenholme.[73] And although women who had worked together for Utah suffrage were separated in partisan politics, many continued their friendships and worked together for national suffrage and for local causes. Capable, intelligent, energetic women formed networks to politically promote self-education, child protection, and urban improvements. One example is the kindergarten movement of the 1890s which resulted in 1903 legislation establishing kindergartens in every Utah town of over 2500 residents.[74] Another is the support led by state legislator Amy Brown Lyman, a future Relief Society general president, for the Federal Maternity and Infancy Act (or the Sheppard-Towner Act, 1921) to provide better maternity and infant care. Both efforts linked Utah women to the national political arena.[75]

Some of the women who ran for political office in Utah prior to 1920 had professional careers—Martha Hughes Cannon and Jane Wilkin Manning Skolfield were medical doctors, Mary Anna Clark Geigus Coulter was a lawyer, Grace Copp Stratton Airey was an osteopath, Cloa Pearl Huffaker Clegg was a school teacher, and Emmeline B. Wells and Kate Hilliard were journalists. All were involved in club work—Eurithe LaBarthe and Antoinette Brown Kinney were presidents of the Ladies Literary Club; Lily Clayton Wolstenholme and Anna Holden King helped found the Women's Republican Club. These politicians organized other women in church or community projects which involved public action. Annie Wells Cannon founded the first Red Cross chapter in Utah. Delora Edith Wilkens Blakely created the Sarah Daft Home for the aged.

Nationally woman suffrage had limited impact on politics. It failed to help women achieve equality of legal, economic, or social rights. Women did not vote as a reform bloc or in any pattern different from men. Woman suffrage simply doubled the electorate. Some scholars argue that anti-suffragist women were perhaps right in predicting a loss of power for women as they lost their place "above" politics, as the force of moral order. But it was a loss which had more to do with changing economics and gender roles than with suffrage. Many men and women rejected domesticity as an ideal. Much of the municipal housekeeping and charity work that had belonged to the woman's sphere was surrendered to government functions. Lacking a sense of common ground, women fragmented politically. In rejecting the woman's sphere as an organizing principle, women did not act as a separate political bloc.[76]

However, the level of organization among women after 1920 remained high. Women still joined women's organizations as they had for generations. And new organizations were created, including the American Association of University Women (AAUW) and the YWCA. The National League of Women Voters evolved into a "good government" rather than a feminist organization, its premise being to ready women for political life. Scores of new associations of women professionals were also founded between 1915 and 1930. Women in Utah joined local affiliates of all these organizations, worked to educate the public, and lobbied for specific bills.

A good example of women who continued to organize for political influence in Utah is the Women's State Legislative Council of Utah. It was organized in 1920 with delegates from women's organizations and Jeannette A. Hyde as president to "investigate and study subjects of state and national interest for the purpose of influencing and bringing to fruition beneficial legislation for the state of Utah."[77] Like the League of Women Voters, it involved many women through the years as researchers, writers, and advocates. In 1926, for example, the tax committee, led by Florence Kimball published its research on *Fundamentals of Utah Taxation.* The committee recommended that some provision should be made whereby financially poor school districts might receive adequate funds to "care properly for the educational needs of children."[78]

During the 1920s, as women continued to be politically active mostly through organizations rather than as individual candidates, the national political parties made appeals to potential women voters by setting up women's divisions which mirrored women's clubs. However, unlike women's clubs, these party organizations were not controlled by women, but rather by male elites. The Republican Party was particularly successful nationally in creating a place for women to gain leadership experience while they did the work of party "housekeeping." By the 1940s the image of the Republican Party club woman had become a stereotype.

One of the most accomplished of these Utah Republican club women was Ivy Baker Priest. She achieved national fame, not through winning an election but through working for the election of others. She got into Republican Party work with her mother, a community activist in Bingham,

Reva Beck Bosone ran for Congress against Ivy Baker Priest in 1950 and won. This election garnered national interest because Bosone entered politics through more traditional male routes (law and public service). Bosone was the eleventh woman admitted to practice law in Utah (1930). Photo, 1954.

Utah. Priest became a delegate to the state Republican convention in 1937 and to the national convention in 1948. She lost her bid for Congress in 1950 but her campaigning, particularly among women voters, for the 1952 election of Dwight D. Eisenhower won her the appointment as U.S. Treasurer, a position in which she served eight years.[79]

In her 1950 run for Congress, Priest lost to the incumbent, Reva Beck Bosone. Although not the first national election in which women were pitted against each other, this election was still unusual enough to generate national attention. Unlike Priest and most women who ran for office in Utah and the nation, Bosone did not enter formal politics through service in community and party organizations. She entered through the routes more traditional for male legislators: law and public service. In 1930 Bosone was the eleventh woman admitted to practice law in Utah. She got involved in Democratic Party politics through Elise Furer Musser,[80] the national committeewoman, and Carolyn Wolfe, the state chair of the party. Bosone was elected to the state legislature and then, in 1936, was elected as Utah's first woman judge. She ended her twelve-year stint on the bench to again run for office and was elected in 1948 as Utah's first woman member of Congress. In Congress she became the first woman to serve as a member of the Interior Committee. Although she won again in 1950, she lost other bids in 1952 and 1954 during the Republican insurgency.[81]

Women in Utah, as well as the nation, continued to be involved in politics much less often through elected office than through the hard work of sisterhood in their own groups and the hard work of sustaining campaigns for their political parties. If women were elected, it was many times more often at the local level than at state and federal levels. Hundreds of thousands more women worked within organizations to bring various issues to public attention and to impact policy rather than to be public and to make policy.[82]

In 1972 Jean M. Westwood from West Jordan, Utah, became the first woman to be elected chair of a national political party. Although not well-known publicly, Westwood had been a "tough, loyal soldier" in the Democratic Party.[83] That same year the U.S. Senate passed and sent on to state legislatures for ratification the Equal Rights Amendment to the Constitution which declared: "Equality of rights under the law shall not be denied or abridged by the United States or any State on account of sex."[84] Spurred by the revival of feminism in the late 1960s and 1970s, the ERA received much early support as thirty states ratified it within one year of its Senate approval. Utah was not one of those states. (Ten of the thirteen western states ratified the ERA by 1974; Idaho voted to rescind its ratification in 1977.)

Women had established Utah branches of the National Organization of Women (1966) and the National Women's Political Caucus (1971), both organizations mobilized to remove legal barriers to women's economic, social, and political equality with men. However, other Utah women joined competing networks of women to oppose those efforts, such as the National Committee to Stop ERA (1972) which became the Eagle Forum (1975), both headed by Phyllis Schafly, who had been a speechwriter for Barry Goldwater. The fight over the Equal Rights Amendment paralleled the fight over woman suffrage with women using political strategies of rallies, publications, lobbying, and demonstrations against each other.[85]

This time, however, LDS Church leadership was critical of "women's liberation." It tasked its Special Affairs Committee in 1974 to work against ratification of the ERA by soliciting Relief Society leaders to publicly oppose the ERA and by funding and directing local efforts to prevent ratification.[86] Thereby, thousands of LDS women again participated in the American political process, albeit with an agenda and direction from a male hierarchy. The First Presidency issued a formal statement against ratification in 1976. The ERA ultimately failed to achieve ratification by the required thirty-eight states, even though the deadline for ratification was extended to June 30, 1982. This defeat, part of the conservative backlash that gained momentum in the mid-1970s, did not reflect national public support for the amendment which never fell below 54 percent.[87]

Organizations formed to oppose the ERA rapidly expanded to organize women in a broader agenda of political and social conservatism. Anxieties about changes in gender roles and about waning male relevance became linked to the larger conservative agenda. Ironically many who defended the importance of women's domestic roles deviated from those roles in the conduct of their own lives as they worked hard to recruit other women to engage in political activities to oppose issues raised by feminists.[88] By the time there was another contest for Congress between two women candidates in Utah, the modern women's movement and its opposition had recruited and trained many women lobbyists and candidates.

In 1994 Enid Greene Waldholtz unseated incumbent Karen Shepherd in the Second Congressional District. Unlike Bosone and Priest's cordial race of 1950, this race was acrimonious and, as it turned out, fraudulent. Although Shepherd was a graduate of BYU, married and the mother of two, she had also been president of the Equal Rights Legal Fund and the owner of *Network* magazine (1978–88), aimed at women progressives. She was labeled "anti-family." Greene, the newcomer to politics, benefitted from the conservative tide. She became the "darling" of the Newt Gingrich Congress, especially when she gave birth to a daughter during her term. However, when it was discovered that her husband had embezzled huge sums of money from her father to finance the campaign, Greene chose not to run for reelection.

Public womanhood continues in Utah and the nation into the twenty-first century. Increasing numbers of women run for public office at every level of government. Women are reelected at close to the same rate as incumbent men. Among all voting-age people, women have voted at higher rates than men in every presidential election since 1984.[89] And in the election year of 2004, no group received more attention than the 22 million unmarried women who were eligible to vote but had not cast ballots in the 2000 presidential election.

Women have always been involved in politics through their own organizations. They have trained themselves about public issues and have worked to impact public policies. Politics is not just about elections, government, and public affairs; it is about the power to influence decisions made within human groups. Politics is about setting an agenda for public debate. This book which declares that women and women's ideas and experiences matter in Utah history is a political act.

NOTES

1. Center for American Women and Politics, *Facts on Women Candidates and Elected Officials,* 1995–2004; retrieved in July 2004 from http://www.cawp.rutgers.edu/Facts/Officeholders/cawpfs.html.

2. Barbara B. Smith and Shirley W. Thomas, "Roles for LDS Women," *Encyclopedia of Mormonism,* 5th ed., vol. 4 (New York: Macmillan, 1992); retrieved in April 2005 from http://www.lightplanet.com/mormons/basic/family/mothers/women_roles_eom.htm.

3. Elizabeth M. Cox, *Women, State, and Territorial Legislators, 1895–1995: A State-by-State Analysis, with Rosters of 6,000 Women* (Jefferson, N.C.: Mcfarland & Co., 1995), 29.

4. See, for example, Amy Calazza, "Does Women's Representation in Elected Office Lead to Women-Friendly Policy?" *Institute for Women's Policy Research Publication* #910, May 2002; retrieved July 2004 from http://www.iwpr.org/pdf/i910.pdf.

5. Utah Department of Health, "Sociodemographics of Utah Women," *Women's Health in Utah, 1996;* retrieved in July 2004 from http://www.health.state.ut.us/action2000/section1.pdf. See also Institute for Women's Policy Research, *The Status of Women in Utah: Highlights*; retrieved in July 2004 from http://iwpr.org/states/pdf/national.pdf.

6. Lori C. Beaman, "Molly Mormons, Mormon Feminists and Moderates: Religious Diversity and the Latter Day Saints Church," *Sociology of Religion,* Spring 2001; on-line version accessed July 2004 via LookSmart at http://www.findarticles.com/p/articles/mi_m0SOR/is_1_62/ai_73692409.

7. See, for example, Lawrence Foster, "From Frontier Activism to Neo-Victorian Domesticity: Mormon Women in the Nineteenth and Twentieth Centuries," *Journal of Mormon History* 6 (1979): 3–22.

8. For an argument that polygamy fostered community loyalty, see Kathryn M. Daynes, *More Wives than One: Transformation of the Mormon Marriage System, 1840–1910* (Urbana: University of Illinois Press, 2001).

9. Martha Sonntag Bradley, The Mormon Relief Society and the IWY," *Journal of Mormon History* 21 (Spring 1995): 105–67.

10. Alan P. Gimes, *The Puritan Ethic and Woman Suffrage* (New York: Oxford, 1967), chap. 2. The description of Mormonism is taken from Leonard J. Arrington, *Great Basin Kingdom: An Economic History of the Latter-day Saints, 1830–1900* (Cambridge, Mass.: Harvard University Press, 1958), 3.

11. A good overview of the political roles of American women to 1900 is Louise M. Young, "Women's Place in American Politics: The Historical Perspective," *Journal of Politics* 38 (August 1976): 295–335. Helpful interpretive studies of woman suffrage are Eleanor Flexner, *A Century of Struggle: The Woman's Rights Movement in the United States* (Cambridge, Mass.: Harvard University Press, 1958); Aileen Kraditor, *The Ideas of the Woman's Suffrage Movement, 1890–1920* (New York: Columbia University Press, 1965). Marjorie Spruill Wheller, ed. *One Woman, One Vote: Rediscovering the Woman Suffrage Movement* (Troutdale, Ohio: NewSage Press, 1995), accompanied the PBS American Experience television program of the same name.

12. *Constitution of the State of Deseret*, Article II, Section 10, 1859, retrieved April 10, 2005, from http://relarchive.byu.edu/19th/descriptions/constitution.html.

13. Klaus J. Hansen, *Quest for Empire: The Political Kingdom of God and the Council of Fifty in Mormon History* (Lincoln: University of Nebraska, 1968).

14. Ralph Lorenzo Jack, "Territorial Politics: 1847–1876" (Ph.D. diss., University of Utah, 1970), 69.

15. Ibid., 75–76.

16. Linda King Newell and Valeen Tippets Avery, *Mormon Enigma: The Biography of Emma Hale Smith* (New York: Doubleday, 1984), 127.

17. For examples of women's organizations in other parts of the country, see Mary Ann Irwin, "'Going About and Doing Good': The Politics of Benevolence, Welfare, and Gender in San Francisco, 1850–1880," *Pacific Historical Review* 68 (Summer 1999): 365–96; and Anne M. Boylan, *The Origins of Women's Activism: New York and Boston, 1797–1840* (Chapel Hill: University of North Carolina Press, 1992).

18. Sarah Barringer Gordon, *The Mormon Question: Polygamy and Constitutional Conflict in Nineteenth-Century America* (Chapel Hill: University of North Carolina Press, 2002), chap. 5. For the richest collection of the scholarship on Utah suffrage, see Carol Cornwall Madsen, *Battle for the Ballot : Essays on Woman Suffrage in Utah, 1870–1896* (Logan: Utah State University Press, 1997).

19. Gerda Lerner, *The Majority Finds Its Past: Placing Women in History* (New York: Oxford University Press, 1979), 112–28.

20. The Supreme Court ruled in a test case in Missouri: "There is no doubt that women may be citizens. They are persons, and by the fourteenth amendment 'all persons born or naturalized in the United States and subject to the jurisdiction thereof' are expressly declared to be 'citizens of the United States and of the State wherein they reside.' But, in our opinion, it did not need this amendment to give them that position. . . . If the right of suffrage is one of the necessary privileges of a citizen of the United States, then the constitution and laws of Missouri confining it to men are in violation of the Constitution of the United States, as amended, and consequently void. The direct question is, therefore, presented whether all citizens are necessarily voters." The court opined that they are not and continued: "No argument as to woman's need of suffrage can be considered. We can only act upon her rights as they exist. It is not for us to look at the hardship of withholding. Our duty is at an end if we find it is within the power of a State to withhold. Being unanimously of the opinion that the Constitution of the United States does not confer the right of suffrage upon any one, and that the constitutions and laws of the several States which commit that important trust to men alone are not necessarily void, we affirm the judgment [made in the lower court that the state of Missouri could lawfully define voters as men only]." *Minor v. Happersett*, U.S. 162, October, 1874.

    While the Missouri case was going through the courts, so was the case of Susan B. Anthony who had registered, cast a ballot in Rochester, New York, in a federal election, and then been arrested for "illegal voting." Anthony's conviction was not appealed. Doug Linder, "The Trial of Susan B. Anthony, 1873," *Famous Trials,* 2004, retrieved July 2004 from http://www.law.umkc.edu/faculty/projects/ftrials/anthony/sbahome.html.

21. Quoted in Ralph C. Jack, "Woman Suffrage in Utah as an Issue in the Mormon-Non-Mormon Press of the Territory, 1870–1887" (M.A. thesis, Brigham Young University, 1954), 35.

22. House Resolution 64: "To discourage polygamy in Utah by granting the right of suffrage to the women of that Territory," was introduced March 15, 1869. *Congressional Globe*, 41st Congress, 1st Session, 1869, 72. The fifteenth amendment to the Constitution which granted suffrage to black males was proposed in February 1869.

23. Edward W. Tullidge, *History of Salt Lake City* (Salt Lake City: Star Publishing, 1886), 435.

24. *Deseret News,* August 6, 1869. See also Thomas G. Alexander, "An Experiment in Progressive Legislation: The Granting of Woman Suffrage in Utah in 1870," *Utah Historical Quarterly* 38 (Winter 1970): 20–30.

25. Edward Tullidge, "Our Woman's Platform," *Utah Magazine* 3 (May 8 and July 31, 1869): 199.

26. For a rich discussion of the role of the New Movement in enfranchising Utah women, see Lola Van Wagenen, *Sister-Wives and Suffragists: Polygamy and the Politics of Woman Suffrage* (Ph.D. diss., New York University, 1994; printed, Provo, Utah: Joseph Fielding Smith Institute for Latter-day Saint History and BYU Studies, Dissertations in LDS History Series, 2003).

27. Ibid., 6–7.

28. Maureen Ursenbach Beecher, "The Leading Sisters: A Female Hierarchy in Nineteenth Century Mormon Society," *Journal of Mormon History* 9 (1982): 25–40.

29. Leonard J. Arrington, *Brigham Young: American Moses* (New York: Alfred A. Knopf), 1985, 364. According to Susa Young Gates: "President Brigham Young called into council the leading men of the legislature, President George A. Smith, Lorenzo Snow, Abram O. Smoot, George Q. Cannon, and William Maughan, and he suggested the advisability of granting the right of suffrage to the women of Utah, committing the responsibility of the whole measure to Abram O. Smoot." Susa Young Gates, "Suffrage in Utah," manuscript, p. 17, in Susa Young Gates Collection, Box 17, Utah State Historical Society.

30. Quoted in Lola Van Wagenen, "In Their Own Behalf: The Politicization of Mormon Women and the 1870 Franchise," *Dialogue: A Journal of Mormon Thought* 24 (Winter 1991): 35. See also Beverly Beeton, *Women Vote in the West* (New York: Garland, 1986).

31. Quoted in Jack, "Woman Suffrage," 72.

32. Van Wagenen, *Sister Wives and Suffragists,* 7.

33. Gates, "Suffrage in Utah," 12; Beeton, "Woman Suffrage," 11.

34. Van Wagenen, *Sister Wives,* 36–37.

35. Gates, "Suffrage in Utah," 12.

36. Beverly Beeton, "Woman Suffrage in Territorial Utah," *Utah Historical Quarterly* 46 (Spring 1976): 2, discusses the concern in both England and the United States for the "surplus women problem."

37. Susan E. Marshall, *Splintered Sisterhood: Gender and Class in the Campaign against Woman Suffrage* (Madison: University of Wisconsin Press, 1997), 19–20.

38. Quoted in Beeton, "Woman Suffrage," 118.

39. "Both Utah women addressed the convention, attended congressional committee meetings, called upon the President of the United States and presented the case of the 'Mormon' women to the Lady of the White House, Mrs. Hayes." Gates, "Suffrage in Utah," 15.

40. Elizabeth Cady Stanton, *Eighty Years and More* (New York: European Press, 1898), 286, hoped that the Mormon women would eventually give up their vigorous

support of the Mormon "arrangement" and come to "understand that governments and religions are human inventions, that the Bible, prayer books, catechisms, and encyclical letters are all emanations from the brain of man." Then they would "no longer be oppressed by the injunctions that come to them with the divine authority of 'Thus saith the Lord.'"

41. Pauline W. Davis, *A History of the National Women Rights Movement* (1871; reprinted New York: Source Book Press, 1970), 25.

42. Quoted in Ileen Ann Waspe LeCheminant, "The Status of Women in the Philosophy of Mormonism from 1830 to 1895" (M.A. thesis, Brigham Young University, 1942); see also Sherilyn Cox Bennion, "The *Woman's Exponent:* 42 Years of Speaking for Women," *Utah Historical Quarterly* 44 (Summer 1976): 222–39. Edward Tullidge was involved with the Mormon dissenters of the New Movement. In 1877 he published *The Women of Mormondom* (New York: Tullidge and Crandall) with help from Joseph Smith's widow, Emma Hale Smith Bidamon.

43. See Mary Isabella Horne, "Appreciative," *Women's Exponent*, January 15, 1874. See also "A resolution expressing appreciation to the women's suffrage associations accepted unanimously at a large meeting of the Senior and Junior Co-operative Retrenchment Association," n.d., manuscript, Susa Young Gates Collection, Box 17, Utah State Historical Society. Under English common law, women were not regarded as legal persons or entities. The Mormons had declared common law not operable in Utah. Members of Congress seemed less concerned that Utah women voted than that they did not vote against LDS candidates. Some members saw woman suffrage in Utah as "another monstrous instance of Mormon craft" by which Mormon leaders could offset their potential loss of power through the influx of non-Mormons by enfranchising women who would vote for Mormon candidates. Mormon male leaders countered with arguments that the majority of women did not vote. Thomas Fitch, *Arguments . . . in Opposition to House Bill 3791* (Washington, D.C.: Gibson Brothers Printers, 1873) 17–19.

44. Quoted in Beverly Beeton and G. Thomas Edwards, "Susan B. Anthony's Woman Suffrage Crusade in the American West," *Women in the West,* edited by Glenda Riley (Manhattan, Kan.: Sunflower University Press, 1982), 11.

45. The Homestead Act (1862) turned over vast amounts of the public domain to private citizens. A homesteader had only to be the head of a household and at least 21 years of age to claim a 160–acre parcel of land. Since married women were not considered heads of households, only unmarried, widowed, or divorced women could claim homestead land.

46. Belva A. Lockwood, "The Disfranchisement of the Women of Utah," *Ogden Daily Herald,* June 9, 1883, 4. For descriptions of the mass meetings of Mormon women in 1870, 1876, and 1886 see Heather Symones Cannon, "Practical Politicians," *Mormon Sisters: Women in Early Utah,* edited by Claudia L. Bushman (1976, reprinted with a new introduction by Ann Firor Scott, Logan: Utah State University, 1997), 162–69.

47. Patricia Lyn Scott, "The Respected Mrs. Cooke: Sarah Ann Sutton Cooke," in *Worth Their Salt Too: More Notable But Often Unnoticed Women of Utah,* edited by Colleen Whitney (Logan: Utah State University Press, 2000), 1–27. See also Barbara

Haywood, "Utah's Anti-Polygamy Society, 1878–1884" (M.A. thesis, Brigham Young University, 1980).

48. Froiseth later used writings from the *Standard* to produce *Women of Mormonism or The Story of Polygamy as Told by the Victims Themselves* (Detroit, Mich.: C. G. G. Paine, 1886); available on-line at http://www.polygamyinfo.com/wom_book.htm. Frances Willard, president of the National Woman's Christian Temperance Union, then largest women's political organization in the country, wrote an introduction to the book.

49. Patricia Lyn Scott, "Jennie Anderson and the Blue Tea," *Utah Historical Quarterly* 71 (Winter 2003): 20–35.

50. Beeton, "Woman Suffrage in the West," 95–96; also Jean Bickmore White, "Gentle Persuaders: Utah's First Women Legislators," *Utah Historical Quarterly* 38 (Winter 1970): 41–42.

51. Sarah Barringer Gordon, "The Liberty of Self Degradation: Polygamy, Woman Suffrage, and Consent in Nineteenth-Century America," *Journal of American History* 83 (December 1996): 815–47.

52. That the Mormon women did vote as a block in support of the Mormon Church candidates and issues is obliquely admitted in the 1886 protest sent to Congress that the women were being deprived of suffrage "for no other reason than that we do not vote to suit our political opponents." *"Mormon" Women's Protest, An Appeal for Freedom, Justice and Equal Rights . . .* (Salt Lake City: Deseret News Co., 1886) 18.

53. Other officers elected were Lydia D. Alder, Nellie R. Weber and Priscilla J. Riter, vice-presidents; Cornelia N. Clayton, secretary; Charlotte I. Cobb Kirby, corresponding secretary; and Margie Dwyer, treasurer; Maria Y. Dougall, Nettie Y. Snell, Ann E. Grosebeck, Phoebe Y. Beatie, Jennie Rowe, members of the executive committee. Gates, "Suffrage in Utah," 15–16.

54. Jean Bickmore White, "Woman's Place Is in the Constitution: The Struggle for Equal Rights in Utah in 1895," *Utah Historical Quarterly* 42 (Fall 1974): 344–45, 347.

55. *Salt Lake Tribune,* March 4, 1895; quoted in White, "Woman's Place," 348. Ruth May Fox, active in the Utah Woman Suffrage Association and the Republican Party, noted in her diary going around several times with petitions, "to find out who [was] . . . willing the suffrage clause should remain in the constitution. Met with very good success." Linda Thatcher, ed., "'I Care Nothing for Politics': Ruth May Fox, Forgotten Suffragist," *Utah Historical Quarterly* 49 (Summer 1981): 249.

56. White, "Women's Place Is in the Constitution," 361.

57. Ibid., 363.

58. Results of the election given by Utah Commission, quoted in White, "Woman's Place Is in the Constitution," 364. Gates, "Suffrage in Utah," 18, lists the results as 28,618 for and 2,687 against.

59. The *Deseret News* comments on the women's participation in the 1896 election is the typical rhetoric about women's nullifying role and the evidence that the role then, as later, also included "domestic service": "In all the precincts, the ladies, who now are exercising the right of franchise for the first time in Utah for many years, were

much in evidence; their presence undoubtedly had much to do with the tranquility that has already been referred to. In addition to having a nullifying influence on . . . disturbances at the polls, they also set good examples of their zeal and activity . . . . Then again, they did much towards keeping the workers in bright cheer by the substantial bands, hot coffee and other good things that they gave to them from time to time." "Fight at Home," *Deseret News,* November 5, 1896, 1. According to the *Salt Lake Tribune Almanac*, 1899, 36, the first woman to vote in Utah after statehood was Mrs. George Mollins, who cast her ballot in the municipal election at the mining town of Mercur, April 21, 1896. The first woman office holder was Mrs. M. J. Atwood who was elected school trustee in Kamas, Summit County, January 9, 1886. Quoted in Jean Bickmore White, "Utah State Elections, 1895–1899" (Ph.D. diss., University of Utah, 1968), 123.

60. "Registration Record," *Deseret News,* October 26, 1896, 5.

61. For example, of the five elected to the state senate from the sixth district, Cannon had 7,868 votes compared to Caine 5,371, Haboor 8,429, Ridout 8,272, Whitaker 9,068. "Election Returns," *Deseret News,* November 3, 1920, 1.

62. For discussion of the shift into national political parties see Thomas G. Alexander, "Political Patterns of Early Statehood, 1896–1919," in *Utah's History,* edited by Richard D. Poll, Thomas G. Alexander, Eugene E. Campbell, and David E. Miller (Provo, Utah: Brigham Young University Press, 1978): 409–28. See also Kenneth G. Stauffer, "Utah Politics, 1912–1918" (M.A. thesis, University of Utah, 1972).

63. Sillito, "Women Socialists," 235–36.

64. Gates, "Suffrage in Utah," 22–23. Statistics compiled by Gates during 1915 show there were in Utah 65,000 men and 75,000 women voters. In 1914 90 percent of the women cast their vote, compared with 65 percent of the men. Gates, "Suffrage in Utah," insert page 11. Since voter surveys were not done, it is not known what percentage of women voters voted for women candidates.

65. Mary W. Howard, "An Example of Women in Politics," *Utah Historical Quarterly* 38 (Winter 1970): 62. Members of the board included Luella McAllister, Blanche Hamblin, Tamar Hamblin, and Ada Seegmiller. Susa Young Gates, *Utah Women in Politics* (Salt Lake City: n.pub., 1914), 16.

66. [Susa Young Gates], "Utah," in *The History of Woman Suffrage,* edited by Susan B. Anthony and Ida Husted Harper (1902; reprinted, New York: Arno Press, 1969), 645.

67. Gayle Gullett, *Becoming Citizens: The Emergence and Development of the California Women's Movement, 1880–1911* (Urbana: University of Illinois Press, 2000), 100.

68. Aileen Kraditor, ed., *Up from the Pedestal: Selected Writings in the History of American Feminism* (New York: Quadrangle Books, 1973), 110–31.

69. Delia M. Abbott and Beverly J. White, comps., *Women Legislators of Utah, 1896–1993* [Salt Lake City: Governor's Commission for Women and Families, 1993], 56.

70. Kathleen Flake, *The Politics of American Religious Identity: The Seating of Senator Reed Smoot, Mormon Apostle* (Chapel Hill: University of North Carolina Press, 2004).

71. *Deseret Evening News,* 22 June 1905; quoted in Jeffrey Nichols, *Prostitution, Polygamy, and Power: Salt Lake City, 1847–1918* (Urbana: University of Illinois Press, 2002).

72. Gary L. Bunker and Carol Bunker, "Woman Suffrage, Popular Art, and Utah," *Utah Historical Quarterly* 59 (Winter 1991): 32–51.

73. For biographical information on Utah women legislators, see Abbott and White, *Women Legislators of Utah.*

74. Carol Cornwall Madsen, "Decade of Détente: The Mormon-Gentile Female Relationship in Nineteenth Century Utah," *Utah Historical Quarterly* 63 (1995): 298–319.

75. Loretta L. Hefner, "The National Women's Relief Society and the U.S. Sheppard-Towner Act," *Utah Historical Quarterly* 50 (Summer 1982): 255–67.

76. Paula Baker, "The Domestication of Politics: Women and American Political Society, 1789–1920," *American Historical Review* 89 (June 1984): 620–47.

77. Women's State Legislative Council of Utah records, Special Collections, Marriott Library, University of Utah.

78. Florence Kimball and Mrs. H. S. Tanner, *Fundamentals of Utah Taxation* (Salt Lake City: Women's State Legislative Committee Tax Committee, 1926).

79. Stanford J. Layton, "Ivy Baker Priest, Treasurer of the U.S.," in *Worth Their Salt: Notable But Often Unnoticed Women of Utah,* edited by Colleen Whitley (Logan: Utah State University Press, 1996), 219–27.

80. Juanita Brooks and Janet G. Butler, eds. "Utah's Peace Advocate, the 'Mormona': Elise Furer Musser," *Utah Historical Quarterly* 46 (Spring 1978): 151–66. Furer Musser began her social service and political career with work in Neighborhood House, a settlement house patterned after Hull House, established in Salt Lake in the 1890s. She became influential in Utah's Democratic Women's Club, served as state senator (1933–34), and was the only woman delegate (appointed by President Franklin D. Roosevelt) to the Buenos Aires Peace Conference in 1936. It was she who responded to a national effort to organize women state legislators. In 1936 she helped organize the Utah Order of Women Legislators. One of their topics of discussion in 1938 was the Equal Rights Amendment then before Congress.

81. Beverly B. Clopton, *Her Honor the Judge: The Story of Reva Beck Bosone* (Ames: Iowa State University Press, 1980).

82. Janet A. Flammang, ed., *Political Women: Current Roles in State and Local Government* (Beverly Hills, Calif.: Sage Publications, 1984); also her *Women's Political Voice: How Women Are Transforming the Study and Practice of Politics* (Philadelphia: Temple University Press, 1997).

83. Jean M. Westwood, "The Political Status of Women—1974," *Wisconsin Academy Review* 20 (Spring 1941): 2–6.

84. The original Equal Rights Amendment was first introduced in Congress in 1923, three years after the Nineteenth Amendment was ratified. The initial language, changed in 1943, provided: "Men and women shall have equal rights throughout the United States and every place subject to its jurisdiction." It had been drafted by the radical suffragist Alice Paul, whose National Woman's Party had split from the

ranks of mainstream suffragism. Some form of the Equal Rights Amendment was introduced in nearly every succeeding session of Congress, but it was a half century before it received any serious attention. Martha Craig Daughtrey, "Women and the Constitution: Where We Are at the End of the Century," *New York University Law Review* 75 (April 2000): 6.

85. In the 1973 legislative session in which Utah lawmakers considered the amendment, members of the Governor's Committee on the Status of Women served as a steering committee for efforts in support of the measure. Other women, such as herbalist Reba Lazenby, were sponsored by the John Birch Society to organize HOTDOGS (Humanitarians Opposed to the Degradation of Our Girls) which succeeded in defeating ratification. Marilyn Warenski, *Patriarchs and Politics, the Plight of the Mormon Woman* (New York: McGraw-Hill, 1978), 182–87.

86. D. Michael Quinn, "The LDS Church's Campaign Against the Equal Rights Amendment," *Journal of Mormon History* 20 (Fall 1994): 85–155. Quinn maintains that "existing evidence verifies a . . . successful effort by the LDS Church to prevent ratification of the ERA in Arizona, Florida, Georgia, Illinois, Missouri, Nevada, North Carolina, Oklahoma, South Carolina, and Virginia." The church was also successful in its campaign to rescind ratification in Idaho. However, Mormons and their "ecumenical allies" were not successful in rescinding ERA ratification in California, Hawaii, Iowa, Montana, Texas, and Wyoming.

87. *The Equal Rights Amendment: Guaranteeing Equal Rights for Women under the Constitution*, United Commission on Civil Rights Clearinghouse Publication 68 (July 1981); retrieved April 2005 from http://www.thelizlibrary.org/suffrage/eracom.htm.

88. Susan E. Marshall, "Marilyn vs. Hillary: Women's Place in New Right Politics," *Women and Politics* 16 (1996): 55–75.

89. For most of the presidential elections since women nationally gained the right to vote, men have proved more likely to vote than women. In 1964, for example, 72 percent of voting-age males participated, versus only 67 percent of voting-age females. However, as more women participated in the workplace, more women voted. (Employed people are more likely to vote.). U.S. Census Bureau, "Women by the Numbers, 2004," retrieved in August 2004 from http://www.infoplease.com/spot/womencensus1.html.

12

Women's Life Cycles

1850 to 1940

Jessie L. Embry

In the twentieth-first century, Utah women can see many examples that they can "have it all." In public life, such examples include a woman governor, women who have served in the state and federal legislature, and women judges. Women are also successful business leaders, educators, entrepreneurs, and blue-collar workers. Professions that belong exclusively to women or men have apparently disappeared. As the chapters in this book have pointed out, there have always been outstanding women in many fields; but until recently, there was a pattern, or life script, that women were expected to follow and many Utah women accepted it. As historian Gerda Lerner explained, historically women's development

> was dependent on her relationship to others and was often determined by them; it moved in wavelike circuitous motion. . . . For the girls such rises were . . . closely connected to distinct stages in the biological life transitions from childhood to adolescence to marriage. . . . [This resulted in] a shifting of domesticity from one household to another and the onset of her serious responsibilities: childbirth, childbearing and the nurture of the family. Finally came the crisis of widowhood and bereavement which could mean, depending on her economic circumstances, increasing freedom or autonomy or a difficult struggle for economic survival.[1]

While other chapters in this book focus on characteristics distinctive to Utah women, this essay makes the point that Utah women were not greatly different from their sisters across the nation. Their lives also followed the expected life cycle. Although it focuses on Mormon women as the dominant majority and makes no effort to duplicate the information in Helen Papanikolas's chapter on ethnic women (see chap. 4), nothing in my research indicates that women of other faiths (see chap. 3) experienced their life stages or life cycles in ways that were dramatically different.

The first part of this chapter surveys the literature of life patterns over time as a vital and important part of understanding women's experience; then I show how the pattern for Utah women remained essentially the same from the frontier period until World War II. The "wavelike circuitous motion" Lerner described—birth, marriage, maternity, widowhood, and death—was the same for all of these generations to a striking degree. World War II gave women more employment options; and significant psychological and social changes developed from the women's movement of the 1960s and 1970s. Although many, perhaps most, Utah women still follow the same basic pattern, they must now do so as a conscious choice instead of growing up and into a script that had not fundamentally changed since their grandmothers' day. For this reason, the chapter focuses on the lifespan experiences of Utah women before World War II, and argues that they were more like other American women than they were different.

WHY STUDY LIFE CYCLES?

Studies like Lerner's consider that the life elements shared by most women are of greatest importance and seek to identify those patterns and their strengths, rather than writing from an assumption of uniqueness. There are advantages in viewing similarities in life patterns over time. As sociologist Tamara K. Hareven explained, "Because of the emphasis on social classes in a narrow, structural approach, more subtle relationships [have] escaped attention. Generations were treated as chronological sequences, rather than as stages in the life cycles."[2] By looking at cycles over several generations rather than seeking isolated patterns within a limited time frame, the historian can ask questions about how daughters used information from their mothers and grandmothers to adjust to new circumstances. As a second advantage, life cycle studies shift "the focus of study of human development from stages and ages to transitions and timing of life events."[3]

Does such an approach ignore individual lives? No, studying life cycles requires studying individual lives—many of them—to find the patterns held in common. The question of how many lives need to be studied to find genuine trends is important, yet social scientists have found that basic patterns become clear with a relatively small number of cases. In a study of bakers and their apprentices, Daniel Bertaux discovered that fifteen life stories gave him a fairly clear picture of the basic life structure. He learned a great deal from the first life story, and the second and third and fourth stressed new information that might have been lost in the first narrative. However, although "each new life brought something new, the proportion of the new versus the already known was getting smaller all the time."[4]

After reading over three hundred oral histories and approximately one hundred published life sketches, I agree with Bertaux about the pervasive power of the life-cycle pattern. The first stories I read provided a great deal of information. As I read the lives of more women, I found differences in each one, but the common pattern became more apparent. Although a significant percentage of these women were Mormons, their religious beliefs seem to have had little direct effect on their life cycles. Being female was more determinant then being Mormon.

Some critics of the life-cycle approach point out that, while women repeat the same patterns, timing of crucial events varies greatly from family to family and time period to time period.[5] Hareven agrees that such variation was especially true during the late nineteenth century when "pressing economic needs and familial obligations took precedence over established norms of timing." But only the timing changed, not the "set of sequences."[6]

Women's Life Stages and Frontier Challenges

During the early frontier period of Utah's settlement—about the first ten or fifteen years of each community—women often stepped out of their traditional roles to do what needed to be done. In 1854, Brigham Young encouraged the women at a conference to help harvest the crops rather than let them rot in the fields, but in 1864 Young told women in another conference that "plowing, raking, and making hay . . . this hard laborious work belongs to men."[7] By the 1870s and 1880s, federal census takers recorded that most women in Utah were "keeping house."[8]

According to Brigham Young, "It is the calling of the wife and mother to know what to do with everything that is brought into the house, laboring to make her home desirable to her husband and children, making herself an Eve in the midst of a little paradise of her creation."[9] Thus, Terrence Heaton, whose mother raised her children in Orderville in the early 1900s, explained that she "never did do any work outside of the home. She was a real homemaker."[10]

The typical pattern of a nineteenth-century woman's life was learning her female identity largely in terms of her future duties as a wife and mother from her own mother at home, receiving some education, and possibly—if school were abbreviated or marriage postponed—working at whatever job or trade her skill level could command. Such employment was almost always relatively unskilled and seen as temporary, even if it continued beyond marriage. Marriage, whatever its timing, came for nearly all women, followed by children, whatever their numbers. A woman trained her own daughters, grew old, contributed aid to her children as they began raising their own children, experienced widowhood, became increasingly dependent on her children for material and emotional support, and died while the cycle repeated itself.

Of course, there were exceptions to this pattern. Some girls died before maturity. Some never married. Some led lives disrupted by criminality (including prostitution), illness, or addiction. Some were widowed when they were young, others when they were older. Some predeceased their husbands, leaving their children to be incorporated into another woman's cycle. The discussion below, however, follows the traditional pattern.

FEMALE CHILDHOOD

Girls and boys in the nineteenth century learned their responsibilities from their mothers; and from childhood, their talents and drives were channeled in different directions. "For boys, the family was the place from which one sprang and to which one returned for comfort and support, but the field of action was the larger world," observed Gerda Lerner. "For girls, the family was to be the world, their field of action, the domestic circle."[11] Mothers were expected to teach "those traits that would ensure success in the domestic sphere—submissiveness, loyalty, gentleness and social grace."[12] Girls of good families learned from their mothers how to manage homemaking duties so that home became a shelter from worldly pressures for the men of the family.

Young girls imitated their mothers, role-playing their future. Reta Bartell, who grew up around the turn of the century in Cedar City, Utah, remembered:

> We imitated adults in our play. We played "mamas" and "daddy's" and at "keeping house." We dressed the cats in doll clothes and wheeled them around in the doll buggy because they were alive like babies were. . . . We used to cook dinner "for the men." We would set the play table with doll dishes and cut potatoes or apples for all the different foods. Then we would ask the boys to come and eat. They always behaved perfectly until all the food was gone; then they would tip the table over and run. We would vow that we would never ask them to eat again, but we always did.[13]

This example may reveal more about men and women's roles than Bartell meant it to.

In their study of nineteenth-century Mormon girls, Leonard J. Arrington and Susan Arrington Madsen asked: "What did these pioneer girls do? Mostly it would seem, they worked. They helped their mothers; they helped their fathers; they helped their grandparents, if one or more were near; they helped their neighbors; they helped their brothers and sisters. The specific tasks of the girl, in most instances, were to help with the housework and gardenwork."[14] As these girls worked with their mothers, they learned what would be expected of them when they became housekeepers in their own homes.

Much of this learning was the transfer of specific skills. Laura Clark Cook, who was born in the 1880s, remembered, "I would help Mother make soap and candles, churn butter, and do other household chores," including the Saturday duty of filling the kerosene lamps, trimming the wicks, and cleaning their chimneys. Yet "with all the work we had making candles, churning butter, making bread, filling the lamps . . . we had time to sit down and sew."[15] Ellis Reynolds Shipp of Pleasant Grove, who later became a physician, also learned

Young girl playing with her doll and buggy, role-playing her future.

to sew from her mother. "I was handy with my needle. I could sew and knit and do anything (I thought) that any woman could do, thanks to a wise mother's early training."[16]

Housekeeping frequently included caring for chickens or milking cows, and almost always meant gardening. Although all the work was necessary, much of it was monotonously routine. Mary Jane Mount Tanner complained in 1878, "I am neglectful of my diary, but there seems so little to write. One day comes and goes, and the next follows; the same routine of work is gone through, and the same remains to be done."[17]

Rhea Hart Grandy recalled that her mother, who lived in Preston, Idaho, just across the Utah state line, "had the garden mostly to herself. She didn't have much help with it. That is the way it is on a farm. The men would do the major work, and the women would take care of the garden."[18] Rhea's brother, Marcus Hart, recalled that his mother took great pride in her chickens.

Woman performing the domestic chore of peeling potatoes, Elfie Huntington, photographer, ca. 1904.

"In fact, we used to think that the chickens came first with mother. But we felt we were sort of a close second."[19] Jonathon S. Cannon explained, "We had cows that were problems, that were hard for anyone to handle and my mother could always handle them."[20]

Maurine Eyring Boyd of Thatcher, Arizona, the daughter of settlers from Utah, remembered milking as "very, very unpleasant . . . getting up early, rain or shine, when it was very cold. When it was warm, we had to contend with flies. I didn't know which was worse, the cold or the flies."[21] Daughters also helped with the extra work of harvest time. Zina Patterson Dunford of Bloomington, Idaho, also on the Utah-Idaho border, reported that, for each of their two crops of hay, "the men folks would do the mowing and raking. When it was time to haul it or stack it, then the rest of the kids would help. The girls would . . . drive the horses to unload [and] . . . help tromp the hay down on the load so that we could get more in."[22] Seneth Hayer Thomson learned how to thin, hoe, and top sugar beets. During World War I, when her brothers went to war, she and her sisters "did things that the boys used to do like pitch hay and shock grain."[23]

But the spheres of men's and women's activities were sharply differentiated; and after the temporary need or emergency was over, girls returned to house-related activities. Furthermore, women helped outside when there was an emergency, but

"Harvest time." The whole family unit was involved in the harvest, ca 1900.

men rarely helped in the home, even when the need was acute, although boys could sometimes be pressed into service. According to Howard Charles Woodfield, who grew up in North Ogden in the 1920s, "On a farm it is necessary for the whole family to work together to make it work. My mother's job was caring for the house. My father or any of us boys very seldom ever helped in the house. I had a sister, and she worked in the house part of the time and then out part of the time. The cleaning, preparing meals and actually drying of fruit and food was done by my mother with what help she could get from the boys."[24]

Mothers also taught their children values. For example, Amy Brown Lyman, later general president of the Mormon women's organization, the Relief Society, identified "loyalty to church leaders, industrious living, and church and community services" as central values" she had learned from her mother.[25] Dorthea F. Parent, also a Mormon, understood that "the main thing our parents wanted for us, especially daughters was to have testimonies of the gospel. They were really staunch in the Church."[26]

Some families stressed education more than others, depending on personal values and also the time period. To some parents, daughters needed only to read and write; others felt they should have some type of vocation, in case they needed to support themselves. According to Dorthea Parent, who lived in Benson, Salt Lake City, and Kamas, between 1900 and 1910, "My folks really wanted us kids to get an education. They tried to help us and encourage us all they could."[27]

Young Adulthood

The typical age at which Utah young women married depended, to some extent, on the decade and community. When a girl married in her teens and moved directly from her parents' home to her husband's home, she usually did the same domestic work, with the differences that it was a beginning household, rather than an established one, and that she now controlled the work rather than helping her mother. Others, however, worked outside the home before they married, although it is not possible to determine which proportion of women followed which pattern.

A study of age at marriage shows an unvarying pattern for Utah women who married between 1870 and 1915: the largest group were married by nineteen, the next largest were married by age twenty-four, and the next largest group married by age twenty-nine.[29] Or, to look at it a different way, 56.7 percent of the Utah women born between 1850–54 were married by age twenty, while 48.6 percent of the women born thirty years later did not marry until they were between twenty and twenty-four.[30] Their work did not, however, generate independence. Rather, according to one scholar, it was "only an extension of traditional values which regarded the family as the fundamental economic unit."[30] All family members were expected to contribute their labor to the family income, including daughters.

Wage-earning Utah girls frequently hired out as mother's helpers or "hired girls" to do housework, thus applying the skills they had learned at home from their mothers. In 1873, twelve-year-old Sarah Endiaette Young Vance of Fairview, Utah, hired out to work in the homes of other families. She "did everything from washing clothes and ironing to fixing meals and general housekeeping." When she was fifteen, she took care of a family in her hometown while the parents went to Salt Lake. "I did all the work and took care of the milk and made butter," she reported, "When they returned at the end of twelve days I had make enough butter to pay my wages."[31]

Other girls expanded their work experience from the home to the office. Loretta M. Rigby, at age nineteen, began work at the Sego Milk Products Company in Richmond in 1910, to help with family finances after her father died.[32] During the 1920s, after Violet Bird Alexander graduated from the eighth grade and attended high school for a part of a year, she worked at the beet dump of the Amalgamated Sugar Company in Mendon. She also clerked at the Mendon Post Office, helped cook for threshing crews, and did housework. She attended one more year of high school in Logan, then began working in the county treasurer's office in 1927. She married in 1931 and continued working until 1935 when the family moved shortly after the birth of her first child.[33]

Most young women chose traditional female jobs such as teaching, nursing, and office work when they had a choice of training. Two Parent sisters, Dorthea and Leonta, attended the LDS Business College during the 1910s.

Roy Winchester and Effie May Miller married at Mill Creek (Salt Lake County) March 25, 1896.

Courtesy Marjorie Winchester Scott.

Myrtle, a third sister, went to the University of Utah and became a teacher. Dorthea ultimately chose that profession as well. Two more sisters, Aurelia and Geneva, became nurses, while the youngest, Vesta, became a stenographer.[34]

Because of her childhood of "economic deprivation and poverty," Mary Jane Mount Tanner of Salt Lake City was determined to have a vocation that would bring her some financial security. She became a teacher in the 1850s.[35] Ada Palmer of Sandy taught in Grand County after she finished her normal education at the University of Utah in 1925. She had decided to become a teacher because "it only took one year to be certified," but while she was in school, the state changed its requirements to two years, thus doubling her projected training time.[36]

Lucile Barlow Clark of Bountiful decided to become a nurse and, in 1916, took a course in Salt Lake City offered by the Relief Society. She supported herself during that time by keeping house for a widower and his family. She graduated in 1918 during the flu epidemic so she had plenty of employment in people's homes. She also worked with Dr. Jane Scofield, one of her instructors, on obstetric cases in Salt Lake City.[37]

Even trained professions like teaching or nursing were seen as temporary, premarriage employment, however. Until World War II shortages forced reappraisal of policy, many school districts in Utah required women to quit teaching once they married, and nearly all of them required women teachers to resign when they became pregnant. Helen Peterson Redd, whom grew up in Wyoming and who was a teacher in San Juan County in the late 1920s, reported, "In our contract it said if we married during the year we forfeited our last month of wages and would not be rehired." Teachers who planned on marrying were also expected not to sign contracts.[38] She taught one year and did not sign a second contract since she planned to marry John Redd whom she had met in Utah. This contractual stipulation did not single out teachers for discrimination. It rather reflected the middle-class assumption that a woman, by choice, nature, and nurture would devote her full time to her husband and future children.

Some husbands felt uneasy about employed wives. Diantha Cox Sherratt worked in hotels and homes in Cedar City; but when she married in 1919, "my husband wouldn't allow me to work."[39] Thressa Lewis Frost, of Monticello, described her work experience "until I got married when I was twenty one."[40]

Courtship and Married Life

Western historian John Mack Faragher in his book on the Overland Trail reminds us, "It is important to remember how dependent rural women were upon marriage. The public world was closed to respectable women; alternative careers to that of housewife and mother were almost inconceivable."[41] Mary Jane Mount's description of her marriage to Myron Tanner probably mirrored the feeling of other women: "I had a strong manly arm to lean on for comfort and support; and his wisdom and good natural intelligence gained him a position of trust and honor in the Church and in society."[42]

Girls under age twenty who married during the 1870s through the 1890s nearly always married men significantly older than themselves. According to Geraldine Mineau, a researcher at the University of Utah, in almost 40 percent of Utah marriages during these three decades, the husband was more than six years older. Only 1 percent of women under twenty married younger men. In contrast, women who married after age twenty-five, married men who were either the same age or younger in 55 percent of the cases.[43]

In 1880, thirteen-year-old Catherine Heggie of Clarkston was clerking in a store when she met sixteen-year-old William Griffiths. They attended sleigh-riding parties and circuses, and eventually she married him in the Logan Temple in 1886.[44] Pearl Bliss met Herm Butt at stake conference in Monticello and saw him occasionally when he came to Moab to celebrations. After a couple of years of courtship, they married in 1932.[45] No women among the 400 that

I looked at for this chapter left a specific record of adjustment to marriage—sexual initiation, decision-making patterns, or discussions (if any) of fertility and child-rearing philosophies.

Childbearing Years

After marriage came "the dictatorial rule of a two-and-a-half-year cycle of childbirth, of which nineteen or twenty months were spent in advanced pregnancy, infant care, and nursing. Until her late thirties, a woman could expect little respite from the physical and emotional wear and tear of nearly constant pregnancy or breastfeeding.[46] This pattern, according to Colleen Whitley, "attracted little attention, even when it carries enormous social import, like the raising of the next generation of human beings."[47]

Geraldine Mineau's study shows that Utah women born in 1840, who would have been raising families during the 1860s, had 9.1 children. By the time women born during 1885–89 had families during the first decade of the twentieth century, they were having, on the average, 6.56 children.[48] For nearly all women born before 1859, the birth of the last child came at age forty, meaning that she had spent at least twenty years of her life had having children. That mother of nine had experienced eighty-one months of pregnancy at about two and a half year intervals, the first baby coming within the first eighteen months.[49] A nineteenth-century Utah woman would be, on average, sixty-two or sixty-three when her last child left home. She would die herself within the next two to seven years.[50] By the end of the century, childbearing was being completed at about the age of thirty-nine, a barely perceptible drop, then thirty-eight.

Although it is probable that some mothers felt overburdened by this cycle and faced a new pregnancy with dismay, most of those who left records reflected the convention that children were a blessing. Mary Jane Mount Tanner, who had nine children in sixteen years, wrote in her journal about the last: "The baby grows nicely and we all think him very sweet." Two years later, she recorded his birthday and called him "a pet with all the family."[51]

Many women had little medical assistance in childbirth. In the nineteenth and early twentieth century, often one midwife would deliver all the babies in the community. Ann Amelia Chamberlain remembered that Aunt Harriet Bowers was called by a Mormon official to be a midwife in Orderville with the promise that, if she went when she was asked, no mother she cared for would die. She delivered over a thousand babies and this promise was fulfilled.[52]

Marie Ekins Redd recalled that the midwife attending her first child's birth in Blanding in 1919 arrived, "just immaculate, hair done up nicely, dressed all in white." Marie was in labor all night with a complicated birth. "The cord was wrapped around the baby's neck, which kept her from being born. I was so exhausted. I had to be urged not to give up. Sister Palmer kept saying, 'Don't you want your baby?' 'Oh, yes,' I would answer but I was too exhausted to stay conscious. The midwife left with her hair all down. The poor dear, she looked like she was the one she had been in the hard labor." The second child was born with only a neighbor's help.[53]

In rural areas, midwives continued to provide almost all the obstetrical care into the late 1920s and 1930s. However, in urban areas, doctors began to take over obstetrical duties by the early 1900s. Mary Elizabeth Lindsay Bennion gave birth to eleven children in three communities, all delivered by physicians: a Dr. Fairbee in Granger, a Dr. Sharp in Salt Lake City, and a Dr. Budge of Logan between 1893 and 1913.[54]

CHILD-REARING

Mothers were responsible for child-care during a youngster's first five or six years virtually alone except for help from a neighbor, a sister, a mother, or a hired girl. When the boys were old enough to help with the fieldwork, the fathers took over responsibility for them. This divisional of emotional responsibility also meant that women bore the primary burden in illness and death of young children, not only of nursing them during illness, but of grieving when they died. Although the deaths of children are underreported, genealogy records available for Utah families indicate that more than 18,000 children died between 1879 and 1899, a mortality rate of 60.5 per thousand.[55] In 1917, the year before the influenza pandemic, the mortality rate was even higher—69.4 per thousand.[56]

Aurelia Spencer Rogers of Farmington had five of her twelve children die in infancy between 1860 and 1871. When Howard, the fourth child and the first to go, died, she recorded, "I have been so happy previous to this; the trials of poverty and sickness that we had passed through were nothing compared to this great sorrow that had overtaken me; and I mourned for my baby incessantly." As four more children died, Rogers almost lost faith in God but reconciled herself to this suffering with the explanation: "Perhaps all the people of God would have to pass through certain ordeals to prove whether they would trust in Him to the end."[57]

Erma Valentine Jacobs recalled a run of scarlet fever in Brigham City when she was eight or nine years old in 1912. All one summer the family was quarantined with the disease. Although none of her family died, others were not as fortunate.[58] Pearl Bliss Butt remembered an epidemic of diphtheria in Moab about 1902. "Several children died that winter; three from one family and two from another. In several families, one child died."[58]

Measles, chicken pox, and polio were other diseases which quarantined and killed children. During the flu epidemic of 1918, children were among the first victims. Many quarantined families had to depend on neighbors to leave food on their doorsteps. When a child or an adult died, the body had to be buried immediately without a funeral for fear of infection. The women consistently provided most of the actual nursing and neighborly care.

In such vulnerability and risk of emotional pain, many women, no doubt, found ways of distancing themselves emotionally from their children while others, like Aurelia Rogers, developed faith in the consolations of religion with its promised reunions. Still others developed especially tender ties with their children, particularly those between mother and daughter. The separate spheres of traditional gender relations fostered such closeness. LaRue Cox Jefferies felt that "Mother was my good friend. I was very close to her. We did many things together in the home like the sewing, the housework and everything. She was my friend and my counselor and helped through all my illnesses. She was just a tremendous help to me all that I did."[60]

Women's Work

Besides caring for children, there was work after marriage and plenty of it, but seldom employment. Between 1870 and 1920, the percentage of women in the Utah labor force was lower than the national average—5.2 percent in 1870 compared to the national average of 14 percent. By 1920, the rates stood at 15.7 percent for Utah and 20.4 percent nationally, a smaller gap.[61] Women could extend their household work into the marketplace in a minor way by selling milk, butter, cheese, poultry, eggs, and/or garden vegetables. Others took in boarders or laundry.[62] When Meda Lucille Jenkins was growing up in Newton during the 1880s through 1910s, the family "had cows to milk, and we separated the milk. [Mother] sold the cream, and that is what she ran the house on."[63] Elna Jonsson Merrill of Richmond, in Cache County, during the 1890s and 1900s, sold fruit from the family orchard and traded eggs at the local mercantile to buy matches, coal oil, and occasionally candy for the children.[64] Outside employment for mothers, as for daughters, was usually seen as temporary and usually required no training. LaRue Cox Jefferies's mother clerked in her husband's store in St. George. Lula Rigby Larsen's mother took over supporting the family financially when her father served a proselytizing mission for the LDS Church in the 1880s. "Those were hard times for my mother," Larsen recalled. By keeping a cow and chickens, she was able to sell eggs and make and sell "a little butter."[65]

For many women of this period, community service or church service supplied much of the sense of connectedness and contribution that employment now provides for some of their daughters. Zora Kay Hansen explained that her mother, raising her family in Mona during the 1900s and 1910s, didn't work outside the home, "but bless her! If there was ever anyone sick in the ward, she was right there with something to eat for them."[66] Pearl Butt's mother worked in the Relief Society in Moab during the 1890s and 1900s. "It seemed to me like she was gone fully half the time taking care of the sick and the dying, helping deliver babies, assisting in emergencies and helping out when there was illnesses."[67]

Even when the exceptional circumstances interrupted the cycle of generation-centered domesticity, it was seldom completely broken. After about 1880, the number of single women increased simultaneously with a gradual decline of polygamy and expanded economic opportunities for women. In 1870, there were 102.4 men for every 100 women; by 1890 the gender ratio had risen to 112.3 men for every 100 women. The balance continued to decline, but Utah women would not outnumber men until 1960.[68] Only 13 percent of Utah's women between ages twenty-five and twenty-eight were single in 1890, compared to the national average of 25.4 percent; by 1910, the figure stood at 17.5 percent for Utah and 24.9 percent nationally.[69]

Still, single women worked at "traditional" jobs as secretaries, and clerks. When they had no means of support, they were often dependent on their relatives.[70] Some postponed marriage to take care of aging parents, thus prolonging the daughter role. Ione Naegle Moss, who married in 1936 at age twenty-nine, described herself as "an old maid schoolteacher. . . . I couldn't get married before because Mother and the family needed my financial help."[71]

English professor Alice Louise Reynolds (1873–1938) never married but probably never described herself as "an old maid schoolteacher." She was proud of being Brigham Young University's first woman professor in a field other than the domestic sciences, achieved a remarkable record of study and travel, oriented her life toward serving others, and balanced her activities around people, profession, country, and church. She wrote to her sister Polly in her declining years: "I am not afraid to die. I have lived the best I could, and I am sure no girl or woman ever had a more wonderful life, with more opportunities, more privileges, more friends."[72]

Stena Scorup of Salina (1888–1950), also centered her single life around service to school and community. She taught school most of her life, served as Salina's mayor, and was a missionary for the Mormon Church. In contrast to Alice, she viewed her life as very ordinary and full of missed opportunities. She wrote:

> to my nieces and nephews and to all the previous and younger generation whom I adore and in whom I am so much interested. Do not follow my example. Get married and make a home of your very own and have as many children as you can educate as they should be. Do not get lost in your profession and work or allow home responsibilities, however urgent and necessary, deprive you of having a family and making a real home of your own for them.[73]

WIDOWHOOD

Another major interruption came when a mother died young and could not complete the cycle. In most cases, the father did not try to take on her tasks but simply "replaced" her, either by remarrying or by assigning the mother's duties to the oldest daughter. In 1861, when Ellis Reynolds Shipp was fourteen, her mother died. Ellis wrote, "I had never known grief. It was my first real sorrow. I became sorrowful and moody. I was no more the gay and lighthearted girl I had been." She became the homemaker for her father, two sisters, and two brothers, responsible for cooking, cleaning, and washing while her brothers took care of the farm.[74]

When Katherine Cannon Thomas's mother died in 1930 in Salt Lake City, Katherine was twenty-eight, the oldest of three children at home. Her father, a polygamist, left Katherine with full responsibility for her seventeen-year-old brother, who had polio, and her twenty-two-year-old sister, Sally, who was attending school. Katherine, a teacher, gave up their house because she didn't think she could keep paying on the mortgage, and rented an apartment for them. She said, "If I were going to pay for the food and rent for the kids, I would do what I could, but I couldn't do the impossible." Later a couple who ran an art store where Sally worked took Sally in.[75]

Widowhood, though a natural, and to some extent, inevitable part of the cycle, was seen as the ultimate disruption. Emmeline B. Wells married three times, twice as a plural wife. Her first husband, James Harris, deserted her in Nauvoo when she was sixteen, and she married Newel K. Whitney in 1845. He died in 1850, and she married Daniel H. Wells in 1852 as his seventh wife. She did not live with the rest of Wells's wives and longed for more attention from him. In 1874, twenty-four years after Whitney's death and while she was married to Wells, she recorded in her diary: "I was very low-spirited, every time anyone spoke to me I was crying. . . . I longed to see my husband who was dead. Why can we not call them to us in our grief and sorrow, why cannot our dead come back to us if only for one sweet hour?"[76]

When Lula Rigby Larsen's father died in 1906 after twenty-five years of marriage, leaving his wife with twelve children, she recounted, "Mother took it hard. She had been president of the Primary and president of the Relief Society and had been very active in the Church. I suppose it was because of the sorrow, strain and all. After that I don't remember her going out too much. Then her health began to fail."[77]

The emotional shock was exacerbated by economic uncertainty for most widows, especially if there were young children. Bernitta Frandsen Bartley's husband died of a heart attack in 1937 when he was thirty-three, leaving her with two preschoolers. When she was interviewed in 1982, she had been a widow for forty-five years. She explained that, despite the problems, "I raised two wonderful U.S. citizens and bought three homes. I did it with a sewing machine."[78] Other young widows received help from other family members. Dorothy Redd Jameson remembered that, after her father died in 1928, leaving ten children, Charles Redd, an uncle and the administrator of her father's estate, provided clothing and treats and gave the children jobs at his ranch as they got older.[79]

Older women who became widows often moved in with a daughter or son, "helping" as they were able. Zina Patterson Dunford remembered her Grandmother Patterson helping with the weaving during the early 1900s by winding the shuttles. Grandmother Patterson "was a dear old soul. She used to always have peppermints in her pocket . . . to reward us for any little thing we would do for her."[80]

Widows also relied heavily on their children for care when they became ill. Lucile Barlow Clark's grandmother moved in with her daughter after a stroke. "My mother was taking care of her in our home [in Bountiful] where she could be with her little family. I can still see her just as plain as I did then sitting in a black wicker chair by the north window in the kitchen.[81]

Sometimes, when timing, opportunity, and personality coincided, widowhood marked the beginning of a new phase. Some women launched into a second marriage. Others developed personal or professional interests. Emmeline B. Wells, after her shattering grief of 1874, editorialized in the *Woman's Exponent,* "Happy the woman who had the foresight to see that through forty years of experience she had matured the ability to commence a grand, useful second half of her life."[82] Sarah Melissa Granger Kimball was such a woman. After her mother and husband passed away in the 1860s, she adopted a daughter, became president of her ward Relief Society in Salt Lake City, and became active in the women's rights movement in the 1880s and 1890s. As her biographer summarized: "The last thirty years of her life would be public rather than private years, during which time her work with the Fifteenth Ward Relief Society would make her realize the value of her strong opinions and her administrative talents."[83]

Divorce

Divorce, though comparatively rare during this period and more a function of divorce laws than of marriage quality, also interrupted the traditional life stages for women. Divorce was always an option in Utah, though for the most part an unwelcome one. Between 1867 and 1909, more women than men sought divorces. The most frequent reasons were, in order of numbers, neglect, desertion, cruelty, and adultery.[84] Susa Young Gates, married at sixteen in 1872, gave birth to two children, and divorced after five years of marriage. She did not plan to remarry but instead decided she had a "destiny in this Church to fulfill" and became a faculty member at Brigham Young Academy. Her resolution lasted only five years. She remarried in 1880 and had eleven more children, only four of whom survived to adulthood, maintained an active life of participation in various LDS and public organizations, and became a voluminous writer.[85]

Summary

Although the economic, linguistic, and cultural settings of ethnic women in Utah meant that they experienced their life stages in different settings (see chap. 4), their major life events were very similar to those of Caucasian women in Utah. They were "dutiful daughters, wives, mothers, and homemakers. They

Four generations of one family visually represent the stages and cycles of women's lives. Martha J. Perkins Howell, Mary Lucille Perkins Bankhead, Ruth H. Jackson, and baby Juanita Spillman, now the mother of a new generation.[86]

nurtured, sustained, and consoled. They maintained order and tranquility and were the fixed point of reference in a chaotic and uncertain world."[86] The women described in this chapter could have lived almost anywhere in the United States. They grew up in homes where their mothers taught them their future responsibilities. While some went to school or found paid employment, at some point most married, had children, and kept house. Very few women in Utah were of a social class that freed them from the physical labor of maintaining a home, and even those affluent few, such as Jennie Judge Kearns, kept amply busy with charities. Mrs. Kearns funded and took an active interest in St. Ann's orphanage and school and also St. Mark's Hospital, both of them Salt Lake City landmarks. Death, divorce, and ill health modified these patterns, but they did not change what was seen as the ideal.

Historian Anne M. Butler and storyteller/editor Ona Siporin captured the similarities in women's life in their study *Uncommon Common Women: Ordinary Lives of the West.* Their summary of western women in general also fits Utah women: "The joys and griefs that enveloped western women transcended

Susa Young Dunford Gates with her daughters Emma Lucy Gates and Leah Dunford and an unidentified granddaughter.

cultural boundaries and brought together as one the common women of the American West. All women exalted [sic] at the first cry of a newborn child, all wept at the last death rattle of a beloved." They saw as a potential tragedy that these universal experiences for "women of all cultures" did not bring them "together in the unity of laughter and tears." Yet they held up the "universal truth—that all women, despite their uncommon lives, are bound together in the commonality of womanhood" and saw in this hope "the threads of unity for modern women of every class and race."[87]

Notes

1. Gerda Lerner, *The Female Experience: An American Documentary* (Indianapolis: Bobbs-Merrill, 1977), xxvi-xxvii.

2. Tamara K. Hareven, *Anonymous Americans: Explorations in Nineteenth Century Social History* (Englewood Cliffs, N.J.: Prentice-Hall, 1971), viii.

3. Tamara K. Hareven and Kathleen Adams, introduction, in *Aging and Life Course Transactions: An Interdisciplinary Perspective,* edited by Tamara K. Hareven and Kathleen Adams (New York: Guilford Press, 1982), xiii.

4.   Daniel Bertaux, "From the Life-History Approach to the Transformation of Sociological Practice," in *Biography and Society: The Life History Approach in the Social Sciencies,* edited by Daniel Bertaux (Beverly Hills, Calif.: Sage Publications, 1981), 133.

5.   Paul C. Glick, "The Life Cycles of American Families: An Expanded Analysis," *Journal of Family History* 5 (Spring 1980): 97–111.

6.   Tamara K. Hareven, "The Life Course and Aging in Historical Perspective," in *Aging and Life Course Transitions,* 22.

7.   Quoted in Carol Cornwall Madsen, "Survey of the Lives of Cache Valley Women in 1890," paper written for the Ronald V. Jensen Living Man-and-His-Bread Museum, 1979, 8.

8.   Julie Roy Jeffreys, *Frontier Women: The Trans-Mississippi West, 1840–1880* (New York: Hill and Wang, 1979), 77.

9.   Quoted in Kimball Young, *Isn't One Wife Enough?* (New York: Henry Holt and Company, 1954), 175.

10.   Terrence Heaton, Oral History, interviewed by Marsha C. Martin, November 11, 1982, 3, LDS Family Life Oral History Project, Charles Redd Center for Western Studies, L. Tom Perry Special Collections and Manuscripts, Harold B. Lee Library, Brigham Young University, Provo, Utah (hereafter Redd Center).

11.   Lerner, *The Female Experience,* xxv-xxvi.

12.   Joyce D. Goodfriend and Claudia M. Christie, *Lives of American Women: A History with Documents* (Boston: Little, Brown, and Company, 1981), 15.

13.   Reta Bartell, Oral History, interviewed by Jessie L. Embry, July 23, 1973, 3, Monticello, Utah, Southeastern Utah Oral History Project, Redd Center.

14.   Leonard J. Arrington and Susan Arrington Madsen, *Sunbonnet Sisters: Stories of Mormon Women and Frontier Life* (Salt Lake City: Bookcraft, 1984), 3–4.

15.   Laura Clark Cook, Oral History, interviewed by Leonard R. Grover, February 7, 1981, Salt Lake City, 23, LDS Polygamy Oral History Project, Redd Center.

16.   Arrington and Madsen, *Sunbonnet Sisters,* 127.

17.   Kenneth W. Godfrey, Audrey M. Godfrey, and Jill Mulvay Derr, eds., *Women's Voices: An Untold History of the Latter-day Saints, 1830–1900* (Salt Lake City: Deseret Book, 1982), 317.

18.   Rhea Hart Grandy, Oral History, interviewed by Leonard R. Grover, February 16, 1980, Smithfield, Utah, 14, LDS Family Life Oral History Project, Redd Center.

19.   Marcus Fielding Hart, Oral History, interviewed by Jessie L. Embry, May 31, 1976, Preston, Idaho, 6, LDS Polygamy Oral History Project, Redd Center.

20.   Jonathan Cannon, Oral History, interviewed by Leonard Grover, December 20, 1979, Salt Lake City, 4–5, LDS Polygamy Oral History Project, Redd Center.

21.   Maurine Eyring Boyd, Oral History, interviewed by Rochelle Fairborn, 1982, 3–4, LDS Polygamy Oral History Project, Redd Center.

22.   Zina Patterson Dunford, Oral History, interviewed by Jessie L. Embry, December 2, 1980, Provo, Utah, 7, LDS Polygamy Oral History Project, Redd Center.

23.   Seneth Hyer Thomson, Oral History, interviewed by Leonard Grover, February 16, 1980, Lewiston, Utah, 2, LDS Polygamy Oral History Project, Redd Center.

24. Howard Charles Woodfield, interviewed by Marsha Martin, May 10, 1985, 3, North Ogden, Utah, LDS Family Life Oral History Project, Redd Center.

25. Loretta L. Hefner. "Amy Brown Lyman: 'Raising the Quality of Life for All,'" in *Sister Saints,* edited by Vicky Burgess-Olson (Provo, Utah: Brigham Young University, 1978), 98.

26. Dorthea F. Parent, Oral History, interviewed by Stevan M. Hales, November 25, 1981, Provo, Utah, 15, LDS Polygamy Oral History Project, Redd Center.

27. Ibid.

28. Geraldine P. Mineau, "Fertility on the Frontier: An Analysis of the Nineteenth-Century Utah Population" (Ph.D. diss., University of Utah, 1980), 123.

29. Ibid., 144; Lee L. Bean, Geraldine P. Mineau, and Douglas L. Anderton, *Fertility Change on the American Frontier: Adaptation and Innovation* (Berkeley: University of California Press, 1990), 123–26.

30. John W. Shaffer, "Family, Class and Young Women: Occupational Expectations in Nineteenth Century," *Journal of Family History* 3 (Spring 1978): 62–77.

31. Arrington and Madsen, *Sunbonnet Sisters,* 101.

32. Loretta M. Rigby, Oral History, interviewed by Kathleen Cook, November 14, 1981, Rexburg, Idaho, 23, LDS Polygamy Oral History Project, Redd Center.

33. Violet Bird Alexander, Oral History, interviewed by Thomas G. Alexander, October 10, 1980, Slaterville, Utah, 1981, 13–14, LDS Family Life Oral History Project, Redd Center.

34. Parent, Oral History, 15.

35. Arrington and Madsen, *Sunbonnet Sisters,* 90.

36. Ada Palmer, Oral History, interviewed by Jessie L. Embry, July 25, 1973, Monticello, Utah, 2, Southeastern Utah Oral History Project, Redd Center. "Normal" in the nineteenth and early twentieth century mean "teacher education," so most colleges had "normal schools" or "normal training" for that purpose.

37. Lucile Barlow Clark, Oral History, interviewed by Jessie L. Embry, December 1, 1980, Farmington, Utah, 17, LDS Polygamy Oral History Project, Redd Center.

38. Helen Redd, Oral History, interviewed by Jessie L. Embry, July 23, 1973, Monticello, Utah, 13, Southeastern Utah Oral History Project, Redd Center.

39. Mary Diantha Cox Sherratt, Oral History, interviewed by Stevan Hales, April 23, 1982, St. George, Utah, 15, LDS Polygamy Oral History Project, Redd Center.

40. Thressa Lewis Frost, Oral History, interviewed by Jessie L. Embry, July 23, 1973, Monticello, Utah, 2. Southeastern Utah Oral History Project.

41. John Mack Faragher, *Women and Men on the Overland Trail* (New Haven, Conn.: Yale University Press, 1979), 158–59.

42. Arrington and Madsen, *Sunbonnet Sisters,* 91.

43. Mineau, "Fertility on the Frontier," 125.

44. Arrington and Madsen, *Sunbonnet Sisters,* 125.

45. Pearl Bliss Butt, Oral History, interviewed by Jessie L. Embry, July 19, 1973, 10, Southeastern Utah Oral History Project.

46. Faragher, *Men and Women on the Overland Trail,* 58.

47. Colleen Whitley, ed., *Worth Their Salt, Too: More Notable but Often Unnoted Women of Utah* (Logan: Utah State University Press, 2000), viii.

48. Mineau, "Fertility on the Frontier," 102.

49. Ibid., 107, 115–16.

50. Ibid., 161.

51. Quoted in Godfrey, Godfrey, and Derr, *Women's Voices,* 310, 315.

52. Ann Amelia Chamberlain, Oral History, Interviewed by Ronald K. Esplin, April 22, 24–25, 1973, Salt Lake City, 3, Archives, Family and Church History Department, Church of Jesus Christ of Latter-day Saints, Salt Lake City (hereafter LDS Church Archives).

53. Marie Ekins Redd, Oral History, interviewed by Jessie L. Embry, July 20, 1973, 8–9, Monticello, Utah, Southeastern Utah Oral History Project.

54. Lora Bennion Nebeker, Oral History, interviewed by Stevan M. Hales, November 21, 1982, Salt Lake City, 17, LDS Family Life Oral History Project, Redd Center. Lora was one of the daughters.

55. Mineau, "Fertility on the Frontier," 55.

56. U.S. Bureau of the Census, *Vital Statistical Rates in the United States, 1900–40* (Washington, D.C.: Government Printing Office, 1941), 578, 601.

57. Aurelia Spencer Rogers, *Life Sketches of Orson Spencer and Others and History of Primary Work* (Salt Lake City: Geo. Q. Cannon and Sons, 1898), 163, 198–99.

58. Erma Valentine Jacobs, Oral History, interviewed by Marsha C. Martin, August 8, 1983, Provo, Utah, 12, LDS Family Life Oral History.

59. Butt, Oral History, 2.

60. LaRue Cox Jefferies, Oral History, interviewed by Marsha C. Martin, August 1, 1983, Orem, Utah, 8–9, LDS Family Life Oral History Project, Redd Center.

61. U.S. Bureau of the Census, *1950 Census of Population, Vol. 11: Characteristics of Population, Part 44–Utah* (Washington, D.C.: Government Printing Office, 1951), 24.

62. Jessie L. Embry, *Master or Slave: The Economic Role of Mormon Polygamous Wives,* Working Paper, No. 15 (Tucson, Ariz.: Southwest Institute for Research on Women, 1982), 5–6.

63. Meda Lucille Jenkins, Oral History, interviewed by Jessie L. Embry, August 30, 1980, Newton, Utah, 7, LDS Polygamy Oral History Project, Redd Center.

64. Rigby, Oral History, 7.

65. Lula Ann Rigby Larsen, Oral History, interviewed by Rochelle Fairbourn, January 30, 1982, Manti, Utah, 4, LDS Family Life Oral History Project, Redd Center.

66. Zora Kay Hansen, Oral History, interviewed by Stevan Hales, December 29, 1981, Pleasant Grove, Utah, 10, LDS Family Life Oral History Project, Redd Center.

67. Butt, Oral History, 2.

68. Mineau, "Fertility on the Frontier," 16; U.S. Bureau of the Census, *1980 General Population Characteristics. Vol. 1: Chap. B; Part 1, U.S. Summary, and Part 46, Utah* (Washington, D.C.: Government Printing Office, 1981).

69. U.S. Census, *1950 Census of Population,* Vol. 11, *Part 44–Utah,* 76.

70. Lavina Fielding Anderson, "Ministering Angels: Single Women in Mormon Society," *Dialogue: A Journal of Mormon Thought* 16 (Autumn 1983): 59–78.

71. Ione Naegle Moss, Oral History, interviewed by Gary Shumway, November 16, 1981, St. George, Utah, 26, LDS Family Life Oral History Project, Redd Center.

72. Reba Keele, "Alice Louise Reynolds: A Woman's Woman," in *Sister Saints,* edited by Vicky Burgess-Olson (Provo, Utah: Brigham Young University, 1978), 276–85.

73. Vicky Burgess-Olson, "Stena Scorup: First Lady of Salina," in ibid., 297–98.

74. Arrington and Madsen, *Sunbonnet Sisters,* 127.

75. Katherine C. Thomas, Oral History, interviewed by Leonard R. Grover, March 28, 1980, Provo, Utah, 14, LDS Polygamy, Oral History Project, Redd Center.

76. Quoted in Godfrey, Godfrey, and Derr, *Women's Voices,* 298.

77. Larsen, Oral History, 8.

78. Bernitta Bartley, Oral History, interviewed by Stevan M. Hales, 1982, 8, LDS Family Life Oral History Project, Redd Center.

79. Dorothy Redd Jameson, Oral History, interviewed by Gregory Maynard, June 7, 1973, Provo, Utah, 2, Charles Redd Oral History Project, Redd Center.

80. Dunford, Oral History, 1980.

81. Clark, Oral History, 1.

82. Maureen Ursenbach Beecher, Carol Cornwall Madsen, and Lavina Fielding Anderson, "Widowhood Among the Mormons: Personal Accounts," in *On Their Own: Widows and Widowhood in the American Southwest, 1845–1939,* edited by Arlene Scadron (Urbana: University of Illinois Press, 1988), 121.

83. Jill Mulvay Derr, "Sarah Melissa Granger Kimball: The Liberal Shall be Blessed," in *Sisters Saints,* edited by Vicky Burgess-Olson (Provo, Utah: Brigham Young University, 1978), 29.

84. U.S. Bureau of the Census, *Special Report on Marriage and Divorce, 1867–1906* (Washington, D.C.: Government Printing Office, 1909), 563.

85. Rebecca Foster Cornwall, "Susa Young Gates: The Thirteenth Apostle," in Sister Saints, edited by Burgess-Olson, 67–74; Derr, *Women's Voices,* 291.

86. Norman Juster, *So Sweet to Labor: Rural Women in America, 1865–1895* (New York: Viking Press, 1979), 13.

87. Anne M. Butler and Ona Siporin, *Uncommon Common Women: Ordinary Lives in the West* (Logan: Utah State University Press, 1996), 122.

Suggested Readings

Armitage, Susan, and Elizabeth Jameson, eds. *The Women's West.* Norman: University of Oklahoma Press, 1987.

Beeton, Beverly. *Women Vote in the West: The Woman Suffrage Movement, 1869–1896.* New York: Garland, 1986.

Blair, Karen. *The Clubwoman as Feminist: True Womanhood Redefined, 1868–1914.* New York: Holmes and Meier Pub., 1980.

Bradley, Martha Sonntag. "The Mormon Relief Society and the IWY." *Journal of Mormon History* 21 (Spring 1995): 105–67.

Burgess-Olsen, Vicky, ed. *Sister Saints.* Provo, Utah: Brigham Young University, 1978.

Bushman, Claudia L., ed. *Mormon Sisters: Women in Early Utah.* Salt Lake City: Olympus Publishing Company, 1980. New edition, Logan: Utah State University Press, 1997.

Butler, Anne M. and Ona Siporin. *Uncommon Common Women: Ordinary Lives in the West.* Logan: Utah State University Press, 1996.

Cott, Nancy F. *The Bonds of Womanhood: Women's Sphere in New England, 1780–1835.* New Haven: Yale University Press, 1969.

———. *Public Vows: A History of Marriage and the Nation.* Cambridge: Harvard University Press, 2000.

———, ed. *No Small Courage: A History of Women in the United States.* New York: Oxford University Press, 2000.

Daynes, Kathryn M. *More Wives Than One: Transformation of the Mormon Marriage System, 1840–1910.* Urbana: University of Illinois Press, 2001.

Degler, Carl N. *At Odds: Women and the Family in America from the Revolution to the Present.* New York: Oxford University Press, 1980.

Embry, Jessie L. *Mormon Polygamous Families: Life in the Principle.* Salt Lake City: University of Utah Press, 1987.

Epstein, Barbara Leslie. *The Politics of Domesticity: Women, Evangelism, and Temperance in Nineteenth-Century America.* Middleton, Conn.: Wesleyan University Press, 1981.

Faragher, John Mack. *Women and Men on the Overland Trail.* New Haven, Conn.: Yale University Press, 1979.

Flexner, Eleanor. *Century of Struggle: The Woman's Rights Movement in the United States.* Cambridge, Mass.: Harvard University, 1958.

Gibbey, Kristina C. "The Hollow Promise?: The Paradoxical Outcome of the Feminization and Professionalization of Teaching in Utah, 1890–1920." Ph.D. diss., University of Utah, 2001.

Godfrey, Kenneth W., Audrey M. Godfrey, and Jill Mulvay Derr. *Women's Voices: An Untold History of the Latter-day Saints, 1830–1900.* Salt Lake City: Deseret Book Company, 1982.

Governor's Committee on the Status of Women in Utah. *Utah Women: Opportunities, Responsibilities: A Report of the Governor's Committee on the Status of Women in Utah, June 15, 1966.* Salt Lake City: The Committee, 1966.

Harris, B. J. *Beyond Her Sphere: Women and the Professions in American History.* Westport, Conn.: Greenwood Press, 1978.

Harvey, Sheridan, et al., eds. *American Women: A Library of Congress Guide for the Study for Women's History and Culture in the United States.* Washington, D.C.: Library of Congress, 2001.

Hine, Darlene Clark, et al. *A Shining Thread of Hope: The History of Black Women in America.* New York: Broadway Books, 1999.

Holt, Marilyn Irwin. *Linoleum Better Babies & the Modern Farm Women, 1890–1930.* Albuquerque: University of New Mexico Press, 1995.

Irwin, Mary Ann, and James F. Brooks. *Women and Gender in the American West: Jensen-Miller Prize Essays from the Coalition for Western Women's History.* Albuquerque: University of New Mexico, 2004.

Iversen, Joan Smyth. *The Antipolygamy Controversy in U.S. Women's Movement, 1880–1925: A Debate on the American Home.* New York and London: Garland Publications., 1997.

Jeffrey, Julie Roy. *Frontier Women: The Trans-Mississippi West, 1840–1880.* New York: Hill and Wang, 1979.

Jensen, Joan. *With These Hands: Women Working on the Land.* New York: McGraw-Hill, c.1981.

Kerber, Linda K. *Women of the Republic: Intellect and Ideology in Revolutionary America.* Chapel Hill: University of North Carolina Press, 1980.

Kerber, Linda K., Alice Kessler-Harris, and Kathryn Kish Sklar. *U.S. History as Woman's History: New Feminist Essays.* Chapel Hill: University of North Carolina Press, 1995.

Kessler-Harris, Alice. *Out to Work: A History of Wage-Earning Women in the United States.* New York: Oxford University Press, 1982.

Kinkaid, Joyce. *A Schoolmarm All My Life: Personal Narratives from Frontier Utah.* Salt Lake City: Signature Books, 1996.

Lerner, Gerda. *The Female Experience: An American Documentary.* New York: Oxford University Press, 1992.

Lobb, Ann Vest, and Jill Mulvay Derr, "Women in Early Utah," in *Utah's History*, edited by Richard D. Poll et al. Provo: Brigham Young University Press, 1978.

Madsen, Carol Cornwall, ed. *Battle for the Ballot: Essays on Woman Suffrage in Utah, 1870–1896.* Logan: Utah State University, 1997.

————. "Decade of Détente: The Mormon-Gentile Female Relationship in Nineteenth-century Utah," *Utah Historical Quarterly* 63 (Fall 1995): 298–319.

Matthews, Glenna. *Just a Housewife: The Rise and Fall of Domesticity in America.* New York: Oxford University Press, 1987.

Murphy, Miriam B. "Women in the Work Force from Statehood to World War II." *Utah Historical Quarterly* 50 (Spring 1982): 139–59.

Myres, Sandra L. *Westering Women and the Frontier Experience, 1800–1915.* Albuquerque: University of New Mexico Press, 1982.

Petrik, Paula. *No Step Backward: Women and Family on the Rocky Mountain Mining Frontier, 1865–1900.* Helena: Montana Historical Society Press, 1987.

Ruiz, Vicki L. and Ellen Carol Dubois. *Unequal Sisters: A Multicultural Reader in U.S. Women's History.* 2d ed. New York: Routledge, 1994.

Ryan, Mary P. *Womanhood in America: From Colonial Times to the Present.* New York: Routledge, 1994.

Scandron, Arlene, ed. *On Their Own: Widows and Widowhood in the American Southwest, 1848–1939.* Urbana: University of Illinois Press, 1988.

Scandron, Arlene, Vicki L. Ruiz, and Janice Monk, eds. *Western Women: Their Land, Their Lives.* Allbubuerque: University of New Mexico Press, 1988.

Scharf, Lois. *To Work and to Wed: Female Employment, Feminism, and the Great Depression.* Westpoint, Conn.: Greenwood, 1980.

Ulrich, Laurel Thatcher. *A Midwife's Tale: The Life of Martha Ballard, Based on Her Diary.* New York: Knopf, 1990.

Van Wagenen, Lola. "Sister-Wives and Suffragists: Polygamy and the Politics of Woman Suffrage, 1870–1896." Ph.D., diss., New York University, 1994. Printed Provo, Utah: Joseph Fielding Smith Institute for Latter-day Saint History and BYU Studies, Dissertations in LDS History Series, 2003.

Van Wagoner, Richard S. *Mormon Polygamy: A History.* Salt Lake City: Signature Books, 1986.

Ware. Susan. *Holding Their Own: American Women of the 1930s.* (Boston: Twayne Publishers, 1982.

Welter, Barbara. "The Cult of True Womanhood, 1820–1860," *American Quarterly* 18 (Summer 1966), 151–74.

Whitley, Colleen, ed. *Worth Their Salt: Notable But Often Unnoted Women of Utah.* Logan: Utah State University Press, 1996.

————, ed. *Worth Their Salt, Too: More Notable But Often Unnoted Women of Utah.* Logan: Utah State University, 2000.

Contributors

Lavina Fielding Anderson, the copy editor of this book, has been with the project from the beginning. The president of Editing, Inc., she earned her Ph.D. in English from the University of Washington. From 1990, she has served as editor of the *Journal of Mormon History* and is the recipient of the Grace F. Arrington Award for Distinguished Service to Mormon History and a past president of the Association for Mormon Letters and editor of its *Annual*. The AML awarded her an Honorary Lifetime Membership Award (2002). With Maureen Ursenbach Beecher, she edited *Sisters in Spirit: Mormon Women in Historical and Cultural Perspective* (Urbana: University of Illinois Press, 1987). She is the author of *Lucy's Book: A Critical Edition of Lucy Mack Smith's Family Memoir* (Salt Lake City: Signature Books, 2002) for which she was awarded the John Whitmer Historical Association's Best Book Award and the Mormon History Association's Christensen Best Documentary Book Award.

Martha Sonntag Bradley-Evans is associate professor in the College of Architecture and Planning at the University of Utah and is director of the university's Honors Program. She is the recipient of numerous teaching awards including the Distinguished University Teaching Award. She is the author of numerous historical articles and, with Mary Brown Firmage Woodward, coauthored *Four Zinas: Mothers and Daughters on the Mormon Frontier* (Salt Lake City: Signature Books, 2000) for which she won the Best Book Award from the Utah Historical Society and the Best Biographical Book Award from the Mormon History Association. Her most recent book is *Pedestals and Podiums: Women, Mormonism, and Equal Rights* (Salt Lake City: Signature Books, July 2005).

Mary Riggs Clark (1928-2000) was born in New York City and grew up in nearby Woodlawn, Yonkers, and Cornwall, New York. She attended the State University of New York at New Palz but left to marry Richard Major Clark in 1947 and to raise a family. In 1960, Dick's job at Sperry-Rand brought them to Salt Lake City, where Mary resumed her studies at the University of Utah. She graduated with honors in English and journalism, and immediately began a career that lasted over twenty years in teaching and educational administration at Rowland Hall-St. Mark's Preparatory School in Salt Lake City. During that time, she earned her M.A. in American literature from Middlebury College and was a Ph.D. candidate in education at the University of Utah. The Clarks retired to Mary's childhood summer home in Ripton, Vermont, in 1986, where she founded the Ripton Historical Society and continued to teach in the adult diploma program. Mary and Dick had been married for fifty-two years at the time of her death in 2000. In retirement, they particularly enjoyed travel, genealogy, and their grandchildren.

JILL MULVAY DERR is the author of numerous articles on Mormon women and coauthor with Janath Russell Cannon and Maureen Ursenbach Beecher of *Women of Covenant: The Story of the Relief Society* (Salt Lake City: Deseret Book, 1992). She is currently coediting for publication with Karen Lynn Davidson nearly five hundred of Eliza R. Snow's poems, and her major work in progress is a biography of Eliza R. Snow. She was the managing director of the Joseph Smith Institute for Latter-day Saint History and associate professor of church history at Brigham Young University, 2003–2005.

JESSIE L. EMBRY is the associate director of the Charles Redd Center for Western Studies at Brigham Young University. She is the author of seven books and more than eighty articles on oral history, western history, women's history, and LDS history. Her publications include: *Mormon Polygamous Families: Life in the Principle* (Salt Lake City: University of Utah Press, 1987), *A History of Wasatch County* (Salt Lake City: Utah State Historical Society, 1996), *Mormon Wards as Community* (Binghamton, NY: Global Publications, Binghamton University, 2001); *Black Saints in a White Church: Contemporary African American Mormons* (Salt Lake City: Signature Books, 1994); and *"In His Own Language": Mormon Spanish-Speaking Congregations in the United States* (Provo, Utah: Charles Redd Center for Western Studies, Brigham Young University, 1997).

LOIS JEAN MILLER KELLEY (1935-90) was a member of the Mormon History Association. She graduated *magna cum laude* with a bachelor of science in history from Utah State University and was near completing her master's degree at the time of her death.

KATHRYN L. MACKAY is associate professor of history, Weber State University and one of the founders of the Utah Women's History Association, which began in the 1970s to work on a collaborative history of Utah women. Kathryn teaches and publishes in American Indian history, women's history, and folklore. Her publications include coauthoring with Floyd A. O'Neil, *A History of the Uintah-Ouray Ute Lands* (Salt Lake City: American West Center, University of Utah, 1979) and co-edited with Floyd A. Neil, *A History of the Northern Ute People* ([s.l.]: Uintah-Ouray Tribe, 1982).

Carol Cornwall Madsen received a Ph.D. in American history from the University of Utah and is presently professor emeritus of history at Brigham Young University and a senior research scholar with the Joseph Fielding Smith Institute for Latter-day Saint History. She is the author/editor of several books including *In Their Own Words: Women and the Story of Nauvoo* (Salt Lake City: Deseret Book, 1994); *Battle for the Ballot: Essays on Woman Suffrage in Utah, 1870-1896* (Logan: Utah State University, 1997); and *Journey to Zion: Voices from the Trail* (Salt Lake City: Deseret Book, 1997). At press is a biography of the public life of Emmeline B. Wells: *"A Fine Soul Who Served Us": Emmeline B. Wells, A Mormon Woman's Advocate.* Carol has written numerous articles on Utah and Mormon women's history and has won seven best-article awards. Her current project is the personal life of Emmeline Wells. She and her daughter Lisa Madsen Pearson, a legal scholar, have brought their two professions together in their essay for this volume.

Miriam Brinton Murphy was born and raised in Salt Lake City. She attended the University of California, Berkeley, and completed a B.A. in English at the University of Utah where she served as editor of the *Daily Utah Chronicle* in her senior year. After working in New York and San Francisco, she returned to Utah and was associate editor of *Utah Historical Quarterly* during 1971-97. She is the author of numerous historical articles and reviews, *A History of Wayne County* (Salt Lake City: Utah State Historical Society, 1999), and *That Green Light That Lingers* (Salt Lake City: City Art, 2001) a collection of poetry. She has a son, Bill.

Helen Zeese Papanikolas (1917-2004) was born in a mining town in Carbon County, Utah. She graduated from the University of Utah in 1939 where she was editor of the *Pen* literary magazine. She became involved in the study of Utah and ethnic history, a passion she pursued for more than fifty years. She wrote numerous articles for the *Utah Historical Quarterly* and in other journals. She was also the author of seven books including *The Time of the Little Black Bird* (Athens: Swallow Press/Ohio University Press, 1999) which won the Utah Fiction Prize for 2000. She edited the classic book on the history of ethnic groups in Utah for the national bicentennial: *Peoples of Utah* (Salt Lake City: Utah State Historical Society, 1976) and most recently: *An Amulet of Greek Earth: Generations of Immigrant Folk Culture* (Athens: Swallow Press/Ohio University Press, 2002). Her posthumous novel *The Rain in the Valley* is forthcoming in 2006 from Utah State University Press.

Lisa Madsen Pearson is a lecturer at Stanford Law School where she teaches federal pretrial litigation and directs the Kirkwood Moot Court program. A member of the Utah and California State Bar Associations, she has practiced law in both states. She received her B.A. and J.D. from the University of Utah and a J.S.M. from Stanford Law School.

PATRICIA LYN SCOTT is the records analysis section manager at the Utah State Archives and was previously the local government records archivist (1984-January 2004) working with all counties and school districts in Utah. She earned an M.S. in library science with a specialization in archival administration from Wayne State University (1977), and a M.A. in the history of the American West from the University of Utah (1983). She is the author of various historical articles, the most recent being, "Jennie Anderson Froiseth and the Blue Tea," *Utah Historical Quarterly* 71 (Winter 2003), 20-36; and "The Widow and the Lion of the Lord: Sarah Ann Cooke vs. Brigham Young," *Journal of Mormon History* 30 (Spring 2004): 189-212.

JOHN SILLITO is university archivist and curator of special collection and professor of libraries at Weber State University in Ogden, where he was named the Nye honors professor of the year for 2002. He is the editor of *The Wilderness of Faith: Essays on Contemporary Mormon Thought* (Salt Lake City: Signature Books, 1991); coeditor with Constance L. Leiber of *Letters from Exile: The Correspondence of Martha Hughes Cannon and Angus M. Cannon, 1886-1888* (Salt Lake City: Signature Books, 1989); co-editor with Susan Staker, *Mormon Mavericks: Essays on Dissenters* (Salt Lake City: Signature Books, 2001; and, with John McCormick, *A World We Thought We Knew: Readings in Utah History* (Salt Lake City: University of Utah Press, 1995) He has also contributed to several anthologies, including *Differing Visions: Dissenters in Mormon History; Expectations for the Millennium: American Socialist Visions of the Future; Socialism and Christianity in Early Twentieth-Century America;* and *The Utah History Encyclopedia.* He edited *History's Apprentice: The Diaries of B. H. Roberts, 1880-1898* (Salt Lake City: Signature Books, 2004), which won the Mormon History Association's Christensen Best Documentary Book Award. His many professional activities include currently serving on the board of editors of the *Utah Historical Quarterly.*

CYNTHIA JANE STURGIS was born and raised in southern California. She graduated from the College of William and Mary in Virginia in 1975, *cum laude,* with honors in history. She earned her M.A. (1978) and Ph.D. (1983) in western and nineteenth/twentieth century U.S. history from the University of Utah. Her dissertation examined Sevier County, Utah, from the 1890s through the 1930s as an example of bureaucratization, systematization, and social change in rural, agricultural communities. During her Utah years, she also worked with the Utah State Historical Society and other organizations on a variety of public history projects, and she edited and contributed to a guide on historical preservation published by the University of Utah. Following four years as an assistant professor at Texas Tech University, she found a home at the Bishop's School in La Jolla, California, one of the premier college preparatory institutions in the nation, where she is responsible for teaching U.S. history (regular and advanced placement), A.P. American government, and California history. She also reviews books for the San Diego Historical Society.

Linda Thatcher has an B.S. and M.Ed. from Utah State University as well as an M.L.S. from Brigham Young University. She has worked at the Utah State Historical Society since 1975 where she is the Historic Collections coordinator. She has served as president of the Utah Women's History Association and second vice-president of the Utah Library Association. Her articles include: "'I Care Nothing for Politics': Ruth May Fox, Forgotten Suffragist," *Utah Historical Quarterly* (Summer 1981); "The 'Gentile Polygamist': Arthur Brown, Ex-Senator from Utah," *Utah Historical Quarterly* (Summer 1984); and "Women Alone: The Economic and Emotional Plight of Early LDS Women," *Dialogue: A Journal of Mormon Thought* (Winter 1992). With Roger D. Launius, she coedited *Differing Visions: Dissenters in Mormon History* (Urbana: University of Illinois Press, 1994).

Gary Topping is professor of history at Salt Lake Community College and archivist of the Roman Catholic Diocese of Salt Lake City. Formerly curator of manuscripts at the Utah State Historical Society, he serves on the Advisory Board of Editors of the *Utah Historical Quarterly.* He is the author and editor of books and articles on the history of the Colorado Plateau and Utah historiography and literature. He has edited *Gila Monsters and Red-Eyed Rattlesnakes: Don Maguire's Arizona Trading Expedition, 1876-1878* (Salt Lake City: University of Utah Press, 1997) and *The Great Salt Lake: An Anthology* (Logan: Utah State University Press, 2002). His most recent book is *Utah Historians and the Reconstruction of Western History* (Norman: University of Oklahoma Press, 2003).

Susan Allred Whetstone attended Eckerd College in St. Petersburg, Florida, the University of Utah, graduated from Brigham Young University with a B.S. in geography (1974), and earned an M.L.S. from Brigham Young University in 1977. Since 1978, she has been curator of photographs at the Utah State Historical Society since 1978. She has continued professional training through the Western Archives Institute, the American Association for State and Local History, and Society of American Archivists. Susan has been a member of Utah Library Association, Utah Cooperative Preservation of Architectural Records, Conference of InterMountain Archivists, and Utah Preservation Consortium. She is the executive secretary for the Utah Committee for Geographic Names. She did technical work for Richard H. Jackson's *Historical Atlas of the United States East of the Mississippi River* ([n.p.] 1979). She was the photograph editor for *Utah, the Right Place: The Official Centennial History* (Salt Lake City: Gibbs Smith, 1996). Susan has assisted in several television documentaries for KUED and Ken Burns.

Index